Bt
9.50

# In Honour of Daniel Jones

IN HONOUR OF

# DANIEL JONES

Papers
contributed on
the occasion of his
eightieth birthday
12 September 1961

*Edited by*

DAVID ABERCROMBIE D. B. FRY
P. A. D. MacCARTHY N. C. SCOTT
J. L. M. TRIM

LONGMANS

LONGMANS, GREEN AND CO LTD
48 Grosvenor Street, London W1
*Associated companies, branches and representatives throughout the world*



*First published 1964*

Made and printed in Great Britain by
William Clowes and Sons, Limited
London and Beccles

# Contributors

David Abercrombie *Edinburgh*
W.S.Allen *Cambridge*
G.F.Arnold *London*
Georges Bertrand *Paris*
E.Blancquaert *Ghent*
J.Carnochan *London*
J.C.Catford *Edinburgh*
Yuen Ren Chao *Berkeley, California*
M.Chapallaz *London*
Suniti Kumar Chatterji *Calcutta*
André Classe *Glasgow*
Hélène N.Coustenoble *London*
Ivar Dahl *Temperley, Argentina*
Pierre Delattre *Boulder, California*
O. von Essen *Hamburg*
G.Faure *Aix-en-Provence*
Piero Fiorelli *Rome*
Charles C.Fries *Ann Arbor, Michigan*
D.B.Fry *London*
Robert H.Gerhard *Tokyo*
A.C.Gimson *London*
Morris Halle *Cambridge, Massachusetts*
Eugénie J.A.Henderson *London*
Beatrice Honikman *Leeds*
Lee S.Hultzén *Urbana, Illinois*
Roman Jakobson *Cambridge, Massachusetts*
Wiktor Jassem *Poznań*
L.Kaiser *Amsterdam*
R.Kingdon *Mexico City*
H.Kökeritz *New Haven, Connecticut*
Hans Kurath *Ann Arbor, Michigan*
W.R.Lee *London*
P.A.D. MacCarthy *Leeds*
Bertil Malmberg *Lund*
André Martinet *Paris*
J.D.O'Connor *London*
Kenneth L.Pike *Ann Arbor, Michigan*
Sir James Pitman *London*
Julian T.Pring *London*
Maria Schubiger *Basel*
N.C.Scott *London*
Alf Sommerfelt *Oslo*
W.F.Stirling *Accra*
Peter Strevens *Leeds*
Olive M.Tooley *London*
George L.Trager *Buffalo, New York*
J.L.M.Trim *Cambridge*
B.Trnka *Prague*
A.N.Tucker *London*
Elizabeth Uldall *Edinburgh*
Josef Vachek *Brno*
Siddheshwar Varma *Chandigarh*
Dennis Ward *Edinburgh*
C.M.Wise *Baton Rouge, Louisiana*

# Contents

## *The Phonetics of English*

CONTENTS

CONTENTS

# Daniel Jones: Bibliography and Discography

## BOOKS

*100 Poésies Enfantines (avec Maximes et Proverbes)*, Teubner, Leipzig, 1907.

(With D.L. Savory) *The Sounds of the French Language*, Clarendon Press, Oxford, 1907. A translation of *Les Sons du Français*, by Paul Passy.

*Phonetic Transcriptions of English Prose*, Clarendon Press, Oxford, 1907.

*Intonation Curves*, Teubner, Leipzig, 1909.

*The Pronunciation of English*, Cambridge University Press, 1909. 3rd ed., rewritten, 1950. 4th ed., revised and enlarged, 1956.

*Phonetic Readings in English*, Carl Winter, Heidelberg, 1912. 31st ed., new and improved version, 1956.

(With Kwing Tong Woo) *A Cantonese Phonetic Reader*, University of London Press, 1912.

(With H. Michaelis) *A Phonetic Dictionary of the English Language*, Carl Meyer (Gustav Prior), Hanover, 1913.

(With S. T. Plaatje) *A Sechuana Phonetic Reader*, University of London Press, 1916.

*An English Pronouncing Dictionary*, Dent, London, 1917. 4th ed., rewritten, 1937. 11th ed., rewritten again, 1956.

*An Outline of English Phonetics*, Teubner, Leipzig, 1918. 3rd ed., rewritten, 1932. 7th ed., with an Appendix on American Pronunciation, Teubner, Leipzig, and Heffer, Cambridge, 1948. 8th ed., revised and re-set, with an Appendix on Types of Phonetic Transcription, Heffer, Cambridge, 1956.

(With H. S. Perera) *A Colloquial Sinhalese Reader*, Manchester University Press, 1919.

(With M. V. Trofimov) *The Pronunciation of Russian*, Cambridge University Press, 1923.

(With E. M. Stéphan) *Colloquial French for the English*, The Gramophone Co., London, 1927.

*The Phoneme, its Nature and Use*, Heffer, Cambridge, 1950. 2nd ed., 1962.

General Editor of the Series of *London Phonetic Readers* published by the University of London Press.

Editor of *Le Maître Phonétique*, 1907–1949 (with Paul Passy until 1939).

(With D. B. Fry) Editor of the *Proceedings of the Second International Congress of Phonetic Sciences*, Cambridge University Press, 1936.

## ARTICLES AND PAMPHLETS

'Implosive Sounds and Clicks', *Maître Phonétique*, Nov.–Dec. 1907, 111–114.

(With Paul Passy) *Alphabet Organique*. Supplement to *Maître Phonétique*, Nov.–Dec. 1907.

'The MF Alphabet and Spelling Reform', *Maître Phonétique*, Nov.–Dec. 1908, 125–128.

*Specimens of Shakespeare in the Pronunciation of the Period*. Supplement to *Maître Phonétique*, July–Aug. 1909.

'The Pronunciation of Early English', *Maître Phonétique*, Sept.–Oct. 1909, 119–123.

'Uniform Spelling for the African Languages (with a Short Analysis of the Chindau Language of Southern Rhodesia)', *Maître Phonétique*, Nov.–Dec. 1910, 148–152.

(With Kwing Tong Woo) 'Specimen of Standard Colloquial Cantonese', *Maître Phonétique*, May–June 1911, 80–84.

*The Pronunciation and Orthography of the Chindau Language*, University of London Press, 1911.

'Specimen of Tyneside Dialect', *Maître Phonétique*, Nov.–Dec. 1911, 184.

(With Kwing Tong Woo) 'Specimen of Cantonese, Colloquial Style', *Maître Phonétique*, Mar.–Apr. 1912, 67–68.

'Note on Syriac', *Maître Phonétique*, Nov.–Dec. 1913, 136–137.

'The Value of Phonetics to the Language Student', *International Review of Missions*, 1917, 196.

'The Phonetic Structure of the Sechuana language', *Transactions of the Philological Society*, 1917–1920, 99–106.

'The Use of Experimental Phonetics to the Linguist', *Modern Language Teaching*, XIV, 1918, 125–132.

'Experimental Phonetics and its Utility to the Linguist', *Proceedings of the Royal Institution*, XXII, 1919, 8–21.

'Specimen of the Hwa Miao Language of Western China (Province of Yünnan)', *Maître Phonétique*, Jan.–Mar. 1923, 4–5.

'Specimen of Cornish Dialect', *Maître Phonétique*, Jan.–Mar. 1923, 7.

(With K. Minn) 'Specimen of Korean, with Notes', *Maître Phonétique*, Apr.–June 1924, 14–15.

'Specimen of Gã, with Notes', *Maître Phonétique*, Jan.–Mar. 1925, 6–9.

'Unstressed English ɪ', *Maître Phonétique*, Jan.–Mar. 1926, 3–4.

'New Signs', *Maître Phonétique*, July–Sept. 1926, 26–27.

(With J. Kabraji) 'Specimen of Gujrati, with Notes', *Maître Phonétique*, Apr.–June 1926, 18–19.

'Words distinguished by Tone in Sechuana', *Festschrift Meinhof*, Hamburg, 1927, 88–98.

'Specimen of Modern Greek, with Notes', *Maître Phonétique*, Apr.–June 1928, 38–39.

(With M. Heepe) 'Das System der Association Phonétique Internationale (Weltlautschriftverein)', *Lautzeichen und ihre Anwendung in verschiedenen Sprachgebieten*, Reichsdruckerei, Berlin, 1928, 18–27.

*The Tones of Sechuana Nouns*, International Institute of African Languages and Cultures, London, 1928.

'Definition of a Phoneme', *Maître Phonétique*, Oct.–Dec. 1929, 43–44.

'On Phonemes', *Travaux du Cercle Linguistique de Prague*, IV, 1931, 74–79.

'The Phonetic Representation of the Swedish Close Vowels', *Maître Phonétique*, Apr.–June 1931, 21–23.

'The "Word" as a Phonetic Entity', *Maître Phonétique*, Oct.–Dec. 1931, 60–65.

'The Theory of Phonemes, and its Importance in Practical Linguistics', *Proceedings of the First International Congress of Phonetic Sciences*, Amsterdam, 1932, 23–24.

'Some Tendencies of Modern English Pronunciation', *Commemorative Volume*, Institute for Research in English Teaching, Tokyo, 1933.

'Specimen of Sindhi, with Notes', *Maître Phonétique*, Oct.–Dec. 1933, 75–77.

(With A. Camilli) *Fondamenti di Grafia Fonética*, International Phonetic Association, 1933.

'Specimen of Assamese, with Notes', *Maître Phonétique*, Oct.–Dec. 1933, 78.

(With B. R. Kolatkar) 'Specimen of Literary Marathi, with Notes', *Maître Phonétique*, Oct.–Dec. 1934, 102–105.

'The Phonetic Aspect (of Speech Training)', *British Journal of Educational Psychology*, v, 1935, 27–30.

(With B. R. Kolatkar) 'Specimen of Colloquial Marathi', *Maître Phonétique*, Apr.–June 1935, 30–32.

'Report presented at the General Meeting of Members of the International Phonetic Association, 27 July 1935', *Maître Phonétique*, July–Sept. 1935, 41–53.

(With I. Moskowska) 'Specimen of Bulgarian, with Notes', *Maître Phonétique*, July–Sept. 1937, 44–45.

(With H. S. Perera) 'The Application of World Orthography to Sinhalese', *Bulletin of the School of Oriental Studies*, IX, 1937, 705–707.

'Specimen of Literary Modern Greek', *Maître Phonétique*, Oct.–Dec. 1937, 71.

*On 'Received Pronunciation'*, International Phonetic Association, 1937.

'Some Notes on the Pronunciation of English at the Time of Shakespeare', *English Pronunciation through the Centuries*, Linguaphone Institute, London, 1937, 38–41.

'The Aim of Phonetics', *Archiv für die gesamte Phonetik*, I, 1937, 4–10.

*The Aims of Phonetics*, International Phonetic Association, 1938.

'Orthophonics (Speech Therapy) in London', *Maître Phonétique*, Jan.–Mar. 1938, 5–6.

*A Passage of Chaucer in Phonetic Transcription*, International Phonetic Association, 1938.

'Concrete and Abstract Sounds', *Proceedings of the Third International Congress of Phonetic Sciences*, Ghent, 1938, 1–7.

'*r*-coloured Vowels', *Maître Phonétique*, Oct.–Dec. 1940, 56–65.

'Specimen of Shan, with Notes', *Maître Phonétique*, Jan.–June 1942, 6–7.

'The letters ɪ and ʊ', *Maître Phonétique*, July–Dec. 1942, 14–15.

*The Problem of a National Script for India*, Department of Phonetics, University College London, 1942.

(With A. Gugushvili) 'Specimen of Georgian, with Notes', *Maître Phonétique*, Jan.–June 1944, 5–6.

*Specimen of Shakespeare in the Original Pronunciation*, International Phonetic Association, 1944.

(With I. Dahl) *Fundamentos de Escritura Fonética*, International Phonetic Association, 1944.

'Chronemes and Tonemes', *Acta Linguistica*, Copenhagen, IV, 1944, 1–10.

*Dhe Fonetik Aspekt ov Speling Reform*, Simplified Spelling Society, London, 1944.

'Some Thoughts on the Phoneme', *Transactions of the Philological Society*, 1945, 119–135.

(With P. C. B. Deo) 'Specimen of Oriya, with Notes', *Maître Phonétique*, July–Dec. 1945, 26–27.

'G(eorge) B(ernard) S(haw) and Phonetics', *G.B.S. 90*, Hutchinson, London, 1946, 158–160.

'ʌ and ə in British English', *Maître Phonétique*, Jan.–June 1946, 2.

(With I. C. Gröndahl) 'Specimen of Norwegian (Bokmål, Eastern Variety), with Notes', *Maître Phonétique*, Jan.–June 1946, 2–3.

(With E. Mesterton) 'Specimen of Swedish, with Notes', *Maître Phonétique*, July–Dec. 1946, 25–26.

(With C. L. Wrenn) *Chart illustrating the Great English Vowel Shift*, Department of Phonetics, University College London, 1947.

*Differences between Spoken and Written Language*, International Phonetic Association, 1948.

'The London School of Phonetics', *Zeitschrift für Phonetik*, II, 1948, 127–135.

'Difficulties of English Pronunciation', *London Calling Europe* (BBC European Bulletin), 1948: I, no. 19 (10 June); II, no. 20 (17 June); III, no. 21 (24 June); IV, no. 22 (1 July).

'The romanization of Japanese', *Zeitschrift für Phonetik*, III, 1949, 68–74.

'The Tongue that Shakespeare Spake', *Radio Times*, 16 Dec. 1949.

'A Romanic Orthography for Oriya', *Siddha-Bhāratī* (Siddheshwar Varma Presentation Volume), Vishveshvaranand Vedic Research Institute, Hoshiarpur, 1950; reprinted in *Zeitschrift für Phonetik*, III, 1949, 74–76.

'A Letter to Professor C. M. Wise, Louisiana State University', *Southern Speech Journal*, University of Texas, XVIII, 1952, 81–86.

'Falling and Rising Diphthongs in Southern English', *Miscellanea Phonetica*, II, International Phonetic Association, 1954, 1–12.

'The Hyphen as a Phonetic Sign', *Zeitschrift für Phonetik*, IX, 1956, 99–107.

*Cardinal Vowels*, Linguaphone Institute, London, 1956.

'Modern Trends in English Pronunciation', *Ici Londres* (BBC), 1957, no. 503 (17 Sept.), 6; shortened version in *London Calling Europe*, 1957, nos. 500 and 501.

*The History and Meaning of the Term 'Phoneme'*, International Phonetic Association, 1957.

(With W.E.Skillend) *Report on the Koreanization of Foreign Words*, presented to the Korean Language Society, Seoul, 1957.

'The Use of Syllabic and Non-syllabic l and n in Derivatives of English Words ending in Syllabic l and n', *Zeitschrift für Phonetik*, XII, 1959, 136–144.

'Arthur Lloyd James' in *Dictionary of National Biography 1941–50*, Oxford, 1959, 430.

'Phonetics', in *Chambers's Encyclopædia*, 1959.

Obituary notices, all in *Maître Phonétique*: Henry Sweet, July–Aug. 1912, 97–99; W. Temple Gairdner, July–Sept. 1928, 49–51; Max Walter, Jan.–Mar. 1935, 2; William Tilly, Oct.–Dec. 1935, 61–63; Lilias Armstrong, Jan.–Mar. 1938, 2; Paul Passy, July–Sept. 1941, 30–39; Christian Cloos, July–Dec. 1942, 13–14; Otto Jespersen, July–Dec. 1943, 17–20; Georges Thudichum (in the same article); Walter Ripman, Jan.–June 1947, 2–3; Sophie Lund, July–Dec. 1948, 18–20; E. R. Edwards, July–Dec. 1948, 20; L. Sčerba (in the same article); Ida Ward, Jan.–June 1950, 2–3; Harold Palmer, Jan.–June 1950, 4–7; Simon Boyanus, July–Dec. 1952, 20–22; H-J. Uldall, July–Dec. 1957, 30–31; (with M. Chapallaz) Amerindo Camilli, July–Dec. 1960, 22.

## REVIEWS

Alexander Graham Bell, *The Mechanism of Speech*, *Maître Phonétique*, May–June 1907, 66–67.

Henry Cecil Wyld, *The Historical Study of the Mother Tongue*, *Maître Phonétique*, Sept.–Oct. 1907, 98–100.

Paul Verrier, *Principes de la Métrique Anglaise*, *Maître Phonétique*, July–Aug. 1910, 111–112.

C. M. Doke, *The Phonetics of the Zulu Language*, *Maître Phonétique*, Oct.–Dec. 1926, 36–37.

C. M. Doke, *The Problem of Word Division in Bantu*, *Maître Phonétique*, Jan.–Mar. 1930, 2–3.

G. Laziczius, *Egy Magyar Mássalhangzóváltozás Phonologiája*, *Maître Phonétique*, Apr.–June 1931, 24–25.

H. J. Melzian, *Die Frage der Mitteltöne im Duala*, *Maître Phonétique*, Apr.–June 1932, 38–39.

Harold E. Palmer, *The Principles of Romanization*, *Maître Phonétique*, Apr.–June 1933, 28–30.

Walter Ripman, *A Pocket Dictionary of English Rhymes*, *Maître Phonétique*, Apr.–June 1933, 31.

A. Barbeau and E. Rodhe, *Dictionnaire Phonétique de la Langue Française*, *Maître Phonétique*, Apr.–June 1933, 33–34.

Otto Jespersen, *Linguistica*, *Maître Phonétique*, Oct.–Dec. 1934, 98–100.

John S. Kenyon and Thomas A. Knott, *A Pronouncing Dictionary of American English*, *Maître Phonétique*, Jan.–June 1944, 7.

R. Curry, *The Mechanism of the Human Voice*, *Maître Phonétique*, July–Dec. 1945, 30–31.

Peter A. D. MacCarthy, *An English Pronouncing Vocabulary*, *Maître Phonétique*, Jan.–June 1946, 4.

A. S. Hornby and E. C. Parnwell, *An English-Reader's Dictionary*, *Maître Phonétique*, Jan.–June 1953, 15.

A. N. Tucker and J. Tompo Ole Mpaayei, *A Maasai Grammar*, *Maître Phonétique*, July–Dec. 1956, 48–50.

## GRAMOPHONE RECORDS

*The Eight Cardinal Vowels* (1917). The Gramophone Company (His Master's Voice). B 804

*The Cardinal Vowels* (1943). Linguaphone Institute. DAJO 1/2

*The Cardinal Vowels* (1955). Linguaphone Institute.
Primary Vowels. ENG 252/253
Secondary Vowels and Cardinal Vowels compared with each other. ENG 254/255

*The English Vowels and Diphthongs; Voiced and Voiceless Consonants* (1921). Odeon, Berlin. A 66084/5

*Kulturkundliche Lautbücherei* (Wilhelm Doegen-Lautverlag) (1921). Extracts from *Phonetic Readings in English* and other English passages. Odeon, Berlin.

| | | | |
|---|---|---|---|
| A 66004 | A 66008/9 | A 66010/1 | A 66014 |
| A 66050/1 | A 66053 | A 66080/1 | A 66082 |

Extracts from *Metodisk Nybörjarbok i Engelska* (Björkelund-Danielsson) (1925). The Gramophone Company (His Master's Voice). X 1977–82

*English Conversational Course* (1929). Linguaphone Institute.

*The English Vowels and Diphthongs* (1932). Otto Sperling, Stuttgart. 3636

*English Spoken Here* (1932). Otto Sperling, Stuttgart. 3651–56

*Phonetic Readings in English* (1932). Otto Sperling, Stuttgart. 3637–43

*Pronunciation of Early XVIIth Century English—Shakespeare.* (1939). Linguaphone Institute. EE 47/48

*The Linguaphone English Course* (1949). Linguaphone Institute. ENG 146/147

*The New Method Records* (1959). Bokförlaget Niloe, Stockholm. HEP 1/2–9/10

PUBLISHED 1920–1930

*Phonetic Readings in English* and extracts from *The Pronunciation of English.* Deutsche Grammophon-Aktiengesellschaft (Sammlung Dr Driesen). 1678–85

Extracts from *Phonetic Readings in English.* Odeon, Berlin. AA 53816–29

Readings from *Hausknecht's Lehrbücher.* Odeon, Berlin. A 66086–123

Extracts from *Lehrbuch Lincke* (M.Diesterweg, Frankfurt-am-Main) Odeon, Berlin. AA 53802/3

# Daniel Jones: A Personal Tribute

A Professor Daniel Jones, hommage, respect, admiration, gratitude et affection.

J'ai l'honneur et le privilège de connaître Professor Daniel Jones depuis 1917.

Ayant été vaguement initiée à la phonétique par un de mes professeurs d'anglais, en France, et ayant vu une annonce relative à l'Association Internationale de Phonétique dans le *Journal of Education*, je me suis mise en rapport avec lui. En avril 1917, je suis venue à Londres suivre un cours de vacances dirigé par lui, et à partir de ce moment, je suis devenue son élève. Depuis, je n'ai jamais cessé de travailler avec lui et pour lui.

Professor Daniel Jones est connu dans le monde entier par ses travaux. Ses dons naturels, sa culture, son souci de l'exactitude, sa clarté dans la pensée et dans l'expression de ses idées, sa générosité, toutes ces qualités ont fait de lui un phonéticien exceptionnel, un chercheur de premier ordre et un maître incomparable. Il est de ceux qui croient que la science n'a sa raison d'être que si elle est appliquée, et le côté pédagogique de la phonétique a également été soigneusement cultivé par lui.

De plus, à côté du phonéticien et du pédagogue, on retrouve toujours le mathématicien, le musicien, l'homme de loi et le philosophe.

Il a su inspirer ses élèves en travaillant uniquement pour le développement de la science. Son but était de former des phonéticiens qui seraient capables de continuer son œuvre.

Si j'ai moi-même contribué quelque peu au développement de la science phonétique par mes recherches et par mon enseignement, c'est à la formation que j'ai reçue de lui, à ses encouragements et à sa direction que je le dois.

*Hélène N. Coustenoble*

# General Phonetics

# On Quantity and Quantitative Verse

W.S.ALLEN

It is common practice to contrast the 'accentual' verse of a modern language such as English with a 'quantitative' type represented by ancient Greek or Latin. 'It is, in fact,' writes Beare,[1] 'almost impossible for us to appreciate a purely quantitative rhythm, a rhythm not of "pulse" but of "pattern".' This hypothesis of 'the delicate ear of the ancients', as Stetson has satirically named it,[2] implies that, whereas in modern verse the rhythms are marked by 'stress', the classical rhythms were expressed solely in terms of time-ratios. It is sometimes felt necessary to support this hypothesis by pointing out that stress is not an essential of musical rhythm, and here the organ provides the consecrated example as an instrument possessing no stress mechanism. It is doubtful whether such an unequivocally stressless and time-measured rhythm can be demonstrated for any living Indo-European verse or language[3] (though the stresses may be linguistically non-significant or relatively unobtrusive); but in any case there is neither necessity nor evidence for drawing such a distinction in order to account for the nature of Greek or Latin prosody.

The purpose of this paper is to approach the matter from a rather more practical standpoint, and so perhaps to dispel a certain amount of spurious mystique. The following basic postulates will be adopted:

(a) The underlying material of verse is language. Therefore we should not attribute to verse phenomena which are not present (albeit in less stylized form) in the language upon which it is founded.[4]

(b) There is no special correlation between the chronological and typological classification of languages. Therefore, unless there is clear evidence to prove it, we should not attribute to a 'dead' language or its verse phenomena which are not observed in any living language or verse.

It is of course also assumed that we are dealing with something composed to be spoken aloud, and not read silently from the written page (a faculty that is in any case comparatively recent).

It is true that from the historical standpoint classical Latin verse is based on Greek models; but since there are certain connections between verse-rhythm and word-accent[5] in Latin, which are lacking in Greek, it is logically and practically preferable to begin by considering the relation between Latin verse and language.

Latin, like Greek, possessed a clearly defined word-accent, but differed from Greek in that the accent was dynamic rather than tonal, i.e. manifested in terms of 'stress' rather than pitch. This does not of course rule out the possibility, indeed probability, that in Latin, as in other 'stress-languages', the accent may, from a phonetic standpoint, have included important pitch-components.[6] The view that the classical Latin accent was tonal, however, in the manner of Greek – a view held mainly by French scholars – must be rejected; the arguments in its support are phonologically[7] unconvincing, but this is not the place for a detailed refutation, and the dynamic nature of the accent will be assumed.

The rules for the *location* of the classical Latin accent are simple and well known. It falls on the penultimate syllable if this is heavy; or on the antepenultimate if the penultimate is light. Obvious exceptions are provided in the case of monosyllables, of syncopated and apocopated forms (e.g. *illíc* < *illíce*), and of disyllables with light penultimate. But the general rule may be interpreted in terms of a preference for the stress to fall on a heavy syllable; it falls elsewhere only *faute de mieux* – thus on a light antepenultimate only because of the over-riding three-syllable rule, which will not permit it to recede further, and on a light penultimate when there is no antepenultimate (in such a case the phenomenon of 'iambic shortening', whereby the final syllable is lightened, gives a hint of its exceptional status[8]); no monosyllables are inherently light.

The rules of syllabic *weight* ('quantity') are similarly well defined. Those syllables are heavy which contain a long vowel (e.g. *pō*-tus), or a consonantal closure (e.g. *pěc*-tus), or both (e.g. *pāc*-tus); all other syllables are light – i.e. which contain a short vowel and are open (e.g. *pě*-cus). The statement of these rules is often confused in traditional and pedagogical accounts by a failure to distinguish 'long' and 'short' as properties of vowels from 'heavy' and 'light' as properties of syllables. This error goes back to the Greek and Latin grammarians; the Greeks, failing to observe the distinction, assumed that only a syllable containing a long vowel could be long 'by nature' (*φύσει*), so that a syllable containing a short vowel could only be considered long 'by convention' (θέσει); confusion is then worse confounded when the Latin translation of θέσει by *positione* is understood as 'by position', and the short vowel as actually becoming long before the consonant-group![9] The confusion is avoidable (and increasingly avoided) by adopting the distinction made by the incomparably more sophisticated ancient Indian grammarians, whereby the terms *guru* (heavy) and *laghu* (light) are applied to syllabic quantity.

In the Latin language the concept of quantity has only one function – to determine which syllable of a word may be stressed. So far as the language is concerned, therefore, *the rules of quantity are rules of stressability*. The nature of these rules is incidentally a strong additional argument in favour of a non-tonal accent for Latin; for whereas in Greek, as befits a tonal accent, the rules governing its location involve only the *intonable*, vocalic elements of the (final) syllable – thus ἀνθρώπου but ἄνθρωπος and even e.g. κῆρυξ—the rules for the location of the Latin accent may involve *non-intonable*, consonantal elements – thus re-*lĭ′c*-tus as re-*lā́*-tus.[10] In Latin, then, heavy syllables are syllables which qualify as potential stress-bearers, and light syllables are syllables which do not thus qualify except under special conditions.

From the classical Latin language we may pass to classical Latin verse. Here we find that in each foot (of a 'dactylic' or 'iambic' line – to take the principal metres common to both Greek and Latin) there is a 'strong' position (initial in the former, final in the latter metre), where the syllable has an almost invariable quantitative value; and an 'ictus', or 'beat', is commonly said to fall upon this syllable. This sense of the term 'ictus' is not entirely in accordance with ancient usage, but it will be convenient to accept it. Now the important point is that the rules for the structure of the syllable in this 'strong' position are the same as for the structure of accented syllables in the Latin language – it must (with the exception in iambics of the final foot and of very limited resolutions[11]) be a heavy syllable, whereas the rest of the foot in a 'dactylic' hexameter consists optionally of a heavy or (except in the final foot) two light, and in an 'iambic trimeter' of a heavy (odd feet only) or a light or occasionally two light.

It has been acknowledged that the classical Latin metrical schemes are based upon Greek patterns; and the phenomenon of the 'syllaba anceps', whereby after a short vowel a stop followed by a liquid may optionally be allotted to the preceding syllable (as *păt*-ris), thereby rendering it heavy, is undoubtedly borrowed from Greek. But it is scarcely credible that the Greek models would ever have been so readily and generally adopted if their conventions had been entirely alien to the phonological structure of the Latin language. It is reasonable therefore to suppose that, since the rules for the placing of the verse ictus are identical in principle with those for the placing of the linguistic accent, the nature of ictus and accent must have been similar, and that the ictus must consequently have been manifested by stress.

Thus in both language and verse, so far as Latin is concerned, the 'rules of quantity' will have been rules of stressability. In verse, as in the language, not every heavy syllable is stressed; it is only *stressable*, subject to the limiting positional rules governing words in the language and feet in verse. The ictus may then be regarded as a stylized culminative accent, bearing to the feet of the verse the same relation as the accent bears to the words of the language – i.e. occurring once and only once in each case, but stylized in verse to the extent that it is only rarely permitted to fall on a light syllable.

Thus far we have been concerned only with Latin. But bearing in mind that we are proceeding logically from the more to the less evident correlations, and not in historical order, we may go on to apply our conclusions to Greek. For the rules governing the placing of the ictus in Greek verse are based on precisely the same principle, i.e. the incidence of heavy quantity, and on the same definition of quantity. If, therefore, the ictus of classical Latin verse was manifested by stress, it is reasonably certain that the same applied to Greek verse – i.e. that here also the rules of quantity are rules of stressability. There is, however, the difference that in Greek the verse ictus would not be of the same nature as the (tonal) culminative accent of Greek words (nor is there any correlation between the two earlier than Babrius and Nonnus[12]: ancient Greek metre entirely disregards the linguistic accent); and we have established the principle that one should not attribute to verse phenomena which are not at least potentially present in the language.

But the fact that a language does not have a dynamic word-accent is no indication that it has no variations of stress; the variation is likely to be less than in a dynamically accented language, and to be a function of sentence rather than word rhythm[13] (as, conversely, intonation in a non-tonal language) – but there is probably no language in which it is entirely lacking. And if, as we presume, the rules of quantity in Greek verse have a basis in the Greek language, then it is reasonable to suppose that it was precisely the heavy syllables which were liable to receive stress in the rhythmic pattern of the sentence. That syllabic quantity, as well as vowel-length, did in fact function as a linguistic feature in

Greek, is shown by the parallelism, for instance, of *λεπτότερος* with *ὠμότερος* (showing short vowel after heavy syllable) as against *σοφώτερος* (showing long vowel after light syllable). And that quantity was not simply a matter of duration was recognized by the Greeks themselves, since e.g. *ἤ* was observed to have the same (heavy) quantity as *σπλήν*, just as the first syllable of *στρόφος* has the same (light) quantity as that of *ὁδός*.[14] The stress-pattern of the Greek verse-line will then represent a stylization of the freer stress-pattern of the Greek sentence.

One may here note incidentally a further argument against the hypothesis of a tonal accent for Latin. If identity of rules implies similarity in the original nature of the phenomenon which they govern, then the Latin accent was similar to the Greek ictus; and if the Latin accent were tonal, then the Greek ictus would be tonal; and since the Greek ictus bears no relation to the Greek accent, we should have to admit for Greek the existence of a double tonality, governed by different sets of rules.

It is now possible to compare Greek and classical Latin verse from the standpoint of its stress element. In Greek, since the linguistic word-accent is tonal and the verse-ictus is dynamic, it is irrelevant to speak either of concord or of conflict between ictus and accent.[15] There may nevertheless have been a certain tension between the rigid stress-pattern of the metre and the stress-pattern normal to the same or similar sequences of words in the course of non-poetic utterance. Such tension however, would not be particularly strong, since any given heavy syllable might in normal speech be sometimes stressed and sometimes unstressed, according to the pattern of the sentence in which it occurred.

In Latin, the fact that both ictus and accent were dynamic served in one sense to bind language and verse more closely – the ictus being simply a stylization of the accent, and the foot in consequence a kind of stylized word. But this very fact provided a source of tension far in excess of anything in Greek; for there could be either direct concord or direct conflict between ictus and accent – a situation that presented the Latin poet with certain difficulties and opportunities entirely unknown to Greek. The ictus might fall on a non-accented syllable, or an accented syllable might bear no ictus. It is well known that in the cadence of the Latin dactylic hexameter the agreement between ictus and accent approaches 100%; it is on the other hand equally notorious that in the rest of the line disagreement is rather the rule – a situation encouraged by preferences regarding caesurae.[16] A consecutive hundred lines chosen at random from the *Aeneid* show the following proportions of cases where the ictus falls on an accented syllable in the various feet:

| 1 | 2 | 3 | 4 | 5 | 6 |
|---|---|---|---|---|---|
| 55% | 28% | 15% | 28% | 97% | 99% |

Thus in the third foot, for example, conflict in the 'strong' position is nearly six times as frequent as concord (85:15). Conflict in the 'weak' position (i.e. the occurrence there of an accented syllable) shows the following proportions:

| | | | | | |
|---|---|---|---|---|---|
| 54% | 82% | 69% | 22% | 2% | 1% |

A typical example of both types of conflict is seen in a line such as:

*ín*de tó*rō* páter *Ae*nḗ*ās* síc *ór*sus ab *ál*tō

(where acutes indicate the word-accent and italics the verse-ictus); the overall pattern of agreement and conflict for weak and strong positions in this line may be indicated as follows (agreement 1, conflict 0):

1 0 / 0 0 / 0 0 / 0 0 / 1 1 / 1 1

For the hundred lines the averaged pattern would be:

1 0 / 0 0 / 0 0 / 0 1 / 1 1 / 1 1

It might appear that where, as commonly in Latin,[17] conflict reaches these proportions, there can be little connection between the prosodies of the language and its poetry. But to accept this conclusion would be to ignore an important feature of Latin phonology. For in the Latin language there are not simply accentually stressed and unstressed syllables, but also a third category of *stressable* syllables[18] – i.e. syllables having precisely the same 'heavy' phonematic structure as accented syllables, but being unaccented in consequence of the positional rules – e.g. the first syllable of a word such as *conténtus* or *dēdicā́tus*, or the last syllable of *plū́rimōs*. Such syllables are likely in many cases to have borne a secondary stress,[19] and may under favourable conditions have received a primary stress (as e.g. *plūrimṓs-que*, with a following enclitic); and on the other hand the accentual stress of the grammatically isolated word is likely to have been partially subordinated in actual speech to the requirements of phrase and sentence rhythm[20] (just as word-tones in tonal languages may be 'perturbed' by their environment). There are in fact clear indications of such tendencies in Plautus and Terence.[21]

Thus when the ictus falls on a syllable which is, in the word-isolate, unaccented, it is nevertheless falling on an accentable *type* of syllable, which may indeed in some circumstances have been stressed in normal speech; the conflict is therefore less violent than it might appear *a priori*.[22] And it is in the recognition of this category of stressable syllables that the real difference between 'quantitative' and 'accentual' verse lies.

Since it has now been suggested that the rules of quantity in classical verse are simply rules of stressability, and since modern 'accentual' verse is also patterned in terms of stress, it might appear that the distinction between the two forms has been blurred. But in fact a clear distinction still remains, though it differs from that traditionally assumed. The nature of accent and ictus in Greek, Latin, and English may be summarized as follows:

| | *Accent* | *Ictus* |
|---|---|---|
| GREEK | tonal | dynamic |
| LATIN | dynamic | dynamic |
| ENGLISH | dynamic | dynamic |

But this tells only half the story. For whereas Latin has stressed, unstressed, and stressable syllables (in the sense defined above), English syllables are either stressed or unstressed (or of a particular degree of stress) relatively to their environment, and there is no structurally defined 'stressable' category; for stress in English is not a direct function of the phonematic structure of syllables.[23]

This has the important consequence that a conflict of ictus and accent in English verse is a much more violent matter than in Latin; and such conflict is comparatively rare, being mainly confined to certain well-defined, 'normal' deviations – such as, for example, in the iambic pentameter, the inverted first foot and the hypermetric final. It is true that in terms of a binary stress-system for the English language (stressed: unstressed) the conflicts might appear to be very frequent; but recent studies working on the basis of a four-stress system[24] have shown (as already Jespersen in his excellent 'Notes on metre'[25]) that in these terms there is very little conflict, the second syllable of each foot in an iambic line being stronger than the first except in comparatively few cases. This agreement between ictus and accent is the more complete if it is accepted that of two successive syllables having the same integral degree of linguistic stress the second is normally fractionally stronger.[26]

This should not be taken to imply an acceptance of the 4-term (Smith-Trager) stress system; but whether one adopts a system of two or more significant degrees of stress, it is certain that there are a number of gradations, significant or otherwise; and we need only concern ourselves with the *relative* strength or weakness of the syllables in a foot – 'In a spoken system where the only absolute value, the ictus, consists only in a relationship, we needlessly pursue a too-close enquiry into the precise strength of the stronger point in the relationship.'[27]

This lack of conflict, on the other hand, does not mean that there is no 'tension' in English verse. But the tension consists not so much in direct clashes between ictus and accent as in the fact of a 2-term ictus-system being imposed upon a widely variable linguistic stress-pattern[28]; in an iambic foot, for example, the ictus relationship of the syllables is absolutely weak : absolutely strong[29]; whereas the corresponding linguistic stress relationship of the same syllables is relatively weak : relatively strong, the actual strengths of the two syllables, and the differences between them, varying from foot to foot – 'There is no line so regular (so *evenly* alternating weak and strong) that it does not show some tension.'[30]

The conclusions that emerge are thus as follows. The distinction between 'accentual' and 'quantitative' verse has nothing to do with the nature of the ictus, which in both cases is manifested by stress – the difference lies in the nature of the interrelation between the metrical and linguistic stress-patterns. An understanding of the nature of quantitative verse involves the recognition of a category of 'stressable' syllables; and the so-called 'rules of quantity' are simply rules of stressability.

At this point it seems advisable to express certain reservations about the nature of what we have been calling 'stress'. We apply this name to the phenomena traditionally so called in reference to English. The precise nature of these phenomena is still a subject of current research; but it is clear that they involve more than mere force of articulation, as has been traditionally assumed; and it may be that duration is in fact one of the most significant components. But whatever may be the final solution of this extremely difficult phonetic problem, the present argument is in no way affected, since the object has been to demonstrate that there is no reason to believe that the phenomena called 'stress' and 'quantity' are substantially different; and if it eventually emerges that English is in fact more 'quantitative' than is generally supposed, this can only help to strengthen their identification.

Finally some tentative suggestions may be made concerning the manner in which classical Latin verse was probably spoken. The point at issue is whether, in cases of conflict, the verse-ictus or the linguistic accent predominated. The modern tendency is to assume the latter, and it is customary to suggest the improbability of the former by reference to modern parallels; it is pointed out that if one were to allow the metre to predominate in a line such as

'Burned after them to the bottomless pit',

the result would be a ridiculous distortion of the language (e.g. *bottómless*); the alternative involves some distortion of the metre, 'but provided there is sufficient general agreement to keep the pattern present in our minds, minor clashes, so far from disturbing our enjoyment, may even lend it a subtler flavour. There is no necessity to alter the normal pronunciation of words merely to bring out the metre.'[31]

But to speak of 'general agreement' and 'minor clashes' in reference, for example, to the Latin dactylic hexameter would be a gross misrepresentation – for conflict is here the more general rule; and if the linguistic accent were permitted everywhere to predominate, there would consequently be no means of indicating the metrical pattern, even on a statistical basis, or of keeping it in mind (apart from the marginal possibility of inferring it for the first four feet from the pattern of the final two). As Wimsatt and Beardsley remark even of English verse,[32] 'A good dramatic, or poetic, reading will tend to bring out the tensions – but note well that in order to do this it must be careful not to override completely and kill the meter. When that is done, the tensions vanish.'

Moreover, so far as Greek is concerned, we have no reason to assume that the verse was read with other than a predominantly metrical rhythm, since there were no positively conflicting linguistic stresses. It would be surprising, therefore, if the Romans, in taking over the conventions of Greek metre, proceeded to ignore the rhythm which those conventions were designed to ensure.

This does not mean to say that in speaking Latin verse the linguistic accent was necessarily completely suppressed. It is possible that an accented syllable in weak position would receive more than a minimum degree of stress, and that an unaccented syllable in strong position would receive less than a maximum degree of stress; one could envisage, for example, a possible scale of stresses somewhat as follows:

(1) ictus on accented syllable;
(2) ictus on unaccented syllable;
(3) accented heavy syllable without ictus;
(4) unaccented heavy syllable without ictus;
(5) accented light syllable;
(6) unaccented light syllable.

But if a clear metrical pattern were to emerge, the ictus must have prevailed over the accent at least relatively and in at least a majority of cases.

From a pedagogical standpoint it has been remarked of English verse-reading[33] that: 'Schoolteachers nowadays . . . probably try much too hard to prevent their students from a "mechanical" or thumped-out scansion. . . . The meter . . . tends to be over-ridden and, if not actually destroyed (as it cannot be in any correct reading), at least obscured.' If this is the result for English verse, how much more so would it be for Latin with its vastly more prevalent conflicts. Admittedly a metrical reading tends to obscure the linguistic accent – but the language as such is not thereby diminished, since its rhythms are maintained in ordinary usage, and continue to provide the norm against which poetic tensions are measured; whereas the metre exists only in the poetry, and if it were there suppressed it would be lost completely, thereby precluding any possibility of tension.[34] It might be objected that the rigorous application of this principle would lead to a 'stilted' and 'unnatural' performance; but it is as well to remember, as A. Y. Winters points out in a chapter on 'The Audible Reading of Poetry',[35] that: 'A poem in the very nature of the case is a formal statement; and the reading of a poem is thus a formal occasion.' And in any case the existence in the Latin language of a category of stressable though unaccented syllables serves to cushion the impact of metrical rigour.

It may nevertheless be prudent to anticipate a possible charge of inconsistency – namely that, even allowing for the existence of this 'buffer' category, there is no other culture whose principal forms of verse show such a marked discrepancy between ictus and dynamic linguistic accent; and that in proposing it we are therefore in a sense betraying the principle (b) assumed on p. 3. On the supposition that Latin is in fact unique in this respect, the objection has some force; but the uniqueness could well be explained as the result of special historical circumstances. We have argued (p. 5) that Latin would not have adopted Greek metrical systems so readily if their conventions had been entirely alien to the Latin language; and we have shown that they were in fact peculiarly appropriate. But one can still admit that, without the influence of the Greek models, Latin would not 'naturally' have evolved such conventions (as in fact its native verse never did); in which case the relationship between classical Latin verse and language is of an abnormal type by comparison with independent developments of poetry from language, and so may well be unique. We could then say that, as a result of adapting itself to Greek conventions, Latin poetry was enabled to realize certain latent potentialities of its own language, which it might otherwise never have discovered.[36]

## *Notes*

[1] W. Beare, *Latin Verse and European Song*, London, 1957, 57; cf. P. Maas, *Griechische Metrik*, Leipzig and Berlin, 1929, § 4.

[2] R. H. Stetson, *Bases of Phonology*, Oberlin, Ohio, 1945, 71.

[3] Cf. F. Crusius, H. Rubenbauer, *Römische Metrik*, 2nd ed., München, 1955, 30; A. Schmitt, 'Musikalischer Akzent und antike Metrik', *Orbis Antiquus*, x, Münster, 1953, 16; A. W. de Groot, 'Phonetics in its Relation to Aesthetics', *Manual of Phonetics*, ed. L. Kaiser, Amsterdam, 1957, 385 ff., 393 ff. This does not, of course, mean to say that duration may not be a common concomitant of stress: cf. R. Jakobson and M. Halle, *Fundamentals of Language*, 's-Gravenhage, 1956, 24 f., and observations on p. 10, below.

[4] Cf. H. L. Smith, 'Towards redefining English Prosody', *Studies in Linguistics*, XIV, 3–4, 1959, 70, and also in E. L. Epstein and T. Hawkes, *Linguistics and English Prosody*, Studies in Linguistics Occasional Papers, VII, Buffalo, 1959, 5; M. Beck, 'Poznámky ke vztahu německého jazyka a verše', *Sborník Prací Filosofické Fakulty Brněnské University*, A VIII, 4, 1960, 69 ff.

[5] 'Accent' is here and subsequently used in its linguistic sense of a culminative feature, without regard to the nature of its manifestation.

[6] See e.g. D. L. Bolinger, 'A Theory of Pitch Accent in English', *Word*, XIV, 1958, 109 ff.; D. B. Fry, 'Experiments in the Perception of Stress', *Language and Speech*, I, 1958, 126 ff.; A. C. Gimson, 'The Linguistic Relevance of Stress', *Zeitschrift für Phonetik*, IX, 1956, 143 ff. (on English); W. Jassem, 'The Phonology of Polish Stress', *Word*, XV, 1959, 252 ff.

On the physiological independence of stress and pitch mechanisms, however, cf. Daniel Jones, *Outline of English Phonetics*, 9th ed., Cambridge, 1960, 246, n; W. F. Twaddell, 'Stetson's Model and the "Supra-segmental Phonemes"', *Language*, XXIX, 1953, 415 ff.

[7] On the phonological typology of accentuation, see especially R. Jakobson, 'Die Betonung und ihre Rolle in der Wort- und Syntagmaphonologie', *Travaux du Cercle Linguistique de Prague*, IV, 1931, 164 ff.

[8] Cf. J. Kuryłowicz, 'Latin and Germanic Metre', *English and German Studies*, II, 1948–1949, 34 ff. (also in *Esquisses Linguistiques*, Wrocław-Kraków, 1960, 294 ff.).

[9] Cf. R. Hiersche, 'Herkunft und Sinn des Terminus "positione longa"', *Forschungen und Fortschritte*, XXXI, 1957, 280 ff.

[10] Note also that whereas in Greek one or other mora of a long vowel or diphthong is accented (with the consequent possibility of contrasts such as οἴκοι = ὀίκοι : οἶκοι = ὄικοι), in Latin it is the syllable as a whole that is the accentual unit, and so does not require the concept of mora. On the phonological significance of these facts as an indication of accentual type see particularly Jakobson, *TCLP*, IV, 1939, 166 ff.; N. Trubetzkoy, *Grundzüge der Phonologie*, *TCLP*, VII, Prague, 1939, 193.

[11] On the question of apparent 'resolutions' (in fact something quite different) in

strong position in early Latin (and Germanic) verse, see Kuryłowicz, 'Latin and Germanic Metre'; cf. also J.Vendryes, *Recherches sur l'histoire et les effets de l'intensité initiale en Latin*, Paris, 1902, 132.

[12] By which time pitch was probably being replaced by stress as a culminative feature.

[13] For such a situation in Georgian cf. H.Vogt, 'Esquisse d'une Grammaire du Géorgien Moderne', *Norsk Tidsskrift for Sprogvidenskap*, IX, 1938, 325. On the possibility, however, of a dynamic culminative (and demarcative) word-accent in a language having (as Greek) a tonal differentiative, but non-demarcative, accent see Jakobson, 'Ueber die Beschaffenheit der prosodischen Gegensätze', *Mélanges van Ginneken*, Paris, 1937, 25 ff.; also C.M.Doke, *The Southern Bantu Languages*, London, 1954, 43.

[14] On lack of correlation between syllabic quantity (or even vowel 'length') and temporal duration cf. M.S.Ruiperez, 'Cantidad silábica y metrica estructural en griego antiguo', *Emerita*, XXIII, 1955, 79 ff.

[15] It might be argued on the basis of later developments that the Greek accent included a stress component; but there is no evidence whatever for this in ancient times: cf. E.Sturtevant, *The Pronunciation of Greek and Latin*, 2nd ed., Philadelphia, 1940, §§ 108 ff.

[16] Cf. Crusius-Rubenbauer, *Römische Metrik*, 54 f.

[17] On attempts by some poets to improve the proportions of agreement elsewhere than in the cadence, and on similar developments in the second verse of the elegiac couplet, see especially Sturtevant, *The Pronunciation of Greek and Latin*, 184 f. and references.

[18] Cf. A.Heusler, *Deutsche Versgeschichte*, Leipzig, 1925–1929, 58.

[19] Cf. E.Fraenkel, *Iktus und Akzent im lateinischen Sprechvers*, Berlin, 1928, 351 f. It may be noted that even in the early Latin period of strong initial stress, short vowels in heavy syllables (as here defined) were less liable to weakening than in light syllables (e.g. *facio*; *reficio*, but *refectus*).

[20] For similar phenomena in English cf. Jones, *Outline*, §§ 931 ff.; Bolinger, 'Intersections of Stress and Intonation', *Word*, XI, 1955, 198 ff.

[21] Cf. Fraenkel, *Iktus u. Akzent*, 3 and references; Sturtevant, *The Pronunciation of Greek and Latin*, 182 f.

[22] Cf. Fraenkel, op. cit., 353.

[23] On correlations of stress with vowel-quality, however, cf. G.F.Arnold, 'Stress in English Words', *Lingua*, VI, 1957, 221–267, 397–441.

[24] Smith, *SIL*, XIV, 70; Epstein and Hawkes, *SIL Occ. Pap.*, VII; H. Whitehall, 'From Linguistics to Criticism', *Kenyon Review*, XVIII, 1956, 411 ff.; S.Chatman, ibid., 421 ff.

[25] First published in Danish in 1900; reprinted in English in O.Jespersen, *Linguistica*, Copenhagen, 1933, 249 f.

[26] Cf. Smith in Epstein and Hawkes, op. cit., 5.

[27] W.K.Wimsatt and M.C.Beardsley, 'The Concept of Meter: an Exercise in Abstraction', *Publications of the Modern Language Association of America*, LXXIV, 2, 1959, 594; cf. Jespersen, 'Notes on Metre', 255 f.; A. Y. Winters, *The Function of Criticism*; *Problems and Exercises*, Denver (Colorado), 1957, 93 f.

[28] These remarks on English verse are intended only to apply to the 'syllable-stress' metres, and not to older (and more recent) forms in which the dominant

factor is the pattern of primary linguistic stresses, with a consequent tendency to isochrony.

[29] In 'dipodic' metres (modern or classical) it would be possible to recognize three metrically significant stress-levels in the dipody (an analysis supported, e.g., by the different rules for odd and even feet in the Greek iambic trimeter); but the binary analysis still applies within each foot.

[30] Wimsatt and Beardsley, *Concept of Meter*, 596; cf. Chatman, *Kenyon Rev.*, XVIII, 421 ff.

[31] Beare, *Latin Verse*, 28.

[32] Wimsatt and Beardsley, *Concept of Meter*, 596; cf. Winters, *Function of Criticism*, 94.

[33] Wimsatt and Beardsley, *Concept of Meter*, 597.

[34] Cf. especially N.I. Herescu, *La Poésie Latine*, Paris, 1960, 27: 'L'accent verbal est donc nécessairement subordonné, dans le vers, à l'accent du pied ou ictus. S'il n'y avait pas d'ictus dans la versification, il n'y aurait pas de versification.'

[35] Winters, *Function of Criticism*, 84. Note also Fraenkel's striking statement (*Iktus und Akzent*, 343): 'Dichter und Zuhörer wissen, dass sie sich in einer ideellen Welt befinden, dass in der in Verse gefassten Sprache sich nicht so sehr ein Abbilden als ein Umsetzen des wirklichen Sprechens vollzieht. Demgemäss ist die Dichtersprache nur zu dem einen verpflichtet: alle ihre Erscheinungsformen müssen von der Art sein *οἷα ἂν γένοιτο*.'

[36] In this connection it may be mentioned that the Latin metrical equivalence of one heavy syllable to two light is most probably taken over from Greek; for such an equation can naturally arise in a language where accentual variation on a long vowel or diphthong gives rise to the concept of mora (cf. n. 10, and Ruiperez, *Cantidad silábica*, 79. It is perhaps significant that this equation does not apply to Aeolic verse – the dialect in this case having, like Latin, a fixed accent (apparent variation, as in *θῦμος* : *θύμου* is only phonetic and not phonological, the circumflex and acute being automatic variants of the same single accent, determined by the length of the vowel in the final syllable).

# Vowel and Consonant: A Phonological Definition Re-examined

G.F.ARNOLD

Following a statement by Bloomfield that phonology 'defines each phoneme by its rôle in the structure of speech forms',[1] O'Connor and Trim have advanced the view that, in phonology, the proper theoretical basis for the establishment of the vowel and consonant classes is the study of phoneme distribution.[2] This view they substantiate by an analysis of Southern British English according to the following method. The distribution of phonemes, the total inventory of which is assumed, is studied in the first two and last two positions in words. All the two-term phoneme combinations occurring initially and finally in words are listed, and every phoneme is compared with every other phoneme so as to determine the total number of contexts which each pair of phonemes share in respect of the four positions considered. This total of contexts common to each pair of phonemes is then expressed as a percentage of the total occurrence of the less widely distributed phoneme of the pair in question. A study of all the percentages thus derived allows the division of the phoneme inventory into two mutually exclusive classes, members of one class sharing more than a critical percentage of their contexts with each other and less than this same critical percentage of their contexts with members of the other class. For English, O'Connor and Trim fix this percentage at 50%. While it is desirable as a general principle that 50% should be the minimum figure, the actual critical percentage set up for any given language is to be the one which yields the fewest anomalous results.[3] Though the possibility is visualized that the two phoneme classes arrived at in this way may differ, perhaps widely, from the vowel and consonant classes as defined phonetically by Daniel Jones,[4] for example, there is none the less a remarkably close correspondence between the latter's phonetic categories and O'Connor and Trim's phonological ones. Since the original paper by O'Connor and Trim, the same method has been applied to French, modern Greek,[5] and Polish.[5] The analysis of

French[6] turns out to be as successful as that of English: two groups of phonemes are distinguished, differing little from the vowel and consonant classes as set up phonetically, for example by Armstrong.[7] The Greek and Polish results are less satisfactory.

For the analysis of Greek the assumed inventory of phonemes consists of 5 vowels[8] and 18 consonants, /i, e, a, o, u/ and /p, t, k, b, d, g, m, n, l, r, f, θ, s, x, v, ð, z, ɣ/. The 253 common context percentages scored by comparing every phoneme with every other phoneme in the four positions range from 32% to 100%. The 10 percentages accruing from V/V comparisons lie between 94% and 100%, the 153 percentages from C/C comparisons between 64% and 100% with only 6 results below 70%, and the 90 percentages from V/C comparisons between 32% and 94% with only 19 results below 70%. In Table 1 these same percentages are regrouped according to whether they fall within a high, middle, or low range; the figures for Polish will be discussed later, while those for French are included for comparison.

TABLE 1

| % RANGE | NUMBER OF PERCENTAGES | | |
|---|---|---|---|
| | *Greek* | *French* | *Polish* |
| 70–100 | 228 | 272 | 126 |
| 40–69 | 24 | 94 | 393 |
| Below 40 | 1 | 264 | 147 |

The actual number of percentages within each range in each language is not in itself important, since this is in some measure dependent on the over-all size of the phoneme inventory, which differs from language to language. What is important is the relationship between the totals in the three ranges in each language. The high percentages are obtained from comparisons of phonemes obviously belonging to the same class, the low percentages from comparisons of phonemes clearly members of different classes. The middle-range percentages on the other hand are provided by comparisons of phonemes which are unquestionably established neither as members of the same class nor as members of different classes. If, therefore, a language is to yield two mutually exclusive groups of phonemes according to the method outlined above, it must concentrate the greater majority of its common context percentages in the high and low ranges and at the same time ensure that its middle range contains fewest percentages. As the above table shows, French conforms to this pattern while Greek, with its virtual absence of percentages in the low range, does not. The conclusion is therefore that, in Greek, no simple dichotomous grouping of the phonemes listed is possible if the analysis is based strictly on the method described by O'Connor and Trim. The analysis does of course throw up certain small-scale differences and similarities of distribution: /u/, for example, is to be classed with /i, e, a, o/, the relevant percentages ranging from 98% to 100%, rather than with the remaining phonemes in comparison with which /u/ never scores more than 64%. Any phoneme groups established on the basis of these minor distributional differences and similarities would, however, be small, numerous, and overlapping.

The phoneme inventory assumed for Polish consists of 8 vowels, /i, e, ɑ, o, u, y, õ, ẽ/, and 29 consonants, /p, t, c, k, b, d, ɟ, g, f, s, ʃ, ɕ, x, v, z, ʒ, ʑ, ʦ, ʣ, ʧ, ʨ, ʥ, l, ɫ, m, n, ɲ, r, j/. The 28 V/V comparisons have a range of from 30% to 100%, the 406 C/C comparisons a range of from 8% to 100% and the 232 V/C comparisons a range of from 0% to 69%. Reference to Table 1 shows that, though Polish does not exhibit the disproportion, noted in Greek, between the high and low ranges – the percentages in these ranges in Polish are in fact roughly equal in number – in no sense can these percentages be said to be concentrated in the high and low ranges: considerably more than half, 393 out of a total of 666, fall within the middle range. Since in any language, analysed according to the O'Connor and Trim method, the critical percentage for the division of its phonemes into two groups must in general be sought between the minimum and maximum of this middle range, it is clear that, when the majority of percentages are concentrated in the middle range, the number of anomalous[3] results is likely to constitute a high proportion of the total results. In Polish the minimum of anomalous results is almost certainly achieved when the phoneme inventory is divided into two classes corresponding exactly to the above vowel and consonant groupings and when the critical common context percentage is fixed at either 36% or 40%: both figures give 144 anomalous results, somewhat more than one-fifth of the total of 666. In this respect Polish compares very unfavourably with both English and French: English has a mere 20 anomalies in a total of 1081 results; and French, with the percentage fixed at 60%, 21 in a total of 630. The comparison is even less favourable if the critical percentage in Polish is set at the more reasonable figure of 50%, the anomalies now numbering 160. The conclusion is that the method, as outlined by O'Connor and Trim, does not lead to a satisfactory division of the assumed phoneme inventory of Polish into two mutually exclusive classes of phonemes. Contrary to what has been noted in the case of Greek, however, a division is possible in Polish, but the high proportion of anomalies which result makes this division unsatisfactory.

The measure of similarity has been the same for all four languages: the total number of contexts shared by any pair of phonemes is expressed as a percentage of the total occurrence in all the four word positions of the less widely distributed phoneme of the pair under consideration. Statistically this is, as O'Connor and Trim say, a rather crude measure of similarity; and certainly it tends to mask certain rather obvious differences of distribution. Such would be the case, for example, in an imaginary language where phonemes /a/ and /b/ occur 20 times and phoneme /c/ 40 times and where all three phonemes share 20 contexts with each other; the three resulting comparisons each score 100%, although phoneme /c/ occurs twice as often as the other two. As the example from the imaginary language shows, this measure of similarity takes no account of the unique occurrences of phonemes: the 20 unique occurrences of phoneme /c/ are in no way reflected by the final general figure of 100%. Nor does the measure of similarity take into account what may be called the spread of any pair of phonemes, that is to say, the total number of different contexts in which either or both occur: for /a/ and /b/ the spread is 20, for /a/ and /c/ and for /b/ and /c/ the spread is 40. Considerations such as these prompt speculation as to whether some other measure of similarity, taking note of unique occurrences of phonemes, the spread of each pair of phonemes, and maybe other features of phoneme distribution, could be devised so that, statistically, it would perhaps be less subject to criticism and would at the same time deal adequately with all four languages. If this were possible, such a measure, so far as the four languages are concerned at any rate, would be preferable to the original measure of similarity which, while satisfactory for English and French, is inadequate for Polish and apparently impossible for Greek.

As yet the present author has been able to apply only one new measure of similarity to all four languages. This measure entails expressing the total unique occurrences of any pair of phonemes as a percentage of the total spread of the same two phonemes. In this measure, unlike the original one, similarity of distribution is shown by low percentages which are obtained when two phonemes have relatively few unique occurrences: 0% would thus indicate two phonemes with identical distributions. The results of applying this new measure to English, French, and Polish are considerably less satisfactory than those obtained by the original measure: the two fairly clear-cut phoneme groupings, provided by the latter in English and French, are now no longer apparent, and the number of anomalous percentages in Polish is somewhat increased. Greek, on the other hand, responds quite well to this new measure: the assumed phoneme inventory is divided into two classes corresponding exactly to the vowel and consonant groupings given above. The 10 V/V comparisons range from 8% to 28%, the 153 C/C comparisons from 0% to 66% with only 2 exceeding 60%, and the 90 V/C comparisons from 60% to 90% with only 10 below 70%. If an admittedly rather high 61% is taken as the critical percentage, the anomalous results number no more than 3.

From the varying responses of English and Greek, for example, to the two measures of similarity so far tried out, it seems clear that, unless and until a measure is set up which will deal adequately with all four languages and any others to be analysed along the same lines, the satisfactory division of the phonemes of a given language into two mutually exclusive classes according to their distribution in the first two and last two positions in words depends to some considerable extent upon the measure of similarity which is employed. As yet too few languages have been analysed in this way and too few measures of similarity tested for us to be able to say whether a single, all-embracing measure of similarity is a possibility. This much, however, can be said. Since the object of any such measure is to enable us to allocate to the same class phonemes which rarely, if ever, display identity of distribution and each of which is often characterized by clearly-marked individual peculiarities of distribution, the best results will probably be provided by a measure which, though perhaps statistically crude, is essentially simple. The more detailed the features of phoneme distribution that are incorporated into a measure of similarity, the more likely it is that the measure will emphasize the individual distributional characteristics of any phoneme and obscure those features which the phoneme may share with any other phoneme; and the phoneme inventory will thereby be divided, not into two mutually exclusive classes, but into smaller, more numerous, and overlapping groups. This is certainly the case with English and French, for which languages the original, simpler measure is so far the best. Only to Greek, of the four languages as yet analysed, does the more complex measure bring improvement; and this improvement may not be as important as it first seems, since Greek presents certain distributional features which run counter to the ideal distribution presupposed by O'Connor and Trim's general thesis. A language exemplifying this ideal distribution would permit only vowel and consonant alternation in the first two and last two positions in words and all possible VC and CV combinations would be found.[9] In Greek, by contrast, the VV occurrence initially in words is relatively high, 12 out of a possible total of 25 occurrences, while the VC occurrence finally in words is unusually low, only 13 out of a maximum of 90. It may therefore be that, rather than seek a measure of similarity which will accommodate the contrasting types of phoneme distribution presented by English, French, and possibly Polish on the one hand and Greek on the other, we should look no further than the measure devised by O'Connor and Trim and conclude that some languages, including Greek, do not respond to the kind of analysis they have outlined. In these circumstances it is important to understand the implications of their measure of similarity. Data from the four languages already analysed are now sufficient to allow us to sketch some of the features of phoneme distribution which, if found in a language, promise a successful application of this original measure of similarity to that language.

Let us first of all assume a model language with two mutually exclusive groups of phonemes: the consonant class contains 10 phonemes, the vowel class 5 phonemes, including /a/. Since this is a model language, all possible VC and CV combinations occur initially and finally in words, but there are no occurrences of VV and CC sequences. Thus every vowel occurs four times the total number of consonants, that is, 40 occurrences, and every consonant four times the total number of vowels, that is, 20 occurrences. When every vowel is compared with every other vowel, the common context percentage is 100% in each case: all 5 vowels have their 40 contexts in common and the minimum total vowel occurrence is also 40. Consonant comparisons likewise score 100%: all 10 consonants share 20 contexts and the minimum total consonant occurrence is 20. On the other hand when any vowel is compared with any consonant 0% results: there are no common contexts and the minimum total phoneme occurrence (in this case, consonant) is 20.

In the vast majority of languages this simple, clearly marked dichotomy will be complicated by the random occurrence of VV or CC sequences or both and/or by the chance absence of any VC or CV sequences or both, whether initially or finally in words. Let us now suppose the occurrence at word beginnings of the VV sequence /aa/.[10] This occurrence of /aa/ adds 2 to /a/ contexts, which now number 42, and 2 to the 0 contexts originally common to /a/ on the one hand and to all the consonants on the other. The effects of the /aa/ occurrence are twofold. Firstly, the percentage scored by /a/ when compared with all other vowels stays at 100%: the total of common contexts is still 40, as is the minimum total vowel occurrence. Secondly, the percentage of contexts shared by /a/ and any consonant is raised from 0% to 10%: common contexts now number 2 and the minimum total phoneme (consonant) occurrence is 20. From the point of view of the general thesis the first effect is unimportant, though the measure of similarity does in fact obscure the difference in distribution now shown by /a/ as compared with all other vowels. More serious, however, is the raising of the percentages scored by /a/ in conjunction with all consonants. Since the general aim of the measure of similarity is to facilitate the assignment of two phonemes to the same class if they share at least a minimum percentage of their contexts and to opposing classes if they do not, the actual figure to which any percentage scored by V/C comparison is raised by the occurrence of any VV or CC sequence can obviously be of the utmost importance. Now the percentage value of the /aa/ occurrence is not invariable. In our model language its value in V/C comparisons is completely dependent on the total occurrence of each consonant, this total being four times the number of vowels. If, however, the model language has nine vowels rather than five, the occurrence of /aa/ raises the percentage scored by /a/ in comparisons with all consonants from 0%, not to 10%, but to 5·5%: the common contexts are now two in number and the minimum total phoneme (consonant) occurrence is 36, that is four times the number of vowels. With the number of vowels increased to 10, that is to say, with the vowel and consonant classes now numerically equal, the occurrence of /aa/ causes /a/ to score 5% in comparisons with any consonant, 40 now being the minimum total phoneme occurrence. With 11 vowels, that is to say, with vowels more numerous than consonants, the percentage in question is lowered to 4·8%: the two common contexts are now to be expressed as a percentage of the total occurrence of /a/ which at 42, that is, four times the number of consonants plus the two additional occurrences derived from /aa/, is now less than the total occurrence of any consonant, that is, 44 or four times the number of vowels. Further reductions of this percentage can be achieved only by increasing simultaneously the number of vowels and the number of consonants. With 11 vowels and 11 consonants, the score is 4·5%, with 11 vowels and 20 consonants still 4·5%, but with 12 vowels and 20 consonants 4·2% and, with 20 vowels and 20 consonants, 2·5%

Though an actual language will present distributional complications considerably more numerous and more far-reaching than this simple case of /aa/ in our imaginary language, some general conclusions can none the less be drawn. In the model language the adverse effect on the final statistics of the random occurrence of the VV sequence /aa/ grows progressively smaller with each simultaneous increase in both the total vowel inventory and the total consonant inventory; and furthermore this adverse effect is at its smallest for any given size of phoneme inventory when the vowel and consonant classes are, numerically, more or less equal. The suggestion is therefore that the type of language which is more likely to respond satisfactorily to the original measure of similarity is one which presents a larger rather than a smaller phoneme inventory and one in which the vowel and consonant classes tend towards equivalence in number. This suggestion is well supported by data supplied by the four languages already analysed. The best results are obtained from English and French. Both languages have relatively large, well-balanced inventories: English 47 phonemes, 23 vowels and 24 consonants; French 36 phonemes, 18 vowels and 18 consonants. Less satisfactory is Polish with its relatively large but ill-balanced inventory, 37 phonemes, 8 vowels and 29 consonants. Least satisfactory is Greek: its inventory of 23 phonemes, 5 vowels and 18 consonants, is both relatively small and ill-balanced.

This failure of Greek, in particular, to respond satisfactorily to the original measure of similarity must not, however, be attributed entirely to these two factors, very important though they obviously are. The conclusions so far have been based on the simplest possible case: the ideal symmetrical distribution of vowel and consonant in the first two and last two positions in words being disturbed by the single occurrence of a VV or a CC[10] sequence but not both. Nor has account been taken of the random absences of CV or VC sequences, absences which sometimes disturb the symmetry of phoneme distribution but which may on other occasions counterbalance, statistically, the random occurrences of VV or CC. What really matters in the analysis of an actual language is the total occurrence of each of its phonemes. The higher the general level of phoneme occurrence in the four positions considered, the less disturbing will be the effect of any VV or CC occurrence or of any CV or VC absence: the percentage increases scored by V/C comparisons in the former case and the percentage decreases scored by V/V and C/C comparisons in the latter are thereby minimized, since, with the general level of phoneme occurrence high, the less widely distributed phoneme of any pair being compared has none the less a relatively high total occurrence. Thus in Greek, with an average occurrence per phoneme of 31, the effects of these disturbing factors are more serious than in Polish with its average phoneme occurrence of 44. Polish in its turn absorbs these effects less well than either English or French, both having averages of 56. Even more significant than these over-all averages is the comparison, in the four languages, of the average total occurrence of vowels and the average total occurrence of consonants.

TABLE 2

| | VOWEL OCCURRENCE | | | CONSONANT OCCURRENCE | | |
|---|---|---|---|---|---|---|
| | *Minimum* | *Maximum* | *Average* | *Minimum* | *Maximum* | *Average* |
| English | 17 | 87 | 55 | 7 | 95 | 57 |
| French | 11 | 88 | 55 | 20 | 85 | 58 |
| Polish | 12 | 90 | 67 | 9 | 56 | 38 |
| Greek | 53 | 71 | 67 | 14 | 33 | 21 |

As Table 2 indicates, best results are obtained when the average total occurrence of vowels and that of consonants are not only high but more or less equal, as in English and French. The above figures are of course to some extent a reflection of the balance, or the lack of balance, in the phoneme inventories of the four languages. In Greek and Polish, for instance, the average consonant occurrence tends to be low and the average vowel occurrence tends to be high owing to the relative smallness of their vowel inventory as compared with their consonant inventory. There can, however, be no doubt that the major cause of the very low average consonant occurrence in Greek is in fact the extreme rarity with which consonants occur finally in Greek words.

Summarizing then, it may be said that the language in which the original measure of similarity devised by O'Connor and Trim is *more likely* to produce satisfactory results is one which presents the following structural features:

(a) a relatively large phoneme inventory;
(b) vowel and consonant classes numerically more or less equal;
(c) a high general level of individual phoneme occurrence;
(d) a level of individual vowel occurrence more or less the same as the level of individual consonant occurrence.

Just how crucial all or any of these features turn out to be in any given language will depend on how far the structure of that language departs from the ideal distribution, vowel and consonant alternation only in the first two and last two positions in words, of the model language, for in the model language these features are of no consequence.

*Notes*

[1] L. Bloomfield, *Language*, New York, 1935, 136.

[2] J. D. O'Connor and J. L. M. Trim, 'Vowel, Consonant and Syllable – A Phonological Definition', *Word*, IX, 2, 1953, 103–122.

[3] In this context an anomalous result is *either* a percentage, higher than the critical percentage, which is scored by two phonemes otherwise generally indicated to belong to different classes *or* a percentage, lower than the critical percentage, which is scored by two phonemes otherwise generally indicated to be members of the same class.

[4] E.g. Daniel Jones, *Outline of English Phonetics*, 8th Ed., Cambridge, 1956, 23.

[5] The present author's thanks are gratefully given both to Mr J. T. Pring, who provided the word material for the analysis of Greek, and also to Mr J. D. O'Connor, who made available the results of a preliminary analysis of Polish.

[6] G. F. Arnold, 'A Phonological Approach to Vowel, Consonant, and Syllable in Modern French', *Lingua*, V, 3, 1956, 253–287.

[7] L. E. Armstrong, *The Phonetics of French*, London, 1932.

[8] One of the purposes of this paper is to determine some of the structural features of a language which promise success if the method summarized above is applied to that language. Consequently, in what follows, the terms *vowel* (V) and *consonant* (C) are used as labels, not for phonological groupings determined by that method, but for the more traditional phonetic groupings.

[9] For such a language an analysis according to the O'Connor and Trim method would in the end turn out to be superfluous: the two phoneme groups could be established quite simply by inspection. This method finds its real usefulness in the analysis of languages the structure of which departs to some extent from the ideal distribution.

[10] For simplicity of presentation we have studied only the effects of the random occurrence of a VV sequence in which both vowels are the same. If the occurrence is considered of a VV sequence consisting of two different vowels, the results are broadly similar: the common context percentages scored by both vowels in V/C comparisons are raised. But the amount of the raising for each of the two vowels is somewhat less than that which the occurrence of /aa/ above brings to /a/ in its comparisons with all consonants. It should also be noted that a random occurrence of a CC sequence in which both consonants are the same has the same effect as the /aa/ sequence above; similarly the effect of the occurrence of a CC sequence in which the consonants are different is identical with the VV sequence in which the vowels are different.

# Phonation Types: The Classification of Some Laryngeal Components of Speech Production

J.C.CATFORD

1. It will be convenient to have a single cover term for the phenomena dealt with here, and *phonation* naturally suggests itself. The term 'phonation' has, it is true, been used in at least two different ways: some linguists have used it in the sense of 'production of sound'. Bloch, for example, says: 'Collectively, the simultaneous articulations of all the vocal organs are a phonation.'[1] Marouzeau defines *phonation* as 'production des phonèmes par le jeu des organes vocaux'.[2] Writers on the anatomy and physiology of the larynx, on the other hand, tend to use the term phonation in the sense of 'production of voice': Negus, it is true, in a chapter headed 'The Mechanism of Phonation', mentions the production of sound at points other than the larynx, but it is clear that for him phonation is essentially 'voice production'.[3] Kaplan entitles a chapter on the larynx 'The Structure for Phonation', while a later chapter entitled 'The Structures for Articulation' opens with the words: 'Articulation refers to the activities of supraglottal structures which modify the phonated air.'[4]

2. This last quotation approximates to the way the terms *phonation* and *articulation* are used here. It is not easy, however, to set up a satisfactory criterion for distinguishing between phonation and articulation. Kaplan's definition seems to supply one: namely, phonation *generates* sound, articulation *modulates* sound generated at the larynx (by phonators). The distinction between generators and modulators is sometimes useful, but it will not serve as criterion here. It is true that in the case of vocoids we have a periodic sound generated at the glottis (the phonator) and modulated by the supraglottal cavities (articulators). But the glottis is not the only generator of sounds – activities which we prefer to call 'articulatory' also generate sounds: in voiceless fricatives, for example, the articulatory stricture *generates* turbulent airflow, and resultant hiss, and does not merely modulate a sound generated else-

where. Again, some laryngeal activities associated with the production of voice are modulatory rather than generative in function: e.g. variations in length and thickness of vocal folds modulate the frequency of the glottal tone: constriction of the upper part of the larynx or vertical displacements of the larynx are also phonatory features, or concomitants of phonation, which modulate, but do not generate, sounds.

3. As with a number of supposedly phonetic categories, it is possible to distinguish between phonation and articulation on grounds which are partly phonological. This criterion might be stated somewhat as follows:

Laryngeal activity which generates a sound which functions as a term in a system of phonematic units is *articulatory*.

Laryngeal activity which generates a sound which is common to two or more terms in a system of phonematic units, differentiated by supraglottal modulation, is *phonatory*.

4. According to this criterion, *glottal stop*, in a language in which glottal stop is a term in a system of stops, would have glottal *articulation*: and [h], as a term in a system of voiceless fricatives, would likewise have glottal articulation. On the other hand, the *breath* component of a 'voiceless vocoid' in languages which have a system of voiceless vowels would be *phonatory*, not articulatory, since here the laryngeal sound, breath, is common to several terms in a phonematic system, these terms being differentiated by supraglottal articulation. And, of course, *voice* is phonatory by this criterion as well.

5. For the purpose of the present paper the term *phonation* is used to mean 'any laryngeal activity which is not initiatory in its phonic, or sound-producing, function – whatever its phonological function may be'. This rules out glottal closure as an initiatory element in the production of sounds with glottalic *initiation* ('air-stream mechanism'), but it includes glottal stop. It also includes breath, voice, whisper, and various types and modifications of these which commonly come under the heading of 'voice qualities'.

6. PHONATION, in this sense, has received much less systematic treatment by phoneticians than other components of speech production. Every textbook of phonetics includes a section dealing at least with 'breath' and 'voice' – that is, with those phonatory activities which

characterize voiceless and voiced sounds. Sometimes other types of phonation are referred to: Sweet describes breath, two types of voice, and three types of whisper,[5] but few of his successors have gone as far as this. An exception is Pike, who describes various types of voice, creak, whisper, etc.[6] Laryngeal activities other than those responsible for voicelessness and voice are sometimes mentioned in passing, or described in *ad hoc* imitation-label terms, and referred to as types of 'voice-quality'.

7. The only attempts I know of to describe, or at least to enumerate, a considerable range of 'voice-quality' types are those of Pike[7] and Trager.[8] Neither of these, however, does much more than propose a few imitation-labels, with a minimum of description and nothing like the systematic classification in terms of 'place and manner' or 'location and stricture type' used in describing supraglottal articulation types. Pike lists a few types of 'modification by quality' presented in the form of imitation labels for contrasting end-points of laryngeal/pharyngeal parameters such as *Tense* vs. *Relaxed* vocal cords, *Small Throat Opening* vs. *Large Throat Opening*, *Normal* vs. *Falsetto*, *Whispered* speech vs. speech *Aloud*, *Breathiness* vs. *Clear* tones. No precise descriptions are given, only hints such as: 'In speaking while sighing, more air escapes than is needed for voice production; *Breathiness* of voice is similar . . .', etc.

8. Trager distinguishes between *Voice Set*, *Voice Qualities*, and *Vocalizations* – the distinction between these being a matter of the utilization in speech of various components of speech-sound production, including phonation-types. Distinctions of this type, in respect of phonation, are dealt with at the end of this paper (section 20). Trager simply lists, with a minimum of description: e.g. 'Vocal lip control ranges from heavy *rasp* or hoarseness through slight rasp to various degrees of *openness*.'

9. The laryngologists, speech-therapists, and voice-production specialists have done little more than the phoneticians. There are many detailed studies of certain aspects of voice: e.g. of the physiology, mechanics, and aerodynamics of ('normal') vocal fold vibration, and the mechanism of pitch-change and 'registers' ('chest', 'head', 'falsetto', etc.), with little more than passing reference to such things as whisper, hoarseness, ventricular voice, etc. Kaplan, for example, has a

section on 'hoarseness' which opens: 'Hoarseness is a rough, harsh quality of the voice, and the pitch is relatively low.'[9] This is followed by a discussion of pathological conditions which give rise to hoarseness, but there is no attempt here, or in other works on voice, to set up a systematic framework of categories for the description of different kinds of voice quality.

10. There are several good reasons for the relative neglect of phonation types. For the phoneticians these include: (i) the difficulty of observing laryngeal activity, particularly by traditional kinaesthetic-auditory techniques; (ii) the fact that phoneticians have always been primarily concerned with setting up descriptive categories for phonic features which are utilized phonologically in languages. Since few languages make phonological use of more than two or three types of phonation, no great delicacy of description or classification has seemed to be called for.

11. Laryngologists have likewise tended to neglect the systematic classification of the full range of laryngeal activities for two main reasons: (i) because they have often been primarily concerned with 'the normal voice' (that is 'normal' in a few Western European languages) or indeed with 'the singing voice', rather than with phonologically pertinent laryngeal activity in a wide range of languages; (ii) in any case, unlike the phoneticians, the laryngologists have no tradition of systematic, even if superficial, differential description of phonologically pertinent sound-types.

12. The present paper, which is no more than a preliminary survey, derives from the belief that phoneticians should be able to classify 'voice-qualities' and other phonatory activities in as systematic a way as they classify supralaryngeal articulation.

The starting point of the tentative investigation on which this paper is based was a systematic kinaesthetic-auditory exploration of phonatory activities, of a kind familiar to phoneticians: that is, an exploration starting from one or two known points of reference and proceeding from the known to the unknown by making minimal laryngeal adjustments, combining known phonation types, and so on. The 'known' points of reference include 'normal' voice, falsetto, two kinds of whisper – for all of which descriptions and laryngoscopic drawings or photographs abound in the literature. The larynx may not be well supplied with sensory nerves, but it is surprising how far one can go by 'introspective' techniques. A precondition for such kinaesthetic-auditory exploration, of course, is a knowledge of laryngeal anatomy and physiology: some knowledge of the potentialities of movement of the laryngeal cartilages, the effects of contraction of laryngeal muscles, etc., is necessary as a corrective to 'unrealistic' interpretation of kinaesthetic-auditory sensations.

13. The findings of direct kinaesthetic-auditory exploration and classification are partly confirmed by

(a) *laryngoscopy*, the most direct and obvious means;
(b) *air-flow* data: maximal, and critical rates of air flow in phonation, were plotted against data (obtained for another purpose) on maximal and critical rates of flow of air blown through tubes and orifices of known dimensions. This enabled inferences to be made about the cross-sectional area of the glottis, and hence also about velocity of air flow through the glottal channel;
(c) *spectrography*: spectrograms give indirect information of limited value.

14. Phonation-types may be classified basically in terms of *type of stricture* and *location of stricture*: additional *modifications* which have to be taken into account include vocal-fold length, thickness, and tension; upper-larynx constriction; and vertical displacements of the larynx.

15. PHONATION STRICTURE TYPES: The articulatory terms 'fricative' and 'trill' could be applied to phonatory strictures, but, since two types of each of these categories must be distinguished, it is more convenient to use the imitation-labels 'breath', 'whisper', 'voice', etc.

15.1. BREATH: Glottis widely open (estimated area of glottis about 60% to 95% of maximal glottal area). Critical rate of air-flow about 25 cl/sec, maximum about 890 cl/sec, estimated critical velocity about 240 cm/sec. Diffuse low-velocity turbulence. Acoustic spectrum: hiss noise from about 500 cycles upwards with some concentration of energy in formant-like bands. Auditory effect: a 'hushing' noise of rather 'thin' quality (as compared with 'whisper'): audible breathing.

With the same configuration of the glottis, but with rates of flow below the critical value of about 25 cl/sec, airflow through the glottis is non-turbulent and consequently silent. This 'silent breath' may be called *nil phonation*.

15.1.1. Both *breath* and *nil phonation* function as the 'voicelessness' component of voiceless sounds. Voiceless vocoids necessarily have *breath*; that is hiss generated at the glottis and modulated in the pharynx and mouth. Voiceless [h] differs from voiceless vocoids only in its occurrence as syllable margin instead of syllable nucleus, and probably in having a rate of flow peaking at a higher value than that of voiceless vocoids. (The mean rate of flow for initial [h] is commonly of the order of 50 to 100 cl/sec in isolated words.) Voiceless fricatives in quiet or normal speech normally have rates of flow below 25 cl/sec, and consequently *nil phonation*: the hiss is entirely generated by turbulent flow at the supraglottal point of articulation.

15.2. WHISPER: Glottis constricted (estimated area, from the smallest possible chink up to about 25% of maximal glottal area). Critical rate of flow about 2·5 cl/sec, estimated critical velocity about 1900 cm/sec.[10] Maximum rate of flow about 500 cl/sec. Turbulent flow, with projection of high-velocity jet into pharynx. Acoustic spectrum similar to breath but with considerably more concentration of acoustic energy into formant-like bands. Auditory effect: a relatively 'rich' hushing sound.

15.3. VOICE: Periodic vibration of vocal folds under pressure from below (normal) or above (inverse).[11] For normal voice the liminal pressure-drop across the glottis is of the order of 3 cm of water. Rates of flow vary according to types of voice ('registers'): for chest voice at about 100 cps the liminal rate of flow is about 5 cl/sec, maximal about 23 cl/sec. These are mean flow-rates: during the open phase of vocal fold vibration flow-rates much in excess of these must occur, and since the glottal area is small the general aerodynamic picture is of a series of high-velocity jets shot into the pharynx. Acoustically, periodic sound of fundamental frequency within the range of about 70 cps to 1100 cps.

Voiced sounds with non-fricative articulation (e.g. vocoids, non-fricative laterals, etc.) consist simply of voice generated at the glottis and modulated in the supraglottal cavities. Voiced fricatives have sound generated at two points: voice, generated at the glottis, and fricative *hiss*, generated at the articulation point (and intensity-modulated by voice: i.e. the trans-glottal air-jets of voice superimpose a periodic fluctuation on the mean air pressure behind the articulatory stricture, resulting in a fluctuation of air-velocity through the articulatory channel and consequent fluctuation of intensity of turbulence and resultant hiss – hence the vertical striations in spectrograms of voiced fricatives).

15.4. CREAK: Low frequency (down to about 40 cps) periodic vibration of a small section of the vocal folds. Mean rates of flow very low – of the order of 1·25 to 2 cl/sec. The precise physiological mechanism of creak is unknown, but only a very small section of the ligamental glottis, near the thyroid end, is involved. The auditory effect is of a rapid series of taps, like a stick being run along a railing.

15.5. STOP: The glottis is tightly closed: pressure (positive or negative) is built up behind the stop (which can be released explosively into breath, whisper, voice, or creak).

15.6. These five major phonatory stricture types can also occur in the following combinations:

*Breathy voice*: Combination of breath + voice: glottis relatively wide open: turbulent airflow as for 'breath' plus vibration of vocal folds. The vocal folds do not meet at the centre line: they simply 'flap in the breeze'. Auditory effect, 'sigh-like' mixture of breath and voice: one form of voiced [h].

*Whispery voice*: Combination of whisper + voice: glottis narrowed as for whisper: vocal folds vibrating, but not occluding, so that whisper hiss continues throughout.

*Whispery creak*: Whisper + creak.

*Voiced creak* ('creaky voice'): Simultaneous voice + creak: a common type of voice in low-toned parts of utterances in RP.

*Whispery voiced creak*: Simultaneous whisper + voice + creak: one form of 'beery' or 'whisky' voice.

16. LOCATION: In the above summary of phonatory stricture types no account has been taken of differences in the location of the phonatory stricture. There are four major locational types. These are:

16.1. GLOTTAL (to use the traditional term): The full glottis, both ligamental and cartilaginous, functioning as a single unit. This is the location of 'normal' voice, and one type (perhaps not the most common) of whisper. Although falsetto voice, falsetto whisper, and (glottal) creak involve only the ligamental glottis they can be considered (full) glottal, except when produced with the active 'medial compression' of *ligamental* phonation.

16.2. LIGAMENTAL: The arytenoid cartilages are tightly occluded both by contraction of the interarytenoid muscles and by the forward pull of the lateral crico-arytenoids, which press the vocal processes together (medial compression). Phonation is thus actively restricted to the ligamental glottis. Laryngoscopy indicates that, in the author's pronunciation, ligamental phonation may often (perhaps always?) be accompanied by upper larynx constriction – the epiglottis tends to be pulled back over the top of the larynx. Ligamental whisper, voice, creak, and stop (i.e. glottal stop with purely ligamental release) can be produced. The auditory effect in voice and creak is a 'sharper', 'clearer' sound than in full glottal phonation, often accompanied by slight 'ainish'([ʕ]-like) quality (due no doubt to upper larynx constriction).[12] Ligamental voice appears to be one of the two phonologically distinct voice-qualities in Logbara, and possibly other Nilotic languages: it is commonly the 'normal' voice (contrasting with whispery voice) in Hindi and other North Indian languages, etc.

16.3. ARYTENOIDAL: The ligamental glottis is tightly closed; the vocal processes of the arytenoids are pressed together, but the bodies of the arytenoids are separated. One type of whisper (perhaps 'normal' whisper for some people), a kind of creak, and glottal stop can probably be produced arytenoidally.

16.4. VENTRICULAR: The ventricular bands are approximated to produce whisper, voice-like, and stop phonations.

17. The various combinations of phonatory stricture-type and location are displayed in Table 1. It should be emphasized that there is more certainty about the nature of the stricture types than about locations.

TABLE 1

| STRICTURE | | NORMAL GLOTTAL | LIGAMENTAL | ARYTENOIDAL | VENTRICULAR |
|---|---|---|---|---|---|
| Voiceless: | Nil phonation | + | | | |
| | Breath | + | | | |
| Whisper | | + | + | + | + |
| Voice | | + | + | | ? |
| Creak | | + | + | ? | |
| Stop | | + | + | + | + |
| Breathy voice | | + | | | |
| Whispery voice | | + | + | | ? |
| Whispery creak | | + | + | ? | |
| Voiced creak | | + | + | | |
| Whispery voiced creak | | + | + | | |

18. Multiple phonations, i.e. involving simultaneous phonation at different locations, can occur. These include *arytenoidal whisper* +

*ligamental voice or creak* (a type of 'whispery voice'), *ventricular* + *glottal whisper*, *ventricular* + *glottal stop*, etc.

19. MODIFICATIONS: Laryngeal modifications of phonation are discussed under three main heads:

19.1. VOCAL FOLD MODIFICATIONS: Variations in the *length*, *thickness*, and *tension* of the vocal folds. It is uncertain how far these are independent. The interaction of thyro-arytenoid, crico-thyroid, and posterior crico-arytenoid muscles singly, in combination, and/or as antagonists permits of great variation in these three factors.

Hollien, Hollien and Moore, and Hollien and Curtis have most clearly shown correlations between both length and thickness of vocal folds on the one hand, and fundamental frequency of voice on the other.[13] From a phonetic point of view, frequency of voice can be dealt with without reference to its physiological correlates. Variations in vocal fold thickness, however, certainly produce qualitative variations in whisper, and in the release-sound of glottal stop: cf. whisper and glottal stop with thick vocal folds (as for 'chest voice') and with thin vocal folds (as for falsetto). 'Register' differences, probably largely variations in vocal fold thickness, are associated with tone-differences in several S.E. Asian languages.

19.2. UPPER LARYNX CONSTRICTION: Contraction of the ary-epiglottic folds with retraction of the epiglottis produces a characteristic ('ainish', cf. 16.2 above) modification of whisper, voice, and creak.

19.3. VERTICAL DISPLACEMENT OF LARYNX: The larynx can be displaced vertically. As is well known, larynx-raising is a common accompaniment of high pitch (presumably because the larynx is braced up to the hyoid bone to withstand the strong pull of the crico-thyroid muscle acting to stretch the vocal folds), and larynx lowering often accompanies the production of (long) voiced stops, serving in this case to increase the volume of the supraglottal cavity, so preventing the supraglottal pressure from increasing to the point where the necessary pressure-drop across the glottis is abolished (cf. 15.3 above).

19.3.1. It is, however, easy to train oneself to raise or lower the larynx, and vertical larynx displacement is a modification which can be applied to most types of phonation. With voiced vocoids the main acoustic effect of larynx raising or lowering is, as one might expect, the raising or lowering of the first formant. Lowered-larynx sounds occur (in phonological opposition to normal or raised-larynx sounds) in Javanese. Here the stops and affricates commonly written b, d, ḍ, dj, g are, like the corresponding series, p, t, ṭ, tj, k, completely voiceless: the series b, d, etc., however, are produced with the larynx considerably lowered (a downward-forward displacement of the hyoid bone of up to about 1 cm can easily be observed). During the stop, this produces no acoustic or auditory effect, but the lowered larynx position persists into the following vowel, where it can be observed acoustically as a downward shift of formant 1, and auditorily as a 'muffled' or 'centralized' vowel-quality.

20. UTILIZATION OF PHONATION IN SPEECH: Phonatory differences are utilized in three distinct ways, or have three different types of function in relation to language: these may be termed (1) *phonological*; (2) *paraphonological*; (3) *non-phonological.*

20.1. By *phonological* function we mean that the phonatory difference can be correlated with a difference between grammatical or lexical forms. Examples are the difference between *voiceless* and *voiced* in most languages, e.g. in English where this distinction correlates with differences between lexical items (exemplified by *fat/vat*, *cease/seize*) or between grammatical classes such as *noun/verb* (exemplified by *house* (n)/ *house* (vb) *mouse* (n)/*mouse* (vb)): the difference between *glottal* or 'normal' and *ligamental* voice in some Nilotic languages, etc.

20.2 By *paraphonological* function we mean that the phonatory difference can be correlated directly (not *via* linguistic form) with contextual differences: an example is the difference between *voice* and *whisper* in English. This difference does not correlate with differences in linguistic form – but it does correlate with a contextual difference: voice is related to 'normal' or 'unmarked' context, whisper to what may be termed 'conspiratorial' context.

In both these types of function, the phonatory difference is *contrastive* in the linguistic sense.

20.3. By *non-phonological* function we mean that the phonatory feature or difference is directly related to the situation – as a characteristic of the speaker as an individual, or of the language or dialect which the speaker is using: in this function, phonatory features may be indicative of the speaker's sex, age, health, social class, place of origin, etc. – but they are not contrastive in the linguistic sense.

21. For the phonetician, phonological utilization of phonation types is of most interest, and we conclude with a few examples, some of which have already been mentioned.

*Breath* and *Voice* are very widely utilized contrastively with consonants, less commonly with vowels. *Whisper* substitutes for *voice* in whispered speech. *Breathy voice* occurs in 'voiced h', and is contrastive only in languages which have both [h] and [ɦ].

*Whispery voice* (or, possibly, *breathy voice*) is utilized contrastively in Hindu, Urdu, and some other North Indian languages after so-called 'aspirated voiced stops' or in syllables which are conventionally written with vowel + [h]. In these languages 'normal' or 'non-whispery' voice is often *ligamental. Voiced creak* may be one form of the 'stød' in Danish: it may also be a concomitant of certain tones in some S.E. Asian languages.

*Ligamental voice*, contrasting with 'normal' voice, is not uncommon. It occurs, for example, in Logbara, and possibly in other Nilotic languages. In some languages, it occurs as an accompaniment to other features, usually involving glottal closure: e.g. in Tagalog, vowel preceding voiceless unreleased oral + glottal stop may have ligamental voice (as opposed to the normal voice of vowel preceding voiced stop): in one variety of Eastern Armenian vowel following lenis ejective has ligamental voice, and this is the most noticeable auditory difference between syllables containing lenis ejectives (conventionally transcribed [p, t, k]) and those containing lenis voiceless stops (conventionally transcribed [b, d, g]). *Larynx-lowered* phonation in Javanese has been mentioned above (19.31). The occurrence of phonation with different *register* modifications in S.E. Asian languages has been mentioned above (19.1).

22. Though many languages make phonological use of only two types of phonation, *breath* (or voicelessness) and *voice*, it is not uncommon to find three types. Such sets of three can consist of at least the following phonation-types:

| | |
|---|---|
| *breath* ~ *voice* ~ *voiced creak* | e.g. Danish |
| *breath* ~ *voice* ~ *whispery voice* | e.g. Hindi (some types) |
| *breath* ~ *ligamental voice* ~ *whispery voice* | e.g. Hindi (some types) |
| *breath* ~ *voice* ~ *ligamental voice* | e.g. Nilotic, etc. |
| *breath* ~ *voice* ~ *lowered larynx voice* | e.g. Javanese |

It is probable that four types of phonation are utilized in some languages, a possible example being Gujarati, in some varieties of which *breath* ~ *voice* ~ *ligamental voice* ~ *whispery voice* perhaps occur.

In any case, the study of such features of languages would be facilitated if phonetics had at its disposal a consistent method of classifying and describing phonation, perhaps along the lines very tentatively sketched in this paper.

*Notes*

[1] B.Bloch, 'A Set of Postulates for Phonemic Analysis', *Language*, xxiv, 1948, 9.

[2] J.Marouzeau, *Lexique de la Terminologie Linguistique*, Paris, 1951, 154.

[3] V.E.Negus, *The Comparative Anatomy and Physiology of the Larynx*, London, 1949, 128–129.

[4] H.M.Kaplan, *Anatomy and Physiology of Speech*, New York, 1960, 113, 232.

[5] H.Sweet, *A Primer of Phonetics*, Oxford, 1906, 9–12.

[6] K.L.Pike, *Phonetics*, Ann Arbor, 1943, 125–128.

[7] Pike, *The Intonation of American English*, Ann Arbor, 1946, 99–100.

[8] G.L.Trager, 'Paralanguage: a First Approximation', *Studies in Linguistics*, xiii 1958, 1–12.

[9] *Anatomy and Physiology of Speech*, 168.

[10] It has been observed that what *feels* like *breath* (i.e. wide-open glottis) begins to *sound* more whisper-like at rates of flow above about 300 cl/sec. It is estimated that at this rate of flow the velocity of the air through the open glottis approaches the critical velocity for whisper.

[11] It will be noted that we do not accept the 'neurochronaxic' theory of vocal fold vibration. Many convincing arguments have been adduced against this theory, particularly by van den Berg: in addition, there is no support for the neurochronaxic theory in the literature of instrumental phonetics. See J. van den Berg, 'Sur les théories myoélastique et neuro-chronaxique de la phonation', *Rev. Laryng.*, lxxiv, Bordeaux, 1954, 494; 'Myoelastic-aerodynamic Theory of Voice Production', *J. Sp. Hrg Res.*, i, 1958, 3.

[12] This appears to be the same as the 'sharp voice' described by T.Chiba and M.Kajiyama in *The Vowel, its Nature and Structure*, Tokyo, 1958, 17, 20.

[13] H.Hollien, 'Some Laryngeal Correlates of Vocal Pitch', *J. Sp. Hrg Res.*, iii, 1960, 52; Hollien, 'Vocal Pitch Variation related to Changes in Vocal Fold Length', *J. Sp. Hrg Res.*, iii, 1960, 150; Hollien and G.P.Moore, 'Measurements of the Vocal Folds during Changes in Pitch', *J. Sp. Hrg Res.*, iii, 1960, 157; Hollien and J.F.Curtis, 'A Laminographic Study of Vocal Pitch', *J. Sp. Hrg Res.*, iii, 1960, 361.

# Some Feed-back Effects of Communication Technology on Styles of Speech

YUEN REN CHAO

Speech being a form of social behaviour, it is natural that what and how a person speaks is constantly being affected, temporarily or permanently, by what the speaker feels about the way his speech is being received. The story is told of the man who, on being offered a bargain in a hearing-aid, said he had a much cheaper one in the form of a wire, one end in one ear and the other in his pocket, since every one noticing his wire talked much more loudly. The well-known opposition and balance between phonetic change through laziness on the one hand and the demand for clear intelligibility on the other is another case of the speaker's response to the hearer's response. Thus, under different conditions of sound transmission and reception, every stage of a language is in a dynamic equilibrium, which is stable for a short period, but a shifting one in the long run.

Under changing conditions of transmission the needs of successful reception will change correspondingly. It is common knowledge that early Germanic lingual [r] was favoured by its greater carrying power in open-air life, as compared with the Gallic uvular [ʁ], which was more suitable for the salons of Paris and that the Germans then imitated and adopted the uvular [ʁ] as they became more civilized – or degenerated, as one may prefer – in any case, more adjusted to the conditions of efficient transmission and reception, since efficiency includes both economy of effort and correct reception. The opposite has also happened for the same reason in the setting up of the so-called *Bühnenaussprache*, with its sounds of greater carrying power, such as [ʃ] instead of [ç] in *ich*, [k] instead of [x] in *tag*, etc., and the lingual [r], back again, instead of the uvular [ʁ], so that the speech could go over the footlights without getting lost on the way or misheard by the audience.

Vowels are of course as much affected by conditions of transmission as consonants. Since English vowels tend to take a neutral quality when weak, more than do those of many other languages, any poor condition for transmission would tend to react on the speaker by making him use the so-called 'strong' forms, sometimes even otherwise non-existent spelling pronunciations. Witness the style of speech at American presidential conventions before the 1920s. That was no *Bühnenaussprache*; that was *platform-ausprache*.

In singing, for reasons of resonance, carrying power, and for other considerations, there are a number of conventional deviations from the pronunciation of everyday speech. It used to be obligatory, and still practised to a large extent, to sing English [æ] as [ɑ], [ɹ] as [r] and to bring back into strong forms words which would have the weak forms in speech. One reason for the requirement of what in singing technique is called 'diction' is that since stress and especially time patterns are often greatly distorted in the melody, especially in lyric songs and operas, an attempt will have to be made to recover some of the lost intelligibility. Such attempts are of course never completely successful, and it is still harder to understand a song sung than a poem read. Witness the common practice, when singing the 'On Top of Old Smoky' type of American song, of first saying each line rapidly in speech intonation before actually singing it.

With the advent of modern acoustical aids to the study and use of speech, the first effect was not always in the direction of natural speech in the so-called intimate style. Thus in the mechanico-acoustic set-up for recording speech on wax masters, one had to speak extremely loud in order to make an impression, as all the energy for cutting the wax with the needle had to come from the voice and the energy could not be concentrated by speaking too close to the horn, as that would distort the quality. I am reporting this from experience, as I had to shout towards the horn when recording for the first set of Chinese National Language Records in 1921. Since the register of natural speech normally occupies the lowest third of one's range of voice, and since the lower register is greatly limited in volume, this implies the necessity of great readjustment of habits of tone and intonation in order to make recordings acoustically.

It was not, however, only the pitch of the fundamental that was concerned here. Because of the relatively low signal-to-noise ratio obtainable, the higher frequencies often got masked and could not get through. On one of the commercial records I possessed, Hamlet seemed to be advising his players to do the following:

'Pick the peach, I pray you, . . . trippingly on the tongue.'

Here the missing [s] was not really missing; on the contrary the whole recording, like most other recordings of those days, had a continuous pedal point covering the upper thousands of cycles, so that an [s] was being heard all the time.

What finally changed the whole situation was of course the introduction of electronic amplification of acoustic energy, and the feed-back effect on the speaker or singer was immediately noticeable. To be sure, some people still use a high register of voice and shout at the receiver when making long-distance calls. Speakers at political conventions still use strong forms of words which they would not use in conversation. But by and large the total effect of the spread of electro-acoustic technology in linguistic life is that of a return to nature. Under present conditions, where most stage plays still depend upon the power of the voice, they are never able to compete with electrically transmitted rendition, with its unlimited possibilities of nuances of pitch and voice quality. To be sure, the knowledge that it is Sarah Bernhardt or Forbes-Robertson or whom have you that is on the stage in person certainly still counts heavily in the spectators' appreciation, but that is a value of a totally different order from that of optimum versatility of expression through the use of speech as speech. The two kinds of value are not commensurable.

Besides the increased efficiency of transmission and reception of speech through improved communication technology, there is also the mass effect of the media of mass communication. Never before have so many of the people heard so much of the same thing so much of the time. This is what the engineer calls elimination of time coupling and space coupling, which contributes greatly to uniformity of speech and levelling of styles. Since the advent of the radio there has probably been more rapid convergence of national standards of speech than at any previous time of conscious effort through normative instruction.

Coming closer to the work of the scholar in whose honour these studies are being written, I am gratified to read that objective studies have shown that there is greater agreement about vowel qualities among linguists trained under the Jonesian cardinal vowels as a set of reference points (permanently established in the form of the cardinal vowel recordings) than any articulatory system of vowels.[1] The cardinal vowels are admittedly arbitrary, but they are objective and accessible and the system works. There is, to be sure, more to the system of cardinal vowels than just the set of recorded sounds, but the recording aspect of it is a necessary link.

Not all effects of modern means of speech transmission are in the direction of more intimate style. Because it is often important for a message to reach a large audience, sometimes under conditions of great noise, noise both in the ordinary and in the communicational sense, it is often necessary to strengthen those aspects of speech which are informationally important but often acoustically weak. Part of this need is met by the equalization (or unequalization, from another point of view) of different parts of the sound spectrum, usually by way of boosting the higher frequencies. But the speaker also learns to meet the demand by modifying his speech. For example, one often has to bite harder into the consonants without raising the pitch or even to increase the volume of some of the voiced elements of one's speech. What is popularly known as 'good diction' often takes the form of putting in junctures and pauses where they do not occur in ordinary speech. For example one often hears over the radio three released [t]'s in the phrase *want to tell you,* which in ordinary speech has only two, or even only one, after an extra-long held [t]. At the San Francisco airport one usually hears the points of departure Concourse C announced with a pause between the two [s]'s and Concourse E with a 'plus juncture', if not a glottal stop, where in ordinary speech the only differences are in the length of the [s] and a hardly audible difference in syllabication.

In this connection recent work in automatic speech recognition (leading to the speech-writer – the 'speakwrite' of George Orwell's '1984' – as the most important practical application) usually runs into problems of word division, and there will not only be demands for 'word, for, word' enunciation,[2] but a premium will also be put on styles approximating spelling pronunciations. For example, you will have to say [ɒftən] instead of [ɒfn̩] if you want the machine to type out 'often', or pronounce *at your convenience* without the usual palatalization and affrication of the [t], and use the strong form for *con-* if you do not want the machine to type 'achoor kunvenyents'.[3] This may not affect the man in the street's manner of speaking, but it will, as speech technology advances, invade the fields of business and journalism, and whose speech is not influenced by those institutions?

Thus, the same complementary factors of economy and clarity which have operated throughout history are operating under changed and changing conditions of communication. High-fidelity amplification permits a return from forced forms of loud speech to a more natural or intimate style; at the same time, increased demands for reaching larger and larger audiences under varying conditions calls for more redundant and more noise-resistant ways of diction – diction in both the literary and the musical sense. In other words, the history of language repeats itself. It, too, has a high degree of redundancy.

*Notes*

[1] Peter Ladefoged, 'The Value of Phonetic Statements', *Language*, XXXVI, 3, 1960, 390.

[2] P. Denes and M. V. Mathews, 'Spoken Digit Recognition using Time-frequency Pattern Matching', *J. acoust. Soc. Amer.*, XXXII, 11, 1960, 1450–1455.

[3] Y. R. Chao, 'Linguistic Prerequisites for a Speechwriter', *J. acoust. Soc. Amer.*, XXVIII, 6, 1956, 1107–1109.

# Redundancy

ANDRÉ CLASSE

Redundancy is a concept well-established in phonology; it can easily be extended, in a slightly modified form, to syntax. For example, in *I shall write to-morrow*, *shall* is redundant in the sense that the future is unambiguously indicated by the words *to-morrow*; in *several times* the *s* is redundant since the plural is already marked by the word *several*. In grammatically complicated languages this type of redundancy can assume major proportions. The investigation of a whistled form of Spanish (Silbo Gomero) where the articulatory technique gives rise to a number of consonantal clashes without attendant ambiguity suggested that the notion of redundancy in modified form might conceivably extend to the lexis, and the problem may be formulated as follows: could the number of consonantal phonemes in Spanish be reduced without giving rise to an inconvenient number of homonyms? Or is there any considerable number of apparent oppositions which are in fact generally redundant? Suppose, for example, that /l/ and /r/ were invariably interchangeable (as they are in many words of the Spanish dialect with which we are concerned), we should be driven to the conclusion that there are not two phonemes /l/ and /r/ but two sounds [l] and [r], realizations of one phoneme. This is not the case: even if the disappearance of the opposition in the minimal pair *pero*/*pelo* was the only example found throughout the lexis it would disprove the hypothesis, and there are many other cases.

But our first question is still valid and interesting. The apparent absence of ambiguities in the Silbo strongly suggests that the realization of several phonemes as one sound does not necessarily impair intelligibility, and we may legitimately attempt to obtain a numerical expression of this kind of redundancy in the Spanish lexis. This is easily done, although a fair amount of tedious labour is involved. We tested one group of consonants which are invariably confused in the Silbo, viz. [l, r, r̄, ð, j, ʎ] and [n] in final and preconsonantal positions. The method consisted in examining a random sample in order to discover whether the substitution of one phoneme /$\pi$/ for every one of these consonants would produce homonyms in significant numbers. To ensure true randomness a list of sampling numbers was used. A preliminary run of 300 through the dictionary failed to produce a single pair of new homonyms. It was of course clearly realized that this procedure would yield misleading results since the confusion of, say, two common tool-words would produce only one ambiguity in the final statistic whereas it might lead to many on every page of a novel. But the test was necessary in the sense that if it had produced a large number of homonyms, it would have shown the futility of going on with this investigation. The procedure was repeated with two modern prose texts, *Las Gafas del Diablo* (Fernandez-Florez) and *Todos los Ombligos son Redondos* (Álvaro de Laiglesia). The bag resulting from two samplings of 600 each was meagre in the extreme, consisting in all of the following clashes: *yo/lo*, *pero/perro/pelo*, *siento/cierto*.[1] This suggests very strongly that *in general* the group of consonants under consideration behaves as if it were one phoneme and that Spanish could therefore make do with a more restricted consonantal system at the cost of an inconsiderable increase in the number of its homonyms and without appreciable loss of efficiency as a means of communication.

Now phonologically redundant does not necessarily mean useless, as far as communication is concerned: the feature of aspiration of the voiceless plosives of English, although strictly non-significant, does facilitate their correct identification by increasing the obviousness of the opposition voiceless-voiced when it would otherwise be hard to perceive. It is the unvoicing of [r] produced by the aspiration of the preceding [t] rather than the voicelessness of the [t] itself, and the voicing of the [r] rather than that of the preceding [d], that make clear the opposition in minimal pairs such as *try/dry*. This is why the native speaker of English will often hear, say, [brei] for [prei] when a foreigner uses a non-aspirated form of [p]. But what we have called lexical redundancy is quite another thing: it does not increase intelligibility; in Spanish there is nothing to choose, from that point of view, between the forms [sur, sul, suð, suj, suʎ]. Here redundant features appear to be truly redundant.

A question immediately poses itself: is this state of affairs peculiar to Spanish? A general answer, involving the examination of the word-structures of many languages, is obviously out of the question at this stage. But even without going to the length of submitting English and French to a statistical test we can state immediately that in this respect they are quite unlike Spanish, since a few seconds' reflection will produce many proofs of the non-interchangeability of any pair of consonants in these languages, with the occasional exception of [θ/ð] in English.

What characteristics of the languages under consideration, then, can account for these differences? Certainly not the number of available consonantal phonemes: there are 17 or 18 in Spanish and French, about 22 in English, and French behaves like English and not like Spanish. What is significantly different, on the other hand, is word length. It can easily be shown that Spanish tends to be more polysyllabic than the other two languages. Three random samplings from the dictionary[2] gave the results shown in Table 1.

TABLE 1

| Words of: | 1 | 2 | 3 | 4 | 5 | 6 | 7 | 8 | syllables. |
|---|---|---|---|---|---|---|---|---|---|
| Spanish | 1 | 60 | 184 | 188 | 119 | 27 | 2 | 2 | mean: 3·8 |
| English | 27 | 68 | 57 | 35 | 11 | 5 | 1 | 0 | mean: 2·77 |
| French | 51 | 90 | 51 | 13 | 0 | 0 | 0 | 0 | mean: 2·0 |

The means for English and French differ significantly from the mean for Spanish ($t_{s,e} = 11{\cdot}4$, $n = 787$; $t_{s,f} = 15{\cdot}8$, $n = 788$) whereas there is no significant difference between the means for French and English ($t_{f,e} = 61$, $n = 409$).[3]

Now, elementary arithmetic shows that we need fewer different sounds to form distinctive combinations with long words than with short ones. We require only two different symbols to express the number twelve in the binary system, where we have to use five digits, whereas one digit will do the work in the duodecimal system, which uses twelve different symbols. The chances of ambiguity will then be fewer, *ceteris paribus*, in languages which tend to polysyllabism than in others, when some circumstance or other leads to the confusion of some of the component sounds.

Phonological redundancy is largely inevitable: it is strictly impossible to articulate in such a way that only pertinent features will appear to the exclusion of the non-significant. Not so in the lexis. But because language is not an artifact it would seem that Zipf's principle of economy does not apply here.

*Notes*

[1] In the context, there was in fact no ambiguity.

[2] As we are concerned with the lexis, this is appropriate.

[3] Even without the help of statistical techniques, inspection of the data leads to the same kind of picture: in Spanish, words of 3, 4, 5 syllables account for some 92% of the total; in English and French, words of 1, 2, 3 syllables account for 75% and 94% of the respective totals.

# Classifying Speech Sounds by their Source

PIERRE DELATTRE

Acoustic theory indicates that the articulatory production of a speech sound essentially depends on two successive events: a source phenomenon and a resonance phenomenon. For a number of years now the acoustic resonances resulting from the articulatory motions have been studied on spectrographs. A great deal has been learned about the rôle of the various acoustic elements in phonetic and phonemic identification. This advance is due to the new technique of synthesis, which permits us to isolate those elements, vary them separately, and subject the results of changes to judgments by ear. Thus a fairly high degree of certainty has been reached in regard to the physical aspect of speech and its perception: formants, formant transitions, and noise bands are rather well known in relation to the sound perceived.

The acoustic resonances are not so well known in relation to the articulatory factors of production. There, little progress has been made. Further study of the source in relation to the resonance is needed. In an attempt to shed some light on the production phase of speech sounds we have found it useful to compare the 'loud' and the 'whispered' articulations.

Our interest in the relation between source and resonances as seen on a spectrogram was once more aroused while attempting to synthesize some allophones of /l/ in the French word *peuple* [pœpl]. First, a voiced [l], with voiced release into an embryo-schwa, had to have a periodic F1[1] steady state and transition as well as periodic F2 and a periodic F3 (this last one is not indispensable, but contributes to naturalness and to the distinction between /l/ and /r/). See 1 (1) in Fig. 1; voiced [l] formants are drawn with horizontal lines representing the harmonics of periodic sound.

Second, a voiceless [l] was produced by drawing turbulent F1, F2, and F3 steady-states and transitions. See 1 (2) in Fig. 1; voiceless [l] formants are drawn with random dots.

Third, another voiceless [l] was produced by drawing turbulent F2 and F3 steady-states and transitions only, omitting the F1 altogether – which may be equivalent to reducing its intensity considerably. See 1 (3) in Fig. 1.

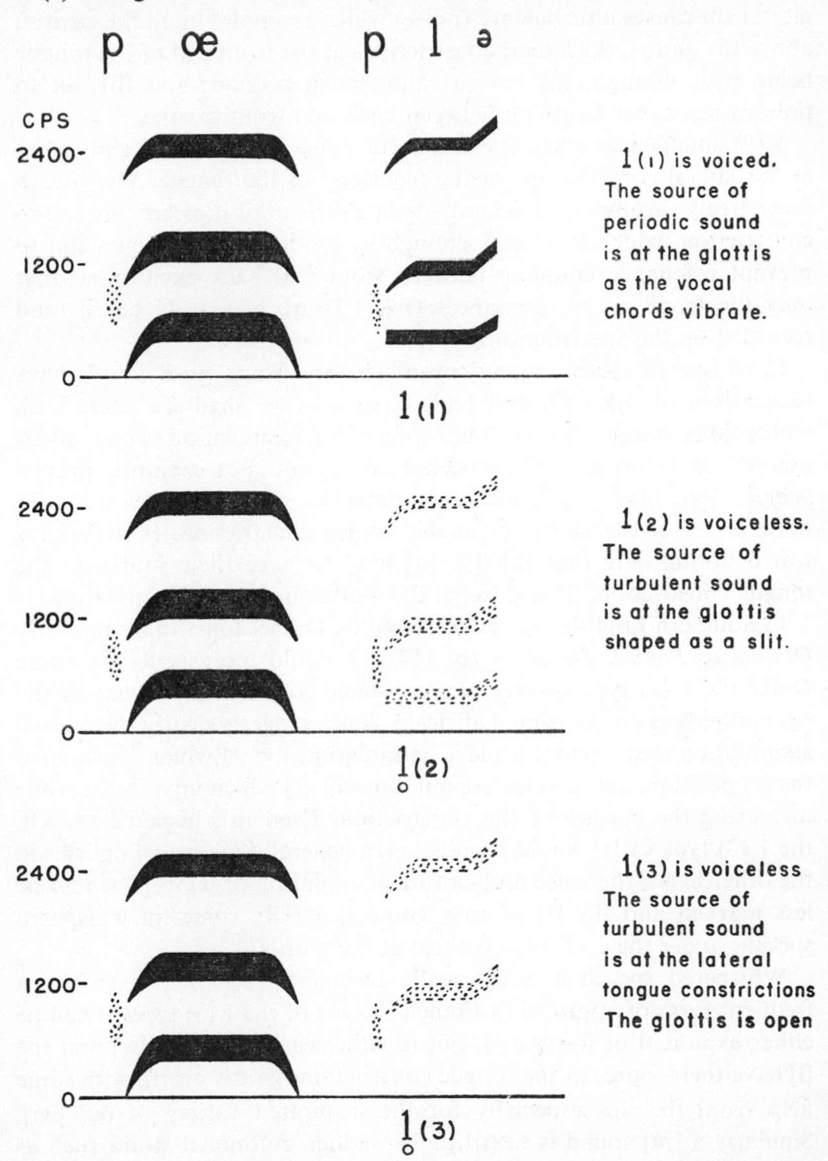
p œ p l ə
CPS
2400-
1200-
0
1 (1)
1 (1) is voiced.
The source of
periodic sound
is at the glottis
as the vocal
chords vibrate.
2400-
1200-
0
l̥ (2)
l (2) is voiceless.
The source of
turbulent sound
is at the glottis
shaped as a slit.
2400-
1200-
0
l̥ (3)
l (3) is voiceless
The source of
turbulent sound
is at the lateral
tongue constrictions
The glottis is open

Fig. 1. Three spectrographic patterns for the synthesis of l in French *peuple*

Now, 1 (2) and 1 (3), although both voiceless, certainly did not sound the same, phonetically speaking: 1 (2) sounded as when the source of noise is at the vocal cords. The flow of breath through a narrow glottal slit causes a turbulence (noise) which resonates in all the cavities above the glottis, the lateral constrictions at the front end of the tongue being wide enough: (a) not to cause much friction; and (b) not to prevent resonance coupling between back and front cavities.

1 (3) sounded as when the source of noise is not at the glottis but at the lateral constrictions of the front end of the tongue. The breath flows freely through a sufficiently open glottis until it meets this lateral constriction, which is narrow enough to produce a turbulence and to prevent resonance coupling between front and back cavities, so that only the front cavity resonances (F2, F3) are effectively heard (and recorded on the spectrogram).

In whispered speech, many consonants and some close vowels have realizations of the 1 (2) and 1 (3) types – as we shall see later. Such realizations occur also in loud speech by assimilation when glides precede or follow a strong voiceless consonant. For example, French *peuple, âpre, pied, poing, tuile* may have the voiceless glide source of noise either at the glottis or at the tongue constriction. It is perhaps worth noting here that [ʀ], [j], [ɥ] tend to have their source at the tongue constriction, [l] and [w] at the glottis, in French assimilation.

In Southern English *tree*, as described by Daniel Jones in his masterly *Outline of English Phonetics* (p. 152) [r] would more generally come under the 1 (3) type (source at the tongue constriction). Treating the /tr/ complex as an occasional affricate, Jones suggests clearly the mutual assimilation that occurs: a place assimilation for [t] which backs it to the [r] position, and a voice assimilation for [r] which unvoices it while increasing the closure of the constriction. Even in whispered speech, the 1 (3) type of [r] would dominate. In general American English, on the other hand, the voice and closure assimilation of [r] to [t] would be less marked and the [r] of *tree* would generally come, in whispered speech, under the 1 (2) type (source at the glottis).

Whispered speech is occasionally normal speech. For example, a frequent form of approval in French is a *oui* of the 1 (3) type. It can be either expirated or inspirated, but in either case, both the [w] and the [i] have their source at the tongue constriction (glottis open), with some help from the lips especially for the inspirated variety of *oui* [wi]. Similarly a [ju] sound is heard under sudden emotional strain such as that caused by a burn. These [j, w, i, u] are effectively resonated in the front cavities only, and show no first formants, or weak ones, on spectrograms. As confirmed by synthesis, *with* the presence of an Fl, [wi] and [ju] sound as when the source is at the glottis and all the mouth tract cavities are used to resonate; *without*, they sound as described above, with the source at the tongue constriction.

The source can have a phonemic function even with glides. The allophonic variations noted above for French become distinctive in English *whispered* speech where the initial glide of *you*, *weal*, have their source at the glottis, whereas *Hugh*, *wheel*, have theirs at the tongue constriction. Note that the vowel following the glide may also have its source at the tongue stricture, but only if it is a close vowel – compare *wheat* and *white*: [i] may, [ai] may not.

This leads us to note that not only consonantal glides but the close vowels as well may have their source either at the glottis or at the tongue constriction in whispered speech: [i, u] can be whispered with the source at either place. They will be understood as [i, u] in either type of articulation in spite of the fact that the acoustic picture differs in two ways: (a) F2 will be higher in frequency for [i], lower for [u]; (b) F2 will be stronger and wider, and F1 weaker or absent, when the source of noise is at the tongue constriction.

Why, one may ask, are such physically different patterns identified correctly? The answer is not unilateral. We find in a study of vowel formants published some ten years ago[2]: (a) that the second formant is more important than the first for identification of [i]: (b) that any narrow formant above 2500 is identified as [i] rather than as any other vowel – probably because there exist no vowels which have a higher F2 (cf. the fact that [i] can be identified by F3 alone). In the same study, we find that a *single* formant at the frequency level of F2 for [u] would sound a little closer than [ɔ]. Therefore, to be heard as [u], a single formant must be somewhat lower than the F2 of a spoken [u].

Besides that of the semivowels and close vowels just mentioned, another analogy to the '1 (2) vs. 1 (3)' types appears in the comparison of 'whispered vowel vs. [h]'. Spectrographic analysis and especially synthesis have well proved that [h] is different from whispered vowels, and that the difference is largely in the first formant. Here is a revealing experiment. A loud vowel is synthesized with three formants composed of harmonics. Then before each formant, at the same frequency as the formants, turbulent sound is added. The sequence 'turbulent formants – periodic formants' is not identified as '[h] plus loud vowel', but as 'whispered vowel plus loud vowel'. It is not until the F1 of the turbulent portion has been removed that the sequence can be identified as '[h] plus vowel'. This absence (or weakness) of F1 in [h] can be seen on spectrograms of natural speech. From this it would appear that the whispered vowel is much like the voiceless 1 (2) in *peuple* – its source is at the glottis, and it uses all the resonance cavities of the vocal tract above the glottis. That is why it has all the formants. Whereas [h] may be much like the 1 (3) of *peuple* – its source is at the tongue constriction, not at the open glottis, and it resonates effectively in the cavities above the source only, hence the lack of F1.

There is one difference, however, between 1 (3) and [h]: in 1 (3) the constriction needs to be narrow because the rate of the flow of breath is slow; in [h] the tongue constriction for the following vowel may be fairly wide because the flow of breath moves at a sufficiently fast rate.

Yet another experiment by synthesis[3] showed that the turbulent portions of formant transitions that appear between the explosion of English [p, t, k] and the loud vowel that follows could not be identified as 'aspiration' (or could not cause the [p, t, k] to be heard as 'aspirated') unless the F1 of the turbulent portion was removed. The inevitable suggestion here is that 'aspiration' is similar to [h] or 1 (3) (it has its source at the tongue constriction) and not to 1 (2) or to a whispered vowel which has its source at the glottis.

If we continue our inventory of oral phones, loud or whispered, in regard to the place of the source, we find that, apart from vowels and glides, they all belong to one of two types.

The voiceless plosives and fricatives have their source at the vocal tract constriction; to this there is no alternative, even in whispered speech. The glottis is always open wide enough to let a flow of breath through noiselessly at moderate rate. The behaviour is that of 1 (3). It explains the absence of any equivalence to an F1 on the acoustic pattern, and the effective resonance of the cavities above the constriction only. This is translated by the appearance on spectrograms of a single frequency region of noise which is lower, from [s] to [x], as the constriction is farther back in the tract and as the cavity in front of it is larger. What is true of fricative noise is true of plosive noise.

Finally, let us consider the *voiced* plosives and fricatives. They differ from the glides in that in voiceless realizations, they cannot choose to have their source at either one of two places (the glottis as in 1 (2) or the constriction above it as in 1 (3)); they must use both sources simultaneously. Similarly, in loud speech the voiced plosives and fricatives – if they are really voiced and not merely non-aspirated – have two sources simultaneously: one at the glottis, which is resonated as a schwa vowel, the other at the constriction, which is resonated as a noise. The schwa vowel runs parallel to the noise. On spectrograms, it shows from 1 to 2 base harmonics, as during the closure of [ba, da, ga], to a two- or three-formant very low-intensity vowel, as during the closure of [za, ʒa, va]. This simultaneous schwa vowel is indispensable in order to produce synthetically a well-voiced fricative in initial position – the only position permitting no substitution effects such as exaggerated shortness of the friction noise. In whispered speech a similar simultaneity exists – a vowel which has its source at the glottis resonates concurrently with an extremely low-intensity noise which has its source at the vocal tract constriction.

Where do the nasal consonants fit in this picture? Surprisingly, with the open vowels, for they are not subject to any friction noise. Their source can only be at the glottis, in loud or in whispered speech, for they have to use the complete naso-oral coupling of cavities in order to produce nasal identification.

The fact that, in whispered speech, consonants that have a source at the glottis can be identified in spite of the near-absence of noise only serves to show how important the rôle of transitions is in recognizing not only the place of articulation but the manner as well.

To summarize, in regard to source, four classes of speech sounds can be distinguished:

(1) The open vowels and the nasal consonants which have only one source – at the glottis – in normal as well as in voiceless realizations.

(2) The glides (oral resonants) and the very close vowels, which have only one source – at the glottis – in normal realization, and a choice of two sources – at the glottis or at the constriction – in voiceless realizations.

(3) The voiced fricatives and plosives, which have two simultaneous sources – at the glottis and at the constriction – in normal as well as in voiceless realizations.

(4) The voiceless fricatives and plosives, including [h], which have only one source – at the constriction – in normal or in voiceless realizations.

*Notes*

[1] F1, F2, and F3 are abbreviations meaning first formant, second formant, and third formant. In addition, the arbitrary term *glides* will comprise liquids and semi-vowels.

[2] P. Delattre, A. M. Liberman, F. S. Cooper, and L. J. Gerstman, 'An Experimental Study of the Acoustic Determinants of Vowel Colour; Observations on One- and Two-formant Vowels Synthesized from Spectrographic Patterning', *Word*, VIII, 1952, 195–210.

[3] Liberman, Delattre, and Cooper, 'Some Cues for the Distinction between Voiced and Voiceless Stops in Initial Position', *Language and Speech*, I, 1958, 153–167.

# An Acoustic Explanation of the Sound Shift [ɫ] > [u] and [l] > [i]

O. VON ESSEN

In linguistic circles it is a well-known fact that in some languages and dialects an original lateral consonant, generally represented by the letter *l*, has been changed into an [u]-sound, in other cases into an [i]-sound.

Daniel Jones, our esteemed colleague and friend, has given a convincing explanation of this phonetic process from the genetic point of view. The problem, however, has also an acoustic aspect, and it is worth while investigating whether the acoustic structures of the sounds mentioned can contribute to the intelligibility of the twofold development.

We know that in the First Modern English there appeared an [u]-sound between a vowel and [l], and that later on the [l] was dropped, so that the [u]-sound remained. Henry Sweet states that: 'Already in First MnE (= Modern English) [l] began to be dropped between [u] and the following consonant, as in *half* [haulf, hauf], *folk* [foulk, fouk]; also in *should* [ʃuuld, ʃuld, ʃud], *would, could,* where the [l] was at first dropped only when these words were weak.'[1] Further we know that late Latin [l] to some extent changed to [u] in Provençal, when, by dropping the final vowel, it became final itself; also in Portuguese [l] before another consonant has often been vocalized, acquiring a strong velar component and approaching the [u]-sound. B. Zauner informs us: 'Portuguese is also on the way to vocalizing the *l*-sound which is becoming strongly velar, taking on a resemblance to [u]. There are also some cases in Portuguese and Spanish of a real replacing of [l] by [u] (or by its further development), the reasons for which are as yet unknown.'[2] Latin [l] changed to [u] and was together with the preceding vowel monophthongized in French: *caballo* became *cheval,* but plural form *chevaux, ascultat* became *écoute,* etc.

It is remarkable that in West Polish a non-syllabic [u̯] is to be traced back to dark [ɫ], whereas clear [l] has not shifted: [ɫan] > [u̯an] 'field'.

A similar phenomenon occurs in the Low German dialect of Vierlanden (E. of Hamburg), where the realization of /l/ is split into two allophones, [l] and [ɫ], the use of which is regulated in exactly the same way as in English. In my early years – I lived there until I was sixteen – we used to pronounce the dark [ɫ] as a non-syllabic [u̯] without lip-rounding: *hell*, 'clear, light', was pronounced [heu̯], *School*, 'school' = [ʃeu̯ʊ], *Kalf*, 'calf' = [kau̯f].

Jones informs us that in English there are also these two varieties of lateral consonants. 'These are known as "clear" *l* and "dark" *l*. They are members of the same phoneme, the principle governing their use being that clear *l* occurs only before vowels and before [j], while dark *l* is only used before all other consonants and finally.'[3]

In some cases an original [l] was changed into an [i]-sound, as for instance in the Latin combination consonant + *l* in Italian: *plenu* > *pieno*, *clave* > *chiave*, *glande* > *ghiande*, *flamma* > *fiamma*, etc. The Bavarian dialect of German often has [i] instead of [l]: *Holz*, 'wood', becomes [hoits]. Sütterlin states: 'Lowering of the back of the tongue and a distinctly *i*-coloured *l* are attributed to . . . some districts of southern Germany, e.g. to those in whose dialects [l] has already been completely changed to [i] as the Munich dialect in *foisch*, "false", and *hoib*, "half".'[4]

The shifting of [l] to [u] on the one hand and to [i] on the other gives rise to the question how this development in different directions could have been possible and how it might be explained phonetically.

As for the dark variety of the lateral consonant, Daniel Jones remarks that its dark quality is achieved by raising the tip of the tongue against the back part of the upper teeth or teeth-ridge, the body of the tongue taking a form and position resembling that for producing an [u]-sound, and leaving a passage for the air-stream on both sides or on one side. In this way [l] will gain a certain similarity to [u], a kind of [u]-quality already being contained in it. When the front part of the tongue fails to touch the teeth or the teeth-ridge, i.e. when a frontal opening is left for the air-stream, a kind of [u]-sound alone will be the result. Jones indicates this species of *l* by the sign $\text{l}^{u}$.

Clear *l*, on the other hand, contains an [i]-component, which can easily be understood by the fact that 'in clear varieties of [l] there is a raising of the front of the tongue in the direction of the hard palate (in addition to the tongue-tip articulation)',[5] the body of the tongue thus approaching the position which is used for pronouncing an [i]-sound. For this variety of *l* Jones writes $\text{l}^{i}$.

Hence we may conjecture that in any case where [l] has been transferred to [u] or a further development of it, the basis was dark [ɫ], and that the [i]-pronunciation is to be traced back to clear [l]. But in addition to the genetic statements it will be of interest to investigate also the acoustic features of the sounds in question and to discover whether there are also physical relations that justify such an assumption.

A good number of acoustic analyses of vowels and consonants has been made recently at the Hamburg Phonetic Laboratory, by means of the *Brüel and Kjaer* combination, i.e. an Automatic Spectrum Recorder linked with a Level Recorder. The spectrum recorder is equipped with 27 third-octave filters which are automatically engaged and disengaged, one after the other, by a switch that runs at a constant speed through its scale, beginning with 40 cps up to 16,000 cps. The filters pass only those frequencies which they are tuned to. Using the slow gear, one analysis takes about five minutes. The speech sound to be analysed must be continued all the time, i.e. a static sound has to be conveyed to the apparatus. In practice, this is realized by first taking a tape recording of the sound continued for some seconds. The middle part of the tape is cut out, and this piece is formed into a loop which now runs uninterruptedly in front of the reproducer. Its magnetic oscillations excite identical oscillations of voltage; these are conducted to the frequency analyser. The level recorder shows the frequencies which can pass the corresponding filters; the sharp point of a delicate stylus scratches the traces of its movements on a running strip of paper covered with wax. In this manner we obtain 'spectrograms', as shown in Figs. 1 and 2.

Among our speech sounds we had clear [l] as well as dark [ɫ], the latter spoken by an Englishman (Mr Kelley) and myself.[6] From the results of the analyses the spectrograms of [l] and [i] are represented in Fig. 1, those of [ɫ] and [u] in Fig. 2.

In each case, the fundamental tone, i.e. the voice-pitch, was about 125 cps. The intensity of voice production was kept constant.

In the [l]-spectrogram (Fig. 1, upper line) the fundamental frequency of 125 cps appears with an amplitude of about 35 db; a second peak is located within the range of the 250 cps-filter, with an amplitude of 40 db. A third strong component stands around 400 cps with 32 db; then a rather extensive depression is to be observed, until another elevation follows on the frequency range of 1600–2000 cps with 13 to 10 db, and again another one around 4000 cps with amplitudes oscillating about

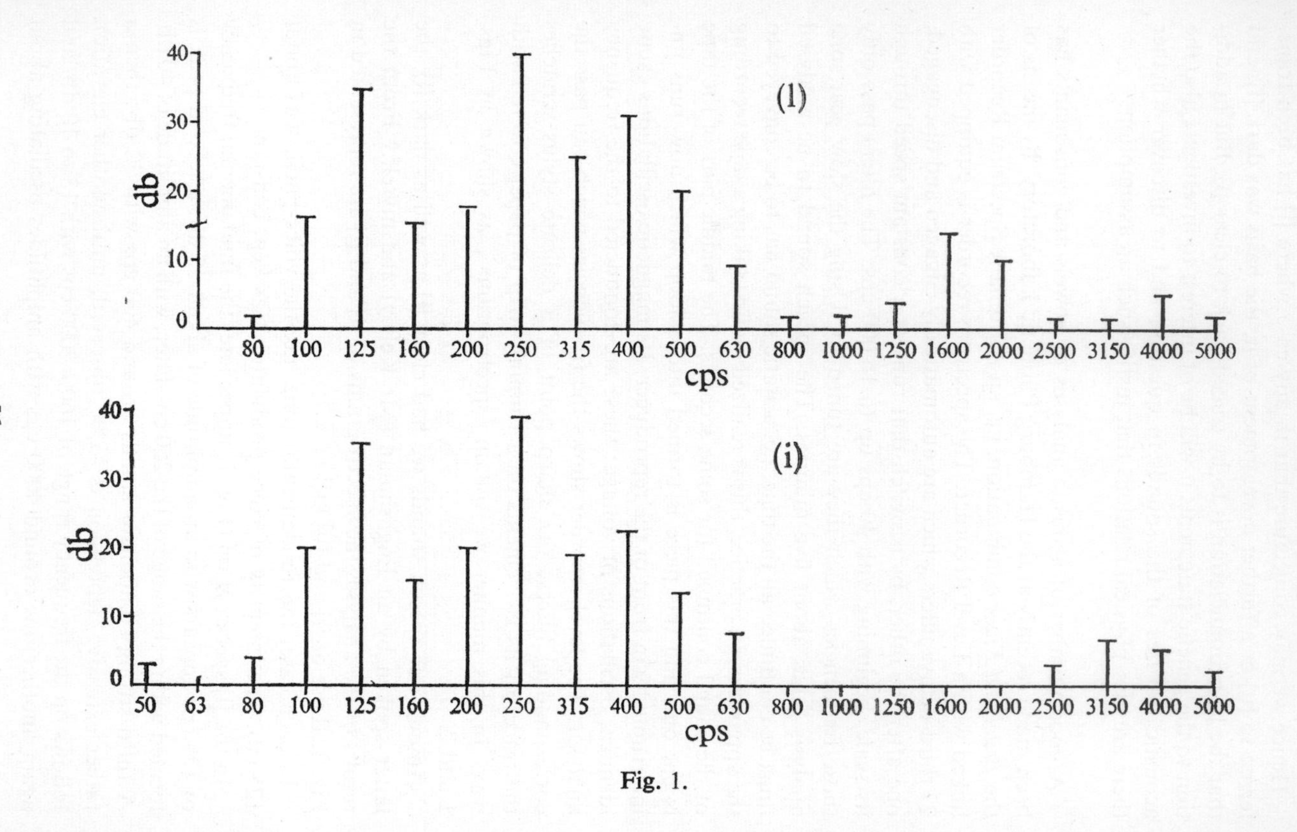
(l)
db
40
30
20
10
0
80 100 125 160 200 250 315 400 500 630 800 1000 1250 1600 2000 2500 3150 4000 5000
cps
(i)
db
40
30
20
10
0
50 63 80 100 125 160 200 250 315 400 500 630 800 1000 1250 1600 2000 2500 3150 4000 5000
cps

Fig. 1.

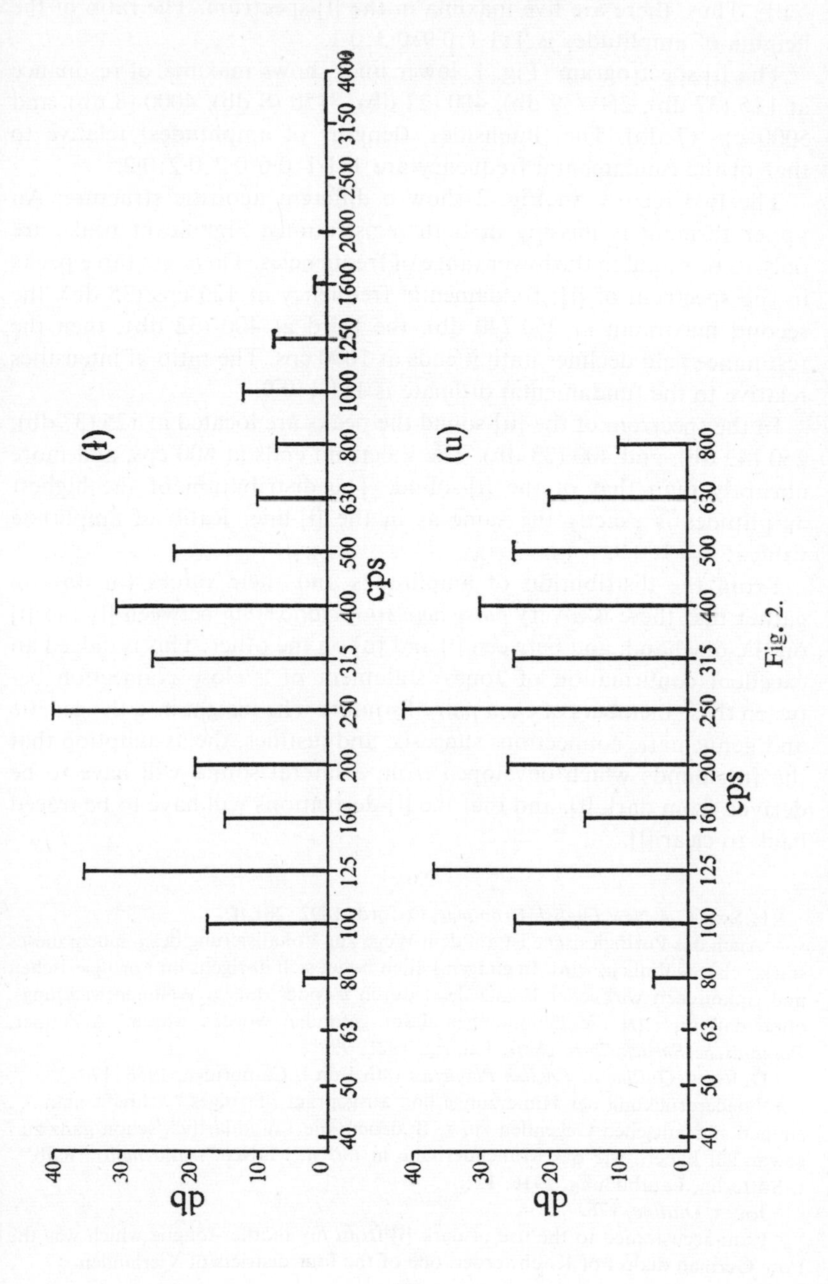
(t)
db
0
10
20
30
40
cps
40
50
63
80
100
125
160
200
250
315
400
500
630
800
1000
1250
1600
2000
2500
3150
4000
(u)
db
0
10
20
30
40
cps
40
50
63
80
100
125
160
200
250
315
400
500
630
800

Fig. 2.

5 db. Thus, there are five maxima in the [l]-spectrum. The ratio of the heights of amplitudes is 1:1·1:0·9:0·3:0·1.

The [i]-spectrogram (Fig. 1, lower line) shows maxima of resonance at 125 (37 db), 250 (39 db), 400 (23 db), 3150 (8 db), 4000 (8 db), and 5000 cps (7 db). The 'intensities' (lengths of amplitudes) relative to that of the fundamental frequency are 1:1·1:0·6:0·2:0·2:0·2.

The two records in Fig. 2 show a different acoustic structure. An upper formant is missing in both registrations. Significant peaks are only to be found in the lower range of frequencies. There are three peaks in the spectrum of [ɫ]: fundamental frequency at 125 cps (35 db), the second maximum at 250 (40 db), the third at 400 (32 db); then the resonance field declines until it ends at 1600 cps. The ratio of intensities relative to the fundamental ordinate is 1:1·1:0·9.

In the spectrum of the [u]-sound the peaks are located at 125 (37 db), 250 (42 db), and 400 (33 db). The spectrum ends at 800 cps, and more abruptly than that of the [ɫ]-sound. The distribution of the highest amplitudes is exactly the same as in the [ɫ]-line. Ratio of amplitude values: 1:1·1:0·9.

From the distribution of amplitudes and their values (in db) we gather that there is a very *close acoustic relationship* between [l] and [i] on the one hand, and between [ɫ] and [u] on the other. This is indeed an excellent confirmation of Jones' statement of a close connection between these members of each pair of sounds. The insight into the genetic and gennematic connections suggests, and justifies, the assumption that the [u]-sounds which developed from a lateral sound will have to be derived from dark [ɫ], and that the [i]-derivations will have to be traced back to clear [l].

*Notes*

1 H. Sweet, *A New English Grammar*, Oxford, 1892, 281 ff.

2 'Auch das Portugiesische ist auf dem Wege zur Vokalisierung des *l*, indem dieses stark velar, *u*-ähnlich, wird. In einigen Fällen findet sich übrigens im Portugiesischen und Spanischen wirklicher Ersatz des *l* durch *u* (oder dessen Weiterentwicklung), ohne daß bis jetzt die Bedingungen dafür gefunden worden wären.' A. Zauner, *Romanische Sprachwissenschaft*, Leipzig, 1921, 99.

3 D. Jones, *Outline of English Phonetics* (8th Edn.), Cambridge, 1956, 173.

4 'Niederdrückung der Hinterzunge und ausgeprägt *i*-farbiges *l* schreibt man ... einigen süddeutschen Gegenden zu, z. B. denen, die *l* mundartlich schon ganz zu *i* gewandelt haben, wie das Münchnerische in *foisch*, "falsch", und *hoib*, "halb".' L. Sütterlin, Lautbildung, 1916, 121.

5 Jones, *Outline*, 176.

6 I am accustomed to the use of dark [ɫ] from my mother-tongue which was the Low German dialect of Kirchwerder, one of the four districts of Vierlanden.

# Experimental Evidence for the Phoneme

## D.B.FRY

Nowhere in the field of linguistics is a cleavage between theory and practice so apparent as in the matter of the phoneme. Although much has been written and many different viewpoints have been expressed about the nature of the phoneme and the way in which it may be defined, when linguists are faced with the task of establishing the phonemes in a given language they all adopt essentially the same procedures and tend to arrive at very much the same phonemic inventories. There can be no doubt that these procedures owe a great deal to the work of Daniel Jones, who as early as 1917 was using the term 'phoneme' and, what is more important, the idea of the phoneme in his analysis of languages. Since his aims have always been of a very practical kind, it is not surprising that he has felt no need to modify his concept of the phoneme with the passage of time; it is other scholars, rather, whose phoneme theories are less closely related to the nature of phonetic data who have felt the necessity for frequent changes. It is no accident that basically common practice should unite Daniel Jones and those who have, over the years, expressed the strongest objections to his theoretical standpoint, for the phonemic type of structure appears to be one of the brute facts about speech and language which cannot be conjured away by any amount of theorizing.

Theoretical difficulties about the phoneme are not likely to be resolved until a great deal more attention is paid to the behaviour of people who use language, the speakers and the listeners, and rather less to theorists who treat language as something whose existence is independent of speakers and listeners. With the recent growth of work in experimental phonetics, we may in fact be entering a period when this balance is likely to be righted, and such a development might lead eventually to the highly desirable situation in which a linguistic category or a feature of a linguistic system would be considered to be justified only when it was shown to be effective in the behaviour of the language users. In the past, suggestions that the phoneme is a unit which can be justified in this way have often been countered by assertions that any evidence suggesting that language users operate with phonemic units is purely the result of literacy. To argue in this way is, however, in some measure to read history backwards: the existence and the widespread use of alphabetic writing are an indication that a phonemic system and segmentation into phonemic units are features which find a ready response in speakers and listeners. In a similar way, in languages where it is the practice to mark word boundaries in writing or printing we should argue that this practice could arise only if segmentation into words appeared a common-sense procedure to the speakers of the language.

Naturally there is interaction between the system of writing any language and the behaviour of the speakers of that language. In English where the correlation between spelling and the phonemic system is not as close as in some languages, the effect of interaction is mainly to blur some features of the phonemic structure and to make it more difficult to find evidence for this structure in the speakers' behaviour. But it is a question of interaction between phonemic system and spelling and not a case of no phonemes without letters. It is equally an error to suppose that when the orthography of a language is based on a particular linguistic level it is no use to look for evidence of other levels in the speakers' behaviour: speakers of a language which uses an ideographic system of writing are just as likely to show the working of a phonemic system in their linguistic behaviour as are speakers of a language with alphabetic writing.

It would be unreasonable to look for evidence of the working of phonemic systems in language behaviour and especially to set up experiments for the purpose unless there were some general observations that appear to demand an explanation of this sort. In fact every phonetician makes such observations very early in his experience. That a pair of utterances may appear indistinguishably the same to a listener of one nationality and indisputably different to a listener of another nationality is a fact that calls for some explanation. Two syllables consisting in one case of a vowel preceded by an aspirated [t] and in the other of the same vowel preceded by an unaspirated [t] will be heard as the same by an English listener yet the speakers of many Indian languages will not only say that they are different but will find it impossible to imagine that there are people to whom they could sound the same. The Englishman and the Indian, when they listen to these syllables, receive the same sound-waves. Moreover, the movements of the peripheral hearing mechanism in response to the sound-waves are mechanical, they are uninfluenced by learning and are certainly approximately the same in the two listeners; hence the information supplied to the brain is the same for each listener and the difference between them must lie in the structuring of the information at the cortical level. This is clearly the result of language learning, and we are faced here with an aspect of human behaviour which requires explanation and which cannot be explained without linking it with language structure, in particular phonemic structure.

It is through the study of this kind of behaviour that a good deal of information has recently been gained and it is the main purpose of this paper to summarize this knowledge and to consider some of its implications.

## PHONEME BOUNDARIES

In the example given above of aspirated and unaspirated [t], there is evidently a division between two classes for the Indian listener which is inoperative for the English listener. If we could produce a range of sound qualities filling, as it were, the space between aspirated and unaspirated [t] and send these one after the other to the Indian listener, we might expect that at some point in the series he would cease identifying the sound as aspirated and begin to identify it as unaspirated; he would, in other words, pass through a boundary between the two classes. In reporting experiments designed to study this phenomenon, Liberman and his co-workers at Haskins Laboratories[1] have used the expression *phoneme boundary*, and this seems to be a convenient term, provided it is clear that it refers to a boundary between classes and is not in any way related to the question of segmenting an utterance along the time dimension.

The first experiments along these lines were intended to discover whether there is in fact any evidence for the existence of phoneme boundaries in listeners' behaviour and they were concerned with distinctions which, unlike that between aspirated and unaspirated [t], are operative for English listeners, namely distinctions between [b], [d], and [g]. Previous research has shown that whenever a listener makes a distinction between two sounds he has several acoustic cues at his disposal to form the basis of his discrimination. In distinguishing between initial [b] and [d], for example, the English listener may rely on the frequency of a short burst of noise occurring before the periodic sound begins and on changes of formant frequency during the first 50 msec or so of the periodic sound. In receiving natural speech, he probably uses both types of information, but in an experimental situation he can make the distinction on the basis of formant frequency alone.

The Haskins experiments consisted in setting up a series of test stimuli by means of a speech synthesizer in which a periodic sound akin to the English vowel [aː] was initiated by a range of second formant transitions. It had been found in earlier experiments that a minus second formant transition with this vowel was taken by most English listeners to form the syllable /baː/, absence of transition or a slight plus transition was generally heard as /daː/, a more pronounced plus transition, as /gaː/. In synthesizing such syllables it was possible to proceed by very small steps through a wide range from a large minus second formant transition through zero transition to a large plus transition. This provides a continuum of sound change which for English listeners passes from [b] through [d] to [g] in a way which cannot be imitated in human speech because of the articulatory discontinuities in the series. The range of synthesized syllables was presented a number of times in random order to listeners whose native language was English and they were asked to register with respect to each syllable whether they heard /b/, /d/, or /g/. Over certain parts of the continuum the labelling, both by individual listeners and by groups of listeners, was very consistent; that is to say, there were some sets of transitions which were labelled with great consistency as /b/, others as /d/, and yet others as /g/. Between these three sets there were parts of the continuum where the stimuli were labelled in a more nearly random fashion: an individual listener hearing them a number of times would label a given stimulus sometimes /b/ and sometimes /d/, or another one sometimes /d/ and sometimes /g/. The same uncertainty was reflected in the results for a group of listeners; there were points in the continuum where the votes of a group added together showed 50% /b/ and 50% /d/, or 50% /d/ and 50% /g/ in contrast to the three stretches where the judgments were consistently 100% /b/, 100% /d/ and 100% /g/. These areas of uncertainty constitute the *phoneme boundaries* with respect to this particular physical dimension, second formant transition.

In the labelling experiment, the listener is placed in a 'forced choice' situation. He is provided with three categories and is told that he must place every test stimulus in one of these. The experimenter chooses the categories to fit the language with which he is dealing, naturally, and the results of the experiment are not relevant, for example, to the question of the number of phonemic categories in English. What they do demonstrate is the correctness of the prediction that, if we can pass smoothly from a sound quality that is typical of one phonemic class to a sound quality that is typical of another, we shall find a place where the listener is in the act of switching his judgment from one class to another and is hence uncertain what decision to make.

## MEASUREMENTS OF DISCRIMINATION

To provide firm evidence of the operation of phonemic grouping in the perception of speech requires experiments in which the phonemic categories are not imposed on the listener by the design of the experiment. This requirement is met by the second series of experiments carried out by Liberman and his fellow workers as a sequel to the labelling experiment just referred to. It was argued that phonemic grouping, if it indeed operates in the perception of speech, must be one result of the language learning process and must involve either the classing together of a number of sounds that are initially distinct from each other (acquired similarity) or else learning by practice to distinguish sounds which are initially perceived as the same (acquired distinctiveness). In either case, we might expect that the listener will not be equally sensitive to sound differences over the whole range of possible variation. In the case of the stimuli used for the labelling experiment, for example, one would predict that there would be less capacity for discrimination over the range of second formant transitions that were all unhesitatingly labelled as /b/ and an ability to make relatively finer discriminations in the neighbourhood of the phoneme boundary between /b/ and /d/ where it was necessary to make a decision between the two. In general terms, listeners were expected to be able to perceive smaller differences between stimuli in the region of the phoneme boundaries than at other points in the continuum.

This hypothesis was tested by using the same stimuli as for the labelling experiment and presenting them to the same subjects in an ABX test. This consists in arranging the stimuli in triads in which stimulus A is one item in the whole series of stimuli; stimulus B is the item, say, one step removed from A; and stimulus X is a repetition of either A or B. The subject is asked simply to say whether X is the same as A or as B. The whole test consists of a larger number of triads in which X is actually B as often as it is A; in addition to the items in which B is one step removed from A, there are others in which B is two steps or three steps removed from A in the series. These test items are presented to the subject in random order and an analysis of his responses provides a measure of the size of the difference that he can perceive at each point in the continuum. Let us suppose that for a particular A and B his answers are correct only 50% of the time; this is not better than the score he could achieve by answering at random, since he has a choice of only one out of two. If, on the other hand, his answers were 100% correct for a given A and B, we should be justified in concluding that he was able to perceive the difference between this particular A and B with certainty. On comparing the responses of one subject for two different points in the continuum, we might find that at one point he answered correctly all the items involving a one-step difference between A and B while at another point he scored only 50% for the one-step differences. We should then infer that the subject was more sensitive to differences at the first point than at the second. The same conclusion would be indicated if at one point the subject was certain in his judgments for the one-step difference but at a second point required a three-step difference in order to reach the same level of certainty.

The second series of Haskins' experiments set out to measure discrimination in this way, and it was found that there was a clear tendency for the subjects to distinguish smaller differences in second formant transition at the places in the continuum where the phoneme boundaries lay than over the stretches where phoneme identification was certain. The importance of this result for linguistics can scarcely be overestimated. Here for the first time was an experiment in which subjects were not asked to do any phonemic labelling or indeed to perform any overtly linguistic task and yet evidence of phonemic structuring is to be found in the results. On this evidence it is likely that our very perceptions are influenced and modified by the language learning process and if this is so, we may hope to find out more about the way in which speech and language work by studying the behaviour of speakers and listeners at this level.

This experiment constitutes only a beginning and cannot be in any sense conclusive. We are bound to ask the question whether this variation in differential sensitivity is truly connected with language or whether we might not find similar fluctuations if we experimented with any other series of stimuli which had no connection with speech, whether in fact it is not just a coincidence that the points of maximum sensitivity in this case happen to be at the same places as the phoneme boundaries. In order to test this and at the same time to throw more light on the question whether the effect, if it exists, is to be considered as an example of acquired similarity or of acquired distinctiveness, a third set of experiments has been carried out.[2] In these experiments stimuli were used which did not impress the subjects as being in any sense speech-like. They were obtained by transposing the sounds used in previous tests concerning the distinction between /t/ and /d/ to a considerably higher frequency range, a change which was sufficient to remove the stimuli from the general class of speech sounds even though the variations used in the new experiments were an exact parallel to those already used. Measures of discrimination were obtained as before by presenting the sounds in ABX triads and analysing the results to determine the differential threshold for each listener. In this case, unlike that of the speech-like sounds, there was no pronounced variation in sensitivity to change throughout the continuum. At succeeding points in the series the mean differential threshold remained the same and there was no sign of the rise in the ability to discriminate which had appeared at the phoneme boundaries. It seems therefore that the features revealed by the previous labelling and discrimination experiments really are associated with language functioning and are a genuine expression of phonemic structuring. It is interesting to note, also, that the size of the minimum perceptible difference in the case of the non-speech stimuli was comparable with that of the differences perceived *within* the /t/ and /d/ phonemes; they were larger, that is, than those perceived at the phoneme boundaries, suggesting that the linguistic distinctions are based on acquired distinctiveness.

## PHONEME BOUNDARIES WITH RESPECT TO DURATION

The language learning process at the phonemic level appears therefore to involve the sharpening of sensitivity to differences wherever necessary, that is to say at appropriate points in the physical dimensions relevant to a given phonemic opposition.

Since several dimensions are likely to be concerned in a single opposition, it will be necessary to explore in this way a variety of dimensions. The /b, d, g/ experiments involved frequency cues, and these are certain to prove important in many phonemic distinctions. The /t, d/ experiments involved a time cue, and there is already plenty of experimental evidence to show that time cues will need to be considered in the same light. The time domain is particularly suitable for this type of experimentation since it is always possible to set up a continuum of change in this dimension and to quantize in steps as small or as large as may be necessary. Since the tempo of speech is variable, duration effects are always a matter of relative times and are generally best expressed in terms of duration ratio, although they may, for a given set of stimuli, be stated in absolute terms. Phoneme boundaries with respect to time have been revealed both in experiments expressly designed to discover them and also in others where the idea of the phoneme boundary is more implicit. In experiments reported by Denes[3] on the distinction between final /s/ and /z/ in English, it was shown that the duration ratio of the periodic and the noise segments of a syllable was a cue for distinguishing the two sounds. The listeners' judgments in these experiments disclose a well-defined phoneme boundary where the ratio of noise to periodic sound is 1·0.

Lisker[4] has examined the importance of duration for the distinction between intervocalic /p/ and /b/ in English. He found that the time occupied by the closure in the middle of the words *rupee*[5] and *ruby* was an important cue for listeners who were asked to distinguish the words in a listening test. He came to the conclusion that for the particular isolated words that he used there was a phoneme boundary with respect to duration of closure in the region between 75 msec and 130 msec, that is to say, all closures shorter than 75 msec were heard as /b/ and all closures longer than 130 msec were heard as /p/.

This conclusion has been supported by further work by Liberman,[6] who obtained both labelling and discrimination data for the pair of words *rapid* and *rabid.* Here it was found once more that the phoneme boundary which was apparent in the labelling data was matched by a maximum in the ability to discriminate as shown in the discrimination experiment. This is further evidence to support the hypothesis that phonemic structuring is to be found in listeners' perceptions and is particularly interesting because it deals with a different physical dimension from that involved in the /b, d, g/ experiments. Since several dimensions are likely to be concerned in a single phonemic opposition, it would be reasonable to expect that the phenomenon of increased differential sensitivity will appear in each of them and one might predict, in fact, that the ability to discriminate would be increased by language learning just to the extent that the particular dimension was important for the opposition. In other words, discrimination experiments might provide a means of estimating the relative weight of various physical cues.

## VOWEL PHONEME BOUNDARIES

The foregoing account of experiments on phoneme boundaries is too brief to represent anything but the merest summary of results and will inevitably give the impression that these results are more simple and more clear-cut than they can by their nature really be. These are psycho-physical experiments, and it is to be expected in general that well-defined trends in the data will appear only after perhaps rather extensive statistical treatment. A surprising feature of the experimental results referred to is that the phoneme boundary effect is seen so readily after little or no statistical treatment. It is clear that this can scarcely be the case for every cue and every phonemic opposition and, if the suggestion made in the previous paragraph is well-founded, the sharpness and stability of a perceptual phoneme boundary may be related to the importance of the particular physical cue.

It is also probable that the distinctness of a phoneme boundary may depend partly on the degree of articulatory difference between one phoneme and another. In the case of [b], [d], and [g] the articulations are so distinct from each other that, as we have said, it is not possible by articulation to produce a smooth change from one to another. This factor undoubtedly has some influence on perception and will be quite strong in the case of most consonants, at least. The case of vowels will be different for a number of reasons. The impression a speaker has of differences in vowel articulation is by no means as clear as that which he gains from consonant articulation, partly because of the tactual sensations that many of the latter give. This fact may tend to make phoneme boundaries for vowels less sharply defined than for consonants. In addition, the degree of redundancy associated with vowels, at least in a language like English, is considerably greater than that of consonants and hence the phonemic identification of vowels is rather less necessary as far as the informatory level of speech is concerned.

Two considerations of equal weight may be set against these facts. Since the speaker has relatively little articulatory impression when he is producing vowel sounds, he may come to rely the more on auditory impression as a means of controlling his articulatory movements and thus develop his sensitivity to vowel differences to a higher degree than is generally the case with consonants. Further, although vowels may not be very important for the point of view of communication because of their redundancy, they none the less carry other kinds of information which are of great value to the listener. In English, for example, vowels are the main vehicle for dialectal differences and also contain important cues as to the speaker's identity. When a listener takes in speech from a variety of speakers he has in each case to adjust his vowel reference system. The difference between vowel allophones is generally speaking smaller than the difference between vowel phonemes and hence these adjustments call for discriminations which are finer than those demanded by the act of distinguishing between vowel phonemes.

The effect of these last two factors therefore would be to sharpen the ability to discriminate vowel qualities despite the less pronounced vowel phoneme boundaries that are to be expected on the grounds indicated above.

Experiments in the labelling and discrimination of vowels have been begun[7] and the first indications are that listeners' reactions to vowels are in fact rather different from their reactions to consonants. If this is borne out by later results, it will be a further indication that study of the behaviour of language users may provide a firm basis for linguistic categories, in this particular case a sign that the vowel-consonant distinction is a fact of linguistic behaviour and not, as some would have us believe, an invention of the linguist.

The stimuli for these vowel experiments were designed primarily for use with subjects whose native language is English. The continuum of physical change was planned with reference to the plot of the frequencies of Formant 1 and Formant 2 (F1/F2). Vowels consisting of a fundamental frequency and F1 and F2 only were synthesized, in the first instance setting the values of F1 and F2 so as to give three vowel qualities which it was thought listeners were most likely to label /ɪ/, /e/, and /æ/ respectively. The points representing these vowels on an F1/F2 plot were joined by a curve, and other vowels were then synthesized whose two formant frequencies lay on this curve. In all, thirteen vowels were made in such a way as to give equal steps between succeeding vowels in the series. The vowels were presented in isolation; the over-all intensity and fundamental frequency were given the same time-course for every vowel, and this was chosen to make the speech sound as natural as possible.

Labelling and discrimination tests with these stimuli are still at an early stage but certain trends in the results are discernible. The vowel phoneme boundaries are clearly to be seen in the labelling data, but they are less sharply defined than in the consonant data in the sense that a greater proportion of the stimuli in the series produce a rather low level of agreement in labelling, between 50% and 75%. This means both that individual subjects were inconsistent in their labelling of the same stimulus when it was repeated in the test and also that the group of listeners as a whole was divided in its judgments about a particular stimulus. An analysis of the test results shows, however, that the main reason for this is to be found in the well-known effect of context on the perception of vowels.[8] The vowel colour perceived on the presentation of one stimulus is very dependent upon the stimulus that immediately preceded it. An item in the labelling test tended to be assigned to the more open category if it were preceded by a close sounding vowel, and to the more close category if preceded by a more open sounding vowel. As the vowels in the test were presented in random order, one vowel in the series was likely to be labelled differently on different occasions and in this way the scatter of the results was increased. The effect of context or sequence is clearly indicated by the fact that while most subjects achieved a consistency of 100% in labelling certain stimuli as /ɪ/ and others as /æ/, no one reached the same level in labelling stimuli as /e/. This can be accounted for by the fact that the whole series contained no vowel which sounded more close than the first stimulus and none which sounded more open than the last. For these two stimuli, therefore, any sequential effect would tend to force stimulus number 1 firmly into the /ɪ/ category and stimulus number 13 into the /æ/ category. For all other stimuli in the series, however, there were always preceding vowels which could make them sound sometimes more open and sometimes more close. As a consequence there was considerable dispersion in the judgments of the stimuli that fell mainly into the /e/ category, the maximum agreement being 89% for stimulus number 8 compared with 98·4% for stimulus number 1 as /ɪ/ and 100% for stimulus number 13 as /æ/.

The same sequential effects took place in the discrimination experiment, but their operation was even more complex since the stimuli were again presented in ABX triads. Here the number of steps between A and B and also the fact that X was actually A or B would help to determine the context effect, as well as the direction of the difference between A and B. Despite the variability inherent in the discrimination test for this reason, the results showed some very interesting features. The A and B comparisons included, as in the previous consonant tests, differences of one, two, and three steps in the series. In the case of the vowels it was only the one-step differences that gave any trouble in discrimination; when the difference between A and B was as great as two steps, most subjects identified X correctly in practically every case. If the differential threshold is between one and two steps in this series, it seems clear that subjects were able to distinguish many sub-phonemic differences. In the consonant experiments it was shown that subjects' ability to distinguish between stimuli was more closely linked with their ability to distinguish /b, d, g/ as phonemes and in this respect the vowel results are markedly different.

A second difference between the results of the two experiments is that the subjects showed no systematic variation in the ability to discriminate between vowels as the phoneme boundaries are passed through. They tended to be equally sensitive to differences throughout the whole range of the stimuli, as indeed one would expect if they are generally able to notice sub-phonemic differences.

These most recent experimental results suggest, therefore, that the language learning process, in English at least, leads the listener to deal with vowels and consonants in different ways. Although a quantitative comparison of the discrimination data for vowels and consonants is scarcely possible, since the dimensions and hence the scales and steps are so different in the two cases, it seems probable nevertheless that language learning increases the sensitivity to consonant differences near the phoneme boundaries but develops a capacity for distinguishing vowel colour which is fairly uniform throughout the possible range of vowels. It is difficult to determine how the ability to distinguish vowels and consonants compares, but it may be worth noting that in the /b, d, g/ and the vowel experiments it happened that thirteen steps were used to cover three phoneme categories; if this can be taken as an indication that the range of stimuli was comparable in the two cases, then there is evidence in the results that discrimination for vowels is equal and possibly superior to discrimination for the consonants /b, d, g/.

## PHONEME LABELLING BY DIFFERENT LANGUAGE GROUPS

Many crucial experiments remain to be done in this field. The first results are promising enough to make it worthwhile to continue the search for evidences of phonemic structuring in perceptual data. The most urgent need at this stage is for experimental demonstration that phonemic labelling of the same set of stimuli will differ with speakers of different languages, and then for an extension of this work to discover whether in discrimination experiments maxima of differential sensitivity go consistently with the phoneme boundary regions.

The first of the questions has already been tackled in experiments reported by Lotz *et al.*,[9] who presented to speakers of four different languages syllables containing fortis aspirated, fortis unaspirated, and lenis unaspirated stops. The stimuli were made by tape-cutting recorded utterances by American English speakers, the fortis unaspirated stops being obtained by removing the initial friction in syllables such as *spill*, *spore*, etc. When the set of eighteen stimuli were presented in random order to a group of American listeners for labelling, the subjects very consistently assigned the fortis aspirated stops to the /p/, /t/, and /k/ phonemes and equally consistently placed both the fortis unaspirated and the lenis unaspirated stops in the /b/, /d/, and /g/ phonemes. This result is interesting, because it throws light on the weight of the various cues which determine the phonemic grouping of plosives. For English-speaking listeners, aspiration is a deciding factor in the labelling of initial stops.

The three other groups of listeners used in the experiment were speakers of Puerto Rican Spanish, Hungarian, and Thai. In Spanish and Hungarian the phonemic systems include an opposition of voiceless and voiced stops where there is no aspiration and the determining factor is generally considered to be voice. Both Spanish and Hungarian speakers labelled the fortis aspirated stops as /p/, /t/, and /k/, and the lenis stops as /b/, /d/, and /g/; the fortis unaspirated stops were most often assigned to the /p, t, k/ category, though the judgments were somewhat divided, particularly when the sound occurred before a back vowel. The Thai system of stops contains three terms, voiceless aspirated, voiceless unaspirated, and voiced. Thai subjects consistently assigned the fortis aspirated stops to the /ph/, /th/, and /kh/ phonemes, the fortis unaspirated ones to /p/, /t/, and /k/, and the lenis bi-labial and alveolar stops to /b/ and /d/. There is no velar-voiced stop in Thai, and although in the test the subjects were offered the possibility of labelling the velar lenis sound as /g/, the majority of them placed it in the /k/ category.

There can be no doubt that in dealing with the same set of stimuli each of these four groups of subjects was applying the criteria demanded by his native phonemic system – we cannot indeed suppose that the case would be otherwise. But experimental work of this kind is extremely valuable, because through its aid we begin to see more exactly how linguistic behaviour is organized. This may lead in its turn to a linguistic science which is firmly grounded in the material which it professes to study. There is certainly no way in which we could make better use of the tremendous capital of phonetic observations which has been amassed by scholars such as Daniel Jones than by allowing it to serve as the basis for such a task.

*Notes*

[1] A. M. Liberman, K. S. Harris, H. S. Hoffman, and B. C. Griffith, 'The Discrimination of Speech Sounds within and across Phoneme Boundaries', *J. exper. Psychol.*, LIV, 1957, 358–368.

[2] Liberman, Harris, J. A. Kinney, and H. Lane, 'The Discrimination of Relative Onset-time of the Components of Certain Speech and Non-speech Patterns', *J. exper. Psychol.*, LXI, 1961, 379–388.

[3] P. Denes, 'Effect of Duration on the Perception of Voicing', *J. acoust. Soc. Amer.*, XXVII, 1955, 761–766.

[4] L. Lisker, 'Closure Duration and the Intervocalic Voiced-Voiceless Distinction in English', *Language*, XXXIII, 1957, 42–49.

[5] This word is a trochee for Lisker.

[6] Liberman, Harris, P. Eimas, Lisker, and J. Bastian, 'An Effect of Learning on Speech Perception', *Language and Speech*, IV, 1961, 175–195.

[7] These experiments have been carried out by the present writer in collaboration with Professor A. M. Liberman, Dr A. S. Abramson and the staff of the Haskins Laboratories, New York.

[8] See, for example, P. Ladefoged and D. E. Broadbent, 'Information conveyed by Vowels', *J. acoust. Soc. Amer.*, XXIX, 1957, 98–104.

[9] J. Lotz, A. S. Abramson, L. Gerstman, F. Ingemann, and W. J. Nemser, 'The Perception of English Stops by Speakers of English, Spanish, Hungarian, and Thai', *Language and Speech*, III, 1960, 71–77.

# Articulatory Settings

BEATRICE HONIKMAN

In the study of spoken language, especially in that branch dealing with pronunciation generally and articulation particularly, it would seem that though in our analyses of numerous languages we have described in great or lesser detail the formation of their individual sounds (as well as intonation, rhythm, stress, and other phonetic features), yet there is an elusive aspect of articulation which, up to the present, if not totally neglected, has not received the attention it merits. I refer to what is here termed the *articulatory setting* of a language.

By articulatory setting is meant the disposition of the parts of the speech mechanism and their composite action, i.e. the just placing of the individual parts, severally and jointly, for articulation according to the phonetic substance[1] of the language concerned. To put this another way, it is the over-all arrangement and manœuvring of the speech organs necessary for the facile accomplishment of natural[2] utterance. Broadly, it is the fundamental groundwork which pervades and, to an extent, determines the phonetic character and specific timbre of a language. It is immanent in all that the organs do.

Articulatory setting does not imply simply the particular articulations of the individual speech sounds[3] of a language, but is rather the nexus of these isolated facts and their assemblage, based on their common, rather than their distinguishing, components. The isolated articulations are mutually related parts of the whole utterance; they are clues, as it were, to the articulatory plan of the whole; the conception of articulatory setting seeks to incorporate the clues or to see them as incorporated in the whole. Thus an articulatory setting is the gross oral posture and mechanics, both external and internal, requisite as a framework for the comfortable, economic, and fluent merging and integrating of the isolated sounds into that harmonious, cognizable whole which constitutes the established pronunciation of a language.

If we are sufficiently expert acoustically and in articulation or endowed with a sufficiently acute linguistic and phonetic sense or insight, we might divine the articulatory setting of a foreign language from the actions required of the speech mechanism. 'Natural mimics' and the gifted do just this; they adopt the articulatory pattern almost unconsciously. Those less gifted can fall into the pattern but must work at it consciously at first, and for this they need help and training. It was in an effort to aid those struggling to improve their pronunciation of a foreign language that it became clear that the field of articulatory settings might well be explored.

Though there is nothing in this article that is not implied in the many good publications on phonetics, the reader will appreciate the necessity for reintroducing here certain details with which he is already familiar.

It is because the student is inclined to interpret the articulations analysed in textbooks, not as events in a moving continuum but as a manifold of detached articulations, that he so often fails to co-ordinate them satisfactorily. To counteract this tendency and to enable him more effectively to correlate these apparently isolated clues and weld them into a consistent whole, some observations concerning the articulatory settings of various languages are given below.

All languages do not have identical articulatory settings: whereas one language may resemble another in this respect, others may differ considerably. Where two languages are disparate in articulatory setting, it is not possible completely to master the pronunciation of one whilst maintaining the articulatory setting of the other.

In this connection, it is enlightening to observe the characteristic movements and lineaments about the lips and jaws of different peoples[4] *during utterance* of their own language.

The cinema or television screen provides a good opportunity for objectively studying these particulars.

Watching the speakers in, say, French, Russian, and English films, it is interesting to note (a) the difference between these in 'look' about the mouth and jaw, and (b) the similarity of 'lip-jaw look' of the individual speakers in any one of them.

Comparing individual speakers in French films, one notices the considerable mobility of the lips which, much of the time, seem to round very energetically.[5] This contrasts markedly with Russian, in which the lips appear to be mostly closely spread, well stretched into an almost horizontal line and only intermittently rounded. And, between these two lip-settings, English, in which on the whole the lips neither round vigorously nor spread very much but mostly remain rather 'neutral' –

slightly and loosely apart, slightly cornered and with only moderate mobility – a sort of compromise between French and Russian.[6]

Furthermore, in French utterance the tongue setting and rather frequent lowering of the jaw allows the tongue to be visible, whereas in English,[7] the jaw-movement is so slight and the internal setting such, that the tongue is hardly ever visible during utterance.

This brings me to a remark made by foreign students from many countries who have studied English at home: when asked for their impressions on first hearing English as spoken in England, one of their replies is invariably either, 'The English don't move their mouths when they speak', or, 'You don't open your mouths when you speak.'

These lay remarks are not empty of significance; they are revealing and worthy of more than just passing notice: on closer consideration, one realizes that implicit in them is the observation that the *external articulatory setting* of English is unexpected and different from their own.

This noticeable lack or, rather, near-lack of activity of almost closed jaws together with relatively unvigorous lip-rounding are essential features of good, unaffected,[7] everyday English utterance: they are part and parcel of the articulatory setting requisite for normal English, just as the vigorous lip-rounding of French and German, the close-spread lips of Russian, the slack lips and loosely apart jaws of Indian languages[8] are essentials of the external articulatory settings for those languages.

So far reference has been sketchily made mainly to the 'external setting', but intimately bound up with this, and to a considerable extent governing it, is the *internal articulatory setting*, i.e. the over-all positioning of the internal mobile organs of the mouth for natural utterance.

Here again languages differ, the setting depending upon the phonetic substance of the language. The articulating organs require to be so placed that all the actions required of them are easy and comfortable and able smoothly to link and merge with their neighbours. The distribution of sounds in one's own language can, to some extent, be ascertained by concentrating on the feel of the oral cavity *during utterance.* For instance, one becomes aware in speaking English of the constant rapping of the tongue-tip against the alveolar ridge and intermittent closing and opening and other slight motions of the lips; whereas this is not the case in French, where the tongue-tip is hardly palpable and certainly less active than the blade and front and the constantly moving (rounding and spreading) lips. In both these languages, as in utterance generally, the sides of the tongue are almost impalpable.

The internal articulatory setting of a language is determined, to a great extent, by the most frequently occurring sounds and sound combinations in that language. Since it is the articulation for consonants that interrupts or impedes the free flow of the air stream through the mouth, the setting required for the most frequent consonants has an important bearing on the articulatory setting as a whole – no less important than that required for the most frequent vowels.[9]

Of the internal oral organs, the tongue, with its wide range of mobility and therefore considerable capacity for altering the shape of the resonance chamber of the mouth, is of paramount importance.

As has been mentioned, during utterance the sides of the tongue, and in some languages, e.g. French, even the apex, are not easily felt. This is probably due to the fact that no pressure is exerted by them or because they are lightly tethered or relatively inert compared with some more active or more tense or more stable organ which dominates the articulation and so masks the more passive parts of the 'articulator'. Nevertheless, these less palpable parts are important to the positioning of the tongue as a whole.

Among the consonants of English, cardinal alveolar articulation occurs, in general, considerably more frequently than any other; for this reason, the anchorage described below, i.e. that required for the cardinal alveolar sounds [t, d, n, ɾ, s, z],[10] should be regarded as the basis of the internal articulatory setting of English utterance.

## THE TONGUE-SETTING FOR ENGLISH

Almost throughout English, the tongue is tethered laterally to the roof of the mouth by allowing the sides to rest along the inner surface of the upper lateral gums and teeth; the lateral rims of the tongue very seldom entirely leave this part of the roof of the mouth, whereas the tip constantly (or some other part of the dorsum, occasionally) moves up and down, periodically touching the central part of the roof, but generally not for very long at a time, before it comes away. Thus, one might regard the tethered part – in this case, the lateral contact – as the *anchorage*, and the untethered part as the *free* or *operative part* of the tongue-setting.

By anchoring the tongue we, naturally, lessen its freedom of movement. Therefore it is important to note the extent of the anchorage, for this prescribes the range of play of the free part as well as of the tongue as a whole. The forward limit(s) of tethering might well serve as points of reference in describing the anchorage.

Thus, the alveolar consonants of English – [t, d, n, ɾ, s, z] and generally [l] – require lateral anchorage as far forward as the upper posterior pre-molars (but never beyond the anterior pre-molars).[11] These teeth on either side of the roof of the mouth serve, as it were, as forward mooring-posts for the tongue, allowing the transverse part of the dorsum between them to operate as a hinge which enables the tip and blade to swing comfortably up and down, towards, to, and away from the alveolar ridge, but preventing the blade and tip from ranging much further forward without strain.[12] This anterior lateral contact is released for a following further back consonant or open or back vowel, and very slightly extended forward for dental sounds.[13]

Since this anchorage is not tensely held, but is rather a pliable cushioning of the tongue-rim, adjustments to it such as lowering, retracting, and advancing are comfortably and smoothly made when required, as for some vowels and the less frequent lingual consonants. For example: for the sounds [θ, ð, t̪, d̪, n̪, l̪] there is a minute advancing of the lateral contact and a concomitant reaching or sliding forward of the tip and blade, enabling the apical-rim of the tongue without effort to reach as far as, but not beyond the upper front teeth, the undersurface of the tongue resting lightly upon the cutting edges of the lower teeth; except in the rare cases of great emphasis, the tip is not exposed beyond the upper teeth. For the sounds [r, tr, dr] there is a release of the foremost part of the lateral contact; for [l], a release of the mid and/or back part but generally not of the fore-part of the lateral anchorage.

With regard to the *free part* of the tongue: for the most frequent English consonants [t, n], as well as for [d, l, ɫ, s, z, ɾ, ʧ, ʤ, ʃ, ʒ] the *tip* is the effective articulator[14]: the tip is somewhat narrowed and tapered by lateral contraction. In [t, d, n, l, ɫ] the tapered tip works energetically up and down as it touches, exerts some pressure on, and comes down away from the rim of the alveolar ridge to or towards the floor of the mouth, thus allowing some other part of the tongue to come comfortably into play for a following vowel or for a following consonant not requiring tip or blade articulation. The upper surface of the tongue just behind the tip, except in clear [l], lies *concave* to the roof; if the jaw were lowered during the stop of these sounds, the underside of the tongue would be clearly visible and seen to be held concave to the roof.

## THE TONGUE-SETTING FOR FRENCH

In French the tongue-setting is in many respects very different from that of English. For the greater part of French utterance, the tongue: (a) remains broad, i.e. the tip is untapered, there being no lateral contraction. (b) It is anchored medianly, albeit lightly, to the floor of the mouth by the tip tethering to the lower front teeth, either cushioned against their inner surface or held so that the underside of the tip rests upon their cutting edges; thus the under-surface of the tongue is not exposed even when the jaw is lowered, but part of the dorsum – the blade (or tip and blade) – is frequently visible during utterance. Adjustment of this anchorage, by very slightly withdrawing the tip along the floor of the mouth, allows the back of the tongue comfortably to assume the positions required for back vowels and for the back consonants [k, g] and the frequent uvular [ʁ]. (c) The body of the tongue is generally held *convex* to the roof of the mouth; it flattens down, however, as the jaw lowers for the frequent vowel [a], and the back part becomes convex for [k, g, ʁ] and back vowels. (d) Of the free, i.e. untethered part of the tongue, the *blade* (or tip and blade) and the *front* are the dominant articulators – the blade and tip in [t, d, n, l], the blade in [s, z, ʃ, ʒ][15]; the front in all front vowels and the consonants [ɲ, j, ɥ] and to some extent in [l] also. In [t, d, n], though the tip and blade completely contact the upper front teeth (and fore-part of the ridge), it is the blade rather than the tip that exerts the pressure. For [s, z, ʃ, ʒ], while the blade slightly recedes to articulate with the alveolar ridge, the tip lowers to the base of the lower teeth.[15] (e) The sides of the tongue are in contact with the upper gums or teeth for much of French utterance; this lateral contact is not as constant as in English, however, probably due to the fact that in French the open vowel [a] occurs very frequently, more frequently relatively than do the most open vowels in English, and so requires more frequent lowering of the jaw and, consequently, more frequent release of the lateral contact. In the frequent consonants [t, d, n] the lateral contact extends as far forward as the upper canines, thus bringing the entire tongue-rim completely into contact with the upper arcade of teeth.[16]

A tongue-setting different from both French and English is required for Turkish and Iranian where dental consonants are frequent but are articulated with the tongue well tapered and the pointed tip the predominating 'articulator'.

Again, the frequent retroflex consonants in the languages of India and Pakistan are produced with the tongue curled back in such a way that the edge of the rim of the tip approximates or touches the hind-part of the alveolar ridge or fore-part of the palate; the open setting of the jaws enables this tongue-setting to be made comfortably.[17]

In Russian, while blade-dental consonants are not infrequent, the profusion of palatalized sounds would seem to require, for ease of articulation, well-spread lips as an accompaniment to the necessary tongue-setting (front – high and spread; body – convex to the palate). In describing articulatory settings, some reference should also be made to: (a) the *muscular tension* of the tongue, lips, cheeks, jaw, and pharynx; (b) the *pressure* exerted by the 'articulator' upon its opposite number in those sounds with median closure; (c) the general *positioning of the jaw*, as these aspects of articulation have some bearing on the general articulatory setting and languages may differ in these features too.

## TENSION

Thus in English, the lateral tongue contraction, mentioned above, gives to those unaccustomed to this setting the impression that the tongue is somewhat tensed, but the Englishman is not aware of any tension and feels the tongue to be relaxed.

In French, there is no lateral tension of the lingual muscles but strong thrust is felt to be given to the convexed dorsum, especially in articulating the front vowels. French people with whom this has been discussed say it feels as if they were 'pushing the words forward out of the mouth'; no doubt, the strong rounding of the lips together with the exertion – drawing-in – of the cheeks contributes to this effect, the contraction of the buccinator muscles (which is reflected in the external setting too) giving a sense of inner rounding, i.e. rounding within the oral cavity. In English on the other hand, there is no sense of tension or contraction of the inside of the cheeks except perhaps when we greatly emphasize an exclamation such as 'Oo!'

With regard to the pharynx, this is generally relaxed in French and English,[18] there being no contraction of the pharyngeal muscle, whereas in Arabic, and frequently in German (especially in men), pharyngeal contraction is usual.

## PRESSURE

In consonants with median closure[19] the pressure exerted by the 'articulator' upon its opposite number is firm in English (perhaps somewhat less firm in aspirated than in unaspirated consonants) and firmer still in emphasis; weakening of the contact produces what is considered 'slipshod speech'; in American English, however, the tendency is to weaken the contact in intervocalic alveolar plosives so that a tapped consonant results. English, German, Italian, Polish, and many other languages resemble English in pressure of contact; Danish, on the other hand, appears to be following in the direction of Spanish, where plosive contact has gradually weakened over the ages to such an extent that, except after nasal consonants, the contact has altogether disappeared, with the result that weak (homorganic) fricatives and even frictionless continuants have resulted and now replace the plosives in these two languages. In many of the languages of India and Pakistan bilabial contact is generally very weak, the lips only just touch but do not press together. This, no doubt, is due to the jaw-setting (see below).

## THE JAWS

In natural colloquial English the jaws are, for the most part, held loosely together but not clenched – no tension is felt; the most frequent vowels appear to be [ɪ] and [ə] which do not require the jaws to be parted. There is from time to time some lowering of the jaw, but relatively infrequent and slight, so that the aperture between the upper and lower teeth is generally never wide – at most about a finger's width, as required for the diphthongs [aɪ, aʊ], less for [æ]. Thus it appears that the greater part of English articulation takes place behind (loosely) closed jaws. It is this feature of English, no doubt, which helps to give foreigners the impression that we do not move or open our mouths when we speak.

In French utterance the jaws, though mostly fairly close, open more often and perhaps more widely than in English, owing to the relatively greater frequency of the most open vowel [a], which is more open than the open English vowels.

The jaw-setting for the languages of India and Pakistan is distinctive: the jaws are held rather inert and loosely apart, so that the aperture between upper and lower teeth is relatively wide and the oral cavity enlarged; this position is appropriate to the frequently occurring retroflex consonants, enabling them to be produced more comfortably than if the jaws were held closer; this setting accounts, too, for the lack of pressure in bilabial stops, and for the characteristic timbre of Indian languages. This distinctive timbre is very noticeable in the English spoken by Indians.

## APPLICATIONS AND CONCLUSIONS

Though superficial observations on several languages are included in this article, only English and French have been investigated in any detail; the main differences in 'set' of the organs for utterance of these two languages are summarized below for comparison.

| | ENGLISH | FRENCH |
|---|---|---|
| Jaws | Loosely closed (not clenched) | Slightly open |
| Lips | Neutral; moderately active | Rounded; vigorously active in spreading and rounding. |
| State of oral cavity | Relaxed | Cheeks contracted |
| Main consonant articulation | Tip – alveolar | Blade – dental |
| Tongue: | | |
| *Anchorage* | To roof laterally | To floor centrally |
| *Tip* | Tapered | Untapered |
| *Body* | Slightly concave to roof | Convex to roof |
| *Underside* | Concave to roof | Neutral |

Perhaps it would not be out of place here to describe an instance or two of the use to which the articulatory setting approach has been put in the teaching of spoken language.

The first opportunity to apply the technique occurred in the course of some private sessions with advanced French students preparing for their finals as teachers of English. They had a considerable knowledge of English phonetics and had achieved a certain proficiency in spoken English, then had come to a standstill. It appeared to me that while speaking English the 'set' of their features was in some elusive way not quite consistent with the English pattern and that English qualities could not possibly eventuate from such setting. To check that they were doing all they should, I, thinking aloud, attempted to express in layman terms what my mouth felt like during utterance of English; as I did so, I noticed them making adjustments here and there to their settings. Whilst I described much of what has been included in the foregoing analysis, they were encouraged to watch closely as I spoke at normal pace, noting the almost motionless jaws and lips and the fact that the tongue is hidden and does not protrude beyond the teeth.

Exercises were devised to taper and concave the tongue, to anchor it correctly, placing it just so, to feel the tip against the rim of the alveolar ridge (many foreign students, misinterpreting the textbooks, are apt to place it too far forward), practising the minute movements required to link sounds such as [θ] or [ð] with [s] and [z] fluently, stilling the lips, a small adjustment here, another there, patient drills and donkey-work, constant reminders to relax the organs. We had been working in this way for about half a dozen sessions, when, one day, while reading aloud, a student suddenly exclaimed, 'I've got it!', and continued with the passage. The difference was dramatic, and of the two of us, I was the more surprised: she really did sound English and knew it, also her features took on an English 'look'. To both of us it was very satisfying. Of course it needed further perseverance to establish the setting; instructions for obtaining the articulatory setting required were finally reduced to the following formula: taper and concave the tongue, draw it as a whole back into the mouth so that the pointed tip presses against the edge of the alveolar ridge: close the jaws, don't clench them; still the lips; swallow to relax; now to limber up, repeat [t, d, n, l].

This technique with, of course, a different formula, has also been used in teaching French to English students. The formula is devised to assist in positioning the organs preparatory to articulation.

Once the description of the setting had been given and the formula devised, it was found that a blanket-term was required to cover all the details included in a formula; for want of a better, the term '*gear*' has been used quite successfully, students, at this stage, finding the expressions 'English gear', 'French gear', etc., readily intelligible. At the beginning of a practical class I would say, 'Are you in English gear?' – and as soon as I hear them dropping back to a foreign accent, I might remark, 'You're out of gear', and it is rewarding to see how well they react and get back 'into gear' again.

I have found that insistence on the articulatory setting as a starting-point does away with the need to practise new articulations by the method of exaggerating them. For example, the [θ] and [ð] of English – the bugbear of many foreign students – are found to be less difficult to make and incorporate when the setting is explained and mastered. So, too, the production of dental consonants, uvular [ʁ], and the rounded front vowels of French and German, usually difficult for English people to make and, once accomplished, to co-ordinate and catenate with others, has been facilitated by this method.

In the past, we have dissected the whole into its parts by analysing and describing the individual features; then the student attempts to put them together but the synthesis falls short of the original and is halting.

I would therefore say, establish the setting first, then the details of articulation.

From one point of view we may look upon utterance of a particular language as the sum-total or synthesis of its constituent parts, i.e. grammar, idiom, articulations and their distribution, intonation, stress, rhythm, tempo, but it is, from another view-point, more than its parts. While it is dependent upon them, it is not exhaustively analysable into them. All the constituent parts are interrelated and interdependent, if you change a part you change its relations. Something which links all these parts is necessary for their integration. The link, so far as articulation goes, is the *articulatory setting*, external and internal.

I am aware that I have touched only the fringe of the subject of articulatory settings. From what has been set down here, it will be readily appreciated that the concept of articulatory settings is applicable not only to the study of pronunciation *per se*, but, in addition, has an important contribution to make in the analysis of language at the phonological level. It is much to be wished that others will undertake further investigation of *articulatory settings*; the results of their researches will add not only to our methods of teaching and learning the spoken word, but also to our comprehension of the past and future development of particular languages.

*Notes*

[1] By *phonetic substance* of a language is meant the assortment of sounds that compose it and their distribution in the context of natural utterance; 'distribution of sounds' includes their 'periodicity', i.e. their recurrence or relative frequency of occurrence; their 'arrangement', i.e. their order of sequence; their 'assembly', i.e. their patterns of sequence in context. An analysis of the substance (noting what does not occur as well as what does) will give one an idea of the *status* of a language, and this would serve as a clue to the articulatory setting.

[2] By 'natural' is here meant 'consonant with the character of the language; instinctively felt and recognized by the native to be right; unexaggerated'.

[3] These have been meticulously investigated and described in their excellent publications by Daniel Jones, Lilias Armstrong, and other phoneticians.

[4] I do not refer here to typical facial features in the genetic sense.

[5] German lip-action is very similar to French, see p. 82.

[6] For other 'settings' see p. 81.

[7] The English described in this article is to be taken as that spoken by natives of England, except when otherwise specified. Over-rounding of the lips is sometimes adopted by English speakers as an affectation, under the impression that it makes English clearer, but it is not usual and, in fact, 'looks' unnatural. English spoken with considerable movement of the lower jaw is sometimes used in entertainment as

a 'humorous turn' on the music-hall stage. It is not natural English and 'looks funny' to, and so elicits laughter from, an English audience.

[8] See p. 80.

[9] Once the main setting is established, adjustments for the lesser used sounds can be comfortably made.

[10] Of these [t, n] and, next, [s] are perhaps the most prevalent.

[11] Direct observation, as well as palatography, shows this clearly.

[12] Watching the tongue repeat quite naturally [t, d, n, l] a number of times in succession, without an intervening vowel, will show the action of the tongue.

[13] Nearly all lingual sounds have a certain amount of lateral contact; the only ones that show none are open or far back vowels, far back consonants and, occasionally, clear [l].

[14] In [s, z, ʧ, ʤ] the tip plus blade constitute the main articulator; some speakers produce their [ʃ, ʒ] with the blade as the effective articulator, the tip being held somewhat lower.

[15] Except in those who use the variety of [l, ʃ, ʒ] with tip raised.

[16] Cf. English, where only in the relatively rare cases of dental stoppage is the entire tongue-rim in contact with all the upper teeth.

[17] See p. 80.

[18] There are individuals who speak with contracted pharynx, but this is not usual.

[19] Plosives, affricates, nasals, laterals.

# Grammatical Intonation

LEE S. HULTZÉN

The matter in hand is that aspect of intonation which is associated with that part of the communication customarily subject to grammatical analysis, i.e. excluding correlation with emotional states. The treatment is primarily at the prosodemic[1] level, related to utterance intonation in the same way that phonemic interpretation is related to segmental pronunciation, but there is some general reference to what I have elsewhere called the formal pattern characteristic of dialects and idiolects.[2] There is no implication of application to other than dialect-accents of standard English, although the possibility is not ruled out.

Whatever the unit of language immediately in hand for consideration in such inquiry as this, it must be considered as based on utterance and in total context. While the sentence appears to be the largest unit from which grammatical patterns of utterance can be abstracted and to which they can be applied, the sentence prosody as whole and as to parts can be completely analysed only in the light of other-sentence and often of non-linguistic context.

Sentence intonation is adequately specified by the intonations of the constituent clauses, being no more than the sum of the clause intonations, whatever the influence on them of position within the sentence. Clauses may be said to be defined by pauses, although an inter-clause pause may be extremely short and a clearly marked clause pattern may be interrupted by pauses. Clauses cannot be specified solely by pauses, inasmuch as the points at which pauses occur are determined or at least limited, barring fortuitous circumstances, by certain types of juncture in the concomitant text. I use the term *text* here and elsewhere for the residue of utterance after the intonation has been abstracted, referring not only to the segmental line but also to the structures as shaped by form-words, inflections, etc., and got at by something like immediate-constituent analysis.[3] Fortunately for the economy of the present argument, it is only necessary to take note of the rôle of the text in defining clauses; the shape and position of the clause text are more important than the specific boundaries.

Whatever the other characteristics of the internal open juncture which marks off sub-clausal phrases, it apparently is not a matter of perceptible pause or of differentiating intonational turns, and for present purposes need not be taken into consideration.[4] An intonation as pattern may be said to have clausal domain. It is only to be remarked that in various styles of utterance and in various idiolects, what in one style or idiolect may be a phrase juncture for a particular text may be in another a clause end.

I use the term intonation in a somewhat different way from that in which it is often used, although I doubt that it makes much difference so far as the general theory is concerned.[5] An intonation is a pattern of accents; an accent is a composite of relative pitch, loudness (= stress in some systems), and length. The argument is to be only briefly sketched here. There is no evidence that loudness is primary among the features of pitch, loudness, and length which are notable accompaniments of the syllable in utterance; indeed there is some evidence that it is not.[6] It is possible to avoid any question of primacy, and incidentally to do away with the distinction between the word stress and sentence stress, by noting only the pitch-loudness-length positions and shapes in utterances and generalizing the basic clause patterns for the language-dialect in question. The accentuation of citation forms, as in a pronouncing dictionary, can then be interpreted as indicating that the syllables have primary, secondary, or weak accented positions, as marked, in whatever clause pattern the form happens to appear in actual utterance.[7]

It is assumed that there are basic clause patterns or intonations for any language-dialect. Such is the underlying assumption of the Tune 1 and Tune 2 of the Jones school.[8] Although their definition of intonation limits it to 'the variations which take place in the pitch of the voice in connected speech', their displays in fact contain specification of the stress, which is primarily loudness, and, under the general rule that vowels are longer under stress, also length. Other systems of analysis also specify a limited number of clause patterns.[9]

It is a matter of no great importance how many basic clause intonations there are in the repertory for a particular language-dialect so long as such correlations as are to be set forth can be made, but the number is probably always small. I find for English, including what dialect-accents of the standard language I am familiar with, only two. One is not-low ending, to be labelled open, and one is low ending, to be labelled closed.[10] There may be differences in the internal arrangements so that the terms open and closed refer to more than the ending. The form of the endings and the internal arrangements vary from one dialect to another and, particularly to be taken into consideration, from one idiolect to another.

Basically the open tune correlates with a text that is, either in its grammatical shape or in the occurrence in it of some foreshadowing word, non-finitive for an English sentence. The closed tune correlates basically with a text that is similarly finitive in the sense that it is a shape appropriate to the completion of an English sentence. In this basic correlation there is no meaning in the intonation that is not also in the text.[11]

The simplest case of non-finitive and finitive text shape is subject and formally completed predicate. A subject of any appreciable length is regularly set off as a separate clause[12] and is non-finitive in the sense that a predicate is expected to follow. Other formally marked non-finitive texts are initial clauses, by chance co-extensive with grammatical clauses in the traditional sense, introduced by *after*, *if*, *when*, etc., the markers controlling as non-finitive all clauses occurring before the promised completion clause appears. And preposed modifiers introduced by certain connectives, prepositions, or *-ing* forms. And parentheses interrupting or appended to non-finitive texts. And certain word orders best pointed out, for all the hazard involved,[13] by exemplification: (1) 'Were they better, they'd be more acceptable.' (2) 'Were they better, or worse, than you expected?' (3) 'Were they better?'[14] Although in (3) the clause is printed with end pointing, the text shape within the clause, the matter in hand, is the same as it is in the other contexts, where obviously non-finitive, and the basic intonation is the same in all three. It is at least surely so that the open intonation has been established in English for this clause shape, occurring very frequently in the (3) setting.[15] In some idiolects this non-finitive text shape has an arrested down-turn or slight up-turn in situations (1) and (2) but an extensive up-turn in situation (3). These forms can be considered positional variants rather than two different intonations.

A predicate text, in the usual sentence order, is finitive if formally completed at any clause end potential as completion of an English sentence, whether or not there are in fact such co-ordinate or subordinate additions as are frequent in the favoured loose sentence construction in English. It is only in this sense that the closed tune can be said to correlate with the finitive text shape without saying anything that is not said in the text. The sense of the text sometimes has to be taken into consideration. Thus a structure like 'Noun phrase – Verb phrase – *the* Noun' has its generally finitive shape negatived if the reference of the last Noun has not already been fixed. So with clauses containing terms indicating some kind of correlation which are finitive if the correlate has already appeared but non-finitive if it has not. All of the text shapes noted in the preceding paragraph as non-finitive when appearing before the completion clause are finitive when following the completion clause, including parentheses.[16] Sentence fragments such as replies to questions or the three *And* fragments in the middle of the last paragraph, are similarly finitive in that the completion has already appeared.

If it is so that basic intonations correlate with text shapes, it may well be that modification of the intonation as a whole, specifiable as reversal of the end not-low or low, although it may include internal rearrangement, suggests that the text is to be interpreted in some other way than as non-completion or completion of an ordinary sentence.[17]

The conspicuous example is that of finitive text shapes occurring early in what the informant intends to be, and what would occur in print as, a sentence.[18] Very simply, if the text is not to be taken in accord with its shape as completed, it may here be taken as incomplete. In eighteen of the twenty examples of 'Tune I. repeated' shown by Armstrong and Ward,[19] the first clause, a finitive text shape, is graphically represented with the end fall arrested above the base line. Such a not-low ending is just as much a reversal of the text-appropriate low ending as is the up-turn reversal for finitive text shape shown in eight of Jones' nine examples of 'Tune 2 . . . First parts of sentences.'[20] The difference between arrested fall as a reversal of text-appropriate closed intonation and up-turn as the form of text-appropriate open intonation, as in Armstrong and Ward,[21] may be formal in the dialect, alloprosodes, or alloproses for anyone who likes such terminology. If Armstrong and Ward and Jones are describing the same dialect, the difference between reversals as arrested down-turn and reversals as up-turn may be in the idiolects, diaprosodic. Such variations are of no importance at the moment.

There is, however, a pertinent difference between an open intonation with a non-finitive text shape not final in the sentence and a reversed intonation for a finitive text shape that happens not to be final in the sentence, even if the intonations are identical in form. The open intonation is predictable from sentence text structure and is always there; the reversal is not predictable on the evidence from sentence text structure in hand at the moment the clause is heard and may or may not occur. Predictable does not here imply any prior coming into being of the text or that intonation is something added, but only that, given the text, one knows what the intonation is and can find no meaning there that is not in the text.

The long context may be found to predict reversal or non-reversal of intonation for finitive text shapes not actually final in the sentence in certain situations. For example, reversal may be highly probable for completion text shapes preceding formally marked non-finitive text shapes such as *if* clauses, etc., and unreversed closed intonations may have a high correlation with finitive text shape when what follows is parenthetical.[22] This is, however, a different kind of prediction from that noted in the preceding paragraph.

Any examination of a fairly large number of cited or observed cases of clause texts and intonations in the position under consideration here will show up many cases that seem quite haphazard. Thus one guesses that Armstrong and Ward's representation of 'The thing didn't move, it had no pulse, no breath, no colour – it was dead' with arrested downturns for the first and second comma-marked clauses and full downturns for the rest,[23] comes out of an actual utterance. No conceivable theory can account for reversal at *pulse* and not at *breath* except that people sometimes reverse, and as it were help the hearer to understand, and sometimes don't.[24] After all, binding together the parts of a loose sentence is not so vital a matter as preoccupation with intonation may lead some to think: the sentence does go on and can be put together, if at some small cost in effort, without intonational signals, as the line of print indicates.

The reversal of intonation at actual sentence end is to be interpreted in exactly the same way, but the interpretation is often not so simple.[25] The most the intonation can be said to say is that this is not exactly the kind of sentence one would expect out of this text. Query rather than statement, requesting rather than commanding, and taking the edge off flat statements are probable interpretations if the context, sometimes material rather than linguistic, specifies. Sometimes the context is ambiguous and the hearer may guess wrong. One of the justifications for calling the sentence-ending text shape exemplified by 'Were they better?' non-finitive is that when such a shape is uttered with what sounds like a closed intonation, the full fall is always felt to be reversal of the text-shape appropriate intonation. It is the insistence, demanding, emotional colouring, etc., that has to be guessed at when low ending, not the fixed query interpretation with not-low ending.

Sentence-end intonations are not absolutely predictable and are communications in themselves at the grammatical level even if they only point to interpretations based on text and context. That is, the speaker is as free to choose between text-shape propriety or reversal as he is to choose a lexical item at any point in the utterance and the probability restraints can be calculated in the same way. The statement early on that unmodified basic intonations have no meaning that cannot be predicted from the text has to be qualified to take into account the significance of no modification where modification is possible. That sentence-end reversals are not dispensable aids to understanding, as internal reversals are, is amply evident from the effort often required for the interpretation of printed texts and the not infrequent disagreements.

Modification of detail in the basic intonation interrupts the simple propriety of intonation to text shape and, according to the same principle, calls attention to the item in the text where the modification occurs without itself contributing any specific meaning to the utterance. Such modification is implicit in Jones' section on 'Emphasis' and Armstrong and Ward's on 'special prominence' and in many other works, and explicit in Bolinger's *obtrusion* and Daneš's *centre of intonation*.[26] I have suggested elsewhere that attention-calling modifications tend to occur, *ceteris paribus*, at points where there is information in the text in the technical sense of possibility of occurrence of a number of items among which choice has to be made.[27] I add here only a few random comments.

The form of pointing modification is a matter of indifference at the prosodemic level. A raising of the pitch and increase in loudness and length and/or down-turn for the accented syllable of the item representing choice, with the intonation continuing from the end of the modification, is the most frequently occurring form. Other forms may occur as intensification markers or formal characteristics of the idiolect or tying in with emotional overplay or accidental.

The point at which there is information may be predictable from the immediate structure, as in shapes such as 'There was a– – – – –.' and 'either – – – – – or – – – – –'. For the most part, however, the location of the information in terms of the text is a matter of text content in reference to context.

Where the antecedent context determines what Daneš calls the *thème*, 'the thing already known and spoken about',[28] there is no information in the thème. But if the thème is a selection from among things already known and spoken about, what is determined is the range of possible choices and the fact that there are possible choices is by definition information. There is regularly information in 'what is said about the thème', Daneš's *propos*.[29] If a sentence of any complexity is to be taken as divided into two continuous parts, thème and propos, the long context will determine the specific point in either where information lies, i.e. will predict what part is not informing. Thus the context and not the structure determines whether the information point and attendant strong accent lies with the adjective or the noun in an adjective-noun construction, or with both.[30]

While it may be said that modification in detail of the basic intonations occurs non-accidentally only at information points, it is not so that there is modification in actual utterance wherever there is an information point, except perhaps where specified in the structure or where several items in an informational range occur, e.g. in explicit contrasts. The fact can be at least partly accounted for. The basic intonations have in them positions of prominence, more conspicuous in some dialects and idiolects than in others, and an information point at such a position is more or less adequately pointed without the frequently occurring intensification. Indeed for American English the usual raising out of line of the last accented syllable is negatived if the item in the text is completely predicted by the text item immediately preceding and at an information point. There is less likely to be intonational pointing where a highly probable item is chosen. Correlation between amount of information and the probability of intonational pointing is impossible, however, because the choice of a very low-probability item at the same point is very likely to be accompanied by intonational modification. It is also to be noted that, while the intonational pointing is more likely when the amount of information is greater because of equiprobable choices, which may amount to consciousness of the alternatives, it is not proportionally more likely when the amount of information is increased by the number of equiprobable choices.[31] Some individuals and perhaps some dialect groups habitually underplay the possibilities of intonational pointing; the habit may be taken as an extension of the formal pattern of their intonations. Often the speaker's mind is not full of what he is saying, and this is not limited to radio announcers and actors and makers of phonograph records. Emotional colourings intrude here, including pseudo-informational pointing with intensification for the thème.

It seems difficult if not impossible to correlate with the scheme of information points certain rhetorical uses of intonational pointing which are not emotional and should probably come within the range of grammatical concern. For example, the repeated strong accent for the iterated thème or propos where there can be no information in the usual sense. Some of the situations in which there is strong accent at the position of a form-word that would have weak accent in an unmodified intonation are readily explained as less probable choices at information points; others are not so easily explained unless one wants to say that the strong accent in itself represents a less probable choice, which is hardly acceptable.[32]

There are no problems of notation involved. For description of basic intonations, some kind of staff notation is of course required. At any point beyond description it is only necessary to note the clauses, the whole intonations, the accents, and the incidence of detailed modification. This can be done with Kingdon's tonetic-stress marks, as recently shown by Trim in *Le Maître Phonétique*.[33] It is necessary to mark predictable as well as non-predictable accents, intonation, and modifications because the absence of a mark denies the occurrence of what the mark indicates. Upsloped marks can be used for not-low endings, leaving the distinction between up-turns and arrested down-turns to formal exposition, and doubled accent marks similarly for pointing modification. Or descriptive detail may be introduced. Intonation reversals are of course shown by reversing the slope of the intonation-indicating tonetic-stress mark.

If, as suggested, the whole-clause intonation can be interpreted separately from the detailed pointing, there is no need for setting up a nucleus for the intonation unit. That is, the intonation is not built around the pointing; the pointing occurs wherever it occurs within the intonation. I doubt that there is much or any grammatical distinction in pre-heads or heads or tails that cannot be taken care of by the general description of clause form and of the forms of modifications, the only marking necessary being that of accents. There is of course a great deal of grammatically non-distinctive variation in utterance.[34]

Nor is there any utility whatever in setting up phonemes of stress and pitch. It is necessary to distinguish accented from unaccented positions because these positions have different functions in definition of the intonational form and to distinguish between primary and secondary accents for the same reason and to mark strong accents at points of modification. It is not necessary to mark three or four degrees of stress = loudness where no differences beyond that between adjacent syllables, if even that, is demonstrably functional, or to mark levels of intonation in order to form contours which can be indicated independently of the levels.[35] The principal advantage, however, in looking at the segmental line and the prosodic line separately is simplicity. The number of marks necessary for notation directly reflects the comparative simplicity.[36] For citation forms the unsloped accent marks may be used for the prosody with the understanding that, as noted earlier, the syllables so marked have appropriate places, with or without turns, in an intonation.

Quite aside from the question of the relative satisfactoriness of this approach as a matter of theory, it has certain advantages in teaching pronunciation. In general there may be some point to including intonation from the beginning, as necessary if there is no stress separate from prosody, and to dealing pretty thoroughly with grammatical intonation before starting on the complexities of emotional nuances to which it must be basic. The drill process of establishing basic forms is not affected. But the matter of correlating intonations with texts can be put on an efficient operating basis, both for the instructor and for the student. The rôle of immediate and long context is especially to be taken into consideration. Texts for practice of the basic intonations should have no information in them or information only at automatically prominent points. The well-known 'He was about the only intelligent man in the country'[37] fits the basic intonation only if everything in the text is predicted, a useless sentence, or everything except *only*. Similarly texts for illustrating the possibilities of various pointings, such as 'I shall alter my green dress tomorrow'[38] can be put into contexts specifying the point or points where there is information. The student dealing with new texts haphazardly come upon has at least helpful rules to guide him, both for choosing basic tune and placing the modification.

## Notes

[1] Cf. Daniel Jones, *Outline of English Phonetics*, Cambridge, 1956, 297 '(prosodies) length, stress and intonation'. I use the term in this sense, incidentally including juncture, not with the extension sometimes given it. Cf. Einar Haugen, 'Phoneme or Prosodeme', *Language*, xxv, 1949, 278–282.

[2] 'Communication in Intonation: General American', *Study of Sounds*, Tokyo, 1957, 317–333, esp. 320 ff.

[3] Charles F. Hockett, *Manual of Phonology*, Baltimore, 1955, 44, has: 'In English,

a macrosegment is known to consist of two immediate constituents . . . an *intonation* [and] . . . a *remainder*.' I speak of course of immediate constituents at the remainder or text level.

[4] What I call phrases are the units marked off by spaces not corresponding to word divisions in J.L.M.Trim's admirable transcription in *Le Maître Phonétique*, 1959, 26–29.

[5] Cf. my 'Communication in Intonation' in general. Some of the statements here represent revision.

[6] Cf. Dwight L.Bolinger, 'A Theory of Pitch Accent in English', *Word*, XIV, 1958, 109–149, especially first part. In this article Bolinger gathers together much experimental evidence, a considerable part of which is pertinent here.

[7] This is exactly what Jones says he is doing when he lists variants 'according to sentence-stress' in his *English Pronouncing Dictionary*, s.v. *outside*, etc.

[8] Jones, *Outline*, 279 ff., definition, 275; Lilias E.Armstrong and Ida C.Ward, *Handbook of English Intonation*, Cambridge, 1931, 4 ff.

[9] Harold E.Palmer, *New Classification of English Tunes*, Tokyo, n.d.; Roger Kingdon, *The Groundwork of English Intonation*, London, 1958; there are tunes as well as tones. Those who believe in pitch phonemes also have more or less basic patterns: Rulon S.Wells, 'Pitch Phonemes of English', *Language*, XXI, 1945, 27–39; nineteen pitch contours (32), with one the favourite contour (34). Kenneth L.Pike, *Intonation of American English*, Ann Arbor, 1945; four most useful contours (108).

[10] Phonetic description is necessary here. On the distinction not-low vs. low, rather than rising vs. falling, see my 'Communication in Intonation', 324–326. František Daneš, in his 'Sentence Intonation from a Functional Point of View', *Word*, XVI, 1960, 34–54, one of the best articles of all time on this subject, finds three contours for Czech, as he would have to for English, but only because he sets up first a functional dichotomy of actual sentence final and continuing and then must split the former (49). Similarly writers on English intonation have been driven to multiplicity by setting up sentence types first, a consequence which Daneš partly avoids in effect by noting that commands have no special intonation (50).

[11] Cf. Daneš, ibid., 44, 'The communicative validity [of sentence utterances] is signalled doubly – by the intonation and by the sentence-pattern.' Robert P.Stockwell, review of Schubiger's *English Intonation* in *Language*, XXXVI, 1960, 546, comments on the possibility of intonation patterns 'morphophonemically predictable by rules constructed in terms of the nonintonational sequence of formatives'.

[12] Whether the subject is phrase or clause depends in borderline cases on the dialect tendency or on individual predilection.

[13] The trouble with examples is that readers insist on sounding them out instead of listening objectively to a hundred spontaneous utterances of the text. Cf. Daneš, 'Sentence Intonation', 38, § 1.32 (a).

[14] Nos. 1 and 3 from Bolinger, 'Theory of Pitch Accent', 147, where the identity of the pitches is shown graphically.

[15] My explanation is at least simpler than Noam Chomsky's conversion to rising intonation for questions and second conversion back to falling intonation for interrogatives not yes-or-no answerable; *Syntactic Structures*, 's Gravenhage, 1957, 71.

[16] It may be theoretically better to take a low ending for a non-finitive text shape following a completion clause as an end reversal such as is discussed in the next paragraph, but obligatory and not significant.

[17] Cf. my 'Information Points in Intonation', *Phonetica*, IV, 1959, 107–120, esp. 109.

[18] Non-accidental reversal for non-final non-finitive text shapes is apparently rare.

[19] *Handbook*, 30–32.

[20] *Outline*, 284–285.

[21] 'Tune II followed by Tune I', seven of nine examples, *Handbook*, 33–34.

[22] Cf. Jones, *Outline*, 289, §1034, with two examples of early completions; 316, § 1071 on parentheses.

[23] *Handbook*, 33. Note also the residue of two examples in the section referred to in fn. 19.

[24] Some Americans think that Englishmen do less than they might to make understanding easy.

[25] More elaborate statement and examples in my 'Information Points'.

[26] Jones, *Outline*, 297–309; Armstrong and Ward, *Handbook*, 48–69; Bolinger, 'Theory of Pitch Accent', 149 et al. loc.; Daneš, 'Sentence Intonation', 46.

[27] 'Information Points.'

[28] 'Sentence Intonation', 45.

[29] Ibid.

[30] Cf. my '"The Poet Burns" Again', *American Speech*, XXXI, 1956, 195–201, last part.

[31] Cf. my 'Information Points', fn. 3.

[32] Cf. Maria Schubiger, *English Intonation*, Tübingen, 1958, 107–108, where 'emotion' may not be total explanation.

[33] 1959, 26–29.

[34] E.g. parentheses may usually be low in overall pitch, not always, and in any case low marking is unnecessary.

[35] Cf. Bolinger, 'Theory of Pitch Accent', mult. loc.

[36] Cf. my 'Stress and Intonation', *General Linguistics*, I, 1955, 35–42, and analytical displays.

[37] Jones, *Outline*, 280.

[38] Schubiger, *English Intonation*, 79. The section is headed 'Variations conditioned by the context', but no context shown.

# Tenseness and Laxness

ROMAN JAKOBSON and MORRIS HALLE

In discussing the opposition of the so-called tense and lax vowel classes, particularly the distinction between the tense /i/ and /u/ and the lax /ɪ/ and /ʊ/, Daniel Jones states that the reference to the different degrees of muscular tension on the part of the tongue is inadequate. 'A description of the English short [i] as a vowel in which the tongue is lowered and retracted from the "close" position is generally sufficiently accurate for ordinary, practical work. The term "lax" may also be used to describe the organic position of the English short [u] (in *put* /put/) as compared with the long "tense" [uː] (in *boot* /buːt/). Here the organic characteristics of short [u] as compared with long [uː] might be more accurately described as a lowering and advancement of the tongue and a wider opening of the lips.'[1] This lowered and *retracted* [i] and the lowered and *advanced* [u] along with all other lax vowels, as observed by Carl Stumpf, 'shift toward the middle of the vocalic triangle'.[2] Any lax vowel 'liegt stets mehr nach der Dreiecksmitte zu' than the corresponding tense vowel (p. 262). Hence, as was noted by Gunnar Fant and ourselves,[3] a tense vowel compared to its lax counterpart is produced with a greater deviation from the neutral position of the vocal tract, i.e. from the position that the vocal tract assumes in producing a very open [æ]; consequently a tense vowel displays a greater deviation from the neutral formant pattern.[4]

In the chapter 'Vowels' in his 'Handbook of Phonetics' (1877), Henry Sweet declared that 'the most important general modifications are those which cause the distinction of narrow and wide' (since renamed 'tense' and 'lax'). Sweet succeeded in demonstrating the autonomy of each of these two series 'from high to low' and the possibility of a division of any vocalic class into pairs of tense and lax vowels. In the following we shall differentiate these two series by employing the exponent ¹ for tense vowels, and the exponent ² for lax vowels, a device that has often been used in dialectology.

This autonomy of the tense-lax distinction is clearly exhibited by those African languages which display vowel harmony based on the opposition of tense and lax. Thus in Bari with its five tense and five corresponding lax vowels – /u$^1$/, /o$^1$/, /a$^1$/, /e$^1$/, /i$^1$/, and /u$^2$/, /o$^2$/, /a$^2$/, /e$^2$/, /i$^2$/ – 'a word with a tense vowel in the stem will have a lax vowel in the prefix or suffix': cf. /to$^1$-gi$^1$rja$^1$/, *to make wipe*, and /to$^2$-gi$^2$rja$^2$/, *to cause to cicatrize*.[5] Likewise in Maasai, stems consist either of tense or of lax vowels which determine the tense or the lax character of the vowels in the affixes; moreover, in some grammatical categories, lax stem vowels alternate with the corresponding tense vowels.[6] In Ibo, with its four tense-lax pairs, namely close (diffuse) /u$^1$/ – /u$^2$/, /i$^1$/ – /i$^2$/, and open (compact) /o$^1$/ – /o$^2$/, /e$^1$/ – /e$^2$/, a peculiar interplay of the lax-tense and compact-diffuse features underlies the vowel harmony: the vowel in the verbal prefixes is diffuse before a tense root vowel, and compact if the root vowel is lax.[7]

While Melville Bell, who first drew attention to the tense-lax distinction ascribed the decisive röle to differences in the behaviour of the pharynx, Sweet put the chief emphasis on the 'shape of the tongue'.[8] Later investigations, however, as summed up in Heffner's *General Phonetics*, have shifted the reference 'from tongue elevations and tongue muscle tensions to laryngeal positions and air pressures'.[9]

Sievers was already aware of the fact that 'along with the lowering mouth tension also the tension of the vocal bands decreases' and 'dies macht sich praktisch in einer entsprechenden "Verdumpfung"... des betreffenden Vokalklangs bemerkbar'.[10] Later, Meyer, in his detailed study of tense vowels, singled out the cardinal rôle of the sound-pressure: 'In dem verschiedenen Grade der Stimmbandpressung und der dadurch bedingten Verschiedenheit des durchstreichenden Atemquantums, der "Luftfüllung" der hervorgebrachten Laute, erblicke ich den wesentlichen Unterschied zwischen den gespannten und ungespannten Vokalen.'[11]

The heightened subglottal air pressure in the production of tense vowels is indissolubly paired with a longer duration. As has been repeatedly stated by different observers, the tense vowels are necessarily lengthened in comparison with the corresponding lax phonemes. Tense vowels have the duration needed for the production of the most clear-cut, optimal vowels; in comparison with them the lax vowels appear as quantitatively and qualitatively *reduced*, obscured and deflected from their tense counterpart toward the neutral formant pattern.

Sweet, who generally retained Bell's terminology as 'admirably clear and concise', preferred in this instance to substitute 'narrow' for the term 'primary', which labelled the tense vowels in Bell's *Visible Speech* of 1867.[12] Sweet's terminological suggestion, however, obscured the relevant fact, so clearly expressed in Bell's nomenclature, that it is the tense vowels which constitute the 'primary', optimal vocalic pattern and that laxness represents a secondary reduction of this pattern.

There exist in language alternative ways of quantitative reduction, both observable, e.g. in the unstressed vocalic patterns; one leads from tenseness to laxness, while the other, from compactness to diffuseness. *Ceteris paribus* a diffuse (closer) vowel is shorter than the corresponding compact (opener) vowel, for example /i/, /u/ vs. /e/, /o/, whereas the lax vowel, notwithstanding its opener articulation, displays a shorter duration than the corresponding tense vowel, as /i$^2$/, /u$^2$/, /e$^2$/, /o$^2$/ vs. /i$^1$/, /u$^1$/, /e$^1$/, /o$^1$/. Sievers rightly warns against the deep-rooted confusion of these two distinctions: 'Man hüte sich auch davor, die Begriffe "gespannt" (oder "eng") und "ungespannt" (oder "weit") mit denen zu verwechseln, welche die althergebrachten Ausdrücke "geschlossen" und "offen" bezeichnen sollen.'[13]

The 'high-narrow' vowels are particularly short, because they are both lax and diffuse; therefore the opposition of tense/lax in the diffuse vowels may be implemented not only by such pairs as [i] – [ɪ] or [u] – [ʊ] but also by pairs syllabic vs. non-syllabic: [i] – [j] and [u] – [w]. The French vocalic pattern with its consistent opposition of tense and lax phonemes exemplifies this type of bifurcation of the diffuse vowels: the distinction [ai] /ai$^1$/ *aï* – [aj] /ai$^2$/ *ail* corresponds to such pairs as /te$^1$t/, *tête* – /te$^2$t/, *tette*. In French, [i], like other tense vowels, displays a longer duration and a greater sum of deviations from the neutral formant pattern than the lax [j].[14]

The cardinal rôle of duration in the opposition tense/lax suggests the question of the relationship between this feature and the prosodic opposition long/short. In *Fundamentals of Language* we sought to delimit two kinds of phonemic features: 'A *prosodic* feature is displayed only by those phonemes which form the crest of the syllable and it may be defined only with reference to the relief of the syllable or of the syllabic chain, whereas the *inherent* feature is displayed by phonemes irrespective of their rôle in the relief of the syllable and the definition of such a feature does not refer to the relief of the syllable or of the syllabic chain.'[15] In Sweet's terms, quantity 'belongs essentially to the synthesis of sounds, for it is always relative, always implying comparison', particularly a comparison 'of two different sounds'.[16] The prosodic length of a vowel is inferred from the contrast of long and *ceteris paribus* short vowels in a syllabic sequence, whereas length as a component of the tenseness feature is intrinsically connected with the other, qualitative manifestations of the given feature within the same phoneme.

In his scrutiny of the Dutch phonemic pattern de Groot[17] notes that compared with their tense counterparts, the lax vowels are not only duller and slacker but also shorter ('ceteris paribus immer kürzer'), yet for the identification of these phonemes shortness is hardly decisive, since however much one stretches /a$^2$/ in/rá$^2$t/, *rad*, 'wheel', it does not change into /rá$^1$t/, *raad*, 'council'. Thus despite a close interrelation and manifold convertibility between the inherent feature tense/lax and the prosodic feature long/short, these features belong to two substantially different kinds of distinctive features.

The attentive analysis of the tense/lax feature discloses, however, an identical tripartition of each of the two classes. The three types of prosodic feature which, following Sweet, we have termed *tone*, *force*, and *quantity*, and which correspond to the main attributes of sound sensation – pitch, loudness, and perceptual duration, find a close analogue in the three types of inherent feature. The 'tonality' and 'sonority' features, which we attempted to outline in *Fundamentals* (§ 3.6), are akin to the prosodic features of tone and force. The tense/lax opposition should, however, be detached from the sonority features and viewed as a separate, 'protensity' feature, which among the inherent features corresponds to the quantity features in the prosodic field.

The neutralization of the pharynx in the production of lax vowels (its contraction and correspondingly the somewhat lowered tonality in the front series of lax vowels and a pharyngeal dilatation with a heightened tonality in the back series) reveals a certain similarity with the formation and structure of the centralized vowels in a few Nilotic, Caucasian, and Hindu languages. Their vocalism seems to present a peculiar implementation of the phonemic opposition tense/lax, and correspondingly such a system as that of Dinka would have to be viewed as composed of seven pairs: /u$^1$/ [u] – /u$^2$/ [ï], /o$^1$/ [o] – /o$^2$/ [ö], /ɔ$^1$/ [ɔ] – /ɔ$^2$/ [ɔ̈], /a$^1$/ [a] – /a$^2$/ [ä], /ɛ$^1$/ [ɛ] – /ɛ$^2$/ [ɛ̈], /e$^1$/ [e] – /e$^2$/ [ë], /i$^1$/ [i] – /i$^2$/ [ɪ].[18] This question, however, requires further investigation.

In analysing the phonemic pattern of Dutch, de Groot tentatively identified the relation between the tense and lax vowels with the consonantal opposition of the fortes and lenes.[19] The common denominator of both relations is now apparent. Fortes are always opposed to lenes by a higher air pressure behind the point of articulation and by a longer duration. This difference may be accompanied by the voicelessness of the fortes and the voicing of the lenes or may lack such concomitant cues.[20] A typical example of tense and lax stops and fricatives, all of them produced without any participation of voice, is provided by the Swiss German consonantal pattern. As its first investigator Winteler stated, the distinctive mark in a fortis-lenis pair is 'das Mass der auf die Bildung der Laute verwendeten Expirations- und Artikulationsenergie oder deutlicher, die Empfindung von der Stärke des Expirationsdruckes und des davon abhängigen Widerstandes der artikulierenden Organe, sowie das Mass der Dauer der beiderlei Laute'.[21] This outstanding forerunner of modern phonology precisely defined the essence of the fortis-lenis opposition: 'Bei der Bildung der Fortes verharren die Sprachwerkzeuge fühlbar in ihrer Kulminationsstellungs', whereas 'diejenigen Artikulationen, welche Lenes erzeugen, in demselben Augenblicke wieder aufgegeben werden, in welchem sie ihre Kulmination erreicht haben'.[22]

The relative duration of the consonant and the antecedent phoneme may remain for certain contextual or optional variants of tense and lax consonants the chief or even the only cue to their distinction.[23]

In producing lax phonemes the vocal tract exhibits the same behaviour as in generating the cognate tense phonemes but with a significant attenuation. This attenuation manifests itself by a lower air pressure in the cavity, a reduction in the size of the cavity (with an effective closure at the glottis), by a smaller deformation of the vocal tract from its neutral, central position, and/or by a more rapid release of the constriction. The tense consonants show primarily a longer time interval spent in a position away from neutral, while the tense vowels not only persevere in such a position optimal for the effectuation of a steady, unfolded, unreduced sound, but also display a greater deformation in the vocal tract.[24]

*Notes*

1 Daniel Jones, *An Outline of English Phonetics*, 8th Ed., Cambridge, 1956, 39.

2 Carl Stumpf, *Die Sprachlaute*, Berlin, 1926, 259.

3 R. Jakobson, C. G. M. Fant, and M. Halle, *Preliminaries to Speech Analysis* 2nd Ed., Cambridge, Mass., May 1952, 2.43.

4 G. Fant, *Acoustic Theory of Speech Production*, 's Gravenhage, 1960, 210.

5 D. Westermann and I. C. Ward, *Practical Phonetics for Students of African Languages*, Oxford, 1933, 388.

6 A. N. Tucker and J. Tompo Ole Mpaayei, *A Maasai Grammar*, London, 1955, 260.

7 I. C. Ward, *An Introduction to the Ibo Language*, Cambridge, 1936, § 388.

8 *Handbook*, 26 ff.

[9] R-M.S. Heffner, *General Phonetics*, Madison, Wis., 1949, 96 ff.

[10] E. Sievers, *Grundzüge der Phonetik*, 5th Ed., Leipzig, 1901, § 256.

[11] E.A. Meyer, *Festschrift Wilhelm Viëtor*, Marburg, 1910, 238.

[12] *Handbook*, XI.

[13] *Grundzüge*, § 258.

[14] Cf. the numerical data in our *Preliminaries*, 36, 46.

[15] Jakobson and Halle, *The Fundamentals of Language*, 's Gravenhage, 1956, 22.

[16] *Handbook*, § 179.

[17] A.W. de Groot, *Donum Natalicium Schrijnen*, Nijmegen-Utrecht, 1929, 549 ff.

[18] Westermann and Ward, *Practical Phonetics*, 207 ff.

[19] de Groot, *Donum*, 549 ff.

[20] As it was observed by Fant, the 'opposition of tense/lax for stops . . . can . . . be maintained by either an open/closed glottis, which is the most effective means, or a slower/faster rate of area increase at the articulatory constriction and by a greater/smaller over-pressure behind the constriction. Any of these factors can cause a prolongation of the decay time. A superimposed breath pulse will also cause a prolongation by the maintenance or, at least, the support of the over-pressure. In case the constriction opening is kept narrow, there results an affrication and if the constriction rapidly opens past the critical width, the breath-pulse will result in a very marked aspirative sound interval' (Op. cit 279).

[21] J. Winteler, *Die Kerenzer Mundart des Kantons Glarus in ihren Grundzügen dargestellt*, Leipzig-Heidelberg, 1876, 25.

[22] Op cit., 27.

[23] Cf. Daniel Jones, *The Phoneme*, Cambridge, 1950, 52 ff.; F. Falc'hun, *Le système consonantique du breton*, Part I, Rennes, 1951; P. Denes, 'The Effect of Duration on the Perception of Voicing', *J. Acoust. Soc. Amer.*, XXVII, 1955, 761 ff.; P. Martens, 'Einige Fälle von sprachlich relevanter Konsonantendauer im Neuehochdeutschen', *Maître Phonétique*, CIII, 1955, 5 ff.; N. Chomsky, Review of Jakobson and Halle, 'The Fundamentals of Language', *Int. J. Am. Ling.*, XXIII, 1957, 238.

[24] G. Fant, *Acoustic Theory*, 244 f.

# Physiological Factors in the Coding and Decoding of Messages

L. KAISER

## INTRODUCTION

The progress of phonetics in the last decades has been achieved largely by comparing and combining the knowledge of speech phenomena obtained by communication engineers and physiologists, as publications of Fletcher, Jakobson and Halle, Peterson, and many others show.

It is true that since the nineteenth century, contributions from physiologists have become less frequent. The process of coding and decoding is usually considered only in regard to the linguistic system. Peterson has even said that nasalizing, sniffling, and all other individual features (indicating that Theophilus Ignatius is speaking) are to be considered as noise. Though this may hold true from the point of view of linguistics, it cannot be defended from the more general viewpoint of physiology. It seems undeniable that extra-linguistic factors contribute to information, the possibility of establishing an extra-linguistic code having been shown by Trojan and others. Ladefoged has discerned three kinds of information: linguistic, socio-linguistic, and personal.

It may be of interest to consider the two normal ways of coding and decoding, i.e. the speaking-listening and the writing-reading processes. Until some fifty years ago the former process was a direct one, limited in time and space. As soon as speech records could be made, storing, which was formerly characteristic of the writing-reading chain, became possible with speech, the most natural means of communication.

Both ways of coding and decoding show a high degree of similarity, psychomotoric patterns based on language leading to neuromuscular activity, which in its turn leads to spatial coding in both cases. Whereas in the case of speaking-listening respiratory, laryngeal and articulatory muscles come into play, hand and arm muscles provide the result in ordinary writing and in processes that replace it: shorthand, typewriting, etc. Decoding of the movements by eye is possible in both cases, being called lip-reading if applied to speech movements. A special possiblity of decoding by the eye is offered by speech records, e.g. oscillograms and spectrograms. (Similar readable patterns may originate from a machine or from a drawing hand.)

In normal circumstances the spatial patterns produced in speaking, the 'gestures', as Sir Richard Paget called these movements, lead to temporal patterns which have to be decoded by ear. In listening and in reading the physiological qualities of the sensory organs determine the process of decoding, perception leading to recognition in special centres in which reference patterns are stored. In audition, spatial patterns enter again into the process by the intervention of the basilar membrane, a complex of spatial and temporal patterns being finally transferred to the brain. In reading, spatial patterns are transferred as such, though time factors are extremely important in reading. In both cases the process of decoding is partially determined by muscular function, but whereas in reading the inner and outer eye muscles have a preponderant rôle, in listening the action of *m. tensor tympani* and *m. stapedius* is a restricted one.

Redundancy in both processes is estimated to amount to at least 50%. An important difference exists as to the relation of the actual message to the linguistic system. In speaking, considerable freedom is present in this respect, whereas the message itself is well defined. In writing, the relation to the linguistic system is close, but the message is more or less undefined, offering the possibility of different interpretations. Prosodic means, used amply in the case of speech, are only poorly represented in the case of writing. Extra-linguistic means almost exclusively are acting during speaking. Direct connections between both processes of coding–decoding are found in spelling, in pronunciation, and more recently in the phonetic typewriter.

Communication engineers are interested in the costs of coding and decoding, and these costs are supposed to depend upon energy and time. It must now be asked how far energy and time are determined by the encoding muscular system, the linguistic system, and the decoding organs.

## QUALITIES OF THE NEUROMUSCULAR CODING SYSTEM

In both cases muscular activity chooses ballistic movement as a base. In this respect the coding processes require a minimum amount of energy in speaking and in writing. The chest pulse, described by Stetson as a ballistic movement of respiratory muscles, is to be recognized in the syllabic structure of speech. Ballistic movements of the fingers, and in some cases of the hand and arm, furnish the up and down strokes in writing. Here an important difference appears, the syllable in speaking corresponding with a group of speech sounds, whereas one stroke in writing generally corresponds with a part of a letter, i.e. the image of a speech sound. Laryngeal and articulatory muscles are most intimately concerned with the formation of speech sounds, but the former also give structure to larger speech units, De Groot stating that the sentence is based on melodic structure.

General influences, such as fatigue, health, age, emotion, will show themselves in speaking and writing. In both cases they give information not based on the linguistic system.

Some articulatory muscles are powerful, like those moving the lower jaw; others are delicate like the mimical and the laryngeal muscles. The total amounts of energy required in speaking are astonishingly large. Reciting for one hour takes the same amount of energy as walking for the same length of time along a road which climbs to over 300 ft. The force exerted by the tongue was found to 1 kg in stretching, 1–8 kg in pressing. The velar muscles may counterbalance a considerable pressure. Zwaardemaker evaluated the muscular energy used in pronouncing certain speech sounds, finding the influence of stress to be greater than the differences between various sounds. Groen has established that only 0·002% of the total energy is transformed into sound. In writing, Kraepelin determined the pressure used by means of the 'Schriftwage'. In some cases the rules of spelling demand a relatively high amount of energy, e.g. in prescribing a double letter to represent a single speech sound.

As time factors determine the costs to a large extent, the movements concerned have to be considered in this respect. Stetson pointed to the fact that the intercostal muscles are able to contract (and relax) about 7 times per second, whereas the abdominal muscles may only contract 2½ times per second. This determines the number of syllables per second, which reaches its maximum value in ordinary conversation. The muscles of the tongue and the lower jaw show similar values of about 7, the laryngeal muscles exceeding this rate. The labial and velar muscles however show values of about 3 per second as found by the present author and by J. W. Kaiser.

In writing about 3 or 4 movements per second are optimal for the fingers, a maximal rate of 10 to 11 being obtainable. In this case relaxation becomes insufficient, leading to pathological conditions. Hand movements optimally show a rate of about 2 per second. It is interesting that the time used in writing one letter hardly differs in large and small handwriting, the movements being much more rapid in the former case. For typewriting values of 8–10 per second are given.

Thus the difference in the time required for coding a linguistic content in speaking and in writing is highly significant, the ratio being 1 to 20, with an intermediate value of about 5 for typewriting.

## REQUIREMENTS OF THE LINGUISTIC SYSTEM

In speaking, the requirements of language concern in the first place the formation of cavities for resonance and of narrow passages for noises. Generally speaking the demands are only relative, though an upper and a lower limit may be indicated. A comparison of different speech sounds in terms of the muscular energy required shows important differences. The neutral vowel [ə] and the nasal consonants need a minimum amount of energy, whereas front rounded vowels and plosives require a large amount. A special rôle is played by the activity of the muscles in the cheeks, the bottom of the mouth, and the velum, which greatly increases selectivity.

Although the rate of speaking shows a high degree of freedom, in some cases temporal relations show an almost mathematical exactness. This may be observed, for example, in languages and dialects possessing long and short vowels of identical quality. Zwirner, in an exhaustive investigation of German dialects, found a remarkable stability in the ratio between the two durations. Italian double consonants show a duration that is almost exactly twice that of the single consonant. Some groups of consonants are easily pronounced within a time equal to the sum of the durations of the components; in other cases language requires the pronunciation of a group in which a svarabhakti vowel is unavoidable.

In accentuation lengthening plays a preponderant rôle, the prolongation of muscular activity augmenting the costs of coding but also those of decoding. It seems very useful to bear in mind the difference made by Jones between prominence and stress, the former concerning the listener, the latter the speaker. Peterson states that it is impossible to indicate the physical correlates of stress. Fry, investigating the influence of certain physical cues on the perception of stress patterns, found duration even more important than intensity. Rousselot, Zwaardemaker, and Stetson showed kymographically the large differences in the activity of articulation muscles in stressed and unstressed syllables. Stetson also drew attention to the rôle of the intercostal and abdominal muscles in stress, the so-called 'expiratory' stress.

In tone languages pitch is prescribed by the linguistic system. In other languages it enjoys a considerable degree of freedom. In these, prominence may be obtained by a higher pitch, the increased activity of a few laryngeal muscles meaning a relatively unimportant mounting of the costs. In writing, punctuation makes certain demands on muscular energy. The consequences of spelling rules have already been mentioned.

## REQUIREMENTS OF EXTRA-LINGUISTIC FACTORS

Each of the four sound qualities may be used to indicate biological factors. A transition to this field is formed by the employment of these means to underline the meaning of spoken words. Here the speech muscles are imitating in a more or less primitive way action of other muscles or even imaginary action. A lengthening of speech sounds may indicate a slow process, a long distance, hence large dimensions, etc. In the affective sphere a low rate indicates all that is difficult, tiresome, etc. Besides, the personality of the speaker will introduce physiological and psychological factors into his motor functions and give information to the listener by means of modifications of speech sounds.

A high level of energy may imitate events in which much energy is expended, such as loud sounds and large dimensions. Affects like anger and also enthusiasm will be represented by it. As to the speaker a high intensity may indicate good health, somatic force, a choleric temperament. A high pitch, the consequence of an augmented activity of some laryngeal muscles, may indicate cheerfulness, youth, or perhaps small dimensions. By means of pitch the listener may receive information concerning the condition of the speaker, his age, his hormonal functions, his temperament, and state of mind.

Timbre works by recalling the gestures which are at the base of it, indicating dimensions and also figurative largeness. It may show the imprint of emotion as may be seen in spectrograms. A shifting of the formants may be explained by mimical expression. In particular, the vowel [a] will be susceptible, rounding of the lips in sadness and unrounding in cheerfulness being the means for a conscious underlining and for a more or less unconscious demonstration of mood as well.

At the infralinguistic level, a code has been recognized by Trojan, who discerned about forty acuemes, taking into account various factors but above all 'Schonstimme' and 'Kraftstimme'. The present author determined six patterns of affect in three vowels, checked by fifty listeners. De Lacerda thoroughly analysed the patterns of one speaker in several affects.

## QUALITIES OF THE DECODING SENSORY ORGANS

It is well known that the ear is not an objective measuring apparatus. There will be hardly any peculiarity of the ear which does not interfere with the decoding of the detailed and complex patterns of speech. As French has stated, in discussing the problem of establishing useful associations between signals and sensations, the latter are hard to describe, even in qualitative terms.

Time proves to be a very important factor in audition, a certain minimum duration being necessary to give an impression. On the other hand considerable parts of a sound may be omitted, the ear nevertheless receiving a complete impression. Gray found large individual differences, some listeners being able to recognize a sound pattern of a duration of only 3 msec or containing only one-quarter of a cycle.

As different sound qualities are only to a certain degree perceived separately, a difference in duration is perceived as a difference in loudness. As early as 1929 Fletcher had chosen a number of different speech units for the measuring of speech power, among which syllabic power seemed to agree with auditory perception. French stated that in sounds of 0·5 to 1·5 sec loudness does not depend on duration, but speech sounds are of course considerably shorter. As early as 1927 Bouman varied the length of vowel fragments, finding that the perception of timbre varied largely with duration. Jones indicated that in the pair *pence-pens* it is the duration of [n] which determines the impression of voicedness of the sibilant. On the other hand Durand gave several examples of an impression of duration depending on a change of intensity, timbre, or pitch within the vowel.

As the sensitivity of the ear shows a maximum at about 1500 cps, the impression of loudness will depend partially on pitch. Hence, the second, or articulatory, formant plays a preponderant rôle, whereas objectively it contains a small part of the total energy. Finally, variations of intensity may be interpreted as variations of pitch, as Broca has shown.

The phenomenon of masking is sure to affect the perception of speech sounds.

As decoding includes also the psychological component of audition, it will be necessary to bear in mind that intelligibility of larger fragments does not depend on intelligibility of speech sounds only. Gemelli and Black found that longer words, words consisting of two syllables, familiar words, words having the accent on the second syllable, meaningful words and especially words in a sentence, possessed advantages for perception as compared to words that were shorter, monosyllabic, unfamiliar, bearing the accent on the first syllable, meaningless, and isolated.

Among the various instances of visual function reading takes a special place. Though the process is spatial in all its stages, a time factor has to be introduced into it. Ajuriaguerra stressed the necessity of linking the perceptive-oculomotor rhythm to the rhythmic melodic aspect of the sentence.

Experience has shown that reading is only possible when there is developed, social speech, containing distinct speech sounds. Several factors may lead to dyslexia, a condition in which the relation indicated by Ajuriaguerra has not been acquired. Attention has been drawn to the dominance of the right hand, which may be undeveloped in the dyslectic child. Probably the functions of the non-dominant hemisphere are also important in connection with reading. The close relation between the written symbols and the positions and movements of articulatory organs, suggested by Peterson, is demonstrated in the primary form of reading in young children.

## DISCUSSION

From the point of view of communication engineering and from that of phonetics as well, it seems of great importance to recognize the smallest units at the different stages of communication. Even in working with larger units for the establishment of average values, it will be necessary to have available data concerning the smallest units and of statistical data concerning their frequency. Generally the phoneme has been accepted, being a linguistic unit. Peterson, when trying to combine the data from different fields, discerned the 'phone', a minimum distinguishable phonetic unit, calling a group of phones a phoneme, a group of phonemes in its turn forming a word. Apart from the danger of using a word 'phone' when 'phon' is already used in a different sense, it seems uncertain whether the advantages of a similar intermixture balance the disadvantages. Jones, for practical purposes and more prudently, says: 'The linguistic conception of the "speech sound" is determined by the possibility of removing a section from a chain and replacing it by a section from another chain (the glides being at the same time replaced by other appropriate glides), the sections being such that the exchange is capable of changing a word into another word.' Jones introduces the concept of the 'abstract sounds' which can be pictured by oneself, concrete sounds being the physical manifestation of abstract sounds. A phoneme is a family of sounds in a given language. It will depend on one's philosophical basis whether these definitions may be accepted. In any case they have the merit of filling the gap between the different aspects of the process.

Jakobson and Halle, by splitting up speech sounds into bundles of distinctive features, surpassed all divisions in time hitherto used, basing the new method on simultaneous articulatory movements and on characteristics of the sound spectrum. Of some twelve pairs of oppositions, most are characterized by the demands they make on muscular energy. Fletcher compared the average power of various English speech sounds, finding the value for the vowel [ɔ] to be 680 times that for [θ], which means a difference of 28 db, the absolute value found in the latter sound being 0·05 microwatt. Generally speaking, most energy is present in the vowels, voiced consonants coming next, and voiceless consonants presenting a minimum. Fletcher also found that the energy of vowels is contained for the greater part in the lower formant, the second formant bearing only one-tenth of the total energy, whereas the third seems unimportant according to Peterson and Barney. Barney and Dunn found small differences between various sounds, taking 40 db above the threshold as an average. In Dutch students the distribution of energy showed important individual variations. As mentioned, a statistical review of the language concerned will be indispensable, including a review of the occurrence of sequences. For most European languages statistical data are available; for the Dutch language Van Ginneken has procured basic data.

One of the most important results seems to be the acknowledgment that not static segments but dynamic patterns determine perception.

This was demonstrated by Potter, Kopp, and Green. Potter and Steinberg recognized basic elements and transitional sounds in speech, the invariants being localized in the vowels, called information bearers (ibes), in consonants the initial build-up rate being important. Kock gave dynamic sound patterns of the word 'one' spoken by a man and by a child, and Davis checked similar results by means of a digit recognizer, composed of twenty-eight tubes providing the squares of the screen. With adaptation to one speaker an accuracy of 98% was reached, without adaptation the value being 50–60%.

Another proof of the dynamic character of signals consists in the recognizing of consonants by means of their influence on the preceding or following vowel. One of the first to state this fact was Stetson, cutting sections out of a magnetic tape recording. Harris, Hoffman, Liberman, Delattre, and Cooper were able to locate phoneme boundaries by observing third formant transitions. These statements were checked by the same group by means of the playback of painted spectrograms.

From these facts it may be understood that spoken language mainly uses words built up of at least three phonemes, putting at least two transitions at the disposal of the listener. Here a certain contrast exists between the two ways of coding-decoding. The isolated position of auditory perception in speaking, writing, and reading explains the desire to establish connections with the physical sound patterns.

The question arises how far these data give us a tool by means of which we may increase the amount of information relative to the cost. Mastery of elocution will be of great use here. The tension of the wall of the mouth ensures a good result at low cost. The surface of the lip opening is of first importance, as stated by Russell. Too great or too small a volume in speaking has to be avoided, the acoustic qualities of the environment determining an adequate loudness. The speaker has to learn that speaking in general and stressing in particular are not egocentric functions, the sound pattern being the main purpose of his activity. Research has shown that a pitch range exceeding the octave is not effective. More interesting than the indications given above is the statement by Fairbanks concerning the results of increasing the rate of listening, i.e. of time compression. The author says that the listener is able to withstand substantial time compression. He bases his judgment on four unpublished theses, including that of Kodman, who reports that a given amount of factual comprehension of an extended connected message was yielded by a rate very much faster than a speaker ordinarily employs.

Despite the admitted advantages of this recent possibility, a restriction has to be made. The higher rate only fits the cortex of the brain, whereas the older parts of the central nervous system are bound to a rate that is much less fast. Hence the emotional processes which might accompany the communication of factual information will be made impossible.

Relatively little attention has been given to the writing-reading process. It seems that the importance of recognizing morphemes in reading has been hitherto underestimated.

# The Representation of Vowels

R. KINGDON

While it cannot be denied that the International Phonetic Alphabet is a reasonably efficient instrument, its method of representing vowels does lack something in orderliness and completeness. This arises from the fact that the system was not thought out as a whole, but grew in rather haphazard fashion as a result of additions made to the meagre vowel representation possessed by the Latin alphabet. These additions were made *ad hoc* whenever research showed the need for more detailed discrimination in vowel quality; and while the process has filled most of the practical needs of phoneticians, it has, from the theoretical point of view, left certain gaps and ambiguities which in turn have led to inconsistencies in the use of the symbols.

A critical examination of the vowel diagram as a whole reveals the rather disturbing fact that it has never been completed; that is to say, it has never been filled out with symbols to an equal degree of precision in all its parts. This, of course, has been due to the fact that vowels pronounced with the tongue in a position near the vowel limits, having acoustic qualities that make them more easily identifiable by the untrained ear, are in more widespread use than the less characteristic vowels made with the tongue occupying a position nearer the centre of the vowel area. There has consequently been a tendency among phoneticians to establish symbols for the former and to neglect the latter.

It is nevertheless desirable that there should be recognized symbols for the more centralized vowels even if they are not so frequently needed. It is also desirable that the IPA should specify and define the limits of the vowel area to which any given symbol applies, and that these limits should normally be observed in research work, in which considerable precision is to be expected. If it were made clear that the set of vowel symbols recognized by the IPA covered in sufficient detail the whole vowel area of the mouth, there would be an incentive for phoneticians to confine themselves to the specified symbols and to be consistent in their use of them, since their exposition of their theories and discoveries would gain in clarity through the more precise and more generally understood significance of the symbols they were using.

The vowel diagram should be divided, then, into what might be called spheres of influence. The areas allotted to the cardinal vowels should have boundaries as equidistant as possible from their theoretically ideal positions, due regard being had to the creation of suitably shaped areas for the centralized and central vowels. Since centralization involves changes in vertical as well as lateral position it is desirable that areas allotted to such vowels as [ɩ, æ, ɤ] and [ɷ] should increase in amplitude as they approach a centralized position, while those of cardinal vowels should diminish correspondingly. This can be provided for by using zigzag dividing lines.

One method of division following these principles would give a diagram containing sixteen areas. Each of these would require two symbols, since provision must be made for vowels pronounced (a) with spread lips and (b) with rounded lips. It would be understood that in the absence of any indication or convention to the contrary the degree of spreading or rounding would be that appropriate to the closeness or openness of the vowel. There should be two diagrams, one for lip-spread vowels and the other for lip-rounded ones.

Towards this total of 32 vowel symbols which would be needed, the IPA at present authorizes the use of 25 (apart from those indicating *r*-colouring). Seven new symbols would therefore be required, and possibly one or two more if certain adjustments were decided upon.

At present no symbols exist for vowels of the following types:

*With spread lips:*

Front to central, between half close and half open. (The symbol shown in the diagrams has been used for a vowel of this type, but seems to have fallen into disuse.)

Back to central, between open and half open.

Back to central, between half open and half close.

Back to central, between half close and close.

*With rounded lips:*

Front to central, between half close and half open.

Front to central, between half open and open. (This area lies between the points for which the symbols [æ] and [ɐ] are now used for unrounded vowels.)

Front, open.

Back, between open and half open.
Back, between half open and half close.

In Figs. 1a and 1b symbols have been tentatively inserted in areas for which no symbol is at present available. Existing symbols, with the single exception of [ɜ], have been placed in the areas that surround the position with which they are now usually associated. The dots on the outer frame lines represent the positions of the cardinal vowels, and from these the position of the lines on the customary diagram can be visualized.

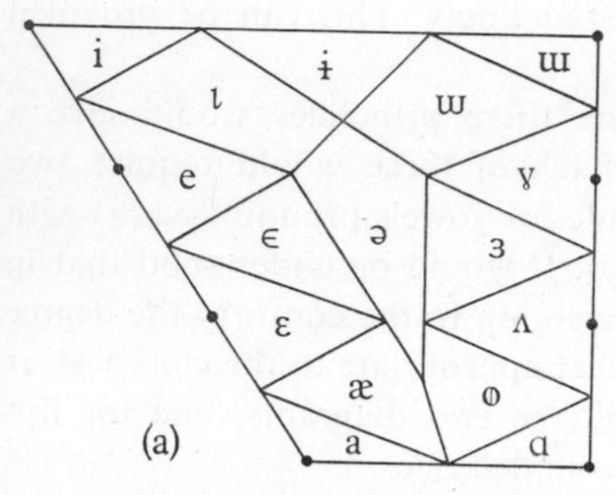

Fig. 1a. With spread lips.

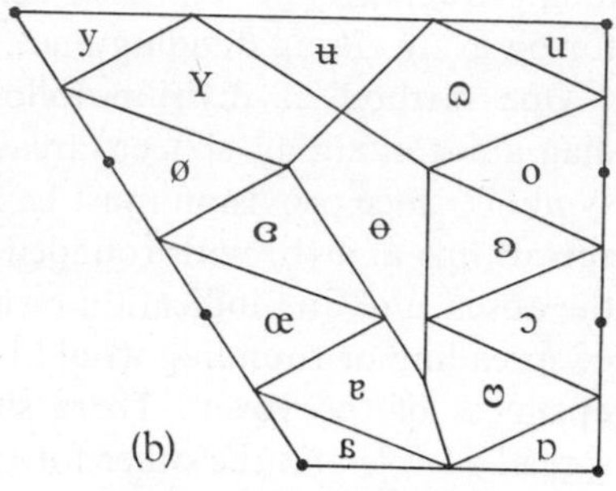

Fig. 1b. With rounded lips.

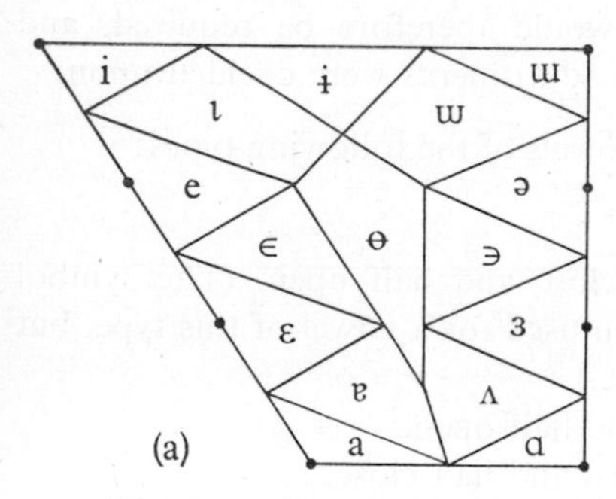

Fig. 2a. With spread lips.

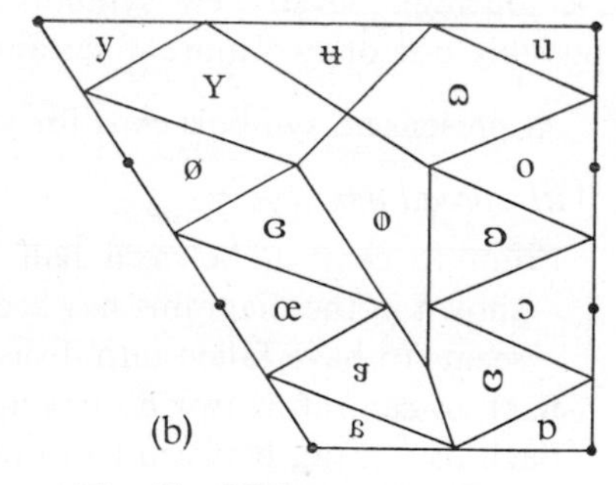

Fig. 2b. With rounded lips.

By making a few adjustments to the values allotted to existing symbols a pair of more logical diagrams could be produced, making the unfamiliar symbols easier to memorize through a more symmetrical arrangement of the shapes used. Figs. 2a and 2b show such an arrangement.

Length marks would of course be used when necessary, and it might be worth while considering the possibility of devising similar substantive symbols to indicate secondary articulations such as palatalization, velarization, retroflexion, and pharyngalization. If these replaced the present modified symbols, the number of symbols in use would be greatly reduced. This would more than offset the modest increase of symbols here proposed – and it is worth remembering that the simpler and more consistent the system can be made to appear without sacrificing its comprehensiveness, the more likely it is to secure widespread acceptance.

These last reforms would lead naturally to one of a much more revolutionary nature: the adoption of a single symbol for each vowel position with auxiliary symbols to indicate lip spreading and lip rounding. However, the time is perhaps hardly ripe for such a drastic reform, which would entail the abandonment of some of the familiar symbols now used for the cardinal vowels. If there were any idea of going so far as this, it would be better to replace the present alphabet by a more purely scientific system of simplified and conventionalized diagrams (which can easily be devised) that would show the trained phonetician at a glance the exact nature of the sounds depicted.

Finally, it must be made quite clear that there is no intention that any more elaborate system of symbols should be used with foreign language students. On the contrary, efforts should be made to simplify the transcriptions at present in use, and to limit them as far as possible to letters of the conventional alphabets with which students may be expected to be familiar.

# Juncture and Syllable Division

BERTIL MALMBERG

We owe to Daniel Jones a number of important remarks on juncture phenomena, in English and in other languages. There is in the first place his article in *Zeitschrift für Phonetik*, IX, 1956 (pp. 99–107), where he mentions distinctions like [mai - ˈtrein] ~ [mait - ˈrein], [ðæt - ˈsiŋk] ~ [ðæts - ˈiŋk], [ðə ˈweitə ˈkʌtit] ~ [ðə ˈwei - tə ˈkʌtit], etc. Another often quoted English example of this type is [ə - ˈneim] [ən - ˈeim]. In German there is supposed to be a similar difference between [ˈ(l)ant - rit] *(L)andritt* and [ˈan - trit] *Antritt*, [kau - ˈflaks] *kau Flachs* and [kauf - ˈlaks] *kauf Lachs*, in French between [trwaptit - ˈru] *trois petites roues* and [trwapti - ˈtru] *trois petits trous* (an example taken over by Jones from Passy[1]).

It would be superfluous to quote further instances – from English or other languages – of a phonemically distinctive syllable division. In fact, many languages have an opposition between explosive (syllable-initial) and implosive (syllable-final) consonant.[2] The main obstacle for phoneticians who have felt inclined to interpret such linguistic distinctions as oppositions of syllable division has been the difficulty of determining the physical correlate of the differences perceived. Some have even gone so far as to deny the existence of syllable boundaries.

In recent years, however, a number of factors have been discovered instrumentally which are of importance for the syllabic segmentation of the speech chain (Stetson's chest pulses, Zwirner's measured intensity variations, Grammont's 'tension musculaire', Strenger's sub-glottic pressure,[3] my own synthetic experiments with variation of the formant transitions[4]). It is not my intention here to discuss these or other findings made recently on the two physical levels of speech, the acoustic and the articulatory. I should, however, like to associate our increasing knowledge of the *phonetic* nature of syllable division with an important result of recent studies of segmental units. I mean the manifold physical manifestations of one and the same linguistic unit and the consequent variation in the so-called relevancy of phonemic differences. Modern phonemicists seem to have accepted – at least more than was usual within the Prague group – the possibility of different relevant characteristics for different contextual allophones of a phoneme. If for instance French /p/ is opposed to /b/ by means of its voicelessness in *pain* ~ *bain*, it is quite evident that the identity of the /p/ in *pain* and in *coupe de champagne* /kup̬ də ʃãpaɲ/ is due to the fortis character of both and that the /b/ in *bain* is identified with that in *absence* /ab̥sãːs/ only through being a lenis. We know that the /p/ in *coupe de* is voiced, the /b/ in *absence* voiceless.[5, 6]

In his book *Eléments de linguistique générale* (Paris, 1960) Martinet mentions French *un grand dadais* /œ̃grã - dadɛ/ with its short /ã/ in final position in the syllable, as opposed to *la grande Adèle* /la grãːd - adɛl/ with a long /ãː/ before a pronounced consonant in the same syllable. But is it the same syllable? This is the problem. I am not going to take up again here the question of a possible opposition between implosive and explosive consonants in French (see in this connection my articles in *Acta Linguistica*, II, 1940–1941, 54–60, and IV, 1944, 61–66). I believe there is a possibility in French of using this difference as a distinctive feature in cases where the meaning demands it, but that in normal speech, where the context is sufficiently clear, the distinction is either given up altogether or replaced by other phonetic differences (e.g. consonant gemination in *il a dit* as opposed to *i(l) l'a dit* with [-l l-],[7] and secondarily also *je l'ai dit* [ʒəl le di]; cf. my article quoted above). We must take into account here the strong tendency in French, as in the other languages of Western Romania, to generalize open syllables.[8] Consequently, originally redundant phenomena take over the rôle of the syllabic boundary and thus become distinctive. They probably always contribute to the identification of this subtle distinction. If, in our French example, the [d] in *grande* becomes explosive, thus following the syllabic tendency of the language, the phonemic distinction *may* be conserved thanks to the length of the nasal vowel.

In fact, Jones' examples in the article quoted are an enumeration of instances of redundant phenomena which have taken over, partly or completely, the responsibility for the identification of the original syllable boundary opposition. Martinet's example /-ã-da-/ ~ /ãːd-a/ is another instance of the same kind. If the syllabic boundary – here marked by a hyphen – loses its distinctive value, or is too subtle to function alone as basis for a phonemic distinction, the contextually conditioned vowel length may take over its function and become the physical correlate to the syllable boundary distinction we are still entitled to account for on the phonemic level. In Martinet's example, the explosive pronunciation of the [-d] in *grande Adèle* is probably the normal realization of it in current speech. Under such conditions, the length of the nasal vowel becomes, or may become, phonemic.[9]

Probably we must take into account in many language systems the possibility of realizing the subtle syllable boundary distinction by means of different so-called juncture phenomena. To what extent distinctions of this kind should be taken into account in setting up the system of segmental phonemes of a language is a matter of convenience. To take them into account would be to increase considerably the number of units (in Martinet's example a distinction between a long and a short nasal /ã/ in French). On the other hand they might be simply interpreted as different manifestations of a phonemic syllable division – with, as a consequence, a splitting up of the whole series of consonant phonemes into two types: explosive and implosive. One interpretation is not *a priori* better than the other. The introduction into the phonemic inventory of a language of a special juncture phoneme – in our case a syllabic frontier – gives a more elegant solution of the phonemic problem but may have the disadvantage, in the opinion of traditional phoneticians, of increasing in very many cases the distance between form and substance, thus creating a striking discrepancy between the structural units and their manifold phonetic manifestations.

*Notes*

[1] P. Passy, *Les sons du français*, Paris, 1913, 61.

[2] See, e.g., A. Sommerfelt, 'Can Syllable Divisions have Phonological Importance?', *Proc. 2nd Int. Cong. Phon. Sci.*, Cambridge, 1935, 30–33.

[3] See *Studia Linguistica*, XIII, 1959, 98–111.

[4] See my articles in *Studia Linguistica*, IX, 1955, 80–87, and X, 1956, 35–37.

[5] In my book *Le système consonantique du français moderne* (Lund, 1943) I expressed the opinion that, in the French consonant system, only the fortis-lenis distinction, not the difference in voice, was phonemically relevant, as it is the only factor which remains unaltered in all possible combinations. Martinet, in his review of my book (*Bulletin de la Société de linguistique de Paris*, XLII, 1942–1943, 106–110) seemed to accept the validity of my arguments, but judging from other works of his (e.g. *La description phonologique*, 1956, 42) he is rather inclined to see force and voice as two features which, apart from the cases of assimilation, jointly characterize the French stops and fricatives in question. It may be seen from what is said here that I nowadays look upon these phenomena in rather a different light. It is one of the many valuable contributions of recent communication research to phonemic theory to have pointed out the importance of redundancy in the communication process. This was completely overlooked by the Prague school.

[6] Such a definition of linguistic units means, of course, the application of negative

criteria – /p/ is /p/ just through not being /b/ or /m/, not because of any positive qualities – and is thus essentially in conformity with the glossematic principle of analysis, according to which the units of speech are defined exclusively in relational terms. It is also in conformity with de Saussure's statement (*Cours*, 166) that 'dans la langue il n'y a que des différences *sans termes positifs*'.

[7] I want to stress the fact that this gemination, which is popular, cannot be explained by the two *l*'s in the spelling, the popular pronunciation of *il* being, since the Middle Ages, [i].

[8] For French, see Gunnar von Proschwitz, *Étude sur la répartition des syllabes ouvertes et fermées en français moderne*, Göteborg, 1953 (*Göteborgs Kungl. Vetenskaps- och Vitterhets-Samhälles Handlingar*, VI, ser. A, Band 4, no. 6), and for Spanish the author's studies in *Boletín de filologia*, IX, 1948, 99–120, and in *Zeitschrift für Phonetik*, II, 1948, 239–255.

[9] It should be added, of course, that in French the distinction of vowel length is valid only in stressed syllables and that, consequently, the length of the nasal vowel in *grande* in Martinet's example quoted above is realized only in an emphatic pronunciation of the word. It is a potential distinction. I refer to my article on vowel length in French (*Acta Linguistica*, III, 1942–1943, 44–56).

# Phonetics, Applied Linguistics, and other Components of Language-Teaching

PETER STREVENS

Notions about how to teach languages, and, in particular, how to teach English to those for whom it is a foreign language, have been transformed in recent years. The changes are many and extreme: new ideas and theories have been developed; old ones have been modified or rejected; new techniques and teaching aids have been devised. Among the most important of these innovations has been the growing use of attitudes and techniques borrowed from descriptive linguistics.

The term 'phonetics' was in common use in relation to language-teaching long before the linguistic revolution began, of course, and it is still in use to-day; but, as might be expected after a period of radical professional change, the popular understanding of what is meant by the term phonetics and of its place in language-teaching now extends so widely as to include events and attitudes that in some cases are barely compatible with each other.

There seem to be two main kinds of use of the term, the first of which relates to practical teaching tasks, and the second to the principles (some would say theories) of language-teaching. That is to say, 'phonetics' for some means 'making sounds', while for others it refers to a component of the discipline of linguistics. It may be of some value to consider each of these kinds of use and to see what relations there may be between them.

The first kind of use of the term 'phonetics' turns out, on close examination, to comprise three main practical teaching activities which are rarely differentiated from each other because they all commonly bear the same pseudo-technical label. Together, these three sub-divisions of teaching make up a large part (though not the whole) of the task loosely described as 'teaching the spoken language', and although no rigorous definitions can be made of any one of them, yet they correspond to sub-routines of the teaching programme that any practitioner will recognize. These three sub-routines might be more easily recognized and better organized if they were given separate labels: the labels here suggested are *pronunciation teaching* and *speech training*, respectively, for two of the categories, retaining *phonetics* for the third, which is now to be more closely defined than is usually the case.

These three labels correspond in a general way to certain teaching activities: pronunciation teaching refers to the initial, basic, preliminary instruction in recognizing and producing the 'sound-system' of the language, and in establishing the most elementary framework of perceptive and productive skills at the phonological level of language; speech training refers to the stage of consolidating these skills, exercising them, recognizing and using them as a carrier for patterns in grammar and lexis, and acquiring the desired degree of social acceptability in speech for the particular educational level; phonetics refers to the academic, intellectual, scientific study of the sounds of speech, appropriate in language teaching only for advanced cases, and usually only for adults. A more detailed discussion of what is involved in each of these activities may make clearer the distinctions between them.

Pronunciation teaching uses above all *mimicry* and *exhortation* as its chief techniques. The direct and deliberate imitation of sounds, either in isolation or in connected utterances that are very short – that is what, for the most part, comprises this form of teaching. Technical terms are not used, although labels may be, as for instance when pupils may be exhorted to 'make their voices buzz', or to 'smile a little as you say that', in order to achieve voicing or lip-spreading, respectively. The lexical and grammatical patterns employed with pronunciation teaching are bound to be highly restricted since this is, by definition, beginners' stuff, at least as far as the spoken language is concerned. Indeed, much of the classroom material used for this stage will consist of games and drills using nonsense or near-nonsense, where all that is required of the pupil is the ability to recognize and perform by imitation the phonological items and systems of the language being taught.

Speech training is different in kind. It deals above all with three distinct aspects of speech: first, with acquiring habits of speech, with fluency, pace, and rhythm; secondly, with expression and interpretation; and thirdly, with what might be called 'social acceptability'. Expression and interpretation are aspects of speech behaviour that phoneticians and linguists have generally ignored, perhaps because the techniques of phonetics need the most skilful adaptation before they can be used for the purpose. Elocutionists and teachers of speech and drama, for their part, have frequently refused to accept phonetics as a useful discipline precisely because it does not deal with expression and interpretation. As far as language-teaching is concerned, there is clearly a need for instruction in expression, but it must come *after* the basic phase of pronunciation teaching, and should not be confused with the discipline of phonetics.

By 'social acceptability' is meant, first, the appropriate use of formulae, greetings, fixed expressions for particular social occasions, and the phonological patterns associated with particular styles and registers; and secondly, the development of accent away from unacceptable and socially rejected patterns and towards those features of accent which constitute the norm in the community whose speech-form has been selected as the model.

In contrast to pronunciation teaching, which might be regarded above all as the acquisition by the pupil of basic patterns of individual behaviour, speech training fosters the development and integration of these individual patterns into the total speech-behaviour of the social group, and the ability to change this behaviour in detail according to fairly subtle features of the context of situation.

Speech training is the phase of language-teaching where it is most appropriate to introduce into the teaching such activities and fields of interest as literary forms, verse, drama, speech-making, debating, and the like. Speech training is almost completely non-linguistic in character, although the material used in it must be carefully graded in relation to other parts of the language course. It belongs to that section of the total course which is reached when the pupil has acquired a fair mastery of the whole phonological system, backed up by a sufficient inventory of grammatical patterns and lexical items.

Phonetics is different yet again. The following proportion may serve as a rough analogy for the purpose of showing how phonetics relates to the other categories so far described:

PRONUNCIATION TEACHING : SPEECH TRAINING : PHONETICS ::
'SUMS' : ARITHMETIC : MATHEMATICS

Phonetics proceeds from observation by way of analysis to classification and description. Technical terms are essential, and labels are used only on sufferance. It is entirely linguistic in its nature, belongs mainly to the advanced study of a language, and is appropriate (in my opinion) only for adult pupils. Of course, a great deal of pronunciation teaching can be described as 'applied phonetics', and certainly the best material for teaching the earliest stages of learning to speak a language is material based on a sound knowledge of phonetic data and techniques. But the point is that it should be *based upon* phonetics: it should not itself *be* phonetics. To return to an example touched on earlier, it is legitimate in pronunciation teaching, remembering that this applies to the earliest stages of learning, to ask the pupil to make a 'buzzing' noise rather than a 'hissing' noise: it is not legitimate to ask him for voiced or voiceless fricatives, respectively. For the advanced adult learner, on the other hand, the opposite course would probably be more appropriate and helpful, granted the necessary background of phonetic categories.

If we may now leave aside those aspects of language-teaching which have been excluded from the purview of phonetics, we can go on to consider what is the function of phonetics in language-teaching operations. Most of what is conventionally called 'teaching the spoken language' turns out to be either pronunciation teaching or speech training, or else it relates to specialized sections of the teaching of grammatical patterns and lexical items. There remain three functions of phonetics: first, as a set of advanced teaching techniques (which includes, of course, transcription and the use of phonetic symbols); secondly, as a background discipline for the writer of textbooks and syllabuses; and thirdly, as a fundamental component of descriptive linguistics, which in turn provides a theoretical rationale for part of the practical job of language-teaching.

The reservation that linguistics forms the basis of only *part* of the job of language-teaching is an important one. The term 'applied linguistics' is an admirable label when it focuses attention on the need to replace many former *ad hoc* procedures by others based on more modern criteria. But when the use of the label 'applied linguistics' begins to excise from language-teaching any and all procedures not based on linguistics, what was virtue has become excess. The activities of pronunciation teaching and (more particularly) speech training are examples of sub-routines that are at once essential to language-teaching and not linguistic: there are other sub-routines that fulfil similar functions in the teaching of other sections of the total programme.

While we are thus involved in terminological hedging-and-ditching around the fields of linguistic pedagogy it may be worth noting that the categories of descriptive linguistics are not always or necessarily the most appropriate ones for use in each and every practical language-teaching task. What *is* essential is that the person who prepares teaching material and syllabuses for teaching should have available to him a description of the language he is teaching, presented in terms of formal descriptive linguistics. It is then part of his task to exercise his professional skill and judgment by selecting, rejecting, or adapting the categories of linguistics, so that the resulting inventory and sequence of teaching items is the one most nearly appropriate to the task in hand.

We have mentioned the case where phonetics functions as a component of descriptive linguistics; to exemplify this we may cite any grammar of English that is based on a description of the spoken language, as well as or instead of the written forms. The necessary techniques for analyzing the difference between (for example) *some* /sʌ́m/ in 'some people think so', and *some* /səm/ in 'some people are coming to dinner' can be found only in phonetics. Whatever the particular phonological analysis, and whatever the grammatical categories invoked to account for contrasts of this and similar types, the analytical and descriptive techniques for identifying the contrasts themselves are a matter of phonetics.

It is worth insisting that grammatical contrasts are best identified and described by the techniques of *general phonetics* (or even, in the phrase used by Ladefoged, 'general linguistic phonetics'). The body of data conventionally known as 'the phonetics of English' includes grammatical, semi-grammatical, and non-grammatical features, all ranged together in an ordering which may well obscure the view when one wishes to observe in particular the grammatical structures and systems of the language. The corpus of 'the phonetics of English' has other functions, especially for teaching an acceptable accent to adult learners, but it should not be confused with general phonetics, which can be applied equally well for the description of any language.

Supposing, however, that the phonetic techniques have been of an impeccable kind and that by further procedures the grammar has been arrived at; it is worth spending a few lines studying the relations between the grammar on the one hand, and the raw material of 'spoken English' on the other. These relations can perhaps help us to understand the directions in which further progress must be made before language-teaching can be said to have acquired an adequate theoretical basis. Our thesis will be more readily understood if we illustrate it by reference to one very important linguistic level, namely, grammar.

We have already sub-divided phonetics into different strata: a somewhat similar division can be applied to grammar. At least four kinds of grammar can be distinguished, perhaps several more. First of all, at one extreme there is the academic study of the theory (or philosophy) of grammar, where the subject of discourse is grammatical categories and relationships, without any necessary reference to 'the grammar' of any specific language. This is a stratum of grammar which has recently been seen to be of great importance, especially when the need arises for the evaluation of such disparate bodies of grammatical theory as those which lie behind phoneme-morpheme-syntax grammar, generative-transformative grammar, and system-structure grammar, respectively.

The next stratum of grammar is the comprehensive, rigorous description of the grammar of a particular language, according to a coherent theory of language. Few such grammars yet exist because dependence on a theory has not until recently been recognized as a criterion for evaluating the worth of a description; but grammars of this complete and rigorous kind are soon to be expected for many languages.

The third stratum might be said to comprise the concise and relatively simple formulations of grammatical 'rules', often accompanied by sets of examples, which we are accustomed to seeing in use for the practical teaching of languages. These are what we might call 'teaching grammars', in the sense that they can be assumed to be a boiling-down of the comprehensive, self-consistent grammatical description of the second stratum in such a way as to provide mnemonic grammatical handbooks for teaching a particular form of a particular language to a particular set of pupils. Most grammars, in the past, have belonged to this stratum, even when they have purported to belong to the stratum above, because they have tended to concentrate on the descriptive task without following any particular theory of language. We may be tempted to say, 'And none the worse for that'. Yet it is likely that teaching grammars in the future, which are derived from a full and rigorous description, will be superior in value and utility to those of the past which have simply been grammar-teaching recipe-books. Some of the most recent teaching grammars give reason for optimism on this point.

A fourth stratum of grammar might be called 'disguised grammar', since it is that body of grammatical statements which underlies the vast majority of modern, practical language-teaching, but which is visible only to the man who prepares the teaching material or operates with it in class. Few teachers would now teach grammar (in the traditional sense) to learners of English before an advanced stage, if at all. But an analysis of modern teaching courses supporting this attitude will show that the most careful preparation of the material has been carried out in order that specific grammatical patterns may be recognized and produced by the pupils in a specific order of presentation. The teaching material exemplifies grammatical categories without making overt grammatical statements. Hence the term 'disguised grammar'.

These four different strata of grammar are not inconsistent with each other. They illustrate some of the relations which exist between, first, the raw, un-analysed data of language; secondly, a theory of language which accounts in an optimum manner for the patterns the language can be shown to exhibit; thirdly, the description of a particular language; and fourthly, the techniques of presentation of a description for different practical purposes. Modern descriptive linguistics operates essentially as any scientific subject does, by working from data to theory and from theory to description, with the data totally accounted for in the description. It is worth insisting on this set of relations, since they are absent from certain other areas of the total field of language-teaching; it may be that some of the major improvements that are to be desired in the field cannot be expected until somewhat similar processes have been carried out for other components of the total task.

If we allow gross over-simplification for the purposes of brevity, we may describe the rough outlines of the steps in abstraction and description in the following way: first, the raw, un-analysed data of language are observed with the aim of discovering what patterns of activity may exist therein. From the first analysis there will be made a number of generalizations about the data, and from these will emerge a set of hypotheses in which large numbers of simple and complex relations will figure. The hypotheses will then be examined in detail and tested for validity by every means available, including experimental methods if these are possible and appropriate. From the corpus of valid hypotheses is derived a theory of language, which is the most abstract stage of the proceedings. Using this theory to the maximum extent, the data are then ordered in a description, which is comprehensive and self-consistent. Finally we distinguish between description in this sense and the more practical matter of descriptive statements prepared for particular purposes: these are specialized *presentations* of the description, a distinction that preserves both the difference between description and presentation and the essential relationship between them.

The distinctions of strata in grammar, in our earlier example, correspond to distinctions between theory, description, and two alternative forms of presentation. At the present time we have at least three theories of language evolved according to the methods sketched above. Two of these, at least (generative-transformative and system-structure theories) seem likely to provide us with sources of new alternative presentations of descriptive statements to meet all our immediate practical needs. Both these theories make use of phonetics as a fundamental component at the theoretical as well as the descriptive and presentational levels.

What of the other areas of language-teaching? Have they, too, produced reliable theories on which we can base our practical teaching operations? It must be admitted that this has not yet happened. The main sub-divisions of language-teaching other than the linguistic are probably these: the process of learning, the process of imparting skills and knowledge, and the practical co-ordination and organization of the various parts of the whole. Understanding what happens during the process of learning falls chiefly within the province of psychology, but it is a branch of the subject which is far from being fully developed. The same applies to the study of the fundamental process of imparting knowledge or skills, although in this field there is a tradition of investigation that has been in existence for a longer period, so that we are probably in possession of a greater quantity of observations and data than in the case of the study of learning. The organization of the various components of language-teaching is often called methodics (to distinguish it from 'The X Method' and from 'methodology'); some brilliant formulations of practical procedure have been made recently by Mackey, Catford, Mackin, and others, which provide a greatly improved programme for preparing teaching material. But it is doubtful whether methodics is a subject best considered in theoretical terms; procedural ones may be more appropriate.

If the foregoing views of the present status of the major components of language-teaching are even approximately valid, we can draft a statement of the ideal situation, seen in terms of our present understanding. What we can hope to work towards, then, will be something along these lines: first, we can hope to possess not only a theory of language but also a theory of language-learning and a theory of language-teaching; these would each be accompanied by descriptive statements arranged in various forms of presentation to suit particular situations; to organize these basic components in the most suitable way for the task in hand we can visualize a framework of methodics which would act as an operational handbook to the whole undertaking and would clinch the relations between theory and practice.

Much of this remains in the future, but it is not necessarily a useless exercise to cast our minds forward, extrapolating from present views.

It seems certain that in the ideal situation, as already at the present time, phonetics will function in two distinct slots in the system: on the one hand as a practical technique for advanced teaching at the phonological level of language; and on the other, as a fundamental component of a theory of language, which itself is but one of the basic ingredients in the theory and practice of language-teaching.

Many of my colleagues, past and present, will recognize portions of this paper as originating with them. My thanks are due to them, and especially to Dr M.A.K. Halliday and Mr J.P. Thorne for ideas about the theoretical basis of linguistics.

# The Phonetics of English

# Phonetic Change and the RP Vowel System

A.C.GIMSON

1

The repercussions of the natural processes of phonetic change, operative over a period of time, may be said to be inhibited by the tendency of phonemic units to remain oppositional and distinctive. Yet too much emphasis should not be laid on the conservative nature and rigidity of the relationship of the phonemic units within a system. The phoneme, even if defined as a minimal contrastive unit, is of only potential contrastive significance; in a language of such high redundancy as English, great tolerance is permitted at the segmental level without loss of intelligibility, the general meaningful significance being provided at a higher level, e.g. that of the context or of the accentual and morphemic patterning of the utterance. Given this tolerance, it is remarkable that phonemic categories remain as stable as they do for so long. The realization of vowel phonemes is in ordinary speech particularly liable to obscuration without loss of efficiency in the act of communication. Indeed, the centralization of vowel articulations in some types of British English reaches such a point that such vocalic oppositions as there are tend to be quantitative rather than qualitative. In earlier periods of the language's development, homophones have frequently emerged as a result of the coalescence of formerly distinct vowel categories, e.g. ME /eː/ and /ɛː/ > ModE /iː/ in *meet, meat*; ME /æi/ and /aː/ > eModE /ɛː/ or /eː/ in *maid, made*; eModE /or/ and /ɔː/ > PresE /ɔː/ in *court, caught*, etc.

2

The present RP system, though a more economical statement may be made of it or imposed upon it, is traditionally expressed in the following categories (typical allophonic realizations being given in terms of the cardinal vowel values):

(a) *relatively pure long vowels* – /iː/ = [ɪi]; /ɑː/ = [ɑ̈ː]; /ɔː/ = [ɔ̝ː]; /uː/ = [ʊu]; /ɜː/ = [əː];

(b) *relatively pure short vowels* – /ɪ/ = [ë̝]; /e/ = [e̝]; /æ/ = [ɛ̝]; /ɒ/ = [ɒ]; /ʊ/ = [ö̝]; /ʌ/ = [ʌ̝̈]; /ə/ = [ə̝] or [ə̞];

(*c*) *glides of falling prominence* (the first element of the glide being markedly shorter in syllables closed by a fortis, voiceless consonant):

*closing* – /eɪ/ = [e̝ˑɪ]; /oʊ/ = [ö̝ˑʊ]; /aɪ/ = [aˑë]; /ɑʊ/ = [ɑ̈ˑö]; /ɔɪ/ = [ɔ̝ˑë];

*centring* – /ɪə/ = [ɪˑə̞]; /ɛə/ = [ɛˑə̞]; /ɔə/ = [ɔ̝ˑə̞]; /ʊə/ = [ʊˑə̞].

In addition, Daniel Jones[1] postulates significant quantitative relationships between /iː/ and /ɪ/, /uː/ and /ʊ/, /ɔː/ and /ɒ/, and /ɜː/ and /ə/.

Such a vowel system, with phonetic realizations of this kind, appears to have had a relatively stable existence for more than a century, a stability which is not at all characteristic of the English vowel system over the last thousand years. If this is the case, reasons for the reduced rate of change, in addition to those provided by the intrinsic tendency to conservation of the system itself, must be sought. Amongst other causes, it may be assumed that the standardization of spelling among the educated during the 18th century and the spread of education and literacy during the 19th century may have served to inhibit to some extent the earlier, freer evolution. More recently, moreover, the exposure of the whole population, through radio and television, to a great deal of speech of an RP kind has provided a normalizing, auditory brake on a mass scale such as has not existed before. RP has become less and less the property of a particular class (as in the 19th century) and, with the increasing blurring of social boundaries in Britain, is adopted or aimed at by a more and more considerable section of the population. If, however, RP forms of speech tend increasingly to be at the disposal of speakers of regional kinds of English, RP is itself exposed to dilution from regional characteristics. Such modifications are naturally not so apparent among speakers of the older generations, whose speech reflects the traditional RP forms current at the end of the 19th century and may be termed *conservative*. The changes as always (e.g. in eModE) are most striking in the speech of the younger generations, who use an *advanced* form of RP. Such speech is often characterized by conservative RP speakers as the result of affectation or vulgarity (cf. the strictures levelled at advanced speech forms of the 17th century by Alexander Gil). The most considerable regional influence at work in advanced RP is, as might be expected, that of the London or South-Eastern area. This influence extends to the RP forms of a wide range of social strata: the younger members of the Royal Family are, for instance, sometimes criticized for speaking 'quasi-Cockney'. Phonetic characteristics of London speech seem, therefore, likely to be adopted more extensively than merely in the South-Eastern corner of England, if, for social reasons, RP continues to serve as a model worthy of imitation. Some of the phonetic changes already existing in advanced RP are sufficiently considerable to warrant an appraisal of their phonemic implications for what may be the general RP system of the near future.

3

A number of divergences from the traditional realization of the RP vowel system have already been noted by Daniel Jones as being current usage among RP speakers for the last thirty or forty years. Notable among these changes are:

(i) Diphthongization of /ɪ, e, æ/ > [ɪᵊ, eᵊ, æᵊ] (*did, head, bad*)[2];

(ii) Lengthening of /æ/ = [æː] (*bad, bag*)[3];

(iii) London dialect /ɔː/ = [o̜ː] (*saw*)[4];

(iv) Southern English unrounding of /ʊ/ = [ɤ̈] (*good*)[5];

(v) London dialect /ɜː/ = [ʌ̈ː] (*fur*)[6];

(vi) Coalescence of Southern English /ɔː/ with /ɔə/ (*more*) and sometimes with /ʊə/ (*poor*)[7];

(vii) London monophthongization of /eɪ/ = [ɛː] (*day*)[8];

(viii) Southern English central first element in /oʊ/ = [əˑʊ] (*go*)[9];

(ix) Reduction of /eɪ, aɪ, ɑʊ/ + /ə/ to [eˑə, aˑə *or* aː, ɑˑə *or* ɑː] (*player, fire, tower*).[10]

From these and other phonetic observations, certain general tendencies and their phonemic implications are noteworthy.

4

INSTABILITY OF THE FINAL ELEMENTS OF CLOSING DIPHTHONGS. The closing diphthongs /eɪ, oʊ, aɪ, ɑʊ, ɔɪ/ have all since eModE had the chief prominence associated with the first element of the glide. At the present time, in advanced RP in the London region, such length is attached to this prominent first element that the second [ɪ] or [ʊ] element is very weak indeed and is liable to be totally lost. This weakening of the second element – and the resultant loss of glide – does not, however, apply to the occurrence of the diphthongs in all contexts: it is, for instance, rather less marked in their relatively short realizations, i.e. when the diphthongs occur in syllables closed by a fortis voiceless consonant (*late, coat, light, shout, voice*) than in those cases where the diphthong is relatively fully long, i.e. in open syllables, in syllables closed by a voiced consonant, and, in particular, in those cases where the syllable is closed by [ɫ] or where an open syllable is followed by /ə/ or another vowel.

(a) /eɪ/ > [e˖ᴵ] or [e̜ː] in *day, made, lay hands*; *player, greyer, layer*; *may end*, with the result that:

(i) the opposition between *men, main*; *edge, age*; *sell, sail*; *tell, tale* may be made chiefly by the length given to a monophthongal vowel [e̜]; it is also to be noted that for some speakers the /eɪ/ of such a sequence as /-eɪʃn/ is levelled qualitatively and quantitatively with /e/, cf. *session, conversation*;

(ii) when /eɪ/ + /ə/ > [e̜˖ə], [ɛ˖ə], it is levelled with /ɛə/, producing homophones such as *they're, there*; *layer, lair*;

(b) /oʊ/ > [ö˖ᵘ], or, with the current complete centralization of the first element in all situations, [ə˖ᵘ] or [əː] in *row, road, low hurdles*; *slower, rower*; *go easy, show up, so early*; *goal, hole*, with the result that:

(i) some confusion between traditional /oʊ/ and /ɜː/ occurs, e.g. *bone, burn*, and especially before [ɫ], *goal, girl*. In word final positions, the confusion between the realization of /oʊ/ as [əː] and /ɜː/ may be lessened, when the following word begins with a vowel, by the potential linking /r/ associated with /ɜː/, cf. *slow up, slur up*; nevertheless, it might be expected that, with the levelling of /oʊ/ and /ɜː/ to [əː], an 'intrusive' /r/ might also apply to the /oʊ/ words, in the same way that it tends to be extended to all /-ə, -ɑː, -ɔː/ endings;

(ii) the sequence /oʊ/ + /ə/ and /ɜː/ become identical (except for the potential /r/ link for /ɜː/), cf. *slower, slur*; *mower, myrrh*;

(iii) if /oʊ/ = [əː] and /ɜː/ do not merge, a qualitative distinction of the sort [əː] (*bone*) and [ə̜ː] or [ʌ̤̈ː] (*burn*) may be maintained. If this happens, [ə̜ː] or [ʌ̤̈ː] comes near to the realization of /ɑː/ (or the reduction of /aɪ, ɑʊ/ + vowel), in which case a qualitative distinction between the vowels of *burn* and *barn* might be maintained, as already in some types of RP, by the use of a very retracted form of /ɑː/.

(c) /aɪ/ > [a˖ᵊ] or [aː] in *sigh, diehard, side*; *fire, society, liable*; *highest, by all means*; *tile, trial.* As a result, a front open long vowel is produced, which in closed syllables has a quantitative relationship with a London realization of /ʌ/ and is opposed to the latter by quantity, cf. *bide, bud*; *sign, sun*.

(d) /ɑʊ/ > [ä˖ˠ] or [ä˖ᵊ] or [äː] in *cow, loud, allow, half*; *tower, nowadays, coward*; *now and then*; *how else, now or never*; *towel, foul.* As a result, /ɑʊ + vowel/ and sometimes /ɑʊ/ may level with /ɑː/, producing such homophones as *tower, tar*; *shower, Shah*; *coward, card*; and even *vows, vase*; *down, darn*; *loud, lard*; more extreme monophthongization may also level /aɪə/, /ɑʊə/, and /ɑː/ as in *shire, shower, Shah*; *tired, towered, tarred.*

(e) /ɔɪ/ > [ɔ̝˖ᴵ] or [ɔ̝˖ë] word finally (*boy, toy horse*), or [ɔ̝ː] followed by a voiced consonant (especially [ɫ]) or vowel as in *void, join*; *toil, royal*; *enjoyable, buoyant, coir*. As a result, the opposition between traditional /ɔː/ and /ɔɪ/ may in many situations be maintained by the relatively closer quality of the former, [o̜ː], cf. *tall, toil*; *gnaws, noise*; moreover, before [ɫ], /ɔɪ/ = [ɔ̝ː] and /ɒ/ may be distinguished chiefly by length, cf. *coil, coll*; *loyal, loll.*

5

THE CENTRING DIPHTHONGS. New phonetic relationships between the centring, falling /ɪə, ɛə, ɔə, ʊə/ and /ɪ, e, æ, ɔː/ may be emerging:

(a) /ɔə/ now rarely exists in RP, having been levelled with /ɔː/, e.g. in *sore, saw*; *pour, paw*; *court, caught* (with the use of a linking /r/ commonly extended to all occurrences of word final /ɔː/). The quality of /ɔː/ appears, under London influence, to be considerably closer, [o̜ː], than at the beginning of the century. This closing of /ɔː/ brings it into increasing qualitative proximity to /ʊə/, so that the levelling of earlier /ʊə/, /ɔə/, and /ɔː/ is now common, e.g. in *poor, pore, paw*; *sure, shore, Shaw*. Moreover, /ʊ/ is now in closer qualitative proximity to /ɔː/ = [o̜ː] than to /uː/ = [ʊu], cf. *could, cord*; *foot, fort.*

(b) The centring diphthongs /ɪə, ɛə/ are frequently in opposition, particularly in open syllables, e.g. *hear, hair*; *fear, fair*; *weary, wary*; and also in *beard, bared*; *peered, paired*, etc., though oppositions in syllables closed by a voiceless consonant or by [ɫ] do not occur, (cf. also the type of RP which renders *really, rarely* as homophones [rɛəlɪ]). But there is a tendency to realize /ɛə/ in non-final syllables as [ɛː] as well as [ɛ˔ᵊ], e.g. in *careful, whereas, scarcely, rarely, paired, bared.* Such a realization is in close phonetic proximity to the long form of /æ/ = [æː] or [æ˔ᵊ], so that *bared, fared, paired* tend in advanced RP to be homophonous with *bad, fad, pad.* There is further confusion with the realization of /eɪ/ + /ə/ in a closed syllable (see p. 134 above), cf. *layered, laird, lad.*

In addition, /ɪə, ɛə/ in their long forms in closed syllables are in opposition with the diphthongized forms of /ɪ, e/ in similar situations, i.e. a 'slow' vs. 'fast' glide, cf. *beard, bid*; *reared, rid*; *hears, his*; *bared, bed*; *fared, fed*; *bairn, Ben.*

6

FRONTING OF /ʌ/. Doubtless under the influence of London speech, /ʌ/ is increasingly fronted to [ä], as opposed to the traditional [ʌ̈]. This fronting of short /ʌ/ may place it in phonetic qualitative proximity and quantitative relationship with *either*

(a) /ɑː/ = [ɑ̈ː], cf. *bun, barn*; *luck, lark*;

*or* (b) the long [ɑ̈ː] realization of non-final /ɑʊ/, cf. *ton, town*; *hull, howl*; *bud, bowed*; *fund, found*; *cud, coward*;

*or* (c) the long [äː] or [ɑ̈ː] realizations of non-final /aɪ/, cf. *bud, bide*; *pun, pine*; *suds, sides*; *dull, dial*.

It is to be noted that /ʌ/ is now no longer similar in quality to even the traditionally opener form of /ɜː/. If, however, /ɜː/ is further lowered in order to remain distinct from [əː] < [ö·ᵘ], a further possibility of qualitative and quantitative relationship for /ʌ/ arises, cf. *bun, burn*; *cull, curl*; *thud, third*.

7

It may be concluded, from the current phonetic changes listed above, that if the language were permitted to develop in an entirely uninhibited way, certain realizations of the traditional vowel categories of RP might exhibit new relationships, which might lead to the fusion of allophones of formerly separate phonemes or to new quantitative rather than qualitative oppositions. Already, for instance, RP listeners tend to interpret [bɛ·ᵊd] as either *bad* or *bared*; [mɛːd] as *made*; [pəːɫ] as either *pole* or *pearl*; [tɑ̈ː] as either *tar, tyre*, or *tower*; [tǫːɫ] as *toil*; [pǫː] as *paw, pour*, or *poor*. The next fifty years should show how effective are the inhibiting influences of literacy, the existence of a broadcast auditory norm, and the self-perpetuating nature of the system itself.

*Notes*

[1] *An Outline of English Phonetics*, 1956.
[2] *Pronunciation of English*, 1956, 35, 36, 37.
[3] *Outline*, 1956, 235.
[4] *Pronunciation*, 40.
[5] Ibid., 42.
[6] Ibid., 47.
[7] Ibid., 65, 66.
[8] Ibid., 53.
[9] Ibid., 54.
[10] Ibid., 59, 61; *Outline*, 125.

# Spelling-Pronunciation in American English

H. KÖKERITZ

When a few years ago Eastern Airlines inaugurated their luxury flights between New York and Miami, Florida, naming them 'The Golden Falcon', and when more recently the Ford Motor Company developed their new compact car 'The Falcon', their respective publicity departments were confronted with what seemed to them a ticklish phonetic problem. In the U.S.A., *falcon* is essentially a book-word, used mainly by ornithologists, for the sport of falconry has few if any practitioners in the country to-day. All American dictionaries record the two time-honoured pronunciations [ˈfɔkən] < ME *faucoun* and [ˈfɔlkən], with an added *l* from Latin *falcōnem*.[1] Despite this unambiguous and unanimous directive, the publicity departments of the two concerns abandoned the traditional American dependence on the dictionary in this case, instructing or permitting their radio and television announcers to say [ˈfælkən]. This obvious spelling-pronunciation, doubtless inspired by [æ] in *balcony*, *talcum*, is now dinned into the ears of those who willy-nilly listen to radio commercials. Upon enquiry one of the concerns defended its choice of pronunciation by saying that although it was not the preferred pronunciation as set forth in the dictionary, the alternative form was decided upon because it appears in larger sections of the country, and by virtue of its common usage is more identifiable.

The answer is an object lesson on how in these days of mass media of communication an obviously erroneous pronunciation – I use the word 'erroneous' here to imply an ignorant deviation from received usage – can be foisted on the public without any regard for the linguistic tradition. It is true that the learned men who once latinized ME *parfit* to *perfect* and changed its pronunciation accordingly, or the schoolmasters who made their pupils spell *s-u-g* [ɛs-ju-dʒi] *sug* [sʌg], *g-e-s-t* [dʒi-i-ɛs-ti] *gest* [dʒɛst], *suggest* [səgˈdʒɛst], seem to have done practically the same thing by inculcating artificial orthographic and phonetic forms. Yet they certainly did not countenance illiterate pronunciations, nor were they insensitive to the linguistic tradition, even though theirs was often a quasi-etymological one. While one cannot admit the argument that substandard [ˈfælkən] is 'more identifiable' than, say, the received secondary form [ˈfɔlkən], there is nevertheless some sense in the letter-writer's insistence on the auditory recognition of a phonetic form. Perhaps it is, after all, a desire to be easily understood that is responsible, at least partially, for the common use of spelling-pronunciation in American platform oratory. Public speakers in America, including clergymen of all denominations, tend almost to spell out their messages to their audience, as if the latter needed the visual image of the spoken word to grasp what is being said. Some of them may actually need such assistance, for in a country with millions of recent immigrants from non-English-speaking countries the audience's comprehension of English may vary from bare literacy to the full mastery of all the subtleties of language and rhetoric. But far greater has been the impact of three centuries of concerted effort by American school-teachers to inculcate a 'correct' pronunciation of English. To them correctness meant two things: the avoidance of provincialisms like *jest* for *just* or *hum* for *home*, and in certain cases the adaptation of the spoken word to its written form. The teacher and the public speaker are probably equally responsible for the monotonous use of [eɪ] and [ði] for the unstressed articles *a* and *the*, for the tiresome final [ɔ˞r] in, e.g. *administrator*, *director*, and for the almost regular [ˈtrɛsˌpæs] in the Lord's Prayer as read by a minister, who, moreover, will say [krɪˈeɪtɔ˞r] (creator), [ˈmidɪˌeɪtɔ˞r] (mediator), and perhaps even [ˈsoʊləs] (solace).

Spelling-pronunciation is not a uniquely American phenomenon, of course, even if it appears to be more widespread here than in England. It definitely antedates the first English settlements of America and it may even antedate the appearance of the first printed books in England. With the growing awareness of the difference between spelling and pronunciation came a desire to adjust one to the other. A fluid orthography tends to favour phonetic spelling, but a fixed, conservative mode of writing, especially one that approaches the ideographic stage, holds the seeds of spelling-pronunciation. The emergence of London English as the written standard in late ME can hardly have failed to exert some influence on the spoken language of the period preceding the introduction of printing. But it is the fossilizing effect of printing that is largely responsible for the wide gap between spelling and pronunciation and for a growing tendency to adapt the latter to the former, despite many futile attempts to reform the antiquated English spelling. Not a few words and groups of words can be shown to have acquired their present pronunciation through the influence of the spelling at some time in the past both in British and American English. We may point to the reappearance of [t] in *pestle*, *often* or of [n] in *kiln*, the use of [l] in British *solder* (American still [ˈsɑdər]), the restoration of [ɪŋ] for [ɪn] or [n̩] in suffixal *-ing* (as in *making*), and the substitution of [ʧə(r)] for earlier [tə(r)] in unstressed *-ture* (as in *picture*) or of [aɪl] for [ɪl] in *fertile*, etc. ([ɪl] remains the standard American form), and so on.[2] Alexander Gill (1564–1635) preferred to pronounce the *l* in *folk*, *fault*, *balm*, *talk*, *walk*, etc., in accordance, he said, with the practice of learned men in reading and sometimes in speaking, although he recognized its non-pronunciation in colloquial speech. Shakespeare satirizes such pedantry when he makes Holofernes condemn the omission not only of *l* in *calf*, *half*, but also of the palatal fricative in *neighbour*.[3]

Most American schoolmasters of the past seem to have been inspired by the same orthoepic ideals as Holofernes or his possible prototype Alexander Gill. No doubt some of them still are. In the seventeenth and eighteenth centuries teachers derived their wisdom from British grammars and spelling-books, some of which they reprinted for colonial consumption, but during the eighteenth they began to compose their own textbooks, relying heavily on their British models. Most famous and most influential of these was Noah Webster's *American Spelling Book* (1783), often referred to as the 'Blue-Back Speller', with an estimated sale of over 70,000,000 in a century of publication. Like its models it divided each disyllabic and polysyllabic word into syllables to be spelled aloud as outlined above, a method that was bound to have a deleterious effect on the natural pronunciation of unstressed vowels while prompting the sounding of historically silent consonants. Some of these little volumes like Benjamin Dearborn's *Columbian Grammar* (1795) contained lists of 'Improprieties, commonly called Vulgarisms, which should never be used in Speaking, Reading, or Writing', e.g. *ax* for *ask*, *done* for *did*, *gal* for *girl*, *larnin* for *learning*, *pint* for *point*, and many others. Of special interest are early nineteenth-century handbooks on elocution like Samuel Worcester's *Third Book of Reading and Spelling* (107th edn., Boston, 1848) and his *Fourth Book of Lessons for Reading, with Rules and Instructions* (Boston, 1847), both of which append to their practice texts short lists of caveats. Thus Worcester objects not only to *close* (clothes), *fort'n* (fortune), *kiver* (cover), *natral* or *natteral* (natural), but also to *evry* (every), *sevral* (several), and *ware* (were).[4] For the correct pronunciation of *-ture* he advises the student to pronounce *creature*, *nature*, and *posture* so as to rhyme with respectively *heat your*, *hate your*, and *cost your* (*Fourth Book*, 42). Such precepts did not pass unheeded. Teachers enforced them and public speakers followed them in the name of correctness and distinctness of delivery.

In his *Lectures on the English Language* (New York, 1860, 670) George P. Marsh touches upon this American predilection for the visual standard. It is typical of the times, I think, that he should interpret it as a manifestation of his fellow-countrymen's high degree of literacy as compared with conditions in England: 'From our universal habit of reading, there results not only a greater distinctness of articulation, but a strong tendency to assimilate the spoken to the written language.' Taking issue with Marsh on this point, Krapp[5] instead regards this preference for an 'eye-standard' as due to the absence in America of a spoken standard of the British type: 'Users of American English have doubtless tended to substitute something for it which seemed equally firm and stable, that is, judgments based upon the visual forms of the printed and written speech.' This may well be so. But the ultimate responsibility for encouraging and perpetuating such forms rests in my opinion with the schools[6] and to a very great extent also with the pulpit or the rostrum in general.

To these two veteran pressure groups, one active and very dynamic, the other rather passive but no less persuasive, must now be added the voice of radio and television. While faithfully echoing its predecessors, it now and then contributes its own cadences, sometimes by analogy but as often out of carelessness or ignorance. An attentive listener is likely to catch both types of spelling-pronunciation in almost any broadcast, accepted variants like [ˈnɛfju] (nephew) or [ˈɔftən] as well as dubious innovations like the above [ˈfælkən] or [ˈfi-æns, fjɑˑns] (fiancé), of which I shall have more to say below. Through their vast coverage – to use an advertising term – these two media can inadvertently give currency to pronunciations that have no *raison d'être* in the language. Fortunately most spelling-pronunciations one hears over the air are not mispronunciations, though some deserve to be labelled as such, e.g. the use of [ju] for *u* in *bilingual.* The majority of them simply reflect a complete reversal of earlier phonological trends. Interestingly, very few of these pronunciations are sanctioned by modern American dictionaries, including Kenyon-Knott's and the *NBC Handbook*. Their social status is not easily defined, but I have the impression that most of them might in Ross's suggestive terminology be classified as U rather than non-U; some of my colleagues have been heard to use several of those to be analysed here, e.g. *provost*, *controversial*, *Durham*, but certainly not *chasm* or *national*.

In the treatment of stressed vowels the tendency seems to be to use the historically long sounds ([eɪ] for *a*, [oʊ] for *o*, etc.) in open syllables, otherwise the short equivalents. Hence [eɪ] appears in *patronage* (the recommended sound in NBC, whereas KN, WCD, and WNW list both [eɪ] and [æ]) by analogy from *patron*, and similarly at times in *bade*, *caste*, *chastity*, and *national*, the last two analogical, of course. *Thames*, the Connecticut river, is regularly [θeɪmz]. *Fakir* is both [fəˈkɪr] and [ˈfeɪkər]. Worcester (*Fourth Book*, 288) disapproves of *sacrifice* with *ā*, i.e. [eɪ], another analogical pronunciation which I have never heard, though it may well be a substandard form. The uneducated [ˈfælkən] for *falcon* is likely to gain wide acceptance because of its use in radio and TV commercials. To the same phonological type belongs [ˈtælbət] for *Talbot*, an unrecorded but not unusual variant of [ˈtɔlbət]. Kenyon-Knott reports [ˈælmənd] (almond) as being frequent in New England instead of [ˈɑmənd] and even rarer [ˈæmənd]; it is commonly heard in grocery stores, as is [ˈsælmən] for *salmon*, which on the other hand tends to become [ˈsɑmən] by hypercorrection. *Trespass* and *harass*, traditionally pronounced [ˈtrɛspəs] and [ˈhærəs], are now usually [ˈtrɛsˌpæs] (in the Eastern states also [-ˌpas, -ˌpɑs], KN) and [həˈræs]; for the latter I have heard the hyperform [həˌrɑs] from a colleague now deceased. *Prelude* is frequently [ˈprilud] and *pretence* sometimes [ˈpritɛns]. More often than not one hears *era* pronounced [ˈɛrə], even by educated speakers, probably on the analogy of *ere*, and [aɪ] is occasionally encountered in *philology* – but not, so far as I know, in *philosophy*. *Lichen*, historically [ˈlaɪkən], tends to become [ˈlɪtʃən] or [ˈlaɪtʃən][7]; according to OED, [ˈlɪtʃən] is the only pronunciation given in Smart (1836), though 'it is now rare in educated speech'. Worcester (*Fourth Book*, 42) repudiates [ju] in *bury*, which apparently was once a pulpit pronunciation but which Walker (1791) calls a Scotticism.[8] To-day one may instead hear [ˈbɜri], perhaps a surviving dialectism (Irish or Northern) rather than a direct spelling-pronunciation; yet it may reflect the same phonetic development as the frequent [ɜ] in *very*. Curiously enough both *turret* and *Durham* often have [ʊ] (probably northern) instead of [ʌ] or [ɜ]; Kenyon-Knott list the variant [ˈtʊrɪt]. *Constable* usually has [ɑ] instead of traditional [ʌ]. And finally we may note the occurrence of [oʊ] in the first syllable of *dolorous* (KN, WNW), obviously from *dolor*, in *sojourn*, pronounced [ˈsoʊdʒɜrn] (KN, WCD, NBC, WNW), *solace*, and *provost*. The last is often [ˈproʊvoʊst] or [ˈprɑvoʊst], though all American dictionaries record only [ˈprɑvəst]; influence from *provost-marshal* [ˈproʊvoʊˌmɑrʃəl] (KN, WNW) should probably be reckoned with.

It is characteristic of spelling-pronunciation that unstressed syllables with historical [ə] or [ɪ] in British English and some types of educated American English, acquire the full pronunciation of the respective vowel symbols. Thus the prefixes *be-* *de-*, *e-*, *re-*, and *se-* are often pronounced with [i] instead of [ɪ], [ɪ], or [ə], while *con-* and *com-* may have [ɑ] or [ɔ] instead of [ə]. Unstressed *-ate* in nouns and adjectives tends to become [eɪt]; during the election of the present pope it was irritating to hear some announcers say [ˈpriˌleɪt] for *prelate* [ˈprɛlɪt], the only dictionary form. *Placate* is [ˈpleɪkeɪt] and [ˈplækeɪt] as against British [pləˈkeɪt], and *vacation* is commonly [veɪˈkeɪʃən] with the verb [ˈveɪkeɪt]. *Saint* followed by a name, as in *St Paul*, is invariably [seɪnt]. The preferred pronunciation of *forehead* appears to be [ˈfɔrˌhɛd] with the alternatives [ˈfɔrɪd, ˈfɑrəd]. Suffixal *-day* in *yesterday*, *Monday*, etc., is mostly [deɪ], while *always* is frequently [ˈɔlweɪz], plus of course [-wəz] or [-wɪz]; *coxswain* is reported to be [ˈkɑkˌsweɪn] (WNW) besides the older [ˈkɑksn̩]. Worcester's rule concerning the pronunciation of *-ture* referred to above is readily followed in polysyllables like *ligature*, *literature*, *temperature*, probably on rhythmical grounds; though NBC and WCD recommend only [ˈlɪtərətʃər], KN's preferred forms are [ˈlɪtərəˌtʃʊr] and [-ˌtjʊr], while WNW gives the former as its second variant. One TV weather forecaster always says [ˈtɛmpərʌˌtʊr]. Occasionally I have heard [tʃʊr] in *nature* but never in *picture*, *scripture*, *feature*, *creature*. For the treatment of final *-or* see above. In the *American Spelling Book*, Noah Webster marks final *-or* as stressed in *appellor*, *donor*, *lessor*, and a few other similar words, corresponding to KN's [ˌæpəˈlɔr] plus [əˈpɛlər] (similarly OED), [ˈlɛsər], adding within parentheses 'lesˈsee and lesˈsor' (cf. [lɛˈsɔː] EPD and OED), [doʊˈni ən doʊˈnɔr], but otherwise [ˈdoʊnər], to be compared with [ˈdoʊnɔː] in EPD and [ˈdoʊnər, -ɔːr] in OED. It is possible that the pronunciation of these legal terms may have been influential to some extent in establishing the current [-ər] for unstressed *-or*.

Since American typography eschews the use of diacritics, at least in newspapers and magazines, the French acute accent rarely appears in *coupé*, *fiancé(e)* with the result that when referring to an automobile the former is regularly pronounced [kup], a form recognized by KN and WNW; the latter actually prints it as a separate entry, spelled *coupe*. As yet no dictionary condones [ˈfi-æns] or [fjɑˑns] for *fiancé*, though this may be heard even from educated speakers[9]; the feminine form *fiancée* always ends in [eɪ], perhaps due to some vague association with *née* [neɪ]. Should this practice become general, American English would acquire a gender distinction unknown to the original language, masculine [fjɑˑns], feminine [ˌfi-ɑnˈseɪ], or [fiˌɑnˈseɪ].

Vowels that are usually syncopated in colloquial British English tend to be reinstated in American English. Medial [ə] therefore may be encountered in *every*, *several*, *separate*, *chocolate*, *interested* (nearly always tetra-syllabic), *vegetable*, and *extraordinary*, which is not seldom [ˌɛkstrəˈɔrdəˌnɛri]. A well-known characteristic of American English is the pronunciation of the suffixes *-ary* and *-ory* with secondary stress and full vowels, e.g. *secretary* [ˈsɛkrəˌtɛri), *auditory* [ˈɔdəˌtɔri]; note also *contrary* [ˈkɑntrɛri].

The most striking consonantal feature is probably the restoration of [l] in *balm, calm, palm, psalm, alms*; about 50% of my students in recent years have been found to pronounce it in these words, and one hears it almost regularly from radio announcers. In *almond* and *salmon* [l] appears, too, preceded by [æ]; Worcester (*Fourth Book*, 329, 366, 387) takes exception to 'cal-um' and 'al-mond(s)'. The use of [t] in *often* and *pestle* is regular, and so is medial [k] in *arctic*, though Kenyon-Knott report [ˈɑrtɪk] (ME *artik* < OFr *artique*) as 'now rare'. On the analogy of *scheme*, *schedule*, *sceptic*, [sk] may be heard in *schism*, *sciatic*, *scintillate*, *Scylla*; like sporadic [ʧ] in *chasm* (repudiated by Worcester, *Fourth Book*, 60), *sepulchre*, and *Charon*,[10] it should doubtless be labelled substandard. Instead of [ʃ(ɪ)] one may hear [sɪ] in *controversial* and *negotiate*, and instead of [k] analogical [ʃ] in *machination*. *Thence* and *thither*, which are book-words in American English, are commonly pronounced with initial [θ]. *Nephew* with [f] and *suggest* with [gdʒ] are the preferred pronunciations (KN, NBC, WCD, WNW); Walker (1791) recommends the latter.

A few names deserve to be mentioned in this connection. In America, *Don Quixote* and *Don Juan* have assumed a pseudo-Spanish pronunciation, viz. [ˌdɑnkɪˈhoʊtɪ] and [dɑnˈ(h)wɑn]; the latter is quite out of place in Byron. English place-names transferred to America have likewise been modified phonetically so as to agree better with the spelling. Those in *-ham*, e.g. *Chatham*, *Nottingham*, *Rockingham*, now end in [hæm] with secondary stress, except *Waltham*, which is [ˈwɔlθæm]; those in *-wich* like *Norwich*, *Harwich*, have become [ˈnɔrwɪʧ] and [ˈhɑrwɪʧ], whereas *Greenwich* is [ˈgrinwɪʧ] as well as [ˈgrɛnɪʧ] and [ˈgrɪnɪʧ], the last two mainly in New England. The suffix *-bury*, as in

*Canterbury*, is usually [bɛrɪ], with secondary stress, while outside New England *-ford* tends to become [fɔrd][11]; New Haven Railroad conductors, however, call out [ˈstæmˌfɝrd] (Stamford), a fine instance of restressing. A very striking case is the German name *Gnadenhütten*, Ohio, which according to Kenyon-Knott is locally pronounced [dʒɪˈneɪdn̩ˌhʌtn̩].

Spelling-pronunciation has already left indelible marks on English speech and will doubtless leave others if present trends prevail. Provided these result in greater distinctness of utterance with consequent improvement of communication, the exit of an earlier usage should cause no more concern than any other linguistic change. The fact is, however, that so far it is extremely difficult to point to a single obvious benefit of this kind. Traditional [kɑm], [səˈdʒɛst], for instance, are no less distinct than the more recent [kɑlm], [səgˈdʒɛst], which are actually inferior in point of linguistic economy. Not even the substitution of [ɪŋ] for [n̩] fully meets the above prerequisite. With [n̩] for *-ing*, confusion of the present and past participle is possible only in a handful of instances like *eating* – *eaten*, *taking* – *taken*; in all other verbs it is syntactically immaterial whether the present participle ends in [ɪŋ] or [n̩]. On the other hand, if we define distinctness of utterance in terms of a tightened relationship of the spoken to the written form, then a reasonable case may be made for trying to adjust the pronunciation to the spelling, at least in less familiar words; after all, there seems to be little likelihood of a reverse adjustment. Nevertheless, it would be irresponsible to encourage, for instance, the phonologically abnormal [ʊ] in *turret*, *Durham*, where, moreover, its use means an added orthoepic complication. Rather than wasting time and effort on such forms and others discussed above, teachers should devote their attention to the important problem of intervocalic *t* and *nt*. When *inter-* becomes almost indistinguishable from *inner* and *winter* from *winner*, or when not even the context helps one to determine whether a speaker says *futile* or *feudal*, *parity* or *parody*, then it is high time for a therapy of spelling-pronunciation.

*Notes*

[1] The phonetic symbols used here are those of Kenyon-Knott, *A Pronouncing Dictionary of American English*, Springfield, 1953, with the exception of [eɪ] in *name*, [oʊ) in *home*, [ɜr] in *bird*, and [ər] in *maker*. The Kenyon-Knott volume will be referred to as KN. Other abbreviations: EPD: Daniel Jones, *An English Pronouncing Dictionary*, London, 1937; NBC: James F. Bender, *NBC Handbook of Pronunciation*, New York, 1943; WCD: *Webster's New Collegiate Dictionary*; WNW: *Webster's New World Dictionary*.

[2] On spelling-pronunciation see further E. Koeppell, *Spelling-Pronunciations: Bemerkungen über den Einfluss des Schriftbildes auf den Laut im Englischen*, Strassburg, 1901; E. Buchmann, *Der Einfluss des Schriftbildes auf die Aussprache im Neuenglischen*, Würzburg, 1940; I. C. Ward, *The Phonetics of English*, Cambridge, 1931, 24–33; S. Kenyon, *American Pronunciation*, Ann Arbor, 1951, 114–121; Horn-Lehnert, *Laut und Leben*, Berlin, 1954, 1212–1235 (principal entry); and A. J. Bronstein, *The Pronunciation of American English*, New York, 1960, 231–236.

[3] See my *Shakespeare's Pronunciation*, New Haven, 1953, 306, 310.

[4] Webster, too, has trisyllabic *every* and *several*, but says that *wear*, *ware*, and *were* are pronounced alike (*American Spelling Book*, Brattleborough, 1824, 26 and 148).

[5] G. P. Krapp, *The English Language in America*, New York, 1925, II, 20 f.

[6] In *An Introduction to Phonetics*, London, 1891, Laura Soames has a list of 'Faults characteristic of teachers, that is to say, pedantic efforts to pronounce as we spell' (114 f.), including [eɪ] in *mountain* and [s] for [ʃ] in *associate*.

[7] Cf. Bronstein, *Pron. Am. Eng.*, 233.

[8] Horn-Lehnert, *Laut u. Leben*, 1219, 1233. In *Dialect Notes*, 1890 (17), N.P. Seymour recalls '*bury* rhyming with *fury*' as a pronunciation formerly used by Connecticut settlers in Ohio.

[9] In a TV sketch a few years ago, the hero, a high-school teacher, introduced his *fiancée* and her father in these words: 'I am the fiancé [fjɑ·ns], she is the fiancée [fjɑ·n'seɪ], and he is the financier.'

[10] Bronstein, *Pron. Am. Eng.*, 233.

[11] See Kenyon, *Am. Pron.*, 118 ff.

# British Sources of Selected Features of American Pronunciation: Problems and Methods

HANS KURATH

1. The phonemic systems of all regional types of cultivated American English (AE) correspond very closely to that of Standard British English (SBE).

There is no difference in the system of consonants, except that unsyllabic /ə̯/, as in *here, four*, etc., appears only in dialects that lack postvocalic /r/. Differences in the incidence of the consonants in the vocabulary, as of /r/ in *four, hard*, /s ~ z/ in *greasy*, /j/ in *due*, /h/ in *white*, are few. Phonic differences in the allophones, as of medial /p, t, k/ in *pepper, bitten, bucket*, of /r/ in *merry*, and of /l/ in *jelly*, are somewhat more numerous, but not very prominent.

In the vowel system the differences between the regional types of AE are greater, but all types have much in common with each other and with SBE, although the phonic character of most of the vowel phonemes varies markedly from dialect to dialect and differences in the lexical incidence of the vowels are rather numerous.

If we choose to interpret diphthongal as well as monophthongal vowels as phonemic units, the vowel phonemes shared by all dialects of AE and by SBE, as well as the phonemes peculiar to one or several dialects (the latter in parentheses), can be conveniently exhibited in a composite table, as shown in Table 1.

TABLE 1

COMPOSITE TABLE OF VOWEL PHONEMES

| Checked | : free | Checked | : free | Checked | : free |
|---|---|---|---|---|---|
| ɪ | : i | | | ʊ | : u |
| ɛ | : e | (ʌ)[1] | : ɜ | (ɵ)[2] | : o |
| æ | : (a)[3] | (ɑ)[4] | : (ɑ)[5] | (ɒ)[6] | : ɔ |
| | ai | | oi | | au |

EXAMPLES

| *Checked* | : *free* | *Checked* | : *free* | *Checked* | : *free* |
|---|---|---|---|---|---|
| crib | : three | | | wood | : two |
| ten | : day | (sun)[1] | : fur | (coat)[2] | : know |
| bag | : (car)[3] | (lot)[4] | : (car)[5] | (lot)[6] | : law |
| | pie | | boy | | now |

*Notes*

[1] Checked /ʌ/, as in *sun*, is lacking in SBE (which has /ɑ/ in *sun*).
[2] Checked /ɵ/, as in *coat*, only in New England.
[3] Free /a/, as in *car*, only in eastern New England.
[4] Checked /ɑ/, as in *hot* (SBE *hut*) is lacking in eastern New England and in western Pennsylvania.
[5] Free /ɑ/, as in *car*, only in dialects that lack postvocalic /r/ (except eastern New England, which has /a/).
[6] Checked /ɒ/, as in *hot*, only in SBE.

*Free* vowels are up-gliding, unless monophthongal; *checked* vowels are in-gliding, unless monophthongal. The phonemic contrast between free and checked vowels in the same phonic range (e.g. high-front, mid-back, etc.) thus rests either on phonic quality alone (if both are monophthongal) or on quality together with 'drift' in quality (if one or both are diphthongal).

The substantial agreement in the phonemic systems of the several regional dialects of AE with that of SBE is a measure of the overwhelming importance of SBE in the development of all varieties of AE spoken in the Atlantic States, and, secondarily, of all regional dialects current in the Middle States and the Far West. Even if the vowel systems of the various regional folk dialects of England, Scotland, and Ireland should turn out to conform largely to that of SBE – which appears to be rather improbable – the dominant influence of SBE upon the systematic features of AE pronunciation could not be questioned.

In view of this unquestionable fact, supported by the practical identity of the systematic aspects of the morphology and syntax of AE and SBE, the chief task of the historian of AE is to account for the divergent features current in the regional dialects. Are they derived from different stages in the phonological development of SBE, or from regional variants of SBE? To what extent do they reflect regional differences in English folk speech, especially in the phonic (subphonemic) characteristics of shared phonemes and in their incidence in the vocabulary? Are they American innovations? Now that an adequate record of usage on the Atlantic seaboard is available, specific questions can be formulated, a procedure can be outlined, and some probable or possible answers can be suggested.

The following examples are intended to illustrate this approach.

2. The consonant /r/ survives in SBE only in prevocalic position. After the high vowel of *here* and the mid-vowels of *care* and *door*, /r/ has become the semivowel /ə̯/; after the low vowel of *car*, *Martha*, and the mid-central vowel of *fur*, *Thursday*, this derivative /ə̯/ is merged with the vowel to produce new vowel phonemes, /ɑ/ and /ɜ/, respectively. SBE shares the types of /hiə̯, kɛə̯, dɔə̯, kɑ, fɜ/ with the folk speech of the eastern counties of England to the north of the Thames. The folk dialects of the south and the west of England, on the other hand, preserve the postvocalic /r/, rather generally as a constricted [ɚ].

In the United States, several dialect areas on the Atlantic seaboard – eastern New England, Metropolitan New York, large parts of Virginia with adjoining sections of Maryland and North Carolina, and most of South Carolina, Georgia, and Florida – and all the states on the Gulf of Mexico as far west as eastern Texas – agree with SBE in lacking postvocalic /r/. Here the high and mid-vowels are normally followed by unsyllabic /ə̯/; *car* has the new phoneme / a ∼ ɑ/, articulated regionally as [a˙ ∼ ɑ˙] or [ɑ˙ ∼ ɑɒ]; *fur* has /ɜ/, pronounced regionally as [ɜ˙ ∼ ɞ· ∼ ɜɪ], with or without partial constriction of the tongue.

Each of the four geographically separated areas on the Atlantic seaboard now lacking postvocalic /r/ had in Colonial times one or more prominent seaports (notably Boston, New York, Richmond, Charleston) through which close contacts with England were maintained until the War for Independence, and gradually resumed thereafter. From the centres of these areas, this feature spread to the hinterland. It must have been rather firmly established in South Carolina and Virginia by c. 1800, since the cotton belt along the Gulf of Mexico, settled from these areas between 1810 and 1840, exhibits this feature.

It is well known that the loss of postvocalic /r/ in SBE, and the consequent emergence of the phoneme /ɑ/ of *car*, *garden*, and the unconstricted /ɜ/ of *fur*, *Thursday*, are of rather late date. They are not noted by orthoepists until the last quarter of the eighteenth century. The fact that landlocked Middle Atlantic States (Upstate New York and Pennsylvania) and the southern Upland universally preserve the postvocalic /r/ and a fully constricted /ɜ/ in *fur*, *Thursday*, supports this chronology. To-day all the Inland and the West of the United States, settled by westward expansion between 1800 and 1850, preserve the /r/ after vowels. Approximately three-fourths of the American people use /r/ in all positions, but about 40 million living in the areas mentioned above do not.

The questions to be raised are these: (1) Did some early settlers on the Atlantic seaboard bring with them the postvocalic unsyllabic /ə̯/ from the folk dialects of the East Midland counties of England, where early loss of postvocalic /r/ is attested? (2) To what extent do the Middle Atlantic States owe the preservation of postvocalic /r/ to settlers from the South and West of England and from Scotland and Northern Ireland? (3) Did all American colonies originally have both /r/ *and* /ə̯/ after vowels, achieving uniformity in usage at a later date? (4) To what extent is the loss of postvocalic /r/ as such in certain coastal areas to be attributed to the cultural influence of SBE *after* the original settlement, especially also after the political separation of the American colonies from England?

To give realistic historical answers to these questions much work remains to be done on both sides of the Atlantic.

3. In SBE, the ME long low vowel /ā/ and the up-gliding diphthong /ai/ are merged in one phoneme, /e/, articulated as an up-gliding diphthong [eɪ ~ ɛɪ], so that *tale* rhymes with *tail*. Merging in an up-gliding [eɪ ~ ɛɪ ~ æɪ ~ aɪ] has also taken place in the folk speech of parts of eastern England (chiefly Middlesex, Essex, Hertfordshire, Bedford, Surrey, and western Kent) in which London is embedded.

In the dialects of western England, on the other hand, these two phonemes are kept apart. ME /ā/ is now represented by an in-gliding [eᵊ ~ ɛᵊ], as in *tale*, *lane*, *April*, ME /ai/ by up-gliding [ɛɪ ~ æɪ ~ aɪ], as in *tail*, *way*. They are also kept apart in Norfolk and Suffolk as well as in coastal Sussex.

On the margin of the area in which coalescence in an up-gliding diphthong occurs, some speakers exhibit merging of the two phonemes in an in-gliding diphthong [eᵊ ~ ɛᵊ].

In conformity with SBE and the folk dialects of eastern England, ME /ā/ and /ai/ are regularly merged in the phoneme /e/ in American English. However, the articulation of this /e/, as in *tale*, *lane*, *April*, and *tail*, *way* varies regionally.

Over large areas /e/ is pronounced [eɪ ~ ɛɪ], as in SBE. Monophthongal [e˔ ~ e] alternating with in-gliding [eᵊ] – the latter in checked position – is widespread in South Carolina and Georgia. Relics of [e˙ ~ eᵊ] survive along Chesapeake Bay in Virginia and Maryland. Monophthongal [e˙] is common in the German settlements of eastern Pennsylvania. Hence, though all dialects of AE share the merging of ME /ā/ and /ai/ with SBE, the phonic character of /e/ derives in part from the folk dialects of the West of England and of East Anglia, and in part from German.

4. Parallel to the coalescence of ME /ā/ and /ai/, SBE has merged ME /ǭ/ and /ou/ into one phoneme, /o/, articulated as an up-gliding diphthong [oʊ ~ ɔʊ ~ ɵʊ], so that *stone* rhymes with *grown*. SBE shares this merging into an up-gliding /o/ with the folk dialects of the Home Counties.

In two widely separated areas, East Anglia, with the valley of the Welland, and the south-western counties (Dorset, Somerset, Devon), ME /ǭ/ and /ou/ coalesce either in an in-gliding [oə ~ uə] or in a short monophthong [ʊ ~ ʌ ~ ɔ].

Elsewhere the two ME phonemes remain distinct in English folk speech: here *stone*, *road*, *clothes* have an in-gliding vowel [oə ~ uə] or monophthongal [ɔ ~ ʊ ~ ʌ], *grown*, *know* an up-gliding [oʊ ~ ɔʊ).

Except for New England, American English conforms to SBE and the folk dialects of the Home Counties, East Anglia, and the south-western counties in merging the two ME phonemes completely.

In conformity with SBE, this /o/ is an up-gliding diphthong over large areas. Coalescence in a monophthongal [oᵊ ~ o], similar to that of the folk dialects of East Anglia and the south-western counties, occurs chiefly in South Carolina and Georgia, whatever the actual historical connections may be.

Only New England preserves the original distinction, though to a limited extent. Here the old monophthong survives in checked position as a short and fronted mid-back vowel /ɵ/, as in *stone*, *road*, *coat* /stɵn, rɵd, kɵt/, contrasting with up-gliding /o/, as in *know*, *grown* (but also, e.g. in *no*, *rode*). This so-called 'New England short *o*' is sharply recessive. This feature of the New England dialect is somehow related to regional English folk speech, perhaps also to early SBE usage.

5. In the greater part of the Eastern States, *law*, *salt*, and *lot*, *crop* have contrasting vowels, the /ɔ/ of *law* ranging phonically from rounded [ɔ˙ ~ ɔ] to [ɒɔ], the /ɑ/ of lot from unrounded low-central [ɑ ~ ɑ˙] to low-back [ɑ ~ ɑ˙]. This distinction corresponds to SBE /ɔ/ as in *law*

vs. /ɒ/ as in *lot*. However, in AE the incidence of /ɔ/ is more extensive than in SBE: it is regular before voiceless fricatives, as in *cough*, *moth*, *frost*, and predominates before the /g/ of *dog*, *log*, etc.

In English folk speech, contrasting /ɔ/ and /ɒ ~ ɑ/ are normal in the eastern counties north of the Thames and in large parts of the Midlands, though their incidence deviates regionally from SBE (e.g. /ɔ/ is usual in *dog*, *frost*, etc., in East Anglia). SBE obviously reflects the folk usage of this area.

South of the Thames and from Bucks westward, on the other hand, the two phonemes are merged in an unrounded [ɑ˖ ~ ɑ] sound. Merging of the two phonemes is found also in two sub-areas of the Atlantic States, eastern New England and western Pennsylvania. Here the resulting vowel, which I shall represent by the phonemic symbol /ɒ/, has a wide range of positional and prosodic allophones running from more or less rounded [ɒ˔ ~ ɒ] to unrounded [ɑ˔ ~ ɑ˖ ~ ɑ].

How shall we interpret this coalescence in two widely separated sub-areas of the Atlantic States? Does western Pennsylvania reflect the usage of the Ulster Scots, since according to Joseph Wright (EDG) *law*, *all*, etc., have an unrounded vowel in Scotland and the northern-most counties of England? What shall we say about the merger in eastern New England? Is it somehow related to English folk usage current in the southern and the western counties, or is this simplification the result of the blending of two English dialectal types? Perhaps we shall see more clearly, when Harold Orton of Leeds publishes the findings of his dialect survey of England.

6. In AE the incidence of the free vowel /u/ of *do* and the checked vowel /ʊ/ of *full* in words like *room*, *coop*, *hoof*, *roof*, *root*, *soot*, *food* varies regionally, socially, and from word to word. For instance, in *room*, *broom* checked /ʊ/ is common in the North and the South Atlantic States, but not in the Middle States and the southern Upland; in *Cooper*, /ʊ/ is regular south of Pennsylvania, but uncommon to rare farther north; in *roof* and *soot*, /ʊ/ is common outside the South; in *food* it is largely confined to Pennsylvania. Moreover, in *soot* the checked vowel /ʌ/ of *hut* occurs extensively in common and in folk speech in most parts of the Eastern States, but in *hoof* only in parts of the South.

This disconcertingly variable incidence of three different derivatives of ME /ǭ/ (and of /ū/ before labials) in AE has its counterpart in English folk speech, and to some extent in SBE (cf. *food*, *good*, *blood*).

Broadly speaking, the eastern counties of England have /ʊ/ in *room*, /ʊ ~ u/ in *hoop, soot*, /u ~ ʊ/ in *root, afternoon*, and /ʊ ~ ʌ/ in *hoof, soot*; the western counties have /u/ in *room*, /ʊ/ in *hoop, soot*, /u ~ ʊ/ in *root, afternoon*, /ʊ ~ u/ in *hoof, soot*; the 'London Corridor' lying in between (widening out into the central Midlands, as so frequently) agrees either with the eastern or the western counties, but generally favours /u/, as does SBE.

It would seem obvious that the complexities in AE reflect the multiple regional variations in English folk speech and the resulting unsettled usage of SBE, especially of earlier times. To trace specific regional variants of AE to particular British sources will remain hazardous until we are better informed about the English dialects and the regional adaptations of SBE, about which we know so little. Nevertheless, it is highly probable that the /ʊ/ in *room, broom*, used primarily in New England, Virginia, and South Carolina, became established in these coastal areas under the influence of SBE of the eighteenth century. In earlier days both /ʊ/ and /u/ must have been current, because the settlers came from western as well as eastern England.

7. In all the Southern states, as far north as the southern boundary of Pennsylvania, the vast majority of speakers on all social levels use the vowel /o/ of *door, boar* also in *poor, sure*. From Pennsylvania northward, *poor, sure* have a high vowel, /u/ or /ʊ/, *door, boar* a mid-vowel, /o/ or /ɔ/, except that in north-eastern New England the high vowel is merged with the mid-vowel /o/, as in the South.

Coalescence of earlier /u/ before a historical /r/ with /o/ (or the derivative /ɔ/), has taken place in SBE and in the folk speech of the eastern counties of England lying north of the Thames, coalescence in an [uᵊ]-like sound (here regular in *stone, road*, etc.) farther west. But distinct vowels are preserved in this position in the folk speech of Kent, Surrey, Hampshire, Oxfordshire, Wiltshire, and Dorset, though not consistently.

The regional differences in AE, therefore, reflect regional differences in the mother country. Shall we attribute them simply to the folk speech of England, or has SBE had some influence? If the latter, why should the Southern States follow the lead of SBE, and Philadelphia, Metropolitan New York, and Boston with their hinterland keep entirely aloof? Should we infer from this diversity in the behaviour of the seaports that SBE usage was as unsettled in the latter part of the eighteenth century as it is today?

8. The diphthongal vowel /au/, as in *cow*, *down*, *out*, has a wide range of phonic variations (diaphones) in the Eastern States. Some variants are regional, some social, others positional or prosodic.

Marked positional allophones are characteristic of Virginia and the Low Country of South Carolina. Before voiceless consonants, as in *house*, *out*, Virginia has a 'fast' diphthong [əu], South Carolina [ɐu]; in other positions, as in *cow*, *down*, *loud*, the former area has a 'slow' diphthong [æ·ʊ], the latter [ɑu]. Elsewhere in the Atlantic States, positional variation is slight.

The phonic type [ɑʊ ~ aʊ], similar to that of SBE, is usual in Pennsylvania, Metropolitan New York, and much of the New England settlement area, where it is regularly used by the better educated. It is also common in the Lower South, especially in South Carolina.

The type of [æʊ ~ ɛʊ] occurs to some extent in all of the Atlantic States, but its social dissemination, hence also its social standing, varies sharply. Virginians of all social levels use it regularly before voiced consonants, and no stigma attaches to it here or in other parts of the South, even where it is not very common. From Pennsylvania northward, however, [æʊ] is rustic or old-fashioned, being avoided by the better educated. The type of [əu ~ ɐu], with centralized beginning, which appears in parts of the South as a positional allophone of /au/, occurs sporadically in old-fashioned speech of the North, especially in north-eastern New England, but without positional restriction.

All of these variants of the phoneme /au/ are current in present-day British folk speech, but the marked positional allophones of Virginia appear to have no counterpart in England and may therefore be an American innovation.

9. In the eastern United States the diphthongal phoneme /ai/, as in *nine* and *twice*, exhibits a wide range of variants. Some of them are regional or social, others positional or prosodic.

Striking positional allophones of /ai/ are confined to two sub-areas of the South. Virginia, with adjoining parts of Maryland and North Carolina, has a 'fast' diphthong [əi] before voiceless consonants, as in *twice*, *light*, and a 'slow' diphthong [a·ᵋ ~ a·ᵊ] in other positions, as in *nine*, *high*. Correspondingly, the Low Country of South Carolina has [ɐɪ] and [ɑ·ɪ ~ ɑɪ] in these positions.

Elsewhere in the Atlantic States positional variation of the phoneme /ai/ is slight, but regional differences in articulation are very marked. Thus the southern Upland has [a·ᵋ ~ a·ᵊ], Pennsylvania, Metropolitan

New York, and southern New England have [aɪ ~ a·ɪ ~ ɑɪ], Upstate New York and north-eastern New England not infrequently [ʌɪ ~ əɪ], though these variants are yielding ground to [aɪ].

The widely used American variants [aɪ ~ a·ɪ ~ ɑɪ ~ ɑ·ɪ] have their counterparts in SBE of to-day and in the folk speech of a corridor leading from Middlesex – Essex through Hertfordshire and Bedfordshire northward into the Midlands.

The variants [ɐɪ ~ ʌɪ ~ əɪ], current positionally in parts of the American South but without positional restriction in parts of the North, correspond rather closely to the variants rather generally used by the folk east, west, and south of the 'London Corridor'. Shall we say that this phonic type of American English is wholly derived from the English dialects of these areas, or should we assume that it was also current in SBE of an earlier day? The narrow corridor to which the phonic type of SBE is now confined in English folk speech makes one suspect that [ɑɪ ~ aɪ] is fairly recent in SBE. Such an inference finds support in the observation that [əɪ ~ ɐɪ] is now current, though positionally restricted, in the cultivated speech of two sub-areas on the Atlantic Seaboard – Virginia and South Carolina – which had intimate contact with England throughout the Colonial Period and after. The positional restriction of these variants, however, may well be an American innovation.

10. My purpose has been to pose specific problems concerning the British sources of some features of American pronunciation restricted to certain sub-areas of the Atlantic States – that section of the United States from which all varieties of American English are ultimately derived – and to suggest probable or possible solutions. I am well aware of the tentative nature of my suggestions. I hope that they may stimulate others to follow them up and to gather further evidence that may lead to firm conclusions. We must learn more about earlier usage in the major focal areas on the Atlantic Seaboard by gathering and interpreting unconventional spellings in local records, so that our historical inferences from present-day usage may be corrected. We need a clearer view of the regional folk dialects of England, Scotland, and Ireland than we now have, before American peculiarities can safely be traced to particular types of English folk speech, if they cannot be reconciled with SBE. We must try to find out more about regional variants in the cultivated speech of England during our Colonial period, before we can decide whether an American regionalism derives from the folk speech or from the cultivated speech of England. It may well be that, in time,

regionally restricted cultivated pronunciations current in America will throw light upon earlier SBE usage and on its regional variants, which otherwise must be largely inferred from the present-day regional folk dialects of England.

11. In accordance with American practice, I cite phonemic units between slants and phonic features in brackets. Since the vowel systems of the various English folk dialects are yet to be worked out, I refrain from phonemicizing the phonic entities of these dialects. For my immediate purpose this procedure is adequate, and in future studies devoted to the British sources of American pronunciation purely phonic data will continue to have considerable importance.[1]

*Note*

[1] Fuller information concerning the data upon which my statements of usage are based will be found in Hans Kurath and Raven I. McDavid, Jr, *The Pronunciation of English in the Atlantic States*, Michigan, 1961. A considerable number of the 1450 field records from the Atlantic States were made by Dr Guy S. Lowman, Jr, who did his doctoral work under Professor Daniel Jones. Dr Lowman also furnished the 60 field records of English folk dialects from which my English data are taken, unless otherwise stated. Daniel Jones' contribution to this paper, though indirect, is therefore quite substantial.

# Criteria for a New Orthography for English

P.A.D.MacCARTHY

An analysis of proposals for a reform of English spelling reveals that would-be reformers are divided into those who advocate the continued use of the roman alphabet, and those who favour its abandonment in favour of some other script. The former subdivide into those who would introduce additional, new characters, and those whose proposed reforms would stop at rearrangement of the existing roman letters.

Let us first examine the roman alphabet in use to-day, viewing it as an instrument for the writing of any language, and for the writing of the English language in particular.

A number of factors or features can be listed in its favour:

(1) It has stood the test of time, and has reached an advanced stage of typographical development, with founts of type, and variations in the design of each letter, that are suited to an immense variety of purposes.

(2) It is in current use for the written representation of numerous languages, in all parts of the world.

(3) With few exceptions the basic shapes of the individual letters are simple – though not, to be sure, as simple as possible; few letters require as many as three downstrokes for their execution, and only m and w take up so much space laterally as to provide a minor problem for the equal-space typewriter. There are perhaps proportionately too many verticals (though the downstroke is the most convenient to execute *by hand*) yet a fair number of diagonals as in *printed* k, v, w, x, y, give differentiation by variety of form, and variety in the distribution of white space between and around sequences of letters.

(4) By and large, the letters are individually distinctive – that is, their basic shapes are sufficiently different not to be confused with one another. But there are notable exceptions: in print, c may look rather like e, and also rather like o. Under adverse conditions, e.g. in very small sizes, or seen in a dim light, or with the blurring of a typewritten carbon copy, gross misspellings such as rcccmmcndaticn, strcctcar, aoocmmcdaticn are hardly noticed. Compare also wccdwcrk and wccd-

killcr. Again, under certain circumstances psssge and paaaage both pass unnoticed for passage. In handwriting, n and u are notoriously alike; and it is only the presence of the dot on i that prevents much greater confusion between such groups as mi, nu, im, un, etc. Compare handwritten impressed with unpressed (e.g. pleats).[1]

(5) The somewhat four-square design of many of the letters leads to sequences of letters being remarkably close-knit; this in turn facilitates the recognition of whole-word patterns, though these are then sufficiently differentiated from one another by horizontal extension, and by variation in the bottom and especially top outline. (It is evident that the resultant easy recognizability of whole words, and even groups of words, compensates in large measure for the non-distinctiveness of some individual letters, referred to under (4) above. In practice, too, immense assistance is of course obtained from context – but this is true of any script, however unsatisfactory typographically.) The distinctiveness of whole-word patterns in turn preserves legibility even in very small sizes, the use of which enables much material to be compressed into little space.

As against the above favourable considerations, the roman alphabet as such carries with it the following disadvantages:

(a) It has too few letters for representing uniliterally the sounds of English – and those of many other languages besides English; this is particularly the case with regard to letters for vowels. The principal devices used in the various languages for making good the deficiency are:

(1) The digraphic representation of simple sounds, as in French – ch, ou, au, eu, German – ch, ee, and on a considerable scale in English – sh, th, ee, and so on; (2) the use of diacritics or 'accents'. These are almost non-existent in English, fairly common in French and in German, ubiquitous in the orthographies of, for instance, Polish, Hungarian, Turkish. (Of these, Polish and Hungarian make in addition extensive use of the digraph, e.g. sz, rz in Polish, sz, zs, ty, gy in Hungarian.[2])

(b) During its long history, usages have grown up that have resulted in a proliferation of forms: of our 26 letters only two (c and o) have a basically unvarying shape in printed lower case, in capitals, and in cursive script. Many letters have to be recognized in three or even four different forms. Compare the following: A, a, ɑ; F, f, 𝔣, ℱ; G, g, ɡ. A person who had never seen roman script might be forgiven for thinking, on first seeing the above forms, that each of them constituted a different letter! The learner, therefore, has not only to master some 60 or 70 different shapes but has to learn to group them appropriately into 'letters', and then has to learn when to use and when not to use each of the shapes, e.g. when to write a capital. Viewed in this light the roman alphabet, however consistently employed, is not so simple a script to learn as one having many more basic, but unchanging, letter-shapes.

A recent and by far the most successful serious attempt to rearrange the existing roman letters to the best advantage is that of the Simplified Spelling Society of Great Britain, see p. 177, in the shape of the system it sponsors known as 'New Spelling'. (Specimen 5 at the end of this article, p. 167). Guiding principles of the Society have always been:

(1) No new letters (not because new letters are necessarily undesirable, but because it was decided that the work of the Society should be directed to showing just how much could be done without them).

(2) Letters to be used as far as possible with their traditional English values, the commonest value of each letter in so far as this can be determined and unless some overriding consideration intervenes (this principle rules out the possible use of the redundant letters c, q and x for vowels, it being felt that spellings such as hct, hqt, or hxt for, say, hot or hut would be too great a departure from established romanic – let alone English – usage to be generally acceptable.[3] For the Society has not approached spelling reform as a mere academic exercise but has always planned with a view to getting some reform actually carried through. Several of its guiding principles were set up with this fact in mind).

(3) Supplementation of roman letters to be by digraphs, as being the lesser evil, in preference to diacritics.

(4) The principle of least disturbance, i.e. the *status quo* should not be disturbed without good reason.

(5) A scheme for thorough-going systematic reform should be put forward (this of course conflicts with, but is held to override, (4) above), no concessions being made for the sake of the living generation, i.e. those who have already learnt the present spelling.

The advantages claimed for 'New Spelling', as compared to other more radical types of reform (augmented roman, non-roman) are:

(1) Greater continuity with the past, and with other languages continuing to use the roman alphabet.

(2) Greater ease of learning *for those who already know roman* – it can be read at sight, and the essentials of the system learnt in a few minutes from information contained on a postcard.

(3) Less *initial* psychological and technological disturbance, and thus (perhaps) more likelihood of gaining acceptance.

On the other hand, advantage (1) above can be in part discounted by the realization that reading from our present spelling would have to be separately learnt in any case, for an indefinite period into the future; and that the conventional allocation of roman letters to the sounds of other languages is so unlike the English, and so lacking in uniformity, that the apparent advantage of continuity with past English tradition would not count for very much outside the English-speaking world. As regards (2), it is only the living generation that could derive benefit from this; and there are millions alive, learners or potential learners of English at any given time, for whom in any case roman script is previously unknown. In reply to (3), it is at least questionable whether rearrangement of the roman letters would prove psychologically more acceptable than something entirely different (see note 3 below). Rearranged, more phonetic, spellings are often suggestive of near-illiteracy (e.g. nollij, elifunt), of sub-standard speech as represented in comic anecdotes (e.g. wot, luv, guv'nor), of commercial catchwords (e.g. Phit-eezi for a brand of footwear, Kumbak for a tennis-trainer having the ball attached to a length of rubber, etc.); these associations all work against the acceptance of a reformed spelling that is liable to evoke them.

In addition, not only are the adverse features inherent in the roman letters (see pp. 157, 158) still present but two other special points should be mentioned: first, the large-scale use of digraphs required in New Spelling almost entirely cancels out the economies achieved by the elimination of 'silent' or redundant letters, e.g. doubled consonants (it must be borne in mind that an economy of something like one letter in six is effected by the uniliteral representation of each sound, coupled with the omission of all unnecessary letters; and this is so regardless of the actual form taken by a reformed script for English).

Second, with the decision, for better or worse, not to employ a single new letter, New Spelling is precluded from dealing radically and satisfactorily with one major problem of English – that of the spelling of vowels in weakly stressed syllables. A high proportion of these being the central, neutral or schwa vowel (for which of course no consistent spelling is available in the current orthography), it follows that in this matter New Spelling is obliged, by its self-imposed terms of reference, to depart from the ideal of spellings that would be deducible from speech.[4] The decision to leave things very largely as they are at present was probably the best in the circumstances. It has this slight compensating advantage: that there can often be greater visual resemblance between cognates than would otherwise be the case, since many vowel quality changes and vowel omissions concomitant with a shift of stress are not recorded in the new spelling. Thus, for example, the retention of the final -or of *ambasador* suggests the proper pronunciation of *ambasadorial*, and the ending -al in *topikal* shows the connection with *topikaliti.*[5]

To sum up, masterly though the New Spelling rearrangement of the existing letters undoubtedly is, some of those people who are convinced of the need for a radical reform may feel that New Spelling does not go far enough.

We come now to the question of supplementing the deficiencies of the roman alphabet by extra letters. This can be tackled by various means: by simply taking over existing letters from other alphabets (e.g. Greek, Cyrillic), with such typographical modifications as may be demanded by the need to harmonize with roman founts; by altering roman letters sufficiently to constitute additional independent shapes; by designing new letters to go with the roman (these might of course have resemblances to existing letters, and so come optionally under the preceding head); and by combinations of the foregoing.[6] Each of these methods has its own problems, which can best be appreciated after a consideration of the requirements to be met. These may be summarized as follows: any new letters must be distinctive, i.e. they must be sufficiently different from roman letters, and from each other, not to cause confusion; they must at the same time satisfy the essential of simplicity – it would be no solution to achieve distinctiveness only by excessive elaboration of form; besides constituting good designs in a variety of sizes and founts of type, they must be satisfactory to form by hand – while of course still retaining their separate identity.

The very number of sounds needing letters is perhaps the chief stumbling-block: distinctiveness is readily achieved when but few distinctions are needed, but with each new letter the difficulty increases by leaps and bounds. (As it is, certain letters resemble one another too closely, see above, p. 156). A further inescapable fact is that the existing letters seem to have used up most of the simplest available shapes, so additional letters are always in danger of bringing added complication of form. Moreover, since the greatest shortage is of letters for vowels, any attempt to preserve traditional usage by having only x-height letters for vowels (surely a desirable aim – not perhaps on theoretical grounds but just because of the roman tradition) runs up against the task of designing a number of new vowel letters without leaving the distinctions between them rather small and inconspicuous.

Most existing romanic orthographies have successfully added at most one or two letters for vowels, e.g. the œ of French, the əe of Icelandic, the ø of Danish. Among consonants Polish ł, Croat Đ, đ, Icelandic ð, are somewhat makeshift devices, involving as they do the small stroke through a letter which is hardly more than a diacritic.

In view of the magnitude of the problem, it is small wonder that romanic orthographies have in general fallen back on accents (diaeresis, cedilla, circumflex, tilde, and the like), yet accents cannot be approved as a device, for the reasons given in note 2 below.

Countless would-be reformers have wrestled with, others toyed with, the designing of augmented roman orthographies. Specimens of three are shown at the end of this paper – Isaac Pitman's Phonetic Alphabet as used for his printed Bibles of 1850 (Specimen 1) and 1892 (Specimen 2), and the Fonetic Alfabet (1958) of the Simpler Spelling Association of America (Specimen 4). These may be compared with New Spelling (Specimen 5).

And so to the consideration of non-roman scripts.[7] It is possible that there exists somewhere in the world a ready-made script that has enough letters, of suitable design, to constitute the ideal, or anyhow an acceptable, solution. If so, it has up till now escaped the notice of reformers far and wide. A cursory examination of exotic scripts commonly reveals in particular an astonishing complexity in the shapes of the letters, which of itself would render them unsuitable. In the absence of an existing script, the reformer falls back on his own inventiveness, assisted no doubt by reminiscences of letter shapes that have come within his experience.

It will naturally be the aim of any designer starting from scratch to avoid most if not all of the adverse features of existing scripts known to him, and at the same time to introduce or retain any features held desirable. In addition, he will need to have an eye to the overall appearance of his design, which must be harmonious and if possible aesthetically pleasing – though here questions of personal taste and individual preference intervene, which are matters incapable of objective assessment or precise handling.

Desiderata mentioned or implied above will not be repeated here. Additional desiderata that might not all earn universal agreement but would probably command a wide measure of approval are the following:

the script should run horizontally from left to right across the line, and from top to bottom of the page – nothing else would be likely to commend itself for English on the grounds of unnecessary and too great departure from tradition; there should be a ribbon- or x-height running through the line, giving a minimum height for the majority of all letters and the remaining letters should extrude above or below this ribbon in the proportion considered desirable,[8] thus ensuring adequate major variation in whole-word outline (but there should also be minor variation of outline along the base and along the top of the ribbon itself); capitals, if provided at all,[9] should not be different in shape from their lower-case counterparts, but only larger or blacker or both; the frequency of occurrence of each sound of the language to be written should be taken into account, the allocation of letters to sounds being guided by this, so that letters having greater complication of line, and greater width, can be relegated normally to the more infrequent sounds – it is particularly important for speed and economy that the very commonest sounds be written with the simplest and narrowest letters; each letter-shape should have only one value, irrespective of size, both absolutely and relative to other letters, and irrespective of its position in relation to other letters, i.e. it should be interpretable in isolation, out of context; and it should preferably not resemble any numeral, mark of punctuation, or other written sign in current use.

The question whether these features, or most of them, together with many more, could be incorporated successfully into a single design ceased to be a matter for mere conjecture with the announcement of the George Bernard Shaw Alphabet Competition in 1958.[10] The terms of reference – to design a new, i.e. non-roman, script for English (Proposed British Alphabet) – gave competitors the opportunity to try their hand at this most difficult exercise. The design chosen has many admirable theoretical and practical features (Specimen 3). Special mention may be made here of the following:

(1) The total number of printer's sorts is 48, but this includes several ligatures: one for [juː],[11] and (incorporating [r]), one for each of the following: [ɑːr, ɔːr, əːr, ər, iər, ɛər]. Diphthongs are uniliteral,[12] but [iə] is combined [i] + [ə]; similarly, [ʧ, ʤ], though single sorts, are plainly constructed from [t] and [ʃ], [d] and [ʒ], respectively.

(2) Four uniliteral 'word-signs' for *the*, *of*, *and*, *to* are standard, the letters being those for the single sounds [ð, v, n, t], respectively.

An estimated 10% of space is saved by this device alone, these four words having very high frequency of occurrence.[13]

(3) Apart from the above four, words having strong and weak forms are regularly written in their strong form, with the exception of the indefinite article(s) *a, an.* Since these two words must be written with a vowel, and since the use of the strong-form vowel in each of them is rare, and since there are advantages in having *a* and *an* resemble one another, the weak form is the one written, namely [ə, ən], respectively.

(4) Ligatures apart, the printed script consists of disjoined letters, and it is intended that handwriting should be similar. The development of cursive forms, that has caused such divergence between roman print and handwriting, is thus automatically discouraged, and could be kept in check, or within fixed limits, without difficulty. It is claimed that in this way the use of the new alphabet would promote legibility, and that the greater ease of reading people's handwriting, and time saved in so doing, would more than compensate for any time lost to the writer in forming sequences of unlinked letters.[14] Any such loss would in any case be far outweighed by time saved through using the PBA as such: the omission of many unwanted letters[15]; the simpler and fewer strokes needed on average to write each letter; the standard use of abbreviation. It is further claimed that the PBA would inculcate habits of good penmanship in early childhood, and actually make it less easy for slovenly and indistinct writers to develop (for the lasting effects of early training, notice how 'script writing' left its mark on the adult hands of the generation brought up on it).

A word, in conclusion, as to the function and possible future of the PBA (Shavian). It goes without saying that it could not and would not be *imposed* on an unwilling public – Shaw realized that it could only make its way on merit, though he himself was confident that it would. It will therefore be seen, and perhaps ultimately used, alongside the roman alphabet for an indefinite period, until one proves the better and the other falls into disuse.[16] But the rate of modern progress and the climate of change are such that, once people were convinced of the superiority of the new, the change-over could be effected within a comparatively short period of time.

As for the transliterated version of *Androcles* (see note 10) this may or may not be the first of a long line of publications in the same script. It had to be made, first, to carry out Shaw's wishes, as expressed in his Will; second, to enable the calculations based upon it to be made, that Shaw believed would prove the feasibility and desirability of reform along these lines by convincing people of the economic advantages resulting from the colossal saving of time, paper, ink, storage, transport, and the rest. In the longer term view, the technological difficulties would be well worth overcoming, the temporary losses on existing printing plant, etc. would be a mere drop in the ocean. And though it might be the pressure of commercial interests that eventually saw the reform through, the possible resultant benefits to the whole English-speaking world, and beyond,[17] are far-reaching and incalculable.

*The phonetic letters in the first column are pronounced like the italic letters in the words that follow.*

*Long Vowels.*

Ɛ ɛ . . *ea*se . . . .
Ꞩ a . . *a*ge . . . .
A ɑ . . *a*lms . . .
Θ ɵ . . *aw*ning. . .
Ꞷ ꞷ . . *o*pe . . . .
Ɯ ɯ . . *oo*ze. . . .

*Short Vowels.*

I i . . *i*s . . . . .
E e . . *e*gg . . . . .
Ʌ ɑ . . *a*m . . . . .
O o . . *o*n . . . . . .
U u . . *u*p . . . .
Ɯ ɯ . . s*u*gar . . .

*Diphthongs.*

Ɨ ɨ . . *i*ce . . . . .
Ơ ơ . . *oy*ster . . . .
Ɣ ɤ . . *ou*nce . . .
Ɥ ɥ . . *u*se . . . .

*Coalescents.*

Y y . . *y*ea . . . .
W w . . *w*ay . . . .

*Breathing.*

H h . . *h*ay . . . .

*Explodents.*

P p . . *p*ole . . . .
B b . . *b*owl . . .
T t . . *t*oe . . . .
D d . . *d*oe . . . . .
Ꞓ ç . . *ch*eer . . .
J j . . *j*eer . . . .
C c . . *c*ame . . .
G g . . *g*ame . . .

*Continuants.*

F f . . *f*ear . . . .
V v . . *v*eer . . .
Ŧ ŧ . . *th*igh . . .
Đ đ . . *th*y . . . .
S s . . *s*eal . . . .
Z z . . *z*eal . . . .
Σ ʃ . . *sh*all . . .
Ʒ ʒ . . vi*s*ion . . .

*Liquids.*

R r . . *r*are . . .
L l . . *l*ull . . . .

*Nasals.*

M m . . *m*um . . .
N n . . *n*un . . . .
Ŋ ŋ . . si*ng* . . .

(') *Vocal*, as in *ab'l*, *siz'm*, *hev'n*, &c.

*A Holy Bible* 1850

*Capter* 1.

1 In đɛ bɛgíniŋ woz đɛ Wurd, ɑnd đɛ Wurd woz wiđ God, ɑnd đɛ Wurd woz God.

2 Đɛ sam woz in đɛ bɛgíniŋ wiđ God.

3 Θl ŧiŋz wer mad bɨ him; ɑnd wiđɤ́t him woz not eni ŧiŋ mad đɑt woz mad.

4 In him woz lɨf; ɑnd đɛ lɨf woz đɛ lɨt ov men.

5 And đɛ lɨt ʃɨneŧ in dɑrcnes, ɑnd đɛ dɑrcnes comprɛhénded it not.

6 ¶ Đar woz a mɑn sent from God, hɯz nam [woz] Jon.

7 Đɛ sam cam fɵr a witnes, tɯ bar witnes ov đɛ Lɨt, đɑt ɵl [men] ŧrɯ him mɨt bɛlɛ́v.

8 Hɛ woz not đát Lɨt, but [woz sent] tɯ bar witnes ov đát Lɨt.

9 [Đát] woz đɛ trɯ Lɨt, hwiç lɨteŧ everi mɑn đɑt cumeŧ intɯ đɛ wurld.

10 Hɛ woz in đɛ wurld, ɑnd đɛ wurld woz mad bɨ him, ɑnd đɛ wurld nɥ him not.

11 Hɛ cam untɯ hiz ꞷn, ɑnd hiz ꞷn rɛsɛ́vd him not.

12 But ɑz meni ɑz rɛsɛ́vd him, tɯ đém gav hɛ pɤer tɯ bɛcúm đɛ sunz ov God, [ɛv'n] tɯ đém đɑt bɛlɛ́v on hiz nam:

13 Hwiç wer bɵrn, not ov blud, nɵr ov đɛ wíl ov đɛ fleʃ, nɵr ov đɛ wíl ov mɑn, but ov God.

14 ¶ And đɛ Wurd woz mad fleʃ, ɑnd dwelt ɑmúŋ us, (ɑnd wɛ bɛhéld hiz glꞷri, đɛ glꞷri ɑz ov đɛ ꞷnli bɛ-gót'n ov đɛ Fɑđer,) fɯl ov gras ɑnd trɯŧ.

A *New Testament* 1849

Specimen 1

*The phonetic letters in the first column are pronounced like the italic letters in the words that follow.*

CONSONANTS.

*Explodents.*

P p.....ro*p*e....
B b.....ro*b*e...
T t.....fa*t*e....
D d.....fa*d*e...
Є ç.....*etch*...
J j.....*edg*e..
K k ...lee*k*...
G g ....lea*gu*e.

*Continuants.*

F f.....sa*f*e.....
V v....sa*v*e.....
Ŧ ŧ...brea*th*.
Đ đ...brea*the*..
S s....hi*ss*....
Z z....hi*s*.....
Σ ʃ.....vi*ci*ous.
Ʒ ʒ.....vi*si*on.

*Nasals.*

M m...see*m*...
N n...see*n*....
Ŋ ŋ...si*ng*.....

*Liquids.*

L l....fa*ll*.......
R r ...*r*a*r*e......

*Coalescents.*

W w....*w*et.....
Y y....*y*et......

*Aspirate.*

H h...*h*ay....aitch

VOWELS.

*Lingual.*

A a......*a*m, f*a*r..
Ɑ ɑ......*a*lms....
E e......*e*ll,f*e*rn..
Ɛ ɛ......*a*le,*ai*r..
I i...... *i*ll.......
Ɨ ɨ......*ee*l,f*ea*r..

*Labial.*

O o..... *o*n, *o*r...
Ꞷ ꞷ......*a*ll......
Ʊ ʊ......*u*p, c*u*r..
Ơ ơ......*o*pe,*o*re..
U u......f*u*ll..
Ų ų...f*oo*d, p*oo*r..

DIPHTHONGS: ei, ou, iu, ai, oi.
*as heard in* by, *now*, *new*, *ay* (yes), *boy*.

CAPTER 1.

IN đe begíniŋ woz đe Wʊrd, and đe Wʊrd woz
2 wiđ God, and đe Wʊrd woz God. Đe sɛm woz in
3 đe begíniŋ wiđ God. Ꞷl ŧiŋz wer mɛd ŧrų him; and
4 wiđout him woz not eniŧiŋ mɛd. Đát whiç haŧ bɨn mɛd
5 woz leif in him; and đe leif woz đe leit ov men. And đe
leit ʃeineŧ in đe darknes; and đe darknes aprehended
6 it not. Đer kɛm a man, sent from God, hųz nɛm woz
7 Jon. Đe sɛm kɛm for witnes, đat hɨ meit bɛr witnes
8 ov đe leit, đat ꞷl meit belɨv ŧrų him. Hɨ woz not đe
9 leit, bʊt kɛm đat hɨ meit bɛr witnes ov đe leit. Đe
trų leit, whiç leiteŧ everi man, woz kʊmiŋ intu đe
10 wʊrld. Hɨ woz in đe wʊrld, and đe wʊrld woz mɛd
11 ŧrų him, and đe wʊrld niú him not. Hɨ kɛm ʊntu
12 hiz ơn, and đe đat wer hiz ơn resɨvd him not. Bʊt az
meni az resɨvd him, tu đem gɛv hɨ đe reit tu bekʊ́m
13 çildren ov God, ɨven tu đem đat belɨv on hiz nɛm: hų
wer born, not ov blʊd, nor ov đe wíl ov đe fleʃ, nor
14 ov đe wíl ov man, bʊt ov God. And đe Wʊrd bekɛm
fleʃ, and dwelt amʊŋ ʊs (and wɨ beheld hiz glơri, glơri
az ov đe ơnli begoten from đe Fɑđer), ful ov grɛs and
trųŧ.

*Niu Testament* 1892
Specimen 2

Specimen 3

but in ə larjər sens, wɛ kanɒt dedikat — wɛ kanɒt kɒnsikrat — wɛ kanɒt halo — ħis graɯnd. ƀ brav men, liviŋ and ded, hɯ strugld hɛr, hav kɒnsikrated it far əbuv aɯr pɯr paɯər tɯ ad ɔr ditrakt. ƀ wərld wil litl not nɔr lɔŋ rimembər ƕɒt wɛ sa hɛr, but it kan nevər fərget ƕɒt ħa did hɛr. it iz fɔr us, ƀ liviŋ, raħər, tɯ bɛ dedikated hɛr tɯ ƀ unfiniʃt wərk ƕić ħa hɯ fɔt hɛr hav ħus far so nobli ədvanst. it iz raħər fɔr us tɯ bɛ hɛr dedikated tɯ ƀ grat task rimaniŋ bifor us — ħat frɒm ħɛz ɒnərd ded wɛ tak inkrɛst divoʃən tɯ ħat kɔz fɔr ƕić ħa gav ƀ last ful meʒər ɒv divoʃən; ħat wɛ hɛr hali rizɒlv ħat ħɛz ded ʃal nɒt hav dad in van; ħat ħis naʃən, undər gɒd, ʃal hav ə nɯ bərħ ɒv frɛdəm; and ħat guvərnmənt ɒv ƀ pɛpl, ba ƀ pɛpl, fɔr ƀ pɛpl, ʃal nɒt periʃ frɒm ƀ ərħ.

Specimen 4

But in a larjer sens, we kanot dedikaet – we kanot konsekraet – we kanot haloe – dhis ground. Dhe braev men, living and ded, huu strugld heer, hav konsekraeted it far abuv our puur pou.er to ad or detrakt. Dhe wurld wil litl noet nor long remember whot we sae heer, but it kan never forget whot dhae did heer. It iz for us, dhe living, radher, to be dedikaeted heer to dhe unfinisht wurk which dhae huu faut heer hav dhus far soe noebli advanst. It is radher for us to be heer dedikaeted to dhe graet task remaening befor us – dhat from dheez onord ded we taek inkreest devoeshon to dhat kauz for which dhae gaev dhe last fool mezher ov devoeshon; dhat we heer hieli rezolv dhat dheez ded shal not hav died in vaen; dhat dhis naeshon, under God, shal have a nue burth ov freedom; and dhat guvernment ov dhe peepl, bie dhe peepl, for dhe peepl, shal not perish from dhe urth.

Specimen 5

*Notes*

[1] In this connection, the Turkish innovation of an undotted i (ı), alongside an ordinary dotted i, has proved of doubtful merit, especially in handwriting.

[2] The theoretical objection to the digraph is that the separate letters that make up each combination have other values when not in combination, thus falling short of the phonetic ideal 'one sound, one symbol' (though, of course it can be maintained that the two letters constitute a single 'symbol'). The practical objections to the digraph are that two letters are likely to take more time to write, and certainly take more time to type or print, than one; and they are also wasteful of space laterally, with increased costs in materials consumed.

As for accents, they are troublesome to write since they interrupt the flow of the writing, either during the writing of a word or after a word has been 'completed'. And they are troublesome for the printer: they get easily broken, they tend to clog, they are a problem where capital letters are concerned. Moreover, when many accents are in use, the visual outline of words tends to get blurred, and the general effect of dazzle is trying to the eye of the reader.

[3] And in this the Society is probably right: many people who might be willing to accept a completely new script seem to be highly resistant to what they would describe as 'tampering' or 'tinkering' with traditional usages.

[4] Not, of course, from the speech of every speaker. Even though a certain choice of alternative spellings would be allowed owing to the large number of current alternative pronunciations of individual words, and to cater perhaps for some major regional differences, yet the existence of many other regional variations would make it inevitable that some speakers would have a number of arbitrary spellings to memorize, i.e. spellings at variance with their own pronunciation. An orthography is unlike a phonetic transcription in that it has to suit many different speakers preferably equally well, so that the more inclusive of various possible spellings of a word has often to be chosen, and this clearly involves some users in arbitrary memorization. (However, if too much has to be memorized, the argument of learning

time saved rather loses its force.) It is for instance unthinkable that an orthography for English intended obviously for world use should be so closely modelled on, for example, RP usage as to omit the many letter r's that are not realized in speech by RP speakers, e.g. before a consonant. And the morphophonemic final r's, that are realized in RP only before a vowel in the next word, must appear (in some form) in the regular spelling for the benefit not only of r-sounders but also of RP speakers themselves, who can then deduce the rule as to the non-sounding of r (as they do now), whereas the reverse process would not work.

5 Linked with the problem of the treatment of vowels in the weakly stressed syllables of longer words, there is the question of the spelling of common monosyllabic words that have different pronunciations according to stress and context – those possessing strong and weak forms. As far as New Spelling is concerned there is no choice, since the weak forms having a schwa vowel could not be separately shown. It is clear that the spelling of such words must therefore be based on the strong form of each. One valid objection to *different* spellings for the various forms would be on account of the extra burden placed on the learner; but in any case the use of a weak form is in many contexts optional, so discrepancies between users, and between writer and reader, would result. (See note 13 below for a further discussion of the matter.)

6 The IPA symbols, cast in a basically romanic mould, have been evolved in all these ways. But such *ad hoc* creations are not all suited to an orthography. One or two letters, e.g. ɛ and ɔ, have been successfully incorporated in the new orthographies of some African languages, but certain European writing habits would need to be changed if these were more widely adopted, since the Greek ɛ shape is now in use also for e, especially as a capital, and one of the cursive forms of s resembles ɔ if joined.

The extensive use of turned, i.e. upside-down, roman letters facilitates the task of the printer already supplied with roman sorts, but many of the result forms cannot be satisfactorily joined to other letters (see note 14 below, for a discussion of joined versus unjoined letters).

Some of the other IPA devices: small capitals; borrowings, mainly from Greek; minor modifications of roman shapes; utilization of cursive or italic forms alongside the usual printed ones, e.g. z/ʒ, a/ɑ; these are all liable to create difficulties of one kind or another if carried over into an orthography.

7 The form of non-roman writing that springs at once to the mind of the layman is that of current systems of shorthand. Now the aims and objects of shorthand are connected firstly with the desire to be short, i.e. go fast, as required for verbatim reporting, and secondly with the end result of being transposed into roman or other orthography. They are thus entirely different from the aims and objects of systems of orthography as such, and many of the features of shorthand systems make them in consequence quite unsuitable for general use as orthographies. Some of these features are: the drastic contraction and abbreviation of words and even phrases, the omission of vowels or their (optional) insertion as diacritics, the use of slight differences in slope or length of stroke, differences in thickness or pressure of stroke, different interpretations of shapes according to their position in relation to the line of writing, e.g. whether above or below it. Other objections are: the difficulty of reading back what has been written when the context is not clear, when time has elapsed since the dictation was taken, or when reader and writer are not the same

person; the difficulty of *printing* shorthand; and the enormous amount of space taken up by the script. In fact, everything is necessarily sacrificed to speed.

[8] English in present roman has a proportion (ignoring capitals, and treating the dot on i as extruding from the ribbon) of about 40% extruders. (Of these, only about one in six descend below the line, the remainder rising above ribbon height. It is doubtless for this reason that experiments have shown the top outline to be the more important for word recognition: it is there that by far the greater amount of information is located). From experience it would seem that this proportion works excellently, and may therefore be held to be about right – though it must be remembered that it is all a matter of training, the eye having learnt to pick out the information it requires from wherever that information happens to be found. Other scripts have entirely different proportions – printed Cyrillic, for instance, has very few extruders, practically everything being contained within the x-height, thus giving to roman alphabet users the effect of a sequence of small capitals. The Devanagari script (e.g. Bengali and Hindi) on the other hand shows a practically unbroken top line, nearly all variation being in the bottom outline of sequences of letters, or within what may be called the ribbon line. Yet readers of all these scripts achieve adequate, indeed striking, fluency (once they have learnt to read). (The degree of eye-strain is a different matter, but this factor is difficult to assess.)

Many other points relating to type design might be mentioned, for instance the effect of extruders on the possible nearness of successive lines of writing, involving in turn considerations of readability. A recent proposal to print all in capitals, in extremely closely spaced lines, may be mentioned in this connection. Even overlapping lines of print, in alternate colours, to be read with complementarily coloured glasses, have been suggested. An almost limitless field of research lies open here, as far too little is known about the reading process, legibility, readability, and the like.

[9] Many important scripts, e.g. Arabic, have nothing corresponding to capitals.

[10] Bernard Shaw died in 1950, and left money in his Will for the alphabet project. After long delays due to legal complications, the Public Trustee was able to advertise the competition in January 1958, and on New Year's Eve 1959 four interim prize-winners were announced (no single design being adjudged entirely satisfactory for use, as it stood, for the stipulated published transliteration of Shaw's play *Androcles and the Lion*). The prize-money was divided equally among these four, who were invited to work on their designs in the light of criticism. The design of Kingsley Read was finally selected, after considerable re-casting, and so becomes Shaw's 'Proposed British Alphabet' (PBA) which has been used to transliterate *Androcles*, now published by Penguin Books Ltd.

[11] The English vowels are here transcribed in the notation used in Daniel Jones' *English Pronouncing Dictionary*.

[12] Besides being more economical, this makes the script more suitable for various types of English, by avoiding the implication of digraphs that certain vowels *are* pronounced diphthongally and others not, since for example [ei] and [ou] may be realized as monophthongal [e, o], and conversely [iː] and [uː] may be diphthongized.

[13] By an extension of this device to other words, e.g. for (f), be (b), with (w), he (h), are (r), so (s), do (d), further economies are possible, but the frequency of occurrence falls off rapidly, so percentage saving is not great. Comparable economies could be made by writing many common words digraphically, omitting the medial vowel, e.g. that (ðt), was (wz), have (hv), not (nt), this (ðs), but (bt), from (fm), had (hd),

has (hz), been (bn), were (wr), etc. If such spellings became standardized, it would have the incidental advantage that these invariable written forms would stand equally well for strong and weak forms in pronunciation (as do the four standard word-signs for *the*, *of*, *and*, *to*), so that neither writer nor reader is visually committed to any one. (Naturally, if for any reason it were desired to indicate a specific form, e.g. for stage dialogue, the script provides everything necessary.) Possibly for private correspondence, note-taking, and the like, more abbreviations might come to be used, the standard for printing being the full, i.e. strong forms (except for *a*, *an* and the four word-signs). Yet the advantages of speed and economy might favour an increase in the number of shortened forms to be used even as standard.

[14] It is doubtful whether disjoined writing is necessarily slower at all: downstrokes of the hand have to be followed by upstrokes in any case, and for the latter to be executed off the paper only a slight adjustment of stroke is needed (which of course would be acquired when first learning to write). Many writers now lift the pen constantly within words (apart from crossing t and dotting i), even if gaps are not always visible between letters afterwards (as in modern 'italic' handwriting of roman). Experience of other scripts (e.g. Arabic, Hebrew, where certain letters *must not* be linked, or where it is inconvenient to do so) shows that sequences of unlinked letters may be formed extremely rapidly. Also relevant are two further facts: for real speed work a genuine shorthand based on the PBA is likely to become available; and professional writers, for whom alone the time spent in writing looms large, are likely to make increasing use of technical aids such as the typewriter and the dictating machine.

[15] One letter in six in roman has been shown by Godfrey Dewey to be superfluous (*Relative Frequency of English Speech Sounds*, Cambridge, Mass., 1923).

[16] The analogy with the roman *numerals* is good up to a point: these were used for centuries for all purposes, even long after our 'arabic' numerals were known; to-day, however, no one would dream of trying to do the simplest addition sum in roman numerals. They are now preserved in archaic usage in dates on gravestones and on the title-pages of some books, and are still current only for the numbering of chapters and paragraphs, and for showing the month in dates, as 12/IX/61.

[17] Though the PBA is designed for English, adaptations to other languages could undoubtedly be worked out. Indeed, it is not impossible that this new alphabet, or something like it, might be in official use for some other language before it gained ultimate acceptance for English.

# The Perceptibility of Certain Word-boundaries

J. D. O'CONNOR and OLIVE M. TOOLEY

Since it was Daniel Jones who first produced an analytic treatment of juncture features,[1] it is perhaps appropriate that two of his students should pay homage to this great phonetician by presenting here the results of an introductory investigation into the perceptibility of some of these features.

The investigation concerns what is widely called plus juncture, or internal open juncture. The features distinguishing such pairs as *plum pie* and *plump eye*, *grey day* and *grade A* have been described by Jones and others. It seems, however, that juncture has almost invariably been approached from the side of the speaker. Because certain phonetic features are – or may be – found at word-boundaries it has been assumed without test that these features are apparent in all cases to a listener. In order to assess the effectiveness of separative phenomena it is necessary to bring the listener into the picture far more than has been the case hitherto.[2] And if it should be found – in the extreme case – that listeners do not perceive word-boundaries at all, then it is difficult to justify reliance upon juncture as an analytical device in a linguistics for which language is a social activity. We do not in fact doubt that some juncture features are regularly present in some styles of speech, yet misunderstandings due to misplaced juncture (by either speaker or listener) do occur,[3] and we have felt that the efficiency of these phenomena as distinctive features in the communication process should be more closely examined.

Our object, then, was to try to determine empirically the degree of correspondence between what the speaker says and what the listener understands. We are not concerned here with the physical features whose presence or absence may correlate with agreement or disagreement between the two parties, though such an investigation would have its own interest. We wanted to establish how often the process of communication succeeds and how often it fails in circumstances where the only phonetic differences would be junctural ones.

We have limited this initial experiment to the case in which a single consonant stands between stressed vowels, the word-boundary occurring either between the first vowel and the consonant or between the consonant and the second vowel, i.e. the type *grey day* vs. *grade A*.

## METHOD

We prepared a list of paired phrases of the above type, including as many consonants as possible in the crucial position. The phrases were of such a kind that they could reasonably stand alone as separate utterances. The list is as follows: *Job Ingham/Joe Bingham, grade A/grey day, to plague Ames/to play games, to barge in/to bar gin, great ape/grey tape, Luke Annan/Lou Cannon, H.Allen/A.Challon, to save Erse/to say verse, to choose ink/to chew zinc, Rafe Elton/Ray Felton, Grace Ealing/grey ceiling, Gail Orde/Gay Lord, more ice/more rice, loam earth/low mirth, Joan Ashe/Joe Nash.* We could find no satisfactory pairs for the consonants /p, θ, ð, ʃ/[4] and the remaining consonants do not occur in this position.

We wished our test to approximate roughly to the normal speech situation and we therefore embedded the phrases in sentences which made them sound as natural as possible. They were so placed in the sentence frames that in every case a final falling intonation was elicited from the speakers chosen to record the material. It was part of our intention to keep these speakers ignorant of the object of the experiment so that they would not make any exceptional effort to distinguish the pairs (e.g. by using glottal stop as a positive juncture marker before stressed vowel); to this end the recordings were made at two different times, only one member of a pair being said in one recording session, the second appearing in a second list recorded a fortnight later. As an additional precaution we inserted between the relevant sentences other sentences calculated to distract the speakers from our true object.

Two RP speakers with no previous experience, one male, one female, recorded all this material on magnetic tape, and our deception plan was apparently successful: neither speaker had realized what the purpose was, though they viewed with some suspicion certain of the more esoteric items. Reading written material into a microphone in an anechoic chamber is obviously a far cry from the conversational situation; in order to achieve some degree of naturalness in the speech we spent a long time over the recordings, allowing the speakers to get used to the (for them) abnormal situation and encouraging them to give a fluent and relaxed rendering. Since we are prepared to concede that the glottal stop before stressed vowel is an unequivocal boundary marker, we rejected any items which showed it and asked for repetitions of the offending sentences until we got an example without the glottal stop. By insisting on 'fluency', and avoiding all specific mention of the glottal stop, we achieved this without making our speakers aware of our purpose. The average rate of delivery was 5·1 syllables per second for the female speaker and 4·8 for the male, over the whole of the recorded material.

We then cut out from the tapes the relevant phrases and reassembled them into two new tapes. Each tape contained thirty single phrases, arranged in random order except that both members of a pair never appeared on the same tape spoken by the same voice (though they might occur spoken by different voices). The purpose of this was again to approximate the speech situation, where a given sequence has to be matched against memory to determine juncture position. Our subjects for the listening tests were 80 first and second year speech therapy students in our department. One tape was played to half the subjects and the other to the other half, so that no subject heard both members of a pair said by the same voice. This was perhaps a needless precaution, and, judging by our subjects' reactions, it is doubtful whether hearing both tapes would have materially affected the over-all picture.

The subjects were provided with an answer sheet showing both members of each pair, and were asked to tick the one which they heard, guessing where necessary. It was essential to make the subjects aware of both items in every case, even though only one of them was presented, because one member of the pair might be a very much more common phrase than the other; so that, if left to themselves it is probable that the subjects, on hearing *to plague Ames*, would not even realize the possibility of this phrase and would assume *to play games* without a second thought. The errors (i.e. failures of communication between speaker and listener) were counted and the data analysed.

## RESULTS

There were 2400 judgments and 797 errors, almost exactly one-third. 385 errors were elicited by the female speaker and 412 by the male.[5] 404 errors came from those hearing only tape 1 (39 subjects) and 393 from those hearing only tape 2 (41 subjects). Table 1 shows details of errors for each item.

TABLE 1

| | STIMULUS | ERRORS | STIMULUS | ERRORS |
|---|---|---|---|---|
| | Job Ingham | 52 | Joe Bingham | 9 |
| *Voiced* | grade A | 30 | grey day | 16 |
| *stops* | to plague Ames | 62 | to play games | 11 |
| | to barge in | 25 | to bar gin | 48 |
| *Voiceless* | great ape | 16 | grey tape | 1 |
| *stops* | Luke Annan | 24 | Lou Cannon | 9 |
| | H. Allen | 14 | A. Challon | 15 |
| *Voiced* | to save Erse | 39 | to say verse | 30 |
| *fricatives* | to choose ink | 18 | to chew zinc | 19 |
| *Voiceless* | Rafe Elton | 57 | Ray Felton | 13 |
| *fricatives* | Grace Ealing | 29 | grey ceiling | 13 |
| | Gail Orde | 53 | Gay Lord | 1 |
| *Voiced* | more ice | 28 | more rice | 15 |
| *continuants* | loam earth | 54 | low mirth | 25 |
| | Joan Ashe | 63 | Joe Nash | 8 |
| | TOTAL | 564 | TOTAL | 233 |

It could be expected *a priori* that different types of consonant would elicit different numbers of errors, but in the event, of the five categories distinguished in Table 1, only the voiceless stops are noticeably different from the rest. Table 2 shows the percentage of errors over judgments in relation to these classes.

TABLE 2

| | VOICED | | | VOICELESS | |
|---|---|---|---|---|---|
| | *Stop* | *Fric.* | *Cont.* | *Stop* | *Fric.* |
| Percentage error | 38 | 33 | 39 | 16 | 35 |

If we define the percentage efficiency of communication *vis à vis* these classes as double the percentage by which the correct answers exceed the chance expectation of 50%, then the voiceless stops are 68% efficient and the other categories vary between 22% and 34%. Very surprising to us was the relatively poor identification when the voiceless fricatives were at the crux, bearing in mind their presumptive effect on the quantity of the preceding vowel. Certainly /f/ provides more errors than /s/ (70:42), but /s/ gives more errors than /z/ (37), and /v/ is little less effective than /f/. The inference seems inescapable that the sibilants perform alike, and better than the non-sibilants /f, v/, irrespective of voicing.

Yet perhaps the most striking feature of the results is the preponderance of errors associated with a C+ stimulus (i.e. one in which the consonant belongs to the first word). 564 errors came from such stimuli, and only 233 from +C stimuli. There are three factors which might account for this: first, the tendency mentioned by Stetson[6] for an arresting consonant to be transformed into a releasing consonant at rates above 3·5 syllables per second, a rate which was exceeded by our speakers over the whole material; second, the relative implausibility of some of the C+ phrases, e.g. *to plague Ames, to save Erse*; third, the statistically greater probability of English words beginning with CV rather than VC.[7] The second and third factors are no doubt connected.

If the first factor is decisive then consonants of all phonetic types should be equally inefficient: there ought not to be so marked a difference between voiceless stops and the rest, nor so large a variation between individual items, ranging smoothly from /t/, which is 78% efficient, to /m/, which is almost totally inefficient (2%). Yet it may be that certain distinctions which are present and effective at the boundaries at lower rates of delivery, become blurred in a proportion of cases at higher rates.

Regarding the second factor, we tried, as explained above, to balance the discrepant plausibility of the two members of certain pairs by providing the subjects with both possible solutions. This seems to have worked reasonably well, for although *Job Ingham* and *to plague Ames* were very frequently heard as their more likely partners, and *to bar gin* as the more common *to barge in*, yet on the other hand *grade A* – which seems about as common as *grey day* – produced double the errors of the latter, whilst *great ape, Gail Orde*, and *Joan Ashe*, all with fairly comparable alternatives, produced far and away more errors, and *to save Erse* gave rise to only a few more errors than *to say verse*.

As to the possibility of influence from the statistically greater likelihood in English of syllables beginning with CV rather than VC, in all but three cases the errors are in this direction, often overwhelmingly so. For /ʧ/ and /z/ the errors are approximately equal in number for the C+ and +C stimuli, whilst for /ʤ/ there are twice as many from the +C stimulus as from the C+. Perhaps this last is a genuine case of the greater plausibility of *to barge in* reversing the general tendency to err on the side of +C judgments. On the whole we are inclined to the view that in most cases of uncertainty the listeners have tended to choose a +C solution in conformity with structural probability.[8]

Because of the small number of speakers used it would be wrong for us to make any firm general pronouncements as a result of this experiment. But within the limits set it is fair to conclude provisionally (a) that word boundaries are not in practice distinguished with an impressive degree of certainty, the level of efficiency being 34% over-all; (b) that correct location of the boundary varies extremely widely with the consonant occurring at the crux; and (c) that factors on linguistic planes other than the phonetic are at work, namely, semantic, collocational, and phonological probability, and may in practice be decisive.

We propose to extend this type of investigation to other word-boundary conditions (e.g. with consonant clusters and both stressed and unstressed vowels at the crux). It would be well if others could take up the same task, in order both to test our methods and conclusions and to provide information which is sadly lacking in an important area.

*Notes*

[1] 'The "word" as a phonetic entity', *Maître Phonétique*, XXXVI, 1931, 60–65.

[2] Lehiste realized this in her *An Acoustic-Phonetic Study of Internal Open Juncture*, Ann Arbor, 1959, but the method of conducting the listening tests for this study was not, in our opinion, likely to answer the questions which we were asking, for the following reasons:

(a) The speakers were directly aware of intended contrasts (2.3). This is not the normal speech situation and would affect the realizations.

(b) Glottal stop and laryngealization before word-initial vowel were accepted and occurred rather frequently. This is probably a consequence of (a) above and of the reading situation. It is much less likely to be found in uninhibited speech.

(c) The minimal pairs were presented *as pairs*, not separately (2.5). This makes identification much easier than in normal speech, where only one item occurs.

[3] E.g., since this paper was first drafted, *she never applied* was taken as *she never replied.*

[4] We rejected, for instance *mar shoes/marsh ooze* on the grounds of implausibility, and *Brie there/breathe air* because the former could hardly stand alone as an intelligible utterance.

[5] It is interesting that slightly fewer errors come from the slightly faster speaker, which suggests that a slower rate of utterance is not *per se* a guarantee of more efficient communication.

[6] R.H.Stetson, *Motor Phonetics*, 2nd Ed., Amsterdam, 1951, 41.

[7] See J.D.O'Connor and J.L.M.Trim, 'Vowel, Consonant, and Syllable: a Phonological Analysis', *Word*, IX, 2, 1953, 121.

[8] We are not greatly impressed by the similarity of the proportions of +C and C+ errors (29%:71%) and of VC and CV initially (33%:67%), see note 7. This resemblance is no doubt coincidental.

# The Simplified Spelling Society

## JAMES PITMAN

The reform of English spelling has been a life-long interest for Daniel Jones, who has been for many years actively concerned in the affairs of the Simplified Spelling Society. The following account of the history of the Society may serve as a tribute to the work he has done to further its objects.

The Simplified Spelling Society was formed at a meeting on 10 September, 1908, held in the Holborn Restaurant, London.

Those present were Mr William Archer (London), Professor James W. Bright (Baltimore), Dr F. J. Furnivall (London), Mr E. P. Gaston (London), Professor I. Gollancz (London), Professor H. Stanley Jevons (Cardiff), Mr J. J. Munro (London), Mr A. W. Pollard (London), Dr Charles P. G. Scott (New York), and Professor Walter Skeat (Cambridge). Professor Skeat was appointed Chairman of the meeting and Mr William Archer was appointed Secretary for the time being.

The principal item in the proposed Constitution and Rules was:

### OBJECTS

> Its objects shall be to recommend simpler spellings of English words than those now in use, to further the use of such simpler spellings by every means in its power, and to co-operate with the Simplified Spelling Board of America, founded and incorporated in New York.

At the next meeting, held on 18 September, 1908, those present agreed that the following gentlemen be asked to form the Committee of the Society: Dr Henry Bradley, Mr W. A. Craigie, Dr Furnivall, Professor W. P. Ker, Professor Jevons, Sir James A. H. Murray, Dr S. A. Napier, Mr Pollard, Mr J. S. Westlake, and Professor Joseph Wright.

At the meeting held on 2 October, 1908, it was reported that Mr Andrew Carnegie, who had been invited to become a Vice-President, had sent a cheque for £1000. Dr Furnivall stated that of the Committee nominated at the previous meeting, five had consented to serve, namely: Dr Furnivall, Professor Jevons, Dr Napier, Mr Pollard, and Mr Westlake. It was agreed that the following five gentlemen should be invited to serve on the Committee: Mr E. Chambers (of University College), Dr Frank Heath, Dr (as he was then) Gilbert Murray, Dr Trechmann, Dr H. C. Wyld. The following were elected to office: Dr Furnivall (Treasurer); Mr Archer (Secretary). The Secretary had been commissioned at the previous meeting to nominate the Assistant Secretary, and he now nominated Professor W. W. Skeat. This nomination was ratified by the Committee.

From 1908 to 1910 the Society was mainly preparing pamphlets for circulation, arranging press notices, and obtaining new members.

On 19 July, 1910, Professor Ripman was elected Hon. Treasurer, owing to the loss of Dr Furnivall. Professor Daniel Jones was first mentioned on 19th December, 1910, when it was agreed that he should be one of the delegates representing the Society at a proposed International Commission or Conference.

On 18 January, 1911, Professor Gilbert Murray was elected President, and in the same year, on 18 September, Professor Jones and Dr Edwards were asked to become members of the Committee. On 28 September it was agreed that Professor Michael Sadler should be asked to serve on the Committee, and, a year later, at a meeting on 10 October, 1912, it was agreed that Dr (later Sir) G. B. Hunter should be asked to serve. At this meeting it was stated that Professor Jones was visiting India that year, and it was agreed to ask him to lecture in as many centres in India as possible, and to bring back a report as to the movement in India.

On 14 November, 1912, it was moved that Professor Grandgent, President of the American Spelling Board, should be asked to become a Vice-President.

At a meeting of the Committee held on 13 March, 1913, Professor Jones gave a brief report on lectures on simplified spelling given during his visit to India. He had lectured in Madras, Bombay, and Lahore, and he reported that the Indians were enthusiastic in regard to the reform of English Spelling. Also at this meeting the Minutes were written in a form of simplified spelling for the first time.

In March 1914, discussion was begun and the details of a petition to the Board of Education were agreed.

At a meeting on 22 September, 1915, Professor Jones gave an interesting account of an experiment carried out by Mr Robert Jackson of Dundee in Clepington Road School. A section of incoming children had been taught to read from the Nursery Rhyme book used in the Society's scheme. At the end of 10 months they were given four months' instruction in conventional spelling, and were then pitted against children who for 19 months had been occupied with the conventional spelling only. It was found that they could read and spell as accurately as the children with the longer training.

Meetings continued regularly during the war years, but there was a certain amount of financial difficulty, and at a meeting on 31 August, 1917, it was decided to appeal for financial support. The question was also raised of whether the Society's publication, the *Pioneer*, should cease publication, and it was decided, on 12 October, that it should be suspended.

On 2 May, 1918, Mr Henry Drummond gave an account of an experiment in spelling at the Lynons School, Hetton, Co. Durham, and on 23 May of the same year, a letter was read from Mr Jackson, informing the Committee of the highly satisfactory result of a Simplified Spelling experiment held at Morgan Academy, Dundee. Among those who attended a meeting on 18 July, 1918, was Miss Walsh, headmistress of the Infants' Department, Honeywell Road School, Battersea, who was conducting an experiment with Simplified Spelling. Also at this meeting a report was read of the excellent results of an experiment with Simplified Spelling at Halesowen Grammar School, Birmingham.

On 29 October, 1920, it was proposed that Lady Astor should be asked to become a Vice-President.

From the end of the war to the transference of the Society's offices to Newcastle, in 1928, the Society was much concerned with the preparation and circulation of literature to teachers and educational bodies, such as the National Union of Teachers, and at educational conferences.

Mr William Archer died in 1925.

Just before the decision was made to remove to Newcastle, at a meeting on 17 June, 1928, the question of a broadcast on Simplified Spelling was discussed, and Professor Jones offered to sound Professor Lloyd James, with a view to his including the subject of Spelling Reform in one of his afternoon talks.

On 30 August, 1928, the Committee agreed that the funds of the Society would no longer permit an office in London, and that the office should be transferred to Newcastle.

The first meeting in Newcastle, on 25 February, 1929, was presided over by Sir G. B. Hunter. Arising from the Minutes, the Chairman explained the reason for removing the office from London, and also proposed that Mr G.H.Richardson and Mr Robertson of Glasgow should be added to the Committee. It was also proposed that Mr Maccall should be added to the Committee, and all three nominations were agreed. Miss Marley was elected as Secretary of the Society.

It was decided at this meeting that the following resolution should be sent to the President of the Turkish Republic:

'The British Simplified Spelling Society desire to congratulate the Rt Hon. Kemal Pasha, President of the Republic of Turkey, and his Government on their wise and courageous step of reforming the National Alphabet. We thank them for showing the way to nations like our own, who, on the path of learning, allow the debris of the past to cumber the children's feet. The Society hopefully anticipate as resulting from this reform, a great advance on the part of the people of Turkey in culture, commerce, and international intercourse.'

On 20 August, 1929, Mr Henry Drummond was elected Hon. Treasurer, in place of Professor Ripman, who had resigned, and it was carried that Mr James Allan should be asked to become a member of the Committee.

On 12 January, 1931, Professor Zachrisson's 'Anglic' proposals for the improvement of English spelling were discussed. Professor Ripman and Professor Jones had written to say that they approved of Professor Zachrisson's proposals, but the rest of the Committee were not wholly in favour.

The next meeting was not until 24 July, 1935. The Chairman, Sir G.B. Hunter referred to the death of Miss Marley, and it was agreed that Mr T.R.Barber should be appointed Secretary. It was also agreed that Professor Lloyd James should be added to the Committee of the Society. The Chairman reported that the main work of the Society since the last meeting had been the promotion of a Memorial to the President of the Board of Education for the appointment of a representative Committee to consider the improvement of English spelling. Considerable support had been secured for this Memorial. It included a great many Vice-Chancellors, Professors, and Lecturers of British Universities, nearly 250 Members of Parliament, a number of Bishops, including the Archbishop of York, a number of educational bodies, and several authors, including Shaw, H.G.Wells, and J.B.Priestley.

On 11 May, 1936, Mr I.J.Pitman the present writer and Mr T. Kingdom were added to the Committee. The appointment of Trustees to the Society was agreed to, these being Sir G.B. Hunter, Mr Barber, and Mr Drummond. It was reported that Mr Kingdom had addressed Rotary Clubs in various parts of the country on Spelling Reform.

The next meeting was held on 2 March, 1937, at which Professor Gilbert Murray presided. He referred to the great loss to the Society by the death of Sir George B. Hunter. The future of the Society was considered, and it was eventually decided, after a long discussion, that a sub-committee should be appointed to consider the matter. This sub-committee consisted of: Professor Murray (Chairman), Professors Jones, Ripman, and Lloyd James, and Messrs Pitman and Walton.

The sub-committee met on 23 March, at the League of Nations Union Headquarters, and the question of a new Chairman was discussed. Mr Walton's name had been put forward, but he had written to say that he could not give the necessary time, owing to pressure of business. Mr Pitman was also asked, but he, too, felt he could not give the necessary time. Professor Murray agreed to act as Chairman until one was appointed.

At a meeting on 25 May, 1937, it was decided to re-write the book *Proposals for a Simplified Spelling of the English Language*, by Walter Ripman and William Archer, and that when the book was re-written it should stand as the handbook of the Society. It was suggested that Mr Orton would be a very useful addition to the Committee.

The next few meetings of the sub-committee were concerned with the details of the re-writing and publication of Ripman and Archer's book.

On 21 July, 1937, there was a conference consisting of Professors Jones and Lloyd James, and Messrs Pitman, Hadley (who was to edit the book), and Barber. Dr Dewey from America was present and gave those present some idea of the American scene. A discussion took place with a view to Dr Dewey's endeavouring to try to get support in America so that both sides of the Atlantic should support one definite system.

On 29 April, 1938 there was a general committee meeting to consider alterations in the Constitution and Rules, and to fix a general meeting of members. This meeting took place on 18 June, 1938. The appointment of Professor Lloyd James, Mr Pitman, Mr Drummond, and Mr Barber as Trustees of the Society was confirmed, and the Chairman (Professor Murray) mentioned that the sub-committee had completed and printed the new edition of the Ripman-Archer proposals for Spelling Reform, and copies of it were handed round to those present.

At the next few meetings there were further discussions of details of the Ripman-Archer book, and it was decided, at a meeting of the sub-committee on 25 October, 1938, that the title of the book should be *New Spelling*.

Sir George Hunter had provided in his Will a considerable sum of money to form a Trust for the Society. The capital was vested in Trustees under the Will who were given power to make payments to the Society out of the income. The Trust Deed provided that in August 1938, at the latest, the Trustees should make a distribution of the capital. Owing to the wording of the Trust Deed, the Trustees had some difficulty in deciding how they should properly make the distribution, and they eventually found it necessary to apply to the High Court for a ruling. On 28 March, 1939, Professor Jones gave a report of the recent hearing in the High Court (which had decided in favour of the Society) to a general committee meeting. A vote of thanks was tendered to Professor Jones for the work he had done regarding the Court case. Professor Jones suggested that, when the funds would permit it, the office of the Society should again be set up in London.

At a sub-committee meeting on 15 December, 1939, it was agreed that a dictionary, *Old Spelling – New Spelling*, should be issued, comprising from 15,000 to 18,000 words. Mr Ripman was invited to undertake the work, and at the meeting on 12 January, 1940, he reported that he had completed about half the work.

Meetings continued more or less regularly throughout the war, and Professor Jones played a prominent part in discussions of pronunciations and transliterations to be adopted in the Society's publications, and in decisions about future publications. In 1942 Professor Sir Douglas Savory was asked to become a Vice-President, and Professor Sidney Chapman, Mr Maurice Harrison (Director of Education for Oldham), and Mr Peter MacCarthy were elected to the Committee.

At a meeting on 20 June, 1942, the question of the revision of the Society's Infant Readers was discussed, and Mr Harrison offered to make enquiries of people he thought might be willing to undertake this. On 2 October, 1942, it was resolved to print a play of Shakespeare (*Hamlet*) in Simplified Spelling, on the motion of Professor Jones, and it was agreed that Mr MacCarthy should be commissioned to make the transcription.

From 1943 to the end of the war, conditions were not very favourable for the work of the Society. It had become increasingly difficult to get printing done, but three publications had been carried through – the collection of essays entitled *Views on Spelling Reform*, a pamphlet on the phonetic aspect of Spelling Reform by Professor Jones and the first of the Infant Readers, *Dhe Litl Red Hen.* Publication of the second and third Infant Readers had been held up, as had Mr MacCarthy's New Spelling version of *Hamlet.* On 14 July, 1945, it was reported that this latter was in print with the exception of its cover, but that its publication was held up owing to paper shortage, and that the same applied to Mr Harrison's Teachers' Manual for Infant Readers.

Dr Dewey attended the meeting on 22 February, 1946, and gave a report of the work of Dr Frank C. Laubach. Dr Dewey stated that he had persuaded Dr Laubach to accept a number of the Society's proposals, but that there were a few details with which he could not agree. Dr Dewey wondered if the Society would agree to modify its scheme of spelling so as to conform in all respects with that of Dr Laubach. However, the view of the Society was that it could not well alter its scheme at the present juncture on account of its existing commitments. It was agreed to ask Dr Dewey to take back an encouraging letter to Dr Laubach.

At a General Meeting held on 6 July, 1946, a letter from Professor Gilbert Murray was read, in which he stated that for reasons of health and on account of other commitments, he felt obliged to resign his position as President and Chairman of the Society. The Committee received his resignation with much regret, and it was unanimously agreed that he should be asked to accept the title of Honorary President. Professor Jones was nominated as President and Chairman of the Committee.

At a meeting held on 3 January, 1947, it was stated that reports of Mr Pitman's meetings in America had been circulated – the chief point was that he (on behalf of the Society) had agreed with the spelling reformers in America that investigations should be made into the method of teaching simplified spelling in infants' schools as a stepping-stone to ordinary current spelling. Mr Pitman further reported that he had a consultation with Professor Jeffery, Director of the University of London Institute of Education, who had expressed provisional and non-committal interest in the idea of school experiments.

At the Annual General Meeting held on 10 July, 1948, it was reported by the Committee that activities had been seriously impeded by the impossibility, under the present conditions of getting anything printed, and by the deferment by the Institute of Education of any action in connection with the projected school experiments on account of impending changes of staff. The printing difficulty seemed likely to persist for some considerable time. The death was announced of Dr Edwards.

On 5 March, 1949, the Chairman, Professor Jones, stated that the Committee would be aware that Mr Follick had obtained a place for his Bill on Spelling Reform, which would accordingly come before the House on 11 March. A discussion then took place on what action the Committee should take. Professor Chapman ultimately proposed: 'That the views of the Committee were that it was prepared to accept an offer of a Departmental Committee if the Minister of Education should offer one during the debate on the Spelling Reform Bill, rather than press the Bill as it now stands.'

The Bill was rejected by a small majority, but the Committee felt that much useful publicity had been achieved by the debate.

At the Annual General Meeting on 22 July, 1950, Sir Graham Savage presided. He announced the resignation of Professor Jones as President and Chairman, owing to ill-health. It was, however, unanimously decided that Professor Jones be asked to retain the office of President.

# On Foreign Phonological Features in Present-day English

B. TRNKA

The Modern English stock of words is divided, from the phonological point of view, into two large groups. One group comprises words implemented by phonological means of purely genuine character (cf. *owe, if, ask, end, low, wine, son, lend, street, strand, utter, fellow, foreign, enough*); the other consists of words characterized by peculiar phonological features not shared by those of the former group. Most of these words (e.g. *vine, vain, zone, general, liquid, examination, idea*) are loans borrowed from Latin and French at different periods in the development of English, but the provenance of words is outside the scope of the present investigation, which is concerned only with their present-day phonological structure. It is obvious that neither the former nor the latter group can be identified simply with the genuine and foreign descent of English vocabulary, respectively. Many words of undoubtedly un-English origin, such as *pit, street, wine, flower, flour, air, aunt, fruit, letter, saint, liquor, pharaoh, phlegm, phase, piquant*, do not exhibit any foreign phonological features, and belong therefore to the former class, even if the spelling or meaning of some of them is still suggestive of their origin (cf. *suite*:*sweet*, *reign*:*rain*, *pharaoh*:*fellow*), whereas some words of English extraction (e.g. *vat, vixen, boy*) in addition to many words of expressive or onomatopoeic character (e.g. *giggle, titter, tehee, blubber, peep, kick, jiffy, twitter*, etc.) must be placed in the latter group. Nor can the relative frequency of words be a reliable criterion for their inclusion in the one or the other group, since many words containing peculiar phonological features may have a frequent occurrence, while some words of purely English phonological structure occur very rarely. If we speak of 'native' and 'foreign' words in preference to 'phonologically unmarked words' and 'phonologically marked words', both terms will be used for brevity's sake only in the sense of their difference in phonological organization. It is understood, of course, that there is no Chinese wall between the two categories in the structural history of the language. In fact, many foreign words lost their foreignisms as a result of the phonological development of English, and joined the group of native words, which constitutes the basic vocabulary of any language.[1] There is, perhaps, no language devoid of phonological deviations from the native patterns, since they serve the needs of speakers in giving a sort of relevance, or a peculiar atmosphere, to the words in question by differentiating them from the common stock of phonologically homogeneous, unmarked words.

What foreign phonological features are to be found in Present-day Standard English? They are many, and may be classified as follows:

(1) *Unusual phonemes*, as the Scottish /x/ in *loch* and the interjection ugh /ʌx/, and the French nasals in the occasionally un-Anglicized pronunciation of Modern French words.

(2) *Unusual position of native phonemes*:

(a) Initial /z/, /v/, and /ʤ/, e.g.

/z/: *xebec, xylem, zeal, zebra, zinc, zone, zoo.*
/v/: *vacant, vague, vase, veal, vein, verb, visit, vision, volley, vote, vowel, vulgar*, etc.
/ʤ/: *jam, jade, gender, germ, giant, George, gipsy, job, juice, jute.*

The initial position of /z/ is a foreign feature both in Standard English and most English dialects, and is utilized, as a phonological peculiarity, for coining new expressive words, as *zoom* and *zip*. The substitution of /w/ for /v/ in some dialects may be due to the tendency of dialectal speakers to assimilate such familiar words as *value, veal, vein, vermin, very, violet, viper, voice, vow*, to the native pattern, whereas the use of /vr/ for /wr/, limited to a small number of dialects, goes back to a genuine sound change. As to the initial position of /ʤ/, its foreignness is clearly indicated by the fact that /ʤ/ did not occur initially in Old English and that there was, later on, no phonemic mutation through which this phoneme would have appeared in this position. Only in Sub-standard English or in English dialects in which initial /ʤ/ arose as a result of the assimilation of /dj-/ (cf. *dew* /ʤuː/), have words like *jade, jam, gin*, etc., lost their peculiar phonological feature. The expressive character of initial /ʤ/ is testified by many words (cf. *jab, jade, jerk, jingle, gib, jiffy, jog, gibber, gibe*, etc.), as well as by the expressive voicing of /ʧ/ which took place in *jaw* (cf. OE *ċēowan* 'to chew'), *jeer* (probably from *cheer*), *jar* (cf. OE *ċeorian*) and some other words in Early Modern English.

(b) Initial /u/: *Uruguay, umlaut, oont* (Anglo-Indian, 'camel').

(c) Initial and final /ʒ/: *gigue, jardinière, mirage, espionage.* The phoneme /ʒ/ occurs only in loan-words, but as it is a product of the genuine change of /zj > ʒ/ (cf. *measure*, *leisure*, *vision*, *occasion*, *luxurious*), which also took place at the juncture of two words (e.g. *as you*), it must be considered a native phoneme, the marked term of the opposition /ʃ/ ~ /ʒ/.

(d) The postvocalic position of the phoneme /j/: *boy*, *coy*, *moist*, *voice*, *void*.

(3) *Monomorphemic consonantal clusters*:

(a) Consisting of two stops or two spirants, or a stop + a homorganic spirant, e.g. *apt*, *act*, *strict*, *smaragd*; *sphere*, *aesthete*, *phthisis*, *naphtha*; *pfennig*. In addition to these there are some other consonantal clusters such as /v/ + a stop or a spirant, /θ/ (or /ð/) + a stop or a spirant, and combinations consisting of two nasals, which do not belong to the inventory of native consonantal combinations.

It is noteworthy that the foreignness of some of these clusters consists only in the absence of the morphemic boundary between their consonantal components, since the same clusters appear in bimorphemic words such as *leap/t*, *robb/ed*, *pick/ed*, *begg/ed*, *cloth/s*, *lath/s*, *cloth/es*, *cup/ful*, *fif/th*, *off/set*, and at the juncture of two contiguous words in a context, e.g. *less five*, *less thin*, *if then*, *up to*. The consciousness of their phonological foreignness varies, therefore, with the extent to which the speakers are conscious of the separate identity of morphemic components of words. Their foreignness is consequently felt more keenly in their initial position than in the final or medial position.

(b) Consisting of three or more homomorphemic consonants, except the clusters /s/ + /pr, tr, kr, kl, kw, mj, pj, tj, kj/; a nasal + /br, dr, gr, bl, gl, dw, pt, sk, zd/; /m, p, l, n/ + /st/, which must be considered native.[2]

(c) Consisting of two monophthongs, e.g. *tiara*, *kiosk*, *piano*, *meander*; *chaos*, *vehicle*, *bivouac*.

(4) *Unusual position of some consonantal clusters*:

(a) Occurrence of /w/ between a consonant and an unstressed vowel, e.g. *sequel*, *sequence*, *liquid*, *colloquy*. The retention of /w/ in *-ward*, *-wards* after a consonant is obviously due to the spelling and/or to the consciousness of the separate morphemic identity of *-ward(s)*. Cf. *conduit* /kʌndit/, *biscuit* /biskit/.

(b) Occurrence of monomorphemic clusters (with the exception of /nt, nd, st/) after an unstressed vowel. Examples: *orange*, *messenger*, *matrix, onyx, herald, ribald.* Consonantal clusters occur in this position only in a few words of Germanic origin, as in *errand, island, husband, thousand, earnest, harvest.* The insertion of /ŋ/ in *nightingale* (OE nihtegale) is undoubtedly due to the need of Middle English speakers for expressiveness.

(5) *Double occurrence of the same consonantal phoneme in monomorphemic words*: /p/: *pip, pepper, poplar, pap, pup, peep, poop, pauper, purple, purpose, paper, pope, pipe, prep, prop, pupil*; /b/: *bib, barb, baby, blab*; /t/: *tilt, tint, tent, tetter, totter, teat, toot, tort, tart, taste, toast, tout, stout, title, tattoo, tomato, trot, tract, treat, trite, twist, twit*; /d/: *dad, dud, dodo, dude*; /k/: *kick, cook, cock, cork, cake, coke, click, clique, clock, cloak, crick, crook, creak, crack, crake, conch, conquer*; /g/: *gig, gag, gargle, goggle, grog*; /f/: *feoff, fife, fluff, forfeit,* /v/: *valve, velvet, verve, vive*; /s/: *cilice, cist, siskin, cess, sense, system, cease, sauce, source, sice, society, slice, sluice, space, sparse, spice, stress*; /ʤ/: *judge*; /r/: *rarity, rearing, roaring, rural*; /l/: *lily, loll, lull, leal, lilac, lapel*; /m/: *memory, malmsey, marmalade, marmot, mine, mimosa, moment, murmur*; /n/: *nun.*

The phonemes /j, w, h, θ, z/ do not re-occur in the same morpheme, and the double occurrence of /ð, ʃ, ʧ/, and /ʤ/ is limited only to a small number of words, such as *thither* /OE þider/, *church, judge, George, backsheesh.* It is remarkable that the re-occurrence of voiceless consonants in the same morpheme is found more frequently than that of the corresponding voiced consonants.[3]

This peculiar distributional feature of consonants occurs in many words of expressive character (cf. *pip, peep, pipit, blab, twitter,* etc.). A few English words of Germanic etymology in which the same phoneme re-occurs go back either to originally bimorphemic words (cf. *hundred, dread, tight, deed, dead, thither, since, sister*), or to reduplicated forms of expressive character (cf. *quick*, from */kwikwaz/, originally */kwiwaz/ from IE */gwiwos/). As far as I can see, only two English words, the numerals *six* and *nine*, are old IE words (monomorphemic?).

(6) *Morphemes consisting of more than two syllables*[4]: e.g. *hospital, paradise, element, pelican,* etc.

(7) *Primary stress* (a) on the non-initial syllable of monomorphemic words, such as *sincere, severe, lapel,* (b) on a suffix, e.g. *trainee, princess, locale, quintet, kitchenette,* and (c) on the second or third stem syllable of words derived by suffixes, cf. *familiarity, photographer, position,* etc. The alternation of stress, conditioned by suffixes or an increase of final syllables, is therefore always a foreign phonological feature in the

structure of morphologically related words. Cf. *prince:princess, photograph: photographer: photographic; family: familiar: familiarity; excel: excellent; convene: convenance.*

(8) *Full vowels and diphthongs in unstressed syllables*: e.g. in *asphalt, chaos, epoch, despot, record.*

(9) *Unusual consonant alternations*: cf. *invade:invasion, social:society, patient:patience.*

The foreign phonological features cited above characterize a large portion of English vocabulary. Their foreignness is obviously on different levels according to their varying remoteness from the native phonological patterns on which they rely. Whereas many of them are felt to be almost imperceptible modifications of native structural and distributional possibilities, others serve the purpose of making words more expressive in contrast to those of ordinary phonological organization, and still others appear unbearably or uselessly foreign, so that they are suppressed or replaced by usual, or less unusual, features (cf. the substitution of a vowel plus a nasal consonant for French nasals, the use of /k/ for /x/, the dropping of initial stops in the initial clusters /gz-/ (in *Xerxes, xebec, xylophone*), /pf-, ps-, tm-, dm-, dv-/ (in *Dvorak*), /kn-, gn-, gm-/, etc.). The extent of adoption and toleration of foreign phonological features is always dependent on the resources of the adopting language. It is obvious, e.g., that Chinese speakers, whose words never begin with consonantal clusters and never end in a consonant (except a nasal), must replace the clusters in loan-words from English by syllables, whereas the English can retain unusual clusters in Latin words without much difficulty, because they have them at the boundaries of morphemes and words in their own language. The elimination of preconsonantal (or final) /r/, which never occurring in Southern English pronunciation is therefore also automatically dropped in loan-words, seems to be the only notable exception.

If we hold that foreign phonological features are reflected against the solid basis of the native phonological pattern irrespective of the origin of words in which they occur, the question may be raised concerning the criteria which enable us to state that, e.g., the cluster /sθ/ is foreign and the cluster /st/ is native. Such criteria, based on the structural analysis of language, do exist and are confirmed by the popular speech-instinct which clearly distinguishes adopted features – even those of long-continued existence – from the basic structural elements of the language, the latter being internalized by all individual speakers on a deeper level than the former. There is no danger for any language, so far as it exists, that the adopted phonological features might destroy its balance and bring the germ of instability or even disintegration to its basic phonological pattern. The never-ceasing phonological fermentation in the history of languages cannot be brought about by adopted foreignisms, but only by the movement of their own structural elements, while the former may be tolerated or assimilated by them. As structural linguistics extends its range, the interaction of these two phonological strata, which necessarily coexist in every language and are especially characteristic of English as a dominant cultural language, will receive increasing attention.

*Notes*

[1] E.g. in Middle English dialects in which the corresponding voiced and voiceless spirants [z] and [s], [v] and [f], [ð] and [θ] belonged to single phonemes, the words containing single [s] or [f] between voiced sounds (cf. *mason, basin, coffin, suffer*) were foreign. As a result of the phonologization of voice of spirants such words lost their foreign phonological feature and became assimilated to the native pattern. The Latinization of the ending *-ive* (for older *-if*, e.g. in *actif, passif*) must have taken place after the phonologization of *f-v*.

[2] Cf. B. Trnka, *Phonological Analysis of Present-day Standard English, studies in English, V, Prague*, 1935, 49–55.

[3] It is tempting to conclude that the double occurrence of the same phoneme in IE morphemes served only for expressive purposes, and that its use for other purposes in Greek and Latin (cf. Gr. *kakós, pápyros*; L. *populus, pōpulus, caecus, bibo, coquo, quinque*, etc.) may have been due to the influence of other languages.

[4] It is noteworthy that most Czech words have monosyllabic or even non-syllabic roots consisting only of one consonant, whereas many English monomorphemic words consist of two syllables, e.g. *father, daughter, river, follow, arrow, barley*, etc. Monosyllabism, characteristic of Modern English, is evidently due to: (1) a small number of productive suffixes, some of which consist of a single consonant or a cluster of consonants; (2) the aversion of the language to the use of multiple suffixes and verbal prefixes; (3) the extensive use of prepositions and other 'small' words which are mostly monosyllabic; and (4) the assimilation of long words to the usual pattern of the domestic ones (e.g. *perambulator* > *pram, examination* > *exam*, etc.).

# Notes on the Phonematic Value of the Modern English [ŋ]-Sound

JOSEF VACHEK

'It goes without saying that no phonemic classification can be made unless the sounds concerned have been analysed with great accuracy and all the conditions concerning their use have been fully established. A superficially made analysis may lead to erroneous classification.' – Daniel Jones.[1]

In explaining the difference between the phoneme and the speech-sound, it has become customary for many writers to adduce the Modern English[2] nasal consonants [n] and [ŋ] as particularly clear and convincing instances of speech-sounds possessing the status of separate phonemes in that language, while in some other languages (such as Italian, Spanish, Czech, Hungarian, etc.) analogous nasal consonants constitute mere variants of one and the same phoneme. As is commonly known, in these latter languages the velar [ŋ] only occurs before the velar consonants [k, g], to the exclusion of the alveolodental [n] which never occurs in such positions, while in ModE both [n] and [ŋ] can be found in perfectly identical environments and, consequently, can differentiate word-meanings.[3]

Although the above phonematic interpretation of ModE [ŋ] has been endorsed by a vast majority of scholars, a closer analysis of the ModE phonematic situation cannot fail to reveal that the real value of [ŋ] within the ModE phonematic system remains a kind of problem. The problem was first envisaged, as early as in 1925, by Edward Sapir,[4] who very aptly pointed out a number of reasons which should make a phonemicist think twice before he subscribes to the traditional interpretation. In view of their basic importance, Sapir's arguments deserve to be quoted here in full. Speaking of 'English sound patterning' (i.e. of the phonematic interpretation) of ModE [ŋ] he says:

'In spite of what phoneticians tell us about this sound ([b : m] as [d : n] as [g : ŋ]), no naïve English-speaking person can be made to feel in his bones that it belongs to a single series with [m] and [n]. Psychologically it cannot be grouped with them because, unlike them, it is not a freely movable consonant (there are no words beginning with [ŋ]). It still *feels* like [ŋg], however little it sounds like it. The relation *ant : and = sink : sing* is psychologically as well as historically correct. Orthography is by no means solely responsible for the '[ŋg] feeling' of [ŋ]. Cases like [-ŋg-] in *finger* and *anger* do not disprove the reality of this feeling, for there is in English a pattern equivalence of [-ŋg- : -ŋ] and [-nd- : -nd]. What cases like *singer* with [-ŋ-] indicate is not so much a pattern difference [-ŋg- : -ŋ-], which is not to be construed as analogous to [-nd- : -n-], (e.g. *window* : *winnow*), as an analogical treatment of medial elements in terms of their final form (*singer* : *sing* like *cutter* : *cut*).'[5]

If Sapir's observations are divested of their psychological garb, they will be found to refer, first of all, to a very important feature of ModE [ŋ], i.e. to what we might call, in terms more common to-day, its limited functional load (or its limited positional distribution).[6] As a matter of fact, there is only one incontestable position in which [ŋ] can be found to function as what appears to be a phoneme, viz. that at the end of a morpheme (that position is exemplified by the commonly known instances of the type [sin : siŋ, sin-ə, siŋ-ə]). In all other positions in which [ŋ] occurs in ModE it might be explained away as a subsidiary variant (or, allophone) of the phoneme /n/ (see instances like [iŋk, tæŋk, fiŋgə, æŋgə]).[7]

The other illuminating observation that phonematic analysis owes to Sapir is his suggestion that, phonematically, ModE [-ŋ] should be associated rather with [ŋg] than with [n]. Should this suggestion prove correct, one would have to interpret the sound [-ŋ] as an implementation of a biphonematic group, viz. of /ng/. On the other hand, the [-ŋ-]-sound of words like *finger*, *anger* should not, in this view, be phonematically identified with the final [-ŋ] of *sing*, *sing-er*; while the latter implements the whole of the phonematic group of /ng/, the former would manifest no more than its first half, viz. /n/. Of equal phonematic value would be, of course, the [ŋ]-sounds of words like *ink*, *tank*. The phonematic structures of the discussed words would be, then, /sing, sing-ə; fingə, ængə, ink, tænk/.

It cannot indeed be denied that a number of facts appear to support the biphonematic interpretation of [-ŋ]. First, this interpretation would do away with the strikingly uneven distribution of the supposedly parallel phonemes /m, n, ŋ/. Second, it would make unnecessary for the morphological analyst of English to establish the highly exceptional, and therefore improbable, suffixal morphemes /-gə/ and /-gist/ for the comparatives *longer*, *stronger* and, respectively, superlatives *longest*, *strongest*. In terms of Sapir's interpretation, the comparison of these adjectives is effected by adding to the stem the ordinary suffixes /-ə/ and /-ist/, found in the overwhelming majority of English comparatives and superlatives: /long : long-ə, long-ist; strong : strong-ə, strong-ist/. Even historical considerations (i.e. the rise of ModE [-ŋ] from Late Middle English [-ng]), though much less important, cannot be wholly overlooked – some attention will be paid to them later on.

On the other hand, of course, one cannot close one's eyes to the objections that may be raised to the biphonematic interpretation of ModE [-ŋ]. First, some methodological misgivings are always associated with a biphonematic interpretation of what is, from the phonetic viewpoint, an unquestionably single speech sound. Although in some circumstances such an interpretation may be found necessary,[8] it should always be resorted to with the utmost caution. Second, analogous doubts regularly accompany those phonematic interpretations which involve the attribution of different phonematic values to one and the same speech-sound placed in different kinds of phonematic environment (such, indeed, would be the case of ModE [ŋ] in words like [iŋk] and [siŋ], which would have to be interpreted, respectively, as /n/ and /ng/). Here again, the utmost caution appears to be indicated: as in any other branch of research work, the validity of the disputed interpretation depends on whether or not it may prove capable of covering all the facts involved, and of giving a better account of them than that provided by the rival interpretation.

Conformity with the facts involved is, indeed, the most essential touchstone of Sapir's biphonematic interpretation of ModE [ŋ]: it might be criticized, that is to say, not only on the two above-mentioned general grounds of methodological character but also on grounds that sound much more concrete, i.e. because some facts of the ModE phonic structure appear to contradict it. It is these facts, therefore, that call for some comment.

As one of such concrete arguments might be quoted here the well-known fact that ModE [ŋ] and [ŋg] can indeed be found in analogous phonetic environments, i.e. in the middle of words (see word-pairs like [fiŋgə : siŋə]). Such instances, however, are easily explained away as due to differences in morphological structure. Sapir himself, in the above-quoted paper of 1925, very aptly attributes the occurrence of [ŋ] in [siŋə] to the high degree of independence enjoyed by the ModE suffix *-er* forming nouns of agents. As a result of this independence, the last phoneme of the preceding stem morpheme follows the same distributional rules as apply to a phoneme standing in the word-final position. As is well known, morphematic limits are often underlined in languages by specific distributional features (N.S. Trubetzkoy's theory of 'Grenzsignale' furnishes rich evidence of the fact).[9] Consequently, word-pairs of the type [fiŋgə : siŋə] cannot invalidate Sapir's interpretation of ModE [ŋ] as /ng/.

Still, differences in morphematic structure cannot easily explain away all concrete arguments contradicting Sapir's theory. A notorious case that cannot be glibly dismissed on the above grounds is the ModE word-pair *longer* [lɔŋgə] (comparative of *long*) : *longer* [lɔŋə] (the noun of agent derived from the verb *to long*).[10] Here one is faced with two words of parallel morphematic structure and, at the same time, clearly differentiated from the semantic viewpoint. The semantic difference is associated with the phonic difference: the phonic feature keeping apart the two words (and thus obviously responsible for the semantic non-identity) is the presence vs. the absence of the sound [g] after [ŋ]. If the criterion of commutation is strictly adhered to, only one conclusion can be drawn from the above opposition, viz. that the speech-sound [g], ranking undoubtedly as a phoneme, by its very absence in the word [lɔŋə] establishes beyond any doubt the phonematic status of ModE [ŋ]. Besides, if [ŋ] can be functionally opposed to [ŋg], it appears impossible to propose the functional identity of the two (such identity is indeed implied by Sapir's thesis, see the word-pair [lɔŋ : lɔŋgə], to be interpreted, in Sapir's terms, as /long : longə/).

But the most important point is that the misgivings aroused by the word-pair [lɔŋgə : lɔŋə] cannot be dispelled by considerations of morphematic structure as in the case of word-pairs like [fiŋgə : siŋə]. It is obvious, that is to say, that the morphematic structures of the two words are perfectly parallel (unless one is prepared to establish the above-mentioned highly improbable comparative morpheme /-gə/. It would appear, therefore, that Sapir's interpretation of ModE [ŋ] as /ng/ can hardly be squared with the existence of the two forms discussed.

Still, the chances of the biphonematic interpretation are not so hopeless as one might be tempted to suppose. Sapir himself was not wholly ignorant of the danger which the comparative forms of the type *stronger*, *longer* (pointed out to him by Bloomfield) constituted to his theory. He faced the trouble by his suggestion that the morpheme /-ə/ forming the comparatives contrasts with the 'agentive' /-ə/ which, as he puts it, 'allows the adjective to keep its radical form in -ŋg-'.[11] Sapir's remark does not develop the contrast any farther; it appears that the reference to it was only annexed to the footnote when the paper was already in print. We may try, however, to follow his argument to its logical conclusion and infer that the comparative *-er* does not enjoy such a degree of independence in ModE as the homophonous 'agentive' *-er*. If this is so, it may be argued that the biphonematic group /ng/ standing before the comparative morpheme is implemented in the same way as when placed inside the morpheme, i.e. as [ŋg]. This suggestion cannot be flatly dismissed: it indeed appears that some ModE affixes (especially the word-formative ones) are more independent, and more easily separable from their word-bases than others (especially those which serve rather grammatical than word-formative purposes).[12] Also some of Trubetzkoy's materials seem to favour the suggestion that the degree of cohesion of the stem and the affixes may vary according to the kind of affix concerned.

Further examination, of course, is needed to prove or disprove the theory that the comparative suffix may not enjoy such a degree of independence as the homophonous agentive suffix. It appears that, unlike some ModE affixes (such as *-ish*, *-able*, *'s*, *pre-*, *anti-*, etc.), neither of the two can ever be joined to a word-group. On the other hand, the fact that the comparative suffix *-er* does not imply the change of the word-category of the basic word, while the agentive *-er* necessarily does so, might speak for the greater cohesion of the comparative *-er* with its stem morpheme. It is also worth pointing out that the comparative (and superlative) suffixes can only be joined to a primary adjective, not to a secondary one (e.g. to one that owes its adjectival status to conversion, e.g. *paper* profits, a *stand-up* collar, his *after* years); this, too, might be regarded as evidence for the relatively close link joining the comparative suffix *-er* to the stem of the primary adjective. But, for all this evidence, the whole question certainly calls for further examination.

The above analysis may not have quite convincingly proved the biphonematic status of the ModE [ŋ]-sound but it will have certainly shown that such biphonematic interpretation is tenable. Besides, it will have also revealed that, whatever the actual functional value of ModE [ŋ] may be, its ascertainment is rendered most difficult by the complexity of the facts to be accounted for. In other words, in this particular point the phonematic system of ModE does not appear to be sufficiently clear. It has been shown above that a number of cogent reasons advocate the interpretation of ModE [ŋ] in terms of a biphonematic group /ng/. On the other hand, it is obvious that the cogency of such an interpretation is outweighed by a number of factors which appear to be opposed to it.

Such factors have been implicitly referred to above in our reference to a double methodological misgiving usually experienced by the students of the functional aspect of speech-sounds: first, the misgiving associated with a biphonematic interpretation of a manifestly single speech-sound, and second, the misgiving accompanying the attribution of different phonematic values to one and the same speech-sound placed in different kinds of phonematic environment. These misgivings originate not only in the saying 'Omne verum simplex', which is an old-established maxim of all scientific methodology, but also in what we know of the actual functioning of language systems considered as wholes. In some of our earlier papers [13] we attempted to show that the numerically limited inventory of the phonemes of a language (usually not exceeding three dozen), faced with the gigantic task of expressing all communicative needs of the given language community, has to be adequately equipped for the task. This means that the phonemes of the language must be well spaced and distinctly kept apart, otherwise the functioning of the higher planes of language (grammatical, lexical, etc.) is bound to be less smooth and the efficiency of the language as a means of communication palpably reduced.

In our papers referred to above we also believe we have furnished some evidence for the operation of a number of tendencies aimed at doing away with some of the sore (i.e. not sufficiently clear) points of the ModE phonematic system, and so making that system less complicated and, consequently, more efficient.[14] Such tendencies, then, may serve as indicators of the presence of such sore points in the system of phonemes of ModE. It may be of some interest, therefore, to see whether any such tendencies can be found operating with regard to the ModE [ŋ]-sound. A reliable answer to this question can only be obtained if the whole of the history of the [ŋ]-sound in English is briefly surveyed, as far as it can be established on the grounds of what we know about the history of the phonic plane of English.

It is generally admitted that in Old English the sound [ŋ] had no phonematic status, being only a combinatory variant (an 'allophone') of the phoneme /n/, whose fundamental variant was an alveolodental sound. The [ŋ]-sound was used in OE 'to the exclusion of [n] before [k] and [g]',[15] i.e. its place in the OE phonematic system was perfectly parallel to that occupied by [ŋ] in the system of Italian, Spanish, Czech, and Hungarian. At that time, the final *-ng* was probably pronounced as [ŋg] (cf. D. Jones, loc. cit.). The fundamental revaluation of the English [ŋ]-sound was not to take place until the latter half of the Middle English period, when the word-final groups [-mb], [-nd], [-ng] were simplified into [-m], [-n], and [-ŋ], respectively.[16]

The changes resulted in the emergence of ModE oppositions like [sin : siŋ, θin : θiŋ, ræn : ræŋ, tʌn : tʌŋ], etc. At first sight, such oppositions seem to furnish clear evidence of the acquirement by [ŋ] of phonematic status. This inference might also be supported by the fact that the alleged new Late ME (or Early ModE) phoneme would have perfectly fitted in with the phonematic structure of the section of the English consonantal system concerned. The newly arisen phoneme, that is, would have remarkably filled the gap ('place vide', to use Martinet's term)[17] that, until then, had existed in that system:

/p/ – /t/ – /k/
/b/ – /d/ – /g/
/m/ – /n/ – ø

It was obviously this congruity of [ŋ] with the general phonematic pattern of English that had led so many scholars to ascribe to that sound the status of a phoneme within that pattern.[18] Still, from the very beginning of its existence in the language the alleged new phoneme was distinctly marked off from all the other phonemes in that section of the system – and particularly from the other two nasal consonant phonemes – by its limited possibilities of distribution (as already noted above, the occurrence of [ŋ] as a genuinely functional phonic item of English is virtually confined to the ends of morphemes). There can hardly be any doubt that this quantitative limitation, coupled with the forementioned close link obviously existing between [-ŋ] and [-ŋg-], from the very beginning considerably obscured the position of the alleged new phoneme in the phonematic system of English. It can be taken for granted, that is, that the combined influence of all the enumerated factors[19] still suggested the possibility of interpreting the sound [ŋ] as an implementation of the biphonematic group [ng]. On the other hand, the congruity of [ŋ] with the English pattern of consonant phonemes, in which it was able to fill the 'place vide', constituted a positive factor working for the definite establishment of [ŋ] as an independent phoneme in the language. It appears that these two kinds of factors (and, consequently, the two opposed possibilities of phonematic interpretation) have been in conflict since the time of the phonetic change of [-ŋg] > [-ŋ], and that even to-day, at least in the standard language, the conflict cannot be said to have been quite definitely settled. It is only in view of this lasting conflict that one can give a satisfactory account of a number of later changes that concerned the *ng*-sound in some way or another. These changes will now have our attention.

The change of [-ŋg-] into [-ŋ-] in words like *singer*, *singing* can, in our opinion, be regarded as an attempt to increase those positions in which the [ŋ] was allowed to occur, and thus as an attempt to consolidate the position of [ŋ] as an independent phoneme of English. Even though the position of [ŋ] in such words was, in principle, of the same kind as in the basic word *sing* (in both words [ŋ] was placed at the end of a morpheme), the very fact that [ŋ] was to emerge there for the first time inside a word before a consonant other than [k] or [g] was of some significance. By their purely phonetic make-up such words might have served as potential models encouraging the rise of other words containing a non-final [ŋ] which was not motivated by the following [k] or [g] and whose existence, at the same time, could *not* be accounted for by the immediately following morphematic limit. The interesting point is, however, that hardly any words of the latter kind are found to emerge in the literary standard. As exceptional instances of the kind might be quoted two words in which [ŋg] > [ŋ] before the following [l], viz. *England* and *English* which may be pronounced either with [-ŋgl-] or with [-ŋl-].[20] But even these two cases can hardly furnish very substantial evidence of the positional expansion of [ŋ]. Not to speak of the fact that the [ŋ] in these two words regularly corresponds to [ŋg] in the pronunciation of other speakers of the standard language (in other 'idiolects', as is sometimes said), the existence of [ŋ] in the word *England* is clearly due to the association of this word with words like *Scotland*, *Finland*, *Netherlands*, etc. This association is responsible for the treatment of the syllable *-land* as a separate morpheme; consequently, the *ng* immediately preceding that morpheme is treated in the manner typical of such positions, i.e. it is pronounced as [ŋ]. In the word *English* the pronunciation containing [-ŋl-] is clearly due to the analogy of the pronunciation [iŋlənd]. As the morphematic motive for the pronunciation of [ŋ] is here missing, this word may really be regarded as evidence, however isolated, for the positional expansion of [ŋ] in ModE. Even here, however, the value of this evidence is rather reduced by the co-existing pronunciation type [ingliʃ], found in other idiolects and following the standard phonematic pattern.

In this connection, it should be added that Dobson[21] points out a large number of instances of words originally containing the group [ŋg]+consonant in which [g] became duly lost and, consequently, the [ŋ]-sound, no longer motivated by the following velar consonant, was placed before some other consonant than [k] or [g] (e.g. *amongst, kingdom, length, strength,* etc.). One might be tempted to interpret this change as evidence of the consolidation of the phonematic status of [ŋ]; such evidence, however, cannot be taken for convincing. For all the (relatively infrequent) vacillations of Early ModE pronunciation registered by Dobson from the writings of early orthoepists and grammarians, it is obvious that in present-day standard language all the quoted words conform to the common structural pattern of ModE: [ŋ] is pronounced in such words when it is separated from the following consonant by a morphematic limit (e.g. *among-st, king-dom, leng-th, streng-th, bring-s, belong-ed,* etc.), while [ŋg] is found in those words in which such a morphematic limit is missing (e.g. *angry, angle, anguish,* etc.). As far as can be seen, the only exceptions to this pattern in present-day standard language are exactly the variant pronunciations [iŋlənd] and [iŋliʃ], commented upon in the preceding paragraph.

Our observations should not be understood as a refutation of Dobson's thesis that in the 14th century the English sound group [ŋg], if followed by an additional consonant, was regularly simplified into [ŋ], while, if followed by a vowel, the same sound-group was preserved unimpaired. Dobson's conclusion, drawn from an ingenious, painstaking analysis of a vast amount of sources, may be perfectly sound (and the same may be said of his thesis that, at the moment of the sound change, morphological analogy played no decisive part in establishing either [ŋ] or [ŋg] as the result of the process). It can even be supposed that the simplification of [ŋg] before a consonant into [ŋ] was actually prompted by the tendency aimed at consolidating the position of [ŋ] as an independent phoneme of the language, and that the vacillations between [ŋ] and [ŋg], which emerge from Dobson's analysis of his Early ModE sources, may be regarded as manifestations of that tendency. Yet the situation in the present-day standard distinctly reveals that, in the long run, the tendency failed to achieve its purpose. The main factor counteracting that tendency was clearly the need to signalize morphematic limits: by its exclusive occurrence at the end of morphemes the [ŋ]-sound (not followed by [k] or [g]) was found to be eminently suited for such signalization. In our opinion, it was for this reason that [ŋ] was introduced into forms like *sing-er, sing-ing*, etc., and that, on the contrary, [ŋg] became the ultimate norm in forms like *angry, angle, anguish*, etc.[22]

All in all, it appears that the rules of the distribution of [ŋ] : [ŋg] in to-day's standard pronunciation can – except for the case of the variant pronunciation of the word *English* – be fully stated in terms of the morphematic structure of the words containing them. As has been shown above (p. 194), the same can be said about the semantically differentiated word pair [lɔŋə] : [lɔŋgə]; it appears that the structural difference existing between the two members of this word-pair can again (though less easily) be accounted for in morphematic terms. In the circumstances, it is hardly an exaggeration to say that the tendency aimed at consolidating the position of [ŋ] as an independent English phoneme has made very little headway, at least in the standard language.

Incidentally, in some of the local dialects [ŋ] seems to have been more successful in its expansion at the expense of [ŋg]. Both Horn-Lehnert (p. 837) and Dobson (p. 973) point to phenomena of this kind, ascertainable in Scotland, Northern and Southern England. It is, however, again rather doubtful whether even this expansion constituted any real consolidation of the phonematic status of [ŋ] in these dialects. It is interesting to learn from Jones[23] that, e.g., '[ng] and [ŋ] form a variphone in the speech of Midland districts of England (Birmingham, Chester, etc.)', i.e. that many English speakers of this area use [ŋ] and [ŋg] promiscuously – indeed, as Jones points out, such speakers 'cannot hear the difference between [ŋ] and [ŋg] nor can they make the difference at will' (l.c.). From the phonematic point of view the [ŋ]-sound in the pronunciation of such speakers cannot be classified as an independent phoneme, but again rather as an implementation of the biphonematic group /ng/, in the quality of what might be called its free variant. It will have to be found out whether the sound [ŋ] of the local dialects referred to above does not, in fact, constitute an analogous variphone of [ŋg]. Obviously, the phonematic status of the non-final [ŋ]-sound could only be admitted in those dialects if no instances of the variphonic relation between such [ŋ] and [ŋg] existed in them.

Our examination has revealed, then, that the development of English between the fourteenth century and the present-day period did not substantially contribute to the consolidation of the phonematic status of [ŋ], although the existence in the Early ModE period of some tendencies aimed at that goal is beyond any doubt. It is now time to give a brief survey of the operation of the opposite tendency, which was directed at clearing the moot point of the English phonematic system in an altogether different manner. Far from consolidating the position of [ŋ], this other tendency attacked exactly that phonic fact which had yielded the most powerful evidence for the phonematic status of the English [ŋ]-sound, viz. the existence of [ŋ] at the end of morphemes. It is clear that if [ŋ] in these positions could have been abolished, the case of the supposed /ŋ/-phoneme would have been unmistakably decided in the negative, because the instances of [ŋ] in all other positions might be easily explained away as implementations of the phoneme /n/.

It is, in our opinion, only by the operation of this tendency that a satisfactory account can be given of the well-known Early ModE change of the unstressed [-iŋ] > [-in] (in some dialects, especially in the North, the change occurred as early as in Late ME).[24] Purely phonetic attempts to account for this change 'by later assimilation of [ŋ] to a dental articulation under the influence of the preceding high-front vowel'[25] are clearly unconvincing. It seems obvious that the *raison d'être* of the change of the unstressed [-iŋ] > [-in] was to manifestly express the persisting functional interpretation of [ŋ] as a combinatory variant of the /n/-phoneme: after the following /g/ had become lost, the use of the velar combinatory variant of /n/ was no longer indicated, and therefore that variant became duly replaced by the fundamental variant of the /n/-phoneme, i.e. by the alveolodental nasal.

Undoubtedly, an objection may be raised to this phonematic interpretation of the change of the unstressed [-iŋ] > [-in]. Why, it may be asked, was the change confined to the unstressed positions and why did it not affect the stressed [-iŋ] as well? But the answer to this question is not difficult to find. Leaving aside for the moment the question of the phonematic relation of [-n] and [-ŋ] in stressed syllables, it is hardly necessary to prove that a fairly large number of new homonyms would arise in English if the latter sound were to be replaced by the former (e.g. word-pairs like *thin* : *thing*, *sin* : *sing*, *kin* : *king*, *win* : *wing*, *ban* : *bang*, *fan* : *fang*, *ran* : *rang*, *run* : *rung*, *sun* : *sung*, *ton* : *tongue*, etc.), while the change of the unstressed [-iŋ] > [-in] only added a very small number of such instances (e.g. word-pairs like *coffin* : *coughing*, *coming* : *cumin*, *jerking* : *jerkin*). It will, besides, be noticed that at least one-half of the last-mentioned six words are items of relatively very low frequency in language utterances of everyday communication, while the frequency of most of the words constituting the former group (*thin* : *thing*, etc.) is relatively high. Under these conditions one can hardly be astonished to find that the language was not particularly disposed to give up the phonic distinction of [-n] and [-ŋ] in stressed syllables in which it had proved so useful. It was certainly for this reason that after the loss of [g][26] the [ŋ]-sound, up to that time a combinatory variant of the /n/-phoneme, was not automatically replaced by [n], its fundamental variant. As a matter of fact, the non-replacement of [ŋ] by [n] after the loss of the following [g] appears to speak most convincingly for the acquirement of phonematic status by the [ŋ]-sound. How, then, could this acknowledgment of the phonematic status of [-ŋ] in stressed syllables be reconciled with the effort to deny its phonematic status in unstressed syllables?

In order to answer this question satisfactorily, one should realize that by the change of the unstressed [-iŋ] > [-in] the positions in which the supposed /n/-phoneme was allowed to occur were again substantially reduced. Before the said change the functionally independent (i.e. not motivated by the following [k] or [g]) [ŋ] already could occur in one position only, i.e. at the end of morpheme, but after the said change its possibilities of occurrence were to be reduced even further, by adding the condition that the concerned morpheme must be a stressed one.[27] This drastic decrease of the functional load of the supposed /ŋ/-phoneme must necessarily have become reflected in a palpable weakening of the position of /ŋ/ within the phonematic system of English. If, in addition to this, one recalls the possibility of interpreting the functionally independent [ŋ]-sound as a biphonematic group /ng/ (see above, pp. 192–196), it will become evident that the change of the unstressed [-iŋ] > [-in] must have considerably increased the probability of that biphonematic interpretation. Indeed, had the change of unstressed [-iŋ] > [-in] taken deeper roots in the standard language (as it actually did in the dialects), it would have most probably played an important part in the process of definitely discarding [ŋ] as a phoneme.

Another well-known dialectal change may be quoted here which reveals another attempt at undermining the phonematic status of EModE /ŋ/. It was the change of the stressed [-iŋ] > [iŋk] (phonematically, /-ink/). But the geographical scope of the change was only a limited one, and the standard language was not appreciably affected by it (see, however, Horn-Lehnert, 847).

But, as is commonly known, the change was not to take deeper roots. The effort of the orthoepists succeeded in restoring the pronunciation of the unstressed [-iŋ] in the standard language by the end of the seventeenth century, although the vulgar (and partly also the conservative aristocratic) pronunciations have preserved the [-in] until the present-day period.[28] Seen from the phonematic angle, the revival of the unstressed [-iŋ] turned the tables again: by restoring some of the ground previously lost by the functionally independent [ŋ]-sound, it also restored the chances of the /ŋ/-phoneme gaining a more solid foothold in English, without, of course, securing this foothold definitely.

The restitution of unstressed [-iŋ] in the standard language calls for another remark, of more general character. On the face of it, the successful intervention of the orthoepists might strike one as inorganic or even destructive, because it invalidated the impending solution of an urgent phonematic problem, i.e. it made impossible the abolition of a slightly charged, peripheral phoneme. Still, a closer look at the systemic situation of Early ModE will reveal that the restoration of [ŋ] in the suffix *-ing* could be only effected because the Early ModE phonematic system had contained an important structural prerequisite that was to make that restoration possible. This prerequisite had again been the 'full integration' of the phoneme /ŋ/. Its full integration is clearly seen from our above scheme (p. 197), revealing that the rise of the phoneme /ŋ/ did, in its time, fill a 'place vide' in the English phonematic system, and that the abolishment of that phoneme would re-establish this 'place vide' again.

Although the position of /ŋ/ in the ModE phonematic pattern has thus been markedly reinforced, it can hardly be said to be particularly firm: in view of its very slight degree of functional utilization, /ŋ/ continues to be evaluated as a peripheral phoneme of the language, and its continued existence in the phonematic pattern is still threatened by the above-discussed alternative, biphonematic evaluation. By way of contrast, this diagnosis is borne out by the situation of /ŋ/ in popular dialects, in which the process aimed at the abolition of the phonematic status of /ŋ/ has reached a fairly advanced stage. In these dialects the factor of the full integration of /ŋ/ alone, uncoupled with the external factor of the impact of orthoepists, has proved to be too weak to enforce an intervention in the phonematic pattern: its potential preservative capacity has never become actualized as it has in the standard language.

*Notes*

[1] *The Phoneme: Its Nature and Use*, Cambridge, 1950, § 156.

[2] Unless otherwise stated, this term refers to the present-day Southern British standard language.

[3] See, e.g., Jones, *The Phoneme*, §§ 75, 116, and also one of our own earlier papers (J. Vachek, 'What is Phonology?', *English Studies*, xv, 1933, 81–92, esp. 81 f.).

[4] E. Sapir, 'Sound Patterns in Language', *Language* I, 1925, 37–51 (reprinted in *Selected Writings of Edward Sapir in Language, Culture, and Personality*, ed. D. G. Mandelbaum, Berkeley and Los Angeles, 1951, 33–45).

[5] 'Sound Patterns', 49.

[6] The explanation of the phonematic terms of the Prague School may be found now in Vachek – J. Dubský, *Dictionnaire de linguistique de l'École de Prague*, Utrecht-Anvers, 1960.

[7] This allophonic interpretation would also hold good for the very few instances of word-initial [ŋ-] that can be found in manifestly foreign proper names, such as *Ngami* [ŋ'gami] and *Nkrumah* [ŋ'krumə].

[8] See, e.g., the case of ModE [ʍ], phonematically interpreted as /hw/ (cf. Vachek, 'On the Phonetic and Phonemic Problems of the Southern English WH-Sounds', *Zeitschrift für Phonetik u. allgemeine Sprachwissenschaft*, VIII, 1954, 165–194).

[9] N. S. Trubetzkoy, 'Grundzüge der Phonologie', *Travaux du Cercle Linguistique de Prague*, VII, 1939, 242 ff.

[10] The latter word has a fairly long history in English: the earliest of its occurrences registered by the Oxford English Dictionary goes back to 1435.

[11] Sapir, 'Sound Patterns', 49.

[12] This subject is developed in some detail in our study 'Some Less Familiar Aspects of the Analytical Trend of English', *Brno Studies in English*, III, 1961; see esp. Chaps. II and III (the latter discusses, among other things, instances of the so-called Group Genitives, which appear to testify to the effect that the 'Possessive Case' of ModE is no longer a paradigmatic case but rather a derived form tending towards full adjectivization).

[13] Vachek, 'Phonemic Remarks on the "Short Mixed Vowel" of Modern English', *Sborník prací filosofické fakulty brněnské university*, A4, Brno, 1956, 81–92 (see esp. p. 88); and 'On the Interplay of Quantitative and Qualitative Aspects in Phonemic Development', *Zeitschrift für Anglistik u. Amerikanistik*, Berlin, V, 1957, 5–28 (see esp. p. 20).

[14] For another tendency of the kind, see Vachek, 'The Decline of the Phoneme /r/ in English', *Sborník prací filosofické fakulty brněnské university*, A8, 1960, 79–93.

[15] Cf. Jones, *The Phoneme*, § 731.

[16] In Jones' opinion, this change took place in the fourteenth century; similarly K. Luick, *Historische Grammatik der englischen Sprache*, I, Leipzig, 1914–1940. 1035 ff.; E. J. Dobson, *English Pronunciation 1500–1700*, Oxford, 1957, 963 ff., places the change in the fourteenth century in vulgar London English, while in the standard speech, in his view, the [-ŋg] was maintained until the late sixteenth century.

[17] A. Martinet, *Économie des changements phonétiques*, Berne, 1955.

[18] The interpretation was backed not only by Jones and Dobson but also by all members of the Prague group who have dealt with the problem (V. Mathesius, B. Trnka, Vachek, and others).

[19] Together with the spelling *-ng*, of course. But the influence of the written norm would hardly have been of any moment, if it had not acted in the same direction as the above-described strong tendencies operating in the spoken norm of the language.

[20] See Jones, *English Pronouncing Dictionary*, 11th Edn., London, 1956; W. Horn-M. Lehnert, *Laut und Leben*, Berlin, 1954, 839, points out that the pronunciation of these two words with [-ŋl-] was already registered by Gill in 1619. Cf. also Dobson, *Engl. Pronunciation, 1500–1700*, 972.

[21] Dobson, *English Pronunciation*, 971–973.

[22] The reasons given by Dobson (p. 972) for the presence of [-ŋg-] in such words are not always convincing. Thus, e.g., in *anguish* the presence of [-ŋg-] is explained as due to the fact that [gw] may function in English as an initial group, as in *Gwen.* This latter word, however, is manifestly a foreign element in the English word stock, in which the initial [gw-] is otherwise unknown. Besides, in words like *angle* the presence of [-ŋg-] is accounted for by the common replacement of the syllabic [l̩] by [əl], so that the group [-ŋg] then becomes intervocalic. Yet the pronunciation with [əl], characteristic of a *lento* style of speech, and occurring therefore rather rarely in common communication, can hardly be credited with exercising a decisive influence on the much more frequent *allegro* form with the syllabic [l̩].

[23] *The Phoneme*, § 631.

[24] The most detailed discussion of the change is given by Horn-Lehnert, 839–847; see also Luick, 1044–1046, and Dobson, 950–951.

[25] Dobson, 950.

[26] The purely phonetic history of that loss was very aptly described by Luick, 1038.

[27] It is certainly remarkable that the unstressed prefixes (and sometimes even the stressed ones), such as *in-*, *un-*, *con-*, etc., regularly preserve their [-n] in pronunciation, even if the initial consonant of the following stem morpheme is [k-] or [g-] (a small number of exceptions may, of course, be found; see Jones, *Eng. Pron. Dict.*).

[28] Cf. Luick, 1045; Horn-Lehnert, 845.

# Thesis and Antithesis in the Evolution of English Linguistics

C. M. WISE

The eightieth birthday of Daniel Jones on 12 September, 1961, and the publication of a commemorative volume in his honour suggest the value of an estimate of how things linguistic stand at this milestone of Professor Jones' magnificent career in linguistic scholarship. An overview of the several phases of current English linguistic thought reveals each of them at some stage of controversy.

It is possible to examine these situations of controversy in the light of the Hegelian philosophy which finds every situation inevitably ambiguous, ambiguity being for the nonce defined as conflict between two mutually opposing trends. Hegel attaches to one of these contradictory drives the label *thesis* (often to be identified with the *status quo*), and to the other, *antithesis* (often to be identified with a revolutionary *Drang* towards change). The outcome of the conflict he labels *synthesis*. This synthesis presently becomes a new thesis, soon to be contradicted by a new antithesis; and so by such recurring circularities of ambiguity, progress in one direction or the other within the situation continually evolves.

It would be supererogatory to undertake a complete summary of all the situations within the purview of the science of linguistics and to define all the theses and antitheses which constitute their ambiguities. Some such situations are large and international, as is suggested by a recent book review which refers to 'American' linguistics in a manner suggesting that it is antithetic to British linguistics or possibly to the linguistics of Europe as a whole; other situations are small and local, as when the linguists in a given university divide into contradictory groups relative to some theory, principle, formulation, or debatable phonemic symbolization. But it is possible to select a limited number of situations, each illustrating how an internally espoused thesis, opposed by its antithesis, promotes the skirmishes and battles of a war, now hot, now cold, a revolution by which the science of linguistics effects its current evolution.

The mention above of applying the thesis-antithesis dichotomy to opinion and practice in phonemic symbolism suggests beginning a selected list of linguistic conflicts with 'The War of the Symbols'. This is particularly appropriate in view of Professor Jones' long years of presiding over the careful evolution of the symbols constituting the alphabet of the International Phonetic Association. Seven related linguistic conflicts may be listed for brief consideration[1]:

(1) The War of the Symbols,
(2) The War of the Phonemes,
(3) The War of Meaning,
(4) The War of Prescription,
(5) The War of Pronunciation,
(6) The War of Grammar,
(7) The War of Syntax.

## THE WAR OF THE SYMBOLS

The War of the Symbols does not loom large in scholarly journals, in the organs of learned societies, or in books composed of selected linguistics articles, all of whose editors accommodate themselves amiably to whatever symbols their authors use. But conflict is evident. Daniel Jones and John S. Kenyon, with their many colleagues, former students, and other followers in England, the Continent, the United States, and other countries generally, adhere almost consistently to IPA; many others, who probably regard their proficiency as phoneticians mainly as implemental to their central interest as structural linguists, use what is often called the linguistic alphabet. Thus *crust* and *mice*, transcribed in IPA as /krʌst/ and /maɪs/, appear in the linguistic alphabet as /krəst/ and /mays/.

It is now over a quarter of a century since Leonard Bloomfield precipitated the War of the Symbols by employing in his book *Language*[2] several symbols which were at the time startling, such as /ij, ej, aj, ɔj, aw, ow, uw/. The reaction of his colleagues may be checked in two long, deferential but heated reviews in the magazine *Language*.[3] Despite all opposition, Bloomfield's symbols were immediately, sometimes excitedly, seized upon and his phonemic inventory modified and expanded by numerous writers. To some extent the process has continued to this day.

Largely through the writings of Bernard Bloch,[4] George L. Trager, and Henry Lee Smith,[5] a hitherto unrecognized phoneme has been added to the English inventory, symbolized /ɨ/, for the vowel of the word *just* when stressed (or perhaps better, restressed), as in *just think* /ǰɨst θiŋk/. Additionally, the second element of the nucleus of the final syllable of *Judea*, or alternately, the second element of the syllable nucleus of the *r*-less pronunciation of *beard*, symbolized /h/, has been re-identified as a voiced postvocalic allophone of the /h/ of *hope*, whence the transcriptions /ǰuwdih/ and /bihd/, corresponding to IPA /ʤudiə/ and /bɪəd/.

Still further, a long-standing opinion (*vide* Henry Sweet[6]) that the syllable nuclei of *mean* and *moon* are diphthongs has been given shape in the transcriptions /miyn/ and /muwn/. Less startlingly, the initial consonant of *yes* has been re-symbolized as /y/, the final consonants of *push* and *rouge* as /š/ and /ž/, and the initial consonants of *chain* and *Jane* as /č/ and /ǰ/, these last two having the effect of advancing the belief that the sounds represented are single consonants, not clusters, as might be suggested by /tʃ/ and /dʒ/ or even /ʧ/ and /ʤ/.

Viewing events from the calmer perspective of twenty-five years, one may venture that the upheaval of the symbols was a set of signals constituting a declaration of independence from anything with which younger scholars might have been impatient – phonetics, the IPA, the past, other places, other people, and other ideas generally. It was such gestures that provoked sporadic accusations of arrogance and withdrawal into a cult on the part of the neo-symbolists, though such accusations have never been applied to the group as a whole, and only occasionally to individuals.

Incidentally, the new alphabet did not actually secede from the IPA; it only used linear or segmental symbols with unaccustomed values. (The invention of suprasegmental and morphemic symbols was largely new achievement.) Such an alphabet might reasonably be called a modified IPA system. The modifications could hardly be said to be necessary, for anything the young scholars may have wished to express could have been expressed in the symbols of the IPA or of any other good alphabet.

The modified alphabet is now a *fait accompli*. Many books and many more scholarly articles have been written employing it. Phonetics is usually still being taught in IPA, and linguistics in the phonemic alphabet.

Many, of whom the present writer is one, have felt that the differences between the alphabets are not really great enough to constitute a *casus belli*, and that the War of the Symbols could now be called off. Others, of whom the present writer is, paradoxically, also one, have inquired whether, before a new run of new texts in linguistics is printed, certain uneasy items in the linguistic alphabet cannot be re-examined with the aim of making adjustments such as the examination may indicate. As to the validity of designating /ɪ/ as a phoneme, inquirers are not oblivious to the fact that much careful argument has been marshalled in justification, as in the following:

> '. . . Speech communities are characterized by a symmetrical arrangement of the total possibilities for contrast, called an over-all frame. From this frame each individual and each dialect select some but not all of the possibilities. The formulation here given has resulted in a modification of the definition of the phoneme. The old concept of the phoneme turned on individual speech, the idiolect. Individual phonemic structures (under this older concept) are structures of idiophones. The newer concept turns on dialect, and to revive and modify an old term used by Jones, can be called a structure of diaphonemes. The over-all frame is not yet universally accepted – Einar Haugen and Hans Kurath are among the objectors – but it has already given interesting results in historical study.'[7]

The reference to dialects in the quotation stems from the fact that stressed /ɪ/ appears in English prominently in dialects, as in Southern American *sister* /sɪstə/, *senator* /sɪnətə/, and constitutes the ninth of the much-debated nine-vowel system.

Some also regard the /w/ of /aw, ow, uw/, the /y/ of /iy, ey, ay, ɔy/, and especially the postvocalic /h/, with uncertainty. They inquire whether it is attested that the constituent sound-waves of a glide, impinging on the tympanic membrane of the ear in reverse time order, produce the same acoustic effect as before the reversal. In other words, they inquire whether the postvocalic /w, y, h/ have been demonstrated to be true allophones of initial /w, y, h/. Gleason, seeing 'no clear evidence that the postvocalic /h/ has a counterpart in (prevocalic) /h/', symbolizes the postvocalic sound as /ʜ/.[8]

Closely related to the expositions of linguistic theory embodied in Bloomfield's *Language*, Bloch and Trager's *Outline of Linguistic Analysis* and Trager and Smith's *Outline of English Structure*, already cited, there has been a notable series of discussions in progress for two decades, touching on numerous innovations, but ultimately bearing heavily on both the nine-vowel system, with its /ɪ/, and the three semi-vowel system, containing /h/. Outstanding have been 'The Syllabic Phonemes of English', by George L. Trager and Bernard Bloch[9]; 'Facts and Phonemics', by Einar Haugen and W. F. Twaddell,[10] opposing Trager and Bloch; 'The Binary Interpretation of English Vowels', by Hans Kurath,[11] attacking particularly the postvocalic /h/; 'Some Questions of English Phonology', by James Sledd,[12] a reply to Kurath; and 'Some Questions of English Phonology: A Reply', by Hans Kurath,[13] answering Sledd.

Probably these questions could not have been answered when the idea of using /w/ and /y/ in diphthongs originated; but with the spectrograph and an increasing number of other electronic instruments now available, the answers should be more easily ascertained. If such answers should be accepted as final, the quite hot War of the Symbols, and with it the War of the Phonemes, may find a quieting synthesis to bridge the period before a new conflict sets in.

## THE WAR OF THE PHONEMES

The War of the Phonemes (and of their constituent allophones) may be said to be essentially co-existent and co-terminous with the War of the Symbols. For present purposes, the comments *ante* on /ɨ, w, y, h/ suggest sufficiently the contradictory tendencies constituting thesis and antithesis in this situation. The War of the Phonemes, equally with the War of the Symbols, is in a state of uneasy truce so far as published books and articles, and so far as the mindsets of many linguists are concerned. But before further major publications are put out, all pertinent questions that can be adduced, including those noted relative to phonemes and their symbols, should be asked and fully answered.

## THE WAR OF MEANING

The War of Meaning rages fiercely from place to place throughout the literature of linguistics. To many linguists, meaning, mentalism, and mentalistic are very nearly wicked words; to most linguists, they are fighting words. Smile when you call anyone a mentalist.

It is not easy to explain the issue in a few words. Charles C. Fries comes near it negatively when he says, 'Note that lexical meaning does not form a part of the apparatus in which to test structural arrangements'.[14] So does George P. Faust when he says, '. . . we tend to think of languages as produced by meaning, and the structuralists regard it as a medium for transmitting "messages". They discriminate between lexical meaning and grammatical meaning, for instance, and concentrate on the grammatical.'[15] The grammatical receives the concentration of attention in Fries' classic set of Jabberwocky-like contrivances of the order of *The uggle wogs a diggle.*[16]

Of the five items in this utterance, three have their lexical meanings erased, while the remaining two particles have but little meaning, being only noun-form (class I) markers. Nevertheless, the structure of the utterance is quite clearly shown, since the morpheme -$Z_3$ (orthographic *s*) in *wogs* locates the verb-form (class II), before which is placed one of the marked noun-forms in the subject position, with the other marked noun-form after it in the complement position.

The writers on linguistics struggle valiantly with meaning. Their efforts are good scientific exposition and make good reading. Perhaps their thinking requires summation, but otherwise we may almost write off the war as all over but the mopping-up operation. The disorder of the battlefield indicates that meaning has sustained terrific assaults, but the evidence appears to be that some fragments of some sorts of meaning, if only in such anaemic bits as enable us to identify the two morphemes in *wogs*, still lurk about awaiting the next assault.

## THE WAR OF PRESCRIPTION

The War of Prescription is still at high temperature. Prescription is even worse than a bad word to most linguists; it is the vilest word they know. One linguist after another slays the wicked fire-drake of prescribed pronunciation or of prescribed grammar, then others rush into the fray to belabour the dead carcass. Simultaneously there are forays against the kindred dragon-words *correct* and *incorrect*, and *right* and *wrong*, which can hardly be mentioned except in quotation marks, and there are threatening gestures towards *sub-standard* and *socially acceptable*.

Let it not be thought that these wars and warriors are not powerfully provoked. The Greco-Latin grammar that has always passed for English grammar, and the hand-books built on earlier hand-books are provocation enough. It is small wonder that, almost suddenly coming to see English grammar as *sui generis*, and pronunciation as ultimately what people make of it, the linguists move in to attack, and often overrun, or seem to overrun, their objectives. It is at this point that their opponents, whom/who they call traditionalists, counter-attack with accusations that 'anything goes' with linguists if any sizeable number of people use it. Even fellow linguists regret the excessive zeal of some other linguists, as when Sumner Ives comments, 'Some of the more junicious [teachers] have complained, and rightly, that the arguments of the linguists have been largely negative and that they have given little to replace that which they have attacked.'[17]

The reader finds it hard not to be confused by the numerous points of view on prescription. Much contemporary writing tends, as Archibald A.Hill suggests, '. . . to add fuel to an already unfortunate blaze'.[18] Perhaps the blaze is not altogether unfortunate. The whole matter is in the discussion stage, and must be talked on out. This is the way thesis and antithesis are resolved into synthesis in situations of this nature. James B.McMillan offers one way to move towards decision, viz., that linguists and rhetoricians keep to their respective levels. To make this plan specific, he defines both linguistics and rhetoric.

'Linguistics is the scientific study of language. It is inductive, objective, tentative, and systematic; it is concerned with reportable facts, methods, and principles; it works by means of observations, hypotheses, experiments, postulates, and inferences; its products are *descriptive* [italics added] verbal or algebraic statements about language.

Rhetoric is the art of speaking or writing effectively. It may be the practical art of communication (with experimental tests) or the fine art of speaking or writing with aesthetic effects.'[19]

In brief the linguist *describes* language as it is at any or all prestige levels and has nothing to suggest relative to choice or change. The rhetorician *manipulates* language for more effective communication, and has, rightfully, many suggestions on choice and change.

Over-simplifying, we may say that the war has been precipitated in two ways: (1) many rhetoricians (including traditional grammarians and many others unfamiliar with recent linguistic progress) have indeed prescribed, sometimes on the basis of tradition (*vide* the split infinitive), and sometimes by reference to alleged laws or principles said to be inherent in the structure or system of the language. Here the rhetoricians have operated on the level reserved for the linguists. On the other hand, (2) many linguists have argued with a passion that gives the effect of prescription, urging the use of disputed features in ways that horrify the other group. In describing these features, they have been on their own level; but in urging their use, they have operated on the level reserved for rhetoricians.

McMillan correctly notes that the same person is often both a linguist and a rhetorician. In such case, the person is obliged to announce which level he is occupying at a given moment, and to give justification, still on the announced level, of his stand regarding a given point.

## THE WARS OF PRONUNCIATION, GRAMMAR, AND SYNTAX

The Wars of Pronunciation and Grammar and Syntax have been treated by implication in the paragraphs on prescription. One item calls for a brief comment, introduced by a brief statement: In most of the English-speaking world there are no fixed classes; even if there is an upper class defined by birth, there are no boundaries of comparable rigidity dividing the majority of the people. In all English-speaking countries there are, to be sure, higher and lower social, economic, and educational groups; but it is possible to move freely from one group to another, given normal capacity for, especially, education. Education has always assumed goals of culture and prestige to which certain acculturated speech habits are appropriate. The lifting of a whole population towards these goals has been a proud purpose in education.

It is saddening to find here and there in the literature of linguistics a writer who appears to believe that people living and speaking and writing at a low level may as well be schooled to continue to speak and write at that level. Along with this expressed belief is an occasional suggestion towards the debatable practice of 'speaking down' to such people. One would like to believe these ideas, if seriously proposed, will not prevail.

Reading in the literature of linguistics leads unerringly to the conclusion that all the best thinking of both the traditionalists and the structuralists should be pooled. Before this can profitably be done, the traditionalists should inform themselves liberally concerning modern linguistics. (The linguists are already informed on the traditionalist side, having been brought up there.) Once both sides are equally informed, learned societies and their committees should set to work to make broad agreements on standards in each of the embattled areas, whereupon new textbooks should be written.

As is evident above, in the situations obtaining in the Wars of Pronunciation, Grammar, and Syntax, we may read for thesis and antithesis the words traditionalist and structuralist. In these wars, as indeed in all seven of the wars named herein, the new appears likely to out-distance the old and traditional. But it will not always displace the old, but rather find a place beside it, or perhaps a bit in front of it.

As a feature of the Wars of the Symbol and the Phoneme, Daniel Jones' years of nurturing IPA will ensure the use of its symbolization for a long time. For many, IPA will be a main dependence, at least until the linguistic alphabet has adjusted convincingly its problems with postvocalic /w, y, h, ɪ/ and some less conspicuous additional other items. IPA too can well do some adjusting, e.g. in the matter of distinguishing between its phonemes and its allophones, and in re-examining the phoneme list itself.

In the War of Prescription, many will find themselves allied with both sides. Language will change – indeed, must change, to maintain its vigour; yet if it changes too fast, it loses connection with its own past through the accelerated obsolescence of its history and literature. The overt espousal of too many new features, and with it the overt lifting of too many hitherto sub-standard features to standard rank may easily constitute too rapid an evolution.

In such matters, it may indeed be best to 'leave your language alone'. For language has a way of sifting and refining its components that is amazingly effective. If a conspicuous new slang item, for instance, meets a felt need, it becomes indispensable and is adopted into the language. If an old sub-standardism works its slow way up through the levels of society to the level where most of the educated people live and speak, it too will be finally accepted. *Al'lies*, as contrasted with *allies'*, reached the upper level in sufficient strength during World War II to become permanently entrenched. Even so radical a change as the reversal of the meaning of a word, if repeated often enough at the highest educational level, may gain permanent acceptance. Before the days of the old League of Nations, the word *sanction*, within the speech community of this writer, carried the ethic meaning of validation and approbation; at about the time the League applied legal sanctions to Italy in the Ethiopian incident, the meaning of the word in that community changed to the legal one of coercion and disapprobation. By tacit compromise, the old meaning survived, however, alongside the new, for occasional use.

Changes of all sorts carry with them their own promotional forces. Language, if left alone, musters its own forces of resistance to change. If an innovation can survive the test of indispensability at the levels of history and literature where language itself chiefly survives, it is 'in'; if it cannot, it is 'out'. Such a resolution of thesis and antithesis into synthesis by gradual acceptance, by denial, or by compromise, is, in language as in politics, good democracy.

Nothing in the foregoing suggests in the least degree the desirability of slackening the exciting programme of research, experiment, and discovery in the field of linguistics, *a science*, which may and should continually exchange information with, but not encroach upon, rhetoric, *an art*. For 'in some respects linguistics has developed more precise methods and attained more definitive results than any other science dealing with human behaviour'.[20]

*Notes*

[1] Cf. C. M. Wise, Review of *Readings in Applied Linguistics* (New York: Appleton-Century-Crofts, 1958, Harold B. Allen, Editor), in *Southern Speech Journal*, XXIV, Summer, 1959, 250–253. Quoted by permission.

[2] Leonard Bloomfield, *Language*, New York, 1933.

[3] R. Kent, Review of Bloomfield, *Language*, *Language*, X, 1934, 40–48; G. M. Bolling, Review of Bloomfield, *Language* (English Edition), *Language*, XI, 1935, 251–252.

[4] Bernard Bloch and George L. Trager, *Outline of Linguistic Analysis*, Special Publication of the Linguistic Society of America, Austin, Texas, 1942.

[5] Trager and Henry Lee Smith, 'An Outline of English Structure', *Studies in Linguistics, Occasional Papers*, III, Norman, Oklahoma, 1951.

[6] Henry Sweet, 'History of English Sounds from the Earliest Period', in Series D, Publications of the English Dialect Society, from the *Transactions of the Philological Society for 1873–1874*, London, 1874, 70.

[7] Archibald A. Hill, 'Linguistics since Bloomfield', *Quarterly Journal of Speech*, XLI, 1955, 253–260.

[8] H. A. Gleason, *An Introduction to Descriptive Linguistics*, New York, 1955, 38.

[9] Trager and Bloch, *Language*, XVII, 1941, 224–246.

[10] E. Haugen and W. F. Twaddell, *Language*, XVIII, 1942, 228–237.

[11] H. Kurath, *Language*, XXXIII, 1957, 111–122.

[12] J. Sledd, *Language*, XXXIV, 1958, 252–258.

[13] Kurath, *Language*, XXXIV, 1958, 259–260.

[14] Charles C. Fries, 'Meaning and Linguistic Analysis', *Language*, XXX, 1954, 57–68.

[15] George P. Faust, 'Basic Tenets of Structural Linguistics', *College Composition and Communication*, IV, 1953, 122–125.

[16] Fries, *The Structure of English*, New York, 1952, 71.

[17] Sumner Ives, 'Linguistics in the Classroom', *College English*, XVII, 1955, 165–172.

[18] Archibald A. Hill, 'Prescriptivism and Linguistics in English', *College English*, XV, 1953–1954, 395–399.

[19] James B. McMillan, 'Summary of Nineteenth-Century Historical and Comparative Linguistics', *College Composition and Communication*, V, 1954, 140–149.

[20] Gleason, *Descriptive Linguistics*, Hartford, Connecticut, 1955, 11.

# Syllable Quantity and Enclitics in English

DAVID ABERCROMBIE

It is a necessary consequence of the fact that English is a language which is spoken with a stress-timed rhythm [1] that its syllables are of uneven length. It is usually held, though, that there is nothing systematic about the way that the length of its syllables varies, and that there are no laws to be discovered behind the variation. As Catherine Ing says, 'English syllables have not in natural speech any consistent relations to each other in quantity.'[2] The present paper is tentative, and deliberately skirts round a number of problems, but it expresses the belief that there *are* consistent relations of quantity to be found between English syllables, and that these relations are quite important in the phonetics and phonology of English.

In spite of the widely-held conviction that English syllable-quantity cannot be systematized, a number of writers have at times, and for various reasons, given fairly precise indications of relative syllable lengths, usually by means of musical notation. Daniel Jones, for instance, has shown certain syllable quantities in his *Outline of English Phonetics* from the first edition onwards.[3] Other writers who have done the same include D. S. MacColl, William Thomson, M. W. Croll, E. A. Sonnenschein, Thomas Taig, A. Classe, N. C. Scott, W. Jassem, W. S. Allen.[4] There is on the whole a remarkable degree of agreement among these writers in the quantities they allot to syllables (though they are not, for the most part, acquainted with each other's works). Most of them, however, make no attempt to work out the factors which determine the quantities, or to classify the patterns they form. Sonnenschein tried to formulate rules from which the quantity of any given syllable could be predicted, but although complex they do not account for many of the quantities he himself adduces. Daniel Jones [5] is an exception, however, and his rather brief discussion of the factors concerned has been well summarized by André Classe.[6] Jones's observations formed the starting point of my investigations, which will, I hope, themselves provide a basis for further research.

The main difficulty in the way of investigation always seems to have been the assumption that if rules are to be found for syllable quantity in English, they must be similar to the rules for syllable quantity in a language such as, say, Latin. In Latin (we are led to believe) the quantity of a syllable is a product of its phonematic structure, and all syllables of the same phonematic structure have the same quantity wherever they occur in the word or the utterance. This is not true of English, however, where, as Jones recognized, the same phonematic structure is by no means always accompanied by the same syllable quantity. Clearly, the factors are not so simple in English; in fact the phonematic structure of the syllable is of small importance, and may at times be quite irrelevant.

We need first, in English, to establish a unit within which, rhythmically, the syllable functions. I shall call this unit the *foot*, using the word as many, though certainly not all, writers on English prosody have. English utterances may be considered as being divided by the isochronous beat of the stress pulse into feet of (approximately) even length. Each foot starts with a stress and contains everything that follows that stress up to, but not including, the next stress. ˈ*This is the* ˈ*house that* ˈ*Jack* ˈ*built* has therefore four feet, and they can be most conveniently indicated by the use of vertical lines:

|This is the|house that|Jack|built|

The quantity of any syllable is a proportion of the total length of the foot within which the syllable occurs, and it is relative to the quantity of any other syllable in the foot. We cannot therefore say anything about the quantity of a syllable until we know its place in the foot.

Perhaps at this point a reminder should be issued, to prevent possible misunderstandings, that (1) syllable quantity is not directly dependent on either (a) vowel quantity or (b) stress; (2) the foot is independent of word boundaries.

It is clear that, since feet are of even length, as they must be if delimited by the isochronous stress pulse, the number of syllables in a given foot will have a direct effect on their length. In a monosyllabic foot the quantity of the syllable and the quantity of the foot coincide; here phonematic structure is totally irrelevant. In

|four|large|black|dogs|

every syllable has the same quantity, though their phonematic structures are very different. In a disyllabic foot it is obvious that neither syllable can be as long as the syllable in a monosyllabic foot; and in a trisyllabic foot some at least of the syllables must of necessity be shorter than those of a disyllabic foot. The number of syllables in the foot is, however, not the only thing which must be taken into account when establishing the quantity of a syllable. The often-quoted minimal pair of sentences produced by Scott[7]

take Grey to London
take Greater London

shows how two disyllabic feet, |*Grey to*| and |*Greater*|, having, moreover, the same phonematic structure /greitə/, may be composed of clearly different syllable quantities. An examination of types of disyllabic feet will provide the simplest illustration of the principles underlying syllable quantity in English (as exemplified in my own pronunciation).

For the purposes of analysis it is convenient to regard disyllabic feet as being in *triple* time; that is to say a foot is to be looked on as containing three units of time, between which the syllables are divided (as compared with *duple* or common time, when the foot contains two or four units of time). This is probably no more than a convenience, largely of notation. (I believe it to be characteristic of prose and conversation that one cannot tell whether the time is duple or triple – it is constantly ambiguous in this respect; whereas the time of verse is usually clearly heard to be either the one or the other, even though occasionally it may be necessary to wait a line or two after the beginning of a poem before being sure.)

There are three types of disyllabic foot. The first, which we may call Type A, has a short syllable followed by a long syllable, that is to say, in musical notation, ♩ 𝅗𝅥, or 1 time-unit followed by 2 time-units. Examples are |*shilling*|, |*never*|, |*atom*|, |*cuckoo*|. I shall represent the syllable quantities of this foot as ∪ —, making use of the symbols of traditional metrical notation, in spite of their misuse these days, and intending that they should be taken literally. A convenient name for it is a 'short-long' foot (it is a pity we cannot call it an 'iamb', which, in the original sense of that word, it is; but it would probably be too confusing).

Many people find the syllable quantities of feet of this type difficult to hear at first, though their existence has often been pointed out (see, e.g., Sweet[8] and many of the writers quoted above in the second paragraph). There is often felt to be something anomalous in a syllable which is stressed and yet short, followed by an unstressed one which is long. Sweet considered (see Sonnenschein[9]) that this relation of quantities goes back a long way in English, and accounts for the retention of the final *u* in OE *scipu* as compared with its loss in *hus* or *word*. My impression is that nowadays there are some types of English where Type A is not found.

The second type of disyllabic foot, Type B, contains two syllables of equal length, ♩. ♩., or 1½ time-units followed by 1½ time-units. Examples are |*greater*|, |*firmly*|, |*centre*|, de|*cisive*|, |*matches*|. The traditional metrical notation does not provide us with a symbol for this syllable quantity, but a satisfactory one can easily be invented by turning the 'short' symbol upside-down, ∩. The foot can thus be represented as ∩ ∩. It is convenient to call this an 'equal-equal' foot (we could not really call it a spondee, even if the term was not spoilt, since a spondee is essentially a foot in duple time).

These two types of feet, therefore, give us three different syllable quantities:

| | | | |
|---|---|---|---|
| ∪ | short | ♩ | 1 time-unit |
| ∩ | medium | ♩. | 1½ time-units |
| — | long | 𝅗𝅥 | 2 time-units |

It is clear, also, that a third type of foot is possible, which we can call Type C, 'long-short', or 𝅗𝅥 ♩. Examples are |*Grey to*|, |*tea for*| two, I'll| see you a|*gain to*|morrow, per|*haps I*| did. (We had better not call this a 'trochee', for the same reason that 'iamb' is best avoided.)

The three types of disyllabic foot, therefore, are:

A ∪ —
B ∩ ∩
C — ∪

We must now consider the factors on which syllable quantities in a disyllabic foot depend. Type C is the simplest case: the quantities — ∪ depend on the presence of a *word-boundary* within the foot, as can be inferred from the examples given above. In this type of disyllabic foot, therefore, the phonematic structure of the syllables plays no part in determining their quantity. (We shall see below that, while the quantities of a Type C foot always imply a word-division between the two syllables, there are certain conditions under which such a word-division does not imply Type C quantities.)

A foot of the two remaining types, Type A and Type B, must consist either of a two-syllable word with the stress on the first syllable, or of the last two syllables of a penultimately-stressed longer word. In these cases the syllable quantities depend on phonematic structure. Three possible phonematic structures of the foot are concerned, and they may be represented in the following formulae, in which C = any consonant; (C) means that the presence or absence of a consonant is immaterial; V = any vowel or diphthong, or a syllabic liquid; $V^1$ = the so-called 'short' vowels (i.e., in the traditional Jones numbering, numbers 2, 3, 4, 6, 8, 10); $V^2$ = the so-called 'long' vowels and the diphthongs (numbers 1, 5, 7, 9, 11, and 13–21):

(i) (C)$V^1$CV(C)
(ii) (C)VCC(C)V(C)
(iii) (C)$V^2$(C)V(C)

Examples of structure (i), which produces a foot of Type A, are *meadow*, *record*, *silly*, together with the other examples of Type A given above. Examples of structure (ii) are *limpid*, *fainting*, *youngster*, and examples of structure (iii) are *drawing*, *open*, *orchard*; both structures produce a foot of Type B, and further examples of both have been given above.

There is a greater variety of syllable-quantity patterns in trisyllabic feet. The syllable quantities can clearly be heard to be different in, for example, each of the following feet:

|*one for the*| road
|*anything*| more
|*seven o'*|clock
|*after the*|war
|*nobody*| knows

The factors which govern these quantities are of the same sort as in the case of disyllabic feet; but there is no need to discuss in detail how they apply. Here too word-division plays an important part, and it does in still longer feet also.

There are times, however, when the presence of a word-boundary within a foot does not produce the syllable quantities expected. |*Stop her*|, for example, is Type A (as Sweet on more than one occasion pointed out), and |*take it*| is Type B: that is to say, the phonematic structure in both of these examples has determined the syllabic quantities, just as if there was no word-boundary. *Her* and *it*, in other words, are *enclitics*, in these particular feet.

The most frequent occasions on which such enclitics are found occur when a verb is immediately followed within a foot by a pronoun of any kind, whether object, as in the two preceding examples, or subject, as in |*did he*|, or indirect object, as in |*tell him*|. *There* seems to be invariably enclitic in |*is there*|, |*may there*|, and similar constructions. *Of* is sometimes enclitic, as for example in |*piece of*|, but the conditions under which this happens are not entirely clear. It is of interest that enclitics may be revealed by factors other than rhythmic ones; for instance in |*feel it*|, where *it* is enclitic and the foot is Type B, the [l] is a 'clear' one as in *feeling*, and clearly distinguished from the [l] in: (I may not look ill but I) |*feel ill*|.

I was led to investigate the problem of syllable quantity as a result of having to lecture to foreign students of English on the structure of verse, and having, because of their mistakes in reading verse, to examine it somewhat more closely than would have been necessary with native English speakers. It now seems to me impossible to give an adequate account of English prosody for any purpose without taking syllable quantities into account – since the rhythm of verse is a rhythm in time. Syllable quantity is of interest in other connections too, however, and a consideration of it may help to throw light on disputed points. It is worth noting, for example, that in my pronunciation *matches* [matʃiz], *fetches* [fetʃiz] are feet of Type B, i.e. for me [tʃ] functions as CC and not C, so that the syllables are of structure (ii) above, and not (i); and the same applies to [dʒ]. (I have observed, moreover, that for a number of people the vowel [a] is $V^2$ and not $V^1$, as shown by the syllable quantities of the feet in which it occurs.)

The difference between $V^1$ and $V^2$ in a monosyllabic foot of the structure (C)VC is, as is well known, a difference which manifests itself over almost the whole word, being apparent in the length of C as much as in the length of V: compare *slip* and *sleep*. It is not so often pointed out that in *slipper* : *sleeper* the difference here too manifests itself over most of the word: it is true that the first vowel in *slipper* is shorter than the first in *sleeper*, but the second vowel in *slipper* is longer than the second in *sleeper* (at least in my pronunciation and that of others who speak like me). The use of the terms 'short vowel' and 'long vowel' for $V^1$ and $V^2$ is thus to some extent misleading, and it is better to think of $V^1$ as producing, when in the first syllable of a structure (C)VCV(C), the quantities ∪ —, and of $V^2$ as producing, in the same structure, the quantities ∩ ∩.

I have found it worth while drawing the attention of foreign learners of English to this point, the common mispronunciation of e.g. *ceasing* as — ∪ being often due to no more than taking 'long' as opposed to 'short' vowel too literally (a misunderstanding which may be reinforced by transcription). More serious rhythmic difficulties, of course, arise for many learners of English. Speakers of syllable-timed languages inevitably have trouble in establishing the foot as a unit in their speech.

Speakers of stress-timed languages too have their difficulties, though the foot itself is not a problem. Many Scandinavian learners, for example, consistently use (following the patterns of their mother tongue) Type B feet instead of Type A. Such a mistake is perhaps not very serious as far as intelligibility goes; more troublesome is the common use by German speakers of Type C feet instead of Type B, which misleads the listener into thinking a word-division is present. Difficulties of this sort seem more easily discussed in terms of syllable quantities than segment quantities.

Finally one might mention that considerable variation is found in syllable-quantity patterns among the various accents of Standard English, and in English dialects. In Yorkshire, for instance, a word such as *Peter* is said with the quantities — ∪, while the same word in Lowland Scots has the quantities ∪ —. It may be that the RP pattern for this and other similar words, ∩ ∩, is one of the most characteristic things about RP.

*Notes*

[1] The earliest person I know to draw attention to this fact is Joshua Steele in *An Essay towards Establishing the Melody and Measure of Speech*, London, 1775. Among later writers Coventry Patmore is noteworthy: 'A simple series of isochronous intervals, marked by accents, is as natural to spoken language as an even pace is to walking' ('English Metrical Critics', *The North British Review*, XXVII, 1857, 127–161). The convenient terms 'syllable-timed' and 'stress-timed' for what Lloyd James (in *Speech Signals in Telephony*, London, 1940, 25) called 'machine-gun rhythm' and 'morse-code rhythm' are due to K. L. Pike (see *The Intonation of American English*, Ann Arbor, 1946, 35).

[2] *Elizabethan Lyrics*, London, 1952, 195. She falls into the common error, when arguing this view, of equating syllable quantity with vowel quantity.

[3] See p. 109 of the first edition (Leipzig, 1918: mostly in print by 1914). In later editions Jones rather guardedly says that the quantities shown 'are not the lengths of the syllables but the lengths separating the "stress-points" or "peaks of prominence" of the syllables'.

[4] D. S. MacColl, 'Rhythm in English Verse, Prose, and Speech', *Essays and Studies*, v, Oxford, 1914; William Thomson, *The Rhythm of Speech*, Glasgow, 1923; M. W. Croll, *The Rhythm of English Verse*, Princeton, 1925; E. A. Sonnenschein, *What is Rhythm?*, Oxford, 1925; Thomas Taig, *Rhythm and Metre*, Cardiff, 1929; A. Classe, *The Rhythm of English Prose*, Oxford, 1939; N. C. Scott, 'Distinctive Rhythm', *Le Maître Phonétique*, 1940, 6; W. Jassem, *Intonation of Conversational English*, Wroclaw, 1952, 41; W. S. Allen, *Living English Speech*, London, 1954.

[5] *Outline of English Phonetics*, 3rd ed., Cambridge, 1932.

[6] *The Rhythm of English Prose*, 102.

[7] 'Distinctive Rhythm', *Le Maître Phonétique*, 1940, 6.

[8] H. Sweet, *A New English Grammar*, Oxford, 1892, 300.

[9] *What is Rhythm?*, 136.

# L'accentuation Lexicale des Polysyllabes Anglais: Finales à Accentuation Fixe[1]

GEORGES BERTRAND

Nous ne nous occuperons que de l'accentuation lexicale (*word-stress*), et nous excluons en principe de notre étude les mots qui sont formés de plusieurs autres mots anglais (*blackbird, seaside, arm-chair, old-fashioned, ill-treat, go on, will-o'-the-wisp*, etc.). Nous nous fonderons sur l'usage des milieux cultivés du sud de l'Angleterre, tel qu'il est enregistré dans le *English Pronouncing Dictionary* (*E P D*).[2]

Certaines terminaisons semblent appeler l'accent à une place déterminée à partir de la fin du mot: dernière syllabe, pénultième, antépénultième, etc. Il s'agit d'une part de finales orthographiques n'ayant guère de sens propre: *..ion, ..eral, ..itive*, etc.; d'autre part de racines grecques ou latines, comme *..fy, ..potent, ..phone, ..scopy*, qui, jointes à d'autres racines de même origine, constituent des composés plus ou moins savants: *qualify, omnipotent, telephone, spectroscopy*.

Pour chaque finale, on trouvera ci-dessous (1) le nombre approximatif des mots qui obéissent à la règle et figurent dans le dictionnaire de Walker et Dawson[3]; (2) (en minuscules) une liste d'exemples[4]; (3) (en MAJUSCULES, et quand il y a lieu) la liste, aussi complète que possible, des exceptions.[5]

Cet ensemble de quelque 150 finales à accentuation fixe est naturellement trop complexe pour être assimilé rapidement: il appartiendra à chaque utilisateur de dégager les éléments les plus intéressants pour lui, compte tenu de ses connaissances ou des connaissances de ses élèves. Des finales comme *-ion, -ical, -ity*, pourront faire l'objet de remarques ou exercices dès le premier cycle de l'enseignement secondaire; d'autres seront réservées aux niveaux supérieurs. L'intérêt pratique de chaque règle n'est d'ailleurs mesuré que très grossièrement par le nombre des mots qu'elle commande; de même, la gravité des exceptions ne dépend pas seulement de leur nombre, mais aussi des coefficients de fréquence, qui sont parfois extrêmement faibles.

## PREMIER GROUPE

Ce groupe comprend des finales 'non signifiantes' qui comportent toutes un *i*, un *e*, ou un *u*, suivis d'une autre voyelle; l'accent frappe la syllabe qui les précède immédiatement.[6]

280 ..ˈ– ia  ˈhernia, ˈfuchsia [ˈfjuːʃə]; Aˈrabia, magˈnolia, (fanˈtasia), neuˈralgia, Tiˈtania, Vicˈtoria, seˈquoia [siˈkwɔiə]; alleˈluia, Oceˈania, Philaˈdelphia, Pennsylˈvania, septiˈcaemia; encycloˈpaedia, pharmacoˈpoeia.

*Exc. en* [.. – ˈiːə] *ou* [.. – ˈiə]: MAˈRIA (*nom latin*), MAˈFIA, RATAˈFIA, LATAˈKIA, AVAˈNIA.

*Exc. en* [.. – ˈaiə]: MAˈRIA (*nom anglais*), SOˈPHIA,[7] THAˈLIA, IPHIGEˈNIA, PERIPEˈT(E)IA.

28 ..ˈ– iac  ˈzodiac, ˈmaniac, amˈmoniac, (ceˈleriac), paraˈnoiac, aphroˈdisiac.

*Exc.:* ELEˈGIAC [eliˈdʒaiək].

350 ..ˈ– ial  ˈgenial (*sympathique*), ˈaerial[8]; proˈvincial, meˈmorial,
19 ..ˈ– ialize  maˈterial, coˈlonial, colˈloquial, inˈdustrial; cir-
18 ..ˈ– ialist  cumˈstantial, testiˈmonial; *et leurs dérivés en ..ize,*
50 ..ˈ– ialism  *..ist, ..ism, quand ils existent.*

*Exc.* (*toutes en* [– ˈaiəl]: GEˈNIAL (*terme anatomique*), DEˈNIAL, REˈTRIAL, MISˈTRIAL, ESˈPIAL.

12 ..ˈ– real  ˈureal; veˈnereal, marˈmoreal; (in)corˈporeal.

*Exc.:* UNˈREAL, (EMPYˈREAL).

60 ..ˈ– ual  ˈusual, ˈequal, conˈtinual, perˈpetual;
10 ..ˈ– ualize  ˈvisual(ize);
8 ..ˈ– ualist  indiˈvidual(ist),
6 ..ˈ– ualism  intelˈlectual(ism).

*Exc.:* ˈSPIRITUAL *et ses dérivés en ..ize, ..ist, ..ism;* SUBˈDUAL.

6 ..ˈ– eant  ˈpageant, ˈsergeant; ˈmiscreant [ˈmiskrĭənt].

520 ..ˈ– ian  ˈFabian; Aˈrabian, muˈsician, Caˈnadian, coˈme-
6 ..ˈ– ianize  dian, liˈbrarian, Eˈgyptian; elecˈtrician, phone-
50 ..ˈ– ianism  ˈtician; necessiˈtarian; valetudiˈnarian; ˈchrist-ianize; tracˈtarianism.

*Exc.:* THAˈLIAN [θəˈlaiən].

8 ..ˈ – iar peˈculiar, faˈmiliar;
3 ..ˈ – iarize faˈmiliarize;
3 ..ˈ – iarist ˈplagiarist;
2 ..ˈ – iarism ˈplagiarism.

40 ..ˈ – iary ˈaviary; auˈxiliary, inˈcendiary; interˈmediary, peniˈtentiary; plenipoˈtentiary.

8 ..ˈ – iery ˈsoldiery, ˈcolliery, ˈhosiery.

16 ..ˈ – uary ˈestuary, ˈsanctuary, ˈJanuary; oˈbituary, voˈluptuary; usuˈfructuary.

*Exc.:* ˈRELIQUARY, ˈANTIQUARY.[9]

110 ..ˈ – iate[10] ˈsatiate, ˈdeviate; apˈpreciate, reˈtaliate, imˈmediate,
25 ..ˈ – iator subˈstantiate; (in)apˈpropriate, interˈmediate; ˈra-
18 ..ˈ – iatory diator, neˈgotiator; ˈexpiatory, proˈpitiatory;
18 ..ˈ – iative ˈpalliative, iˈnitiative.

28 ..ˈ – uate[10] ˈgraduate; exˈtenuate, acˈcentuate; supeˈrannuate;
5 ..ˈ – uator conˈtinuator, eˈvacuator;
4 ..ˈ – uative conˈtinuative.

*Exc.:* ˈANTIQUATE(D), (IN)ˈADEQUATE, LIˈQUATE, EˈQUATE; EˈQUATOR.

75 ..ˈ – ient ˈorient, omˈniscient, (in)efˈficient, (in)conˈvenient;
36 ..ˈ – ience ˈprescience [ˈpresĭəns], oˈbedience, (in)exˈperience;
22 ..ˈ – iency ˈpruriency, efˈficiency.

30 ..ˈ – io ˈstudio, ˈratio, ˈradio; Onˈtario, portˈfolio; impreˈsario, oraˈtorio.

*Exc.:* OˈHIO, ˈCHEERIˈO.

2300 ..ˈ – ion[11] ˈration, ˈnation; batˈtalion, comˈpanion, ocˈcasion,
6 ..ˈ – ionize dicˈtation, diˈvision, oˈpinion, doˈminion, con-
80 ..ˈ – ionist ˈfusion; eduˈcation, appreˈhension; pronunciˈa-
19 ..ˈ – ionism tion, examiˈnation, infatuˈation, accentuˈation;
multipliˈcation; demoraliˈzation; Americaniˈzation; revoˈlution(ize); ilˈlusion(ist), eloˈcution(ist); imˈpression(ism).

*Exc.:* OˈRION, ˈDANDELION, (ˈTELEVISION).

18 ..ˈ–ioner ˈstationer; paˈrishioner; exeˈcutioner; ˈstationery;
2 ..ˈ–ionery conˈfectionery.

40 ..ˈ–ionary ˈdictionary, ˈstationary; preˈcautionary; revoˈlutionary.

16 ..ˈ–ionable ˈfashionable; (un)ˈconscionable; (un)exˈceptionable; ˈquestionably; obˈjectionably.
8 ..ˈ–ionably

140 ..ˈ–ional ˈnational, ˈregional; ocˈcasional, meˈridional;
11 ..ˈ–ionalize constiˈtutional; (un)denomiˈnational; (inter)-
12 ..ˈ–ionalist ˈnational(ize); ˈrational(ist);
15 ..ˈ–ionalism senˈsational(ism).

9 ..ˈ–ionate[10] (com)ˈpassionate; (dis)proˈportionate;
1 ..ˈ–ionative oˈpinionative.

25 ..ˈ–eon ˈgalleon, ˈOdeon, chaˈmeleon, Naˈpoleon; ˈpigeon, ˈluncheon, esˈcutcheon.

*Exc.:* ˈHABERGEON, (PANˈTHEON).

10 ..ˈ–ior ˈjunior; suˈperior;

4 ..ˈ–iour ˈsaviour; (mis)beˈhaviour.

240 ..ˈ–ious ˈspecious, ˈobvious, ˈimpious [ˈimpĭəs]; obˈsequious, deˈlicious; consciˈentious, sacriˈlegious [ˌsækriˈlidʒəs]; supposiˈtitious [səˌpəziˈtiʃəs].

180 ..ˈ–eous ˈhideous; erˈroneous, couˈrageous; advanˈtageous [ˌædvənˈteidʒəs], simulˈtaneous; contempoˈraneous.

40 ..ˈ–uous ˈarduous; inˈgenuous, temˈpestuous, suˈperfluous; (in)conˈspicuous.

*Exc.:* ˈSPIRITUOUS; ˈSILIQUOUS; VENˈTRILOQUOUS, SOMˈNILOQUOUS.

10 ..ˈ–ius ˈgenius, deˈnarius, Stradiˈvarius.

200 ..ˈ–ium ˈmedium; geˈranium, aˈquarium; aluˈminium[12]; epithaˈlamium.

3 ..ˈ–uum ˈvacuum, reˈsiduum.

## DEUXIÈME GROUPE

Nous y classons les finales 'non-signifiantes' qui ne relèvent pas du premier groupe: ou bien (et c'est le cas général) elles ne comportent ni *i*, ni *e*, ni *u* prévocaliques, ou bien (comme ..ˈ *iacal*) elles fixent l'accent ailleurs que sur la syllabe qui précède *i*, *e*, ou *u* prévocaliques.

### *Sous-groupe A*

(Accent sur la dernière syllabe)

40 ..ˈeer caˈreer; engiˈneer, pioˈneer, volunˈteer, auctioˈneer, mountaiˈneer; electioˈneer.
*Exc.:* ˈMAHSEER; ˈREINDEER, ˈKILLDEER; ˈOVERSEER

15 ..ˈesce acquiˈesce.[13]

20 ..ˈese[14] oˈbese [ouˈbiːs], ˈChiˈnese, Japaˈnese, ˈjournaˈlese, (mangaˈnese).
*Exc.:* ˈDIOCESE [ˈdaiəsis] *ou* [ˈdaiəsiːs]; ˈCHERSONESE [ˈkəːsəniːs]; ˈPELOPONNESE.

20 ..ˈesque groˈtesque, burlesque; araˈbesque, pictuˈresque.

70 ..ˈette bruˈnette, gaˈzette; suffraˈgette, cigaˈrette, chemiˈsette.
*Exc.:* ˈPALETTE; ˈOMELETTE (*qui s'écrit aussi* omelet).

20 ..ˈelle gaˈzelle, aquaˈrelle, immorˈtelle, mademoiˈselle.
*Exc.:* ˈFILOSELLE.

15 ..ˈique oˈblique, uˈnique, anˈtique; Martiˈnique.

3 ..ˈigue faˈtigue, inˈtrigue.

20 ..ˈoo bamˈboo, yaˈhoo, shamˈpoo, tatˈtoo; cockaˈtoo, kangaˈroo.[15]
*Exc.:* ˈCUCKOO, ˈIGLOO, ˈBABOO, ˈKOODOO, ˈVOODOO, ˈHOODOO, ˈGOO-GOO.

60 ..ˈoon bufˈfoon, tyˈphoon, saˈloon, balˈloon, Walˈloon, carˈtoon; pantaˈloon.
*Exc.:* PROTOˈZOON [ˌproutəˈzouən] *et autres mots en* ..ZOON; *composés comme* ˈTEASPOON, ˈHONEYMOON.

25 ..ˈain *seulement pour les verbes, prononcé* [..ˈein]; obˈtain, mainˈtain, resˈtrain, enˈgrain; enterˈtain, ascerˈtain, apperˈtain.

*Exc.:* ˈBARGAIN, ˈCAPTAIN, ˈCURTAIN.[16]

120 ..ˈade *généralement prononcé* [ɑːd] *dans* chaˈrade, (promeˈnade), fanfaroˈnade;

*généralement prononcé* [eid] *dans* cruˈsade, perˈsuade [pəˈsweid], sereˈnade, (esplaˈnade), harlequiˈnade.

*Exc.:* ˈMARMALADE, ˈRENEGADE, ˈALIDADE, (ˈDECADE); ˈCOMRADE; ˈCENTIGRADE *et autres mots en* ..GRADE; ˈSUNSHADE *et autres composés.*

*Sous-groupe B*

(Accent sur la pénultième)

15 ..ˈator *pour les trisyllabes*[17]: creˈator, Eˈquator, tesˈtator, narˈrator.

*Exc.:* ˈORATOR, ˈSENATOR, ˈBARRATOR.

12 ..ˈato poˈtato; toˈmato, pizziˈcato, inamoˈrato.

8 ..ˈatum ˈdatum, poˈmatum, (ˈsubˈstratum), ultiˈmatum.

12 ..ˈatus ˈstatus; hiˈatus; appaˈratus.

60 ..ˈitis bronˈchitis; meninˈgitis, tonsilˈlitis; appendiˈcitis; ˈpoliomyeˈlitis.

70 ..ˈosis neuˈrosis, hypˈnosis; diagˈnosis; apotheˈosis, tubercuˈlosis.

*Exc.:* AˈPODOSIS; ANAˈMORPHOSIS, (METAˈMORPHOSIS).

30 ..ˈoma ˈcoma; aˈroma, diˈploma, carciˈnoma.

60 ..ˈescence[18] acquiˈescence, adoˈlescence, acquiˈescent, ado-
60 ..ˈescent ˈlescent; *cf.* ..ˈ*esce, s.-gr. A.*

30 ..ˈoidal colˈloidal, (heliˈcoidal).

60 ..ˈental ˈmental; paˈrental; oriˈental, acciˈdental, departˈmental; (co)inciˈdental, experiˈmental.

15 ..ˈernal ˈvernal; eˈternal, maˈternal; sempiˈternal.

8 ..ˈetive[19] exˈpletive, (seˈcretive).

4 ..ˈotive ˈvotive, (e)ˈmotive.
*Exc.:* (ˈLOCOMOTIVE).

150 ..ˈ–(C)tive[20] obˈjective, atˈtractive, vinˈdictive, olˈfactive, persˈpective; atˈtentive, conˈsumptive, aˈbortive, exˈhaustive.
*Exc.:* ˈADJECTIVE, ˈSUBSTANTIVE,[21] ˈARCHITECTIVE; ˈSTUPEFACTIVE, ˈRAREFACTIVE, ˈPUTREFACTIVE, ˈLIQUEFACTIVE.

130 ..ˈ–sive (ex)ˈplosive; deˈcisive, ofˈfensive, exˈpensive; appreˈhensive; (in)compreˈhensive.
*Exc.:* ˈPURPOSIVE.

40 ..ˈ–sal ˈnasal; reˈprisal, proˈposal; uniˈversal.

40 ..ˈ(V)val[20] ˈoval; priˈmeval, apˈproval, arˈrival, aesˈtival, ginˈgival; adjecˈtival.
*Exc.:* ˈFESTIVAL, ˈCARNIVAL, ˈROUNCIVAL.

110 ..ˈ–(CC)ence[20] ˈabsence; conˈtingence, inˈsistence; corresˈpondence, adoˈlescence; (inter)deˈpendence.
*Exc.:* ˈEXCELLENCE; COMˈMENCE.

47 ..ˈ–ish *seulement pour les verbes*[22]: ˈvanquish; esˈtablish, diˈminish, deˈmolish, aˈbolish, reˈlinquish.
*Exc.:* IMˈPOVERISH.

1850 ..ˈ–ic[23] *seulement pour les adjectifs*[24]: ˈepic; arˈchaic, meˈlodic, paˈcific, terˈrific, straˈtegic, orˈganic, laˈconic, heˈroic, eˈlectric, draˈmatic, faˈnatic, aˈquatic, eˈxotic, giˈgantic, roˈmantic, aˈcoustic; teleˈgraphic, melanˈcholic, aposˈtolic, optiˈmistic; Napoleˈonic, characteˈristic.
*Exc.:* ˈCATHOLIC, (IM)ˈPOLITIC, ˈLUNATIC, ˈHERETIC, ˈARABIC, ˈCHIVALRIC, ˈCHOLERIC, THEˈODORIC, (CLIˈMACTERIC).

110 ..ˈ–ics ˈphysics; euˈgenics, phoˈnetics, staˈtistics; metaˈphysics, matheˈmatics.
*Exc.:* ˈPOLITICS.

60 ..ˈ-lla Valˈhalla, umˈbrella, ceˈdilla, coˈrolla, Abˈdulla; Cindeˈrella; sarsapaˈrilla.

20 ..ˈ-nna anˈtenna, hoˈsanna; bellaˈdonna.

*Sous-groupe C*

(Accent sur l'antépénultième)

20 ..ˈmentary[25] *s'il y a plus d'une syllabe avant cette terminaison*[26]: eleˈmentary, compliˈmentary, parliaˈmentary; integuˈmentary.

10 ..ˈiacal danˈdiacal; demoˈniacal; paradiˈsiacal.

50 ..ˈ-inal ˈcardinal, ˈvirginal; (pro)ˈnominal, abˈdominal, (inˈtestinal); (ab)oˈriginal.
*Exc.:* VAˈGINAL, ˈDISCIPLINAL, (DOCˈTRINAL), (OFFIˈCINAL); SYNˈCLINAL *et autres mots en* ..CLINAL.

23 ..ˈ-tural ˈguttural, conˈjectural, (super)ˈnatural, archiˈtectural.

50 ..ˈ-eral[25] ˈfederal, ˈvisceral; eˈphemeral; uniˈlateral.

25 ..ˈ-era[25] ˈcamera, ˈopera, eˈphemera, lepiˈdoptera.
*Exc.:* CHIˈMERA, CORDILˈLERA, (PHYLLOˈXERA).

9 ..ˈ-erent[25] ˈdeferent, (in)ˈdifferent, belˈligerent;
12 ..ˈ-erence ˈpreference, (in)ˈdifference, cirˈcumference.
*Exc.:* ˈVICEˈGERENT; INTERˈFERENCE; ADˈHERENT, ADˈHERENCE, *et les autres mots en* ..HERENT, ..HERENCE.

35 ..ˈ-(V)lent[20] ˈprevalent, ˈredolent, ˈinsolent, pulˈverulent;
25 ..ˈ-(V)lence ˈviolence, ˈindolence, ˈopulence, eˈquivalence.
*Exc.:* CONˈDOLENT, (CONˈDOLENCE); QUADRIˈVALENT, (TETRAˈVALENT); TRIˈVALENCE, QUADRIˈVALENCE, (TETRAˈVALENCE).

13 ..ˈ-ulant ˈstimulant; coˈagulant, nocˈtambulant;
3 ..ˈ-ulance ˈambulance, ˈpetulance.

9 ..ˈ-ola ˈcupola, ˈgondola, (ˈviola), roˈseola, paˈrabola.
*Exc.:* ANˈGOLA, PIAˈNOLA, SCAGˈLIOLA, GORGONˈZOLA.

36 ..ˈ–ula ˈformula; peˈninsula; aniˈmalcula; ˈregular, mo-
160 ..ˈ–ular ˈlecular, parˈticular, recˈtangular, perpenˈdicu-
120 ..ˈ–ulate[10] lar; ˈconsulate, ˈcalculate, gesˈticulate, arˈticulate, imˈmaculate.

7 ..ˈ–(C)uble[20] ˈchasuble, (in)ˈsoluble, (reˈsoluble), (indisˈsoluble).

160 ..ˈ–ible ˈedible, (im)ˈpossible, (il)ˈlegible, iˈrascible, perˈmissible, (ir)resˈponsible, (in)comˈpatible; (in)compreˈhensible.

*Exc.: les mots en* ..IGIBLE (*voir sous-groupe D*).

14 ..ˈ–acle ˈoracle, ˈmiracle, ˈobstacle, ˈspectacle; reˈceptacle.

*Exc.:* ˈTABERNACLE, DÉˈBÂCLE.

37 ..ˈ–icle ˈicicle, ˈvehicle, ˈarticle; conˈventicle, ciˈcatricle.

360 ..ˈ–ical[27] ˈmedical; theˈatrical, poˈlitical, gramˈmatical; umˈbilical (*comme terme mathématique*); psychoˈlogical, paraˈdoxical; architecˈtonical.

*Exc.:* UMBIˈLICAL [ˌʌmbiˈlaikl] (*comme terme médical*).

15 ..ˈ–ican[28] ˈpelican, ˈAnglican; Aˈmerican, reˈpublican.

16 ..ˈ–icant ˈapplicant, comˈmunicant, (in)siˈgnificant;

2 ..ˈ–icance (in)siˈgnificance.

10 ..ˈ–icist[27] ˈpublicist, emˈpyricist.

70 ..ˈ–icate[10] ˈabdicate, ˈsyndicate, (re)ˈduplicate, (ex)comˈmunicate, intercomˈmunicate.

75 ..ˈ–inate[10] ˈvaccinate, abominate, oˈriginate, (in)suˈbordinate, (in)disˈcriminate.

*Exc.:* ˈPEREGRINATE, ˈGLYCERINATE.

35 ..ˈ–itate[10] ˈimitate; haˈbilitate, preˈcipitate.

15 ..ˈ–itant (in)ˈhabitant, conˈcomitant, anˈnuitant; inˈheri-
7 ..ˈ–itance tance.

25 ..ˈ-itor[29] ˈeditor, ˈvisitor; soˈlicitor; primoˈgenitor;

50 ..ˈ-itive ˈpositive; inˈfinitive, inˈquisitive, comˈpetitive, inˈtuitive; philoproˈgenitive.

12 ..ˈ-(C)iture[30] ˈfurniture, disˈcomfiture, primoˈgeniture.

13 ..ˈ-(C)ury ˈcentury, ˈinjury.

5 ..ˈ-oury ˈarmoury, ˈsavoury; ˈbistoury [ˈbisturi].

1000 ..ˈ-ity[31] ˈbrevity; simˈplicity, uˈbiquity; spontaˈneity, intreˈpidity, elecˈtricity; superˈfluity; potentiˈality; (in)-comprehensiˈbility.

40 ..ˈ-ety[25] ˈfidgety, ˈrickety, ˈpiety; vaˈriety, saˈtiety, perˈnickety, enˈtirety; notoˈriety.

30 ..ˈ-asis ˈemphasis, peˈriphrasis; psoˈriasis, elephanˈtiasis.
*Exc.:* OˈASIS, OSTEOˈCLASIS.

7 ..ˈ-ison ˈvenison [ˈvenzn], ˈunison, comˈparison.
*Exc.:* IMˈPRISON.

13 ..ˈ--ene ˈgasolene, (ˈdamascene), aˈcetylene.
*Exc.:* NAZAˈRENE. Cf. ˈhygiene [ˈhaidʒiːn].

660 ..ˈ-(VC)ous *c'est-à-dire ..ous précédé d'une seule consonne*[32] ˈinfamous, (ˈdecorous), ˈvaporous, ˈmischievous; riˈdiculous, moˈnotonous, feˈlicitous, cirˈcuitous,[31] uˈbiquitous,[31] coˈniferous, carˈnivorous; multiˈtudinous, pusilˈlanimous.

*Exc. en* [..əs]: DEˈSIROUS, (SOˈNOROUS), CAˈNOROUS, MULTIˈFLOROUS *et autres mots en* ..FLOROUS, AˈNOUROUS, DEˈCLIVOUS, CAˈDUCOUS, TRIˈJUGOUS, POLYˈCHROMOUS, ˈPORCELAINOUS, STEATOˈPYGOUS, *et quelques autres mots très peu usités.*

*Exc. en* [..ouəs]: ANTIˈNOUS.

160 ..ˈ--ite *prononcé* [..ˈ--ait] *dans* ˈappetite, ˈsatellite, ˈanthracite, ˈIsraelite [ˈizriəlait], ˈaerolite [ˈɛərəlait], ˈMuscovite, cosˈmopolite, herˈmaphrodite, toˈxophilite, (ento)ˈparasite;

*généralement prononcé* [..ˈ--it] *dans* ˈapposite, ˈhypocrite, (ˈexquisite), ˈcomposite, ˈpreterite, ˈplebiscite; (in)ˈdefinite, (pre)ˈrequisite.

*Exc. en* [..ait] (*ou* [..it]): IMPOˈLITE; ˈREUˈNITE, ˈDISUˈNITE; (REˈCONDITE), INˈCONDITE; (ˈBIPARTITE), (ˈTRIPARTITE), ˈQUADRIˈPARTITE; ˈHETEROCLITE, ARCHIˈMANDRITE; *et quelques autres mots très peu usités.*
*Exc. en* [..iːt]: MARGUEˈRITE.
*Exc. en* [..aiti]: ˈAMPHITRITE, APHROˈDITE.
*Exc. en* [..iti]: BENEˈDICITE.

20 ..ˈ– – ute ˈabsolute, ˈprosecute, an ˈattribute, ˈconstitute, ˈprostitute, (ir)ˈresolute, eˈlectrocute.
*Exc.:* ˈDISREˈPUTE; CONˈTRIBUTE, (RE)DISˈTRIBUTE, to ATˈTRIBUTE.

50 ..ˈ– – ude ˈinterlude; ˈquietude, ˈmansuetude [ˈmænswitjuːd]; ˈsolitude, viˈcissitude, (in)eˈxactitude, (veri)siˈmilitude.

100 ..ˈ– – my ˈinfamy, poˈlygamy, aˈcademy, hoˈmonymy; physiˈognomy, (Deuteˈronomy).
*Exc.:* ˈTAXIDERMY; ˈPOLYCHROMY, ˈPHOTOCHROMY.

100 ..ˈ– – ny ˈagony, ˈebony, ˈcalumny; (ac)ˈcompany, moˈnotony, Eˈpiphany, caˈcophony, (misˈcellany); anthroˈpogeny.
*Exc.:* POˈLONY, GAˈLEENY, UNˈCANNY, MULLIGAˈTAWNY, ˈPICCANINNY; MNEMOˈTECHNY, PYROˈTECHNY; ˈIGNOMINY; ˈCEREMONY *et autres mots en* -MONY (*voir sous-groupe D*).

40 ..ˈ– – py philˈlanthropy, miˈsanthropy, alˈlotropy, enˈdoscopy, radiˈoscopy, radioˈtherapy.
*Exc.:* UNˈHAPPY, (ˈORTHOEPY), ˈPHOTOTYPY *et quelques autres mots très peu usités.*

120 ..ˈ– – try ˈindustry, ˈinfantry, ˈchemistry; iˈdolatry, psyˈchiatry, geˈometry; trigoˈnometry.
*Exc.:* RE-ˈENTRY; ˈCASUISTRY, ˈJESUITRY.

*Sous-groupe D*
(Accent sur la pré-antépénultième)

5 ..ˈ– mentary[25] *s'il y a une seule syllabe avant ..mentary.*[33] ˈmomentary, ˈcommentary, (ˈfragmentary).

8 ..ˈ-igible[34] ˈnegligible, (in)ˈeligible, (un)inˈtelligible.

2 ..ˈ-icanize[35] Aˈmericanize.

300 ..ˈ-ically[36] ˈlogically, ˈpractically; caˈtholically,[37] gramˈmatically; alleˈgorically, paraˈdoxically.

50 ..ˈ-icism[38] ˈcynicism, ˈcriticism; roˈmanticism, faˈnaticism, caˈtholicism.[37]

22 ..ˈ-itory[25] ˈdormitory, ˈterritory, (pre)ˈmonitory, supˈpository.

7 ..ˈ-utory[25] ˈstatutory, eˈxecutory, (circum)ˈlocutory.

5 ..ˈ-ulency ˈtruculency, ˈcorpulency.

8 ..ˈ--ature ˈliterature, ˈtemperature, (ˈjudicature).

*Exc.:* (CARICAˈTURE), (NOˈMENCLATURE), ENˈTABLATURE.

90 ..ˈ--ator *pour les mots de plus de 3 syllabes*[39]: ˈeducator, ˈalligator, ˈgladiator, (ˈconservator); peˈrambulator, conˈtinuator, deˈnominator.

*Exc.:* CONˈSPIRATOR, REˈMONSTRATOR; ˈMULTIPLICATOR, ˈVERSIFICATOR *et autres mots en* ..FICATOR.

40 ..ˈ--acy ˈintimacy, (ˈintricacy), (in)ˈefficacy,[40] (in)ˈaccuracy, (in)ˈdelicacy, eˈpiscopacy, (il)leˈgitimacy.

*Exc.:* SUˈPREMACY, DIˈPLOMACY, CONˈSPIRACY, INˈTESTACY; *et les mots en* ..CRACY.[41]

10 ..ˈ--mony[42] ˈacrimony, ˈpatrimony, ˈceremony.

*Exc.:* ˈDISˈHARMONY, (HEˈGEMONY).

*Sous-groupe E*

(Accent sur la 5ème syllabe à partir de la fin du mot)

4 ..ˈ-icanism[43] ˈAnglicanism, reˈpublicanism.

## TROISIÈME GROUPE

Beaucoup de mots plus ou moins savants sont formés de deux racines grecques (*telegram*, *philosophy*) ou latines (*qualify*, *agriculture*). C'est parfois leur premier élément qui détermine la place de l'accent (cf. ˈ*platinotype* à côté de *e*ˈ*lectrotype*), mais le deuxième élément est souvent décisif, et nous nous trouvons devant un troisième groupe de finales à accentuation fixe. Il s'agit cette fois de finales 'signifiantes' et non plus de groupes de lettres considérés indépendamment de leur valeur sémantique: *ˈhemisphere*, bien que terminé par *..here*, ne relève pas de la finale *..here* (coller), ni *acˈcustom*, *ˈChrysostom* ou *ˈplagiostome* de la finale *..tom(e)* (couper), ni *leafy* de la finale *..fy* (faire). Mais les risques de méprise sont restreints, la plupart des finales de ce groupe étant assez individualisées pour que de telles rencontres soient exceptionnelles.

Notons d'ailleurs que les règles relatives aux finales des premier et deuxième groupes restent valables (sauf exceptions déjà signalées) pour les mots dont nous nous occupons maintenant.[44] Bon nombre de finales du troisième groupe sont des cas particuliers de finales des deux autres groupes; nous ne chercherons pas à les relever toutes.

*Sous-groupe A*

(Accent sur la dernière syllabe)

3 ..ˈhere[45] adˈhere, coˈhere, inˈhere.

*Sous-groupe B*

(Accent sur la pénultième)

4 .. oˈrama dioˈrama, panoˈrama.

24 ..ˈmania
5 ..ˈmaniac klepto ˈmania(c), ˈangloˈmania, potichoˈmania, ˈmegaloˈmania(c), eˈleutheroˈmania.

15 ..ˈcidal[46] homiˈcidal, suiˈcidal; infantiˈcidal.

9 ..ˈhedral diˈhedral, tetraˈhedral;
13 ..ˈhedron rhomboˈhedron; dodecaˈhedron, icosaˈhedron.

4 ..ˈherent[47] inˈherent, (in)coˈherent;
4 ..ˈherence adˈherence, (in)coˈherence.

6 ..ˈflorous[48] triˈflorous, noctiˈflorous, calyciˈflorous.

13 ..ˈmorphous aˈmorphous, polyˈmorphous, anthropoˈmorphous.

4 ..ˈsaurus brontoˈsaurus, megaloˈsaurus, plesioˈsaurus.

8 ..ˈzoon [..zouən][49] protoˈzoon, spermatoˈzoon;
8 ..ˈzoa [..zouə] polyˈzoa, h(a)ematoˈzoa.

9 ..ˈrhoea diarˈrhoea, leucorˈrhoea, spermatorˈrhoea.

*Sous-groupe C*

(Accent sur l'antépénultième)

4 ..ˈcultural agriˈcultural, arboriˈcultural;
4 ..ˈculturist agriˈculturist, arboriˈculturist.

40 ..ˈgenesis ontoˈgenesis, epiˈgenesis, osteoˈgenesis;
24 ..ˈ– geny ˈprogeny, hisˈtogeny;
5 ..ˈ– genist abiˈogenist.
26 ..ˈ– genous inˈdigenous, auˈtogenous.

8 ..ˈonymy meˈtonymy, syˈnonymy, polyˈonymy;
9 ..ˈonymous aˈnonymous, syˈnonymous, eˈponymous;
10 ..ˈ– onym ˈhomonym, ˈsynonym, ˈpseudonym.

4 ..ˈpolitan metroˈpolitan, cosmoˈpolitan, Neaˈpolitan;
5 ..ˈ– polis meˈtropolis, neˈcropolis, Anˈnapolis, Indiaˈnapolis.

30 ..ˈ– cracy[50] deˈmocracy, buˈreaucracy, arisˈtocracy;
10 ..ˈ– – crat ˈdemocrat, ˈbureaucrat, ˈphysiocrat.
*Exc.:* (ˈARISTOCRAT).

130 ..ˈ– ferous coˈniferous, pesˈtiferous, odoˈriferous.

9 ..ˈ– gonal diˈagonal, poˈlygonal, ocˈtagonal;
13 ..ˈ– – gon ˈpolygon, ˈpentagon, doˈdecagon.

140 ..ˈ– graphy orˈthography, phoˈtography, dactyˈlography,
5 ..ˈ– graphist autobiˈography; teˈlegraphist, calˈligraphist;
21 ..ˈ– grapher biˈographer, phoˈtographer, lexiˈcographer;
80 ..ˈ– – graph ˈtelegraph, ˈparagraph, ˈphotograph, (tel)-
30 ..ˈ– – gram ˈautograph; ˈtelegram, ˈanagram, marˈconi-
gram; paralˈlelogram.
*Exc.:* ˈMETEOROGRAPH, (ˈIDEOGRAPH), (ˈIDEOGRAM).[51]

23 ..ˈ– latry iˈdolatry, Mariˈolatry, icoˈnolatry;
5 ..ˈ– latrous iˈdolatrous, bibliˈolatrous;
6 ..ˈ– later iˈdolater, ophiˈolater.

290 ..ˈ– logy biˈology, aˈnalogy, mineˈralogy, etyˈmology,
17 ..ˈ– logize pal(a)eonˈtology, epidemiˈology; ˈeulogize,
40 ..ˈ– logist aˈpologize; ˈeulogist, phiˈlologist, archaeˈologist,
4 ..ˈ– loger bacteriˈologist; asˈtrologer, hoˈrologer; aˈna-
13 ..ˈ– logous logous, hoˈmologous; ˈepilogue, ˈcatalogue,
11 ..ˈ– – logue ˈmonologue.[52]

5 ..ˈ– loquy ˈobloquy, soˈliloquy, venˈtriloquy;
2 ..ˈ– loquize soˈliloquize;
4 ..ˈ– loquist venˈtriloquist;
4 ..ˈ– loquent ˈeloquent, granˈdiloquent;
6 ..ˈ– loquence ˈeloquence, granˈdiloquence;
2 ..ˈ– loquous somˈniloquous.

170 ..ˈ– meter ˈammeter [ˈæmitə], diˈameter, therˈmometer, gal-
40 ..ˈ– metry vaˈnometer, potentiˈometer; ˈsymmetry, geˈometry, anthroˈpometry.

*Exc.:* ˈTAXIMETER, *et les multiples ou sous-multiples du mètre, qui d'ailleurs s'écrivent plutôt ..metre.*

22 ..ˈ– nomy eˈconomy, asˈtronomy, physiˈognomy, (Deute-
2 ..ˈ– nomize ˈronomy); eˈconomize;
8 ..ˈ– nomist auˈtonomist, aˈgronomist;
2 ..ˈ– nomer[53] asˈtronomer, gasˈtronomer;
2 ..ˈ– nomous auˈtonomous.

20 ..ˈ– pathy ˈsympathy, anˈtipathy, alˈlopathy, homoeˈopathy;
2 ..ˈ– pathize ˈsympathize, teˈlepathize; teˈlepathist, hyˈdro-
7 ..ˈ– pathist pathist, osteˈopathist; ˈneuropath, ˈpsychopath,
5 ..ˈ– – path (ˈhomeopath [ˈhoumjəpæθ]).

10 ..ˈ– phony ˈsymphony, caˈcophony, poˈlyphony;
2 ..ˈ– phonize ˈeuphonize;
3 ..ˈ– phonist teˈlephonist;
3 ..ˈ– phonous caˈcophonous, poˈlyphonous;
15 ..ˈ– – phone ˈtelephone, ˈxylophone, ˈhomophone, kaˈleido-
phone [kəˈlaidəfoun].

4 ..ˈ– potent ˈimpotent, omˈnipotent;
3 ..ˈ– potence ˈimpotence, omˈnipotence.[54]

*Exc.:* PREˈPOTENT, PREˈPOTENCE.

20 ..ˈ– scopy neˈcroscopy, specˈtroscopy, ophthalˈmoscopy;
2 ..ˈ– scopist miˈcroscopist;
50 ..ˈ– – scope ˈtelescope, ˈgyroscope, kaˈleidoscope [kəˈlaidəs-
koup], laˈryngoscope, poˈlariscope.

*Exc.: Quelques mots en ..scope qui sont très peu usités et ne se trouvent ni dans EPD, ni dans le Concise Oxford Dictionary.*[55]

5 ..ˈ – sophy   phiˈlosophy, theˈosophy;
2 ..ˈ – sophize   phiˈlosophize;
4 ..ˈ – sophist   gymˈnosophist;
3 ..ˈ – sopher   phiˈlosopher.

5 ..ˈ – strophe[56]   aˈpostrophe, caˈtastrophe.

10 ..ˈ – thesis   ˈsynthesis, ˈpro(s)thesis, anˈtithesis, paˈrenthesis.

50 ..ˈ – tomy   aˈnatomy, diˈchotomy, larynˈgotomy, arteriˈo-
5 ..ˈ – tomize   tomy; ˈatomize, eˈpitomize, phleˈbotomize;
6 ..ˈ – tomist   ˈatomist, aˈnatomist, liˈthotomist;
1 ..ˈ – tome[56]   eˈpitome;
6 ..ˈ – – tome[57]   ˈmicrotome;
1 ..ˈ – – tom   ˈdiatom.

28 ..ˈ – – cide[58]   ˈfratricide, ˈsuicide, inˈsecticide, paraˈsiticide.

150 ..ˈ – – fy[59]   ˈpurify, ˈjustify, (dis)ˈsatisfy, perˈsonify, diˈversify, eˈlectrify, soˈlidify, sylˈlabify.

*Sous-groupe* D
(Accent sur l'anté-prépénultième)

4 ..ˈ culturalist[60]   agriˈculturalist, arboriˈculturalist.

On aura remarqué que l'accent reste généralement au même endroit dans les membres *parisyllabiques* d'une même famille qui se terminent en *..ist*, *..ize*, *..y*, *..er*, et souvent *..ous*, alors qu'il se déplace par rapport aux racines quand certains suffixes viennent allonger le mot: *ˈphotograph, phoˈtographer*; *ˈtelegraph, teˈlegraphy*; *ˈmicroscope, miˈcroscopist*.

Les suffixes *..ly*, *..ness*, *..ing*, n'entraînent pas de tels déplacements d'accent: *diˈagonally*, *aˈnonymously*, *voˈciferousness*, *aˈpostrophizing*. De même, *..ism* laisse l'accent sur la même syllabe que dans le mot apparenté en *..ist*, *..ize*, ou *..y*: *cosmoˈpolitanism*, *paˈralogism*, *anˈtagonism*, *caˈtastrophism*.

*Notes*

[1] Nous espérons publier ultérieurement les chapîtres qui concernent (a) les finales sans influence sur la place de l'accent, (b) les préfixes, (c) les mots à accentuation variable selon le sens, (d) la signification accentuelle de certains redoublements consonantiques, (e) l'accent secondaire prétonique.

[2] Daniel Jones, *English Pronouncing Dictionary*, 11th Edn., London, 1958. Nous avons aussi consulté le *Concise Oxford Dictionary*, et le *Harrap's*.

[3] *The Rhyming Dictionary of the English Language, in which the whole language is arranged according to its terminations*, (Routledge & Kegan Paul, London). C'est grâce à ce dictionnaire, où les mots sont classés alphabétiquement selon leur orthographe inversée, que nous avons pu procéder à un contrôle assez sérieux de l'influence des différentes terminaisons sur la place de l'accent. Le contrôle eût été plus efficace si l'ouvrage de référence avait été moins imparfait, et nous nous permettons d'attirer l'attention des érudits et des éditeurs sur les services inappréciables qu'on pourrait attendre du Walker et Dawson s'il était révisé avec autant de soin que le EPD.

[4] *Emploi des parenthèses*: (a) lorsqu'un mot donné comme *exemple* est entre parenthèses, cela signifie que sa prononciation la plus usitée est conforme à la règle, bien qu'une ou plusieurs variantes y échappent; (b) lorsqu'une *exception* est entre parenthèses, c'est qu'il existe une variante conforme à la règle, mais relativement peu fréquente; (c) quand une *partie de mot* est entre parenthèses, il s'agit de deux formes orthographiques, ou de deux mots étroitement apparentés: *'visual(ize)* est mis pour *'visual, 'visualize.*

[5] Nous ne relèverons cependant pas comme exceptions les mots qui sont manifestement hors du champ d'application de la règle: *via* et *pious* ne peuvent évidemment pas être accentués sur la syllabe qui précède . . *ia* ou . . *ious.*

[6] De façon générale, l'accent porte souvent sur la syllabe qui précède un *i* prévocalique. Cette constatation a été présentée par F. Novion (*Les Mots Anglais*, Hachette, 1940) sous le nom de Règle CiV (Consonne + i + Voyelle). Mais ce n'est pas, à beaucoup près, une règle absolue; cf. *al'liance, re'liance, pro'prietor, Mes'siah, psy'chiatrist, 'justifiable, demo'niacal, so'ciety, an'xiety, cordi'ality, curi'osity, acqui'esce, scoli'osis, servi'ette...*

[7] *Sofia*, autrefois prononcé comme *Sophia*, est maintenant plus souvent accentué sur l'initiale.

[8] Normalement ['ɛərĭəl] en Angleterre; [ei'iːrĭəl] est archaïque, littéraire ou américain.

[9] Ce sont les seuls mots en *-quary* dans Walker et Dawson.

[10] La finale . . *ate* non accentuée se prononce [. . eit] dans les verbes, et aussi dans les noms ou adjectifs plus ou moins savants; elle se prononce [. . it] dans les noms et adjectifs du langage courant.

[11] Il semble que la syllabe qui précède le groupe . . *ion* . ., même non final, porte toujours un accent: accent secondaire si le mot se termine par . . *ic* (*ˌhistri'onic, imˌpressio'nistic, traˌditiona'listic*), par . . *ity* (*imˌpressiona'bility*) ou par un deuxième groupe . . *ion* (ˌfractio'nation, ˌnationali'zation); accent principal dans les autres cas.

[12] La forme américaine *a'luminum* ne se termine pas en . . *ium.*

[13] Les autres mots en . . *esce* sont peu usités, mais ont d'intéressants dérivés en . .*'escence*, . .*'escent* (voir s-gr. *B*).

[14] Cette finale se prononce généralement [. . iːz]; les mots ainsi terminés ont souvent deux syllabes accentuables, l'une ou l'autre pouvant prédominer selon le rythme de la phrase.

[15] *Cockatoo, kangaroo*, ont des variantes avec double accentuation; l'accentuation de *'Hin'doo* varie selon le rythme de la phrase.

[16] D'autre part, *overstrain*, et *re-strain* ont double accentuation.

[17] Les mots de plus de 3 syllabes relèvent du s.-gr. *D* (p. 233).

[18] ..'*escence* est un cas particulier de ..'-(*CC*)*ence* (s. gr. *B*).

[19] Cf. ..*itive*, s. gr. *C*, p. 232.

[20] (V) = lettre-voyelle quelconque. (C) = lettre-consonne quelconque.

[21] Avec variante *sub'stantive* en ce qui concerne l'adjectif; voir *EPD*.

[22] ..*ish* des adjectifs est sans influence sur la place de l'accent; ex. '*yellowish*, comme '*yellow*.

[23] L'accent porte sur la syllabe qui précède ..*ic*.. dans ..'–*ical*, ..'– *icist*, et 5 autres finales du s. gr. *C*, p. 231, dans ..'– *icanize*, ..'– *ically*, ..'– *icism* (s. gr. *D*), dans ..'– *icanism* (s. gr. *E*).

[24] Cf. les noms '*rhetoric*, '*bishopric*; et '*Homeric* (nom de bateau), '*arsenic* ['ɑːsnik], *a'rithmetic*, à côté des adjectifs *Ho'meric*, *ar'senic*(*al*), *arith'metic*(*al*).

[25] Pour la répartition des finales du deuxième groupe dans les sous-groupes, nous comptons pour une syllabe toute lettre-voyelle qui *peut* être syllabique dans la finale considérée, même si elle est souvent (voire toujours) élidée dans certains mots.

C'est le cas de *a* dans ..MENT*a*RY; de *e* dans ..*e*RA(L), ..*e*RENT, ..*e*RENCE, ..*e*TY (cf. *ninety*); de *o* dans ..IT*o*RY.

[26] Voir s. gr. *D* pour ..*mentary* précédé d'une seule syllabe.

[27] Cf. ..'– *ic*, s. gr. *B*. p. 229.

[28] Cf. ..'– *icanize*, (s. gr. *D*), et ..'– *icanism* (s. gr. *E*).

[29] Voir au s. gr. *D* la terminaison ..*itory*.

[30] Les seuls mots en ..(V)*iture* donnés par Walker et Dawson, '*forfeiture* et '*portraiture*, sont également accentués sur l'antépénultième, la voyelle précédant ..*iture* ne formant pas syllabe.

[31] Dans ..*uity*, ..*uitous*, *u* a valeur de voyelle, et forme syllabe, sauf pour ..*quity*, ..*quitous*. *Fruity* fait ['fruːti].

[32] Les mots en ..(CC)*ous* sont en majorité accentués sur la pénultième; (cf. *mo'mentous*, malgré '*moment*), mais il y a une importante minorité de mots accentués sur l'antépénultième (ex.: '*marvellous*). Pour ..(*V*)*ous*, voir 1er groupe, p. 226.

[33] Voir s. gr. *C*, p. 230, pour ..*mentary* précédé de plusieurs syllabes.

[34] Ce sont les seuls mots en ..*ible* qui ne soient pas accentués sur l'antépénultième (cf. s. gr. *C*, p. 231).

[35] Cf. ..' – *ican* (s. gr. *C*) et ..' – *icanism* (s. gr. *E*).

[36] Terminaison d'adverbes qui ne correspondent pas tous aux adjectifs en ..*ical* du s. gr. *C* (p. 231): l'adjectif en ..*ic* (cf. s. gr. *B*, p. 229) est parfois le seul usité.

[37] Malgré '*catholic*.

[38] Cf. ..' – *ic* (s. gr. *B*, p. 229) et ..' – *icist* (s. gr. *C*, p. 231).

[39] Cf. s. gr. *B*, p. 228, pour les mots de 3 syllabes; pour ..*iator* ..*uator*, voir 1er groupe p. 225.

[40] *Inefficacy*, *inaccuracy*, *indelicacy*, et *illegitimacy* ont dans *EPD* une variante avec deux accents principaux, dont un sur le préfixe.

[41] Voir groupe III *C*, p. 236.

[42] Cf. .. ' – *ny* (s. gr. *C*, p. 233).

[43] Cf. .. ' – *ican* (s. gr. *C*, p. 231), et .. ' – *icanize* (s. gr. *D*).

[44] L'accent porte donc sur la syllabe qui précède *i*, *e*, ou *u* prévocaliques dans *claustro'phobia*, *onomato'poeia*, *quin'quennial*, *super'ficial*, *rube'facient*, *tume'faction*, *animad'version*, *eu'phonious*, *mel'lifluous*, *mil'lennium*, etc. L'accent frappe la pénultième dans, *osteomye'litis*, *anasto'mosis*, *anachro'nistic*, *demo'cratic*, *anthropo-*

*'morphic..*; l'antépénultième dans *'chrysolite, a'nachronous, o'viparous, cos'mogony ge'otropy, ico'nolatry..*; la pré-antépénultième *dans 'pacificism.*

[45] Cf. *..'herent, ..'herence* (s. gr. *B*).

[46] Cf. ..' *-- cide*, s. gr. *C.*, p. 238.

[47] Cf. *..'here*, s. gr. *A*, et ..' *- erent*, ..' *- erence*, II*C* (p. 230).

[48] Cf. ..' - (*V*)*ous*, II*C*, p. 232.

[49] Cf. *..'oon*, II*A*, p. 227.

[50] Cf. ..' *-- acy*, II*D*, p. 234.

[51] 'MIMEOGRAPH fait aussi exception si on compte -EO- pour deux syllabes; cf. *EPD.*

[52] *Ideologue* s'accentue sur la première (*Concise Oxford*) ou sur la deuxième syllabe.

[53] Exception apparente: MIS'NOMER (de l'ancien française *mesnommer*).

[54] Cf. *'omni'presence.*

[55] Dans *'stereoscope, 'helioscope, ..eo.., ..io..*, ne comptent que pour une syllabe.

[56] Avec *e* syllabique.

[57] Avec *e* muet.

[58] Cf. *..'cidal*, III*B*, p. 235.

[59] Les dérivés en *..fier, ..fiable, ..fiably, ..ficative, ..ficator, ..ficatory*, sont généralement accentués sur la même syllabe que le verbe en *..fy*.

[60] Cf. *..'cultural*, s. gr. *C*, p. 236.

# On the Intonation of 'Yes-No' Questions in English

CHARLES C.FRIES

The comments on the 'tunes' of English reach back to the middle of the sixteenth century when John Hart pointed out that

> ... 'their [the interrogative and admirative] tunes doe differ from our other maner of pronunciation at the beginning of the sentence.'[1]
> '... thus ? to signifie that the sentence before yt is a question, which at the begining is sharp, and so falleth lower, according to the length of the sentence: as thus, what doo you know? how long sleap you? in lyk wise, though the question be but one word, yt is sharp: as, whie? when? how? wherefore? and souch lyke.'[2]

Although the voluminous discussions of the tunes of our intonation since the sixteenth century contain a great variety of descriptive approaches, we do not yet have a familiar, well-tried, and thoroughly learned system of notation by which to pin down for description and discussion the significant matters of these 'tunes'.[3]

Many, however, have tried meticulously to show the many differences of tone that characterize English utterances – from single word 'calls' and the formulas of 'greeting' to sentences of considerable length and complexity.[4] Very frequently the procedure has been to use a system of dots – a single dot above each syllable, at such a height as to show the relative pitch of the tone in which the syllable is uttered. The series of dots over the successive syllables of an utterance thus marks the sequence of tones which constitute the 'tune' of that utterance.[5] Some investigators have used great care in placing such dots in order to make the graphic record of the sequence of tones represent accurately the actual musical tones of the pronunciation of English speakers who have produced the specimens for analysis.[6] Much has been learned from these and later instrumental records concerning the physical details of the sequences of tone or pitch in the pronunciation of English.

Throughout the many efforts to ascertain and describe the 'intonation' of English speech there have been many attempts to go beyond the records of the physical details of these tones, and to identify the precise significant features of the sequences of tone that constitute its special 'tunes', or 'patterns', and to correlate these special 'patterns' with definite meanings or types of meanings. It seems to have been quite generally assumed without question that such correlations of intonation features with meanings do exist and that the meanings so conveyed are especially strong, although very difficult to isolate and describe precisely. But very few have succeeded in finding and describing, in the great variety of tone sequences that show themselves in English utterances, any set of regularly recurring contrastive patterns of pitch sequences that can be convincingly correlated with either formal grammatical meanings or specific responses of emotion and feeling.

In America, the work of Kenneth L. Pike in 1942[7] started the study of the problems of English intonation in terms of the assumptions and principles of the new developments in linguistics that were especially stimulated by Edward Sapir and Leonard Bloomfield. Pike sought to find in the procedures and techniques of phonemic analysis a sound practical approach to the problems of identifying *the minimum contrastive units of tone sequences that function as the means of differentiating structurally significant intonation patterns* – i.e. the contrastive units that are *intonemes*.

The chief features of the results of Pike's investigations of 1941–1942 have been corroborated by further study,[8] especially the results as they appeared in the expanded form of his book *The Intonation of American English*, (1945). For eighteen years they have been applied practically in the teaching of English as a foreign language in a wide range of situations in many countries. It is this general view of the intonation of American English that constitutes the set of frames within which this study has been developed.

This study centres attention upon the intonation patterns that occur with those questions that are very often called 'yes or no' questions – those that elicit the responses *yes* or *no*. They are often given the name 'general' questions as distinct from 'repeat' questions and 'information' questions.

Perhaps the most commonly repeated statement concerning the intonation of English (both British and American) is the assertion that interrogative utterances of the yes-no type are marked by a rising intonation. Quotations are abundant, both in the practical materials for the teaching of English and in the more scientific descriptive statements.

The following examples are typical.

(A) 'Questions are shown to be such by intonation, by word-order, by a special interrogative word, or, finally, by two or three of these means in the same sentence. . . .

'The rising tone characteristic of questions is, of course, most pronounced in questions which are not marked as such by any other means, e.g. *Tom? Alone? At night?*'[9]

(B) 'In English and many other languages, sentences are marked off by modulation, the use of secondary phonemes. In English secondary phonemes of pitch mark the end of sentences, and distinguish three main sentence types: *John ran away* [.] *John ran away* [?] *Who ran away* [¿] . . .

'Further within our explicit action type we distinguish a sub-type in which the verb *do, does, did* precedes the actor. This inverted type occurs in formal yes-or-no questions, along with question-pitch; *Did John run away? Didn't John run away?* in contrast with the uninverted (informal) types: *John ran away? John didn't run away?*'[10]

(C) 'TONE-GROUP 2 [↗]. . . . In *General Questions* in their most normal form without any special implication beyond "Is it true?" ". . . do you mean?" or ". . . please answer yes or no".'[11]

(D) 'The commonest kinds of sentence pronounced with an unmodified Tune 2 [rising intonation] in final position are *ordinary requests* and *questions* requiring the answer "yes" or "no". . . . Questions requiring the answer "yes" or "no" have this intonation because they imply the continuation "or not".'[12]

(E) 'We notice that there are limitations upon the distribution of these segments. For instance, after a sequence of segments in which each loud-stressed segment is higher-pitched than the preceding, we never get a low-pitched segment: after *Is your brother?* we never get a low *going*, but only a *going* which is pitched even higher than *brother*. And in *Is your brother going?* we do not get a low-pitched *ing*.'[13]

(F) 'This transformation generates simple yes-no interrogatives with a rising intonation:

/Is he going ↑ /. /Won't he eat ↑ /.'[14]

Statements which include assertions such as the following imply quantitative information of some kind.

'The rising tone characteristic of questions . . .'

'A rising pitch at the end usually marks this type of sentence [the yes-no question].'

'After *Is your brother?* we never get a low *going*, but only a *going* which is pitched even higher than *brother*. And in *Is your brother going?* we do not get a low pitched *-ing*.'

Assertions with 'characteristic of', 'usually', 'never', or their equivalents assume a numerical basis or quantitative comparison. To be justified they should have as their foundation adequate counts of some kind. General impressions without the support of any actual counting of the instances in even a small corpus provide no satisfactory ground for generalizing concerning comparative frequency of occurrence. Unfortunately, so far as the evidence goes, the many assertions concerning *the rising intonation as the usual mark of yes-no questions in English* have not been based on any adequate body of quantitative information.

In the past it has not been easy to procure even a small corpus of satisfactory materials upon which to base detailed studies of English intonation. Because of the fact that a tremendous number of emotional features, as well as situational features, affect the intonation patterns of utterances as they are produced, it is extremely difficult for naïve speakers to repeat exactly, in isolation, the intonation patterns they have used in continuous conversation. On the other hand, those who have been trained to a conscious control of their intonation patterns cannot provide the body of spontaneous utterances from which to discover exactly what the patterns are and the relative frequency of their use.

There must be mechanical records of a substantial body of materials which can provide any number of exact repetitions for analytical study. But we no longer believe that we can accept as satisfactory evidence the recordings, made in a laboratory, of specially constructed conversations read or recited by those who are aware that their language is being recorded. Such conscious recordings inevitably show many important differences from those of live conversations, made when the participants do not at all suspect that recordings are in progress.

The mechanical devices for recording, for linguistic study, live conversations outside the laboratory, without the knowledge of the participants, are now available. The chief problems now centre upon the finding of satisfactory occasions where one may reasonably expect a large concentration of the type of expression that is to be the special subject of the investigation. Even the fifty hours of live conversation that formed the corpus of material upon which my *Structure of English* (1952) was based did not provide a sufficient number of yes-no questions to make the quantitative facts concerning the intonation patterns there used really significant.

It has been assumed here that the absolute frequency of occurrence of any individual linguistic item by itself, in any corpus, no matter how big, has little or no significance. Nor does the comparison of items chosen at random. It is assumed too that quantitative significance is limited to systematic comparisons of the frequency of alternate forms within the same structural pattern, or to the relative frequency of the structural patterns themselves as parts of a larger frame.

In making the counts for this study, attention was centred solely on a single feature of the primary contours of the yes-no questions in the corpus recorded – i.e. the direction of the second and final movement of the tone in the peg-post-peg intonation pattern. [See the description given below in note 7(7)(c)]. For example, in the following utterance it is the 'direction' of the tone from 2 to 4 after the word *want*.

I'll go if you want me to go

In the first of the following examples it is the 'direction' of tone from 2 to 1 on the word *hand*. In the second it is the direction of the tone from 2 to 4 on the same word *hand*.

(a) Could I hold it in my hand

(b) Could I hold it in my hand

In these two utterances it is this difference in the direction of the tone on the word *hand*, *after the rise from tone level 3 on the word my to level 2*, that constitutes the difference between the 'rising' intonation of question (a) and the 'falling' intonation of question (b). In the following examples, question (c) had a falling intonation from 2 to 4 after the word *non-profit*, and the repetition of the question in (d) had a rising intonation from tone level 2 to 1.

(c) Have we established the fact that it is a non-profit organization

(d) Have we established the fact that it is a non-profit organization

Question (e) had a falling intonation from 2 to 4 within the word *automobile*. The high tone level 2 continued only through one syllable.

(e) Is it bigger than an automobile

In question (f) the high tone level 2 continued through the word *work* and the first syllable of *indoors* and then fell from 2 to 4.

(f) Do you work indoors

Two other examples of final rising tones were:

(g) Do you give advice or teach anything

(h) Is it some kind of a musical instrument

Two other examples of final falling tones are:

(i) Is it anything with moving parts

(j) Does it carry people

All the yes-no questions in the corpus of the material gathered were examined (by two investigators working independently) for the direction of the tone at this particular part of the intonation pattern used as a primary contour for each question, and the results tabulated.

The corpus of materials thus examined for this study consisted of thirty-nine television-radio programmes in which a panel of four persons, using, in turn,[15] only yes-no questions, attempted to discover the precise vocation, occupation, or special activity of each of several 'contestants' who provided no information other than the *yes* or *no* answers, which the questions elicited. It was therefore the language practice of the 'panellists', not that of the many 'contestants', that was examined. The circumstances in which the programmes were carried on made the speech forms used by these panellists the actual live conversation of language actively fulfilling its communicative function. The speed and spontaneity of the language activity of these panellists reduced to practical zero the chance that the intonation forms of that language activity could have been premeditated or deliberately chosen.

Of the four panellists, on each of the thirty-nine programmes from which all the questions were recorded and examined, three appeared very regularly. The fourth was a 'guest'. The three 'regulars', who, therefore, provided approximately three-fourths of the questions recorded, were the following:

(1) The founder and president of a well-known publishing company in New York for more than thirty years, and himself an author of distinction. Born in New York, N.Y.

(2) A well-known columnist and reporter for one of the leading New York papers for twenty years; a star of radio and television and an active writer. Born in Chicago, Illinois.

(3) A well-known actress starring in a variety of excellent stage plays since 1937; also on radio and television. Born in Boston, Massachusetts.

The 'guest' panellists have usually been those of similar professions as the regular panellists – among them a few British. Altogether, in the programmes here recorded there were twenty-five 'guests', – some of them appearing several times. The thirty-nine programmes recorded were not those of thirty-nine consecutive weeks. They were taken at irregular intervals during a period of two years beginning early in 1959.

The gross quantitative information from the analysis here carried out seems to have particular significance as a commentary upon the validity of the usual assertions concerning the intonation pattern of yes-no questions. The following statements summarize briefly the information.

(1) Altogether the recorded materials contained 2561 questions of the yes-no type.

(2) Of these 2561 yes-no questions, 1580 had a falling intonation pattern, 981 had a rising intonation pattern. In other words, of these more than two thousand five hundred instances of yes-no questions uttered by native speakers of Standard English in the United States, 61·7% had a falling intonation pattern and only 38·3% had a rising intonation pattern.

(3) Of the 39 programmes recorded, in only four programmes did the percentage of the instances of falling intonation fall below 50%. The lowest was 31·6% of falling intonation as against 68·4% of rising intonation. The other three, of the four below 50%, were 43%, 43·2%, and 43·3%.

(4) Of the thirty-nine programmes, eight had more than 70% of falling intonation. The highest was 77·5% of falling intonation with only 22·5% of rising intonation.

(5) In sixteen of the programmes, the percentage of falling intonation ranged from 61·1% to 69·7%, with rising intonations in these programmes ranging from 30·3% to 38·9%.

(6) In eleven of the programmes, the percentage of falling intonation patterns ranged from 50% to 58·6%, with rising intonations ranging from 41·4% to 50%.

(7) Of the total thirty-nine programmes, thirty-five or 89·5% had more falling intonation patterns than rising intonation patterns.

(8) Among the three individual 'regular' panellists there appears to be some difference. But they all used substantially more 'falling' intonation patterns with their yes-no questions than rising intonations. They ranged from 57·2% falling intonations, for the total of 463 yes-no questions, for number 3 of the list of panellists (given above on p. 248) through 63·75% of falling intonations, for a total of 367 yes-no questions, for number 1 of the list of panellists; to 72·7% of falling intonations, for a total of 671 yes-no questions, for number 2 of the list of panellists.

(9) The twenty-five 'guest' panellists together had 58% of falling intonations out of a total of 472 yes-no questions.

(10) Of the three regular panellists one was a man, the other two were women. Of these, one of the women had 57·2% of falling intonation patterns; the other had 72·7% of falling patterns. The man stood between, with 63·75% of falling patterns.

(11) There were some occasions when a question was repeated because it was not heard clearly or not understood. On these occasions it was *the same question, asked twice by the same panellist*, and *directed to the same person*, almost immediately after the first had been put. The point of special interest here is the fact that in many of these instances *the intonation pattern of the question as uttered the second time was the opposite of that used the first time*. If this change had all been in one direction – if, for example, a question with rising intonation had always received a falling intonation in repetition, one would suspect that the repetition itself constituted an instance of the 'special circumstances' that are said to attach to the falling intonation used with yes-no questions. But this was not the case. Questions with falling intonations were repeated with rising intonations, questions with rising intonations were repeated with falling intonations, and some questions were repeated with the same intonations.

As shown above most of those who have commented upon the intonation contours of questions have insisted that a rising intonation marks yes-no questions. A few have pointed out that yes-no questions do occasionally have a falling intonation, but have insisted that these falling intonations on yes-no questions always imply some special meanings apart from the question itself.

> 'Tune 1 [a falling intonation] with or without an emphatic word is sometimes applied to questions requiring the answer "yes" or "no". When said in this way the questions embody the idea of some statement or invitation.'[16]

'Thus . . . the use of the falling contour (which is primarily the non-special final contour) with a yes-or-no question instead of the special interrogative contour that would be used in this case produces an intonationally marked utterance. *Will you come with us?* with falling pitch suggests "I invite you to come with us", it is not a normal question at all but rather a kind of invitation or request.'[17]

The quantitative information derived from the corpus examined for this study does not support the much repeated assertion that yes-no questions 'regularly', 'usually', 'characteristically' have a rising intonation pattern. In this concentration of 2561 yes-no questions 61·7% were produced with a falling intonation pattern. Of course, even with these figures it is still possible to maintain that a primary falling intonation pattern occurs at the ends of yes-no questions only in 'special' circumstances. But then, in the light of the figures, one must also maintain that these 'special' circumstances do occur in more than 60% of the instances. Perhaps we must conclude that the 'circumstances' that determine the primary intonation patterns used in English are all 'special', in the sense that such distinctions as the difference between 'general' questions of the yes-no type and 'information' questions have no part in these 'circumstances'. To put the matter a bit differently, we must perhaps conclude that no special intonation pattern constitutes the signal of a distinction between yes-no questions and other types of questions or other types of utterances. The intonation patterns of English are a highly complex system, signalling features of a range of structural relationships other than the differentiation of question types or even of utterance kinds, and of a range of attitudes that have not yet been clearly identified.

The facts seem to support the conclusion that in English (at least in American English) there is no *question intonation pattern* as such. When one brings together a large number of instances of all types of questions – that is, all the utterance patterns for which we can 'predict with considerable regularity' one of a very limited list of oral response patterns – the proportion of falling intonation patterns they will bear is overwhelming. Of course, when one compares the intonation patterns of all yes-no questions with the intonation patterns of all other types of questions, he will find that, even with the ratio of 3 to 2 in favour of falling intonation patterns for yes-no questions, which the evidence here supports, there will be a higher proportion of rising intonation patterns on yes-no questions than on other question types. But there seem to be no intonation sequences on questions as a whole that are not also found on other types of utterances, and no intonation sequences on other types of utterances that are not found on questions.

*Notes*

1 John Hart, *An Orthographie, conteyning the due order and reason, howe to write or paint thimage of mannes voice, most like to the life or nature*, 1569, 45b (Texts and Index Verborum, ed. Bror Danielson, Stockholm, 1955, 200).

2 Hart, *The Opening of the unreasonable writing of our inglish toung*, 1551, 213, 214 (Danielson, Stockholm, 1955, 147, 160).

See also 164–165 (Danielson, 147), *A table conteyning thaccents*, for the meaning of *sharp*. 'Tunes 2, [sharp and flat] the sharp, wherby the voel is higher and sharper tuned then others the mark wherof is thus ⁄ *and* flat, wherby the voel is lower and flatter tuned then others and is marked ⧵.'

3 The most complete critical survey of the publications dealing with matters concerning intonation has been given by Kenneth L. Pike in the following books: (1) *The Intonation of American English* (first printing of the first edition, in the spring of 1945), 3–19, which must be combined with the notes, 173–190, and the alphabetically arranged bibliography, 191–200. (2) *Language: In Relation to a Unified Theory of the Structure of Human Behaviour, Part III*, 1960, 53–55; (3) *Tone Languages: A Technique for Determining the Number and Type of Pitch Contrasts in a Language, with Studies in Tonemic Substitution and Fusion*, 1948, 1–17, especially the thirty-five footnotes, and the bibliography, 167–174.

4 As early as 1909 Daniel Jones (to whom all of us owe a tremendous debt for a large portion of our phonetic knowledge of English) used an ingenious approach to the practical problem of recording and analysing texts of sufficient length to furnish an adequate basis for the study of intonation sequences. See Daniel Jones, *Intonation Curves: A collection of phonetic texts, in which intonation is marked throughout by means of curved lines on a musical stave*, Leipzig and Berlin, 1909, v–vii, § 6 and § 7.

5 See, for example, the following quotations from Daniel Jones, *An Outline of English Phonetics* (8th edition, reprint, with minor alterations), 1957, 275–326. 'When the pitch of the voice rises we have *a rising intonation*; when it falls we have *a falling intonation* (§ 1010). . . . A good way of representing intonation for practical teaching purposes is a system of dots (denoting approximately level pitches) and curves (denoting rising and falling intonations) placed above each syllable of a phonetic transcription. It is convenient to place these marks on a stave of three lines, the upper and lower lines representing the upper and lower limits of the voice and the middle line representing an intermediate pitch (§ 1014). . . . The two fundamental tunes are generally known as "Tune 1" and "Tune 2" respectively. Their particular features are shown by the following graphical illustrations:

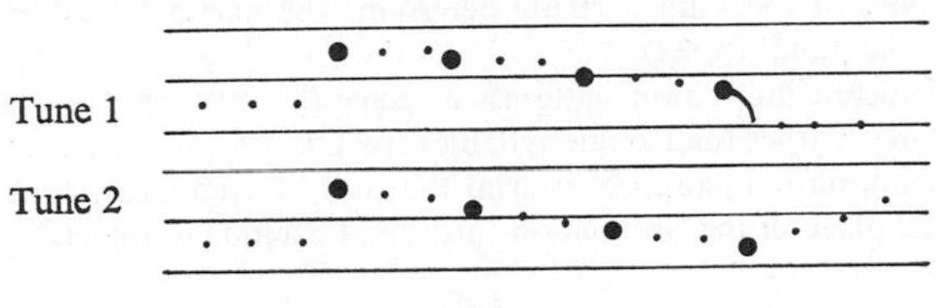

'These tunes may be spread over a large number of syllables, or they may be compressed into smaller spaces. All the essential features of the tunes are shown in the above graphical illustrations. When the tunes are applied to small groups of syllables or to the extreme case of monosyllables, several of these features disappear. I find it therefore a good plan in teaching English intonation to start with the intonation of long sentences and proceed subsequently to the intonation of short sentences' (§ 1020).

[6] See Wiktor Jassem, *Intonation of Conversational English* (*Educated Southern British*), Wroclaw, 1952, 108. 'The intonation of selected sentences (records 5–8) has been measured by picking up the needle of the reproducing machine at the beginning and at the end of the voiced part of every syllable containing at least one voiced sound, and dialing the perceived pitch on a pure-tone generator. In the case of rising–falling tone-segments, a third measurement was taken at the moment of highest pitch. In this way, the pitch of every syllable was taken several times to secure reliability of measurement, but in practically all cases the results were the same within the auditory difference limen.' Compare this procedure with that used by Daniel Jones in 1909, *Intonation Curves*, v–vii.

[7] The results of Pike's ground-breaking study of the intonation of American English carried out from October 1941 to May 1942, were published in a book entitled *Pronunciation* which he contributed as Volume I of the three volume *Intensive Course in English* mimeographed and copyrighted in June 1942 by the English Language Institute of the University of Michigan. Because of this new material on Intonation, which constituted more than half of the book (pp. 26–97), this volume on *Pronunciation* had considerable independent distribution quite apart from the other two volumes of the *Intensive Course.* This intonation material (with a new technique for marking intonation patterns), was used throughout the revised *Intensive Course*, published in 1943. In an expanded and revised form the same basic materials were published in the spring of 1945, with the title *The Intonation of American English.*

In the book of 1942, Pike had arrived at the following significant conclusions among many others (see his structure sketch, pp. 68–86). Here, these few are stated very briefly, and with over-simplification.

(1) The absolute pitch of a syllable (the number of vibrations per second) as such, is not significant. The relative pitch of one syllable to another is all important (p. 31).

(2) English has four significant contrastive levels:

1. extra-high (two steps above the usual voice level);
2. high (one step above the usual voice level);
3. mid (the usual level of the speaker's voice);
4. low (one step below the usual voice level).

'It makes no difference how far apart 1 and 4 may be; English intonation will come out quite satisfactorily if 2 and 3 are spaced between. Personal habits and differences, and various styles of speaking partially determine the particular set of intervals in use at a particular time' (p. 33).

(3) The significant intonation patterns, in general, cover phrases, i.e. groups of syllables or words, rather than single syllables (p. 32).

(4) Primary intonation patterns occur at the ends of utterances. A pattern begins at the 'peg', the place of the 'intonation turn', and extends to the end of the phrase (p. 35).

(5) The syllables immediately following the 'peg' form the 'post-peg' section of the intonation pattern. The semantic feature is expressed only as a result of the total peg-post-peg effect. It demands the complete peg-post-peg intonation phrase (p. 35).

(6) 'Pre-peg' variations of pitch are not structurally significant for the primary contours.

(7) The marking of the significant intonation patterns can thus be schematic and relative rather than an attempt to represent the precise tones of each of the syllables. For the primary contours or intonation patterns, the notation can, therefore, be limited to the following:

(a) the direction of the tone immediately following the beginning of the 'peg' or intonation 'turn';
(b) the tone level reached by this change;
(c) the direction of the final change from this tone level;
(d) the tone level reached by the final movement of tone.

(8) Such a schematic representation can ignore the variations of tone in the material preceding the peg syllable and identify only the distinctive features of the intonation pattern, as listed in the preceding paragraph (§ 7). The following are examples marked with the notation developed in 1943 for the intonation material of the *Intensive Course*.

| | Pattern |
|---|---|
| He went to the of fice | 3–2–4 |
| What did you tell him | 3–2–4 |
| When will he come | 3–2–4 |
| Do you know him | 3–2–1 |
| Is he a young man | 3–2–4 |
| You have no books | 3–2 |

8 'Extensive testing of spoken English material has convinced us of the correctness of the independent conclusions of Pike and Wells that there are four phonemes in English', Smith and Trager, *English Structure*, 1951, 41.

9 Otto Jespersen, *Essentials of English Grammar*, 1933, p. 306.

10 Leonard Bloomfield, *Language*, 1933, 170, 174.

11 Harold E. Palmer, *English Intonation*, 1922, 80, 81.

12 Daniel Jones, *An Outline of English Phonetics*, 1957, 293 (§ 1040). See also examples given 282 (§ 1023) and 294 (§ 1042).

13 Zellig S. Harris, 'Simultaneous Components in Phonology' in *Language*, XX, 1944, 202, note 22a.

14 Robert Stockwell, 'The Place of Intonation in a Generative Grammar of English', *Language*, XXXVI, 1960, 366. The examples appear in the original text in a

phonemic notation as follows, /$^{12}$iziy g$^{3}$owi$^{3}$ŋ ↑/, /w$^{12}$ontiy $^{33}$iyt ↑/. The superscript numbers to indicate pitch levels in the original text follows that introduced by Wells in 1945, which is just the opposite of that introduced by Pike in 1942 and used in all the Michigan materials and many others ever since 1942. The 2 and 3 as used by Stockwell are respectively 3 and 2 of our numbering as used in this paper.

[15] Each of the panellists asked questions 'in turn'; but for only one 'contestant' on each programme were the questions limited to 'a turn' of one question each in succession. For the other 'contestants' on each programme each panellist continued his questioning as long as he received 'yes' answers, and the next panellist took over whenever there was a 'no' answer.

[16] See Jones, *Outline*, 307 and 308, § 1058.

Daniel Jones very early pointed out this falling intonation on yes-no questions. He divides his examples of these falling intonations on yes-no questions into two groups: those 'Without contrast-emphasis' and those 'With contrast-emphasis'.

[17] František Daneš. 'Sentence Intonation from a Functional Point of View', in *Word*, XVI, 1960, 54.

# The Interplay and Co-operation of Word-Order and Intonation in English

MARIA SCHUBIGER

## 1

Modern English word-order (WO) is comparatively fixed. It forms a number of patterns, which the learner must master, in order to speak idiomatically – and in certain cases even in order to be understood. In languages with freer WO, e.g. German, this means of expression, in close co-operation with intonation, can serve to give more or less communicative weight to the elements of the sentence. In English, intonation alone often has to perform this function. In utterances with only one full stress the nuclear glide points to the weightiest element, wherever it may be placed, e.g. *ˋJohn ˌtold me about ˌthat. ˌJohn told ˋme about ˌthat* (Mir hat . . .). *ˌJohn ˌtold me about ˋthat* (Das hat mir . . .). In utterances with several full stresses, however, the rigidity of English WO is a limitation. A comparison with German will elucidate also this point. There is no exact English equivalent to utterances like ‹Interessant war der fünfte Akt›. *The ˈfifth ˈact was ˎinteresting* makes *interesting* too prominent with regard to *fifth act. The ˈfifth ˎact was ˌinteresting*, on the other hand, does not do full justice to *interesting*. The same holds good with ‹Glücklich ist niemand. Zurückkehren konnte er nicht. Das darfst du nicht sagen›. A translator must resort to another construction, e.g. *ˈGoing ˈback was imˎpossible*. Sometimes he can use straight WO, as in the sentences with only one full stress, and rely on the reader's intoning the sentences as intended, e.g. with a fall-rise nuclear glide: *You ˋmustn't say ˇthat*. In print italics often help to guide the reader. But in a good many cases there is no equivalent in English. Even in English, however, WO is not absolutely fixed. The adverbial elements of the sentence have fairly free play, and subject-verb inversion is in many cases optional. Consequently, like in German, the speaker gives preference to a WO that favours co-operation with intonation.

2

Of prime importance for the subject here under discussion is the *head.*[1] It can easily be given additional prominence (gliding tone, extra-strong stress) and is then as weighty as the nucleus.[2] This double-peaked tone-pattern occurs even in sentences without any movable elements and characterizes the utterance as one of a sequence (a). The word that forms the first peak of prominence is sometimes a repetition of an item in the preceding sentence (b). Double contrast is often expressed in this way, the two peaks of prominence marking the items contrasted with two others, mentioned before or afterwards (c).

(a) (From a biographical sketch) *His ˇfather was an ˋartist.*
(From Trollope's denunciation of the old Tories) *The ˈmeddling with the ·Uni‿versities has been ˋgrievous; the ˈtreatment of the ˈIrish ‿Church has been Saˋtanic.*[3]
(b) (You can't use 'or' at the end of a sentence) *ˇOr is a conˋjunction.*
(What does abbreviation mean? – Shortening, really) *To abˇbreviate means to ˋshorten.*[4]
(c) (What are you giving her?) *ˇMary is giving ˋspoons.*
(Where are you going for your holidays?) *ˇWe are going to ˋEastbourne.*[5]

The *self-pronoun*, when placed immediately after the subject, has a similar function. Even without extra tonetic prominence, it increases the weight of the head. Contrast can be suggested by this means, e.g. *The ˈhouse itˏself looks ˈmodest eˎnough* (but the estate as a whole is impressive). Or the self-pronoun gives more volume and therefore more weight to a pronominal subject, e.g. (I'm quite sure Jack was here) *ˈI myˎself ˈopened the ˎdoor for him.*[6]

The place of those elements of the sentence that have relatively free wo must be viewed in the light of the preceding remarks. *Adverbs of definite place and time* in front position can be given prominence in the same way, with the same connotation, e.g.

(a) (From a biography) *In the ˇthirties he became a ˋCatholic.*
(From a traveller's report) *In Deˇcember we went to ˋRome.*
(b) (Don't tell me your sick friend went to the tropics) *In the ˇtropics he will ˋnever reˌcover.*

(c) (When travelling abroad, he moved in the most exclusive circles) *At ˅home he was a ˋSocialist.*

Many *adverbs of indefinite time*, or rather *frequency adverbs*, whose normal position is pre-verbal, sometimes stand in front, in which position they can more easily be made prominent by means of intonation, e.g.

*˅Sometimes we ˈdine in ˋtown.*
*˅Presently I shall have ˈnothing ˋleft.*
*˅Generally I have ˈbreakfast in ˋbed.*

The same position is possible with *sentence-adverbs*, i.e. pronouncements upon the contents of the sentence, e.g.

*Un˅fortunately he ˈdied without having ˈmade a ˎwill.*
*˅Luckily I knew ˈnothing aˋbout it.*[7]

The tonetic prominence that is easily given to these adverbs when in front-position probably accounts for the fact that we rarely place two of them in immediate succession. Especially if the adverbs, or adverb phrases are short, this would upset the balance of the sentence. Although we often say *˅Sometimes I ˈget up at ˋeight*, we hesitate to say *In ˅winter ˈsometimes I ˈget up at ˋnine*; we prefer *In ˅winter I ˈsometimes ˈget up at ˋnine.* An initial adverbial clause can have the same effect on the WO of the main clause. We say *˅Usually I ˈget up at ˎeight*, but *When I am ˅tired I ˈusually ˈget up at ˋnine.* When the finite verb of the sentence is an auxiliary, the frequency adverb normally comes after this light element of the sentence and therefore has a certain amount of prominence, e.g. *It is ˈalways ˈcarefully ˎdone. She will ˈnever ˎlearn it.* But it precedes when the auxiliary carries the nuclear stress, e.g. *It ˈalways ˎis ˌcarefully ˌdone. She ˈnever ˎwill ˌlearn it*; for only in this position can it be given the same tonetic status.

Not only adverbial elements but also *other predicative parts of the sentence* are occasionally placed in front.[8] This exceptional WO, often thrown into relief by intonation, has the same function as the double-peaked tone-pattern in sentences with normal WO.

(a) (From a biography) *ˌHow he ˌspent the ˋnext few ˏyears, ˈnobody ˎknows. ˋMoney he had ˋnone.*
(b) (Don't speak to me about invalids) *ˋInvalids we've no ˋuse for.* (I can't lend you my dictionary) *ˌBooks of ˎthat sort you should poˌssess yourˎself.*

Here belong sentences of corroboration, e.g.
(He suspected it to be whisky) *ˏWhisky it ˎwas.*
(She said she would go to Paris) *And to ˏParis she ˎwent.*
(Well, well; sleep was more important than these vague ruminations) *And to ˏsleep he ˎwent.*

(c) (Put on your coats) *Your ˈhats you can ˈleave at ˎhome.*
(Her get-up was astonishing) *But ˋmore asˏtonishing was her beˋhaviour.*
Even if the related sentence is left unuttered, this WO, often coupled with a fall-rise glide on the first element, helps to suggest it, e.g.
(There are two of them, Bunter, two ladies) *The ˇparlour-maid you've ˋseen.*
(At last Armand appeared with a letter and the papers) *The ˇletter she ˋread.*[9]
Out of context, and with no guidance from intonation, sentences like those above would probably be interpreted as restrictive relative clauses preceded by their head-words. *ˈBooks I ˎlike, ˈfilms ˈeverybody enˎjoys* might be headings. But if the first element is said with a glide, the phrase becomes a sentence.

Of a very different kind are utterances with the same inverted WO, but with the nuclear glide on the initial predicative element, e.g.

*ˈQuite upˎset he was. Fanˋtastic it ˌlooked. ˋStrange they ˌsounded. ˈVery ˎstill he ˌsat. ˈTen ˎchildren they ˌhad. ˎWaste I ˌcall ˌthis. ˋCousins I ˌthink they ˌwere.*

Here the inverted order is due to an urge to blurt out the idea uppermost in one's mind. It is characteristic of popular speech.[10] It is evident from these examples that a given WO does not automatically engender a correlative tonetic stress-pattern. WO and intonation co-operate in more than one way and produce the most varied effects.

Two more remarks belong here:

(1) In the sentence: (God to Adam: Paradise with all its delights belongs to you, you are the master here) *Yet ˈone ˏtree you ˈmust not ˎtouch* – there is no possibility of putting the object in its 'normal' place. *You ˈmust not ˈtouch ˈone ˎtree* has another meaning. In this particular case WO is semantic. In German the position of the negative particle has the same function: . . . einen nicht . . . and . . . nicht einen. . . .[11]

(2) Front-position of the word *much* (or one of its colloquial synonyms), followed by a low nuclear rise-fall on the subject, is not connective but ironical. This WO and intonation underlines the ironical use of the word *much*. It heightens the effect if the first peak of prominence is also a low rise-fall glide. This intonation gives a tinge of sarcasm even to a sentence with no irony in the wording (last of the following examples).

(Peggy sniffed:) *‸Much ‸Vivian will ˌcare.*

*A ‸fat lot ‸you care.*

*‸Nice thing it would have ˌbeen for ˌme, if ‸you'd ˌpassed ˌout in this ˌtaxi*

*‸Little ‸he cares what I ˌsay.*[12]

3

*Subject-verb inversion* must be considered next. While connective WO makes use of the prominence that can be given to the head of the tone-group, inversion is a means of placing a weighty subject at the end, where it forms the *nucleus*. The light verb (*to be*, *come*, *go*, etc.) immediately precedes. Not in all cases, however, does the preponderance of the subject over the verb bring about inversion. Italian 'Viene il papà', Spanish 'Viene Juan', have no equivalent in English. In sentences of this type intonation alone points to the heavier word, e.g. *\`Father is ˏcoming. The \`Browns have arˏrived.* But an initial adverb can engender inversion, e.g. *ˈHere comes ˎJohn. ˈNow is the ˈtime to ˎdo it. ˈOff went the ˏbus.* Cf. also the alternative: *ˈSo I ˎam* and *ˈSo am ˎI*, where WO is semantic.[13]

In literary English, especially in descriptive prose, inversion after an initial adverb phrase is quite frequent, e.g.

*ˈRound the ˏcorner . . . stood the ˎlawcourts.*

*But at ˈthat ˏmoment ˈcame Dr ˎSykes.*

*Aˈcross the ˏroad, behind a . . . lay ˎBrookfield.*

Predicative adjectives, too, can have front-position in literary English. This is why there is inversion in the following sentences:

*ˈGreat is the ˈmystery of ˎgodliness.*

*ˈTall and ˏspectral stood the ˈwhite ˈstatues on the ˎbridge.*

*ˈGreat was my asˏtonishment, when . . .*

In argumentative prose an initial predicative adjective has connective function, e.g.

(The general characteristics of a collection of stories have been stated) ˈ*Typical is the ˏstory which ˈgives the ˈbook its ˎtitle.*
(One sort of valuation has been discussed) ˈ*Very ˏdifferent is the ˇother and more ˋgenuine valuˌation of ˌamateur ˌstatus.*

Here the length of the subject causes it to gravitate to the end.

The subject-verb inversion considered above must be distinguished from another type, which is only partial: the auxiliary precedes the subject; the main verb follows and therefore retains its stress. Sentences beginning with a negative or restrictive element, mostly an adverb, have this inversion. The pattern is purely literary.

ˈ*Never have I ˏseen a more ˈbeautiful ˎspectacle.*
ˈ*Nor did I ˈsee the ˎend.*
*Not a ˈword did he ˎsay.*
ˈ*Little did he iˏmagine that ...*
ˈ*Scarcely had he ˈleft the ˏhouse, when ...*
ˈ*Not till I had ˈreached the ˏsummit, did I ˈrealize ...*

Sometimes partial inversion follows an initial element that is not negative or restrictive in meaning, but which has a similar emotional appeal, e.g.

ˈ*Bitterly did he reˎsent it.*
ˈ*Well do I reˈmember the ˏday, when ...*
ˈ*So ˎdangerous has this ˌwork beˏcome, that ...*
ˈ*Seven ˎtimes did this inˌtrepid ˌgeneral reˌpeat the atˌtack.*

So far only declarative sentences have been considered. When dealing with inversion, however, other types must also be taken into account. With *interrogative sentences* one point is of special interest. While in direct questions asking for the subject or a predicative noun the noun is at the end and bears the nuclear stress irrespective of its communicative weight, which is greater with the predicative noun than with the subject (ˈ*Who is that ˎman?* ˈ*Who is the inˋventor of that ˌstory?*), there is in reported questions, which occupy a position of transition between statements and direct questions, a possibility of differentiation, e.g.

(An anecdote about a lawyer has been told.) ˈ*Do you ˈknow who that ˈlawyer ˏwas?* But, ˈ*Do you ˈknow who is the inˏventor of that ˊstory?*[14]

In *exclamatory sentences* old inversion has practically been superseded by straight WO in current modern English. Only in poetry and in lofty prose do we occasionally come across sentences like:

*How ˈvery ˈbeautiful is the ˎlane!*
*How ˈsplendidly does he ˎride!*
*How ˈgreen was my ˎvalley!*

From what has been said about the driving force in determining WO, it would appear that here inversion was appropriate even to-day; for exclamatory sentences mostly begin with a weighty predicative element and often have a light verb. The modern tendency to abandon inverted order may have been favoured by the fact that most exclamatory sentences – if they *are* complete sentences, and not just nominal phrases like: *ˈWhat ˎluck! ˈHow ˎlovely!* – have the nuclear glide on the initial element, e.g. *ˈHow ˎlovely it ˌall ˌlooks! ˈWhat a ˎnuisance that ˌboy ˌis!*[15] As subject and verb form the low-pitched tail of the tone-group, it does not very much matter which comes first.[16]

*Tags of direct speech* must be mentioned here. In the past, inversion was their established WO. As they are preceded by a heavy element (the quotation) and usually have a light verb (to say), this WO would seem to be appropriate even now. But here, too, straight WO has been gaining ground, without, however, supplanting the older pattern as completely as with exclamations. *I ˈquite aˎgree with you, ˌsaid his ˌfather*, and . . . *his ˌfather ˌsaid* are both current English. As the pitch-pattern is the same in both cases, it does not very much matter which form we use. When the subject is a pronoun, straight WO prevails to-day: *The ˈman's a ˎfraud, I ˌsaid (he ˌsaid)* rather than . . . *said ˌI (said ˌhe)*.[17]

4

It remains to consider the *tail* of the tone-group. When does the adverbial element follow the nucleus and how does the connotation of this position compare with that of others? The theme is very vast. Many adverbs would have to be considered individually. Moreover the possibility of a pause between nucleus and tail would have to be taken into account. Within the limited space of this article only one aspect of the problem can be touched upon.

*The nominal object of a transitive phrasal verb* can be placed either before or after the adverbial particle, e.g. *I ˈput on my ˎhat* and *I ˈput my ˎhat on.* In both cases the noun bears the nucleus and the particle is weak-stressed. According to our school grammars the two patterns are on a par with each other. Yet when we observe current usage, we cannot help noticing that they are not used quite indiscriminately. A few sentences will illustrate this.[18]

(a) To a boy who forgets to observe the rules of politeness one would probably say: *ˈTake your ˎhat off*,[19] or in a different situation: *ˈTake your muddy ˎshoes off beˌfore you ˌcome into the ˌhouse.*[20] At the dinner-table the mistress of the house might be heard to say: *The ˈmaid will ˈtake these ˎplates away ˌnow and ˈbring the ˎpudding in*[21].

(b) While consulting a dictionary, to somebody asking what I am doing: *I'm ˈlooking up a ˎword.* Telling an adventure: *He ˈpicked up a ˏstone and ˈthrew it ˎat me.* Motorist: *I ˈpicked up ˈtwo ˎhikers as I was ˌdriving across ˌSalisbury ˌPlain.* What are you doing to that letter? *I'm ˈrubbing out a ˎword.* It was quite a business to send that letter to Paris; *I had to ˈfill ˈin ˈthree ˎforms.* (ab) *The ˈfirst thing to ˏdo is to ˈput up the ˎtent.* (Here follows a brief description of the operation.) *ˈHaving ˈput the ˏtent up . . .*[22]

As will be seen from these examples, an item which is not new to the context or situation, which, if it stands for something concrete, the speaker and his interlocutor see and could even touch, tends to precede the particle, while a new item is apt to follow. It will also be observed – and this is the grammatical counterpart of the difference – that substantives preceded by the indefinite article or a numeral gravitate more forcibly to the end than those preceded by the definite article or a similar grammatical form-word (possessive or demonstrative pronoun) expressing familiarity rather than novelty. As both with (a) and with (b) the nuclear glide is on the substantive, the weakening of this word in the sentences under (a) must be due to the tail. This is indeed the case. When the particle, which is a component part of the verb, forms the tail, the nucleus throws into prominence the whole group (verb + object); while the nuclear glide on the object in final position bears upon this word alone. With (a) much more than with (b) verb and object form a single unit of communication. In a note on the problem here under discussion[23] F.T.Wood remarks that in some cases 'end-position of the object suggests an activity . . . If we wished to suggest an activity to occupy a person who was at a loss what to do . . . we might ask: *Have you fetched up the coal? Have you made up the fire?* But if we merely wished to know whether the coal is up and whether the fire is made up . . . we should probably ask: *Have you fetched the coal up? Have you made the fire up?*' But why, one will ask, does end-position suggest an activity, mid-position a state or situation? I submit the following answer: if the group verb + object is to suggest an activity, the verb must preserve its independence, not merge its identity in that of the object, which is likely to happen when the adverbial particle forms the tail of the tone-group.[24]

It would be interesting to follow up this line of investigation. Is the communicative weight of the verb one of the factors determining the place of the preposition, which can stand either before the relative/interrogative pronoun or at the end of the sentence?[25] Can the difference between complete and partial inversion in interrogative sentences with the verb *to be* in a compound tense (*Who will be the president? Who will the president be?*) be accounted for in the same way? I feel inclined to answer the second question in the affirmative.[26]

*Notes*

1 I am using the term head for the first stressed element pitched high.

2 Prenuclear glides can also express emotional intensity, e.g. *It's an ex˅traordinary ˎsight*. But this function of intonation does not concern us here.

3 R. Kingdon, *English Intonation Practice*, London, 1960, 89. When the first prominent item consists of several stressed words, and is therefore apt to form a separate, non-final tone-group, the glide occurs on the last stress (*the 'meddling with the ˙Uni˅versities . . .*). This forms a parallel to the nuclear part comprising more than one stressed word, the last of which then bears the nuclear glide. Examples at the bottom of p. 257.

4 P. A. D. MacCarthy, *English Conversation Reader*, London, 1956, 36, where many more examples of this argumentative intonation can be found.

5 Kingdon, *Practice*, 67.

6 The same effect is produced by a turn of syntax: *It was I who. . . .* Occasionally the nucleus falls on the self pronoun. In an appropriate context such an utterance conveys concession, e.g. (The lessons are very dull) *The 'teacher himˎself ˌsometimes ˌfalls aˌsleep*. Cf D. L. Bolinger, 'Linear Modification' Publ. of Mod. Lang. Assn of America LXII, 1952, 1141.

7 W O and intonation of utterances comprising a word-modifying adverb cannot be dealt with here.

8 Jespersen, *A Modern English Grammar on Historical Principles*, VII, London, 1949, 76, calls this a stylistic trick, which for more than a century has been gaining ground in literature.

9 With straight W O the fall-rise nucleus is more essential; for here it is the only bearer of the idea of implication: *She 'read the ˅letter.*

10 Kruisinga's two examples of the W O: predicative adjective + pronominal subject + copula are adapted to illustrate the difference (*A Handbook of Present-Day English*, II, Utrecht, 1925, § 2194): 1. (His fame may have been accidental.) *ˌNever-theˊless 'famous he ˎwas.* 2. (But she appeared to be in no hurry.) *ˋThoughtful*

*she* ˌ*was*. (The tone-marks are mine.) With the nucleus on the copula (1) this w o expresses corroboration, with the nucleus on the predicative adjective (2) it betrays emotional involvement. Britta M. Charleston, from whose book, *Studies on the Emotional and Affective Means of Expression in Modern English*, Berne, 1960, many of the specimen sentences in this and the next section have been taken, does not make this distinction either (146): *Intimi*ˈ*dation there un*ˈ*doubtedly* ˎ*was* is an example of (1), *Eu*ˋ*génie her* ˌ*name* ˌ*was* of (2). (The tone-marks are mine.)

[11] The distinction is similar to that between, *You needn't go there either* (= auch nicht), and, *You needn't go there too* (= nicht auch); or between, *He gets impatient when he does not understand anything* (= nichts), and, *He gets impatient when he doesn't understand something* (= etwas nicht).

[12] The last three of these sentences are quoted from Bengt Jacobsson, 'Inversion in English, with Special Reference to the Early modern English Period,' Uppsala, 1951, 48 and 162. Jacobsson speaks of ironical front-position (136), but does not mention the concomitant intonation, which is largely responsible for the effect. It is especially the *low* rise-fall, as Mr P. A. D. MacCarthy informs me, that has an ironical connotation here.

[13] In German the position of the adverb, in co-operation with tonetic stress, expresses the difference: *Das* ˈ*bin ich auch* and *Das bin auch* ˈ*ich*.

[14] Another distinction regarding interrogative sentences is mentioned at the end of section 4.

[15] If we want to stress also the subject, we prefer the interrogative form: ˈ*Isn't* ˈ*Jimmy a* ˬ*nuisance?*

[16] Cf. Bengt Jacobsson: *Inversion in English*, 185–186.

[17] F. T. Wood ('Subject-Verb Inversion in Modern English', *Moderna Språk*, 1956, 28), says that the choice between *I* (*he*) *said* and *said I* (*he*) depends on whether the pronoun is expected or not. As *he* is practically always expected, *said he* is rarer than *said I*. To D. L. Bolinger ('Linear Modification'), *says he* suggests a contrast between *he* and *others*, and the effect may be sarcasm or disbelief. These two remarks go to show that in a diffuse way rhythmical stress in the tail of the tone-pattern has the same function as tonetic stress in the tone-pattern as a whole.

[18] In all the sentences quoted the adverbial particle can either precede or follow the object, and the latter bears the nuclear stress in both cases.

[19] Quoted from Wood ('Verb-Adverb Combinations: The Position of the Adverb', *English Language Teaching*, x, 1955, 24), who says that mid-position of the object is the current wo with this utterance. Bolinger, commenting upon *Put your hat on/ Put on your hat*, says that a terminal adverb weakens a contrast on some other element, even when that element bears contrastive stress. (*Linear Modification*, 1128, Footnote 23.)

[20] From Ronald Mackin, *Exercises in English Patterns and Usage*, Book I, Oxford 1960, 50.

[21] This sentence is from C. E. Eckersley and J. M. Eckersley, *A Comprehensive English Grammar for Foreign Students*, London 1960, 293, who add in brackets *bring in the pudding*, while they suggest no alternative to *take the plates away*.

[22] This example is quoted from Wood, *Verb-Adverb Combinations*, 24.

[23] Wood, 'Points of Modern English Syntax', 124, *English Studies*, XLII, 1961, 59.

[24] In this connection it is interesting to note that in the collocation nominal

subject + verb this unifying tonetic stress-pattern occurs most frequently when the verb is in the passive, or when the active form expresses a state or an emergence on the scene rather than an activity, e.g. *Our ˋkitchen is being ˌdone ˌup. We had our ˋkitchen ˌdone ˌup. I must ˈget my ˎhair ˌcut. I had my ˋphotograph ˌtaken ˏyesterday. Then a ˋlight apˌpeared on the hoˌrizon. ˈShall we have the ˏfire lighted?* The last example is from Henry Sweet (*A New English Grammar*, Oxford, 1898, §1904), who uses the term *grouping stress*. I myself have treated collocations like *to ˈlet the ˎdog loose, to ˈmake the ˎkettle hot*, contrasted with *to ˈpaint the ˈdoor ˎgreen, to ˈroll the ˈgrass ˎsmooth* under the title *Unity stress* (M. Schubiger, *English Intonation, its Form and Function*, Tübingen, 1956, 84–85). In his article on 'Non-Thematic Subjects (= subjects bearing the nuclear glide) in Contemporary English, (*Časopis pro Moderni Filologii*, Prague, 1957, English summary, 171–173) Jan Firbas points out that subjects with the non-generic indefinite article easily have this tone-pattern, *A ˋhaze ˌhovered over the ˌprospect. A ˋfly ˌsettled on his ˌhair. The ˈdoor ˏopened and a ˌyoung ˎgirl came in.* But: *The ˈdoor ˏopened and the ˌyoung ˈgirl ˈcame ˎin.* (The tone-marks are mine.) Compare with this what was said above about the indefinite article with objects of phrasal verbs.

[25] Poutsma seems inclined to answer this question in the affirmative. There is a remark to this effect in *A Grammar of Late Modern English*, I, 1 Groningen, 1928, 472 (3).

[26] Wood (*MSpråk*, 1956, 25) gives the example: *Who will be the new bishop? Who will the new bishop be?* saying that in the first instance the personality is the centre of interest, in the second the vacancy.

# The Intonation System of American English

## GEORGE L. TRAGER

In the system of linguistic analysis practised by the present author, the intonation system of English, whether American or any other variety, functions as part of the syntax, delimiting stretches of utterance – clauses – that are examined in order to determine their structure, that is, their syntactic structure. But the intonation patterns that make up the system are themselves composed of certain kinds of phonological elements. And it therefore seems appropriate, in a volume dedicated to Daniel Jones, to describe the various aspects of these phonological elements as the author and many of his colleagues use and interpret them.

It is the intention to make this description succinct, and no discussion of other interpretations and of criticisms is given, nor is there much bibliography. This is a presentation of a position, and a statement of conclusions. It is believed that it will be useful, since no similar statement that is up to date has yet been published anywhere.

(1) In *An Outline of English Structure*, hereafter referred to as *OES*,[1] we discussed pitch and terminal junctures in sections 1.71 and 1.72 (pp. 41–48), and in the discussion of syntax (sections 4.0 to 4.5, pp. 67–80) there was some treatment of intonation patterns. Shortly after the publication of *OES*, the group of linguists working on the preparation of English-teaching materials at Cornell University in 1952 and 1953 (and at various other places for some years following), and including such excellent observers as Welmers and Hockett, noted certain omissions and difficulties in our presentation. Smith and I immediately recognized the correctness of the criticisms, and made the needed restatements; these were not published as such, but have been mentioned or alluded to in various publications by Smith and others. A couple of years later Sledd pointed out, in personal communications and oral presentations, that still further details were unaccounted for. Again Smith and I were able to see how these fitted into the total picture, and to make a workable restatement. Since about 1957 Smith especially

has extensively studied the use of intonation patterns in English as markers of the boundaries of syntactic units, and he has in various stages of completion a series of statements about English syntax and semology, based strictly on phonologically bounded units. In this connection it is also pertinent to note that it has become possible to separate out paralinguistic pitch phenomena from those of language proper.[2] It is our hope eventually to publish this material either in a series of articles or in the form of a total revision and expansion of *OES*.

(2) In *OES* we accepted and started from the basic analysis of English pitch made by R. S. Wells and extensively applied by K. L. Pike.[3]

There are four pitch phonemes (in most American usage a distinctive phonological unit is called a phoneme whether it is a vowel or a consonant or a stress or a pitch or something else). We call these 'low' $/^{1}/$, 'middle' $/^{2}/$, 'high' $/^{3}/$, 'extra high' $/^{4}/$. They are found to have allophones that vary in height in terms of the stress (primary /ˊ/, secondary /ˆ/, tertiary /ˋ/, weak /˘/ [or unmarked]) of the syllabic that they accompany. A detailed examination of such allophones is given in *OES*, 1.71, pp. 42–44. Other allophones, involving contour or direction (sustained, rising, falling) are found at terminal points (*OES*, 1.72, pp. 44–49) and involve the amount of segmental material covered by the pitch.

From the material presented in *OES*, the following statement of intonation patterns can be constructed (examples will be given in (3) below): American English intonation patterns consist typically of three pitches and a terminal contour. The initial pitch of the three is most often $/^{2}/$, but may be any of the others. The central pitch accompanies the primary stress of a phrase or clause, is most often $/^{3}/$ in all kinds of material – statements, questions, or the like, but is frequently $/^{4}/$ when there is what is usually called emphasis, and may often be $/^{2}/$ or $/^{1}/$. The final pitch is most often $/^{1}/$ at the ends of statements, $/^{2}/$ at the ends of clauses that do not end sentences, $/^{3}/$ at the ends of certain kinds of questions, but may be any one of the four. The final pitch is modified by the terminal contour, being sustained /|/, rising /||/, or falling /#/; sustained occurs most often in clauses that do not end sentences, falling in statements and interrogative-word questions, rising in other questions and in many non-final clauses. When a clause begins with the primary-stressed syllabic, there are only two pitches, the central and the final, the initial being absent.

The modification necessitated by the observations of Welmers and

Hockett involved the possibility of a fourth pitch in a clause, appearing after the initial and before the central. It has become clear that this pitch, when it occurs, always accompanies the secondary-stressed syllabic nearest to the primary, or, if there is no secondary-stressed syllabic, it falls on the tertiary nearest the primary. Any of the four pitches can appear in this position, /²/ being most frequent.

Sledd's observations indicated that there are also clauses containing four pitches in which there is a pitch after the central one and before the final one. Again, it seems to fall on secondary-stressed syllabics, or on tertiary-stressed ones if there is no secondary, but there are instances where it accompanies weak syllables when there are no stronger ones present.

Putting all these statements together, we now say: an intonation-pattern contains five pitch positions, which we designate as *a, b, c, d, e.* No occurrence of all five is known, and we believe it is not possible; the occurring forms are *a-c-e*, *abc-e*, *a-cde*, and, when the clause begins with a primary, *c-e* and *cde*. The primary stress always accompanies *c*. If a clause begins with a secondary, immediately followed by a primary, it may be asked whether the pattern is *a-c-e* or *bc-e*; we know of no way to answer this question as yet, but believe that *bc-e* may well be the answer; of course, if the clause ends as . . . *cde*, then the pattern can only be, we hold, *a-cde*, since we do not believe that *b* and *d* can occur in the same clause. The clause ends in a terminal contour (*T*). The intonation-patterns are then of these forms:

*a-c-eT*
*abc-eT*
*a-cdeT*
*-bc-eT*
*--c-eT*
*--cdeT*

Any of the positions may be filled by any one of the four pitches, and *T* is any of the three contours. It is not known whether all the possible combinations occur; but a good many of them have actually been observed in material spoken naturally and recorded on tape.

In *OES* the examples given implied that rather long stretches of material could be single clauses with one intonation pattern only. This is probably possible in continued discourse of an oratorical or other literary or technical nature, but we believe that in most ordinary speech the clauses are rather short, and that most long sentences contain many pre-final clauses ending most usually in sustained /|/.

(3) A few examples may now be given. These are as ordinarily spoken by the present author.

*a-c-eT* $^{2}$Ì'm gôing $^{3}$hóme$^{1}$ #
$^{2}$Ì'm gôing $^{4}$hóme$^{1}$ # (definitely not somewhere else)
$^{2}$Ì'm gôing $^{3}$hóme$^{2}$|$^{2}$bùt Ì'll bè $^{3}$báck$^{1}$ #
$^{2}$Àre yŏu gôing $^{3}$hóme$^{3}$‖
$^{2}$Ì'm gôing $^{3}$hóme nôw$^{2}$‖ . . . (doubtful, or reticent)
$^{2}$Whêre ăre yŏu $^{3}$góing$^{2}$|$^{2}$E$^{2}$lízabeth$^{2}$‖
$^{2}$Whêre ăre yŏu $^{3}$góing$^{2}$|$^{1}$E$^{1}$lízabeth$^{1}$‖ (less polite)
$^{2}$Whô(m) ăre yŏu $^{3}$cálling$^{3}$ #$^{2}$E$^{3}$lízabeth$^{3}$‖

*abc-eT* $^{2}$Ìt's ĭn $^{2}$châpter $^{3}$óne$^{1}$ #
$^{2}$Hè's ă $^{3}$gôod $^{3}$bóy$^{1}$ #
$^{2}$Hè's ă $^{3}$gôod $^{2}$bóy$^{2}$|$^{2}$but . . .
$^{2}$Ìt's ă $^{2}$lông $^{2}$stóry$^{2}$|$^{2}$ănd ìt'll $^{1}$bóre yŏu$^{1}$ #

*a-cdeT* $^{2}$Ì'm $^{3}$góing $^{1}$hôme$^{1}$ #
$^{2}$Ì'm gôing $^{2}$hóme $^{2}$nôw$^{1}$ #
$^{2}$It's $^{2}$wón$^{3}$derful$^{1}$ #

*-bc-eT* $^{2}$Châpter $^{2}$Óne$^{1}$ #

*--c-eT* $^{3}$Álways$^{1}$ #
$^{4}$Néver$^{1}$ #

*--cdeT* $^{2}$Éat $^{3}$yôur lûnch$^{1}$ #

A succession of short clauses:

$^{2}$Wéll$^{2}$‖$^{2}$Ì $^{2}$thínk$^{2}$|$^{2}$ìt'd bè $^{2}$àll $^{3}$ríght$^{2}$|$^{2}$tŏ $^{3}$gó $^{1}$nôw$^{1}$ #

(4) This systematization is based on American English. We have heard enough other varieties, however, and have examined enough of the reported intonation data for them, to be convinced that the system set forth here holds for the whole of the English language. The seeming great differences in the way different kinds of English sound in respect to intonation are due, we believe, to different distributions and occurrences of the pitches and terminals, within the same system. Thus American

$^{2}$Whô's $^{3}$thére$^{1}$ #

and Southern British

$^{3}$Whô's $^{2}$thére$^{1}$ #

are different exemplifications of *a-c-eT*.

*Notes*

[1] George L. Trager and Henry Lee Smith, Jr, *Studies in Linguistics*, Occasional Papers, 3, Norman, Oklahoma, 1951; reprinted Washington, D.C., 1956 and 1957.

[2] G. L. Trager, 'Paralanguage: a first approximation', *Studies in Linguistics*, XII, 1958, 1–12.

[3] R. S. Wells, *Language*, XXI, 1945, 27–39; K. L. Pike, *The Intonation of American English*, Ann Arbor, 1946.

# Dimensions of Meaning in Intonation [1]

ELIZABETH ULDALL

Since my first encounters with the study of intonation, under Professor Daniel Jones, the questions of what kind of 'meanings' intonation carries, how these vary from one speech community to another, and in what terms the meanings may be described have interested me. I would not wish to maintain that the three dimensions hypothesized in this paper are the only kinds of meaning carried by intonation, but they obviously bulk large in it. At the outset, my intention was to look for some way of reducing the large number of terms used in describing the meanings of intonations, reducing them preferably to a small closed set.

The experiment described here consisted in offering to a group of subjects a number of sentences on each of which 16 intonation contours had been imposed synthetically, and asking them to rate these on a set of scales consisting of opposed adjectives, with a view to investigating the attitudes or emotional meanings conveyed by the various contours.[2] Professor Osgood's 'semantic differential' appears to be a suitable technique for investigating the emotional meanings of intonation contours, since it is precisely 'emotional meaning' which is strongly present in intonation, and with this aspect of meaning the semantic differential deals most successfully.

The 15 subjects were speakers of American English, and the original recording on which the contours were synthesized was spoken by an American. The contours, shown in Fig. 1, were the same as those used in an earlier experiment.[3] They were intended to cover all the kinds of variation which differentiate intonation contours, though of course nothing like all the possible combinations of variables were represented. The variables are:

Range: wide/narrow.

Pitch reached at end of contour: high/mid/low.

Shape of contour: one direction/with a change of direction.

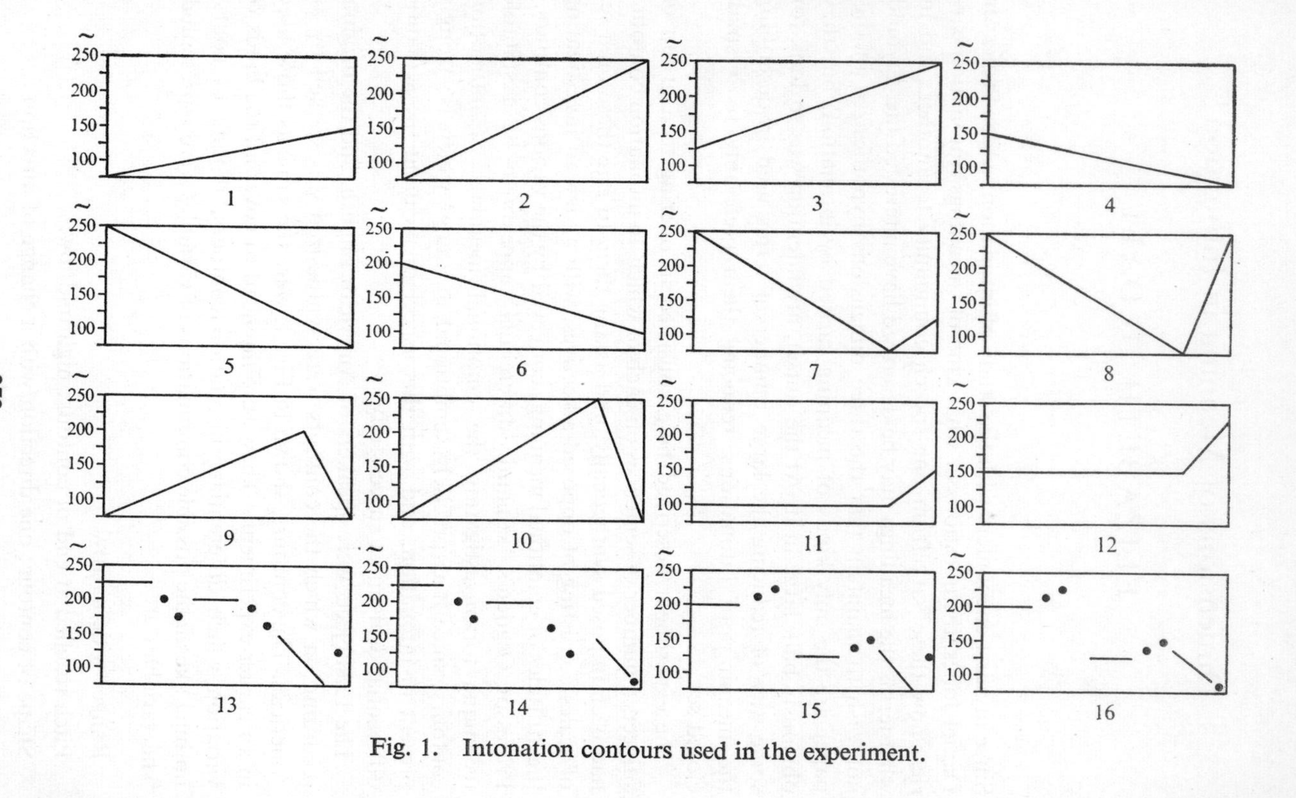


Fig. 1. Intonation contours used in the experiment.

Treatment of weak syllables:

(a) continuing the line of the strong syllables;
(b) rising above the line of the strong syllables;
(c) falling below the line of the strong syllables.

The 'scales' used were the same as in the earlier experiment, with the addition of *authoritative/submissive*, *unpleasant/pleasant*, *genuine/pretended* (feeling) and *weak/strong* (feeling), so that the page on which the subjects were asked to rate each contour on each sentence appeared thus:

| | | |
|---:|---|---|
| bored | — — — — — — — | interested |
| polite | — — — — — — — | rude |
| timid | — — — — — — — | confident |
| sincere | — — — — — — — | insincere |
| tense | — — — — — — — | relaxed |
| disapproving | — — — — — — — | approving |
| deferential | — — — — — — — | arrogant |
| impatient | — — — — — — — | patient |
| emphatic | — — — — — — — | unemphatic |
| agreeable | — — — — — — — | disagreeable |
| authoritative | — — — — — — — | submissive |
| unpleasant | — — — — — — — | pleasant |
| genuine | — — — — — — — | pretended |
| weak | — — — — — — — | strong |

These terms were arranged with seven places between them; the subjects were instructed that the places next to the terms should be checked to indicate 'extremely' (bored or interested, etc.), the two places a little farther in from the terms to indicate 'quite' (bored or interested, etc.), the two places flanking the middle to indicate 'slightly' (bored or interested, etc.), and the middle space to indicate 'neutral' or 'neither' in relation to the scale under consideration.

The extra scales mentioned were added to the original ten in an effort to find more 'central' terms for the dimensions of emotional meaning which appear to be most strongly represented in intonation: 'pleasant/unpleasant', 'authoritative/submissive', and 'strong/weak' (feeling expressed). In the material on which diagrams A, B, C, D, E are based, three of the new scales were in fact used as being suitable characteristic terms in these dimensions. The addition 'genuine (feeling)/pretended (feeling)' was not successful; 'pretended' feeling must either not be expressed in intonation, or be a function of intonation in context; all the contours presented were rated as expressing 'genuine' feeling.

The four sentences were as follows:

A. Statement: 'None of the members are going.'
B. Yes-or-no question: 'Was it arranged at the meeting?'
C. Question-word question: 'What did he think they were doing?'
D. Command: 'Bring it along to the meeting.'

To these was added a nonsense-sequence:

E. [ˈsoɷməvə ˈpaɩθərɔ ˈzɛnɩŋ]

All of these sentences consisted of the same number and arrangement of strong and weak syllables. The real sentences were intended to be suitable as remarks between social equals. They were recorded by Dr Alvin Liberman of the Haskins Laboratories, New York. It was found necessary to have them all recorded on a rising contour in order that the final syllables should not be so low in intensity as to make synthesis difficult. The contours were 'applied' to the sentences by means of the Voback synthesizer.

Each subject took each test twice, some in the same order both times, and some in the reverse order. This was done partly in order to increase the number of judgments to be averaged, and partly to see whether the judgments appeared to be affected by the order in which the contours were presented: were the subjects judging the contours in relation to their whole experience of intonation, or in relation to the preceding contours? It is clear that the former is the case; the variability in judgment was more or less constant for each subject as a person, from two-thirds of a scale unit for the 'best' subject, to one and two-thirds scale units for the 'worst' one ('Scale unit': the difference between, e.g., 'slightly bored' and 'quite bored'.) The average variation over all the texts was 1·12 scale units on test/retest.

These are larger 'errors' than Osgood found on test/retest for subjects judging word 'concepts' in similar tests: '. . . average errors . . . always less than a single scale unit . . . and for evaluative [pleasant/unpleasant] scales average about half of a scale unit.'[4]

The contours themselves also varied in the amount of test/retest variability in the judgments made of them: e.g. contour No. 15 (raised weak syllables, final rise) is usually near the most variable end of a list of the contours arranged to show this characteristic. 'Raised weak syllables', though they certainly occur in American intonation, in the speech of men as well as women, are sometimes said to be a 'woman's intonation'. The variability of the judgments in this case may indicate that this contour was less familiar to the subjects than the other contours were, or that it was unfamiliar to some of the subjects.

There were also differences in the amount of variability on the various scale terms: the subjects were least variable on the scales expressing the 'pleasant/unpleasant' dimension, and most variable on those expressing the 'strong/weak' one. In other words, they were more consistent about their own reactions to the contours than about what they judged the 'speaker's' intention to be.

Factor analyses of the correlations between the various scales for each part of the experiment – A, B, C, D, E – were carried out with a view to extracting the main 'dimensions of meaning' conveyed by these intonations. As in the previous experiment, the 'pleasant/unpleasant' factor was by far the strongest. The grouping of the scale terms in the factor analyses made it clear, however, that this time the 'authoritative/ submissive' factor came second and the 'strong (feeling)/weak (feeling)' factor third. This was the reverse of the earlier experiment, though there were some indications in the earlier one that the arrangement might not be the same for all four sentence types. It is possible that the uniform emergence of the factors on all the sentences this time is related to a larger and better choice of scale terms.

Two scales were chosen to represent each factor in the construction of the 'semantic space'[5] diagrams, Fig. 2 – A, B, C, D, E, which show the relations of the various contours to the three 'dimensions' and to

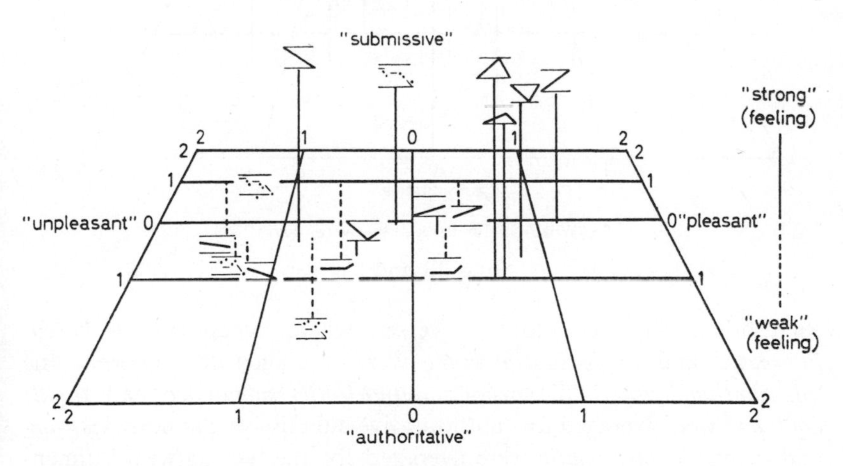


Fig. 2A.

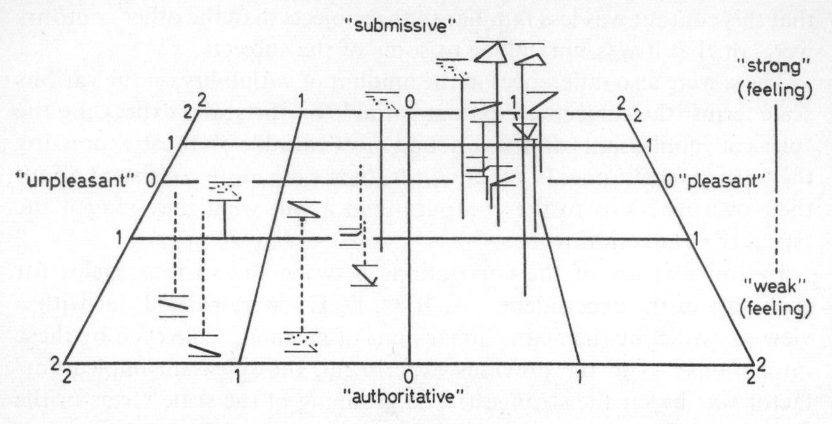


B: "Was it arranged at the meeting?"

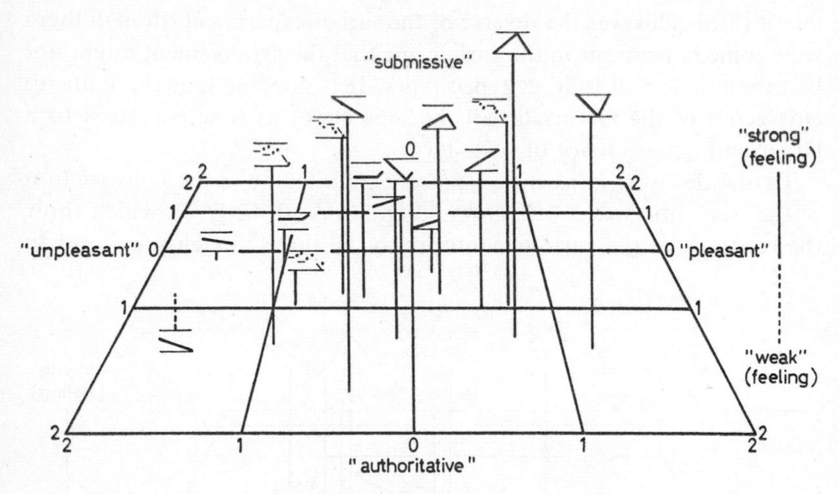


C: "What did he think they were doing?"

Figs 2B and C.

each other. Subjects' scores (reversed where necessary) on *bored/interested* and *unpleasant/pleasant* were averaged to represent the '*pleasant/unpleasant*' dimension; *authoritative/submissive* and *timid/confident* were averaged for 'authoritative/submissive'; and *weak/strong* and *emphatic/unemphatic* were averaged for the 'strong/weak' dimension.

The diagrams display, for each sentence-type and the nonsense-

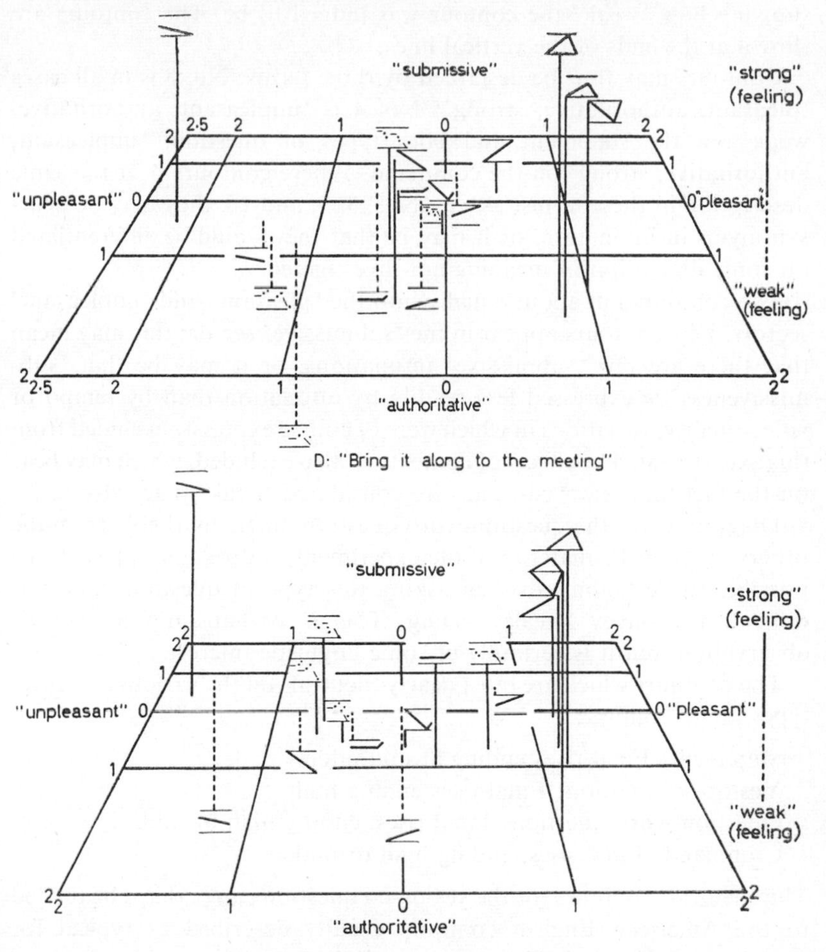


Figs 2D and E.

sequence, three dimensions: the right half of the diagram shows contours judged 'pleasant', the left half 'unpleasant'. The near half shows those judged 'authoritative', the far half 'submissive'. Solid lines rising from the point of intersection of these two scores show 'strong' judgments, the height of the line being proportional to the 'strength' of the feeling; dotted lines descending from the point of intersection of the first two scores show 'weak' judgments, with the length of the line showing how 'weak' the contour was judged to be. The contours are shown at the ends of the vertical lines.

Contours may thus be described by three terms: No. 8 is in all cases 'pleasant, authoritative, strong'; No. 4 is 'unpleasant, authoritative, weak' on the statement and both types of question, 'unpleasant, authoritative, strong' on the command. Where contours bear the same description in these terms, as e.g., Nos. 8, 9, and 10, they may be near-synonyms in intonation, or it may be that they would be differentiated on some dimension of meaning not investigated.

The contours fall about equally into the 'pleasant' and 'unpleasant' sectors. Few contours appear in the 'submissive' sector; this may mean that there are few 'submissive' intonations, or it may be that 'submissiveness' is expressed less readily by intonation than by tempo or voice-quality, variations in which were of course expressly excluded from this experiment. The effects of context are also excluded, which may bear on the fact that fewer contours are considered 'weak' than 'strong'.

Diagram C for the question-word question differs markedly from the others. Within the material of the experiment, it does not appear to be possible to be 'submissive' in asking this type of question, and it is difficult to convey 'weak' feeling. This is perhaps not a *phonetic* observation, but it is certainly of some linguistic interest.

The contours which are most nearly 'neutral' on the various sentence-types are as follows:

Statement: Final rises ending at mid pitch.
Yes-or-no question: Final rises ending high.
Question-word question: Final rises, ending high or mid.
Command: Final rises, ending high or mid.

The 'neutral' contours for the yes-or-no question can perhaps be related to the American English contours usually described as typical for questions of this kind. The others are difficult to relate to any norm.

Generalizing over the five tests, the three 'dimensions of meaning' postulated here are associated with the elements in contour variation in the following ways: (terms in parentheses show less consistent connection with the dimension)

| | |
|---|---|
| 'pleasant' | rises ending high |
| | change of direction [excluding No. 7] |
| 'unpleasant' | raised weak syllables |
| | (lowered weak syllables) |
| | (narrow range) |

| | |
|---|---|
| 'authoritative' | wide range |
| | change of direction |
| | rises ending at mid |
| | raised or lowered weak syllables |
| | (final fall) |
| 'submissive' | (rises ending high [excluding No. 8]) |
| 'strong' feeling | wide range |
| | change of direction |
| | lowered weak syllables |
| | (rises ending at mid) |
| 'weak' feeling | (narrow range) |
| | (raised weak syllables) |

The 'positive' ends of the dimensions are more easily characterized than the 'negative' ones.

Where the contours are rated differently on the different sentences, it can be seen that the less 'lively' a contour is, the more variable it is in meaning. The narrow-range 'smooth' contours Nos. 1, 3, 4, and 6, vary most often from one sentence to another. The two rising contours, 1 and 3, vary on all three dimensions; the two falls, 4 and 6, are always very 'unpleasant', but can be 'authoritative' or 'submissive', 'strong' or 'weak'.

The more 'lively' the contour is, the more stable is its position in the 'semantic space' over the different sentences. Contours Nos. 8, 9, and 10, involving wide range and a change of direction, always occupy the same sector of the space, the 'pleasant, authoritative, strong' one.

The less 'interesting' the intonation contour is, the more influential the sentence itself is in the judgment of the total effect, and vice versa.

*Notes*

[1] The work described here was carried out with the benefit of research funds from the Haskins Laboratories, New York, in connection with a grant from the Carnegie Corporation of New York.

I am much indebted to Dr Boris Semeonoff of the Department of Psychology of Edinburgh University for statistical advice.

[2] See *The Measurement of Meaning*, Osgood, Suci, and Tannenbaum, Urbana, 1957.

[3] E. T. Uldall, 'Attitudinal Meanings conveyed by Intonation Contours', *Language and Speech*, III, 1960, 223–234.

[4] *The Measurement of Meaning*, 131.

[5] Ibid., 114.

# A Suggested Simple System of Transcription for Use by Foreign Students of Standard American English

R. H. GERHARD

To-day, when talk in linguistic circles seems to be preoccupied so largely with supra-segmentals, morphemics, word classes, and the like, it may appear almost reactionary to choose as subject for a paper such as this the old-fashioned matter of phonetic transcription – especially a transcription which dares to disregard many unquestionably important aspects of connected speech.

For most of thirty years, however, I have been directly involved in the absorbing and constantly challenging problems of helping foreign students to a more satisfactory pronunciation of (American) English speech, and, though I have encountered innumerable varying techniques and experimented personally with many, for practical and tangible results in improved performance on the part of my students I still know of nothing more effective than extensive careful reading aloud of simple phonetic transcriptions.

But for this purpose a satisfactory system of notation is essential, and there are various criteria to be considered.

I candidly believe that much of the most significant progress in linguistic thinking during the past quarter-century has taken place in the United States, but it is regrettable, I feel, that so many of my countrymen have tended to draw away, in transcriptional practice, from the accepted conventions of the International Phonetic Association. Even where strong arguments may be advanced for claimed superiority or greater practicality, the benefits affirmed would scarcely seem to compensate for less widespread familiarity. I therefore put basic adherence to the tenets – and symbolization – of the IPA high on my list of requirements for a satisfactory notation.

But even this 'first principle' must be tempered with reason. There is justification I am sure, for the IPA convention of marking accentuation by a sign *before* the syllable concerned. It is certainly preferable to the usual dictionary practice of marking it *after* the syllable. But in some languages (and notably so in Japanese, with which I have my major student contacts) the concept and connotations of the word 'syllable' are so different from ours that much confusion may result from this procedure. With foreign students, therefore, I have come to prefer a mark above the symbol representing the syllabic nucleus. I use an acute accent [ˊ] to indicate full stress, and a grave accent [ˋ] to indicate secondary or half stress, leaving syllables with weak stress unmarked as in the accepted IPA usage, and feel that this adaptation is justified in easier interpretation by my students. (This is, however, a question, so to speak, of 'local ground rules', and strict adherence to IPA usage would seem preferable in case the special problem did not arise.)

Another question sure to raise a storm of argument is whether – and, if so, how – to record intonation. Of the many different systems extant, I personally prefer and use an adaptation[1] of that originally, I believe, worked out by Kenneth L. Pike of the University of Michigan. This very considerably messes up a page of text, but is graphic and easily interpreted, and I find it more practical than any other I know of for the necessary drill work in establishing unfamiliar intonational habits. For the contextual and rather rapid type of reading I am here concerned with, however, and once the basic intonational patterns have been acquired, I find it conducive to better results to discard all tonetic markings and to have my students concentrate upon the sufficiently demanding task of learning to use English sounds in English ways. If the sounds pass muster and the indicated stress pattern is strictly followed I find, at this stage, that few noticeable mistakes in intonational usage tend to occur.

And then there is the final problem of selecting that specific type of notation which is best adapted to the particular requirements. Phonemic? Yes, if only we could all agree upon exactly what that term implies. There is undeniably much to be said in support of a twelve-vowel system for Standard American English, such as that suggested by Daniel Jones[2] and others. In addition to the disadvantages resulting from the relatively large number of different signs required, however, some of us feel that the idea of representing monographically the vowels of *go* and *gay* – particularly when another vowel follows, as in *going*, *gayer*, etc. – necessitates a more involved and less acceptable explanation than do digraphic representations such as [ij], [ər], and [uw] for the vowels of *easy*, *murmur*, and *hoodoo*, respectively. Besides, for many foreign learners of English one of the commonest faults in trying to make any of these five pronunciations is in producing too short and static an articulation, and my experience would indicate that Japanese students respond as readily and more accurately to digraphic than to monographic symbolization for them.

The most satisfactory vocalic analysis I have found for standard American English, then, is one postulating four[3] categories or classes of syllabics, namely: 7 'pure' vowel phonemes; 5 'narrow' diphthongs; 8 'wide' or 'obvious' diphthongs; and 4 'consonantal vowels'. Without at all attempting to describe the sounds in detail, I shall here only identify them and indicate the transcription I use.

The seven sounds in the first group are represented monographically by the symbols [i], [e], [æ], [ə], [a], [o], and [u], and are the vowels I use in, e.g., *bid, bed, bad, bud, bomb, ball,* and *bull,* respectively. All of the remaining pronunciations are represented digraphically. The five narrow diphthongs, written [ij], [ej], [ər], [ow], and [uw], are the vowels I use in such words as *beet* or *easy*, *bait* or *melee*, *Bert* or *murmur*, *boat* or *solo*, and *boot* or *hoodoo*, respectively. The wide or obvious diphthongs, written [ir], [er], [aj], [ar], [aw], [oj], [or], and [ur], are the vowels I use in *dear*, *dare*, *sky*, *scar*, *scow*, *boy*, *bore*, and *poor*, respectively. The final group consists of the syllabic 'vowelized' consonants in, for example, the following pronunciations: *(tab)le*, *(stop)'em*, *(butt)on*, and *(chick)en (gizzard)*, and are represented by the notations [əl], [əm], [ən], and [əŋ], respectively. It will be noted that, in this transcription, every vocalic nucleus is represented by a vowel symbol, and every vowel symbol always indicates a (separate) syllable.

Those persons who believe that a satisfactory analysis of standard American vowels requires more than seven phonemes have only to so designate whichever of the remaining sounds in the above list they deem proper, with the convention of a digraphic instead of a monographic symbolization.[4] I myself often find that a merging of the first two categories makes a more easily explained system for presentation to beginning students, particularly at the secondary school level. But I prefer to regard the acoustically quite distinct quality of pronunciation represented by each of these digraphic symbolizations, in comparison with that of each monographic vowel symbol, respectively,[5] as an allophonic variation of the vowel due entirely to the influence of its phonetic context, and therefore exactly analogous to the variant values of /k/ in, e.g., *keel* and *cool*, of /t/ in *top*, *stop*, *little*, *chop*, etc., or, for that matter, of /j/ in *yes* and *say*, of /r/ in *red*, *tread*, *dare*, etc., of /w/ in *watt*, *what*, *now*, *tower*, etc., and, to a greater or less degree, of practically every sound of human speech in differing phonetic environment.

In this connection, a word may be in order in regard to the representation of diphthongs by means of vowel + glide instead of vowel + vowel symbolization. Occasional experimentation with this convention has been carried on since the earliest days of scientific phonetic alphabets, but it was Leonard Bloomfield who first adopted it 'whole hog' and who is largely responsible for its growing acceptance by linguistic scholars in the United States. And I have assurance in writing from no less an authority than Daniel Jones himself that it in no way violates the basic principles of IPA transcription. In addition to the very considerable advantages accruing from the fact, earlier referred to, that the same symbol is never used to represent at one time a syllabic nucleus and at another a non-syllabic element, however, this transcription is decidedly superior in dealing with students from a linguistic background that does not include the same sort of monosyllabic gliding pronunciations. Japanese contains no true diphthongs, and so a pedagogically valuable contrast can be shown by means of this notation between, e.g., [uisu̥kiː] and [wískij], or between [kau] (to buy) and [kaw] (*cow*), which would be quite impossible with a vowel + vowel representation of the English diphthongs. Neither the acoustic nor the articulatory values of the Japanese and English sounds in these examples are, to be sure, identical, but they are close enough to afford a valid phonetic comparison.

This use of the glide symbols, however, necessitates an extension of the traditional definition, limited to prevocalic occurrence. I shall illustrate this by discussion of the sound /r/.

In the variety of English speech I use and teach, /r/ is unquestionably a glide, analogous in all respects to /j/ or /w/. As /j/ is related to a high front vowel position, or /w/ to a high back vowel position, the /r/ of my speech is a glide from (as in *raw*), toward (as in *ore*), or through (as in *arrow*[6]) a high central vowel position in which the centre of the tongue is raised close to the rear part of the hard palate, the tip is 'bunched' or pulled back into the main body of the tongue[7] and there is both lateral contraction and a considerable degree of tensing in the muscles at the back and base of the tongue. The phoneme /r/ probably has as many variant values in different forms of English speech as any consonant, and the transcription here employed would not, presumably, fit them all. But it appears to me by far the best for representing standard American speech.

With a restatement of my adherence to the approved notation of the IPA, the transcription of consonant sounds requires little additional comment. As implied above, I prefer to explain the pronunciations of, e.g., *chew* and *Jew* as composed of four phonemes each – but will not seriously quarrel with a stand for three – or two. If this be deemed a failure to stand up for principles, I can only plead that I am more concerned with end than means, and that I care less about terminology than I do about pronunciation.

My colleagues and I at International Christian University in Tokyo agreed sometime ago to this transcription for American English, as well as to notations of basically the same type for use in work with other languages taught here, and are currently preparing text and reference materials employing it. Personally, I have found it by far the most satisfying system I have ever encountered for a simple and easily read representation of the variety of English speech I use, and strongly recommend a trial of it by anyone in similar circumstances.

I conclude with a brief transcription illustrating the notation I here advocate, using for this purpose a paragraph[8] which contains all the sounds of English speech in just about every possible phonetic situation.

its júwʒuwəlij rǽðər íjzij tə rìjʧ ðə vərʤínjə θíjətər. bórd kár nəmbər fìftij-síks sə́m(h)wer əloŋ ʧə́rtʃil strìjt ən rájd tə ðə hájwej. trǽntsfər ðèr tə ðə mísəsipij bə́s.[9] wen juw ərájv ət ʤə́ʤ ǽvən(j)uw, bigìn wókiŋ tord ðə bíznəs zòwn. juwl pǽs ə gíft ʃàp displejiŋ lítəl ʧíldrənz pléjθiŋz ðət ófən luk sòw klévər juwl wíʃ jərself jə́ŋ əgèn: sətʃ θíŋz əz búks ən tójz, ǽnd, bihàjnd ðə káwntər, ə pléjru(w)m wið ən éləgənt réd rə́g ən smúwð ʃájniŋ mírərz. bijànd ðíʃ ʃáp ar ðə nǽʃənəl bǽŋk ən ðə glówb gəráʒ. tə̀rn sáwθ ət ðə néks(t) kórnər; ðə θíjətər iz tə jər léft.

*Notes*

1 Dispensing with any marking for the 'normal' second level, I use underlining to indicate the low first level, overlining for the third level, and double overlining to mark the rare syllables when high fourth level pitch is called for. E.g.: Now $\overline{\overline{\text{what}}}$ in the $\overline{\text{world}}$ did I $\overline{\text{do}}$ with that $\overline{\text{t}}\text{ick}\underline{\text{e}}\text{t}$? Oh, $\overline{\text{here}}$ it $\overline{\text{i}}\text{s}$, $\overline{\text{right}}$ in my $\overline{\text{po}}\text{cket}$ all the $\overline{\text{t}}\text{im}\underline{\text{e}}$.

2 In *An Outline of English Phonetics*, 8th Edn. (1956), App. D. The so-called 'Michigan system' is similar, but inconsistently requires the use of a digraph for the vowel of *bird*, *murmur*, etc.

3 See below for an alternative classification.

4 Cf. the universally accepted practice in chemistry (e.g. Al, Cu, Mo, Th, etc. along with H, O, U, etc.).

5 E.g., [e(j)] with [e] or [ə(r)] with [ə], etc.

[6] The articulation of /r/ in this instance is one continuous glide which participates in both syllables of the word. Contrastingly, in *earring* or *near Rome*, there is a glide toward the vowel position, then a lessening of prominence clearly indicating the syllabic boundary, and next a prevocalic glide distinct from the preceding similar, but postvocalic, glide. Transcription /írrìŋ/, etc. Cf. *loyal* with *toy yacht*, *fuel* with *few words*, etc.

[7] An alternative articulation, used by many Americans, has the tip raised toward the alveolar ridge back of the upper front teeth or toward the forward part of the hard palate.

[8] Prepared by Miss Louise M. Linton, as quoted in *Training the Speaking Voice*, by Virgil A. Anderson, New York, 1942.

[9] Intonational pattern: Transfer there to the Mississippi bus.

# Linguistics and Phonetics in the Training of Teachers of English

W. R. LEE

## 1

As a label on the school time-table, 'English' in an English-speaking country and 'English' in a country where the language is little spoken stands for two different things – a fact which those broadly interested in the better teaching of English everywhere often overlook: a fact, also, which is sometimes obscured by attempts to make foreign syllabuses resemble home syllabuses. In an English-speaking country children generally learn English at home, as a first language; abroad, it is usually a foreign language, acquired at school.

Teaching English to pupils who have learnt to think and speak in another language and teaching English to pupils who have learnt to think and speak in English are tasks so dissimilar that we cannot label them alike. To say that pupils who have learnt English at home know English and therefore *cannot* be taught it is an exaggeration, but the exaggeration is useful if it shocks us into acknowledging that the home-English teacher and the English-as-a-foreign-language teacher must have different aims. This does not, of course, mean that there is nothing in common. Both want their pupils to speak and write clearly and in a widely acceptable manner, and to interpret accurately the spoken and written forms of the language. Furthermore, they are both concerned with the language as a whole, including subtleties of usage: the home-English teacher makes his pupils aware of these, while abroad it is mainly the teacher who needs such awareness, without which he cannot distinguish the relatively difficult from the relatively easy.

'Everyone who is not deaf or idiotic has fully mastered his native language by the end of his fifth year', declare B. Bloch and G. L. Trager, 'no matter how difficult or complex it may be to foreigners'.[1] The truth of this pronouncement depends on what is meant by 'mastered', and objection ought to be raised to 'fully'. A five-year-old makes free use of a variety of common syntactic patterns, but will he have mastered more than a small proportion of the vocabulary or of usage in situations unfamiliar to him? Can anyone be said to have 'mastered' a language who cannot read or write it? And if contemporary English only is under discussion, we may ask what is contemporary for the reader: for literature written before the present day is still widely read.

It would be unprofitable to pursue the point. Guilty of distortion though Bloch and Trager may be, they suggest the home-English teacher's two main tasks: to broaden and to refine. Some of the five-year-old's usages are thought 'uneducated' or 'incorrect' and other usages must be acquired. 'Dialect' has to be put in its place, preference being at times given to more 'standard' forms. On the whole the range of linguistic ability expands rather than shifts, since local or class pronunciations and turns of phrase survive education. A still greater broadening comes with the ability to read and write, first what is orally familiar and then what is orally unfamiliar, and this can develop into concern for printed literature and written style.[2] Here comes in the refining process. An attempt is made at educating home-English pupils to read literature critically.

The foreign-language pupil, on the other hand, will not have got so far in five years of an English course as the five-year-old before starting school. He may know and use some words unknown to the latter, but his grasp of basic sentence-patterns will be imperfect and his vocabulary relatively small. The thoughtless English-speaking infant will be untroubled by, for instance, the several uses of the so-called Simple Past and Present Perfect forms, employing them as occasion demands. The older and possibly more thoughtful learner of English as a foreign language, lacking in experience of English speech and everyday situations combined, may find these uses difficult.

A child learning to read his home language should find in print what he is familiar with already in speech, and thus reading becomes a voyage of re-discovery.[3] None the less the home-English teacher has to proceed systematically with reading, and the same applies to handwriting and composition, and indeed to the presentation and discussion of literature. But whereas the pupil who has learnt English at home is taught a new *form* of the language (its visual form), the English teacher's task otherwise being to improve the pupils' spoken (and later on written) usage and to make him sensitive to literature, it is *the language itself* which the foreign pupil has to master. Teaching thus needs to be still more methodical. There are the associated problems of what to teach, of the order in which to teach it, of *how* to teach it. Nor are pupils proficient who are merely able to construct good sentences, without awareness of the situations in which they are used: this is an ability which soon comes to be regarded as a school exercise having little connection with 'real life'.

Unless foreign learners are to be confronted with several types of difficulty at the same time, reading and writing will come later. To grasp something of a new language in its spoken form is hard enough without having to learn simultaneously a strange alphabet and perhaps an unfamiliar direction of reading. Even when these things are the same, there are various letter-shapes to grasp, and often little in common between the shapes of small and capital letters, printed and cursive: witness, for instance, F, f, $\mathscr{F}$, and $f$; L, l, $\mathscr{L}$, and $\ell$.[4] Where the ultimate aim is to produce school-leavers who can read English rather than speak it,[5] oral work is still the most effective way of laying the foundations. If the language is *seen* from the beginning, letters and letter-sequences can exercise an almost hypnotic effect: there is a tendency to give them the sound-values they possess in the learner's mother tongue.[6] Some pupils' speech will be strongly affected also by the visual separation of words on the page. All this hampers the teaching of pronunciation. Oral command of an appreciable amount of the language should be established first, but how long the introduction of reading and writing should be postponed depends on several factors, such as the pupils' ages, ability to read the mother tongue, and the total length of the course. Above all, oral work saves time. Much more practice of a given language-item can be obtained in *x* minutes orally than by other means, and if there is collective as well as individual speaking every pupil speaks for a good many minutes every language-period. Lastly, an oral first stage enables the material taught to be vividly contextualized by means of actions in the classroom.

The home language is poured in profusion over the very young child's head. There is little attempt to simplify, but many utterances occur in situations the relevance of which is clear: *Look*, *Don't touch*, *Hullo*, *Where are you going?*, etc., belong to and are explained by their contexts of occurrence. In the teaching of a foreign language the contexts need to be devised to fit the language-items chosen for teaching, and, contrariwise, the items to some extent chosen because of available contexts. Teaching English contextually means that minimum time is given to *mechanical* sentence-pattern drill, and none to the learning of mere word-lists. If *I am drawing* is the sentence, then it is spoken while the speaker draws; and if it is *Maria is drawing* there should be a real

*Maria* seen in the very act. The result of presenting language-material out of context can only be that its meaning is not well taught and that lack of interest soon sets in.

Usages which cannot be clearly demonstrated by means of actions or pictures do not belong to the oral first stage. The policy affects the grading of courses, which should be governed by class-room considerations as well as by language analysis. But there is no shortage of language-items by which to lay the foundations firmly through oral contextual teaching, the pupils taking a full and interested part.

If the foreign-language course is poorly graded, confusion and discouragement are sown. There is confusion, of course, in the pre-school child's learning of the mother tongue, but because the learner's experience of it is rich he finds his way through in the end. Opportunities of observing the foreign language in use, and of using it, are vastly fewer and should not be wasted. 'One difficulty at a time' seems the ideal to aim at, and the steps of the course must lead on as smoothly and consequentially as possible, so that skill in handling the language is built up from day to day. The progression is not a logical one of the kind to be found in grammar-books or a systematic description of the language: it is a teaching progression, founded on the view that learning is most likely to take place if traps and snares are not laid, intentionally or unintentionally. Choosing the language-material which can best be taught during the oral first stage is one problem, and deciding upon the best order in which to teach it another. There is perhaps no one best order, even in a single area, and certainly not enough considered experiment has anywhere been carried out to determine what that order might be. The systems and structures of the mother tongue and the difficulties the foreign language presents to its speakers have to be borne in mind, as well as the limitations of particular kinds of class-room. Grading is not a linguist's affair alone: it calls for imaginative reflection on class-room experience and an acquaintance with the sort of pupils for whose benefit the grading is done. Yet knowledge of the principles of language analysis does help, because wrong assumptions as to the nature of language (the assumptions, for example, that the written language is the 'real' one, or that the meaning of a word is to be found by examining its derivation) may lead to perversity in practice (for instance, to neglect of context and to the teaching of word-lists). What helps still more is familiarity with a description of the foreign language and, preferably, of the home language too: unreflective fluency in the two languages concerned is not enough, especially for the teacher who aspires to make a syllabus and plan out an order of lessons. Unfortunately we still have no comprehensive description of English, but only the partial and unsystematic descriptions which are all that scholars working alone have had time to make. We have no definitive statement, covering the various aspects of the language, of *what there is to teach*, i.e. of what the systems and structures of English are. Choice of teaching-material ought to be made from such a description: in its absence some guesswork is unavoidable, though a teacher grounded in linguistics is better able to see what is involved than one who is not. Grading, then, is partly determined by the nature of the language-material to be graded and partly by class-room considerations.[7]

Summing up, therefore, the home-English teacher goes to work on something which already exists, on the English his pupils bring with them on starting school. For them English has long been a part of daily life and a means of learning and communication, and with the teacher's help it becomes a more serviceable means and often the gateway to English literature. It is otherwise with the teacher of English as a foreign language. He also may wish to cultivate a taste for English literature in due course[8] and will almost certainly want his pupils to read English and write English: but his first and main task always will be to give them an active grasp of the fundamental usages of the very language.

2

Since their tasks differ, the home-language and the foreign-language teacher must be differently trained. This does not mean that there is no denominator common to the two types of training, or that linguistics and phonetics can be excluded from either. On the contrary, they have an essential part to play in both.

We should have in mind a teacher's training and *education* as a whole, and not merely a language-teacher's. Doubtless 'the student of education is concerned only secondarily with extending his knowledge and accumulating information; his first concern is with cultivating personal quality, with deepening his power of discernment, with increasing the nervousness and relevance of his response, with forming a standard which is personally significant and of more than personal validity.'[9] We may admit the importance also of the 'vivifying' and 'civilizing' influence of literature,[10] particularly where language-teachers are concerned. At the same time no-one can deny that a teacher may be educated in the sense these quotations suggest and yet be ineffective in his teaching. What he also needs is a certain viability, arising from skill in personal relationships (especially with his pupils) and from technical competence. Without this he feels lost, and is lost, and is unable effectively to transmit either his 'personal quality' or his knowledge. Such skill and competence does not belong to an inferior 'tips-and-hints' level the serious educationist can afford to despise: it has its theoretical foundation in analysis of teaching matter and teaching methods, a foundation which research seeks to strengthen and extend; and it has its practical basis in carefully arranged experience intended to yield understanding of class-room problems.

As far as technical competence is concerned, teacher training has to be centred on the class-room. If it is not, the teacher may have extensive knowledge and even some kinds of relevant skill, and yet be a poor teacher.[11] Nevertheless it is not only a question of providing suitable teaching practice but of integrating the elements of training into a coherent plan. Thus if study of audio-visual aids is an element, it should be neither a general study nor a tinkering with apparatus: the clear purpose is to see in what manner aids can subserve language-teaching. The same applies to dramatization, or puppetry, or activity methods, or whatever it may be. And the same applies to linguistics and phonetics, which similarly ought not to be dabbled in or studied in too general a way. How can they be brought into service?

Admittedly the vocational aspects of training can never bc quite separated from the broadly educational. Study of linguistics and phonetics, or for that matter of dramatization or other elements in the training programme, can deepen the student's 'power of discernment' and bring fresh human insights. We can ask, furthermore, how language-teaching aims subserve those of education, as well as how a given element in the language-teacher's training subserves language-teaching aims. Teaching always involves a great deal more than technical competence, though this is undoubtedly a condition of success.

We are not, of course, considering in any detail here either education taken broadly or the English-teacher's training as a whole, but only whether a study of linguistics and phonetics can help the class-room teacher. Yet the background must be noticed if a reasonable perspective is to be kept.

3

Phonetic knowledge and ability are plainly essential to the teacher of English as a foreign language, whether or not English is his mother tongue, and this is widely though by no means universally acknowledged. It is one thing to hear something wrong with a pupil's pronunciation, another to put one's finger unerringly on the faults, another still to define those faults in terms of (say) movements of the speech-organs, and another again to invent remedial exercises when the pupil's imitation of the teacher fails, as it often does. Moreover, the teacher should himself be able to imitate accurately and pronounce the 'right' side by side with the 'wrong'. Possession of these skills presupposes a rigorous phonetic training, and this will include a study of phonetic theory as well as regular practical work, continuing for a year or more, to loosen the grip of mother-tongue listening and speaking habits. Voice-production work, which has a different character, can go on at the same time.

The training ought not to be focused too narrowly on the phonetics of English, or even on the phonetics of English and the mother tongue. Those who are to teach in one country only, where there is one mother tongue, should understand the speech habits of both languages, and need not concern themselves with another; but even they will inevitably be involved with sounds and sound-features which belong to neither language but which the floundering learner will produce. Training in the phonetics of the foreign language and the mother tongue is not enough. What is required also is to develop the skills of identifying and producing sounds and sound-features in general; and this is essential for those who are to teach in a number of countries or whose pupils will speak a number of different mother tongues.

It is perhaps unnecessary to point out that in acquiring the phonetic skills the foreign teacher does much to improve his pronunciation of English. The improvement is brought about mainly by systematic practical work, which should be guided by a phonetician or a well-constructed series of recordings, or by both.

In the training of teachers of English as a home language phonetics has also an important part to play. Striving to establish clear and pleasant speech, free alike of slovenliness and affectation, the English teacher in any part of the school is likely to be helped by knowledge of the way speech is produced and of what the speech-organs can and cannot do. Although he is not concerned with types of sound or phonetic features which do not occur in English, he should be aware of the main differences between one form or style of English speech and another. The teacher of elementary reading should be aware of the rhythmic and tonal features of normal speech, and this awareness would help him in combating the word-by-word (almost letter-by-letter) apology for reading-aloud which is still allowed to drone on in some schools. A phonetically trained teacher of reading would also be able to avoid crude misconceptions as to the relationships of sounds and letters.

4

One of the advantages to a foreign-language teacher of a study of linguistics has been mentioned. Understanding of the principles of linguistic analysis helps understanding of the systems and structures of languages at different levels of analysis, and vice versa.[12] A better assessment can then be made of such part-descriptions of languages as are available. Unless the teacher of English abroad is blindly to follow texts and handbooks, he needs, as we have pointed out, as clear a realization as possible of what there is to teach: that is, of the oppositions, contrasts, and structures characterizing the language.[13] Without this he is imperfectly qualified to grade a course or even to work out a way of teaching each item of the language, though such matters cannot be settled in the light of linguistics alone. A teacher who takes up linguistics is thus better equipped to cope with teaching problems, and should come to exercise more influence, than one who does not. He can assess the value of textbooks and syllabuses better and re-shape them. He is better able to advise other teachers of the same language.

The effect on language-teaching of wrong beliefs about the nature of language has also been referred to. A study of linguistics has negative value in reducing the strength and number of such ideas. Respect for the so-called rules of grammar, for instance, assumes reasonable proportions once it is seen that most 'rules' are but roughly descriptive and that users of the language are under no obligation to conform to them. Understanding of words is likely to be juster once the belief is abandoned that in whatever context a word is found it is the graven image of one and the same idea. Central to the linguistics course are concepts such as system and structure, pattern and variant, difference and sameness, substitution, level of analysis, kinds of meaning, context, and probability.

The negative value of linguistics is equally evident when we consider the training of home-English teachers. For very long the study and description of contemporary English was seriously handicapped by terminology and notions applicable to the description of Greek, and this handicap has not everywhere been overcome: modern linguistics has yet to find its expression, for example, in English grammars for use in schools.[14] The cultivation of a sense of style and of fine shades of meaning in English – one of the home-English teacher's tasks – is also furthered by study of language in its various modes, of ways of analysing and describing language, and of the main ways in which language has been studied: all without prejudice to the view that methodical analysis and would-be scientific description do not exhaust everything that is 'there', everything of interest and value in the human use of language. This is part of a liberal education, though a somewhat neglected part. Schools have devoted their attention, as far as linguistics is concerned, mainly to the historical development of language. It is high time for a linguistics course to be established in training colleges, and then in schools, which would bring to the fore the contemporary language, viewed chiefly as a means of communication. From such a course the students should derive some idea of what the main sub-divisions of linguistics deal with and of the kind of linguistic thought and investigation that is still going on.

## 5

As a general rule the English-teacher should not think of passing on his linguistic and phonetic knowledge to pupils, and certainly not (again with exceptions) in the form in which he acquired it. It is for incidental use during the course of his work. Taking 'teacher' broadly, as one who can make and re-make courses as well as give them, we can say that linguistics and phonetics have an essential rôle to play in the training of English-teachers, whether at home or abroad, and that all teachers of English need training in the phonetic skills. As much as use of a language, however, it is pupils who are taught. A language-teacher's training should not be based *mainly* on linguistic study, and must be primarily a training to *teach* a language. Linguistics and phonetics make vital contributions to that training programme, but there is no place in the class-room for the linguist or phonetician who is nothing else but these. Nor, in the writer's view, are there born teachers who do not need training.

### *Notes*

[1] B. Bloch and G. L. Trager, *Outline of Linguistic Analysis*, Baltimore, 1942, 7.

[2] Concern for *spoken* literature should, of course, develop out of oral work.

[3] If, of course, first reading books contain words and sentence-patterns which are strange to the child, this will not happen.

[4] For this reason the earliest reading-material is probably best printed in only one form of the letters.

[5] It is tempting to declare roundly that in the modern world such an aim is out of date.

[6] This is so, at least, if both languages use the same alphabet.

[7] The material to be graded will not look the same in all countries, some features appearing strange and difficult in one which do not in another. The details of the 'conflict' with the mother tongue should also affect grading to some extent, determining sometimes the easiest 'lead in' to correct use of a given sentence-structure.

[8] Rhymes and simple stories of literary value may indeed be introduced into the language-course from an early stage.

[9] W. Walsh, *The Use of Imagination*, London, 1959, 10.

[10] Ibid., 10.

[11] Still less will he be competent, on returning to his own country, to train other teachers.

[12] The terms 'system', 'structure' and 'levels' are used in the senses made well known by J. R. Firth.

[13] This is not in any way to decry textbooks and handbooks, which most teachers need – the more detailed and definite the better.

[14] Cf. R. Quirk, 'English Language and the Structural Approach', in *The Teaching of English – Studies in Communication 3*, 1959, 17.

# The Phonetics of European Languages

# English Words in Spoken Flemish

E. BLANCQUAERT

Three authors are to be mentioned in connection with the English influence on Dutch vocabulary, namely C. G. N. de Vooys,[1] G. Worgt,[2] and A. Kolsteren.[3]

De Vooys has written several papers on the subject, the chief of which is an essay published by the Royal Dutch Academy of Sciences. Approximately 500 words are treated and classified under headings such as victuals and drinks, dressing, traffic, business, amusement and games, sports, navigation, army, politics, industry, etc. Modern Dutch provides the material: all examples are taken from dictionaries, novels, periodicals, and newspapers. De Vooys paid but little attention to the Flemish part of the Dutch area. Worgt takes his material from the dictionaries. This list of words comprises over 1600 items; he recognizes the necessity of including Flemish in the study of English loan-words, but he declares that he was not able to do so, for practical reasons.

Summing up the desiderata of a more complete study of the English influence on the vocabulary of the Netherlands, De Vooys also admits that a complementary inquiry by a South Netherlands philologist does not seem superfluous.[4] I cannot think of filling such a gap in this note. My purpose is to illustrate, by a limited number of instances, some aspects of this influence in Flanders, confining my remarks to spoken Flemish. My material consists of information provided by students and former students of the University of Ghent, who are familiar with the popular language. I am glad to associate them in this way with the homage to Professor Daniel Jones.

It is not quite possible to delimit precisely the different sorts of language involved in an enquiry of this kind. As to English, I do not distinguish American English from British English; as to Flemish, there is the whole gamut between educated speech and downright dialect. The loan-words listed by De Vooys and Worgt are confined to, or originate in, the written language of dictionaries, etc., as I have already said. When used orally by people who have learned English, they are pronounced in the English way, or approximately so, in Holland and in Flanders. It should be mentioned, however, that even English-speaking Dutch and Flemish people neglect a number of details of the English pronunciation. For instance, English final voiced consonants or consonant-groups such as /d, dz, ʤ, b, bz, g, gz/[5] in the loan-words *week-end(s)*, *porridge*, *club(s)*, *bull-dog(s)*, are treated in the Dutch or Flemish way, i.e. as /t, ts, ʧ, p, ps, χ, χs/. Whereas /r/ is dropped in English in final position, and in some other cases it is pronounced in words borrowed by Dutch and Flemish, e.g. in *teenager*, *manager*, *corner*. We do not, as a rule, aspirate [p, t, k] as in English. The diphthongization of English /ou/ and /ei/ is stronger in the Northern than in the Southern Netherlands. The unrounded pronunciation of English /u/ and /ou/ exists only locally in Holland and Flanders. English weakened syllables are pronounced unreduced, following the English spelling, e.g. /ˈɔksfɔrt/. But all details of this kind cannot be described here; we have to deal with more important differences. For English *tram*, Holland says /trem/ in the English way; most people in Flanders say /tram/, maybe as a result of the influence of French *tram(way)*, or simply as a 'spelling pronunciation', or owing to both factors working at the same time. By 'spelling pronunciation' I mean the pronunciation of the *a* in *tram* as /ɑ/, i.e. in the Flemish way. I will use the same term for all similar cases further on in this note: so /meːtiŋ/ is the semi-popular spelling-pronunciation for English *meeting*. Dutch and Flemish people who know better will say /miːtiŋ/. But the real popular Flemish pronunciation is /meːtiŋk/ or anything approaching this, because the suffix *-ing* is pronounced *-ink* (and var.) in the Flemish dialects. A great many English loan-words occur both in French and in Flemish. The Flemish pronunciation of these loan-words is, more often than in Holland, influenced by their French counterparts, as suggested above in the case of *tram(way)*; this influence is quite certain, or most probable, in many other cases, e.g. in the Flemish and French dog's name /miˈlɔːr/, English *milord*; in Flemish /pikpɔˈket/, French /pikpɔˈke/, where the Flemish has the French stress, but keeps the final /t/ of the original.

In a number of cases, the Flemish loan-word is taken from English, but has been provided with a Flemish compounding or derivating element; so for instance in *cocktailkleed*, /ˈkɔkteːlkleːt/, the first element is English, the second Flemish; *kleed* = *dress, gown*; *fixen*, /fiksə(n)/ = *to fix* (a date, etc.) has taken the Flemish-Dutch suffix of the infinitive; the second element of *beefsteak* is sometimes pronounced /stʌk/ or /styk/ and suggests *stuk* = *piece*.

And this brings us to a final group of loan-words, where popular etymology has been at work (examples in sub-group IV).

In accordance with the preceding remarks, we will classify a limited number of loan-words into four groups: (I) Loan-words with an English – or approximately English – pronunciation; they are generally used by more or less well-educated people who have learned English. (II) Loan-words whose pronunciation is influenced by the spelling in such a way that they are pronounced as if they were Flemish. We include in this group the words that are pronounced in the French way. (III) Loan-words with Flemish compounding element or affixes. (IV) Loan-words assimilated to Flemish by popular etymology, or translated, or transformed to such a degree that their English origin is hardly to be recognized. Here again, it is not possible to draw sharp lines between the groups; some words are pronounced in different ways, so that they belong to more than one group. The reader will find in Group I the words that are pronounced as in English, but with variants belonging to Group II, etc. The notes, *Flemish dialect of Ghent*, or *Antwerp harbour dialect*, or *dialect of Aalst*, are used when the word or the pronunciation is typical for those places; other dialect-quotations apply to more or less general dialect phenomena. I have not listed the items within each group alphabetically because I preferred not to separate some smaller groups belonging to the same semantic area. The entries are the English words; meanings are added only when necessary; the phonetic transcriptions render Flemish pronunciations.

## GROUP I

Loan-words pronounced as in English, or in an approximately similar way.

*Tom(my)*, /ˈtʊmi/, name for a British soldier.
*Eddy*, /ˈedi/; /ˈeːdi/, dial. of Ghent.
*Winston*, /winstʊn/.
*Jack(y)*,/ ˈdʒæk(i)/, /ˈʒak(i)/ (Fr. infl.); /dʒɛk/ in older Flem. dial. = an Englishman.
*Puck(y)*, /ˈpʌk(i)/, /ˈpyk(i)/, dog's name.
*Black*, /blæk/, /blɑk/, dog's name.
*bull-dog*, /ˈbuldɔχ/, /ˈbyldɔχ/.
*Rolls-Royce*, /ˈrʊlsrɔːis/.
*Austin*, /ˈɑustin/; /ɔsˈtɛ̃/. (Fr. infl.).
*Morris*, /ˈmɔris/, /ˈmouris/.
*Rover*, /ˈruːvər/.
*jeep*, /dʒiːp/.
*power-glide*, /ˈpɑuwərglɑit/.
*main line*, /mɑinlɑːin/.
*standing*, /ˈstændiŋ/, /ˈstɑndiŋ/.
*week-end*, /ˈwiːkent/, /ˈweːkent/.
*welfare*, /welfɛːr/.
*hobby*, /ˈ(h)ɔbi/.
*puzzle*, /ˈpʌzəl/, /ˈpyzəl/.
*close-up*, /kloːzˈʌp/.
*tape*, /teːp/.
*pick-up*, /pikˈʌp/, /pikˈyp/.
*drink* (s.), /driŋk/.
*stout* (ale), /stɑut/, /stut/ (Fr. infl.; also dial. of West Flanders).
*Christmas* (ale), /ˈkris(t)mɑs/.
*cocktail*, /ˈkɔkteːl/.
*whisky*, /ˈwiski/.
*bar*, /bɑːr/.
*boy*, /bɔːi/, native servant in Africa.
*jukebox*, /ˈdʒugbɔks/, /ˈjukəbɔks/.
*fifty-fifty*, /ˈfifti-ˈfifti/.
*tennis*, 1. /tenis/, 2. /ˈteːnis/, 3. /teːnys/. (2 and 3: dial. of Ghent, popular).
*set*, /set/.
*fair play*, /fɛːrˈpleː/.
*dumping*, /ˈdʌmpiŋ/, /ˈdympiŋ/.
*doping*, /ˈduːpiŋ/, /ˈdoːpiŋk/.
*outsider*, /ˈɑutsɑidər/.
*nurse*, /nʌrs/.
*Sloan* (liniment), /sloːn/, /sloˈɑn/ (pop.).
*teenager*, /ˈtiːneːdʒər/; for fun also /ˈteːnɑːgər/, spelling pron.
*swing*, /swiŋ/.
*rock and roll*, /rɔk en roːl/, /rɔk en rɔl/.
*Charleston*, /ˈʃɑrləstʊn/.
*jumper*, /ˈdʒʌmpər/.
*blazer*, /bleːzər/.
*pullover*, /pulˈoːvər/, /ˈpyloːvər/.
*step-in*, /stepˈin/.
*tweed*, /twiːt/.
*Oxford*, /ˈɔksfɔrt/.
*Shetland*, /ˈʃetlɑnt/.
*trench-coat*, /ˈtrenʃkoːt/.
*auto-coat*, /ˈɔtokoːt/.
*overall*, /oːvərˈʊːl/, /oːvərˈɑl/.
*porridge*, /ˈpɔritʃ/.
*kipper*, /ˈkipər/.
*cake*, /keːk/.
*container*, /kʊnteːnər/.
*shackle*, /ˈʃekəl/ (Antwerp-harbour dialect).
*boiler*, /ˈbɔːilər/.
*building*, /ˈbildiŋ/; popular: /ˈbildiŋk/, /ˈbyldink/.

*bunker*, /ˈbʌŋkər/, /ˈbyŋkər/.
*timekeeper*, /ˈtaːimkipər/ (harbour dialect of Antwerp).
*wiper*, /ˈwaipər/, id.
*fitter*, /ˈfitər/, id.
*tarpaulin*, /ˈtæːrpəliŋ/, id.
*sling*, /slæŋ/, id.
*winch*, /wiŋs/, id.
*derrick*, /derk/, id.
*wire*, /ˈwaːiər/ (cable), id.

## GROUP II

Spelling-pronunciation, French influence and other anomalies.

Instances of spelling-pronunciation and French influence have already been given in Group I, e.g. the second (and third) pronunciation of *Eddy*, *Jack(y)*, *Puck(y)*, *Black*, *bull-dog*, *Austin*, *Morris*, *standing*, *week-end*, *puzzle*, *pick-up*, *stout*, *Christmas*, *jukebox*, *tennis*, *dumping*, *doping*, *Sloan*, *teenager*, *overall*, *building*, *bunker*. Other instances are:

*pickpocket*, /pikpəˈket/, French stress, Engl. /t/.
*beachcomber*, /ˈbitskumər/, vulg., harbour dialect of Antwerp.
*sandwich*, /ˈsandwitʃ/, /saŋdwis/, dial. Ghent.
*pale ale*, /pelˈel/, Fr. infl.
*fancy-fair*, /fa(ŋ)sifɛːr/ or /ˈfã(ŋ)sifɛːr/, dial. Ghent, Fr. infl.
*macadam*, /makaˈdam/; Fr. infl.
*chamberlain*, /ˈ(t)ʃamberlɛ̃ː/; Fr. infl.
*fair line*, /ˈfairlain/, dial. Ghent.
*choke*, /ʃɔk/ (air vent).
*short*, /ʃɔrt/.
*back* (football), /bak/.
*goal*, /ˈgoːl(ə)/.
*goalkeeper*, /ˈgoːlkiːpər/.
*corner*, /ˈkɔrnər/.
*penalty*, /ˈpenalti/, cf. Group IV.
*Sunlight* (soap), /ˈsynliχt/.
*carnation caps*, /karnasiõ kaps/, dial. Ghent, Fr. infl.
*shampoo*, /ˈʃampuː/.
*shampooing*, /ʃamˈpwɔ̃ĩ/, Fr. infl.
*catgut*, /kadˈgyt/, Fr. infl.
*halfpenny*, /ˈɔːpəniŋk/ (small coin), coast dial., arch.
*beefsteak*, /ˈbifstek/, /ˈbifstʌk/, /ˈbyfstʌk/ (2 and 3: dial.).
*roast beef*, /rɔzˈbif/, /ˈrɔzbyf/.
*battle-dress*, /ˈbatəldres/.
*tank*, /taŋk/.
*jazz-band*, /(d)ˈʒazbãnt/.
*joule*, /ˈjulə/ (school-word).
*(kilo)watt*, /(ˈkilo)wat/.
*bungalow*, /ˈbyŋgaloː/.
*club*, /klyp/.
*pony*, /ˈpʊːneː/, /pʊˈneː/.
*derby*, /ˈderbi/.
*nothing*, /ˈnʊːtẽŋk/, Ghent dial., vulgar.
*foreman*, /ˈfɔːrman/, harbour-dial. of Antwerp.
*butler*, /ˈbytlər/.
*shrapnel*, /sχrapˈnel/.
*knock-out*, /ˈknəkaut/, /knəkˈaut/.

## GROUP III

English words with Flemish suffixes or prefixes; compounds with Flemish element.

*fix*, v., e.g. to fix a date, /ˈfiksə(n)/,
*pullover*, /ˈpyləkə/ = spell. pron. of *pull.* + dim. suffix /-əkə/.
*centre*, v. (football), /ˈsentərə(n)/, with Flem. infinitive suffix.
*picnic*, v. /pikˈnikə(n)/, id.
*tennis*, (to play –), /ˈtenisə(n)/, id. (cf. Group I).
*whist*, (to play –), /ˈwiːzə(n)/, id.
*bridge* (to play –), /ˈbritʃə(n)/, id.
*shift*, v. /ˈʃiftə(n)/, id. (Antwerp harbour-dialect).
*type*, v., /ˈtipə(n)/, imperf. /ˈtiptə/, past participle /gəˈtipt/, also /ˈtaːipə(n)/, /ˈtaiptə/, /gəˈtaːipt/.
*job*, /dʒɔp/, dim.: /dʒɔpkə/.
*stack*, s. + Flem. *-er* suffix: /ˈstækər/, Antwerp harbour-dialect.
*cocktail-dress* (ladies), Flem. /ˈkɔkteːlkleːt/, Dutch /ˈkɔkteːljʌrk/; /kleːt/, /jʌrk/ = *gown.*
*linesman*, Flem. (Aalst) /ˈliɲəkəsmaːn/; /liɲəkəs/: dim. plur. of /ˈliɲə/ = line; /maːn/: local pron. of /man/ = *man.*
*life-boat*, /ˈlaːivbuːət/; /buːət/: Antwerp dial. for Dutch *boot* = Engl. *boat.*
*backstay*, /ˈbakstaːiχ/, Antwerp dial.

## GROUP IV

Popular etymology, translation or extensive transformation.

*bren-carrier*, /ˈbrenkæːrəkən/, Flem. dial (Aalst); /bren/ = machine-gun; /kæːrəkən/ = dimin. to /kæːrə/ = cart.
*scooter*, 2nd component of Flemish /ˈɔtosχəkər/ = kind of small automobile circling within booths, or fair; *scooter* is replaced by the more familiar Flem. *schokker*, nomen agentis from the verb *schokken* = to shock; the more educated use /ˈautoskuːtər/.
*Andrews salt*, dial. of Ghent, pop.: /ˈʊndəræːtsæːt/. English /ˈændruːs/ has suggested /ˈʊndəræt/ = preserving; /zæːt/, /sæːt/ by assimilation = salt.
*Kruschen-salt*, dial. of Ghent, pop.: 1) /ˈkrɔːəskəsæːt/; /ˈkrɔːəskəs/ = dim. plur. of /ˈkrɔːəs/ = cross; /zæːt/, vide supra. (2) /ˈkriːstəsæːt/; /ˈkriːstəs/ = Christ.
*football*, translated into Flem.: *voetbal*, /ˈvuṭbal/, first pronounced /fuṭbal/, as it is still now in some cases where assimilation is excluded: I go to the football = Ik ga naar de /ˈfuṭbal/.
*skyscraper*, /ˈwɔlkərabər/; wolk = cloud; krabber = scraper.
*penalty*, /ˈpenalti/, pop. dial. of Ghent: /ˈpeilanti/, /ˈpenanti/, transformations without sense.

*jam(pot)*, name given by Flemish soldiers to the comrade Tommies in 1914–1918, alluding to their abundant jam rations; pronounced /ˈdjempɔt/, /ˈ(d)ʒɑmpot/; pot = tin.

It appears from the four groups of loan-words dealt with above that the distance from the English originals increases from Group I to Group IV. From the Flemish point of view, they represent increasing degrees of assimilation to the native language or dialect. This conclusion should be subjected to further enquiry; but this is only possible by accurate phonetic observation at various levels and in different areas of the Netherlandic territory.

*Notes*

1 C. G. N. de Vooys, *Engelse invloed op de Nederlandse woordvoorrand*, Amsterdam, 1951.

2 G. Worgt, *Der Englische Einfluss auf das Niederländische*, Diss, Leipzig, not yet published, but summarized by De Vooys in *De Nieuwe Taalgids*, 49, 3–9.

3 A. Kolsteren, *Prisma-vreemde-woordenboek*, Utrecht-Antwerp, 1956. (A dictionary of 'foreigners', among which a great many English loan-words in Dutch occur; no indications of pronunciation; only the stress is given.)

4 De Vooys, *De Nieuwe Taalgids*, 49, 7.

5 The phonetic symbols are those used in Jones's *English Pronouncing Dictionary*, 11th Edn.; key-words on p. xlii.

# Notes on the Intonation of Questions in Italian

M. CHAPALLAZ

Short interrogative sentences have the intonation of one or other of two basic intonation patterns of Italian, viz. the Falling and the Falling-Rising, referred to respectively as Basic Pattern I (BP I) and Basic Pattern II (BP II).

## BASIC PATTERN I

This is similar to Tune I of English described by Armstrong and Ward,[1] except that the last stressed syllable has only a very slight fall of pitch to a low level. If unstressed syllables, or a short group of a parenthetical nature follow, these syllables are on a low level pitch. Any initial unstressed syllables form an ascending scale going up to the first stressed syllable.

BP I is the most usual pattern for X-questions, that is, questions beginning with a specific interrogative word, in their simplest form; as, for instance in:

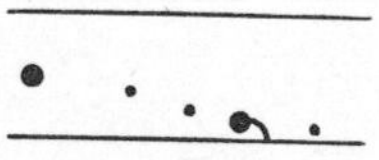

Come ha fatto?

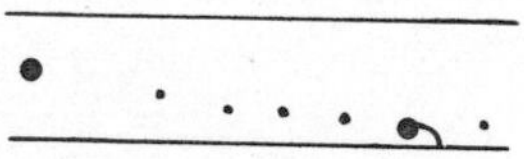

Quando ci rivedremo?

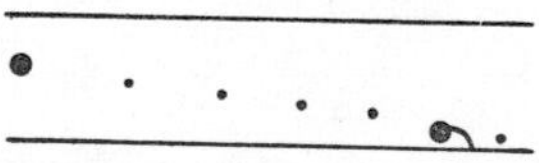

Chi dovrei annunziare?

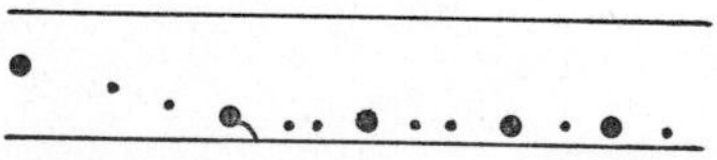

Quali lezioni avete avuto oggi?

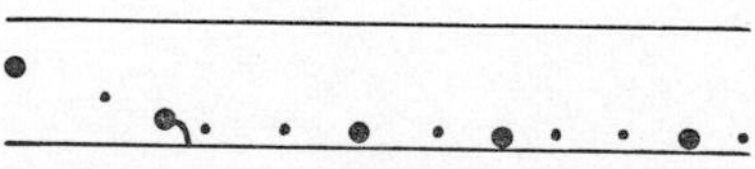

Dove vai? gli chiese il suo amico.

## BASIC PATTERN II

Similarly, Italian BP II is like English Tune II described by Armstrong and Ward.[1] It is the common pattern for Yes-No questions, that is, for questions expecting the answer 'Yes' or 'No', as in the questions:

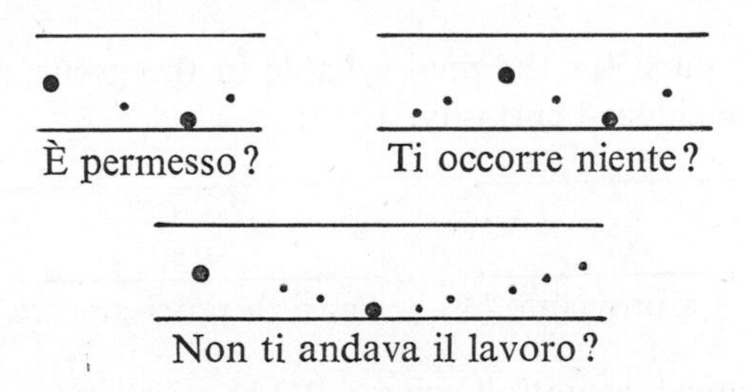

È permesso? Ti occorre niente?

Non ti andava il lavoro?

There is, however, a great deal of variety in the treatment of the final part of a BP II question group especially when the final word has penultimate stress. I have noted the following examples:

(a) The last stressed syllable may be on low level pitch with a rise of pitch in the following unstressed syllable, as in:

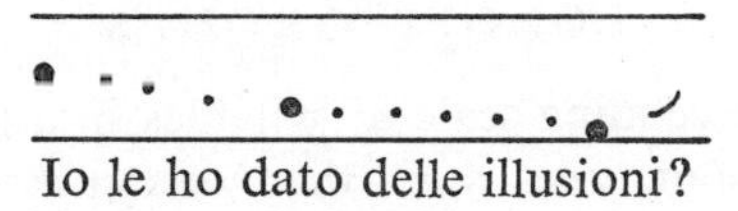

Io le ho dato delle illusioni?

(b) There may be a fall of pitch in the last stressed syllable and a rise in the following unstressed syllable, as in:

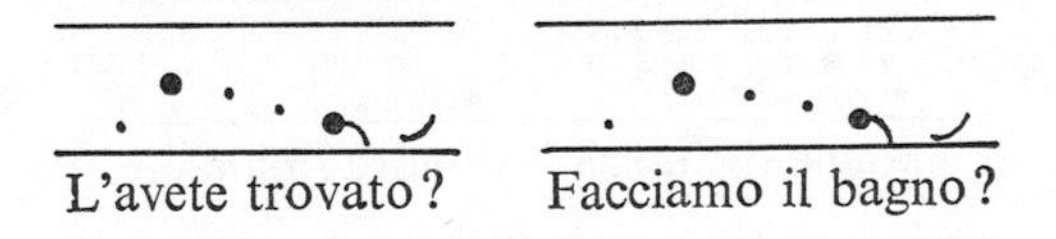

L'avete trovato? Facciamo il bagno?

(c) The rise in pitch may be spread over the two syllables, as in:

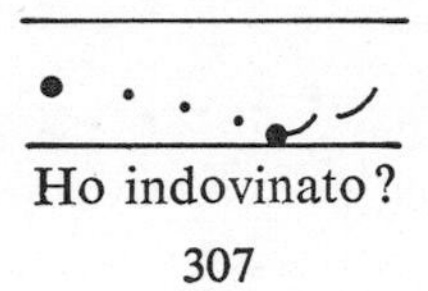

Ho indovinato?

(d) When it is the final syllable which is stressed, there may be a fall-rise within that syllable, thus:

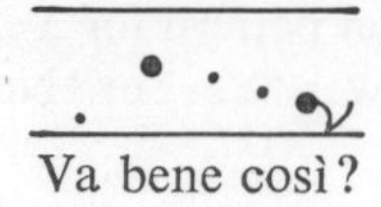

Va bene così?

(e) A high pitch for the final syllable in the group creates the impression of heightened curiosity. Thus:

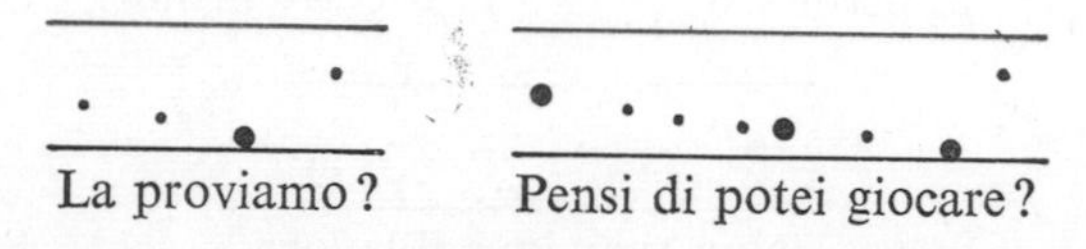

La proviamo? Pensi di potei giocare?

A parenthetical group following a BP II question, as for instance in reported speech, often has a BP I intonation, but with a narrower pitch range than that of the main group. An example is:

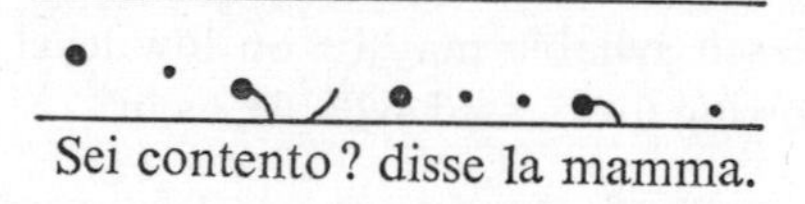

Sei contento? disse la mamma.

## LONGER GROUPS

In the gradually descending scale of syllables in a long BP I or BP II question, one, or sometimes more than one stressed syllable, is pronounced higher than the preceding syllable, the descent continuing after this raised syllable as before. There is thus a break in the gradual descent, the raised syllable forming a 'peak'. (In the text of the examples below an arrow shows the raised syllable.)

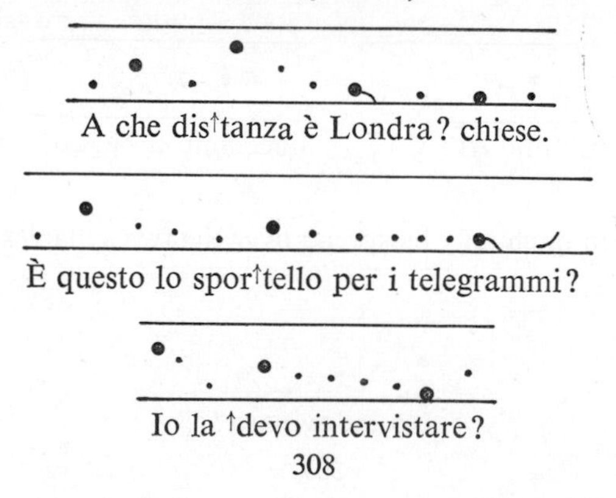

A che dis↑tanza è Londra? chiese.

È questo lo spor↑tello per i telegrammi?

Io la ↑devo intervistare?

## X-QUESTIONS WITH BASIC PATTERN II

Where an answer is courteously requested rather than insisted upon, an X-question is commonly spoken with BP II, as in these examples:

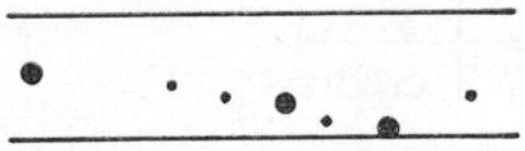

Quando potete farlo? 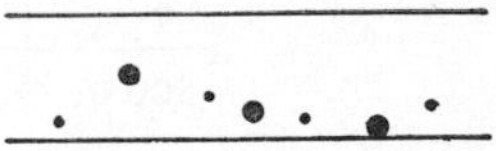    Da che paese viene?

## YES-NO QUESTIONS WITH BASIC PATTERN I

Italian has no special grammatical written forms corresponding to *est-ce que* or to the inversion of the subject in French, nor to the anomalous finites in question forms in English; so that a Yes-No question must be spoken with BP II or it will have the intonation as well as the grammatical form of a statement.

The following examples with BP II are Yes-No questions:

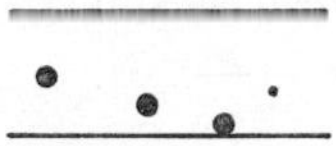

Non è vero? 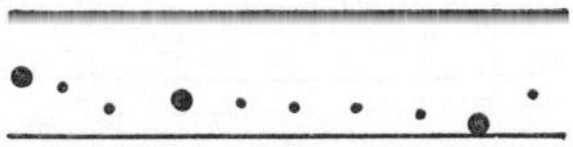    Io la ↑devo intervistare?

With BP I the same examples are turned into statements, thus:

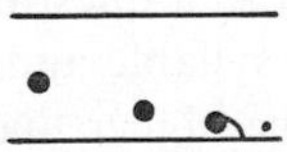

Non è vero 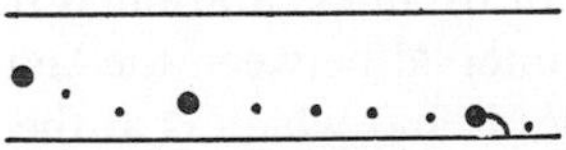    Io la ↑devo intervistare.

Under certain circumstances, however, Yes-No questions can be heard spoken with BP I. This is when either the context is sufficient to indicate that the group is an interrogative one, or a short phrase or 'tag' preceding or following the main group gives the clue. Examples:

## ALTERNATIVE QUESTIONS

Basic Pattern II is general for alternative questions, as in the examples below, but if these are spoken in a more peremptory manner then BP I may be heard.

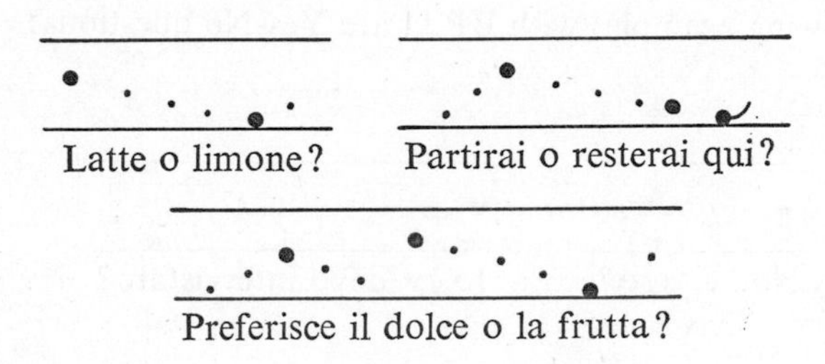


## A COMMON MODIFICATION IN BP I AND BP II

Some degree of liveliness and interest is added to a question if there is a wide pitch interval between the last stressed syllable and the syllable which precedes it and which is at the same time higher than any other syllable in the group. Thus:

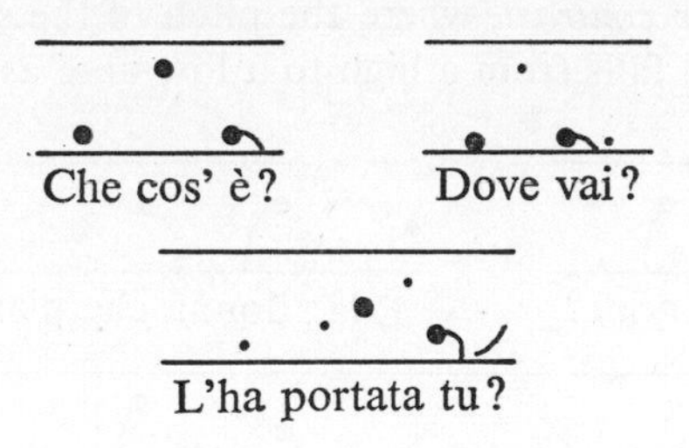


## EMPHATIC INTONATION

Apart from the modifications to BP I and BP II already mentioned in the preceding notes and which add a certain degree of liveliness or interest, ways of giving extra emphasis to questions resemble those used in English. To illustrate this I conclude with a few examples of:

(1) *emphasis for intensity* where the pitch range is widened and the stressed syllables are pronounced with increased stress. (In the text the marks " show intensity stress and ″ contrast stress.) Thus:

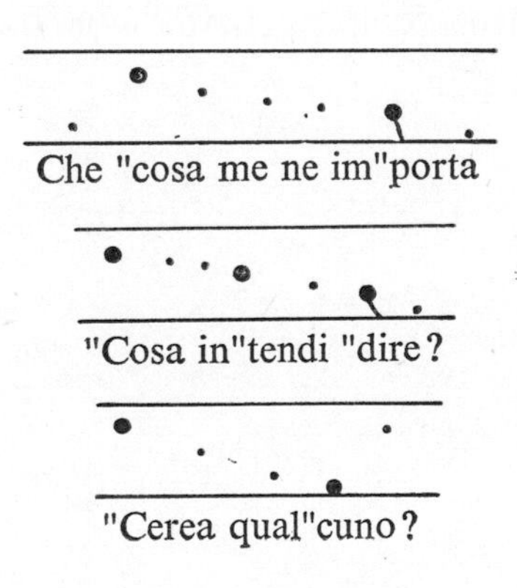

Che "cosa me ne im"porta
"Cosa in"tendi "dire?
"Cerca qual"cuno?

(2) *emphasis for contrast*, where the pitch of the stressed syllable of the contrast word falls from a high to a low note as in:

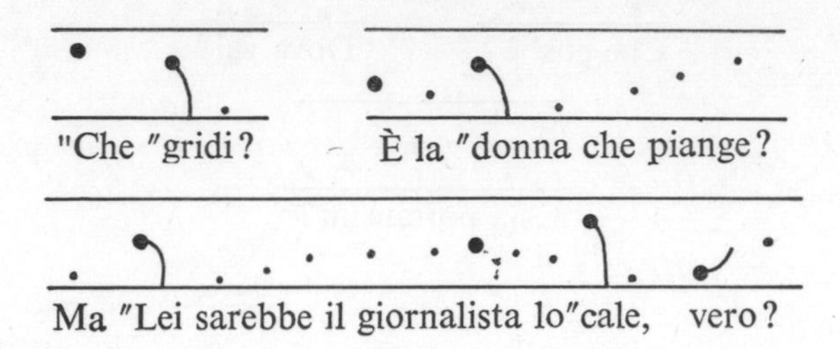

"Che "gridi?
È la "donna che piange?
Ma "Lei sarebbe il giornalista lo"cale, vero?


*Note*

[1] L. E. Armstrong and I. C. Ward, *A Handbook of English Intonation*, Cambridge, 1950, 4 and 19–20.

# The Pronunciation of Brazilian Portuguese

IVAR DAHL

The differences in syntax, vocabulary, and pronunciation between cultured Brazilian Portuguese and cultured Portuguese of the Old Country are not very great, nor are they likely to widen, because of the intense two-way literary traffic and because both countries are fully aware of the importance of linguistic unity. The spelling of Portuguese was standardized by mutual agreement between the two countries in 1943.

There seems to be a good degree of uniformity of speech throughout Brazil. The two twin varieties that enjoy equal prestige are that of Rio de Janeiro (pop. 3,123,980) and that of São Paulo (pop. 3,440,350 – 1956 est.). Their main differences are mostly consonantal, and from them a standard speech is gradually finding its own level by a process of natural gravitation and blending.

The following study is based on analyses of the pronunciation of two skilled teachers of Brazilian Portuguese, Mrs Lygia Fonseca de Ras and Mrs Rosa Nahuys de Ipola. These ladies approached me because they were interested in obtaining knowledge of: (a) the phonetic and phonemic structure of the language; (b) the relation between the pronunciation of Brazilian Portuguese and Spanish; and (c) the use of phonetic transcription for teaching purposes.[1] Long sessions and recordings ensued.

In these notes attention is drawn, when necessary, to the characteristics of the Rio and the São Paulo pronunciations and reference is often made to ordinary writing, the one fixed criterion among the Portuguese-speaking peoples of Europe, Africa, America, and Asia.

As in Spanish, stress usually falls on the penultimate syllable and most syllables are open.

The number of oral and nasalized simple and composite vowel sounds is the most impressive feature of Brazilian Portuguese. Intonation is largely governed by stress. Assimilation is regressive.

CONSONANTS

p b t d c ɟ k g
w f v s z ʃ ʒ j x̥ ʁ
m ɱ n ɲ ŋ
l ɫ ʎ
cʃ ɟʒ
r rr R

NOTES ON THE CONSONANTS. [p, t, k] have no aspiration. [t, d] are dental. It would appear that intervocalic *d* is pronounced [ð] in Portugal; this is unusual in Brazil.

[c, ɟ] are post-alveolar and are currently used in São Paulo and in other parts of Brazil when *t* or *d* are followed by *i* or unstressed *e* (pronounced [ɪ]).

Examples: [ˈpera] *pera*, [ˈbɛla] *bela*, [ˈtela] *tela*, [ˈdɛla] *dela*, [ˈcia] *tia*, [aˈcivu] *ativo*, [ˈsɔrci] *sorte*, [aˈɟidu] *adido*, [ˈtarɟi] *tarde*.

FRICATIVES. [w, j] are pronounced as in English [əˈwei] *away*, [jes] *yes*. Examples: [kaˈwĩɲ] *cauim*, [jaˈja] *Iaiá*.

[f, v] are pronounced as in English. Examples: [ˈfɛra] *fera*, [ˈvɛla] *vela*.

[s, z] are alveolar and made with the tip down.

[ʃ, ʒ] are post-alveolar and made with the tip down.

[s] is represented in ordinary writing in the following ways:

initial *s* [ˈsala] *sala*
medial *ss* [ˈmasa] *massa*
medial *ç* [ˈkasa] *caça*
*c* before *i* or *e* [aˈsima] *acima*, [voˈse] *você*
final *z* [nɔs] *noz*
*x* [ˈprɔsimu] *próximo*

In São Paulo, [s] is represented by final *s* and *s* before a voiceless consonant [nɔs] *nós*, [ˈfresku] *fresco*, [us ˈkarrus] *os carros*.

[z] is represented by:

non-final *z* [beˈleza] *beleza*
final *s* when the next word begins with a vowel [az ˈavis] *as aves*
*x* [eˈzatu] *exato*

In São Paulo, [z] is represented by *s* followed by a voiced consonant [ˈmezmu] *mesmo*, [ˈdezɟi] *desde*, [az ˈbalas] *as balas*, [uz ˈdedus] *os dedos*, [uz ˈʒelus] *os gelos*.

[ʃ] is represented by:

*ch* [ˈʃatu] *chato*
*x* [ˈʃali] *xale*

In Rio, [ʃ] is represented by final *s* and *s* followed by a voiceless consonant [ˈkoizaʃ] *coisas*, [ˈmoʃka] *mosca*, [ˈʁiʃka] *risca*, [uʃ ˈkaʁuʃ] *os carros*.

[ʒ] is represented by:

*g* followed by *i* or *e* [ˈʒelu] *gelo*
*j* [ˈʒarra] *jarra*, [ˈʒatu] *jato*

In Rio, [ʒ] is represented by *s* or *z* followed by a voiced consonant [ˈmeʒmu] *mesmo*, [ˈpaʒ mũŋˈɟʒial] *paz mundial*.

[ʁ] is the normal pronunciation in Rio of initial and final *r*, *r* followed by another consonant, and *rr*. Some people make it voiceless [ʁ̥], except between voiced sounds. Examples: [ˈʁatu] *rato*, [ˈkɔʁda] *corda*, [meˈteʁ] *meter*, [ˈkaʁu] *carro*.

NASALS. Vowel sounds followed by a final nasal are usually – not always – nasalized. Nasalization is fairly strong. Some trace of the nasalizing consonant (*m* or *n*) always persists, mainly with a palatal or velar quality, but their use is not easy to define because regressive assimilation with the following consonant often takes place in the speech of some people. *m* before *p b* is a short [m]. [n] occurs at the beginning of a syllable and sometimes before [t] or [d]. [ɲ] is the usual pronunciation of final *m* or *n* preceded by [ĩ]. [ɱ] occurs before *f* or *v*. [ŋ] is the normal pronunciation of *n* after all nasalized vowels except [ĩ] and sometimes [ẽ]. Examples: [ˈmala] *mala*, [ˈkõmpra] *compra*, [ˈkambiu] *câmbio*, [ˈkãŋtu] or [ˈkãntu] *canto*, [ˈdãŋdu] or [ˈdãndu] *dando*, [koɱˈvɛs] *convés*, [koɱˈfĩɲ] *confim*, [ˈnata] *nata*, [ˈleɲa] *lenha*, [ˈsaɲa] *sanha*, [ˈpuɲu] *punho*, [lõŋgu] *longo*, [ˈfraŋku] *franco*, [ẽɲtreˈtãŋtu] *entretanto*, [sẽɲˈtarsi] *sentar-se*.

LATERALS. [l] is used before all vowels, and [ɫ] finally or before another consonant. There are no signs of delateralization of [ʎ] in Brazil. Examples: [ˈlima] *lima*, [ˈfaɫta] *falta*, [faˈtaɫ] *fatal*, [ˈmaʎa] *malha*.

Most people in Rio omit the alveolar articulation of [ɫ] and substitute [ɷ] [braˈzĩɷ] *Brasil*.

AFFRICATES. [cʃ], [ɟʒ] in the speech of Rio perform the same duties as [c] [ɟ] in the speech of São Paulo. They are also post-alveolar.

Examples: [ˈɟʒia] *dia,* [aˈɟʒidu] *adido,* [ˈtaʁɟʒi] *tarde,* [ˈcʃia] *tia,* [ˈsɔʁcʃi] *sorte.*

ROLLED. A great variety of [r]-sounds are heard in Brazil. In Rio, [ʀ] often occurs as an alternative pronunciation of [ʁ] for initial and final *r*, *rr*, and *r* followed by another consonant, [ˈʀatu] *rato,* [ˈkɔʀda] *corda,* [meˈteʀ] *meter,* [ˈkaʀu] *carro.* A one-flap [r] is used in other positions, [ˈfreʃku] *fresco,* [ˈkaru] *caro.* In São Paulo *r* and *rr* are lingual and pronounced exactly as in Spanish. In other parts of Brazil there is a tendency among certain speakers to velarize [r] and [rr].

In quick colloquial speech final *r* is often elided, [aˈma] *amar,* [beˈbe] *beber,* [paʁˈcʃi] *partir.* In these cases the vowel at the end is lengthened.

## VOWELS

There are seven oral vowel phonemes: /i, e, ɛ, a, ɔ, o, u/. They are all marginal in stressed syllables; in unstressed syllables they are slightly centralized but they are not slurred or indistinct. Vowel alternation need not be shown in phonetic texts except [ə], a subsidiary vowel value of [a].

[i] almost cardinal
[e] and [ɛ] somewhat opener than cardinal
[a] slightly retracted
[ɔ] and [o] somewhat opener than cardinal
[u] almost cardinal

Examples: [ˈliga] *liga,* [ˈpera] *pera,* [ˈseɟʒi] *sêde,* [ˈtɛla] *tela,* [ˈsɛɟʒi] *sede,* [ˈnɔta] *nota,* [aˈvɔ] *avó,* [ˈgota] *gota,* [aˈvo] *avo,* [ˈmula] *mula,* [ˈkəma] *cama.*

[ə] stands for a slightly advanced and lowered [ɤ]. It only occurs when *a* is followed by [m], [n], [ɲ], or [ŋ], as in [ˈfəma] *fama,* [kɔpakaˈbəna] *Copacabana,* [ˈbəɲa] *banha.*

[i] and [u] in unstressed syllables and finally in falling diphthongs equal [ɪ] [ɷ], [ˈtorrɪ] *torre,* [pɪˈkenɷ] *pequeno,* [ˈmatɷ] *mato,* [pɷˈɛta] *poeta,* [paɪ] *pai,* [ˈpəɪna] *paina,* [sɛɷ] *céu.* Before [ɫ] and in the falling diphthong [aŭ], [a] stands for [ɑ], [mɑɫˈvadɷ] *malvado,* [ˈfɑɷna] *fauna.*

NASALIZED VOWELS. /ĩ, ẽ, ã, õ, ũ/. /ĩ/ in ordinary spelling *im* and *in*; /ẽ/ *em* or *en*; /ã/, *a*, *am*, or *an*; /õ/, *õ*, *om*, or *on*; /ŭ/, *um* or *un*.

/ã/ stands for [ə̃] or really [ɤ̃].

Examples: [lĩmpu] *limpo*, [ˈlẽɲtu] *lento*, [ˈkãmpu] *campo*, [ˈkõntu] *conto*, [ˈmũndu] *mundo*.

FALLING ORAL DIPHTHONGS. [aĭ], [əĭ], [aŭ], [ɛĭ], [eĭ], [ɛŭ], [eŭ], [ɔĭ], [oĭ], [uĭ], [iŭ). Examples: [paĭ] *pai*, [ˈpəĭnə] *paina*, [maŭ] *mau*, [rrɛĭs] *réis*, [rreĭs] *reis*, [sɛŭ] *céu*, [seŭ] *seu*, [dɔĭ] *doi*, [boĭ] *boi*, [doŭ] *dou*, [fuĭ] *fui*, [ˈtenuĭ] *tênue*, [rriŭ] *riu*.

Some speakers substitute [eː], [aː], [oː] for [eĭ], [aŭ], [oŭ], [mãnˈteːga] *manteiga*, [kaˈdeːra] *cadeira*, [bãnˈdeːra] *bandeira*, [aˈbaːʃu] *abaxo*, [ˈfaːʃa] *faixa*, [doː] *dou*, [ˈoːru] *ouro*, [ˈkoːru] *couro*.

RISING ORAL DIPHTHONGS. [ĭa], [ĭu], [ĭe], [ŭa], [ŭe], [ŭɔ], [ŭo], [ŭɛ] [ŭe], [ŭi], ([jə]). Examples: [ˈarĭa] *area ária*, [ˈɔlĭu] *oleo*, [ˈvisĭu] *vício*, [serĭe] *série*, [ˈkŭadru] *quadro*, [eˈkŭanime] *equânime*, [ˈkŭɔta] *quota*, [iˈnɔkŭo] *inóquo*, [eˈkŭɛstre] *eqüestre*, [kŭ̃ĩɲˈkŭenĭu] *qüinqüênio*, [eˈkŭinu] *eqüino*, [baˈjəna] *baiana*.

FALLING NASALIZED DIPHTHONGS. [ãĩ̯], [ãũ̯], [ẽĩ̯], [õĩ̯], [ũĩ̯], [õũ̯]. Examples: [mãĩ̯] *mãe*, [ˈkãĩ̯mbra], *caimbra*, [kãũ̯] *cão*, [aˈmarãũ̯] *amaram*, [bẽĩ̯] *bem*, [ˈsabẽĩ̯] *sabem*, [laˈdrõĩ̯ns] *ladrões*, [ˈmũĩ̯ɲtu] *muito*, [kõũ̯] *com*. All these diphthongs are followed by a nasal; [ɲ] after [ĩ] and [ŋ] after [ũ], [sẽĩ̯ɲ ˈeli] *sem êle*, [kõũ̯ŋ ˈeli] *com êle*. At the end of a diphthong [ĩ], [ũ] stand for [ĩ], [ɷ̃].

RISING NASALIZED DIPHTHONGS. [ũ̯ã], [ũ̯ẽ], [ũ̯ĩ]. Examples: [ˈkũ̯ãndu] *quando*, [freˈkũ̯ẽɲci] *frequente*, [arˈgũ̯ĩndo] *arguindo*.

TRIPHTHONGS. [ŭaĭ], [ŭeĭ], [ŭoŭ], [ŭiŭ], [jaĭ], [jeĭ]. Examples: [uruˈgŭaĭ] *Uruguai*, [averiˈgŭeĭ] *averigüei*, [averiˈgŭoŭ] *averigou*, [delĩɲˈkŭiŭ] *delinqüiu*, [vaˈjaĭs] *vaiais*, [vaˈjeĭs] *vaieis*.

The following are two versions of a fine sonnet by Olavo Bilac (1865–1918), who is called *o principe dos poetas brasileiros*. The reader will at once recognize in these lines the beauty and musicality of the language. The first rendering belongs to the Head of the Centre of Brazilian Studies in Buenos Aires, Professor Ney Strauch, who comes from Rio de Janeiro; and the second to Dr Helio Scarabotolo, Cultural Attaché to the Brazilian Embassy, who comes from São Paulo.

nɛɫ ˈmɛzu dɛɫ kaˈmĩɲ . . .

ʃeˈgeĭ. ʃeˈgaʃcʃi. ˈvĩɲaʃ facʃiˈgada
i ˈtriʃcʃi, i ˈtriʃcʃi i facʃiˈgadu eŭ ˈvĩɲa.
ˈcʃĩɲaz a ˈałma ɟʒi ˈsõɲuʃ povuˈada,
i a ˈałma ɟʒi ˈsõɲuʃ povuˈada eŭ ˈcʃĩɲa . . .

i paˈrəmuʒ ɟʒi ˈsubitu na iʃˈtrada
da ˈvida: ˈlõɲguz ˈənuʃ ˈpreza a ˈmĩɲa
a ˈtua ˈmãũŋ, a ˈviʃta ɟʒiʒlũmˈbrada
ˈcʃivi da ˈluʃ ki teŭ oˈʎaʁ kõŋˈcʃĩɲa.

ˈoʒi, ˈsɛgiʒ ɟʒi ˈnovu . . . na paʁˈcʃida
ˈnẽĩɲ u ˈprãntu uʃ teŭz ˈɔʎuz umiˈdɛsi,
ˈnẽĩɲ cʃi koˈməvi a ˈdoʁ da ɟʒiʃpiˈɟʒida.

i ˈj eŭ, soliˈtarĭu, ˈvəłtu a ˈfasi, i ˈtremu,
ˈvẽɲdu u ˈteŭ ˈvułtu ki ɟʒizapaˈrɛsi
na iʃˈtrema ˈkuʁva du kaˈmĩɲu iʃˈtremu.

ʃeˈgeĭ. ʃeˈgasci. ˈvĩɲas faciˈgada
i ˈtrisci, i ˈtrisci i faciˈgadu eŭ ˈvĩɲa.
ˈcĩɲaz a ˈałma ɟi ˈsõɲus povuˈada,
i a ˈałma ɟi ˈsõɲus povuˈada eŭ ˈciɲa . . .

i paˈrəmuz ɟi ˈsubitu na isˈtrada
da ˈvida: ˈlõŋguz ˈənus ˈpreza a ˈmĩɲa
a ˈtua mãũŋ a ˈvista ɟizlũmˈbrada
ˈcivi da ˈlus ki teŭ oˈʎar kõŋˈcĩɲa

ˈoʒi, ˈsɛgiz ɟi ˈnovu . . . na parˈcida
ˈnẽĩɲ u ˈprãŋtu us teŭz ˈɔʎuz umiˈdɛsi,
ˈnẽĩɲ ci koˈməvi a ˈdor da despeˈɟida.

i ˈj eŭ, soliˈtariu ˈvəłtu a ˈfasi, i ˈtremu,
ˈvẽɲdu u ˈteŭ ˈvułtu ki dizapaˈrɛsi
na isˈtrema ˈkurva du kaˈmĩɲu isˈtremu.

*'Nel mezzo del camin . . .'*

*Cheguei. Chegaste. Vinhas fatigada*
*E triste, e triste e fatigado eu vinha.*
*Tinhas a alma de sonhos povoada,*
*E a alma de sonhos povoada eu tinha . . .*

*E parámos de súbito na estrada*
*Da vida: longos anos, presa à minha*
*A tua mão, a vista deslumbrada*
*Tive da luz que teu olhar continha.*

*Hoje, segues de noro . . . Na partida*
*Nem o pranto os teus olhos umedece,*
*Nem te comove a dor da despedida.*

*E eu, solitário, volto a face, e tremo,*
*Vendo o teu vulto que desaparece*
*Na extrema curva do caminho extremo.*

*Note*

[1] Mrs Ras and Mrs Ipola have since produced the second edition of their *Liçõês de Portugues,* Editorial Kapelusz, Buenos Aires. Though intended for learners of Portuguese whose mother tongue is Spanish, this book, however, is likely to be helpful to learners of other nationalities.

# Le Rôle du Rendement Fonctionnel dans la Perception des Oppositions Vocaliques Distinctives du Français

G. FAURE

L'objet des quelques réflexions qui vont suivre est d'essayer d'illustrer le rôle joué par le rendement fonctionnel dans la perception et dans le maintien des unités distinctives d'une langue donnée.

Force nous étant de choisir, nous limiterons notre examen aux oppositions distinctives susceptibles d'intervenir dans le cadre des sept archiphonèmes généralement admis comme constituant l'armature du système vocalique oral du français contemporain.[1]

La meilleure représentation de ce système d'archiphonèmes nous paraît être constitué, sur le plan acoustique, par le diagramme ci-contre que nous tirons, en le simplifiant, du schéma proposé par Delattre[2] et obtenu en portant les fréquences du formant haut horizontalement et celles du formant bas verticalement sur du papier logarithmique.[3]

Ce diagramme, on le voit, diffère assez peu des diagrammes que l'on trouve dans la plupart des ouvrages de phonétique, et auxquels leurs auteurs ont voulu donner une signification physiologique, le degré de relèvement de la langue étant indiqué par les lignes horizontales et le degré d'antériorité par les lignes verticales.

Nous admettrons qu'un phonème peut être considéré, du point de vue fonctionnel, comme un ensemble de traits dont chacun est capable d'assumer à lui seul, une fonction distinctive, c'est-à-dire de changer l'identité d'un mot, s'il lui arrive de disparaître ou d'être remplacé par un autre trait distinctif. Tel serait, par exemple, le cas du phonème: /i/ (ex. *nid*) que l'on peut définir par les traits suivants:

(1) sonorité,
(2) résonance pharyngo-buccale,
(3) absence de bruit d'écoulement,
(4) non nasalité,
(5) articulation antérieure et fermée,
(6) absence de labialisation.

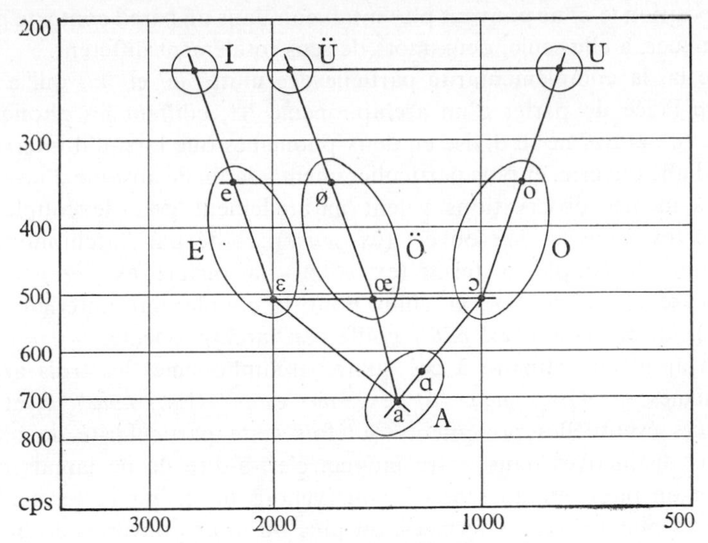


Fig. 1. Système vocalique oral.

Cet ensemble de traits, dont le premier est seul à ne pas avoir de valeur distinctive sur le plan phonologique, assure, sur le plan acoustique, le renforcement des fréquences formancielles situées aux environs de 240 c/s et de 2500 c/s, dont les effets combinés permettent à notre oreille d'identifier ce phonème, comme correspondant à: /ı/ Une articulation plus ouverte ferait, à elle seule, passer ces chiffres à 350 c/s et à 2200 c/s environ, et le timbre perçu serait celui de /e/ ouvert, que l'on entend, par exemple, dans '*blé*'.

Cette définition étant posée, nous entendrons essentiellement par archiphonèmes l'ensemble des traits distinctifs communs à deux phonèmes, dont l'opposition, réduite à un seul trait distinctif, est susceptible d'être neutralisé, c'est-à-dire de disparaître sous l'effet du contexte phonique qui, imposant au locuteur un timbre spécifique, élimine de ce fait même, toute possibilité de choix en fonction d'une signification donnée.

C'est ainsi, par exemple, que le caractère mi-fermé de [e] (ex. *blé*) et le caractère mi-ouvert de [ε] (ex. *père*), qui suffit à distinguer, pour l'oreille, le mot *pré* du mot *prêt*, se neutralise, et perd toute valeur distinctive en syllabe fermée, c'est-à-dire terminée par une consonne, et dans laquelle la voyelle ouverte: [ε] est obligatoire en français, à l'exclusion absolue de la voyelle fermée (ex. *fer*, *plaine*, *chef*, *net*, etc. ...)

l'opposition /e-ɛ/ ne pouvant plus intervenir dans un pareil contexte pour distinguer, à elle seule, deux mots de sens totalement différent.

De là, la complémentarité partielle des unités /e/ et /ɛ/, qui a fait naître l'idée de parler d'un archiphonème /E/, coiffant les phonèmes /e/ et /ɛ/, et qui ne se divise en deux phonèmes que lorsqu'il intervient en syllabe ouverte, et plus particulièrement à la finale absolue d'un mot.

Les mêmes observations valent naturellement pour le couple /ø/ fermé (ex. *jeûne*) – /œ/ ouvert (ex. *jeune*), coiffé par l'archiphonème /Ö/, pour le couple /o/ fermé (ex. *côte*) – /ɔ/ ouvert (ex. *cote*), coiffé par l'archiphonème /O/, et enfin pour le couple: /a/ antérieur (ex. *patte*), /ɑ/ postérieur (ex. *pâte*), coiffé par l'archiphonème: /A/.

On ajoute d'ordinaire à ces quatre archiphonèmes les trois archiphonèmes: /I/ (Ex.: *nid*), /Ü/ (ex.: *nu*) et /U/ (Ex.: *nous*), dont les nuances éventuelles présentent toutefois cette particularité de n'être jamais distinctives dans notre langue, c'est-à-dire de ne jamais constituer un phonème au sens où nous venons de définir ce terme. Les nuances plus ou moins fermées, ou plus ou moins ouvertes de /i/ par exemple, étant toujours comprises, par un français, comme correspondant au même phonème, alors que l'opposition: /i/ fermé–/i/ ouvert, distinctive dans la langue anglaise, où *feel* et *fill* sont deux mots différents, fait que dans cette langue: /i/ fermé et /i/ ouvert sont deux phonèmes différents.

Ces quelques réflexions nous aideront sans doute à nous faire une idée plus nette du rôle, selon nous très important, que le rendement fonctionnel des oppositions distinctives (au sens où nous venons d'entendre ce mot, c'est-à-dire en nous plaçant sur le plan strictement objectif et notionnel) est amené à jouer dans la perception et le maintien des phonèmes d'une langue donnée.

Nous ne dirons que peu de chose des phonèmes totalement indépendants, c'est-à-dire de ceux dont les oppositions distinctives, même avec leurs plus proches voisins, ne sont jamais susceptibles d'être neutralisées sous l'effet du contexte phonique. Cette absence de neutralisation leur confère, du fait du haut rendement fonctionnel qui en est le résultat, un degré d'autonomie tout à fait remarquable dans la conscience linguistique de ceux qui les emploient.

C'est ainsi, par exemple, qu'en dépit de leur contiguité, tant sur le plan physiologique que sur le plan acoustique, il ne viendrait jamais à un français l'idée d'apparenter le /i/ (ex. *nid*) avec le /e/ fermé (ex. *nez*), et de considérer ce /e/ comme un /i/ ouvert, alors que ces deux timbres sont au moins aussi voisins, comme nous allons le voir plus loin, que le sont /e/ et /ɛ/, dans lesquels nous voyons spontanément les deux degrés – ouvert et fermé – d'un même archiphonème /E/, parce que l'opposition physiologique et acoustique qui les sépare est très souvent privée de toute valeur distinctive par le contexte phonique dans lequel ils sont insérés.

Comme l'a fortement souligné Martinet dans sa *Description Phonologique*, déjà évoquée dans la présente étude, 'La neutralisation réalise entre deux phonèmes un apparentement phonologique particulièrement étroit qui a des retentissements profonds dans la conscience des sujets', et même, peut-on dire, dans leur aptitude à percevoir, avec plus ou moins de facilité, les nuances qui distinguent, pour l'oreille, deux phonèmes déterminés.

C'est ce que nous voudrions essayer de montrer en examinant de plus près le comportement sur le plan fonctionnel, et sur celui de la perception, de l'unique opposition qui distingue, sur le plan phonologique, les deux membres d'un même archiphonème.

Nous commencerons cet examen par un rapide retour sur les oppositions /i-e/ et /e-ɛ/ que nous avons déjà évoquées ci-dessus.

Une étude physiologique attentive, à l'aide par exemple de radiophotographies ou de séquences radio-cinématographiques, comme nous avons essayé d'en réaliser nous-même quelques-unes avec la collaboration des services d'oto-rhino-laryngologie de la Faculté de Médecine de Marseille, sous la direction du professeur Appaix, montre que les différences d'articulation qui séparent /i/ et /e/, d'une part, et /e/ et /ɛ/, d'autre part, *sont pratiquement les mêmes*; ces différences se réduisant essentiellement à un changement d'ouverture qui situe notre /e/ fermé à peu près à mi-chemin entre /i/ et /ɛ/, toutes choses parfaitement identiques par ailleurs, c'est-à-dire les autres traits distinctifs (non-nasalité, absence de bruit d'écoulement, absence de labialisation, articulation antérieure...) demeurant communes à ces trois phonèmes.

Ce fait est entièrement confirmé lorsqu'on se place non plus sur le plan physiologique, ou, pour être plus précis, sur le plan génétique, mais sur celui de l'analyse acoustique à l'aide du spectrographe.

On s'aperçoit alors que le timbre de notre /i/ français est essentiellement assuré par la combinaison de deux formants dont les fréquences respectives se situent aux environs de 240 c/s et de 2500 c/s, les fréquences correspondantes étant de 350 c/s et 2200 c/s pour /e/ et de 510 c/s et 1950 c/s pour /ɛ/.

Les différences de fréquence en fonction desquelles l'oreille distingue /i/ de /e/ sont donc de: 350 c/s − 240 c/s = 110 c/s pour le formant bas, et de 2500 – 2200 = 300 c/s pour le formant haut. Celles qui permettent la distinction acoustique entre /e/ et /ɛ/ sont de 510 c/s – 350 c/s = 160 c/s pour le formant bas, soit 50 c/s de plus que pour l'opposition /i-e/, et de 2200 c/s – 1950 c/s = 250 c/s, soit 50 c/s de moins que pour l'opposition /i-e/.

Ces chiffres nous apportent la confirmation du fait que sur le plan strictement objectif, c'est-à-dire sur celui de *l'excitation physique* qui est à l'origine de la perception sonore, /e/ n'est pas plus différent de /i/ que de /ɛ/.

Sur le plan de la *sensation auditive*, qui est celui qui nous intéresse ici le plus directement, on sait que la sensation de hauteur varie en progression arithmétique quand la fréquence varie en progression géométrique, ou qu'en d'autres termes, la hauteur varie comme le logarithme de la fréquence. C'est ce dont a tenu compte Delattre dans l'établissement du schéma dont nous nous sommes inspiré pour la présentation de notre diagramme des archiphonèmes. Or, on constatera précisément, à l'examen de ce diagramme, que les intervalles *perçus*, tels qu'ils s'y trouvent représentés, sont *pratiquement les mêmes* lors du passage de /i/ à /e/ que lors du passage de /e/ à /ɛ/, qu'il s'agisse des formants hauts ou qu'il s'agisse des formants bas.

Mais le fait que l'opposition entre /e/ et /ɛ/ soit neutralisable, c'est-à-dire amenée à perdre toute valeur distinctive sous l'effet du contexte phonique, dans la très grande majorité des cas – ce qui réduit le rendement fonctionnel de l'opposition /e-ɛ/ à la quasi-insignifiance – fait que, pour un français, ces deux timbres font l'impression d'être très étroitement apparentés; alors que ce même français ne sent aucune parenté entre /i/ et /e/, dont l'opposition, non neutralisable, suffit à distinguer une infinité de couples de mots du type: *nid, nez – ici, essai – dix, dé* – etc., ... etc., ...

Les mêmes remarques peuvent être appliquées à l'opposition: /o/ fermé (ex.: *flot*) – /ɔ/ ouvert (ex.: *flotte*). Du point de vue *génétique*, en effet, ces deux phonèmes sont distingués par une différence d'ouverture au moins égale à celle qui sépare /o/ fermé de /u/ (ex.: *chou*) ou /ɔ/ ouvert de /ɑ/ (ex.: *pâte*).

Du point de vue *acoustique*, les formants de ces deux membres de l'archiphonème /o/ correspondent respectivement, à peu de chose près, aux fréquences:

350 c/s et 865 c/s pour /o/ fermé,
et 510 c/s et 1000 c/s pour /ɔ/ ouvert.

La distance qui sépare ces deux phonèmes sur le plan auditif est donc de :

510 – 350 = 160 c/s pour le formant bas,
et de 1000 – 865 = 135 c/s pour le formant haut.

Cette distance est de :

650 c/s – 510 c/s = 140 c/s pour le formant bas,
et de 1200 c/s – 1000 c/s = 200 c/s pour le formant haut lorsqu'on passe de /ɔ/ à /ɑ/.

Elle est donc plus grande pour le formant haut et plus faible pour le formant bas que lorsqu'on passe de /o/ à /ɔ/, sans que l'on puisse dire, cependant, que la différence soit considérable.

Du point de vue de la *perception auditive*, l'examen de notre diagramme prouve que l'intervalle perçu entre /o/ et /ɔ/ est nettement plus grand que l'intervalle perçu entre /ɔ/ et /ɑ/ pour les formants bas, et légèrement plus petit pour les formants hauts.

Pour l'opposition /o/ fermé–/u/ (ex. *chou*), les chiffres sont approximativement les suivants :

350 c/s et 865 c/s pour /o/ fermé,
240 c/s et 750 c/s pour /u/.

La distance entre ces deux phonèmes étant marquée par une différence de :

350 c/s – 240 c/s = 110 c/s pour le formant bas,
et de 865 c/s – 750 c/s = 115 c/s pour le formant haut.

on voit qu'elle est nettement inférieure à celle qui sépare /o/ fermé de /ɔ/ ouvert.

Sur le plan auditif, les intervalles séparant /o/ de /ɔ/ et de /u/ *sont perçus comme strictement égaux* (cf. diagramme).

Or, comme pour le couple : /e-ɛ/, un lien de parenté très étroit s'établit dans la conscience linguistique d'un français entre /ɔ/ ouvert et /o/ fermé, dans lesquels il voit les deux degrés d'un même archiphonème alors qu'il ne lui viendrait pas à l'idée d'associer de la même façon, /o/ fermé et /u/, et de considérer par exemple, /o/ fermé comme un /u/ ouvert.

L'opposition /ø/ fermé (ex. *feu*) – /œ/ ouvert (ex. *fleur*) donne lieu aux mêmes remarques que les oppositions ci-dessus du point de vue articulatoire.

Sur le plan objectif, les fréquences formancielles se situent respectivement aux environs de:

350 c/s et 1600 c/s pour /ø/,
et de 510 c/s et 1400 c/s pour /œ/.

Les fréquences correspondantes étant à peu près:

240 c/s et 1850 c/s pour /ü/ (ex. *vue*),
725 c/s et 1300 c/s pour /a/ (ex. *patte*).

On voit que ces chiffres conduisent aux mêmes conclusions que ceux qui les précèdent. Et ces conclusions se trouvent confirmées sur le plan auditif par l'examen de notre diagramme. C'est pourquoi nous ne nous y attarderons pas.

Enfin, pour l'opposition /a/ antérieur (ex. *patte*), /ɑ/ postérieur (ex. *pâte*), les fréquences formancielles sont d'environ:

725 c/s et 1300 c/s pour /a/,
650 c/s et 1200 c/s pour /ɑ/,

d'où une différence de:

725 c/s − 650 c/s = 75 c/s pour le formant bas,
et de 1300 c/s − 1200 c/s = 100 c/s pour le formant haut.

On remarquera que ces deux derniers chiffres sont exceptionnellement faibles. L'examen du diagramme confirme, sur le plan auditif, l'étroite parenté qui en est le résultat.

Cette faiblesse est sans doute pour quelque chose dans le fait que, sur le plan phonologique, le rendement de l'opposition /a-ɑ/ est extrêmement faible, et surtout dans le fait que l'emploi de ces deux phonèmes est de plus en plus flottant en français moderne. 'La répartition de (a) et (ɑ) dans le français correct d'aujourd'hui est assez délicate à établir' écrit à cet égard Fouché.[4] Il est, sur ce point, parfaitement d'accord avec Grammont, qui affirme, de son côté, dans son *Traité de prononciation française*[5] que: 'c'est pour l'*a* que les divergences individuelles de prononciation ou le flottement sont les plus fréquents'. Il y a environ vingt-cinq ans, Pernot était même allé, sur ce point, jusqu'à prévoir la mort du /ɑ/ postérieur.[6] On sait toutefois que dans la *Prononciation du français contemporain*, Martinet[7] considérait, à juste titre d'ailleurs, que cet auteur semblait 'se presser un peu trop de sonner le glas de *a* postérieur'. Il signale cependant lui-même, dans un ouvrage tout récent[8] que si '66 parisiens nés avant 1920 réunis par le hasard, ont tous deux voyelles distinctes dans *patte* et *pâte*, parmi quelques centaines de parisiennes nées après 1940, plus de 60% ont, dans ces mots, une même voyelle *a* (c'est-à-dire la voyelle antérieure de *patte*)'. Un test analogue nous a personnellement révélé que cette proportion pouvait atteindre 75% dans un groupe d'une cinquantaine de jeunes étudiants dont certains faisaient toutefois intervenir une légère différence de *durée*, mais non de *timbre* entre /a/ et /ɑ/.

Il est incontestable que cette progressive disparition de /ɑ/ au bénéfice de /a/, que Straka souligne, lui aussi,[9] a été facilitée par la parenté acoustique de ces deux phonèmes qui pousse l'oreille à les confondre.

Et il est certain, inversement, que nous avons intérêt à conserver, toutes choses égales d'ailleurs, les phonèmes que notre oreille a le moins de peine à distinguer clairement.

Mais cela ne doit pas nous faire oublier le fait qu'à distance acoustique égale, notre conscience linguistique distingue spontanément les phonèmes dont les oppositions ne sont pas neutralisables sur le plan phonologique et apparente au contraire, sans aucune raison valable, ni sur le plan objectif, ni sur le plan auditif, des phonèmes dont l'unique opposition distinctive peut éventuellement être neutralisée. *Et il peut même se faire que deux phonèmes extrèmement voisins sur les plans articulatoire et acoustique soient nettement dissociés dans notre conscience linguistique, alors que des phonèmes beaucoup plus éloignés l'un de l'autre sur ces deux plans, sont apparentés au point d'être parfois confondus*, parce que les différences physiologiques et acoustiques qui les séparent ne suffisent pas, si importantes soient-elles, à assurer à leur opposition une valeur distinctive sur le plan phonologique. Tel serait, par exemple, le cas en anglais, de /i/ fermé (ex. *feel*) et /ɪ/ ouvert (ex. *fill*) qui ne sont séparés sur le plan articulatoire et sur le plan auditif que par des nuances relativement légères (/ɪ/ ouvert se situant à peu près à mi-chemin entre notre /i/ français et notre /e/ fermé) et dont la commutation incorrecte risque de troubler gravement la compréhension du message, *fill*, par exemple, étant identifié à *feel* si la voyelle tend à se fermer comme cela lui arrive si souvent dans une bouche française! Un sujet anglais est, par contre, très peu sensible à l'opposition /e-ɛ/, bien que la distance qui sépare ces deux sons, pour la bouche, comme pour l'oreille, soit bien plus considérable que celle qui sépare /ɪ/ ouvert de /i/ fermé.

S'il est vrai, comme l'ont précisé des études récentes[10] que 'l'on parle comme on entend', non seulement parce que c'est par l'oreille que nous sont assurées ces réserves d'images acoustiques en fonction desquelles nous formulons nos messages, et nous interprétons ceux que nous recevons, mais encore parce que notre phonation semble bien être soumise à un contrôle auditif *direct* et *permanent* de l'une de nos deux oreilles, il importe de préciser que nous sommes, dès notre enfance, *conditionnés physiquement par les exigences du système phonique que le hasard de notre naissance nous a imposé* et qui, nous sensibilisant à l'extrême aux nuances de timbres, de rythme et de mélodie dont ce système nécessite la parfaite maîtrise, nous rend, par contre, indifférents et, par suite, quasi insensibles à celles qui n'y jouent qu'un rôle négligeable, alors qu'elles peuvent au contraire, intervenir d'une façon décisive dans une autre langue que la nôtre.

Nous avons voulu illustrer par ces quelques remarques le très grand intérêt qu'il convient d'attacher à une collaboration toujours plus poussée entre la description phonétique et la description phonologique. La première s'attachant à une analyse aussi précise que possible des réalités physiques et physiologiques du langage parlé, fournit à la seconde une matière de choix, scientifiquement authentique et inattaquable, faute de laquelle elle risquerait d'aboutir à des conclusions discutables; et la seconde donne un sens et une valeur humaine à la première qui s'exposerait, si elle devait rester gratuite, à une dispersion stérile et décourageante, les éléments pertinents d'un système phonologique donné risquant de se perdre dans un foisonnement de 'variantes' pratiquement dépourvues d'intérêt linguistique et qui déroberaient à nos regards ce qui doit être le véritable objet de nos efforts, à savoir, une connaissance toujours plus profonde de tout ce qui peut contribuer à la claire manifestation, par la parole, des plus délicates nuances de nos pensées ou de nos sentiments.

*Notes*

[1] Cf., en particulier, Gougenheim, *Eléments de phonologie française*, Paris, 1935; A. Martinet, *La prononciation du français contemporain*, Paris, 1945; *La description phonologique*, Genève-Paris, 1956; *Eléments de linguistique générale*, Paris, 1960.

[2] P. Delattre, 'Un triangle acoustique des voyelles orales du français', *French Review*, XXI, 6, May 1948.

[3] On sait que cette échelle établit une compensation telle que *des intervalles égaux pour l'oreille sont représentés par des distances égales*.

[4] *Traité de prononciation française*, Paris, 1956.

[5] *La prononciation française – Traité pratique*, Paris, 1954.

[6] *Revue de Phonétique*, V, 1928, 301.

[7] Paris, 1945.

[8] A. Martinet, *Eléments de linguistique générale*, Paris, 1960.

[9] 'La prononciation parisienne', *Bulletin de la Faculté des Lettres de Strasbourg*, 1951.

[10] Cf., en particulier, Dr A. Tomatis, 'Relations entre l'audition et la phonation', *Ann. Télécomm.*, II, 7–8, Juillet/Août 1956.

# La Prononciation des Plus Anciens Textes Italiens

P. FIORELLI

On vient de célébrer ce qu'on a voulu appeler, avec quelque peu d'arbitraire, le millénaire de la langue italienne: à proprement parler, le millénaire d'un document judiciaire en latin dont quelques lignes, pour la première fois dans l'histoire de la péninsule, ont été écrites résolument, consciemment en langue vulgaire.

Il s'agit, comme on sait, d'un *iudicatum* délivré au mois de mars 960 par Arechisi, juge de la ville de Capoue, en faveur de l'abbé du Mont-Cassin, Aligernus, à qui un certain Rodelgrimus (un homme de paille, selon quelqu'un) contestait, tout en étant dépourvu d'arguments, la propriété d'environ vingt-mille hectares de terre, placés dans le bassin du Garigliano.[1] La preuve qui trancha toute question fut portée par trois témoins, qui répétèrent, *de verbo ad verbum*, la formule que leur avait proposée le juge. Elle disait: 'Sao ko kelle terre, per kelle fini que ki contene, trenta anni le possette parte sancti Benedicti.'[2]

Trois ans après, nous trouvons trois documents encore qui contiennent une formule de témoignage en langue vulgaire. Ils nous viennent tous de la même région, ils concernent tous des questions de propriété foncière, ils sont tous conservés, comme le premier, aux archives de l'abbaye du Mont-Cassin: le *iudicatum* de Sessa Aurunca du mois de mars 963,[3] le *memoratorium* de Teano du 26 juillet 963,[4] le *iudicatum* de Teano du mois d'octobre 963.[5] Voici la formule du premier: 'Sao cco kelle terre, per kelle fini que tebe monstrai, Pergoaldi foro, quc ki contene, et trenta anni le possette'[6]; celle du deuxième: 'Kella terra, per kelle fini que bobe mostrai, sancte Marie e, et trenta anni la posset parte sancte Marie'[7]; celle du troisième: 'Sao cco kelle terre, per kelle fini que tebe mostrai, trenta anni le possette parte sancte Marie.'[8]

On voit d'abord que ces quatre formules ont été écrites dans un langage bien éloigné de ce dialecte florentin, dont les premiers documents ne dépassent guère le commencement du XIIIe siècle, et qui dès le siècle suivant atteindra le rang de langue nationale grâce au prestige de Dante, de Pétrarque et de Boccace. Elles ont été écrites, en effet, dans le dialecte qu'on parlait au Xe siècle parmi les gens cultivés de la principauté longobarde de Capoue et Bénévent, en particulier de la Terre de Labour, qui en formait la partie occidentale. C'est donc un dialecte du type napolitain, qui se ressent de certaines influences du latin de l'école et de l'église, influences illusoires quelquefois, étant bornées à l'orthographe, quelquefois plus substantielles. C'est bien sur ces fondements que la langue des formules de témoignage du Mont-Cassin a été analysée une première fois par Pio Rajna, il y a soixante-dix ans,[9] ensuite par Matteo Bartoli,[10] qui, ayant comparé les formules avec leurs versions dans les dialectes actuels de la campagne et de la ville de Naples, crut devoir y reconnaître, à côté des éléments dialectaux et des latinismes, aussi des éléments vulgaires interrégionaux, en première ligne le *sao* initial.[11] Cette thèse hardie a été vivement discutée.[12] En tout cas, elle ne pourrait point toucher à la phonétique des formules, qui est celle des dialectes locaux: les latinismes, même les formes interrégionales, s'il y en a, ont été soumis tous, évidemment, à ses règles.

Or, la prononciation courante des formules, parmi les savants italiens, s'appuie exclusivement sur l'écriture, lui donnant la même valeur qu'elle aurait selon l'orthographe italienne moderne, sans tenir compte ni des habitudes graphiques des notaires du moyen âge, ni de la phonétique dialectale de la Terre de Labour. Dans la pratique, on ne saurait condamner cette façon de lire. Toutefois, il n'est pas difficile de reconstruire celle qui a dû être la prononciation effective, avec un certain degré de vraisemblance. C'est ce que nous allons essayer de faire.

L'orthographe, en premier lieu, n'avait pas le moyen de représenter certains phénomènes syntactiques. Nous trouvons quatre fois *trenta anni*, mais l'hiatus aura été sûrement évité avec l'élision du premier *-a*; c'est là l'usage de tous les dialectes italiens (sauf peut-être dans quelques zones du Nord), de même que celui de la langue littéraire. Nous trouvons *sao ko kelle*, *que ki contene*, *que tebe*, *que bobe*, mais il y aura eu le redoublement (ou gémination, si l'on veut) du *k-*, du *t-*, du *b-* respectivement, selon des règles qui sont communes à la langue littéraire et aux dialectes en dehors de ceux du Nord, mais qui ne sont pas reflétées par l'orthographe constituée, sauf dans le cas des mots composés. En particulier, le redoublement exceptionnel de la consonne initiale de *co* dans *sao cco* (à Sessa Aurunca et à Teano) nous assure de la gémination dans ce premier cas[13]; dans les autres, elle est déterminée régulièrement par le mot qui précède, dont la consonne finale, disparue mais toujours latente, s'assimile à la consonne initiale qui la suit.[14] Ajoutons que les graphies *per kelle, et trenta,* cachent elles aussi, sous leur aspect latinisant, des géminations syntactiques plus ou moins évidentes.[15]

Encore: l'orthographe est muette au sujet du degré d'ouverture des voyelles *e* et *o*. En général, on pourra supposer une prononciation ouverte dans *terre* et *terra, contene, possette, foro, e,* fermée dans *kelle* et *kella, trenta, tebe, bobe,* conformément à la quantité latine aussi bien qu'à la prononciation italienne actuelle[16]; les voyelles atones auront été plutôt fermées, y compris les voyelles des mots proclitiques, à l'exception de la conjonction *et*.[17] On peut se demander si certaines voyelles finales n'étaient pas affaiblies, phénomène qui est normal en napolitain moderne; mais sur ce point nous ne pouvons disposer d'aucun renseignement.

En ce qui concerne les consonnes, il faut remarquer que la graphie *nt* (dans les mots *contene, trenta, sancti*) correspond certainement à une prononciation [nd]: en effet, dans cette région, les sourdes précédées d'une nasale se sont sonorisées à une époque très ancienne.[18] De même, la prononciation de *b* et *d* intervocaliques était très probablement constrictive.[19] On ne saurait dire si le *s* préconsonantique de *mostrai* avait déjà, au Xe siècle, la même articulation chuintante qu'on lui connaît en napolitain moderne. En tout cas, il s'agit de variétés de position: ces trois phénomènes n'ont pas de valeur phonologique.

Enfin, il faut tenir compte des latinismes purement graphiques, tels que *sancti, Benedicti, monstrai, sancte,* avec des lettres étymologiques qu'on ne prononçait pas; *que,* déguisement de [ke][20]; *posset,* hypercorrection pour *possette*.[21]

Cela posé, nous pourrons reconstruire ainsi la prononciation vraisemblable de la formule de témoignage contenue dans le *iudicatum* de Capoue:

*Sao ko kelle terre, per kelle fini que ki contene, trenta anni le possette parte sancti Benedicti* [ˈsaŏ kko kˌkelle ˈtɛrre, pe kˌkelle ˈfiːni ke kˌki kkonˈdɛːne, trenˈd anni ˌle posˈsɛtte ˈparte ˌsandi ˌβeneˈðitti];

celle de la formule contenue dans le *iudicatum* de Sessa Aurunca:

*Sao cco kelle terre, per kelle fini que tebe monstrai, Pergoaldi foro, que ki contene, et trenta anni le possette* [ˈsaŏ kko kˌkelle ˈtɛrre, pe kˌkelle ˈfiːni ke tˌteβe mosˈtraːi, ˌpergoˈaldi ˈfɔːro, ke kˌki kkonˈdɛːne, ˈɛ ttrenˈd anni ˌle posˈsɛtte];

celle de la formule contenue dans le *memoratorium* de Teano:

*Kella terra, per kelle fini que bobe mostrai, sancte Marie e, et trenta anni la posset parte sancte Marie* [ˌkella ˈtɛrra, pe kˌkelle ˈfiːni ke bˌboβe mosˈtraːi, ˌsande maˈriːe ˈɛ, ˌɛ ttrenˈd anni ˌla posˈsɛtte ˈparte ˌsande maˈriːe];

celle de la formule contenue dans le *iudicatum* de Teano:

*Sao cco kelle terre, per kelle fini que tebe mostrai, trenta anni le possette parte sancte Marie* [ˈsaŏ kko kˌkelle ˈtɛrre, pe kˌkelle ˈfiːni ke tˌteβe mosˈtraːi, trenˈd anni ˌle posˈsɛtte ˈparte ˌsande maˈriːe].

*Notes*

1 Éditions: E. Gattola (Gattula), *Ad Historiam Abbatiae Cassinensis accessiones*, I, Venise, 1734, 68–69; L. Tosti, *Storia della badia di Montecassino* [1ère éd. 1842–1843], 2e éd., I, Rome, 1888, 331–334; E. Monaci, *Crestomazia italiana dei primi secoli* [1ère éd. 1889–1912], 2e éd., par les soins de F. Arese, Rome – Naples – Città di Castello, 1955, 1–4; M. Inguanez, *I placiti cassinesi del secolo X con periodi in volgare* [1ère éd. 1929], 4e éd., Mont-Cassin, 1942, 13–15; A. Monteverdi, *Testi volgari italiani anteriori al Duecento*, Rome, 1935, 10–17; Id., *Testi volgari italiani dei primi tempi* [1ère éd. 1941], 2e éd., Modène, 1948, 18–23; G. Lazzeri, *Antologia dei primi secoli della letteratura italiana*, Milan, 1942, 5–11; A. Camilli, 'Il placito di Arechisi, giudice di Capua', dans *Studi di filologia italiana*, VII (1944), 183–188; C. Dionisotti et C. Grayson, *Early Italian Texts*, Oxford, 1949, 4–9; *Il placito di Capua del marzo 960*, par les soins de P. Fiorelli, Trieste, 1960, 10–21; *I documenti cassinesi del secolo X con formule in volgare*, par les soins d'A. Mancone, Rome, 1960, 9–10; A. Schiaffini, *I mille anni della lingua italiana*, (1ère éd. 1961), 2e éd., Milan, 1962, 61–67.

2 Traduction littérale: 'Je sais que ces terres-là, dans les confins qui sont contenus ici [c'est-à-dire dans un document que le témoin touche de sa main], trente ans les a possédées la partie [au sens judiciaire du mot ou mieux dans celui de 'domaine'] de saint Benoît [le monastère bénédictin du Mont-Cassin].'

3 Éditions: E. Gattola (Gattula), *Historia Abbatiae Cassinensis*, I, Venise, 1733, 308–310; Inguanez, op. cit., 16–19; Lazzeri, op. cit., 11–19; *I doc. cass.*, 11–12.

4 Éditions: Inguanez, op. cit., 19–20; Lazzeri, op. cit., 20–23; G. Muzzioli, *La formula testimoniale del memoratorio di Teano*, Rome, 1950, 6–8; *I doc. cass.*, 13–14.

5 Éditions: Gattola, *Hist. Abb. Cass.*, t. cit., 39–40; J. Ficker, *Urkunden zur Reichs- und Rechtsgeschichte Italiens*, Innsbruck, 1874, 31–33; Inguanez, op. cit., 20–23; Lazzeri, op. cit., 23–30; *I doc. cass.*, 15–16.

6 Traduction littérale: 'Je sais que ces terres-là, dans les confins que je t'ai montrés [à l'occasion d'une descente sur les lieux], et qui sont contenus ici, ont été à Pergoald, et il les a possédées trente ans.'

7 Traduction littérale: 'Cette terre-là, dans les confins que je vous ai montrés, est à sainte Marie [le monastère de Sainte-Marie-de-Cengla], et trente ans les a possédées la partie de sainte Marie.'

8 Traduction littérale: 'Je sais que ces terres-là, dans les confins que je t'ai montrés, trente ans les a possédées la partie de sainte Marie.'

[9] P. Rajna, *I più antichi periodi risolutamente volgari nel dominio italiano*, dans *Romania*, XX (1891), 385–402.

[10] M. Bartoli, *Sao ko kelle terre . . .*, dans *Lingua nostra*, VI (1944–1945), 1–6.

[11] Dans le dialecte actuel de la région, on dit *saccio*.

[12] Selon Bartoli, la forme *sao* aurait été importée du Nord; selon d'autres (déjà Rajna, et aujourd'hui Castellani, Folena, Migliorini), elle serait due à l'analogie de la seconde personne *sai*.

[13] Dans la langue littéraire, le redoublement syntactique est toujours déterminé par le mot qui précède; il n'y a qu'une exception, *Dio*. Dans les dialectes, ces exceptions peuvent être assez nombreuses.

[14] Ainsi, *ko* est le latin *quod*, *ki* est *eccum hic*, *que* [ke] est le continuateur de *quid* aussi bien que d'autres formes pronominales.

[15] On devait prononcer *per* [pe], *et* [ɛ], du moins devant une consonne. Celle-ci, dans le cas de *et trenta*, est un *t-*, et pour cela le *-t* de *et* est conservé apparemment dans la prononciation.

[16] Aujourd'hui, cependant, *trenta* a l'*e* ouvert dans la prononciation napolitaine.

[17] La prononciation [ɛ] a subsisté en Toscane jusqu'au XVIIIe siècle; ailleurs, elle survit encore.

[18] 'Probabilmente fino dall'età romana' (Bartoli, op. cit., 5).

[19] Aujourd'hui, *b* et *d* intervocaliques sont devenus [v] et [ð] ou [r] respectivement. Au moyen âge, on peut supposer que la prononciation de *b* était encore bilabiale (I. Baldelli, 'Glosse in volgare cassinese del secolo XIII', dans *Studi di filologia italiana*, XVI, 1958, 127–129).

[20] On écrivait *ki* et *kella*, mais pour *que* on disposait d'un modèle bien plus évident dans l'orthographe du latin.

[21] Si, tout en écrivant *et* (conjonction latine), on prononçait ['ɛtte], on pouvait de la même manière écrire *posset* le mot vulgaire qu'on prononçait [pos'sɛtte].

# A Spectrographic Study of Polish Speech Sounds

WIKTOR JASSEM

The present is a pilot study of those acoustic (mainly spectral) properties of Polish speech sounds which can be detected by means of the Kay Electric Sonagraph Type 661.[1]

The material is a word list containing 44 items, pronounced by three native speakers of Educated Polish[2]: BP (rather low male voice), KD (fairly high male voice), and BK (low female voice). The word list was so constructed that those phonemes which previous experience had shown to require more extensive exemplification should be more frequent than those whose analysis is relatively simple. Within the scope of the material all allophonic variations due to the interdependencies between contiguous phonemes could not be investigated, but it is hoped that the more important acoustic features of the individual phonemes have been discovered. Extensive research is now urgently needed to establish, in acoustic terms, the distinctive features of the Polish phonemes and to describe all the conditioned and free variants, as well as the characteristics distinguishing individual voices.

When the speech wave is so analysed and portrayed that energy is distributed both in frequency and time, the following types of acoustic events can be distinguished (a) *near-periodic*, (b) *aperiodic* (noise-like), (c) *aperiodic superimposed on near-periodic*, (d) *pulse-like*, and (e) *zero-energy gaps* of limited duration. Some phonemes are represented by only one event, others by sequences of different events. A speech-wave signal occurring between two consecutive pauses (e.g. when words are pronounced in isolation, as they are in our material) can be split up into consecutive *segments*. The boundaries between segments are marked by (a) rapid change from one type of event to another, and (b) relatively fast change of overall amplitude level and/or energy-frequency distribution. An event of a given type, e.g. a near-periodic, may therefore represent two consecutive segments, if within that event a fairly well-defined point along the time scale can be indicated at which the

| VOWELS | | | | | |
|---|---|---|---|---|---|
| | | syllabic | | non-syllabic | |
| | | open | close | | |
| unrounded | front | e | i | palatal | j |
| | central | a | ɨ | | |
| rounded (back) | | o | u | velar | w |

| CONSONANTS | continuant | | | | | non-continuant | | | | |
|---|---|---|---|---|---|---|---|---|---|---|
| | non-fricative | | | fricative | | affricate | | stop | | |
| | non-nasal | | nasal | voiced | voiceless | voiced | voiceless | voiced | voiceless | |
| | lateral | non-lateral | | | | | | | | |
| | | | m | v | f | – | – | b | p | labial |
| | | | n | z | s | d͡z | t͡s | d | t | dental |
| | l | r | – | ʒ | ʃ | d͡ʒ | t͡ʃ | – | – | alveolar |
| | | | ɲ | ʑ | ɕ | d͡ʑ | t͡ɕ | ɟ | c | palatal |
| | | | ŋ | x | | – | – | g | k | velar |

Fig. 1. The phonemes of educated Polish.

rate of change of overall amplitude level or the rate of change of the spectral envelope (or that of both) is maximum.

The sounds of Educated Polish as spoken by the younger generation can, in the present writer's view, be interpreted as representing the phonemic system shown in Fig. 1.[3]

The data which follow have been extracted from sonagrams made with the broad-band filter, amplitude sections made either with the broad or the narrow band filter, and from traces obtained with the amplitude-display unit.

SYLLABIC VOWELS. All syllabic vowels are represented by near-periodic segments. Their formants can be specified most simply if their frequencies are established at points where the rate of change of all, or most of, the formants is minimum. In very nearly all cases the frequencies of the first three formants could be established. Formant 4 could be satisfactorily determined in approximately 90% of the cases. The following table shows figures relating to the 'principal' allophones. They represent mean values for each of the three voices.

TABLE 1

| | PB | | | | KD | | | | BK | | | | |
|---|---|---|---|---|---|---|---|---|---|---|---|---|---|
| | 1 | 2 | 3 | 4 | 1 | 2 | 3 | 4 | 1 | 2 | 3 | 4 | |
| i | 250 | 2250 | 2850 | 3600 | 250 | 2500 | 3400 | 3900 | 320 | 3500 | 4300 | 5100 | i |
| ɨ | 340 | 1850 | 2650 | 3600 | 300 | 2100 | 2650 | 3600 | 350 | 2250 | 3300 | 5150 | ɨ |
| u | 340 | 950 | 2350 | 3300 | 300 | 1000 | 2500 | 3500 | 320 | 1100 | 3000 | 4000 | u |
| e | 500 | 1750 | 2750 | 3750 | 550 | 1800 | 2700 | 3700 | 550 | 2200 | 3250 | 4200 | e |
| a | 750 | 1350 | 2400 | 3750 | 800 | 1350 | 2500 | 3650 | 800 | 1750 | 2600 | 3700 | a |
| o | 500 | 950 | 2700 | 3700 | 700 | 1150 | 2550 | 3700 | 750 | 1250 | 3000 | 4000 | o |

Table 1 and the corresponding Fig. 2 show regularities in the frequencies of formants 1, 2, and 3 similar to those found in other languages.[4] Thus in the *close* vowels /i, ɨ, u/ the frequency of the first formant, $F_1$, is lower than the frequency of $F_1$ in the *open* vowels /e, a, o/. Among the close vowels the *front* /i/ has a greater distance between $F_1$ and $F_2$ than the *central* /ɨ/, and in the *back* /u/ this distance is smaller still. Also among the open vowels the distance between $F_1$

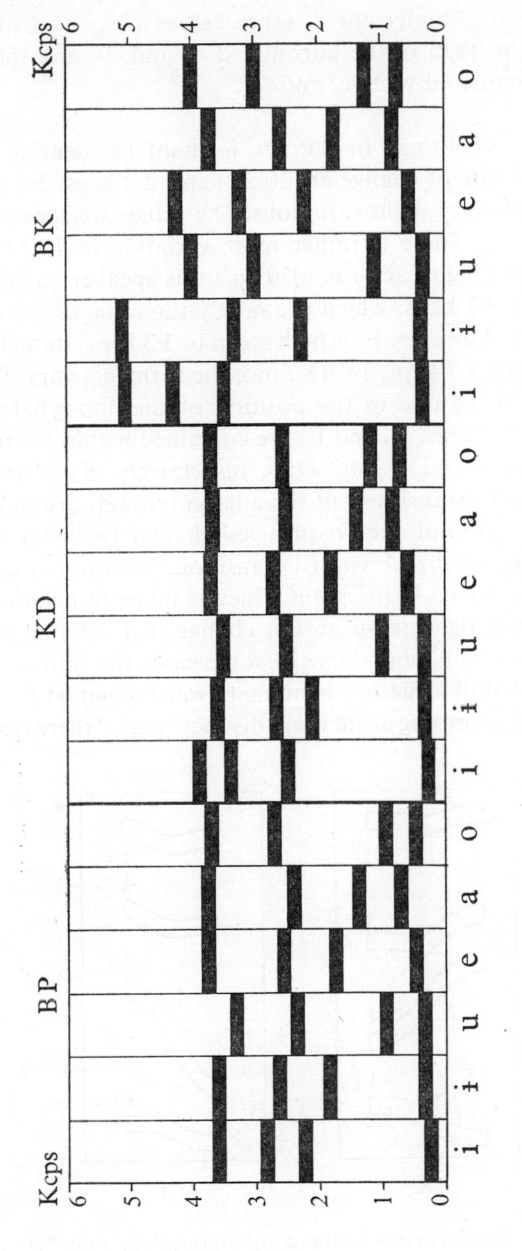


Fig. 2 The vowel formants.

and $F_2$ is greater in the front /e/, smaller in the central /a/, and smaller still in the back /o/. Finally, the distance between $F_2$ and $F_3$ is greater in the rounded /u/ than in the unrounded /i/ and /ɨ/, and the same is true for /o/ as compared with /e/ and /a/.

NON-SYLLABIC VOWELS. In BP the formant frequencies of /j/ at points of slowest rate of change are: 0·25 kcps, 2·2 kcps, 2·8 kcps, and 3·7 kcps, with only very slight variations. The values are here practically the same as for /i/. There is rather more variation in KD. In *wióry* /ˈvjurɨ/ (before the high back-rounded /u/) this speaker has the values 0·3, 2·1, 2·6, and 3·7 kcps, which are nearly the same as those for /ɨ/. In other positions, however, $F_3$ is higher (up to 3·3 kcps) though $F_4$ does not seem to exceed 3·7 kcps. In BK, too, the formants vary, the variations appearing to be due to the position of the non-syllabic vowel. With $F_4$ around 0·3 kcps, $F_2$ and $F_3$ are contained within the frequency ranges 3·0–3·3 kcps and 3·5–4·2 kcps, respectively. $F_4$ is around 5·0 kcps. The $F_1$ and $F_2$ transitions of the adjacent vowels are smooth and continue within /j/ until the frequencies characteristic for the non-syllabic vowel are reached.[5] The $F_3$ transition, however, is completed within the non-syllabic. At the point which is taken to delimit /j/ from the adjacent vowel there is an abrupt change in $F_3$. Often there is a weakening of $F_3$ at this boundary. In some cases the transition of the syllabic is even slightly negative, bending upwards again at the segment boundary and thus forming a still more distinct 'angle' there (see Fig. 3).

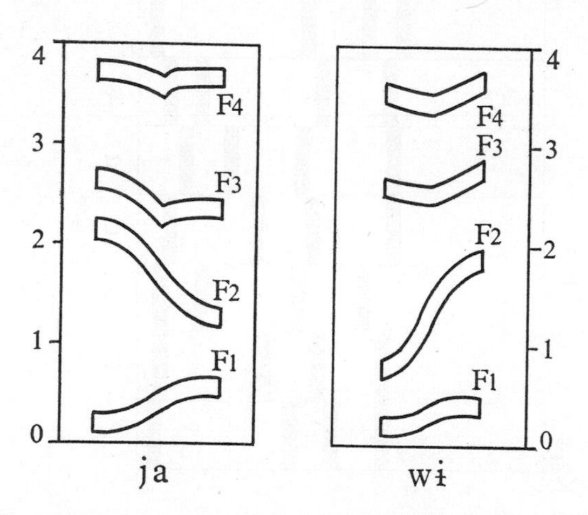


Fig. 3. The formants in the combinations /ja/ and /wɨ/.

The formants of /w/ are, in BP and KD, at 0·3, 0·8, 2·6, and 3·6 kcps. $F_2$ of /w/ is thus distinctly lower than it usually is in /u/, and $F_1$ also tends to be lower. Whilst $F_3$ is about the same as in /u/, $F_4$ tends to be higher. Those relationships are no doubt due to the fact that /w/ is closer and more rounded than /u/. (In BK the $F_1$ and $F_2$ frequencies of /w/ are about the same as in BP and KD, and $F_3$ and $F_4$ are about the same as in her /u/.) As in the case of /j/, the $F_1$ and $F_2$ transitions of an adjacent vowel are smooth and continue within /w/, $F_3$ showing an abrupt change at the junction between the syllabic and the non-syllabic.

THE NON-FRICATIVE CONTINUANTS. Four formant regions have been found in the male voices for the lateral /l/: 0·3–0·5, 1·4–1·8, 2·0–3·0, and 2·7–3·8 kcps; and three in BK; 0·3–0·4, 1·6–2·0, and 2·6–3·7 kcps. In one case, a fourth formant appears in BK at 5·0 kcps. The formant frequencies depend on the spectral properties of neighbouring sounds. The lowest values have been encountered in the word *kolumna* /koˈlumna/ between the back vowels /o/ and /u/. There are no examples of /l/ next to /i/ and /ɨ/, so the upper limits of the formant regions may actually be somewhat higher than the values quoted. The transitions of $F_1$ and $F_2$ in the neighbouring vowels are gradual, but $F_3$ and $F_4$ either have a decrease of level at the segment boundaries, or show abrupt changes of direction. The segments constituting /l/ sounds are near-periodic.

Articulatorily, the Polish /r/ may be described as either 'flapped' or 'rolled', on the assumption that two 'taps' are sufficient for a sound to be labelled 'rolled'. In the material only one-tap or two-tap /r/s have been found, and it would appear that in ordinary speech (except for purposes of emphasis) Polish /r/ is not usually given more than two 'taps'. Our /r/s then consist acoustically of between one and four segments, all of which are the near-periodic type. If there is only one segment (this variety appears to occur between vowels only) it is contoidal and corresponds to the oral closure. Otherwise there is an alternation of vocoidal and contoidal segments. In a non-intervocalic position the contoidal segment is separated from a pause or a neighbouring consonant by the vocoidal segment which is a variety of [ə]. The contoidal segment shows a distinct drop of the overall intensity curve. If its intensity is very low, it appears on spectrograms as one or more small voicing striations near the base-line. Its duration is very short – it does not exceed some 40 msec – and it may extend over just one period of the fundamental frequency. If it has more intensity, however, it shows

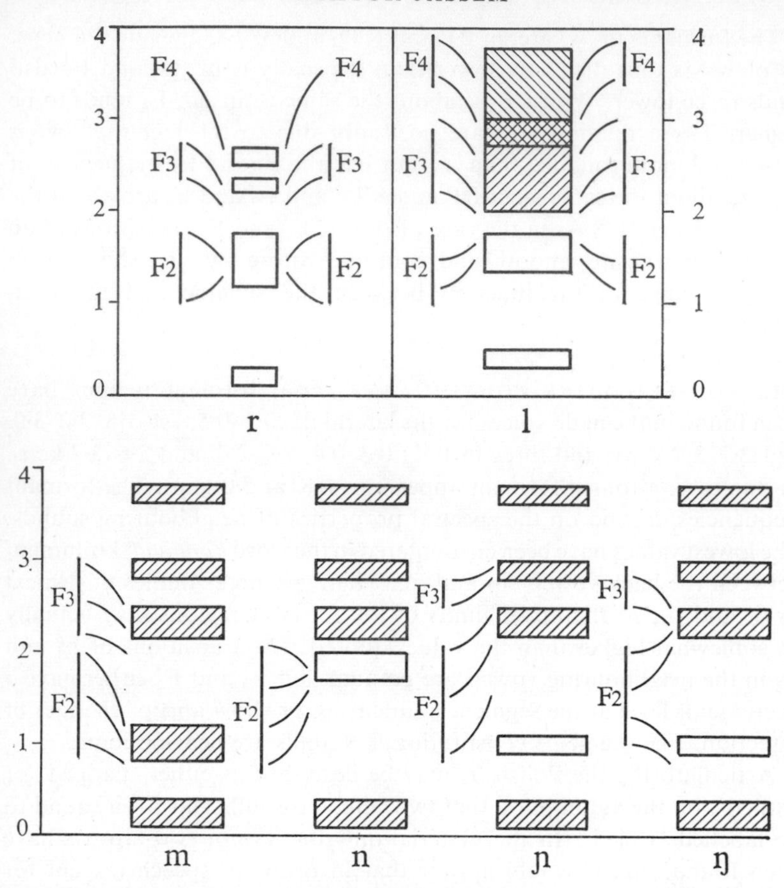


Fig. 4. Formant regions of non-fricative continuants with typical vowel formant transitions.

traces of formants (1) near the fundamental, and in the male voices, (2) at 1·2–1·8 kcps, (3) 2·2–2·4 kcps, and (4) at approximately 2·6 kcps. The last two often coalesce, and the values for BK are typically 0·5, 1·7, 3·0, and 3·2 kcps. The corresponding formants of the neighbouring vocoidal segments (including [ə] if any), bend towards those frequencies, if they differ from them. $F_3$ and $F_4$ of a neighbouring vocoid tend to, or actually do, converge at 2·5 kcps. The formants of the [ə] segment, which in our material has a duration of between 30 and 80 msec, are variable, but are contained within the ranges: 0·35–0·6, 1·5–1·8, 2·5–2·8 kcps and around 3·7 kcps for BP and KD, the upper limits of these ranges being typical for BK. $F_4$ of [ə] in BK could not be satisfactorily established.

The nasal consonant phonemes are also represented by near-periodic segments having a formant-structure similar to vowels. Five formant frequency regions are represented in BP and KD: (1) around 0·3 kcps, (2) between 0·7 and 1·7 kcps, (3) between 2·2 and 2·5 kcps, (4) between 2·7 and 3·0 kcps, and (5) between 3·7 and 4·1 kcps. Region (1) is equally well represented in all nasals. Region (2) is more prominent (i.e. the level of the formant is relatively higher) in /m/ than in the others. The frequency of (2) in /m/ tends to depend on the adjacent vowel. It is higher next to vowels with a higher $F_2$ and lower next to vowels with a lower $F_2$. The lowest figure for /m/ has been found at 0·8 kcps and the highest at 1·2 kcps. In a word like *momentalny* /momenˈtalnɨ/ where the second /m/ is preceded by a back vowel and followed by a front vowel, the formant at (2) changes within the segment corresponding to the nasal phoneme. For /n/ the values for (2) are at about 1·7 kcps, but this formant has been found only in a few cases of /n/. It is extremely weak

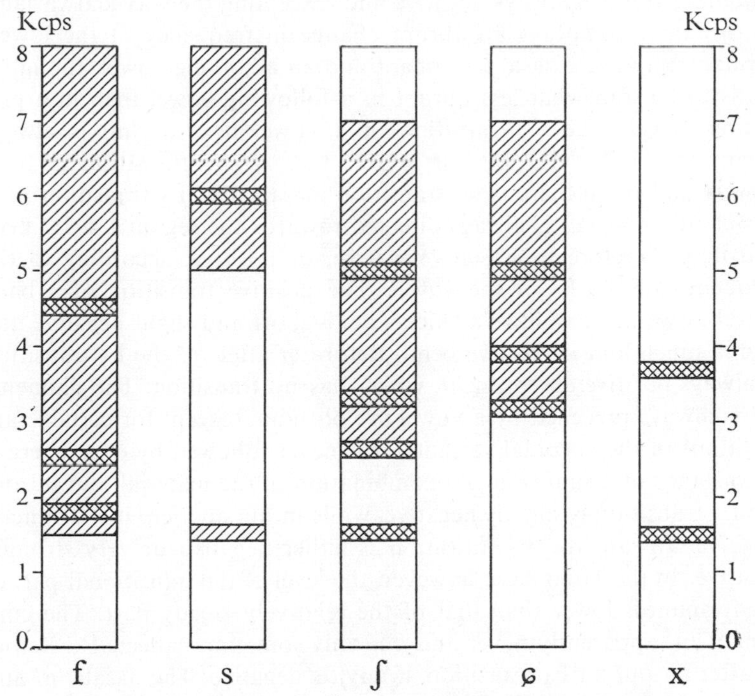


Fig. 5. Energy distribution in the fricatives (schematized).

in this nasal. The level of the higher formants tends to be higher in /ɲ/ and /ŋ/ than in the other nasals. No definite decision as to the difference in formant-structure between /ɲ/ and /ŋ/ could be reached, but it would appear that it is the relative level rather than the frequency of the formants that distinguishes /ɲ/ from /ŋ/ (apart from the transitions: see below). Region (3) tends to be more pronounced in /ɲ/ and region (4) in /ŋ/. There are also, in Polish, non-syllabic nasal vocoids of the [ɯ̃] or [ɤ̃] type. Their phonemic status is a matter of controversy, but in the present writer's view they belong to the [ŋ] phoneme. They differ from the other nasals by showing higher frequencies in region (1) – between 0·3 and 0·5 kcps. The frequency of the formant at (2) varies in these sounds between 0·7 and 1·2 kcps.

The corresponding values in BK are higher in each of the regions 1–4 by approximately 15–20%. Region (5) could not be satisfactorily established for BK.

The frequency of the lowest formant remains perfectly steady all through the length of a nasal consonant. The transition of the $F_1$ of an adjoining vowel is always negative and (excepting the vocoidal variants of /ŋ/) there is always an abrupt change in frequency of the lowest formant between a nasal consonant and an adjoining vowel, though it tends to be somewhat less abrupt in a following vowel than in a preceding vowel. The $F_2$ transition of a vowel next to /m/ is always negative in BP and KD, but in BK there is no transition in back vowels and often there is no transition in /a/. The $F_2$ transition of a vowel adjoining /n/ is always directed towards the region 1·4–1·7 kcps and may therefore be absent, negative, or positive, according to the frequency of the $F_2$ of the vowel. The positive transition of a back vowel or an /a/ may have a 'kick', i.e. a short and slight negative and then a much longer positive bend. Before or after /ɲ/ the $F_2$ transition is always positive except in /i/, which has no transition. The phoneme /ŋ/ is always preceded by a vowel in Polish but (except for certain rare positions of the vocoidal variants) it is never followed by one. There is no instance of a /uŋ/ or a /ɨŋ/ combination in the material, but in /oŋ/ the $F_2$ transition is slightly negative, while in /iŋ/ and /eŋ/ it is distinctly positive. In /aŋ/ the $F_2$ transition is either negative or very strongly positive. In the latter case, however, the level of the transitional part of the formant is lower than that of the relatively steady part. The consonant /n/ apparently never and /m/ only sometimes affects $F_3$. Before or after an /m/ an $F_3$ transition, if any, is negative. The nasals /ɲ/ and /ŋ/ are consistently distinguished from each other by their effect on the

$F_3$ transition which is positive for the palatal and negative for the velar. Thus at the end of a front vowel $F_2$ and $F_3$ often converge before /ŋ/. The nasal /n/ often produces a very rapid negative $F_4$ transition of a preceding or a following vowel. Within a few periods of the fundamental this decreases by as much as 1 kcps. No distinct effects on $F_4$ have been observed in the case of the other nasals. A vowel adjoining a nasal consonant is always nasalized in Polish. This appears on the sonagrams as an extension of the nasal formants, especially the higher ones. A nasalized vowel may therefore be found to have a large number of formants, some of which are due to the oral articulation, and some to nasality. Between the two consecutive nasals in the word *kolumna* /koˈlumna/ all three speakers have a short [ə]-like vowel (approximately 40 msec in duration). This also appears between /g/ and /ɲ/ in the word *gniew* /gɲef/. A statement of the conditions under which a non-phonemic [ə] appears in Polish requires further investigation.

FRICATIVES. With one exception which is discussed later in this section, the consonant phonemes currently described as fricative are shown by periodic segments, aperiodic segments and segments representing a superposition of aperiodic vibrations on periodic. As shown in Table 1 there are four pairs of voiced vs. voiceless phonemes, and one phoneme lacks the distinctive feature of voicing.

That part of the spectrum which corresponds to the aperiodic vibrations lies, in all fricatives, above 1·5 kcps. Below this frequency energy is only found in the voiced fricatives, at the frequencies of the first few harmonic components. When voiced fricatives occur in an initial position a periodic-aperiodic segment is almost invariably preceded by a purely periodic segment of about 80 msec showing energy at the low end of the frequency scale. This segment is therefore similar to the one which is commonly known to constitute part of voiced plosives (see below, p. 346). A careful listener can hear this segment as a 'colourless' murmur.

Both /f/ and /v/ have very low over-all level, and the spectral properties of the noise are distinct enough in BK and in some of the specimens of KD, but no reliable data has been obtained for PB. The noise spectrum extends from about 1·5 or 2·0 kcps to the end of the analysed range of frequencies. Maximum amplitude can, however, be observed at 1·8, 2·5, and 4·5 kcps for KD and 2·0, 3·2, and 5·0 kcps for BK with slight variations probably dependent on the adjoining sounds. In two instances BK has, instead of an expected periodic-aperiodic segment, a pulse-like segment for /v/, and the corresponding sound indeed gives a distinct impression of a labio-dental plosive. The pulse is represented by a broken vertical line consisting of sections which centre around the frequencies typical for /v/. If this is not a personal idiosyncrasy, it poses an interesting phonemic problem, since friction is believed to be distinctive in /v/, distinguishing it phonematically from /b/.

The main noise spectrum of the dental (more strictly, postdental) sounds is higher in frequency than that of all the other fricatives. Practically all the energy of the noise is contained above the frequency of 5 kcps. Energy maxima can easily be detected between 5 and 8 kcps, but their position along the frequency scale appear to vary rather freely. A maximum at about 6·0 kcps appears to be typical and to possess the highest level. Other maxima may appear slightly lower or at higher frequencies. There is also a separate energy concentration, with a very narrow band-width, at 1·5 kcps in BP and KD and at 2·0 kcps in BK. The level of this low-frequency noise in the spectrum is 20–25 db below the peak at the higher frequencies. Although /ʃ/ and /ʒ/ appear to be the most practical symbols for the third pair of Polish fricatives, it should be noted that the sounds are purely alveolar.[6] The main noise spectrum for /ʃ, ʒ/ extends from about 2·5 kcps to approximately 7 kcps with a strong energy concentration at the lower end (about 3·5 kcps in BK) and a lesser one between 3·0 and 3·5 kcps for BP and KD (about 5·0 kcps in BK). Between 4 and 7 kcps there is always at least one other maximum at 5·0 kcps for BP, 6·0–7·0 kcps for KD, and 6·5 kcps for BK. There is also a separate energy concentration of narrow band-width below 2·5 kcps whose centre frequency is largely dependent on the adjoining sounds. Without a neighbouring vowel this noise lies at 1·5 kcps in BP and KD, and slightly higher in BK. In a word like *cisza* /ˈtɕiʃa/ this narrow-band noise forms, on a spectrogram, a connection between the $F_2$ of /i/ and $F_2$ of /a/ with a nearly straight downward slope within the /ʃ/ segment. This low-frequency energy concentration is not present in /ɕ, ʑ/. The maximum at the high frequency is about the same in /ɕ, ʑ/ as in /ʃ, ʒ/, but the middle two maxima are higher in/ɕ, ʑ/ than in /ʃ, ʒ/, the difference being approximately 0·6 kcps in BP and KD and 0·3 kcps in BK.

There is only one velar fricative phoneme. It has an occasional conditioned voiced variant which does not appear in our material. Otherwise the allophones are voiceless. There are two distinct and separate, rather narrow frequency bands of noise. If there is no vowel next to /x/ (the example in our material being *chrząszcz* /xʃoŋʃtʃ/), the lower frequency noise lies at 1·5 kcps in BP, 1·7 kcps in KD, and 2·0 kcps in BK, and the higher frequency noise at 3·3 kcps in BP, 3·7 kcps in KD, and 5·0 kcps in BK. Except for a following /i/, an adjoining vowel does not appear to affect the higher frequency noise. The centre of the lower-frequency noise, however, depends largely on the frequency of the $F_2$ of the vowel. It is slightly above the $F_2$ of a neighbouring /a, o/ or /u/ and slightly below the $F_2$ of a neighbouring /ɨ/. No examples of /ex/ or /xe/ are contained in the material. Before /i/ the 'lower /x/-noise' covers a broader frequency range in the region of $F_2$, $F_3$, and $F_4$ of the vowel with slight maxima at about the formant frequencies of the /i/.

The $F_1$ of a vowel adjoining a fricative always has a distinct, gradual negative transition. The $F_2$ regularly bends towards the frequency of the 'low noise' in /s, z/, and /ʃ, ʒ/. $F_3$ is not affected. The /f, v/ pair produce negative $F_2$ and $F_3$ transitions whilst /ɕ, ʑ/ produce positive transitions of $F_2$ and $F_3$. The $F_2$ of a vowel next to /ʃ, ʒ/ links up with the 'low noise' described above and $F_3$ may tend to have a negative transition, but the evidence is not conclusive.

AFFRICATES. The affricates /ts, ʣ, ʧ, ʤ/ and /tɕ, ʥ/ are essentially combinations of the respective plosives with the respective fricatives. The duration of the aperiodic (or periodic-aperiodic) segment is regularly shorter here than it is in the fricatives, in comparable positions. The aperiodic segment follows the pulse-like segment almost immediately. In /tɕ, ʥ/ the higher-frequency parts of the pulse stripe tend to show better than in the other fricatives. A curious phenomenon has been observed in the majority of cases where an affricative follows a homorganic fricative as in the words *ściana* /ˈɕtɕana/ *drożdże* /ˈdroʒʤe/, or *chrząszcz* /xʃoŋʃʧ/. There is a gradual decrease of the noise level in the fricative followed by a gradual increase for the fricative portion of the affricative, with the boundaries of the 'stop' (i.e. the zero energy) portion in between much less clear-cut than in other positions.

STOPS. Various types of segments represent the stop phonemes. The pulse is represented by a broken (rarely by an unbroken) vertical line on the spectrograms. The individual parts of the broken line tend to occur at the following frequencies: (1) below 1 kcps, (2) between 1·1 kcps (or slightly lower) and 2·5 kcps, (3) about 3 kcps, and (4) between

4 and 4·5 kcps in BP and KD (KD tending to show slightly higher values than BP). Those regions will be referred to as $N_1$, $N_2$, $N_3$, and $N_4$ in the specified order. In BK the corresponding values for $N_1$ and $N_2$ are somewhat above those for BP and KD; $N_3$ is contained between 3·2 and 3·7 kcps and $N_4$ between 5 and 5·5 kcps. The pulse shows clearly in all cases of the voiceless stops, but it is sometimes absent from the spectrograms in the voiced stops, this being obviously due to the lower level of the pulse in this latter category. If a voiceless stop occurs in a non-initial position, the pulse is preceded by a gap of between approximately 70 and 120 msec. In an initial voiceless stop the pulse is the first constituent segment. In the voiced stops the pulse is (apart from one or two exceptions) preceded by a periodic segment with all energy concentrated at the lowest end of the frequency range. In these periodic segments no energy is registered above approximately 0·6 kcps in BP and KD and above 1·0 kcps in BK. The Polish voiceless stops are currently described as unaspirated. However, a distinct aperiodic segment has been found after the pulse in about 80% of the voiceless stops in BP and KD and in about 90% in BK. The duration of the aperiodic segment ranges from 20 to 100 msec, but as a rule values above 60 msec only occur in /c/, which generally shows a tendency to 'affrication'. BK tends to have longer aperiodic segments ('bursts') following a pulse and one case of 80 msec in a final /k/ has been found in this voice. It is probable that if the aperiodic segment following a pulse has a duration of less than some 50 msec, the stop consonant is not perceived as being 'aspirated'. Among the voiced stops distinct 'bursts' have only been found in /ɟ/. In the 'bursts' of the labial, dental, and velar stops the energy is concentrated in rather narrow frequency bands. In the palatal stops the energy is spread over a wider range of frequency, occasionally extending from some 3·0 kcps to the top end of the scale covered by the spectrograph. A final voiceless stop invariably shows an aperiodic segment, which is sometimes missing before a vowel (voiced stops do not occur utterance-finally in Polish). In both types of stops the aperiodic segment is sometimes replaced by a second pulse which may probably be regarded as a 'reduced burst'. On the other hand, in a few cases several (up to 7) distinct separate pulses have been found either preceding or replacing an aperiodic segment. These differ from the striations of periodic segments by not having any appreciable concentration of energy in the lowest frequencies and by being unevenly spaced. If a stop is followed by a vowel and there is no aperiodic segment, the pulse is separated from the following periodic segment by a

gap of between 20 and 30 msec (with occasional slightly higher values). The 'bursts', if any, appear at the same frequencies as the sections of the pulse 'line' except that no bursts have been found at $N_1$.

The pairs /p, b/, /t, d/, /c, ɟ/ and /k, g/ differ from one another chiefly in two respects: the relative levels of energy concentrations in the individual N regions in pulses and aperiodic segments, and if there are adjoining vocoids, in the formant transitions. An energy concentration at $N_1$ has been found in nearly all cases of /p, b/ which show any pulses. A trace of this occasionally occurs in the other stops. At $N_2$ some energy is contained in all the stops in the material which have a pulse or a 'burst', but /c/ and /ɟ/ have less than the remaining stops. In /p, b/ and /k, g/ $N_2$ is sometimes split into a lower and a higher range. At $N_3$ the level is highest in /c, ɟ/. The other stops quite often do not show any measurable energy in this region. A 'pulse section' or 'burst' at $N_4$ is best represented in /t, d/ and /c, ɟ/, worse in /k, g/, and /p, b/ have very little energy in that range. The middle frequency of the pulse or 'burst' in the $N_2$ range is very stable for /t, d/. It is 1·8 kcps for BP and between 2·0 kcps and 2·2 kcps for KD and BK, whatever the adjoining sounds. But for /k, g/ and, to a lesser degree, for /p, b/ this middle frequency varies according to the phonetic environment. Before pause the typical frequency for /k/ is 1·5 kcps in BP and 1·8 kcps in KD and BK. In prevocalic position the $N_2$ pulse section (and 'burst') for /k, g/ lies at about the frequency of $F_2$ of the following vowel or (especially in BP and KD) up to 0·3 kcps higher. In the combination /ko/ the frequency of the $N_2$ 'pulse section' is as low as 0·8 kcps in PB, 1·1 in KD, and 1·2 kcps in BK.

In /p, b/ the transitions of both $F_2$ and $F_3$ in a preceding vowel as well as a following vowel tend to be negative. The /t, d/ pair appears to have no effect on the formants of an adjoining /e/ whilst /a, o, u/ have positive and /ɨ/ a slightly negative transition of $F_2$. Next to /t, d/ an $F_3$ usually has a slightly positive transition, though BK's $F_3$ is not appreciably affected in this position. Quite often the $F_2$ and $F_3$ of /a, o, u/ following a /t/ have a 'kick', i.e. the transition consisting of a short negative bend followed by a longer positive bend. The vowel formants $F_1$ and $F_2$ preceding /c, ɟ/ or /k, g/ strongly tend to converge at about 2 kcps, and in most instances actually do converge at that frequency. In the combination /ka/ the vowel regularly has a positive transition in BP and KD, but no transition in BK. In /ko/ the $F_2$ of the vowel has no transition. The combinations /ke/ and /ku/ are not represented in the material; /ki/ and /gi/ do not exist in Polish. The $F_3$ of an /a/ or /o/

following /k, g/ has a slightly negative transition, but it may remain unaffected. The Polish stops /c/ and /ɟ/ are only followed by /i/ or /e/. There are no transitions in the combinations /ci/ and /ɟi/. In /ce/ and /ɟe/ the $F_2$ and $F_3$ transitions are both positive, see Fig. 6.

*Notes*

[1] The investigation was carried out in the Department of Phonetics, University of Edinburgh. I wish to thank Mr David Abercrombie, Head of the Department, for the opportunity of working there, and Mr John Dignan, Electronics Specialist in the Department, and the laboratory staff for their technical assistance. I am also indebted to Mr James Anthony, Senior Research Fellow in the Department, for help in the preparation of this article.

[2] The voices were tape-recorded in the Acoustic Phonetics Laboratory of the Polish Academy of Sciences in Poznań, in a studio sound-treated to have a reverberation of less than 50 msec over most of the audio-frequency range. The recording and reproduction corresponded to the CCIR standard, and the response was flat within ±2db between 40 cps and 12 kcps.

[3] Some controversial problems connected with the phonemicization of Educated Polish have been treated in W. Jassem, 'Phonologic and Acoustic Classification of Polish Vowels', *Zeitschrift für Phonetik*, XI, 4, 1958, 299–319.

[4] Cf. E. Fischer-Jørgensen, 'What Can the New Techniques of Acoustic Phonetics Contribute to Linguistics?', *Proc. 8th Int. Cong. Ling.*, Oslo, 1958, 433–477; C. G. M. Fant, 'Modern Instruments and Methods for Acoustic Studies of Speech', ibid., 282–358; Fant, *Acoustic Theory of Speech Production*, 's Gravenhage, 1960.

[5] In BK there is no connection between $F_2$ of /j/ and the second formant of an adjacent vowel. At the frequency at which the transition of the syllabic starts (or finishes), which is around 2·5 kcps, no energy concentration has been found within the /j/ segment. In most cases there is a partial overlap in time between what is doubtless a positive $F_2$ transition of the syllabic and what seems to be a negative $F_2$ transition of /j/, so that the two run parallel for about 100 msec, after which the latter ceases in /j/+ vowel and the former in vowel + /j/. 'Amplitude sections' give no ground for a suspicion that what is taken to be an $F_2$ transition of /j/ might in fact be an $F_3$ transition. The problem requires further investigation.

[6] All varieties of the English /ʃ, ʒ/ are distinctly more palatal than Polish /ʃ, ʒ/. The auditory effect as well as the acoustic spectrum of Polish /ʃ/ is not unlike that of Swedish /ʂ/, though the former has stronger friction.

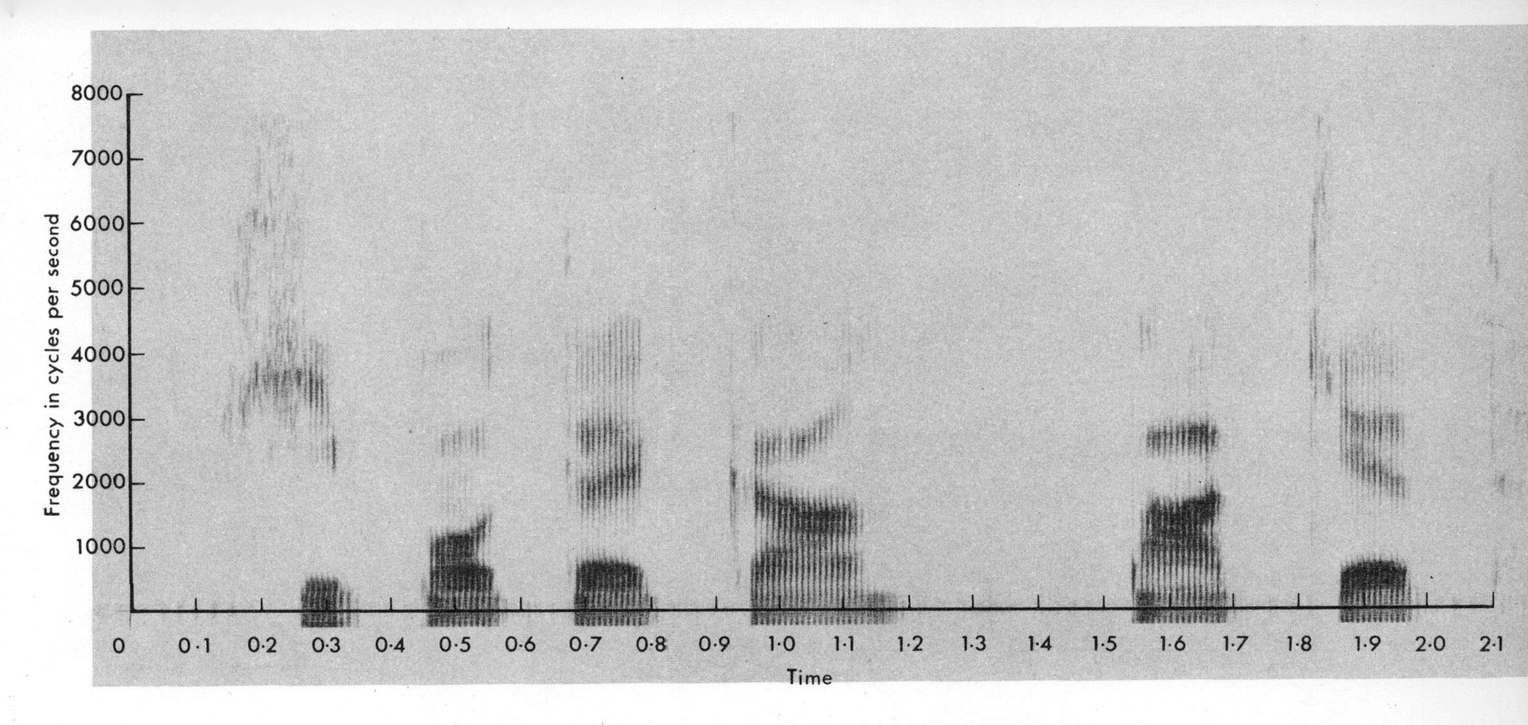


Fig. 6. Spectrograms of the words *hitoteka* /xitoˈteka/ and *pakiet* /ˈpacet/.

# Pour un Dictionnaire de la Prononciation Française

ANDRÉ MARTINET

De tous les ouvrages de Daniel Jones, son *English Pronouncing Dictionary* est probablement celui qui a eu la plus vaste diffusion et qui, plus que tout autre, a contribué à faire connaître son nom et son œuvre hors du cercle des spécialistes et des enseignants. Il est inutile de refaire ici l'éloge de ce classique qui est de ceux dont on ne discute pas l'autorité, parce que l'usager sait qu'il y trouvera un guide toujours sûr et parfaitement adapté à ses besoins.

On peut légitimement s'étonner que l'éclatante réussite de ce dictionnaire n'ait pas suscité plus d'imitateurs sur le continent européen et en France, en particulier. Avant de publier son *Pronouncing Dictionary*, Daniel Jones avait composé, en collaboration avec H. Michaelis, un *Phonetic Dictionary of the English Language*, paru à Hannovre en 1913, qui s'inspirait directement du *Dictionnaire phonétique de la langue française* de H. Michaelis et P. Passy. On regrette que ce précédent n'ait pas amorcé, en France, une réelle émulation. Si l'on met à part le petit *Dictionnaire phonétique de la langue française* d'Alfred Barbeau et Emil Rodhe qui, certes, ne mérite pas l'oubli dans lequel il semble tombé, mais dont l'autorité est discutable, on s'est contenté, pour le français, de recueillir les mots dont l'orthographe ne permettait pas de retrouver à coup sûr la prononciation, et de les ranger selon un plan qui varie d'un auteur à un autre. Mais rien ne nous permet jamais de savoir si les mots qui ont été passés sous silence l'ont été parce qu'ils ne présentent réellement pas de difficulté, parce qu'ils n'ont, du fait d'une faible fréquence, pas paru dignes d'être retenus, ou encore parce qu'ils ont été purement et simplement oubliés. Rien, à cet égard, ne peut remplacer un dictionnaire, un bon dictionnaire.

La solution qui consisterait à reproduire mécaniquement la dernière édition du Michaelis et Passy est à rejeter absolument: on a aujourd'hui de la peine à comprendre et à partager l'esprit de prosélytisme phonétique qui a entraîné les premiers auteurs de dictionnaires de prononciation à placer, dans l'ordre alphabétique, non les formes orthographiques universellement connues, mais les transcriptions phonétiques, celles précisément sur lesquelles on désire obtenir des éclaicissements. Le succès du *Pronouncing Dictionary* de Daniel Jones a été largement conditionné par la rectitude du jugement de l'auteur qui lui a fait choisir le seul ordre pragmatiquement correct: celui qui mène du connu à l'inconnu.

On pourrait certes envisager de reclasser, à partir des formes orthographiques, les éléments qu'on trouve chez Michaelis et Passy. On aimerait qu'un travail aussi soigné survive sous une forme mieux adaptée aux besoins réels du public. Mais un examen un peu poussé des données de ce dictionnaire convainc que l'entreprise ne serait recommandable qu'accompagnée d'un travail de révision considérable; bien des choses ont changé depuis 1897 et même 1913: les théories et la pratique des phonéticiens, aussi bien que les habitudes de prononciation, qu'il s'agisse de l'articulation des phonèmes ou de leur distribution, sans parler des changements qui ont affecté le système dans son ensemble. On a, en fait, intérêt à repenser complètement l'ouvrage, en s'inspirant largement, certes, de tous les précédents, dans la mesure où ils restent valables, mais dans un cadre qui tienne compte de tous les développements de la linguistique contemporaine.

Il ne saurait être question de calquer l'ouvrage sur celui de Daniel Jones, et ceci pour des raisons aussi bien linguistiques que sociolinguistiques: il n'y a, en France, rien qui corresponde à l'usage des 'Public Schools' anglaises, qui est celui que présente Jones dans son ouvrage. Il est incontestable que le fait d'avoir fait ses études dans ces établissements longtemps réservés à une aristocratie nobiliaire ou d'argent confère, en Angleterre, un prestige indiscuté qui tend à imposer à l'admiration et à l'imitation des classes moins favorisées les manières et le comportement des privilégiés. Il n'y a rien de semblable en France. On ne peut pas dire, par exemple, que le fait d'avoir fait ses études dans un lycée parisien mette, une fois pour toutes, un jeune Français dans une classe à part. Les anciens élèves du Lycée Janson de Sailly et du Lycée Pasteur qui, dans l'ensemble, se recrutent parmi la bourgeoisie aisée, ont peut-être le sentiment d'appartenir à une élite sociale. Mais, si élite il y a, elle ne jouit d'aucun prestige auprès des élèves des khâgnes de la Rive Gauche qui représentent, à leurs propres yeux, l'élite intellectuelle du pays. Le grand public ignore tout de tels conflits et si, en matière de modes et de distractions, il est tenté d'imiter le comportement des privilégiés de la fortune, il n'est probablement pas conscient d'une nécessité d'améliorer sa langue par imitation d'un groupe social particulier.

Ceci s'explique aisément du fait que les Français sont beaucoup plus sensibles au maniement défectueux de la grammaire qu'aux aberrances de prononciation. Aucun 'accent' reconnu comme français ne saurait déclasser personne, pourvu qu'il ait, par frottement, perdu de son agressivité: qu'il roule les *r* ou qu'il grasseye, qu'il distingue *un* de *in* ou qu'il les confonde, qu'il fasse on non sentir certains *e* 'muets', un Français sera toujours 'distingué' si sa syntaxe est impeccable et s'il choisit immanquablement le mot juste. On consulte le dictionnaire pour vérifier le sens ou la construction d'un mot, mais guère pour s'assurer que sa prononciation est correcte. Les dictionnaires sont, bien entendu, rédigés en conséquence; les indications orthoépiques y sont ou à peu près inexistantes, ou fondées sur on ne sait quel usage. C'est cet évident désintéressement qui explique, en fait, que nous n'ayons encore aucun répertoire exhaustif de la prononciation française. En pratique, les Français font confiance à la graphie traditionnelle pour leur suggérer la prononciation des mots qu'ils n'ont guère l'occasion d'entendre. Là où la graphie est ambiguë règne l'arbitraire. C'est le cas, par exemple, de la graphie par *a* qui n'indique qu'assez exceptionnellement si l'on a affaire à un *a* d'avant (/a/) ou un *a* d'arrière (/ɑ/). La phonologie historique suggère que la finale orthographiée *-as* devrait se prononcer avec un *a* d'arrière. Mais comme ceci n'est pas enseigné aux enfants quand ils apprennent à lire, les gens ne s'accordent guère sur la qualité de la dernière voyelle de *matelas* et de *cadenas*, ceci dans la mesure, de plus en plus réduite, où ils restent capables de distinguer entre deux *a*.

Ceci ne veut pas dire qu'il faille reconcer à décrire la prononciation française. Il faut le faire, sinon pour les Français eux-mêmes qui, jusqu'ici, ne se posent guère de questions, du moins pour les francophones, moins sûrs d'eux-mêmes, de Belgique, du Canada et d'ailleurs, et, bien entendu, pour tous ceux qui apprennent le français comme langue seconde. Cette description exhaustive qu'il faut présenter ne saurait être celle qui convient pour une langue où il est possible de se mettre d'accord sur un type relativement uniforme de prononciation, aussi bien en matière de distribution que de système phonologique. Il faudra soigneusement y marquer les latitudes de façon à ne pas imposer une norme tyrannique là où l'usager français en prend, en fait, à son aise. Proposer à l'imitation du public la prononciation d'un Français unique, quel que soit le prestige dont cet individu jouisse sur tous les plans et quelque châtié que soit considéré son emploi parlé de la langue, aboutirait à consacrer des bizarreries qui seraient récusées par ceux qui jouissent d'un égal prestige, et qui viendraient compliquer, sans aucun avantage, l'apprentissage de la langue. Qu'on songe, par exemple, à l'enseignement de Grammont relatif à la prononciation du *oi* de la graphie[1] et aux heures perdues par tous ceux qui ont tenu à répartir, dans ce cas, les timbres d'avant et d'arrière selon ses indications, alors que d'innombrables Français cultivés, à la satisfaction de tous leurs compatriotes, prononcent, dans tous les cas considérés, le même timbre de *a*.

On est assez bien renseigné sur ce qu'on pourrait appeler le dénominateur commun des systèmes phonologiques valables pour la première moitié du XXème siècle. On constate, en effet, une coïncidence remarquable des résultats fournis, d'une part, par le témoignage des orthoépistes qui ont cherché à présenter ce qu'ils estimaient être la prononciation correcte, et, d'autre part, par l'enquête phonologique réalisée en 1941 au Camp de prisonniers de Weinsberg[2]: si l'on groupe les distinctions que tous les orthoépistes en cause s'accordent à recommander, on constate qu'elles coïncident avec celles qu'une majorité des sujets de la France non-méridionale et de la Région parisienne s'accordent à identifier chez eux-mêmes. Voici les traits principaux de ce qu'on pourrait appeler le système vocalique moyen du français d'entre les deux guerres mondiales:

1⁰ la seule opposition de longueur qui se maintienne est celle de /ɛ/ ~ /ɛ·/ (*mètre* ~ *maître*) et ceci en syllabe finale couverte seulement;

2⁰ on ne distingue, en toutes positions, qu'un seul /i/, un seul /y/ et un seul /u/;

3⁰ à la finale absolue, on distingue un /e/ d'un /ɛ/, un /a/ d'un /ɑ/, mais /ø/ et /o/ sont seuls attestés à l'exclusion de /œ/ et de /ɔ/;

4⁰ en position couverte, on oppose /œ/ à /ø/, /ɔ/ à /o/, /a/ à /ɑ/, mais /ɛ/ (et /ɛ·/) sont seuls attestés à l'exclusion de /e/; ces distinctions de timbre peuvent être accompagnées de distinctions de longueur, mais les sujets sont normalement sensibles au timbre qui est le seul trait qui distingue /a/ et /ɑ/ à la finale;

5⁰ en syllabes ouvertes non finales, on relève les oppositions /ø/ ~ /œ/, /o/ ~ /ɔ/, /a/ ~ /ɑ/, mais celle de /e/ à /ɛ/ tend à se neutraliser;

6⁰ on distingue quatre voyelles nasales: /ɛ̃/, /œ̃/, /ɑ̃/ et /õ/, encore que l'opposition /ɛ̃/ ~ /œ̃/ soit sérieusement atteinte.

De façon générale, les voyelles orales se rattachent à sept types parfaitement distincts dans toutes les variétés de français. Les oppositions à l'intérieur de chaque type (/o/ ~ /ɔ/ ou /ø/ ~ /œ/ par exemple) peuvent être à recommander, mais elles ne sont pas le fait de l'ensemble des francophones.

Les données les plus récentes remettent dès aujourd'hui en cause certains traits de ce système.[3] Sans qu'on puisse se référer à un comportement majoritaire des Français des deux tiers septentrionaux du territoire, on constate que ce qui ne représentait que des tendances, aboutit, sur un rythme accéléré, à l'élimination des distinctions de faible rendement: l'opposition /ɛ̃/ ~ /œ̃/ disparaît par désarrondissement de /œ̃/, et l'on peut, dès aujourd'hui, poser que quiconque a la moindre difficulté à distinguer /ɛ̃/ de /œ̃/, lorsqu'il apprend le français comme langue seconde, peut, sans remords, prononcer /ɛ̃/ dans *lundi* et dans *brun*; l'opposition de deux phonèmes /a/ et /ɑ/, encore universelle chez les enquêtés de 1941, n'existe plus que chez le tiers des jeunes Parisiennes touchées par l'enquête de Ruth Reichstein en 1957. Il ne faut pas hésiter à recommander, dans tous les cas, une prononciation par /a/ moyen plutôt antérieur qui tend à se généraliser chez les jeunes. L'opposition /ɛ/ ~ /ɛ·/, qui représente le résidu d'une ancienne corrélation de longueur, est si atteinte qu'il serait ridicule de l'exiger de gens pour lesquels elle n'est pas, dès l'abord, une seconde nature. On obtient donc les systèmes que voici:

| POSITION FINALE | | | POSITION COUVERTE | | |
|---|---|---|---|---|---|
| i | y | u | i | y | u |
| e | | | | ø | o |
| ɛ | ø | o | ɛ | œ | ɔ |
| | a | | | a | |

Quant aux nasales, la représentation la plus adéquate du système serait sans doute la suivante:

| | õ |
|---|---|
| œ̃ | ɑ̃ |

La distinction entre /ɑ̃/ et /õ/ semble se maintenir du fait du rendement considérable de l'opposition, mais, probablement, avec des réalisations qui diffèrent aussi peu qu'il est possible sans que l'opposition disparaisse.

Dans maintes positions où l'opposition /ɛ/ ~ /e/ se neutralise, le résultat est, le plus souvent, intermédiaire entre [ɛ] et [e] ou variable selon le style. On aurait intérêt à utiliser le signe /e/ là où la distinction ne se maintient guère (par ex. pour *maison* /mezõ/), et à faire usage de diacritiques pour distinguer [ɛ] et [e] là où la chose est nécessaire (par exemple /bɔnè/ ou /bɔnẹ/ *bonnet* et /ʃé/ ou /ʃẹ/ *chez*). On pourrait être tenté d'utiliser les mêmes diacritiques pour distinguer /ø/ de /œ/ et /o/ de /ɔ/ de façon à pouvoir utiliser le signe nu (/ø/, /o/) là où les deux prononciations peuvent s'entendre (par ex. /nøtr/ *neutre*, /oby/ *obus*). Toutefois, il vaudrait mieux, dans ce cas, donner les deux prononciations comme concurrentes (/nœtr/ ou /nøtr/, /oby/ ou /ɔby/).

Le système consonantique français pose peu de problèmes: on a probablement toujours intérêt à présenter comme normale la distinction entre [-nj-] et [-ɲ-], et la prononciation [-lj-] de *-li*+voyelle, même dans *million* ou *filière*.

Une fois les phonèmes établis, il reste à déterminer quels sont ceux qu'on rencontre dans tel ou tel mot. En cette matière, nous ne disposons d'aucune documentation sérieuse: les orthoépistes ont ou bien proposé leur propre usage comme norme, ou bien copié leurs prédécesseurs, ou peut-être reproduit ce qu'il avaient relevé, mais sans préciser leur sources. Il conviendrait, avant toute chose, de procéder sur ce point à une vaste enquête. Dans l'absolu, cette enquête devrait porter sur tous les mots de la langue française, y-compris les noms propres des pays francophones (*Marie*, *Durand*, *Paris*, *Bruxelles*) et ceux d'autres pays qui se trouvent avoir une forme française ou francisée (*Gengis Khan*, *Londres*, *Copenhague*). En pratique, il y a des milliers de mots français dont la prononciation ne soulève aucun problème: [plym] n'est pas la seule prononciation du mot *plume* qu'on puisse entendre en France, mais c'est certainement /plym/ qui sera recommandé; il y a bien des Français du Nord qui prononcent *avion* en trois syllabes, mais personne n'hésiterait à retenir la prononciation [avjõ] comme la seule recommandable. A considérer les objets qui m'entourent alors que j'écris ces lignes, je constate que *lampe*, *lunettes*, *colle*, *stylo*, *livre*, *bureau*, *crayon* ne sauraient poser aucun problème et seraient certainement interprétés comme /lãp, lynet, kɔl, stilo, livr, byro, krejõ/. *Encrier* et *cendrier* soulèvent la question de savoir si l'élément noté *-rier* s'y prononce exactement comme le *-riller* de *griller*, c'est-à-dire /-rije/, ou avec un élément de liaison moins net que [j]. Je noterais et recommanderais, pour ma part, /ãkrijé/ et /sãdrijé/, mais, de préférence, après avoir recherché quelle extension peut encore avoir une prononciation comme /ãkrié/, /sãdrié/. Restent *cahier* et *carnet* pour lesquels je recommanderais volontiers ma propre prononciation /kajé/, /karnè/ plutôt que /kajè/ et /karné/ qui s'entendent. Mais il conviendrait de vérifier si ces prononciations, que je serais tenté de considérer comme 'populaires' et, en fait, peu recommandables, ne sont pas, à mon insu, en train de changer de statut.

On pourrait donc prévoir un dictionnaire dans lequel l'auteur, ou mieux, les auteurs indiqueraient, pour les mots qui ne leur paraissent poser aucun problème orthoépique, la seule prononciation qu'ils connaissent. Ces mots devraient, bien entendu, être signalés comme tels par l'emploi d'une typographie particulière. La prononciation de mots comme *encrier*, *cendrier*, étant moins un fait de distribution qu'un trait du système choisi comme le plus recommandable, devrait faire l'objet d'une remarque dans l'introduction à l'ouvrage, et, dans le corps du dictionnaire, ces mots devraient avoir la même forme que ceux dont la prononciation ne soulève aucun problème. Le même traitement pourrait valoir pour *carnet* (mots en *-et*), mais non pour *cahier* que tel sujet prononcera avec /-è/, alors qu'il a /-é/ dans *soulier*. Il faudrait donc soumettre individuellement à l'enquête les mots du type *cahier* dont on se doute qu'ils présentent, selon les gens, des phonèmes différents. Une première liste de tels vocables pourrait être dressée par référence aux index des traités d'orthoépie existants.

Une fois établie la liste définitive – sans doute après rédaction de tous ceux des articles du dictionnaire que les auteurs estimeraient pouvoir rédiger antérieurement à l'enquête – il s'agirait d'obtenir des informateurs qu'ils en prononcent chacun des éléments. Il pourrait être utile de dégager tout d'abord le système phonologique de chacun des sujets choisis, et ceci pourrait amener à reconsidérer les conclusions exposées ci-dessus relativement au dénominateur commun phonologique. En tout cas, on pourrait utiliser, pour noter la prononciation des informateurs, une transcription plus 'serrée' que celle qu'on retiendrait pour présenter les prononciations recommandées.

Les articles correspondant aux mots et aux formes de la liste des cas d'espèce comporteraient chacun, outre la forme orthographique et son identification grammaticale (*cahier* sm. ...), la forme ou les formes recommandées selon le système phonologique standardisé (... kajé ...) suivies d'indications relatives aux réactions des informateurs (par ex.: ..., -é 9, -è 1 ... à supposer qu'un informateur sur dix se soit prononcé pour /kajè/, ou encore ..., -é 4p 5d, -è 1p ... si l'on doit distinguer entre informateurs parisiens: p, et informateurs des départements: d).

Il est difficile de se prononcer ici sur le nombre et la nature des informateurs dont il faudrait solliciter le concours. Il va sans dire que l'enquête ne pourrait que gagner à ce qu'on en étendît le nombre. Celui-ci dépendrait nécessairement du personnel enquêteur et des ressources disponibles. Dans les conditions les moins favorables, il faudrait se contenter de cinq ou six sujets choisis dans les couches de la population dont on peut penser qu'elles ont un certain prestige, probablement les milieux cultivés de la bourgeoisie parisienne. Mais on devrait accorder la préférence aux personnes d'origine et d'attaches provinciales, car une certaine mobilité géographique est susceptible d'éliminer les bizarreries et les 'localismes'. Si l'on peut se le permettre, il faudrait élargir le recrutement et l'étendre jusqu'aux milieux populaires et provinciaux. Ceci ne veux pas dire qu'on devrait nécessairement donner, en fin de compte, autant de poids aux données provenant de ces milieux qu'à celles relevées dans l'usage des bourgeois parisiens.

On pourrait, dans chaque cas, indiquer l'opinion des orthoépistes du passé, mais à titre purement documentaire.

Il est difficile de savoir dans quelle mesure la prononciation des speakers de la radio et de la télévision peut, à la longue, influencer celle des auditeurs. Il pourrait être intéressant de relever certains traits de cette prononciation pour autant qu'on y pourrait observer des faits de distribution particuliers.

Parmi les faits de liaison, il faudrait noter ceux qui caractérisent certains mots, comme *quand* pour lequel on doit sans doute recommander une prononciation /kãt/ devant voyelle suivante. Mais c'est dans l'introduction qu'il faudrait traiter de tous les faits de liaison dont le rôle est proprement morphologique, comme la liaison en /-z/ en tant que marque du pluriel. Ceci figurerait dans la section qu'il faudrait nécessairement consacrer aux formes grammaticales, trop nombreuses et variées, en français, pour qu'on puisse les reproduire après chacun des mots auxquels elles sont susceptibles de se joindre. Seuls les différents radicaux verbaux devraient figurer dans le corps du dictionnaire, probablement groupés après l'infinitif.

Un tel dictionnaire pourrait être le premier tome d'une série d'ouvrages où l'on s'efforcerait, non de compliquer à loisir l'enseignement du français en insistant chaque fois sur toutes les nuances, même les plus insignifiantes, mais de montrer comment, en dépit de l'effort conjugué de générations de grammairiens et de beaux esprits, les Français arrivent à se servir de leur langue pour satisfaire à leurs besoins de tous les jours.

*Notes*

[1] Cf. Maurice Grammont, *La Prononciation française*, Paris, 1930, 26 et 27.

[2] Cf. André Martinet, *La Prononciation du français contemporain*, Paris, 1945.

[3] Cf. Ruth Reichstein, 'Etude des variations sociales et géographiques des faits linguistiques', *Word*, XVI, 1960, 55–99.

# Spelling Reform in Modern Greek

JULIAN T. PRING

Although anchored to the past by the great weight and influence of the classical tradition, modern Greek offers one of the comparatively rare examples of a radically reformed spelling having been put into effect for a whole linguistic community (the Greek-speaking minority in Russia). This striking contrast is one of many interesting features of Greek in relation to orthography. But let us first glance at the general setting.

There is only one Greek language. Like other languages with a long history, it is well equipped to serve the various needs of religious ritual, ceremonial, law, technology, literature, as well as everyday life in town and country. But the course of history since the fall of Constantinople (1453) has hindered a harmonious development and integration of the formal and vernacular elements of the language. When Greece found freedom and independence early in the nineteenth century, the somewhat stiff, scholastic form of language that had been fostered by Byzantine conservatism was adopted for official use, and predominated in writing. This contrasted strongly with demotic, or common, Greek, which had served the humble needs of the people, and found expression in their folk-songs, during their four hundred years of subjection to Turkish rule without material or intellectual advancement of any kind. The division between the two was soon turned into a matter of national controversy; but the cause of strife has been rather the ambition and rivalry of individuals and parties than any serious lack of coherence in the language itself.

At first the purists prevailed; and until 1917 only puristic Greek (*katharevusa*) was allowed to be taught in schools. Now it is the partisans of demotic who are to the fore; and demotic has become the language of primary education. These disputes have fostered an idea that either katharevusa or demotic ought to be recognized, to the exclusion of the other, as the only proper form of modern Greek. But the truth is that the language is developing in two dimensions. A study of present-day usage in speech and writing will show that the two traditions are established with equal firmness. Both flourish; and between the extremes of formal and vernacular there is increasingly found a blended idiom which is the natural, and indeed inevitable, result of growing linguistic sophistication. Could anyone suppose that the nimble Greek mind would not exploit to the full, in its new-found freedom, the rich possibilities that the genius of the language offers? However, the 'language question' dies hard, and some are at pains to keep it alive. It therefore forms an important element in the background to spelling reform. Most of the advocates of revised orthography have been demoticists, partly owing to their anti-conservative outlook, and partly because, although, broadly speaking, ancient Greek is pronounced like modern and modern Greek is spelt like ancient, there is a good deal of instability in the spelling of demotic, especially in loan-words and transliterated foreign names. Demotic hesitates between some different types of inflexion; and its extremist supporters, who wish to impose uniform types at any price, are also those who desire the most revolutionary changes in spelling.

## METHODS OF REFORM

The following kinds of orthographic change are possible for Greek:

(i) Revaluation of the letters and abolition of superfluous ones.
(ii) Simplification or abolition of breathings, accents, and other diacritics (diæresis, iota subscript, etc.).
(iii) Introduction of new letters or modifiers.
(iv) Total substitution of the Roman alphabet.

Type (iii) is commonly used in Greece for writing dialect texts. These are often interspersed with Roman letters (especially *b*, *d*, *g*) and accents to show palatalization, etc., with results that are generally inadequate and always unsightly. Most spelling reformers have adopted changes of type (i) or (ii), or a combination of both.

Outstanding among the earlier reformers of the nineteenth century was Yannis Vilaras (1770–1823), physician to Ali Pasha at Yanina, whose ideas are embodied in his *Μηκρη ορμηνια για τα γραματα κε ορθογραφηα της ρομεηκης γλοσας* [*Μικρὴ ὁρμήνεια γιὰ τὰ γράμματα καὶ ὀρθογραφία τῆς Ρωμαιικῆς γλώσσας*] and *Φηλολογηκες γραφες* [*Φιλολογικὲς γραφές*] and other works. His main changes are: /e/ written always with epsilon; /i/ written with eta, but iota is used in 'diphthongs' such as *αιτος* [*αϊτός*], *λει* [*λέει*], *ακουι* [*ἀκούει*]; omega is abolished; *αυ* becomes *αβ* or *αφ*; *ευ* becomes *εβ* or *εφ*. Breathings and accents are dispensed with, but an accent may be used to distinguish between such pairs as *άλα* (*other*) and *αλά* (*but*), or *πόλη* (*city*) and *πολή* (*much*, *many*). Here is a specimen passage: *Κε γιατη; Επηδης στοχαζοντε οτη το γενος μας γλοσα δεν εχη· κε αφτη εμαθαν το σκελεθρο, κε θελουν τη γλοσα οπου εχη το γενος, την οπηαν τη στοχαζοντε χηδεα κε χαλασμενη, να τη μπολιασουν με τα στεγναδια κε ξεραδια του σκελεθρου τους για να ξεχηδαηση.* [*Καὶ γιατί; Ἐπειδὴς στοχάζονται ὅτι τὸ γένος μας γλῶσσα δὲν ἔχει· καὶ αὐτοὶ ἔμαθαν τὸ σκέλεθρο, καὶ θέλουν τὴ γλῶσσα ὅπου ἔχει τὸ γένος, τὴν ὁποίαν τὴ στοχάζονται χυδαία καὶ χαλασμένη, νὰ τὴ μπολιάσουν μὲ τὰ στεγνάδια καὶ ξεράδια τοῦ σκέλεθροῦ τους γιὰ νὰ ξεχυδαΐση*].

Another native of Yanina, the philosopher Athanasios Psalidhas (1760–1833), held radical views on spelling similar to those of Vilaras. He wrote: 'The Greeks were Greeks before eta and omega were invented. They will again show themselves to be Greeks, not by keeping them when they are unnecessary, but by discarding them as superfluous.' In 1879 a Greek priest in Liverpool, Timotheos Kustas, produced a pamphlet urging the need for simpler spelling as an aid to the learning of Greek. It is remarkable as being written in katharevusa, and also because it foreshadows very closely the system later used in Russia. Here is the title-page of his work: *Πάντες ι 'Ελινες εγγράματι, τυτέστι πος ι καθομιλυμένι ελινικὶ γλόσα δύνατε, διὰ καταλίλυ διδασκαλίας κε απλοπιίσεος επυσιόδυς τυ ορθογραφικὺ αφτὶς μέρυς, κε ζοὶν πλίονα ιθικίν τε κε κινονικὶν ν αποκτίσι, κε εφκολομάθιτος να καταστὶ προς πάντας ομογενὶς κε αλογενίς.* [*Πάντες οἱ Ἕλληνες ἐγγράματοι, τουτέστι πῶς ἡ καθομιλουμένη ἑλληνικὴ γλῶσσα δύναται, διὰ καταλλήλου διδασκαλίας καὶ ἁπλοποιήσεως ἐπουσιώδους τοῦ ὀρθογραφικοῦ αὐτῆς μέρους, καὶ ζωὴν πλείονα ἠθικήν τε καὶ κοινωνικὴν ν' ἀποκτήση, καὶ εὐκολομάθητος νὰ καταστῆ πρὸς πάντας ὁμογενεῖς καὶ ἀλλογενεῖς*].

Some others confined themselves entirely or mainly to changes of the second kind (accents, etc.). Nikolaos Fardhis wrote a monograph (Marseilles, 1884) proposing to abolish all accents and breathings. In a later tract (1889) he accepted an acute accent to mark the stress of all words except monosyllables in order to 'avoid difficulty in reading'. I. Skilitsis proposed (1886) to omit the smooth breathing and grave accent, on the ground that they are rendered superfluous by the placement of the other breathing and accents. Alexandros Pallis employed for his modern versions of the New Testament (1910) and the Iliad

(1917) a form of type resembling capitals, which somewhat mitigates for the eye the absence of all breathings and accents. Yannis Psiharis (1854–1929), the most famous champion of demotic, used various simplifications of spelling, but did not keep to all of them. He felt that there was little point in making modern accentuation differ from its classical form; but later he came to favour no breathings and no accents on monosyllables as an intermediate stage, leading to more radical changes of the sort already made by Kustas. Thus he hopes that ψυχή will come to be written as ψιχί and παίζω as πέζο.[1]

## THE CHANGES IN RUSSIA

The most far-reaching and interesting reform is that which has been carried out in Russia (though, unfortunately, little material has been available for the preparation of these notes). Greeks of the dispersion have been settled in Russia for many centuries, in Crimea, Ukraine, and the Caucasus. Preliminary figures from the U.S.S.R. census of 1959 give the total Greek-speaking element of the population as 120,000; but detailed information is lacking about the living conditions of these people.

Between 1920 and 1930 steps were taken to introduce a revised orthography of Greek for this minority. The texts examined here were all published at Rostov-on-Don between 1928 and 1935. Among them are an elementary grammar; translated extracts from nineteenth-century Russian literature; a school reader (poems and stories by Russian authors, with one poem by Drosinis); a book on the history of writing; the story of a polar expedition; a novel about partisan warfare. All are in a form of common Greek (but containing a number of Russian words). Some publications in local dialect are also known to have been issued, but are not here referred to. The main features of this orthography can be summarized as follows (making allowance for errors and misprints).

The letters η, ξ, σ, ψ, ω are dispensed with, leaving an alphabet of 20 letters.

The vowel phonemes /i, e, a, o, u/ are written as ι, ϵ, α, ο, υ.

Doubled consonants are reduced to single, e.g. *άλος (ἄλλος) θάλασα (θάλασσα), Γιάνις (Γιάννης)*. But two new signs, double sigma and double zeta, are provided to represent Russian /š/ and /ž/, e.g.: *Πύssκιν* (*Pushkin*), *μαρss* (*musical march*), *μπυρζζυας* (*bourgeois*).

Sigma is replaced by zeta where it represents a voiced sound within the word: *κόζμος (κόσμος), ενθυςιαζμος (ἐνθουσιασμός).*

The digraphs *αυ* and *ευ* are replaced by *αφ*, *αβ* and *εφ*, *εβ*.

No attempt is made to settle the ambiguities connected with /b, d, g/. The digraphs *μπ*, *ντ* are preserved, but *γκ*, *γγ* are replaced by *νκ*, e.g., *μπένο (μπαίνω)*, *κομπάιν* (*combine*), *Μπαμπύςςκιν* (*Babushkin*), *Ντον* (*Don*), *εντολι (ἐντολή)*, *νκρινιάρις (γκρινιάρης)*, *ςπάνκος (σπάγγος)*.

Fluctuations of a kind familiar in conventional spelling turn up again here, as in these variations between *μπ*, *ντ* and *π*, *τ*:

| | | |
|---|---|---|
| *μπριγάτα* | and | *πριγάτα* |
| *μπάντα* | and | *πάνκα* |
| *Τμπίςςενςκ* | and | *φυτπολ* |
| *να λικβινταριςτι* | and | *να λικβιταριςτι* |

Similar variation occurs between *φθ*, *χθ* and *φτ*, *χτ*, etc.:

| | | |
|---|---|---|
| *να θεραπεφθίτε* | and | *να γιατρεφτίτε* |
| *να προζλιφθι* | and | *διεφτίνο* |
| *εχθρος* | and | *εχτρος* |
| *εκπέδεπςι* | and | *εχτέλεςι* |

We find, too, such inconsistencies as *δένδρο* (for *δέντρο*) and *βαμπάκι* (for *βαμβάκι* or *μπαμπάκι*). A nasal letter is often dropped before a fricative, e.g. *ςιφονο* (*συμφωνῶ*), *ςιφορα* (*συμφορά*), *ςιδεζμος* (*σύνδεσμος*), *ςιγραφέας* (*συγγραφέας*). But *ν* prevails in *ςίνχρονα (σύγχρονα).*

Accents are omitted on monosyllables and terminal syllables. The acute is used in penultimate and antepenultimate position, grave and circumflex being abolished. But different functions of a monosyllable can be signalled by accent. Thus, *ί* (*or*), *τί* (*what?*), *πύ* (*where?*) are distinct from *ι* (*the*), *τι* (*the*), *πυ* (*who*, *that*, etc.). Breathings, iota subscript, and diæresis are dropped; but an enclitic is hyphenated with its prop-word (whose final syllable can then bear an accent), e.g: *τιν ὄπςι-τυς (τὴν ὄψη τους), τυς θεύς-ςυ (τοὺς θεούς σου).*

Extract from the translated novel *Armoured Train No. 14–69*.

*Το θορακιζμένο τρένο* No. 14,69 *ςταμάτιςε ςτιν τάγια ςτο ςταθμο Νικόλ-ςκαγια, όχι μακρια απ᾽ τιν πόλι Τμπίςςενςκ, με τιν οπία ίχε διακοπι ι ςινκι-νονία. Το θορακιζμένο τρένο ίχε εντολι να διαςκορπίςι τις παρτιζάνικες ςιμορίες, πυ δρύςαν ιπό τι διίκιςι τυ Βερςςίνιν. Ι παραθαλάςια πόλι Βλαδι-βοςτοκ, απ᾽ όπυ αναχόριςε το τρένο, ίτανε ςτο έπακρο ανίςιχι κι αναςτα-τομένι, λόγο τον μεγάλον διαςτάςεον πυ πίρε το παρτιζάνικο κίνιμα, κιρίος απ' τι μέρα πυ ανέλαβε τι διίκιsί-τυ ο Βερssίνιν, χορικος πsαρος, με μεγάλες sτρατιοτικες ικανότιτες . . .*

*Ο λοχαγος Νεζελάsοφ καθότανε sτο κυπέ-τυ δίπλα sτο ορθάνιχτο παράθιρο, ακατάπαφτα κάπνιζε, sινάζοντας τι sτάχτι sτιν κιλια sπαζμένυ τsυγυνένιυ κινέζυ θευ.*

*— Έτsι, πυ λες, ι sίνδεsι με το Τμπίssενsκ διακόπικε, ανθιπολοχαγε.*

*— Μάλιsτα, διακόπικε, λέγι ο ανθιπολοχαγος.*

*— Να το κόπsυμε λάsπι, ε; Αμε τι . . . Καταρέομε sαν έμπιο πλιγις . . . sτα πέρικς . . . εμιs . . . όλι . . . κε πρόsφιγες κε πνιγμένες πια sτα χιόνια κιβερνίsιs. Αλα-α! Εγο ο ίδιοs sας λέγο, ανθιπολοχαγε. Μα ίsτερα, πύ; Στι θάλαsα; . . .*

*Ο Ομπαμπ έρικsε λοκsι ματια sτα ζαρομένα μιόνια τυ προsόπυ τυ λοχαγυ.*

*— Δεν θα κάνατε άsκιμα να θεραπεφθίτε. Νε, λοχαγε . . . Σαs χριάζετε, το δίχοs άλο, θεραπία, κίριε λοχαγε. Γιατρεφτίτε.*

*Ο Νεζελάsοφ βιαsτικα έβγαλε απ' το sτόμα το τsιγάρο.*

*— Κλιsτίκατε κιριολεκτικα sτο καβύκι-sαs, Ομπομπ . . . Τίποτε δε νιόθετε.*

The first paragraph of this passage is here transcribed conventionally, with non-Greek words abbreviated:

*Τὸ θωρακισμένο τραῖνο ἀρ. 14,69 σταμάτησε στὴν τ. στὸ σταθμὸ N, ὄχι μακριὰ ἀπ' τὴν πόλι T, μὲ τὴν ὁποία εἶχε διακοπῆ ἡ συγκοινωνία. Τὸ θωρακισμένο τραῖνο εἶχε ἐντολὴ νὰ διασκορπίση τὶς παρτιζάνικες συμμορίες, ποὺ δροῦσαν ὑπὸ τὴ διοίκηση τοῦ B. Ἡ παραθαλάσσια πόλι B, ἀπ' ὅπου ἀναχώρησε τὸ τραῖνο, ἤτανε στὸ ἔπακρο ἀνήσυχη κι' ἀναστατωμένη, λόγω τῶν μεγάλων διαστάσεων ποὺ πῆρε τὸ παρτιζάνικο κίνημα, κυρίως ἀπ' τὴ μέρα ποὺ ἀνέλαβε τὴ διοίκησή του ὁ B, χωρικὸς ψαρός, μὲ μεγάλες στρατιωτικὲς ἱκανότητες.*[2]

## ROMANIZATION

The complete replacement of Greek by Roman characters has been discussed in various articles, notably by Kartheos.[3] Among the advantages of such reform, he counts the following: (i) Ancient Greek spelling would be much easier to learn if a different alphabet were in use for modern Greek, whereas it is confusing if the same characters have to serve for two different spellings of the same word. Thus it would be better to reform the modern equivalents of *γλῶσσα* and *μοιραῖος* to *glosa* and *mireos* rather than to *γλόσα* and *μιρέος*. (ii) Foreign names would have one definite form instead of many variants as at present.

He illustrates this by giving the possible variations of the name Baudelaire in Greek:

> *Μποντελέρ, Μποντλέρ, Μπωντελαίρ, Μπωντλαίρ, Μποδελέρ, Βωδελαίρ, Βωδλαίρ, Βοδελέρ, Βοδλέρ,* etc.

The proposed alphabet is based on an imperfect phonological analysis of Greek, and contains a number of undesirable features. I will quote only from the treatment of unstressed /i/, which may or may not undergo synizesis with a following vowel. 'Cette synizèse du *i* . . . est toujours pratiquée dans le grec moderne. C'est seulement dans les mots qui ont été empruntés au grec ancien ou à la langue érudite que le *i* est séparé de la voyelle qui le suit (*ὁπλοποιός ἀρτοποιός*). C'est une prononciation *bâtarde* pour le grec moderne. . . .' Special letters will be used for foreign names. Thus the French /š, ž, y, ø/ are to be written as sh, zh, ü, ö. The penultimate syllable being the most frequently accented, accent need only be shown when it occurs elsewhere.

The following specimen is given:

Ston Psarón tin olómavri rachi
perpatondas i Doxa monachi
meletá ta lamprá palicaria,
ce stin comi stefani forí
ginomeno apó liga chortaria
pu ichan mini stin érimi gi.

[*Στῶν Ψαρῶν τὴν ὁλόμαυρη ράχη
περπατώντας ἡ Δόξα μονάχη
μελετᾶ τὰ λαμπρὰ παλικάρια
καὶ στὴν κόμη στεφάνι φορεῖ
γινομένο ἀπὸ λίγα χορτάρια
ποὺ εἶχαν μείνει στὴν ἔρημη γῆ.*]

This same book reproduces a letter from L. Roussel, advocating a romanized orthography based on the one he uses in his *Grammaire du Roméique littéraire* (1922), which contains an assortment of letters and diacritics with little or nothing to commend it.

Long before it had been discussed by theoreticians, a romanized form of Greek was in use in various parts of the Greek world that were more especially under Frankish (and particularly Italian) influence. Merchants in Smyrna and Chios and elsewhere were long in the habit of using, in their business correspondence, an orthography that came to be known as *francochiotica* (which might also serve for official documents). The history of this term is obscure, but according to Falbos,[4] the first Greek book to be written in this way was a religious work published in 1595, entitled 'Didaskalia christianiki, is tin opian o Didascalos erota, che o mathitis apilogate, Camomeni apo ton patera Jacobon Ledesma theologon tis sintrofias tu Iisu, chie girismeni is to Romaecon dia mesu tu patros Vincentiu tu Castagniola tis omias sintrofias.' Other books with similar titles followed. Falbos also quotes a document relating to an inheritance, dated at Smyrna in 1834, of which the following is an extract: '... emis oli omoghnomis esterchthicame ke edhechthicame to zitima tu kiriu J. Maltass peri to meridhio ghnorizondas to dhikeotato, ke acomi oti aftos echi telia exusia na matachiristi (sic) to anothen meridhion tu cathos thelisi ke tu fani evlogho.'[5]

A similar spelling of Greek was commonly used in Crete under Venetian occupation. *Erofili*, a verse drama by the Cretan Hortadzis, was first published in Venice (1637) from a manuscript in Latin characters. Another such text was printed by Legrand in his *Bibliothèque Grecque Vulgaire* (1881), from which this passage is taken (Act ii, Scene vi):

> Ci frognimus to risico chie olus ci procomenus
> pada ghieramenus crati chie calocardhismenus,
> ch' i afediassu anamelos dhe carteri na pari
> apu stan egiegnithichie chiamia apochino ghari,
> ma me ci strates ci aretis to cagnis chie gireugi
> ci copussu ci eugiegnicus dhichia na su adimeugi.

This Greek version of the passage is from *Δημοτικὴ Δραματικὴ Βιβλιοθήκη* (Athens, 1898):

> *Τσοὶ φρόνιμους τὸ ριζικὸ κι' ὅλους τσοὶ προκυμμένους*
> *πάντα χαιράμενους κρατεῖ καὶ καλοκαρδισμένους·*
> *κι' ἡ ἀφεντιά σου ἀνάμελος δὲν καρτερεῖ νὰ πάρη*
> *ἀπ' ὥστ' ἂν ἐγεννήθηκε καμμιὰ 'πὸ κεῖνο χάρι,*
> *μὰ μὲ τσῆ στράταις τσ' ἀρετῆς τὸ κάμνεις καὶ γυρεύγει*
> *τσοὶ κόπους σου τσ' εὐγενικοὺς δίκηα νὰ σ' ἀντιμεύγει.*

## CONCLUSIONS

There is no likelihood of any radical change in Greek spelling in the oreseea ble future. Such changes are only found when the community exists in isolation, or in conditions of restricted liberty. Thus the Greeks of Russia got a new spelling after they had become completely separated from the mainstream of Hellenism, and subject to authoritarian control. *Francochiotica*, which developed under foreign domination, declined once Greece had become an independent sovereign state, and is now limited to telegrams between Greece and foreign countries. The bulk of present-day opinion is reflected in the recommendation of the Academy of Athens that, in principle, historical orthography should be the basis of modern spelling. A good many people favour dropping the smooth breathing and having a single accent (the acute). Ancient Greek would keep its traditional form. (If a phonetically based spelling of modern Greek were introduced, it would have the startling effect of necessitating Erasmian pronunciation of ancient Greek. This alone rules it out of court.)

What is needed is not a new system of spelling, but a standardized spelling, instead of the multiplicity of variant forms now in use, which have gained wide currency in print. Each word should have not a changed form, but a fixed form. Thus /i/ will continue to be written as ι, η, υ, ει, or οι, but μαζί must be only so written, and not as μαζῆ or μαζύ. In view of the large scale on which foreign words are borrowed or quoted, some inconsistencies are likely to remain. It rests with individuals to make a beginning by adopting the rules of consistent spelling set out in books such as Triandafillidhis' *Grammar*.[6]

The question of diacritics is simpler. Breathings and iota subscript can be abolished. The diæresis may be kept, marking as it does such distinctions as παιδάκι (*child*) and παϊδάκι (*cutlet*). A written stress-accent is not indispensable for the mother-tongue. English and Russian make do without it. In Greece, learning the rules of accents is one of the most burdensome and time-wasting tasks of the school pupil, and a reform would benefit the curriculum. But if we take account of the vast range of the Greek vocabulary, and the value of simple visual aids in teaching, there seems to be a good case for keeping one uniform accent-symbol to mark the stress of words.

The placement of word-stress is shown approximately by the figures given in Table 1, based on six passages of contemporary prose, each of 250 words, three in katharevusa and three in demotic. (Synizesis of /i/ with final vowel is not taken into account.)

TABLE 1

| | % |
|---|---|
| Antepenultimate stress | 16·2 |
| Penultimate stress | 30·0 |
| Final stress | 17·3 |
| Monosyllables | 36·5 |

It is agreed that monosyllables need not bear an accent. Exceptions to this have been proposed (i) to separate a few pairs of the type *πού* (interrogative) and *που* (relative); (ii) to distinguish between proclitics and enclitics, e.g., *το λάδι μάς φτάνει* (*the oil is enough for us*) and *το λάδι μας φτάνει* (*our oil is enough*). Others would distinguish these last by hyphenating the enclitic with its prop-word (as in Russian Greek).

Some have proposed an economy in writing non-monosyllables by leaving unaccented either the penultimate syllable (Kartheos) or the final syllable (Russian Greek). But Greek does not show a sufficient preponderance of any one stress-position to justify this; and the economy of mechanical recognition is not necessarily that of the human eye. A few texts have been printed according to a different scheme (supported by Filindas and others), in which an accent is written on every syllable which the reader feels to be stressed as he reads it. This subjective method, which amounts to a form of phonetic transcription, must be dismissed as contrary to sound principles of orthography.

It should be noted that, if any stress is to be left unmarked, we must calculate stress-placement by counting written syllables, and not allow synizesis to confuse the issue. Kartheos failed to observe this, and in his specimen quoted above, *palicaria* and *chortaria* ought to be written *palicária*, *chortária*. Otherwise there is no way of distinguishing this stress-pattern from one in which penultimate /i/ is stressed, e.g., *fliaria* (*φλυαρία*), or of separating pairs like *télia* (*τέλια*) and *telia* (*τελεία*).

Finally, the reduction of diacritics is an urgent typographical need. Triandafillidhis has calculated that, whereas the German case comprises 73 items, the Greek case has over 180, of which 120 are combinations of vowel letters with diacritics. With simplification, the number could be reduced to 58.[7]

*Notes*

[1] The quotations given in this section are from: *Μ. Τριανταφυλλίδης, Τὸ Πρόβλημα τῆς 'Ορθογραφίας μας*, Athens, 1932; and *Γ. Π. 'Αναγνωστόπουλος, 'Ορθογραφία* in *Μεγάλη 'Ελληνικὴ 'Εγκυκλοπαιδεία*, Athens, 1926–34.

[2] The Russian Greek texts are from the Dawkins collection, now in the Taylor Institution, Oxford.

[3] K. Kartheos, *L'adoption universelle des caractères latins*, Société des Nations, Geneva, 1934.

[4] *Φ. Φάλμπος, 'Ο Φραγκομαχαλᾶς τῆς Σμύρνης* (*Μικρασιάτικα Χρονικά, Τομ.* H, 1959).
I am indebted to Mr Philip Argenti for bringing the article by Falbos to my notice, and for other information about *francochiotica*.

[5] L. Missir, *Bollettino della Badia Greca di Grottaferrata*, XII, 1958.

[6] *M. Τριανταφυλλίδης, Νεοελληνικὴ Γραμματική*, Athens, 1938–1941.

[7] Some questions of orthography are briefly referred to in my article 'The Romanization of Greek', *Le Maître Phonétique*, LXXV, 113, 1960, 1–4.

# Consonant Clusters or Single Phonemes in Northern Irish

ALF SOMMERFELT

Northern Irish as it was spoken some 40 to 50 years ago when it was described by Quiggin, Seámus Ó'Searcaigh, and myself, is remarkable in that it has retained the old Celtic binary division between tense and lax consonants (in many cases long versus short).[1] It has further another binary opposition between plain and sharp consonants (neutral or velarized consonants versus palatal or palatalized). It also, according to the traditional point of view, opposes voiceless to voiced consonants. It has even a whole series of liquids, nasals, and vibrants which are voiceless and strongly aspirated. They were first described by Quiggin in his excellent book *A Dialect of Donegal* (1906). In this article I shall use the material I collected in Torr in Gweedore in 1915–1916 and 1921.

TABLE 1

| PLAIN (*Neutral or velarized*) | | | | SHARP (*Palatal or palatalized*) | | | |
|---|---|---|---|---|---|---|---|
| Tense | | Lax | | Tense | | Lax | |
| Voiced | Voiceless | Voiced | Voiceless | Voiced | Voiceless | Voiced | Voiceless |
| b | pʰ | w | f(w̥) | bˈ | pˈʰ | vˈ | fˈ |
| d | tʰ | | h | dˈ | tˈʰ | | |
| | | ɡ | | | | j | ç(hˈ) |
| g | kʰ | | x | gˈ | kˈʰ | | |
| | sʰ | | h | | sˈʰ | | hˈ(ç) |
| L | L̥ʰ | l | l̥ʰ | Lˈ | L̥ˈʰ | lˈ | l̥ˈʰ |
| m | m̥ʰ | w̃ | w̥̃ʰ | mˈ | m̥ˈʰ | ṽˈ | f̃ˈ |
| N | N̥ʰ | n | n̥ʰ | Nˈ | N̥ˈʰ | nˈ | n̥ˈʰ |
| | | r | r̥ʰ | | | rˈ | r̥ˈʰ |

*Note:* w̥, m̥, *etc., denote voiceless* [w], *voiceless* [m], *etc.*

The language makes extensive use of these oppositions in its morphonemic alternations, that of tense and lax in the verbs and the nouns, that of plain and sharp mainly in the noun, and that of voiced and voiceless both in the verb and the noun.

If all the voiceless articulations are regarded as phonemes and the morphonemic alternations are taken into account, we get the overall system shown in Table 1.[2]

The phonemes [ŋ] and [ŋˡ] have no lax opponents, but [ŋ̥ʰ] occurs. [ʀ] appears as a traditional allophone in a few words.

The vocalic system is simple but it has a series of allophones:

| | | |
|---|---|---|
| i, i: | ʎ: | u, u: |
| e, e: | ʌ: | o̤, o: |
| a, a: | | ɔ, ɔ: |

In unstressed syllables we have:

| | | |
|---|---|---|
| i | ə | u |
| a | | ɔ |

[o̤] is a low-in-mixed-narrow vowel from the phonetic point of view. An allophone [o] of short [ɔ] corresponds in articulation approximately to the articulation of [o:]; it occurs in some few words in labial surroundings. [i] and [ə] are distinct only in absolute word end and in proclitic positions, e.g. [tˡaxtirˡə] *messenger*, pl. [tˡaxtirˡi].

In the consonant system the lax phonemes are realized as spirants except in the case of nasals, liquids, and vibrants ([w] and [v] can in this connection be classed with the spirants).[3]

The morphonemic alternations are of several kinds: (1) tense vs. lax; (2) non-nasal vs. nasal; (3) plain (velarized or neutral) vs. sharp (palatal or palatalized); (4) voiced vs. unvoiced; (5) vocalic initial vs. initial beginning in [t, d] or in [h], and initial in [s] vs. initial in [t].

The morphonemic oppositions of the first group have the following aspect:

| | | | | | | | | | | | |
|---|---|---|---|---|---|---|---|---|---|---|---|
| b | : | w | bˡ | : | vˡ | p | : | f | pˡ | : | fˡ |
| d } g | : | g | dˡ } gˡ | : | j | t | : | h | tˡ } kˡ | : | ç(hˡ) |
| | | | | | | k | : | x | | | |
| | | | | | | s | : | h | sˡ | : | hˡ(ç) |
| L | : | l | Lˡ | : | lˡ | f | : | zero | fˡ | : | zero |
| m | : | w̃ | mˡ | : | ṽˡ | | | | | | |
| N | : | n | Nˡ | : | nˡ | | | | | | |

The vibrant and the guttural nasal are outside these alternations.

The second group of alternations consist of oppositions between voiced stops and nasals or between unvoiced and voiced ones and of vocalic initial vs. initial beginning with a dental nasal. All these consonants have the tense quality. The only exception is [f] which in this connection is opposed to [w̃] (and [fˡ] to [ṽˡ]). The [f, fˡ] is in a peculiar position as it acts as the lax opposition to [p, pˡ], but also appears in positions where the tense quality is the rule in the case of other consonants, and then its 'lax' counterpart is zero. We therefore have:

| | | | | | |
|---|---|---|---|---|---|
| b | : | m | bˡ | : | mˡ |
| d | : | ɴ | dˡ | : | ɴˡ |
| g | : | ŋ | gˡ | : | ŋˡ |
| p | : | b | pˡ | : | bˡ |
| t | : | d | tˡ | : | dˡ |
| k | : | g | kˡ | : | gˡ |
| f | : | w̃ | fˡ | : | ṽˡ |
| vowel | : | ɴ + vowel | | | |

The third group has plain (neutral or velarized) consonants as opposed to sharp (palatal or palatalized), e.g. [baːd] *boat*, gen. [baːdˡ], [brɔːg] *shoe*, dat. [brɔːgˡ], [fˡar] *man*, gen. [fˡirˡ], etc.

The alternations of the fourth group take place between voiced and voiceless phonemes, e.g. [ʟuːbəm] *I bend* : fut. [ʟuːpi mˡe]; [dɔːjəm] *I burn* : fut. [dɔːçi mˡe]; [pˡiʟˡəm] *I turn* : fut. [pˡiʟ̥ˡi]; [mˡeːtʰaŋi] *tongue* : gen. [tˡaŋ̊ə]; [kar̥ˡaxi], pl. of [kaharˡ] *city*, etc.

Examples of the last group are: [ə t-uan] *the lamb*; [ə tigərtˡ] *the priest's* from [sigərt]; [ɴa h-aːtˡə] *of the place*, from [aːtˡ]; [d-ɔːl mˡe] *I drank* from [ɔːləm] *I drink*.

The devices are often redundant, cf. such oppositions as [ə fˡar] *the man*, gen. [ə ɴˡirˡ], where the genitive is marked both by the vowel and the sharp quality of the final consonant.[4] But there exist also minimal pairs in which the consonant alternation is the only distinguishing element, e.g. [tˡimpaitˡ sˡe], *let him turn* : [himpaitˡ sˡe], *he used to turn*.

It would be possible to regard the voiceless liquids, nasals, and vibrants as clusters containing [h] as their second element. Their limited distribution would be in favour of this view as they occur only internally, with the exception of [l̥ˡ-] and [r̥] which stand in morphonemic alternation with [tˡlˡ-] and [tr-], respectively. In this case we would get a more regular future in [-hi] of many verbs, and similarly a more regular declension of some nouns. But it must be borne in mind that voiceless liquids, nasals, and vibrants may also be parts of the lexical segment of the word, e.g. [fˈar̥inˈ] *rain*, [ka:l̥ˈax] *husk*, [krin̥əm] *I miss.*

In an article published in *Celtica*, vol. V, I have pointed to the possibility of regarding all the voiceless articulations as clusters containing [h]. As has been pointed out already, the voiceless stops and also [s], somewhat less [f], are aspirated in all positions when the position after [s] is excepted. It is significant that the grammarians of Modern Irish have quarrelled about the nature of the stop in [sp, st, sk], some using this orthography, others writing [sb, sd, sg].

If all the voiceless consonants are regarded as clusters containing [h], the morphonemic alternations appear in a new light. The binary opposition voiced : voiceless would have no place in the system, the consonants being neutral from the point of view of voice. For the transcription I use the symbols which usually indicate a voiced type on the understanding that the question of voice is irrelevant.

In the first group of morphonemic alternations there would be no change in those which according to the usual interpretation are classified as voiced. But the other half of the alternations would take the following aspect:

| Plain | | Sharp | |
|---|---|---|---|
| Tense | Lax | Tense | Lax |
| bh | wh | bˈhˈ | vˈhˈ |
| dh | h | dˈhˈ } | |
| | | | jhˈ |
| gh | gh | gˈhˈ } | |
| zh | h | zˈhˈ | hˈ |
| ʟh | lh | ʟˈhˈ | lˈhˈ |
| mh | w̃h | mˈhˈ | vˈhˈ |
| ɴh | nh | ɴˈhˈ | nˈhˈ |
| | rh | | rˈhˈ |
| | wh : zero | | vˈhˈ : zero |

In the second group we should have:

| | | | | | | |
|---|---|---|---|---|---|---|
| bh | : | b | (instead of | p | : | b) |
| dh | : | d | (instead of | t | : | d) |
| gh | : | g | (instead of | k | : | g) |
| wh | : | w | (instead of | f | : | w) |

Similarly for the sharp series where in the fourth case there would be an alternation between [vˡhˡ] and [vˡ]. The remaining alternations would not be altered.

In the third group we would get such alternations as:

dh : dˡhˡ, e.g. [ghadh] *cat* : gen. [ghidˡhˡ] (for [kat : kitˡ])
gh : gˡhˡ, e.g. (zhagh] *sac* : gen. [zhigˡhˡ] (for [sak : sikˡ])
bh : bˡhˡ, e.g. [zhabh] *wisp* : gen. [zhibˡhˡ] (for [sap : sip]).

In the fourth group we would have:

b : bh, e.g. [ʟuːbəm] *I bend*, fut. [ʟuːbhi], etc.

Finally in the fifth group:

zh : dh, e.g. [zhigərdh] *priest*, gen. [ə dhigərdˡhˡ] *the priest's* for [sigərt, sigərtˡ].
vocalic initial : dh, e.g. [uan] *lamb* : [ə dh-uan] *the lamb*, for [ə t-uan].

It would not be necessary to posit complicated groups such as [ghdh], as there is no alternation between voiced and voiceless before [t].

Voiceless liquids, nasals, and vibrants must then be interpreted as consonants + [h]. Phonetically there is a difference between a voiceless liquid, nasal, or vibrant and one preceded by [x] or [ç]. The latter are not unvoiced, e.g. [krɔ : xrəɴ (ghrɔ : ghrəɴ)] *a vision of a funeral* or [çrˡian, hˡrˡian (jhˡrˡian)] from [tˡrˡian (dˡhˡrˡian)] *a third part.* Such forms as [kriṋuw] *to miss* where the [ṋ] belongs to the stem will therefore have to be interpreted as [ghrinhuw] although the literary form, which is etymological, is *cruthnuighim.*

By adopting the hypothesis that all phonetically voiceless consonants are clusters containing [h] one reduces the dichotomy of the consonant system to two binary oppositions, that between tense and lax and that between plain and sharp. If one, on the other hand, regards all the phonetically voiceless articulations as single phonemes, one gets a language which has carried the binary opposition voiced : voiceless to its extreme limits. Finally, if only the voiceless liquids, nasals, and vibrants are regarded as clusters one is able to simplify certain grammatical forms, but makes the phonemic system less systematic. However, as the morphological point of view ought to have preference the most rational point of view, it seems to me, will be to operate with an opposition between voiced and voiceless in the system of stops and spirants ([s] included) and to regard the phonetically voiceless liquids, nasals, and vibrants as clusters containing a final [h].

### *Notes*

[1] The opposition might perhaps be called one between fortes and lenes, but the articulation of the series here called tense is very different from that of ordinary lenes (cf. *The Dialect of Torr*, and E. C. Quiggin, *A Dialect of Donegal*), and corresponds more to what Jakobson and Halle in their *Fundamentals of Language* call tense.

[2] The voiceless consonants are aspirated in all positions except after [s, s']. In Table 1 I have marked the voiceless consonants by a small [h], but do not find it necessary to do so in the other tables nor in the examples. The unvoicing of a lax consonant at the end of a monosyllable having a short vowel occurs only before the pause and is therefore a prosodic phenomenon, cf. my *Dialect of Torr*, 133 ff.

[3] The labial spirants are bilabial (or were in the speech of the old generation). The plain labials are strongly velarized with a [w]-glide, the sharp labials have no [j]-element, but the lips are tightly drawn to the teeth. The lax plain labial spirant was originally a velarized bilabial [v] which occurs in other Irish dialects.

[4] The [ɴ'] in [ə ɴ'ir'] has its palatality from the consonant it replaces, cf. [ə ɴɔːd'] *of the sod*, gen. of [fɔːd]. In words with vocalic initial it follows, as a main rule, the character of the vowel in former times, e.g. [əɴ' aspik'], gen. of [aspək] *bishop*, O. Ir. [epscop], [əɴ ɪʟ'əɴ], gen. of [iʟ'ə] *elbow*, M. Ir. [ule].

# Tonetic Stress-marks for German

J.L.M.TRIM

The 'tonetic stress-marks' introduced by Kingdon in 1939[1] have provided teachers of English intonation with a powerful tool. The spirit of Kingdon's conventions has since established itself in practical teaching and has been employed in most of the principal textbooks and phonetic readers published in the last decade.[2] The advantages of such a system are readily apparent, being closely related to those of broad (simple phonemic) transcription as developed and established by Daniel Jones,[3] which they may be considered to complement. In both cases the attention of the student is concentrated upon making, at the relevant 'information points',[4] the appropriate choices from a limited set of possibilities. These possibilities alone are symbolized, using a set of marks designed for simplicity and mnemonic value, while the material import of the choices is relegated from the text to a body of accompanying conventions. In this way, the student can function much more effectively, whether as speaker, writer, listener, or reader, than if his attention is dispersed over a shifting continuum in which some features represent free choices, some automatic consequences of these choices, while the rest are irrelevant to choice.

Several years' experience teaching English and German pronunciation at University College, London, convinced me that tonetic stress-marks could be used with equal advantage for the notation of German intonation, since in that language, too, relevance attaches to choices made in connection with certain stressed syllables. It is not, of course, a question of transferring the system, complete with symbols and conventions *en bloc*, but rather of applying the same principles of representation to a body of behaviour which is rather differently organized.

From the point of view of intonation, German texts can be divided into tone-groups. As in English, major and minor tone-groups may be distinguished.[5] Major tone-groups are of about the same length as in English, that is normally co-extensive with the clause, but longer in rapid speech and shorter in a slow, deliberate style. They are followed by a pause, or pause-substitute. The boundaries of major tone-groups are marked with a double bar: /‖/.

Within each major tone-group, certain syllables are stressed, and the remainder unstressed. In the notation, unstressed syllables are left unmarked. Of the stressed syllables, some are intonationally prominent and the remainder intonationally non-prominent. The latter are marked with a prefixed raised dot /·/. Alternatively, the subscript 'secondary stress' mark /ˌ/ may be used, but perhaps this is best reserved for low prominences if these should be observed.

The selection of prominent stressed syllables is principally related to information value and hence inversely to predictability. This in itself entails a fairly close correlation with syntactic categories, since members of 'open' word-classes are generally less predictable than members of 'closed' ones. There appears, however, to be a degree of syntactic biassing beyond simple information value. Common nouns, for instance, are given greater weight than verbs and adjectives of seemingly comparable frequency. All prominent syllables in the major tone-group are made the nuclei of minor tone-groups, the boundaries between which are being marked with a single bar /|/.

The last intonationally prominent syllable in each major tone-group bears a tone which characterizes the major tone-group as a whole, though to a more restricted extent, it seems, than in English. The completive fall, the continuative low rise, the interrogative high rise, have been repeatedly described.[6] Their functions seem to be very much those of punctuation: to define a sentence-type, to mark major boundaries, to define the relation of the group to others in a larger discourse. The expression of attitude is rudimentary, this function being performed rather by word-order and particles.[7] Nevertheless, the difference between a neutral low fall and an exclamatory high fall is of this kind, as are the mid-low-high fall-rise for (one kind of) emphatic interrogative and the high level for impersonal public address. Undoubtedly there are more, awaiting discovery. It may be found that intonation plays a more prominent part in single-word utterances, in which word-order and use of particles are by definition inoperative.

Perhaps the greatest difference between English and German in this respect is the almost total absence from German of any counterpart of the English implicatory fall-rise. The nearest equivalent would seem to be a kind of divided rise-fall. The key component is shifted to initial positions with rising pitch and strong stress, with a low fall on the last stressed syllable. One may for instance compare: I'm ˇtired (but I can carry on) with ˊMüde | ˎbin ich‖, and ˋI'm ˏtired (I don't know about you) with ˊIch | bin ˎmüde‖.

The formal characteristics of the nuclei are as follows:

(a) falling /ˎ/ and /ˋ/. The pitch falls on the nucleus from a higher to a low pitch. All succeeding non-prominent stressed and unstressed syllables (tail) follow on the same low pitch. There seems to be also a variant in which the nucleus is level, and the tail descends gradually to a low pitch.

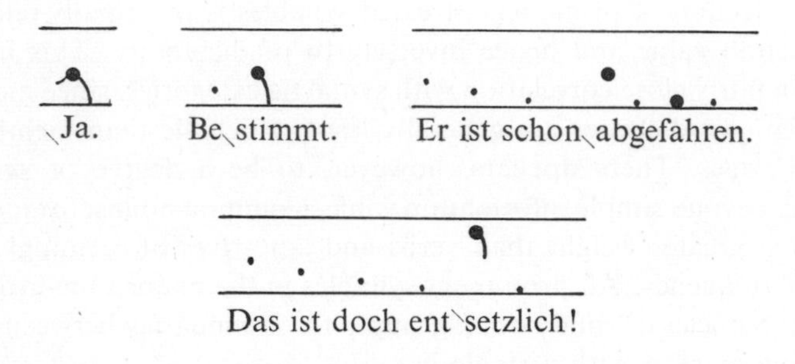


(b) low rise /ˏ/. The nucleus, if final, glides from a low pitch to a somewhat higher pitch, still below middle pitch. If a tail follows, this may contain minor tone-groups, within which all syllables up to the prominent syllable are placed on the same pitch as the last syllable in the tail of the preceding group; there is then a continuous rise from the prominent syllable throughout the tail.

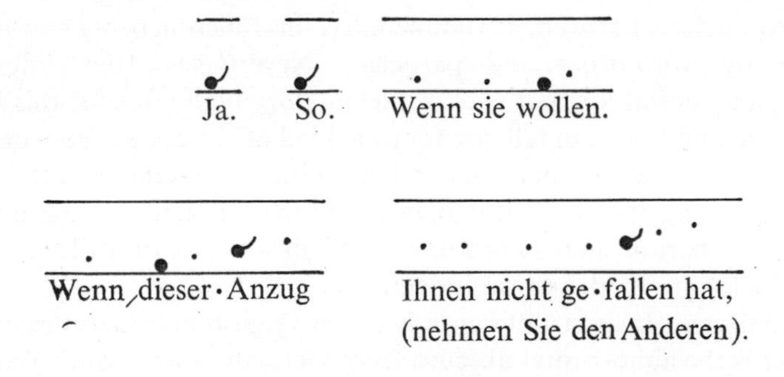


(c) high rise /ˊ/. The pattern is similar to that for the low rise, except that the nucleus starts anywhere between low and middle pitch, but rises well above middle pitch, with a slight upward glide on the final syllable.

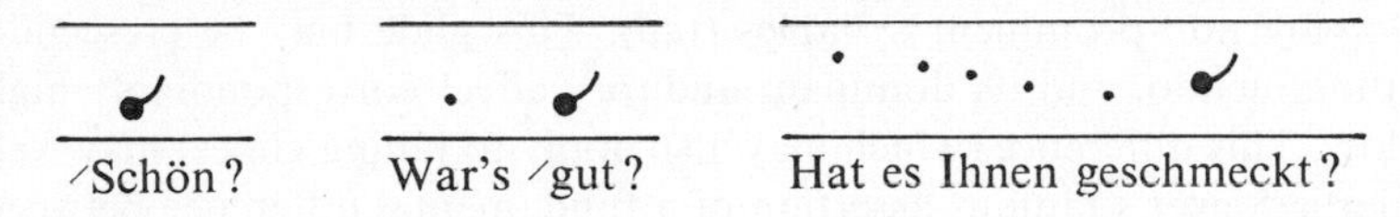


(d) fall-rise /˅/. If final, the nucleus starts on a middle pitch, falls to a low pitch and rises to, or above, the initial middle pitch. Where there is a tail, the nucleus is mid-level, and the tail contains a rise from a lower pitch.

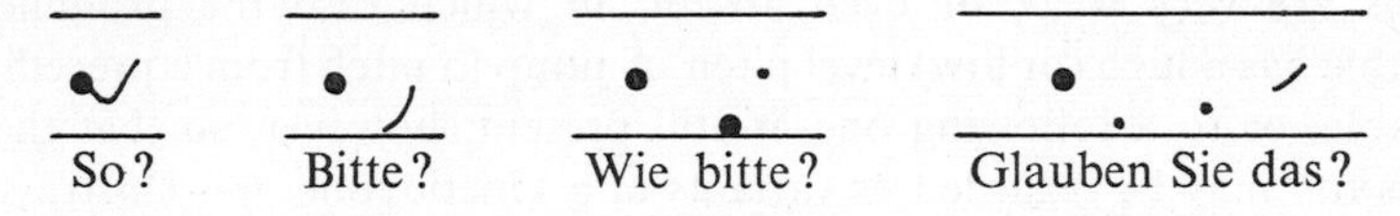


(e) rise-fall /˄/. If final, the nucleus starts on a middle pitch, rises somewhat and then falls to a low pitch. Where there is a tail, the nucleus glides from a middle pitch to a somewhat higher pitch and the tail follows on a low level pitch.

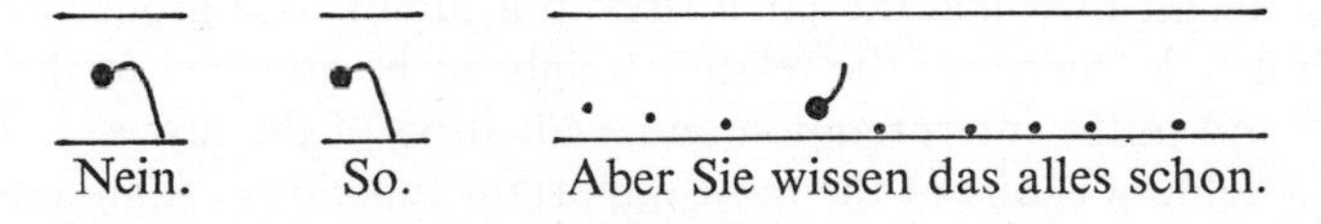


(f) high level /¯/. The nucleus is placed on a high level pitch and the tail, if any, follows on the same pitch.

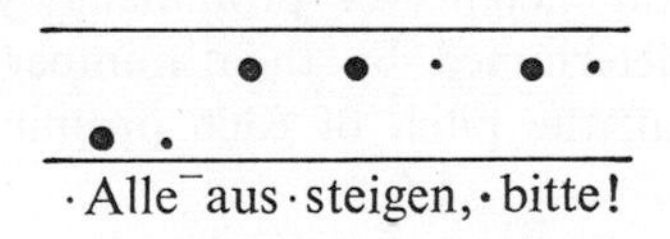


In all minor tone-groups, any initial non-prominent syllables are pronounced as a level or slightly descending sequence somewhat lower than middle pitch; except that in a final minor tone-group, non-prominent syllables preceding a low falling nucleus continue at the same height as the end of the preceding group.

The nuclei of all minor tone groups other than the last bear either a falling or a rising tone. The pattern for the falling tone is no different from that described in (a) above. In the case of the much more frequent rising tone, however, the prominent syllable generally contains a glide from a low to a higher pitch, irrespective of the presence or absence of following non-prominent syllables (tail). This glide may be crescendo or diminuendo, and its dominant auditory effect correspondingly high or low. This difference (which may also apply to falling glides) may well underlie Siever's famous assertion of a fundamental difference between North and South German intonation in their respective employment of high and low pitches for emphasis.[8] If so, they would both be referable to this system, requiring some different conventions for its interpretation.

In some cases (with some speakers always, with others in certain phonetic contexts, e.g. before voiceless consonants) the on- and off-glides are very weak or even absent, in which case the prominent syllable has a high (or low) level pitch. A jump in pitch from a preceding syllable, or to a following one, is still present, however, so that these cases too may be regarded as variants of a kinetic tone, /ˊ/. Unstressed syllables which follow a rising nucleus in a non-final minor tone-group are placed on a high level pitch, the exact height being determined by the 'weight' of the nucleus (see below). Non-prominent stressed syllables, however, are placed one step lower than the preceding syllables, and subsequent unstressed syllables follow on this pitch.

The height to which the pitch rises in a minor tone-group, or from which it falls, indicates the relative weight to be attached to the word (or group) in the interpretation and evaluation of the text as a whole. This weighting is one of the most important functions of intonation in German, and differentiates it sharply from English where this is true only in some cases of contrast. Normally, the pitch heights of head and nucleus in English are relevant to the interpretation of the tone-group as a whole, while the heights of prominent syllables in the body are bound, being determined by their number and the height of the head. In German, the pitch of each prominent syllable is freely variable.

The height of the prominent syllable of a minor tone-group in German, like the height of the head in English, appears to be a clear case of the representation of some kind of semantic continuum by a parallel phonetic continuum established in a particular phonetic dimension. Such systems are familiar in other spheres – most measuring devices work in this way – but many theorists have denied that a system of this kind can properly be treated as a 'linguistic'.[9] It is difficult to see why the phonetician, at any rate, should accept such a limitation upon his studies. Here, after all, are regular systematic, meaningful features of human speech, which his methods are adequate to handle. Nevertheless, there are obvious difficulties of notation. Where an analysis yields clear-cut, discrete categories, it is a relatively simple matter to devise appropriate symbols: if, however, analysis reveals the absence of clear-cut categories, representation is more difficult. For practical reasons, the continuum has to be treated as though it were categorizable – as with the scale of measuring instruments. Since the number is indeterminate, the number of categories established is a matter of convenience. The differences between units must be fine enough for the purpose in hand, but coarse enough to be well above the threshold of discrimination, readily learnt and remembered. It is possible to record simply the presence of rising or falling prominent syllables by the use of /ˊ/ or /ˋ/ in all cases. Or the 'kernel' of the sentence can be picked out from other prominent syllables by the use of /ˊ/ as opposed to /ˏ/ or of /ˋ/ as opposed to /ˎ/. If more differentiation is needed, a number system is convenient,[10] using the numbers to represent either quasi-absolute categories, or else relative height in a particular group. The numbers 1 to 4 are convenient (which is not, of course, to propose four 'pitch phonemes' or tonemes for German). In teaching, it is probably best to start with a coarse system and refine it as the student progresses.

The German minor tone-group has affinities with the English foot, but whereas feet consist of a stressed syllable together with any following unstressed syllables and are isochronous, German minor tone-groups correlate highly with syntactic groups, vary widely in length, both as to the amount of textual material included and the time taken. The boundary between one minor tone-group and the next coincides with the highest level syntactic boundary available – most generally a phrase boundary. It is this boundary, marked by a switch from a post-nuclear pattern to a pre-nuclear one, and occurring often in the middle of a series of unstressed syllables, that necessitates the analysis into minor tone-groups, whereas the English foot requires no delimitation beyond the marking of stress. In those kinds of German in which non-prominent syllables form a smooth unbroken descending sequence from one prominent syllable to the next, the concept of the minor tone-group is superfluous, unless demanded by the presence of some rhythmic or other junctural feature. The resulting tone-group (apparently regarded as normal by most writers) can be simply symbolized using the nuclear tones (a) to (f) above together with /ˈ/ for the head and any breaks within the general descending sequence, and /·/ for other stressed syllables since these are all non-prominent.

How widely applicable the system described above may be, I do not know. It appears to deal adequately with the material I have hitherto collected, consisting of passages in different styles read by educated speakers from North German cities. The notation is, in addition, an 'inclusive' one, and may be usable, with different conventions, in connection with a wider range of speakers. In any case, it has proved effective in teaching English students an acceptable pronunciation of German. In addition to readings from prepared texts, I have found it useful to follow this procedure for preparing a text (phonetic or orthographic) for reading:

(a) Divide the text into major tone-groups.
(b) Select the prominent syllables.
(c) Select the appropriate nuclear tone and mark it before the last prominent syllable.
(d) Mark the remaining prominent syllables according to degree of delicacy desired.
(e) Mark the divisions between minor tone-groups.
(f) Mark all non-prominent stressed syllables.

In taking the series of decisions required by this procedure, the student rapidly becomes aware of the significant differences between his native language and German.

The following passage may give some impression of the appearance of texts using this system. It is taken from Viëtor.[11] Very little alteration is needed to Viëtor's text, other than the replacement of his stress-mark by an appropriate tone-mark, and the marking of non-prominent stress. Concerning his own practice, Viëtor says of *Ton* (*Nachdruck*): 'In zusammenhängender Rede wird der Wortton jedesmal dann bezeichnet, wenn er zugleich Satzton ist, gleichviel, welche Silbe des Wortes er trifft; z.B. /das ˈkɛtsçən/ ˈliːf/ˀin ˈʃneː (Das Kätzchen lief in Schnee). Die Sprachtakte (Satzteile mit je einem Satzton) werden durch Taktstriche [|] getrennt. Bei stärkeren Einschnitten (wo Atempausen oder auch Sinnpausen moglich sind) stehen doppelte Taktstriche [‖].[12]

di: ˊklu:ge | ˎmaus ‖

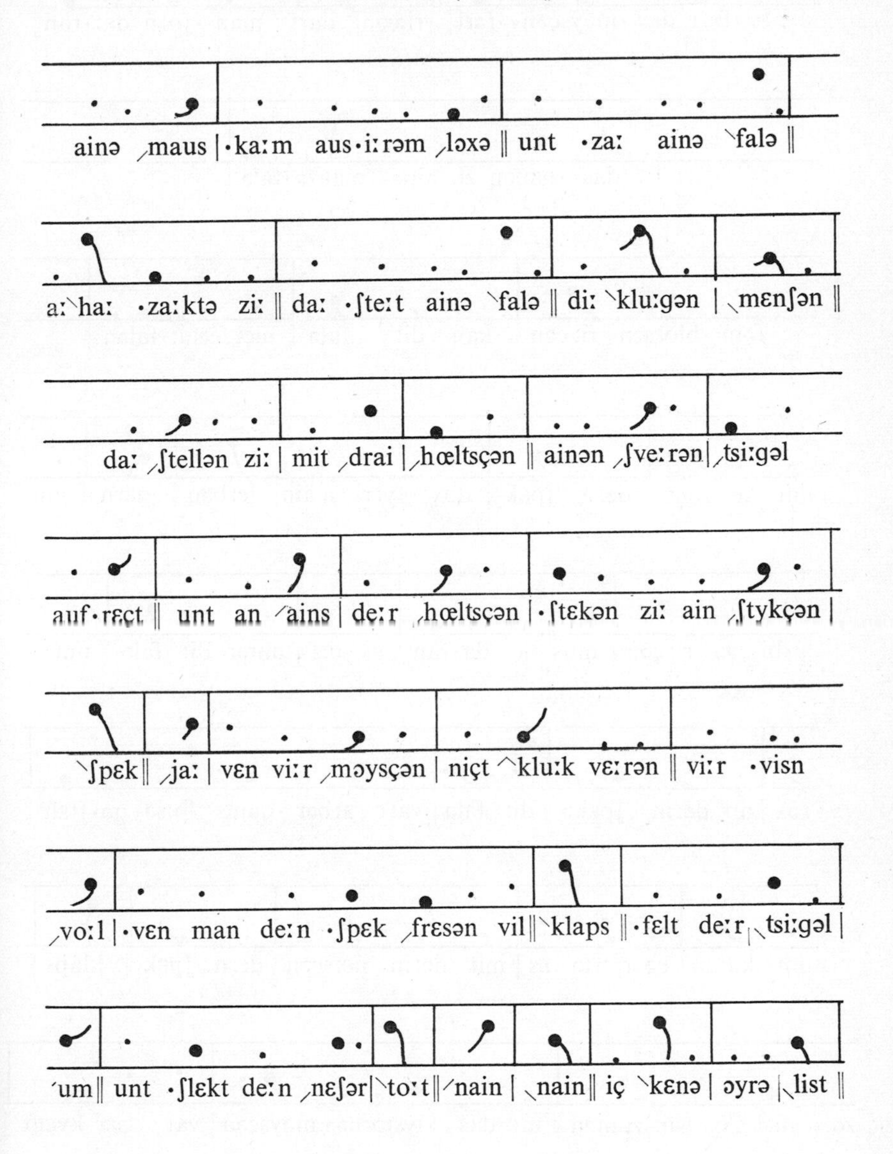

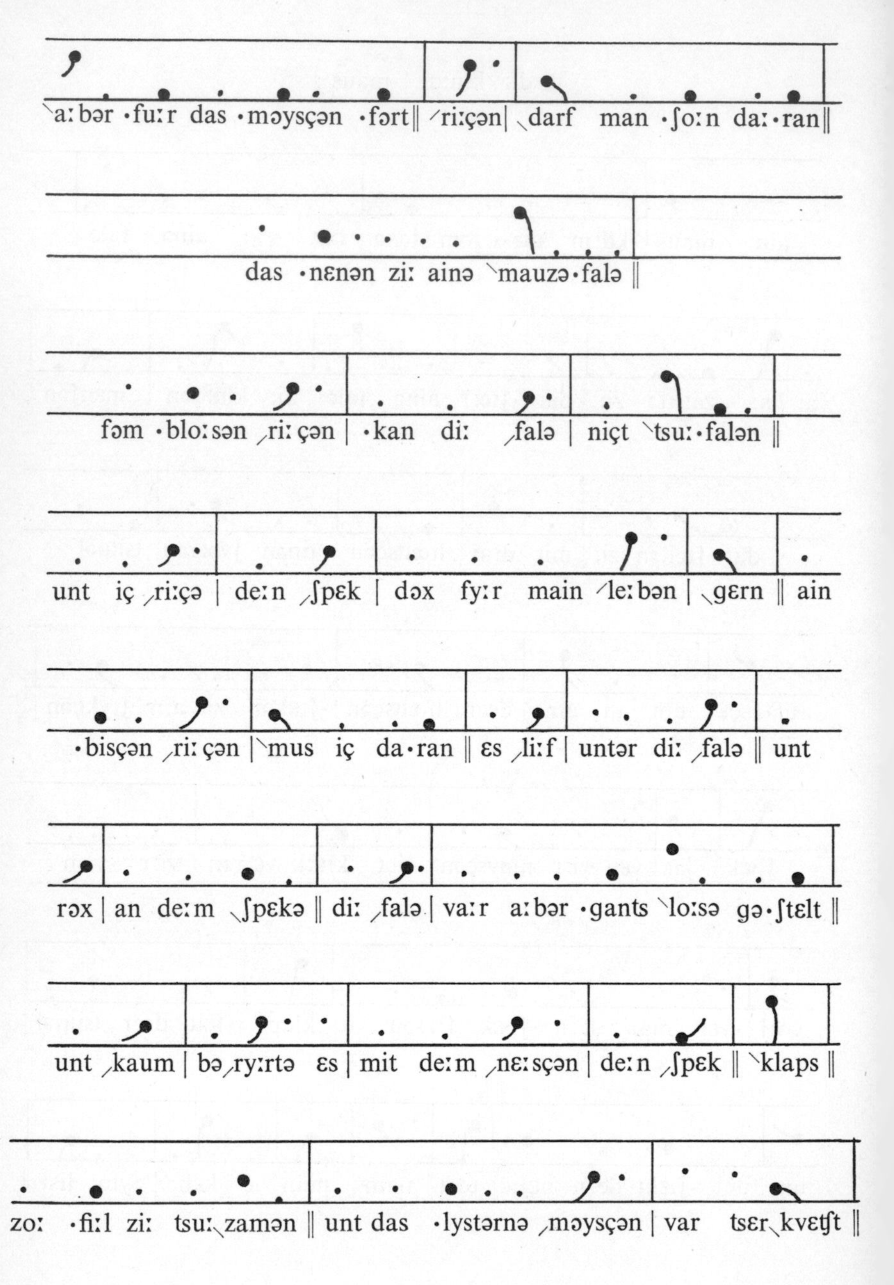
ˋaːbər ·fuːr das ·mɔysçən ·fɔrt‖ ˊriːçən| ˎdarf man ·ʃoːn daː·ran‖
das ·nɛnən ziː ainə ˋmauzə·falə ‖
fɔm ·bloːsən ˏriːçən | ·kan diː ˏfalə | niçt ˋtsuː·falən ‖
unt iç ˏriːçə | deːn ˏʃpɛk | dɔx fyːr main ˊleːbən | ˎgɛrn ‖ ain
·bisçən ˏriːçən | ˋmus iç da·ran ‖ ɛs ˏliːf | untər diː ˏfalə ‖ unt
rɔx | an deːm ˎʃpɛkə ‖ diː ˏfalə | vaːr aːbər ·gants ˋloːsə gə·ʃtɛlt ‖
unt ˏkaum | bəˏryːrtə ɛs | mit deːm ˏnɛːsçən | deːn ˏʃpɛk ‖ ˋklaps ‖
zoː ·fiːl ziː tsuːˎzamən ‖ unt das ·lystərnə ˏmɔysçən | var tsɛrˎkvɛtʃt ‖

## *Notes*

[1] R. Kingdon, 'Tonetic Stress-marks in English' *Le Maître Phonétique III*, 68, 1939, 60–64; also Kingdon, *The Teaching of English Intonation*, London, 1942, and *The Groundwork of English Intonation*, London, 1958. The practice of using conventional marks in texts is, of course, much older, different systems having been developed by Sweet, Palmer, and Coleman.

[2] Such as J. D. O'Connor and G. F. Arnold, *Intonation of Colloquial English*, London, 1961; M. Schubiger, *English Intonation, its Form and Function*, Tübingen, 1958; P. A. D. MacCarthy, *English Conversation Reader in Phonetic Transcription, with Intonation Marks*, London, 1958; W. R. Lee, *An English Intonation Reader*, London, 1960.

[3] D. Jones, *An Outline of English Phonetics*, 9th Edn., Cambridge, 1960, Appendix A.

[4] L. S. Hultzén, 'Information Points in Intonation', *Phonetica*, IV, 1959, 107 ff.

[5] J. L. M. Trim, 'Major and Minor Tone-groups in English', *Le Maître Phonétique*, 1959, 26.

[6] E.g. H. Klinghard, *Übungen im deutschen Tonfall*, Leipzig, 1927; M. Barker, *A Handbook of German Intonation for University Students*, Cambridge, 1925; J. Bithell, *German Pronunciation and Phonology*, London, 1952; W. Kuhlmann, *Tonhöhebewegung des Aussagesatzes*, Heidelberg, 1931; Von Essen, *Grundzüge der hochdeutschen Satzintonation*, Ratingen, 1956.

[7] See numerous remarks in Schubiger, *English Intonation*; also the same author's contribution to the present volume.

[8] E. Sievers, *Rhythmisch – melodische Studien*, Heidelberg, 1912; for later discussion and an experimental (qualified) confirmation, see P. Martens, *Vergleichende Untersuchung der Sprachmelodie in der Hamburger und Müncher Umgangssprache*, Diss, Hamburg, 1952. (Unpublished, but available in duplicated form.)

[9] Cf. H. Ebeling, *Linguistic Units*, 's Gravenhage, 1960, 12.

[10] Cf. H. O. Coleman, 'Intonation and Emphasis', *Miscellanea Phonetica*, I, London, 1914.

[11] W. Viëtor, *Deutsches Lesebuch in Lautschrift*, I, Leipzig, 1914, 100 f.

[12] Ibid., 147.

# A Critique of Russian Orthography

DENNIS WARD

Before examining the orthography of Russian it is necessary to state briefly what the phonemes of the language are and how the phonemes are interconnected in the morphophonematic system.

Russian has five vowel phonemes and each has a range of allophones. The occurrence of a particular vowel allophone x′ is therefore determined by the following factors: the structural unit at a certain point is the vowel phoneme X, and the occurrence of any one allophone of the entire range $x$–$x^n$ is limited by: (a) the phonetic context; and (b) the position of the syllable in relation to the nodal position.[1] Each of these two factors leads to a restricted range of allophones, and the two restricted ranges have only one member in common, namely x′. Of the five vowel phonemes /i, e, a, o, u/, one, /e/, occurs only in nodal position, being replaced elsewhere by /i/. The phoneme /o/ occurs in non-nodal position only in a few loan-words, being replaced after palatalized consonants, j, ʃ, ʒ, and ts by /i/, otherwise by /a/. /a/ itself occurs in non-nodal position; but if the preceding consonant is palatalized or is j, then, in pre-nodal position, /a/ is replaced by /i/.

The bulk of the consonant stock is made up of pairs of consonants distinguished one from the other by the presence or absence of palatalization:

/p, b, m, f, v, t, d, n, s, z, r, l, k/
/p̡, b̡, m̡, f̡, v̡, t̡, d̡, n̡, s̡, z̡, r̡, l̡, k̡/

The palatalized (fronted) velars [g̡] and [x̡] occur, but they are allophones of /g/ and /x/, respectively. There are two hard fricatives /ʃ/ and /ʒ/, a hard affricate /ts/ and a soft affricate /tʃ/. The palatal /j/ also serves as the end term of diphthongs. In one type of pronunciation there is a sequence [ʃ̡tʃ] with a weak stop element, [ʃ̡] here being an allophone of /ʃ/. In another type there is the sequence [ʃ̡ʃ̡], which is an independent phoneme and may be symbolized by a single symbol /ʃ̡/.[2] There are therefore 33 or 34 consonant phonemes.

Consonant substitutions are of three types: phonatory, articulatory, and a combination of the two. By phonatory substitutions is meant the substitution of corresponding voiceless phonemes for all voiced phonemes except sonants in word-final position and word-internally before voiceless consonants, and also the substitution of corresponding voiced phonemes for voiceless phonemes before all voiced consonants except the sonants, /v/ and /v̡/. Articulatory substitutions include the phenomenon of 'palatalization in juxtaposition', or the spread of the palatalization feature from one consonant to a preceding consonant, and also the substitution of /ʃ/ for /s/ before /ʃ/ and of /ʒ/ for /z/ before /ʒ/. Where /s/ + /ʧ/ would occur the sequence [ʆʧ] ( = /ʃ + ʧ/) or the sequence [ʆʆ] (= /ʆ/) arises, depending on the type of pronunciation. The combination of phonatory and articulatory substitutions leads to /ʒʒ/ from /s/ + /ʒ/, to /ʃʃ/ from /z/ + /ʃ/, and to /ʃʧ/ or /ʆ/ from /z/ + /ʧ/.

Hence, most of the consonant phonemes are interlocked in a system of substitutions which hinges in part on phonatory factors, in part on articulatory factors, is much more complex with regard to some phonemes than others, is at some points 'ill-defined',[3] and may be represented by the following table, in which horizontal lines signify articulatory substitutions and vertical lines phonatory substitutions:

```
ʃ         s — s̡     t — t̡     f — f̡     p — p̡     k — k̡
  (ʆ)←—   |   |     |   |     |   |     |   |     |
| ←———    |   |     |   |     |   |     |   |     |
ʒ         z — z̡     d — d̡     v — v̡     b — b̡     g

m — m̡     n — n̡
```

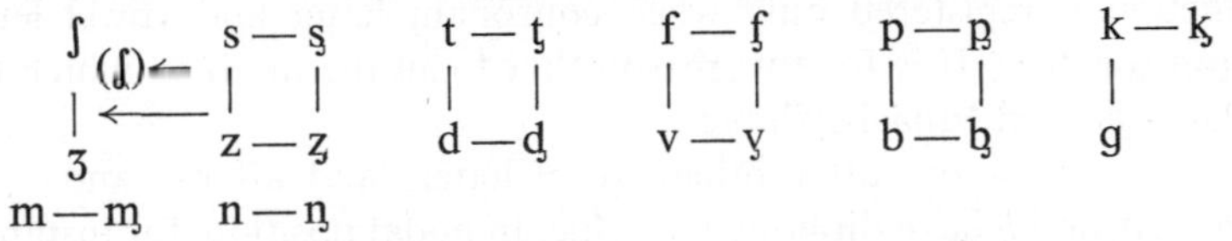

To register its 38 (39) phonemes, Russian has an alphabet of 32 letters[4]:

9 vowel letters:

| а | я | е | э | и | ы | о | у | ю |
|---|---|---|---|---|---|---|---|---|
| *a* | *ä* | *e* | *ê* | *i* | *y* | *o* | *u* | *ü* |
| a | ja | jɛ | ɛ | i | ɨ | o | u | ju |

21 consonant letters:

| п | б | м | ф | в | т | д | н | с | з | р |
|---|---|---|---|---|---|---|---|---|---|---|
| *p* | *b* | *m* | *f* | *v* | *t* | *d* | *n* | *s* | *z* | *r* |
| pə | bə | m | f | v | tə | də | n | s | z | r |

| л | ш | ж | к | г | х | ц | ч | щ | й |
|---|---|---|---|---|---|---|---|---|---|
| *l* | *š* | *ž* | *k* | *g* | *x* | *c* | *č* | *ŝ* | *î* |
| l | ʃ | ʒ | kə | gə | x | ts | ʧ | ʃʧ/ʆʆ | jə[5] |

In addition there are two auxiliary letters, ъ and ь, which do not on their own represent any sound, are known respectively as the 'hard sign' and the 'soft sign' and are transliterated here as ″ and ′.[6]

Russian spelling is, in about 70% of cases,[7] phonetically 'lucid', that is to say that it is at once evident from the written forms, without the application of any substitution rules, what their phonemic make-up is. There is, as it were, no intervening stage between grapheme and phoneme. This is achieved, in the face of an apparent deficiency of letters in one category (21 consonant letters for 33/34 consonant phonemes), by making use of the apparent superfluity of letters in another category (9 vowel letters for only 5 vowel phonemes). The letters of the alphabet are used in what I shall call a 'quasi-syllabic mode'.[8] In this quasi-syllabic mode the nine vowel letters are divided into two sets: (i) *y*, *ê*, *a*, *o*, *u*; and (ii) *i*, *e*, *ä*, *ü*. When one of the consonant letters *p*, *b*, *m*, *f*, *v*, *t*, *d*, *n*, *s*, *z*, *r*, *l*, or *k* is followed by *y*, *ê*, *a*, *o*, or *u* the consonant letter represents a hard consonant, whereas when followed by *i*, *e*, *ä*, or *ü* it represents a soft consonant. This means that the hard-soft distinction of the paired hard-soft consonants is marked not by the consonant letter but by the vowel letter. However, since the hard-soft distinction is not, phonetically, a feature of the vowel, the distinction is registered only when consonant letter and vowel letter are put together. It is for this reason that I call the mode in which the alphabet is used 'quasi-syllabic'.

In initial position, after other vowel letters and after ″ and ′ the letters *e*, *ä*, and *ü* have diphonemic value. In nodal position, for instance, *e* = je, *ä* = ja, and *ü* = ju. The letter *i* has diphonemic value after the soft sign and may also have such value after other vowel letters, though the j element here is weak and frequently absent; it does not have diphonemic value in initial position.[9] The 'softening vowel letter' corresponding to *o* in normal usage is *e*, which thus has a double function. In its second function *e* may be written with a diæresis (*ë*), but this is used in normal printed and written matter only in the rare instances when it is necessary to avoid ambiguity (e.g. *vse* 'everybody', *vsë* 'everything') and *ë* is not regarded as a letter of the alphabet independent of *e*. Hence *tem* = /ţem/, whereas *tetka* = /ţotka/. Although *e*, *ä*, and *ü* have the phonetic value j + V in certain positions (see above), the first is not used in foreign words having the sequence jo, nor in derivatives of these words. Instead, the letters *îo* are used, *î* otherwise being used to indicate the end-term of diphthongs. Thus, one writes *äxta* [ˈjaxtə] yacht, *ünga* [ˈjungə] cabin-boy but *raîon* [raˈjon] region, *maîor* [maˈjor] major, *îod* [jot] iodine, *îotaciä* [joˈtatsɨjə] jotation.[10]

As we have seen, two of the velar phonemes, /x/ and /g/, have soft allophones. These are registered in writing in the same way as soft phonemes, as for example in *doxi* [ˈdox̡i], *nogi* [ˈnog̡i]. Here, therefore, allophonic differences are registered by the orthography. The allophonic divergence of /i/, into [i, ɩ] and [ɨ, ɨ] is also registered orthographically, as it happens, since this front ~ non-front divergence of /i/ is correlated with the absence or presence of preceding hard consonant and therefore the letter *y* signifies preceding hard consonant *and* non-front quality ([ɨ] or [ɨ]). The orthographic rendering of /ʃi/, /ʒi/, and /tsi/, however, is discrepant here. Since the consonants in these sequences are all hard, one might expect the letters *š*, *ž*, and *c* to be followed by *y*, *ê*, *a*, *o*, and *u*, just as one might expect *č*, denoting soft [ʧ], and *ŝ* denoting soft [ʃʧ/ʆʆ], to be followed *either* by the 'softening vowel letters' *i*, *e*, *ä*, and *ü*, *or* by *y*, *ê*, *a*, *o*, and *u* (since softness is, as it were, immanent in the letters *č* and *ŝ*). What one actually finds, however, are the following letter sequences: *š*, *ž*, *c*, *č*, *ŝ* + *i*, *e*, *a*, *o*, *u* and also *cy* (having the same value as *ci*).[11] Both *e* and *o* are written after *š*, *ž*, and *č* to indicate /o/, the present rules for their usage[12] being unnecessarily complicated.

The soft sign is used with a preceding consonant letter in a digraphic mode to indicate the softness of a consonant when the latter is final, or has softness independently of the following consonant (as in *gor'kiî* [ˈgoɽk̡i], *svad'ba* [ˈsvaɖbə]), or is followed by jV. In this last context the soft sign is followed by *i*, *e*, *ä*, or *ü*, and in such a sequence as, for example, *t'ä* all three letters are closely bound in an indissoluble complex: the value of none of them is known without the others.[13] This convention for representing C'jV is broken once again where /o/ in loan-words is concerned. Thus, one has on the one hand *bel'em* [b̡ɩl̡ˈjom] 'linen' inst. sg., but on the other hand *počtal'on* [pəʧtʌl̡ˈjon] 'postman'.

In this prevocalic position the soft sign is said by Russians to have the function of 'separating sign',[14] though it still has its basic function of indicating palatalization. When the preceding consonant letter is *š*, *ž*, or *č*, however, the soft sign functions purely as 'separating sign', since *š* and *ž* represent hard consonants[15] and *č* represents a soft consonant whatever follows. Thus *š'et* represents [ʃjot], *muž'ä* – [muʒˈja], *č'ä* – [ʧja]. The soft sign also occurs finally after *š*, *ž*, *č*, and *ŝ* with no phonetic function at all. Its function here is that of a graphic marker having various grammatical meanings.

The occurrence of the hard sign is much more restricted than that of the soft sign: it occurs only between final *s, z, t, d, v, b* of prefixes and initial *e, ä, ü* of roots[16]. Its function is that of a separating sign, the sequence *C″V* meaning, phonetically, hard consonant + [j] + vowel except in the case of *s* and *z*, which may in this context represent, optionally, [s] or [ş] and [z] or [ʐ], respectively. Thus *ot″exat′* [ʌtˈjɛxəţ] 'to ride away', *v″exat′* [ˈvjɛxəţ] 'to ride in', *s″exat′* [ˈşjɛxəţ] or [ˈsjɛxəţ] 'to ride down from'.

What has been described so far belongs to the field of what Russian writers call *grafika* [ˈgraţıkə], by which they mean the fundamental mode in which the letters of the alphabet are used. *Grafika* is distinguished from orthography proper in that it deals with the methods whereby a language represents its sounds with the alphabet or system of writing at its disposal, whereas orthography deals with the representation of words as bearers of particular meanings.[17] Russian writers say that while the *grafika* of Russian is 'syllabic' (my 'quasi-syllabic'), the orthography is 'morphological', since it represents morphemes in their 'fundamental' form rather than allomorphs. I prefer the term morphophonematic and would say that there is a morphophonematic principle superimposed on the quasi-syllabic mode. Even this formulation, however, does not seem to cover some of the uses of the soft sign which have been examined in immediately preceding paragraphs, and one must therefore conclude that some written forms in Russian are, as was indicated above, purely graphic devices designating grammatical categories with no phonetic, phonemic, or morphophonematic reflex.[18]

The morphophonematic principle in Russian operates so that the orthography, by and large, does not record vowel or consonant substitutions arising from changes in the phonetic context. It does not, therefore, record vowel substitutions arising from shifting of the nodal position nor the 'devoicing' of final consonants, nor, in general, consonant changes of the 'assimilation' type. It records all the elements of a morpheme in 'strong' position, i.e. as if they had not been subjected to any automatic phonetic substitutions. Moreover, because of the quasi-syllabic mode, it frequently preserves the graphic identity of a phonetically varied morpheme. To illustrate this briefly I shall set down a series of words with a common root-morpheme and various affixes, giving first a phonetic transcription, then a phonemic transcription, then the orthography, and finally the meaning. Thus:

(1) [ˈnoskə] /ˈnoska/ *noska* ‘carrying’
(2) [ˈnoᶊɪƫ] /ˈnoᶊit/ *nosit* ‘carries’
(3) [nʌˈᶊiƫ] /naˈᶊiƫ/ *nosit′* ‘to carry’
(4) [ˈvɨnəs] /ˈvinas/ *vynos* ‘carrying out’
(5) [ˈvɨnəᶊɪƫ] /ˈvinaᶊiƫ/ *vynosit′* ‘to give birth to’
(6) [ˈnoʃə] /ˈnoʃa/ *noša* ‘burden’
(7) [nʌˈʃu] /naˈʃu/ *nošu* ‘I carry’
(8) [ɪzˈnaʃᵻvəƫ] /izˈnaʃivaƫ/ *iznašivat′* ‘to wear out’

Here we have eight phonetic versions of a root, resolving into six phonemic versions, which the orthography records as three versions. The substitution of /a/ for /o/ because of a shift in nodal position is not registered – *o* remains – and the regular change of hard to soft consonant before the verbal stem i is registered in the vowel letter by virtue of the quasi-syllabic mode, so the first four phonemic versions resolve into one orthographic version *nos*. The vowel alternation /a/ ~ /o/ again is not registered in the next two versions of the root, but the non-automatic substitution of [ʃ] for [s] *is* registered, so the two phonemic versions /noʃ/ and /naʃ/ resolve into one orthographic version *noš*. Finally, the /a/ in /izˈnaʃivaƫ/, being in nodal position and therefore ‘independent’, is registered in the orthography and the third orthographic version *naš* arises.

A prosodic analysis of these same words should, as I understand it, arrive at a single root-morpheme, modified by the effect of a number of prosodies which would be construed as ‘part’ of the suffixes.[19] Thus /naˈᶊiƫ/ would be interpreted as {nos$^{y}$ít$^{y}$}, where the first ‘y-prosody’ is ‘part’ of the verbal stem i realized as palatalization (‘softening’) of the preceding consonant. The forms /ˈnoʃa/ and /naˈʃu/ would be interpreted respectively as {nós$^{y2}$a} and {nos$^{y2}$ú}, where the ‘y$^{2}$-prosody’ is in each case part of the suffix and is realized as palatalization of the tongue-tip /s/ into the blade /ʃ/. Even the /naʃ/ of /izˈnaʃivaƫ/ can, by this means, be resolved into {nos} plus prosodies, thus: {iznos$^{y2x}$ivat$^{y}$}, where by the x prosody is meant that feature of the morpheme iv which locates the nodal position at the preceding syllable and requires that /o/ shall be replaced by /a/.[20] It would be possible to base an orthography for Russian on the results of such analyses as those illustrated in the preceding lines. One would then write, in the case of the words quoted above, *nos* throughout, leaving some of the prosodies to be indicated by means of the quasi-syllabic mode (as is at present the case with *nosit*, for example) and others to be indicated by special devices *or not at all.* It is for instance quite feasible to write *iznosivat'* for what is phonemically /izˈnaʃivaţ/ if one knows – as one would know – that the morpheme iv carries the prosodies named above. Gvozdev follows a similar line of thought when he says[21] that it would seem completely unnatural to write *drugba, mostën* for the present orthography *družba, mošën*, 'but really the ingrained habit of one's own orthography creates the illusion that such graphemes would be completely impossible, whereas it is not so difficult to imagine such graphemes'. He goes on to point out that such a system would lead to far more instances of discrepancy between written and spoken forms and would create many graphic homonyms. And, one might add, the ultimate result would be an orthography not unlike that of English in respect of the wide gap between sound and symbol and one which would, at very many points, appear to be registering the reconstructed language, Common Slavonic.

Such a system of orthography could perhaps be called 'morphological' (which is how Russian writers do in fact describe the orthography of Russian), since it would strip the graphic representation of morphemes not only of phonetically automatic modifications, but also of morphematically conditioned modifications. Since Russian orthography does not in fact do that, the term 'morphophonematic' has been preferred here. The application of the morphophonematic principle to Russian orthography has this in its favour – that it results in an orthography which disregards phonetically automatic, hence predictable, and, as it were, superficial or trivial modifications but records those modifications of the morpheme which, were they not recorded, would necessitate a rather complicated set of orthographic rules.[22] That such an orthography as the one current for Russian is not the only possible, efficient one for a language with such a phonology as Russian is, of course, self-evident and is illustrated by the case of White Russian, which, with a similar phonology to that of Russian registers automatic vowel-substitutions in its orthography.

There are some departures from the morphophonematic principle in Russian, including such sporadic ones as, for example, *nozdri* 'nostrils' (cp. *nos* 'nose'). The many instances of etymological graphemes which cannot now be justified by means of a morphophonematic analysis amount to about 8% of all graphemes, according to Gvozdev.[23] This count presumably includes the presence of *g* where [v] is pronounced in the genitive singular, masculine and neuter, of adjectives and most pronouns, as in *krasnogo*, *sinevo*, which are phonetically [ˈkrasnəvə, ˈʂiɲɩvə], phonemically /ˈkrasnava/, /ˈʂiɲiva/, and morphophonematically {krásnovo}, {ʂíɲovo}. Another departure from the morphophonematic principle was introduced in 1917 and came into general practice the following year.[24] This was the variable spelling of some prefixes ending in tongue-tip sibilants. Thus, one writes *ras*, *vos/vs*, *is*, and *(o)bes* before *p*, *f*, *t*, *s*, *c*, *č*, *š*, *ŝ*, and *x* but *raz*, *voz/vz*, *iz* *(o)bez* before other consonants, vowels, and the hard sign. This was an unnecessary violation of the morphophonematic principle, whereby 'the latest orthography has gone back to thirteenth-century principles'.[25] A rationalization of the orthography on the basis of strict adherence to the morphophonematic principle would remove this and other anomalies and give a phonemic spelling to the 8% or so of non-verifiable ('*neproäsnimye*') graphemes. The discussion of the reform of the orthography which was carried on in the columns of *Russkiî äzyk v ŝkole* and *Učitel'skaä gazeta* in 1954 led not to a reform of the orthography but to regularization and improvement.[26] That the orthography is still in need of considerable 'regularization and improvement,' to say nothing of reform, is revealed by a quick perusal of the '*Pravila*'.

The quasi-syllabic mode for Russian is peculiarly apt, because it is not only to a considerable extent unambiguous but also economical. It avoids the necessity of either a double set of consonant letters for the hard-soft pairs or a separate palatalization mark, which would be liberally scattered about the printed page. From what has been said above, however, it is clear that there are certain flaws and deficiencies in the Russian quasi-syllabic mode too.

A completely rationalized quasi-syllabic mode would need an extra vowel letter – let us say, arbitrarily, *ö* – to act as 'softening vowel letter' corresponding to *o* and to relieve *e* of its dual rôle. One would then use the vowel letters *y*, *ê*, *a*, *o*, *u* after hard consonants (including those symbolized by *š*, *ž*, and *c*) and the letters *i*, *e*, *ä*, *ö*, and *ü* after soft consonants (including that symbolized by *č*). Applying the morphophonematic principle one would then write the vowel letter symbolizing, where possible, the phoneme occurring in nodal position. Thus, the morpheme at present written *žen* as in nom. sg. *žena* [ʒɨˈna] would be *žon*, in view of nom. pl. [ˈʒonɨ] and gen. pl. [ʒon]. To write nom. sg. *žona* with the phonetic value of [ʒɨˈna] is, in terms of the morphophonematic principle, just as reasonable as, for example, the present orthography's *časa* with the phonetic value [ʧɩˈsa]. Similarly, the present *okonce*, for example, with phonetic value ʌˈkontsɨ would become *okonco* since the nom. sg. neut. morpheme is {o} (cp. kʌl̦ˈtso), which in this rationalized system would be written *o* after hard consonants, *ö* otherwise (as in *kop'ö* [kʌp̦ˈjo]).

Though, in a rationalized system, an additional vowel letter becomes necessary, it turns out that three letters at present in the alphabet are superfluous. The affricates [ts] and [tʃ] stand in the same relationship one to the other as do [t] – [ț], [d] – [d̦], [s] – [ș], etc., in that [ts] is hard, [tʃ] is soft; there is no soft [ts], there is no hard [tʃ]; both occur before all the vowel phonemes and after [ts] only the non-front allophones of /i/ occur whereas after [tʃ] only the front allophones occur. In other words [ts] and [tʃ] are another hard-soft pair and could, in terms of the quasi-syllabic mode, be symbolized by one consonant letter (let us say, arbitrarily, *c*) followed by the appropriate vowel letter and, in some instances, the soft sign. Thus, the present orthography's *caplä* [ˈtsapl̦ə] remains *caplä*, but *čas* [tʃas] becomes *cäs*; the present *cista* [ˈtsɨstə] becomes *cysta* and *čisto* [ˈtʃistə] becomes *cisto*; *bac* [bats] remains *bac* but *grač* [gratʃ] becomes *grac'* and *bočka* [ˈbotʃkə] becomes *boc'ka*; the present *cvet* [tsv̦ɛt] remains *cvet* but *čvannyî* [ˈtʃvannɨ] becomes *c'vannyî*. All these contrasting graphemes have their parallels in the graphemes denoting [t] – [ț], etc.

It also becomes apparent that the letter *ŝ*, denoting a sequence of consonants or, in certain very restricted circumstances, a single [ʃ̦], is superfluous. It is the only consonant letter which, of itself, signifies a sequence of consonants and, for this reason alone, is 'alien' to the rest of the alphabet. Moreover, the letter sequences *sč*, *šč*, *zč*, and *žč* in the present orthography also have the same phonetic value as *ŝ*, so that one of these letter sequences, followed by *i*, *e*, *ä*, *ö*, *ü*, or ', would adequately perform the function at present fulfilled by *ŝ*.[27] Another 'rational' solution would be to treat [ʃ] and [ʃ̦ʃ̦] as another hard-soft pair, discard *ŝ*, and write *š* followed by *i*, *e*, *ä*, *ö*, *ü*, or '.

Finally, it becomes apparent that either " or ' is superfluous, the former recurring only with 'separating function' between prefix and root, where the latter does not occur. It could therefore be replaced here by ', it being understood that preceding *s* or *z* may represent soft consonants but that other consonant letters represent hard consonants.

Russian orthography at present, being a historically evolved orthography has numerous flaws. It is in part 'phonetic', i.e. phonetically lucid, in part purely etymological, and in large part morphophonematic. It operates in a quasi-syllabic mode with thirty-two letters. A completely rationalized orthography, in a quasi-syllabic mode, following the morphophonematic principle, could be carried out with 30 letters.[28]

*y, i, e, ê, a, ä, o, ö, u, ü, p, b, m, f, v, t, d, n, s, z, r, l, c, š, ž, k, g, x, î,* and *′*.

## *Notes*

[1] Nodal position means that position (syllable) in a word from which the restricted range (b) of vowel allophones in all the syllables of the word is determined. Certain allophones and only these occur in nodal position, certain others in non-nodal position and this latter range may itself subdivide. 'Word' here means 'phonetic word' – a set of syllables grouped around and including a 'node' and which may consist of more than one lexical item. In most, but not all, cases nodal position coincides with the position of 'lexical stress', though in the sentence there may be no stress at a nodal position. By using this concept of nodal position we avoid the difficulty of talking about an ostensibly phonetic reality – lexical stress – which may in fact not be present in speech. Stress, whatever it is, thus remains in the field of purely phonetic concepts, whereas nodal position is simply the name of a position where certain things may or may not occur. Words with so-called 'secondary stress' have in fact two 'nodes', and hence two sets of syllables grouped around them. The term 'accent' has been avoided because it already has several meanings.

[2] See my 'Russian [ʆ] and [ʒ]', *Le Maître Phonétique*, 1958, 26–28, from which it should be clear that one cannot phonemicize [ʆʆ] as /ʃ/ + /ʧ/ because, apart from all other considerations, there also occurs, in limited contexts, the single [ʆ].

[3] Notably in the matter of 'regressive palatalization', the details of which could not be given in this article.

[4] For the convenience of readers not familiar with Cyrillic a single-letter transliteration system is given (in the second line of the table) and this will be used for orthographic items instead of Cyrillic. The third line shows in IPA symbols the phonetic value which each letter has when spoken in isolation, the plosives and j being registered with a following shwa vowel for present purposes. With the sole exception of ɨ the vowel letter-sounds are in fact the names of the vowels (ы/*y* is called еры jɩ'rɨ). The order of the letters here is *not* that of the Russian alphabet.

[5] The *name* of this letter is *i kratkoe* [i 'kratkəjɩ], 'short i'.

[6] Two of the three Latin letters not used in the consonant transliterations (h, q, w) could be used instead of apostrophes, but I have avoided them and retained the 'traditional' ″ and ′ so as to emphasize that they represent no sound on their own.

[7] A calculation made by A.N.Gvozdev in *Osnovy russkoi orfografii*, Moscow, 1951.

[8] This mode must have been present at the very beginning of Russian literacy, about a thousand years ago. Indeed at that time, discounting certain superfluous letters and foreign spellings, it must have been very nearly perfect. Phonetic changes during the following centuries have given rise to certain 'flaws' in the system, which will become apparent below.

[9] An alternative pronunciation of the plural cases of the 3rd pers. pron. has initial ji where the orthography has *i* – *ix*, *im*, *imi* = [ix, im, 'imʝɩ] or [jix, jim, 'jimʝɩ].

[10] Note also *îemenskiî* [jɩmʝɛnskʝɩ] *Yemeni*. The sequence *îa* occurs in the name of the Maya people and language, *maîä* (indeclinable), and also in the name of a fabric

*maîä* (presumably pronounced ['majjə] or ['majə]), which, according to the orthographical dictionary *orfograficeskiî slovar' russkogo äzyka* (Moscow, 1957), is declinable, so that one would expect to find, for example, genitive *maîi*. I have not met this word other than in dictionaries.

11 *cy* is written in suffixes, grammatical endings, and a few roots, while *ci* is written in most roots and in the endings of words of the type *revolüciä* [ṛɩvʌ'ḷutsɨjə] and *revolücionnyî* [rɩvəḷutsɨ'onnɨ]. *šü and žü* occur in a very few loan-words, where they have the same phonetic value as *šu* and *žu* but are written simply to show the foreign origin of the words: *brošüra* (brʌ'ʃurə], *parašüt* [pərʌ'ʃut], *žüri* [ʒu'ṛi].

12 As laid down on pp. 7–9 of the current *Pravila russkoî orfografii i punktuacii*, 'Rules of Russian Orthography and Pronunciation'.

13 And the value of *ä* is further dependent on its relation to the nodal position.

14 *razdelitel'nyî znak* [rəẓḍɩ'ḷiṭɩḷnɨ znak].

15 Except when followed by *č*.

16 And in some loan-words, such as *ad"ütant* [ʌdju'tant] 'adjutant' *ob"ekt* [ʌ'bjɛkt] 'object'.

17 See Gvozdev, *Osnovy russkoi orfografii*, p. 48, and V.A.Trofimov, *Sovremennyî russkiî literaturnyî äzyk*, Leningrad, 1957, 114.

18 Though, it must be admitted, if one postulates morphemes consisting simply of a phonetic feature – in this case 'palatalization' – then one may say that such forms as *rež'* are also morphophonematic since the morpheme which is normally realized phonetically as 'palatalization feature' is here phonetically zero. It seems better to avoid this: the concept of zero elements is useful in linguistics but leads to absurdities if overworked.

19 K.H.Albrow, of the Department of Phonetics, University of Edinburgh, has read a paper to the Phonetics Seminar at Edinburgh in which he gave a prosodic analysis of the Russian conjugation and which, as I write this, he is preparing for publication. In what follows, all except the x prosody is an adaptation of Albrow's terminology which, I understand, is common to the Firth school of linguistics.

20 These phenomena occur regularly with this verbal suffix. Historically, /a/ here is the reflex of a lengthened *o, so that the prosody originally implied 'lengthening', and the shifting of the nodal position is a reflex of differing tonal configurations.

21 *Osnovy russkoi orfografii*, 84.

22 Rules which would in fact amount to a statement of a prosodic analysis.

23 *Osnovy russkoi orfografii*, 67.

24 The decree introducing the orthographic reforms prepared before the Revolution was promulgated on 23 December, 1917, and its scope extended on 10 October, 1918.

25 W.J.Entwistle and W.A.Morison, *Russian and the Slavonic Languages*, London, 1949, 202.

26 See the preface to *Pravila russkoî orfografii i punktuacii*.

27 It is interesting to note that V.K.Trediakovskiî (1703–1769) consistently used *šč* (шч) instead of *ŝ* (щ) and justified this in his *apologia* for Russian orthography *Razgovor ... ob ortografii starinnoî i novoî ...*, 'Dialogue ... concerning the Old and the New Orthography ...' (St Petersburg, 1748).

28 To take this rationalization to its limit, one could in fact justify the discarding of *î* or ', the remaining letter then being a general 'auxiliary' letter, acting as separating sign, palatalization sign and diphthong sign (and there would be no ambiguities).

# The Phonetics of Non-European Languages

# Pitch, Tone, and Intonation in Yoruba

J. CARNOCHAN

Professor Jones's active interest in African languages goes back at least half a century, to *The Pronunciation and Orthography of the Chindau Language.*[1] Indeed, his approach to tone in 'The Tones of Sechuana Nouns',[2] particularly in his setting up of A-forms, B-forms, and C-forms, without priority, but directly relatable to sentence types (command, and statement of fact) and to place in the sentence (not final) is a procedure with which the present author is in sympathy, and which he is trying to develop in this article.

Yoruba is one of the best documented languages of Nigeria, and others have already investigated a number of its tonal problems.[3] Up to now, writers have chosen to give an over-all system for the tonal phenomena observed. One result has been that perhaps too much importance has been attached to the pronunciation of the word in isolation, longer stretches are looked on as being built up by putting words together, the tonal phenomena being allocated to the words with suitable rules to account for changes from the 'inherent tone' of the word as pronounced in isolation. The present writer considers that perhaps new light can be thrown on tone in Yoruba by drawing attention to regularly recurring tonal phenomena of examples sharing the same grammatical structure.

Investigators into the language have already given accounts of the parts of speech, with sub-classifications of words based on tonal criteria. Some progress indeed has been made by Ward, Rowlands, and Siertsema in dealing with longer stretches of speech, but the relation of intonation to grammar has not been developed to any great extent. Ward recognized that intonation is a feature of the grammatical piece. 'There are in Yoruba a number of gliding tones which do not belong to the syllable itself, but which are incidental to the juxtaposition of certain types of words',[4] and of a particular glide she says, 'It is part of the *pattern of the group*, not of the two words.'[5] In considering tone, Miss Siertsema writes: 'Only "lexical" glides are considered here, that is to say glides within the word unit; in the combination of words in the sentence, several other features appear which it would take us too far into grammar to discuss now.'[6] The present article attempts to take the study of tone and intonation in Yoruba further into grammar than has been done before, in the belief that it is only within the grammatical framework that the facts of tone and intonation can be adequately stated.

Pitch and tone are to be distinguished. Pitch is a sensation, perceived by the listener, and referable to a scale, as well as being related to the frequency with which the vocal cords of the speaker open and close during the utterance, and which is measurable by instrumental techniques.[7] Tone on the other hand is considered here as a prosodic element, in the phonological structure of the syllable. It is an abstraction, and only measurable in the sense that the number of terms in a tonal system set up for any given place in structure can be stated. Intonation is here used for the sequence of the tones of the syllables corresponding to the pronunciation of the example. Some sentences are spoken using a much higher range of pitches than others, and these features are also referred to the intonation of the sentences, or of parts of the sentences, in terms of high register and normal register.

The first sets of examples illustrate differences of intonation corresponding to three different types of sentences, namely, Statement, Question, and Linked Answer. The examples are intransitive affirmative[8] verbal sentences, third person singular, past tense. There are formal criteria for establishing the grammatical categories mentioned, and these are assumed for the purpose of this article.

| | STATEMENT | | QUESTION | | LINKED ANSWER | |
|---|---|---|---|---|---|---|
| 1. | O wa.[9]<br>'He came.' | nr(HH)[10] | O wa?<br>'Did he come?' | hr(HH) | O wa.<br>'Yes.' | nr($HF_1$) |
| 2. | O lọ.<br>'He went.' | nr(HM) | O lọ?<br>'Did he go?' | hr(HM) | O lọ.<br>'Yes.' | nr($HF_2$) |
| 3. | O bọ.<br>'He returned.' | nr(HL) | O bọ?<br>'Did he return?' | hr(HL) | O bọ.<br>'Yes.' | nr(HM) |

The vocal cords are vibrating throughout the pronunciation of each of these sentences, giving the listener a continuous sensation of pitch. The Questions are perceived as spoken with a generally higher range of pitch than the others, their intonation is characterized as being on a higher register, and the notation has hr outside the brackets to indicate this. The higher range of pitch or the normal range is considered as

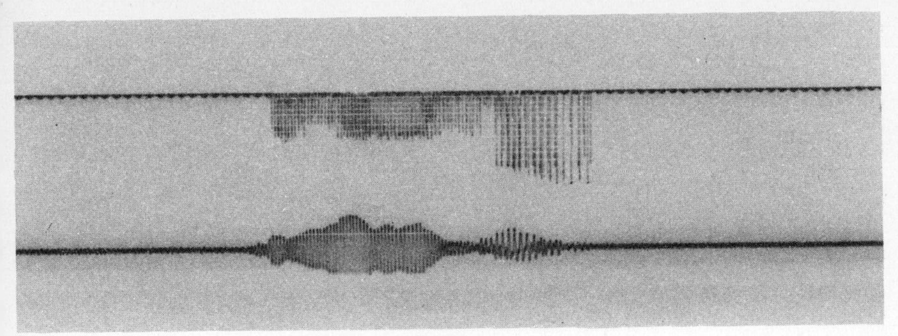

Fig. 1. Statement ó bɔ̀.

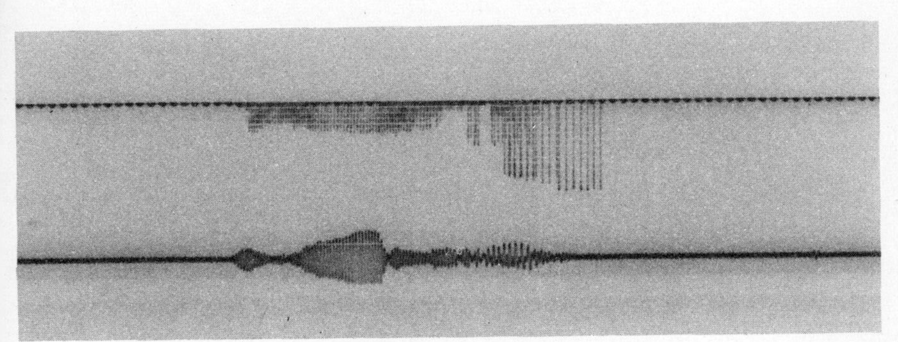

Fig. 2. Question o bɔ?

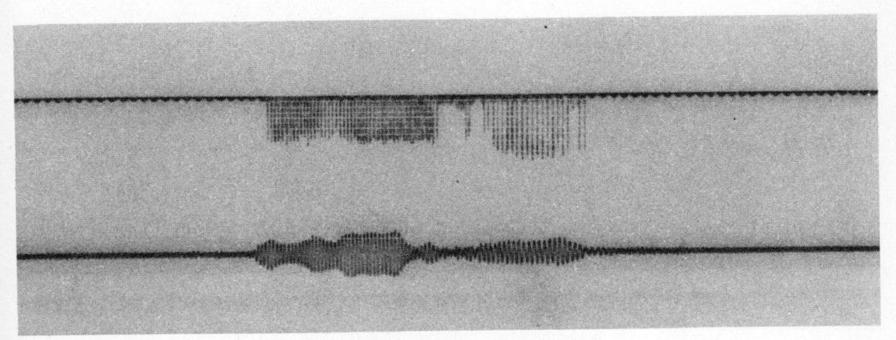

Fig. 3. Linked Answer o bɔ.

characterizing the whole sentence and not any one syllable. The use of the brackets is to indicate this. There is considerable overlap of the pitch ranges, but the general higher range of an hr sentence can easily be appreciated by contrasting it with an nr sentence. At the phonological level of statement, hr and nr are prosodic elements of structure of the sentence as a whole.

Reference may be made to Fig. 1, in comparing the 'tonogram' of *O bọ*, Statement and *O bọ*, Question. The beginning of the Statement was said on a fundamental of just over 140 cps, and that of the Question just below 180 cps. For the Linked Answer it was above 140 cps. The regular wave form at the top of each tonogram is of 50 cycle periodicity, and serves as a Time Marker.

The tonograms were obtained from a pitch meter developed by Mr H.J.F.Adam, during the time he was Chief Technician at the School of Oriental and African Studies and improved by his successor, Mr A. W. Stone. The apparatus consists of the amplifier to provide the signal, the pitch meter which reacts to the fundamental, and a double-beam oscilloscope for the visual display of the analysed signal, and for the display simultaneously of the oscillogram of the signal. The signal is fed to a voice cone in the pitch meter, to the front surface of which is connected a flexible bar holding a series of pre-tuned reeds, giving a response to frequencies from 30 to 230 cycles per second. In front a second bar is mounted, holding a series of silver contact blades, allowing only one vibrating reed to make contact at a time, and thus having the effect of a switch for this one circuit. From the contacts a series of leads is taken to a series of equal resistors mounted in four banks in absolute series. A varying voltage will be available to be taken to the oscilloscope, having the effect of deflecting the beam a given amount according to the voltage produced. Interference from strong harmonics has been largely eliminated by making the lower frequencies give greater deflection of the beam than the higher ones. Thus, on the tonograms, the longer the vertical black line, the lower was the fundamental frequency of the voice. The top thin white line touching the 50 cycle time marker is the 220 cycle line, the next white line is the 210 cycle line, and the third is the 200 cycle line. Because of the inertia of the pitch meter mechanism, the tonogram and the oscillogram for each example do not begin simultaneously. The fact that the tonograms occasionally ends before the corresponding oscillograms may be due either to the presence of a fundamental below 30 cps, or to energy so diminished that the vibration of the reed was insufficiently strong to make the contact. In spite of its imperfections, the apparatus gives instrumental data which are of considerable value in the study of the pitch features of spoken language.

The three Statement examples show three different pitch sequences.[11] The pitch of the voice throughout the first example, *O wa*, is perceived as level, and fairly high; for the second, *O lọ*, the voice begins on almost the same pitch as for the first, but the second syllable is pronounced on a rather lower pitch; for the third, *O bọ*, the first syllable is pronounced on a pitch rather lower than for the first example, and with a slight but perceptible rise at the beginning, and the pitch of the voice falls on the second syllable to the base of the normal register. Since there is voicing without a break throughout the articulation of the sentence, there must be a continuous fall in pitch, even though this is not so perceptible at the upper range of the fall as towards the lower range. My phonological notation for these sentences, nr(HH), nr(HM), and nr(HL) is in keeping with the usual tonal description, which leads to the usual sub-classification of the verbs as high-tone verbs, mid-tone verbs, and low-tone verbs. The sub-classification is based on phonological criteria, but the use of such phonological labels as 'low-tone' verb is confusing, as it entails statements like, 'The low-tone verb becomes mid when followed by a noun object.'[12] All Yoruba Statements of this grammatical structure – and they are numerous – have similar pitch characteristics, except in so far as some have voiceless consonant articulation, e.g. *O ko* 'it's a pity'. All the verbs in such sentences fall into one of the three groups classified above.

Similar distinctions of pitch are made between the three Question examples and the three Statements, but the fundamental reaches a much higher range. Phonologically, the tones are the same for the Questions as for the Statements, the differences of pitch being stated in terms of high and normal registers.

The Linked Answer is in reply to the Question, and the one given in each case is not the only answer; instead of *O wa* 'yes', one may have *Ko wa*, 'no', with similar negative answers for the others, and different pitch features from the affirmative linked answers.

In the case of *O wa* 'yes', the first syllable is on a fairly high pitch of the voice, and the second starts on the same pitch and then falls to a mid pitch. This syllable is considerably prolonged. In the case of *O lọ* 'yes', the first syllable is on a fairly high pitch, and the second is prolonged and falls to the lowest point of the voice, not, however, from the high pitch of the *O* but from a mid pitch. In the case of *O bọ* 'yes', the first syllable is on a fairly high pitch, and the second is prolonged on a rather lower pitch, and does not fall continuously (see Fig. 1, Example 3). The intonation of the three linked answers is given as nr($HF_1$) for *O wa*, (the $F_1$ referring to a falling pitch from a high to a mid range of the voice); nr($HF_2$) for *O lọ* (the $F_2$ tone referring to a falling pitch from a mid-range to the lowest point of the voice); and nr(HM) for *O bọ*.

This analysis recognizes five tones for these nine sentences, H, M, L, $F_1$, and $F_2$. The items *wa*, *lọ*, and *bọ* are each associated with different tones in different types of sentences, and the different types of sentences are given different phonological structures.

An alternative analysis would recognize three tones only, 1, 2, and 3. The intonation of the Statement, Question, and Linked Answer forms of *O wa*, *O lọ*, and *O bọ* would be:

| | | | |
|---|---|---|---|
| 1. nr(1 1) | hr(1 1) | nr(1 1) | (O wa.) |
| 2. nr(1 2) | hr(1 2) | nr(1 2) | (O lọ.) |
| 3. nr(1 3) | hr(1 3) | nr(1 3) | (O bọ.) |

Apart from those phonetic differences which are dealt with in terms of register, the phonological structures are the same for each horizontal set, and pitch differences between *O wa* Statement, and *O wa* Linked Answer, for instance, would be treated purely as different phonetic exponents of Tone 1 in different types of sentence. *Wa* would be a Tone 1 verb, *lọ* Tone 2, and *bọ* Tone 3. This would be an improvement on the present position, with *wa*, *lọ*, and *bọ* regarded as high-tone, mid-tone, and low-tone verbs, respectively, in so far as it is more reasonable to speak of the different pitch exponents of Tone 1 than to consider a low tone becoming a mid tone. It seems best to reserve tone for a phonological element of syllable structure, and to discontinue the practice of using it as a label for sub-classes of word items. I should prefer to number the sub-classes of verbs.

The number of tonal distinctions varies from one grammatical structure to another, and varies according to the place in structure. For instance, there is only one tone set up for the first syllable of all the nine examples so far presented, and three tones for the second syllable, and these three vary as systems from one sentence type to another. If additional sentences varying only in person and number from those already presented are examined, then a system of two tones is set up for the first syllable; these correspond to the pitch differences observed in comparing *O wa* 'he came', and *Mo wa* 'I came', or *O wa* 'you came'.

The phonological notation for the intonation of these two new examples is nr(MH). The two term system for the first syllable is H/M, H going with third person examples, and M with the others.

A two-tone system is set up for the first syllable in the continuous or progressive tense sentences, illustrated by *O nwa* 'he is coming', with intonation nr(HHH) and *Mo nwa* 'I am coming', nr(LHH). Here again, the first formula goes with third person examples, singular and plural, and the second with all examples that are not third person.[13] For such sentences, there is a two-term alternance for the first syllable, no alternance for the second (a syllabic nasal), and a three-term alternance for the third syllable. The pronouns (the first syllable) are associated in the continuous tense sentences with H and with L, while in the past tense sentences they are associated with H and M. This method of analysis enables a partial correlation between the grammatical category of person and the phonological category of intonation to be brought out.

Within the context of language investigation, Yorubas are willing to pronounce words in isolation, and the pitch distinctions in the pronunciation of nouns in this context afford phonetic data on which to base the classification of Yoruba nouns. For other languages, Chaga, for instance,[14] the one-word sentence context is not adequate for determining the tonal classification of words, but it happens to be adequate for Yoruba. The two-syllable nouns give ten intonations as one-word sentences, but the first four classes given have few items, and appear to exclude vowel-initial nouns.

| | | |
|---|---|---|
| 1. nr(HH) | papa 'field' | Ward's Class I |
| 2. nr(HL) | pako 'chewing stick' | |
| 3. nr(LF) | malu 'cow' (Only example found) | |
| 4. nr(FL) | mẹli 'mile' (Only example found) | |
| 5. nr(MM) | ọmọ 'child' | Ward's Class II |
| 6. nr(MH) | ile 'house' | Ward's Class IV |
| 7. nr(ML) | ọja 'market' | Ward's Class VI |
| 8, nr(LL) | ẹhin 'back' | Ward's Class IV |
| 9. nr(LH) | ilu 'town' | Ward's Class V |
| 10. nr(LM) | ode 'street' | Ward's Class VII |

The presentation of the intonation in this way, to include the nr and the brackets, emphasizes that the author regards the examples not as words but as one-word sentences, spoken as statements, with the normal register of statements. Two tones are recognized for each example, corresponding to the two syllables, and to the two syllable-places of the phonological structure. For each of these places in structure there is an alternance system of four terms, shown here as H/M/L/F, called high, mid, low, and falling. The pitch exponents of the tones in the pronunciation of any example are related both to the tonal structure of the example as a whole, that is to the intonation, and also to the tonal system for each place in the structure. For example, the exponents of the high tone of the first syllable of examples 1 and 2 differ from each other. In example 1, the pitch is perceived as high and level, and in example 2 there is a perceptible rise at the beginning, and the voice does not seem to reach quite so high a pitch. The exponents of a high tone are thus different in the intonation nr(HH) and nr(HL). The pitch exponents of H in the second syllable of example 6 sounds level, but slightly lower than that of the second syllable of 1; the exponent of H in example 9 is rising pitch. The exponent of M in example 10 is regularly lower in pitch than in example 5. These remarks serve to show once again the difference in the author's use of pitch, at the phonetic level, and tone at the phonological level.

Nouns may be elements of larger grammatical structures, and it is proposed to consider next the intonations of one such larger structure, namely the prepositional phrase. There are two prepositions in Yoruba, *si* and *ni*, and phrases with *si* and *ni* have the same sets of intonations. The set given below is with *si*, and includes items from seven tonal groups only (Ward's seven classes) as items from the others have not been found in prepositional phrases. The intonation given is for the prepositional phrase only in each sentence, i.e. *si* or *s*' and the following word.

| | | |
|---|---|---|
| 1. O lọ si papa | nr(HHH) | 'he went to the field' |
| 2. O lọ s'oko | nr(HM) | 'he went to the farm' |
| 3. O lọ s'ẹhin | nr(HL) | 'he went to the back' |
| 4. O lọ s'ile | nr(HH) | 'he went home' |
| 5. O lọ s'ilu | nr(HR) | 'he went to the town' |
| 6. O lọ s'ọja | nr(HL) | 'he went to market' |
| 7. O lọ s'ode | nr(HM-L) | 'he went out' |

It seems necessary to set up a five-term tonal system for the last syllable of examples of this grammatical structure, H/M/L/R/M-L, called high, mid, low, rising, and mid-low, since all these examples have a high-tone initial syllable, and there are five alternances for the final syllable. In a one-word sentence context, the rising pitch for the second syllable of *ilu* (and other items of the same tonal class) is regarded as an exponent of H, high tone. In the context of the prepositional phrase, however, there is a distinction between *s'ile*, nr(HH), and *s'ilu*, nr(HR), with a high level pitch of the voice for the second syllable of the former, and a rising pitch for the latter. A fifth term, M-L, mid-low, is also necessary for this context, as there is a pitch distinction between *s'oko*, and *s'ode*, the second syllable in the latter being appreciably lower in pitch than the former, and still contrasting with the low-falling pitch of the last syllable in *s'ẹhin*, and *s'ọja*. It should be noted that a prepositional phrase including a Class III noun item has the same intonation and similar pitch features as one including a Class VI item.

This context has shown the set of intonations corresponding to the syntactic relation of preposition and noun, in the prepositional phrase. It is proposed next to deal with the relation of the nominal subject piece and the verbal piece in verbal sentences. All affirmative verbal sentences having as part of their structure a nominal subject piece (word, phrase, or clause) are characterized by a high-tone syllable. The high tone of this syllable, at the particular place in structure for which it is set up is related to the fact that the sentence is verbal, is affirmative, is of at least two pieces, a nominal subject piece, and a verbal piece; it is, indeed a sentence prosody. Up to now, the phenomenon has only been recognized in part, and Abraham[15] has followed Ward[16] in regarding it as a relation between words. It is a feature of the sentence, and could be considered as a junction prosody, of subject and verb, in specified conditions. Examples are given below, of sentences that are generalized as [(NP)(VP)]h where h outside the square brackets is the sentence prosody; and NP and VP are the nominal and verbal pieces; these elements are placed within round brackets because in the more complex sentences, the nominal and verbal pieces are subject to further analysis. In the texts that follow, round brackets divide the pieces, the high tone syllable referred to is followed by a raised h, and the verb word is followed by a raised v.

1. (Ọmọ$^{h}$) (lọ$^{v}$) (s'ile) 'the child went home' nr (MHM)...[17]
2. (Ọmọ$^{h}$) (wa$^{v}$) (s'ile) 'the child came home' nr(MHH)...
3. (Ọmọ$^{h}$) (bọ$^{v}$) (s'ile) 'the child returned home' nr(MHL)...
4. (Agbẹ$^{h}$) (lọ$^{v}$) (s'ile) 'the farmer went home' nr (LHM)...
5. (Ayọ$^{h}$) (lọ$^{v}$) (s'ile) 'Ayọ went home' nr(MRM)...

Differences in pitch in the pronunciation of examples 1 and 5 are reflected in the intonation, where the second syllable of the noun is H for 1 and R for 5; the exponent of R is a rising inflection of the voice from a low pitch to a high. In view of the fact that the other tone elements of the intonation are the same for both examples, and that the pitch features are different for both sentences, it is necessary to maintain the distinction in the phonological notation of the intonation.

6. (Gbogbo Ẹgba ti ngbe oko$^h$) (gba$^v$ ogun jọ) 'all the Egbas who were living on farms gathered together for war'.
7. (Ige$^h$) (ba$^v$ mi gbe e) 'Ige helped me carry it'.

This last sentence may be compared with *Mo ba Ige gbe e* 'I helped Ige carry it', to show that the tonal relationship being dealt with is not a matter of mere sequence of noun and verb. Here, the noun *Ige* is not in subject relation with the verb *gbe*, which would have demanded high pitch of the voice for *-ge*, as (Ige$^h$) (gbe$^v$e), 'Ige carried it'.

Regular tonal relations between subject and verb may be illustrated from other tenses, the perfect (e.g. *Ọmọ ti lọ s'ile* 'the child has gone home'; where *ti lọ* is the verb, and the last syllable of the nominal piece is on a high pitch of the voice), the progressive (e.g. *Ọmọ nlọ s'ile* 'the child is going home'; where the last syllable of the nominal piece is on a high pitch of the voice), and the future (e.g. *Ọmọ o lọ s'ile* 'the child will go home'; where the particle *o* is regularly on a high pitch of the voice, or on a rising pitch, both being exponents of H, high tone).

All negative sentences also have a regular tonal sentence prosody; but in the negative sentences, the tone is low except in negative linked answers with Class III verbs, where it is mid. This low-tone feature may be associated with the particle *ko*, or *o* or with prolongation of the vowel sound of the last syllable of the nominal subject piece.

It is hoped that enough has been said in this paper to show how close the correspondences in Yoruba[18] between the grammatical statements and the phonological statements involving tone may be. There is every indication that the correspondence extends much further than has been shown in this paper, and that the very large number of different pitch features can be schematized into a small number of tones, relatable partly to the grammatical structure of the piece, and partly to the phonological classification of the items.

*Notes*

[1] London, 1911.

[2] *International Institute of African Languages and Cultures, Memorandum VI*, London, 1928.

[3] I. C. Ward, *Introduction to the Yoruba Language*, Cambridge, 1952; B. Siertsema 'Some Notes on Yoruba Phonetics and Spelling', *Bull. Inst. franç. Afr. noire*, XX, sér. B, nos. 3–4, 1958; H. J. Melzian, 'Beobachtungen über die Verwendung der Töne in der Yoruba-Sprache', *Mitteilungen des Seminars für Orientalische Sprachen zu Berlin*, XXXVII, III, Berlin, 1934; A. Lloyd James, 'The Tones of Yoruba', *Bull.*

*Sch. Orient. Stud. Lond. Univ.*, 1925; E.C.Rowlands, 'Types of Word Junction in Yoruba', *Bull. Sch. Orient. Stud. Lond. Univ.*, XVI, 2, 1954; R.C.Abraham, *Dictionary of Modern Yoruba*, London, 1958.

[4] Ward, *Introduction*, 5.

[5] Ibid., 30.

[6] Siertsema, 'Some Notes', 584.

[7] See Fig. 1 for examples.

[8] Affirmative is used here in contradistinction to negative.

[9] Examples are given in standard Yoruba orthography.

[10] See the next paragraphs for an explanation of the formulaic notation.

[11] The descriptions that follow are of tonograms from examples spoken by Chief I.O.Delano. He had already returned to Nigeria before the improved pitch meter was available, and the three examples on the Figure are from sentences spoken by his son, Akin. There are considerable differences of duration between the two speakers but the pitch characteristics are very similar, and permit the same phonological statements to be made for both.

[12] See also A.E.Sharp, 'A Tonal Analysis of the Disyllabic Noun in the Machame Dialect of Chaga', *Bull. Sch. Orient. Stud. Lond. Univ.*, XVI, 1, 1954.

[13] The other persons are distinguished from each other by criteria other than intonation.

[14] See Sharp, 'Tonal Analysis'.

[15] Abraham, *Dictionary*, 19.

[16] Ward, *Introduction*, 177.

[17] The intonation given for each example here is for the nominal and verbal pieces only, and excludes the prepositional phrase.

[18] Similar facts can be stated for Igbo, where up to now the tonal relationship has only been considered with reference to the sequence of words. See also the author's 'Glottalization in Hausa' for the relation between tonal features and the grammatical categories of Tense and Aspect, *Transactions of the Philological Society*, 1953, and Sharp, 'Stress and Juncture in English', TPS, 1960, for indication of the necessity of relating intonational features as well as stress and juncture to grammatical statements of the larger piece: 'Perhaps the basic trouble has been that our analysis has been geared too much to the word, too little to the sentence.'

# Glottal Spirants and the Glottal Stop in the Aspirates in New Indo-Aryan

SUNITI KUMAR CHATTERJI

Primitive Indo-European, as it had evolved out of the earlier primitive Indo-Hittite, had a characteristic set of sounds which were well established, and their occurrence is made quite clear not only from their actual existence in some of the ancient and modern Indo-European languages but also from the phonetic pre-history of Indo-European itself in very early times. Sanskrit has a full set of aspirates *kh, gh*; *ch, jh*; *ṭh, ḍh*; *th, dh*; and *ph, bh*, and these rest upon an earlier series which have been re-constructed as follows: *qh, Gh*; *qwh, Gwh*; *kh, gh*; *th, dh*; and *ph, bh*.

Greek has preserved the aspirates *kh, th, ph*, which represent the unvoiced aspirates as well as the voiced ones of Primitive Indo-European. From the phonetic history of all the ancient Indo-European languages, particularly of the Germanic and Armenian, the presence of these very specialized sounds in Indo-European is made clear.

We need not go into that phonetic history in the present context. It is enough to say that Sanskrit in India began with the set of 10 aspirated sounds as indicated above, 5 unvoiced and 5 voiced. The character of these, as described by the Sanskrit grammarians, from at least the middle of the first millennium B.C., and as preserved in the tradition of pronunciation as maintained in India, is quite clear in establishing for Indo-Aryan from very ancient times the existence of a series of these modified sounds. In these sounds, we have a stop or occlusive, and immediately after its release there is an accompanying release of breath. This breath was just the spirant sound (occurring as both voiced and unvoiced) which is made in the glottal region. We have the unvoiced *k, c, ṭ, t*, and *p*, which are pure stops without aspiration, and we have also *kh, ch, ṭh, th, ph*, which are completed with an accompaniment of breath. This breath is a spirant sound, unvoiced, which is produced in the glottal region. Similarly we have the voiced *g, j ḍ, d, b*, unaspirated pure stops, and then the corresponding set of aspirates *gh*, *jh*, *ḍh*, *dh*, *bh*, which have the accompaniment of a voiced glottal spirant, the voiced *h* [ɦ]. These sounds were well established in Old Indo-Aryan, and they have been continued through Middle Indo-Aryan right down to New Indo-Aryan.

But in making a close study of the articulation of these sounds in New Indo-Aryan, we meet with a series of unexpected and disturbing facts, which show that the proper aspirated sounds are not universal, at least in New Indo-Aryan. Over considerable parts of the country, in the various language-areas, we have either complete loss of aspiration, leading to the occurrence only of pure stops, or substitution of some other kind of articulation in place of the aspirated one. The *h*-element, or the element of a glottal spirant, in the Indo-Aryan aspirated stops, is so very clear that careful foreigners (or Indian speakers themselves) who wanted to employ a totally different alphabet for the Indian languages, like the Perso-Arabic and the Roman, immediately realized that these aspirate sounds formed a combination of the stops *plus* the glottal spirant *h*, whether voiced or unvoiced. Accordingly, to represent the 10 single letters which the Indian system of writing has for these aspirated sounds, scholars, with the comparatively meagre resources at their disposal in the Perso-Arabic and Roman alphabets, most naturally hit upon the device of indicating these aspirates by means of the letters for the pure stop sounds, followed by the letter for *h*. Perhaps the influence of some standard forms of speech as current in the Upper Ganges Valley, in which the aspirates were clear and precise sounds which were carefully preserved, was responsible for neglect or inattention in respect of the substitute pronunciation for the aspirates.

A proper scientific study of modern Indo-Aryan languages, particularly with reference to their phonetic basis, is a comparatively new thing in Indian linguistics, although this matter has not been wholly missed by workers like G.A.Grierson, T.Grahame Bailey, and R.L. Turner during the last forty years and more. It is now quite clear that the modern Indo-Aryan languages range themselves into two main groups. In one, the aspirates are more or less well preserved. But in the other group, the aspirates are modified in various ways, and other and different types of articulation occur in place of pure aspiration in which the ejected breath or glottal spirant follows or accompanies the stop. In certain languages like the Western Hindi dialects, the dialects of Kosali (the so-called Eastern Hindi), and the various kinds of Bihari speech, and also in West Bengali, Oriya, and Marathi, we have the aspirates more or less preserved, in what may be called their proper Old

Indo-Aryan character. But in a surrounding group of languages like Panjabi (or Eastern Panjabi), Hindki (Western Panjabi or Lahndi), Rajasthani, Gujarati (partly), and the Himalayan dialects (partly), we have these new substitutes for aspirates. They are not uniform throughout these 'outer region' languages surrounding the central or Gangetic ones which have proper aspiration. Thus, in certain important matters, the Hindki or West Panjabi dialects differ materially from the East Panjabi ones. In East Bengali we have regular transformation of these aspirates into stops accompanied, not by the glottal spirant *h* but by the glottal stop (['] = [ʔ]). In Rajasthani and Gujarati, this is also the case. In these languages, the glottal aspirate *h*, which is a voiced sound [ɦ] in Indo-Aryan, is changed to the glottal stop [ʔ] when it stands by itself. In practice, therefore, it may be laid down as a general rule that there has been in these languages a substitution of the glottal stop for the glottal spirant as the necessary accompaniment of the simple stop sounds to produce this distinct class which has had a separate existence from the pure stops from earliest times in the history of Indo-European.

The situation is indicated by means of a number of transliterated passages with phonetic transcriptions, the transliterations being in the current or Geneva system of transliteration nowadays almost universally adopted for Sanskrit and all connected languages of India, whether Indo-Aryan or Dravidian.

Thus, to take a sentence like the following in Standard Khariboli Hindustani:

*us-kā bhāī ghar-mēn̠ nahīn̠ rahā* (*thā*): *dūdh lēkar us-kī bahin* (*bahan*) *bāhar āī*

'His brother was not in the house, his sister came out bringing milk.'

In the above passage in Standard Hindustani (Hindi or Urdu), we have a number of aspirated stops, as well as the single glottal spirant or *h*, in some words. In Standard Hindustani pronunciation, all these aspirates would be pronounced fully, and there is no mistake about them. The above can be transcribed phonetically as follows:

[uskaː bɦaːiː gɦʌrmẽː nʌɦĩː rʌɦaː (thaː), duːdɦ leːkʌr uskiː bʌɦən baːɦər aːiː]

This same passage rendered into a closely connected dialect, the Braj-bhasha, would be as follows:

*wā-kau bhāī ghara-mān̠hi nahīn̠ rahyau* (*hatau*): *dūdh lēi-kari wā-kī bhainī bāhar āī.*

In this dialect also the aspirated sounds are quite clear, as we can see from the phonetic transcription, given below:

[βaːkəŏ bɦaːiː gɦʌrəmãːɦi nʌɦĩː rʌɦjəŏ (ɦʌtəŏ), duːdɦ leːjkʌrĩ βaːkiː bɦæẽniː baːɦər aːiː]

Passing further towards the East, we find the equivalent or translation of the above passage would be as follows, in ordinary Roman transliteration and in phonetic transcription; and from the transcriptions, it will be seen that the aspirates are fully retained. Thus, for example, in the Awadhi form of Kosali (Eastern Hindi):

*ō-kar (ō-kē) bhāi ghar-ma nahīn̲ rahīs : dūdh lē-kai ō-kē bahin bāhar āis.*

Phonetic transcription:

[okər (oke) bɦaːi gɦʌrmə nʌɦĩː rʌɦiːs, duːdɦ leːkʌi oke bʌɦin baːɦər aːis]

and in Bhojpuri:

*ōh-kē bhāī ghar-mēn̲ nahīn̲ rahal : dūdh lēi-kē ōh-kē bahinī bāhir āilī.*
[oɦke bɦaːiː gɦʌrmẽ nʌɦĩː rʌɦəl, duːdɦ leike oɦke bʌɦiniː baːɦir aːiliː]

When we come to Bengal, we find in West Bengal these aspirated stops are preserved as such in initial positions only. But they are modified in various ways when they are intervocalic or final, and the spirant *h*, when not initial – particularly when it is intervocalic – also suffers total loss in the language. Thus the same sentence translated into Standard Colloquial Bengali of Calcutta would run thus:

*ōr bhāi gharē chila nā : dudh niyē ōr bōn bāirē ēla.*

In phonetic transcription:

[or bɦai gɦɔre cʃhilòna, dud nie or bon baire elò]

In Standard Written Bengali, which embraces all the dialects (and largely indicates the situation for the Bengali of four to five hundred years ago), the above sentence would be as follows:

*uhār bhāi gharē chila nā (rahila nā) : dudh laiyā uhār bahin bāhirē āila (āsila).*

The above will be pronounced by a Standard Bengali speaker as follows in quick articulation:

[uɦar bɦai gɦɔre cʃhilòna (ro[ɦ]ilòna) : dud[ɦ] loia uɦar bòɦin ba[ɦ]ire ailò (aʃilò)]

This may be compared with the pronunciation of the same passage by a person from a typical East Bengal area like Dacca (for whom this passage in the Standard Bengali would be as much his own language as for a speaker of the Standard Colloquial from Calcutta): we note some very remarkable differences in the articulation of the same passage by a West Bengal person and one from East Bengal. The points of difference will be noted below.

The Marathi version of the same passage will run as follows:

*hyā-cā bhāū gharāṉt nāhīṉ jhālā* (*rāhilā*) : *dūdh ghēūn hyā-cī bahiṇ bāhēr ālī.*

This would be pronounced as follows, in the Standard Marathi pronunciation of Poona:

[ɦjat͡sa bɦau gɦɐrãt nɐɦĩ zala (raɦila), dudɦ gɦeun ɦjacʃi bɐɦeɳ baɦer ali]

All the above kinds of articulation, namely in the Western Hindi, in the Kosali (or Eastern Hindi), in the Bihari, and in the Western Bengali dialects as well as in Oriya (the Oriya version is not given), we find a similar state of things, except in East Bengali. There is the general preservation of the aspirates, particularly when they are in an initial position – only in spoken West Bengali (as for example in and around Calcutta), the aspiration is dropped, together with the single *h*, in the middle or at the end of a word. (It is to be noted also that in Bengali, the aspirates *ph*, *bh* are normally spirantized to [ɸ, β].

We may now take up some typical examples of the group of New Indo-Ayran in which the aspirates are no longer kept intact. Thus we have in East Bengali:

*ōr bhāi gharē chila nā* (*rahila nā*) : *dudh laiyā ōr buin bāirē āila.*

Phonetically the above will be pronounced:

[or b'ai g'ɔre silòna (r'oilòna), d'ud loia (loiɛ) or b'uin b'aire ailò]

It is to be noted that in the two words [b'uin] and [b'aire], which phonetically are transcribed with a [b'], i.e. with a *b* with an accompanying glottal stop, this modified pronunciation with the glottal stop is a substitute for the *h*, which occurred in the words originally – the earlier forms were *bahin* and *bāhirē*, as in the standard language.

In Gujarati, the sentence will be:

*tē-nō bhāi ghēr-māṉ rahyō nahīṉ* : *dūdh laī-nē tē-nī b-hēn* (*bahēn, bēn*) *b-hār* (*bahār*) *āvī.*

In phonetic transcription:

[teno bɦaːi (b'aːi) gɦermãː (g'ermãː) r'ʌjo n'ʌĩː, dud' lʌiːne tenĩ b'en b'aːr aːβiː]

In Rajasthani, which is so closely connected with Gujarati, the passage will be as follows (in the Marwari dialect):

*uṇ-rō bhāī ghar-mē̱n rahyō nahi̱n : dūdh lēi-kar uṇ-rī bahēn (baiṇ, bhaiṇ) bārai āī.*

In phonetic transcription:

[uɳroː b'aːiː g'ʌrmẽː r'ʌjoː (rʌˀjoː) n'ʌĩː (nʌˀĩː), d'uːd leikər uɳriː b'ɛːɳ b'aːrɛ aːiː]

Sindhi is an important language of Western India, and it is contiguous to Gujarati, Rajasthani as well as Western Panjabi. The above passage in Sindhi will be:

*huna-jō bhāū ghara-ma̱njhē na huō : dūdha nēī (naī) huna-jī bhēṇa bāhara āī.*

The phonetic transcription of the above passage in Sindhi:

[ɦunədʒoː bɦaːuː gɦʌrəmʌ̃ʤɦe nʌ ɦuwo : – duːdɦə neiː (nʌiː) ɦunəʤiː bɦeːɳə baːɦərə ɑːjiː]

Here in Sindhi the aspirates are not interfered with, they remain intact, as well as the letter *h*. But Sindhi has developed (from other groups of sounds) a series of stops accompanied by glottal stops, which are exactly like the East Bengali, Gujarati and Rajasthani, and West Panjabi substitutes for the aspirates.

The Hindki or Western Panjabi version of the passage given above would be:

*us-dā bhrā ghar-vicca na rehā : duddh ghinn-kē us-dī bhaïṇ (bhai̯ṇ) bāhar āī.*

In pronunciation:

[usda b'raː g'ʌrəβiccʃə nʌ r'eaː, d'udd g'innke usdiː b'ʌiɳ (b'æɳ) b'aər aːiː]

The widest deviation we find in the Eastern Panjabi dialects. The Standard Hindustani passage first given will be as follows, in Standard Eastern Panjabi:

*uh-dā (os-dā) bharā (bhrā, bhāī) ghara-vicca nahī̱n sī (na rihā) : duddh lai-kar uh-dī bhai̱ṇṇ bāhar āī.*

In pronunciation, the above passage shows a two-fold treatment of the aspirates, including the single *h*. There is in the first instance an unvoicing of the voiced aspirates like *bh*, *gh*, and *dh*. Then, as a substitute for the aspiration, i.e. the *h* accompanying the stop consonant, and for *h* occurring by itself, there is a modification in tone. As a result of these changes, Eastern Panjabi has virtually become a 'tone language', in which the distinction between words in their meanings is shown in the change of tone, the vowel and consonant sounds remaining the same. The above passage can be transcribed phonetically as follows:

[u⁀daː (osdaː) p‿əraː (p‿aːiː) k‿ʌr βiccʃɔ n⁀ʌĩː siː (nʌ ri⁀aː): d⁀udː lækʌr u⁀diː p‿æɳ b⁀aːr aːiː]

The nature of this Eastern Panjabi modification of common Indo-Aryan aspirated consonants and the aspirate has been discussed fully by several scholars like T. Grahame Bailey and Banarasi Das Jain. To put it briefly, it is a case of change of the glottal spirant into the glottal stop *plus* devoicing in the case of the voiced aspirates *plus* a new element of tone as a concomitant of this change of aspiration. Single *h*, when it occurs initially, or between vowels, or at the end of a word, is not found to occur as a glottal stop, as in East Bengali; it only brings about the introduction of a musical pitch or tone. It is also to be noted that in East Bengali also, whenever there is a change of the *h* in the aspirated stop to a glottal stop, or of independent *h* to the glottal stop, there is an accompanying high tone. Thus in East Bengali *gā*, 'body', and *ghā*, 'wound', 'sore', are pronounced as [gaː] and [g'aː], respectively. But the second word, meaning 'sore' or 'wound', would be pronounced with a rising tone [ˊg'aː]. So [ani] 'I bring' or 'a one-anna coin': but *hāni*, 'loss', becomes [ˊʔani], and here also we have a rising tone on the first syllable as an accompaniment of the glottal stop articulation.

Then, again, in East Bengali we have regular instances of throwing back the glottal stop, as the substitute for the *h* in an aspirated stop, or of the *h* when it occurs independently, upon the initial consonant of the word. Thus *bhāg* = 'division' or 'share' becomes normally in East Bengali [ˊb'aːg], with rising tone or accent; but *bāgh* = 'tiger' evidently first became [baːg'], and then the glottal stop was taken over, so to say, to the first letter *b*, and so to speak combined with it, to give the glottal articulation [b'] – as [b'aːg]. So that these two words, owing to this noteworthy phonetic habit, became identical in East Bengali – as [b'aːg]; whereas in West Bengali they occur as [baːg] = 'tiger', and [bɦaːg] = 'division', 'share'. Careful speakers in West Bengali sometimes seek to preserve the aspiration intervocalically, e.g. in a word like *māthā*, 'head', as differentiated from *mātā*, 'mother'. But commonly the aspiration would be dropped, and both would be pronounced as *mātā* [mata]. In East Bengali the unvoiced aspirates are generally preserved both initially and in the middle of words. But they are accompanied by a rising tone. Thus East Bengali *āṭā* = 'flour', but *āṭhā*, 'gum', has the second syllable pronounced at a higher pitch [aṭa, aṭ'a]).

The behaviour of the aspirates and of the *h* sound in New Indo-Aryan thus presents one of the most interesting, although intricate, problems of Indo-Aryan Phonology; and as yet, full attention has not been paid to this question. It frequently happens that linguistic investigators lack the proper feeling for phonetic phenomena, and unless trained phoneticians, they are very commonly guided by the written word – the orthography giving the 'correct' aspirated letters. It is certain that in this matter of aspiration, full sets of laws can be deduced, as it has been possible to do for East Bengali. Over and above this, certain correspondences in these laws of aspiration and substitution of the glottal stop for the *h*, with the attendant tonic modification, among the various New Indo-Aryan languages, whether they are of Eastern India or of Western India, will come out.

The question has also been posed: how old are these types of articulation as substitutes for the aspirate and the aspirated stops? Orthographic evidence in the connected languages would appear to take it back at least a thousand years. Probably this type of glottal stop pronunciation is much earlier still.

We can look forward to having a new aspect of Comparative and Historical Phonology of the New Indo-Aryan languages – Glottal Aspirate and Glottal Stop Changes with Tonetic Modifications in Middle (and even Old?) Indo-Aryan dialects. It is to be hoped that the younger generation of Indian investigators into the history of their own languages will be able to find out these correspondences and formulate these laws, and trace back the history of this kind of phonetic background in dialectal Indo-Aryan to its early development and origin.

# Marginalia to Siamese Phonetic Studies

EUGÉNIE J.A.HENDERSON

It is almost a quarter of a century since Professor Daniel Jones suggested to me that I should investigate the pronunciation of Siamese, of which at that time no detailed phonetic description existed. He had himself in 1918 undertaken a brief study of the pronunciation of a Siamese speaker at the invitation of Sir George Grierson, in order to provide an authoritative account of the Siamese tones for the first volume of the Linguistic Survey of India,[1] and he very generously passed on to me the phonetic notes he had made on that occasion. Since then a great deal of work, published and unpublished, has been done on the subject, notably that of Mary Haas, and the main phonetic characteristics of the language are now widely known. There nevertheless remain certain interesting features which appear to have escaped notice in print so far, and the present occasion would seem to be a most suitable one on which to bring them to general notice.

Over the past few years I have had the good fortune to work with a succession of young Siamese graduates, a number of whom have been engaged upon phonetic research of one kind or another in their own language. As a result of their keenness of perception and skill in self-analysis, and of the experience accumulated through teaching Siamese phonetics to non-Siamese students, I have come to reconsider or to amplify earlier statements on points of phonetic detail, especially as regards pitch behaviour, consonant articulation, variations in breath-force, and the phonetic properties of particles and running speech. None of the points raised calls for any change in the phonemic or near-phonemic transcriptions currently in use, which probably explains why they have, by and large, been neglected. If the final aim of phonetics were to provide an inventory of phonemes and an unambiguous transcription of a language, as one might sometimes be tempted to conclude when reading some of the literature on the subject, they must, therefore, be regarded as 'irrelevant'. The English phonetic tradition has, however, always regarded phonetics as the 'indispensable foundation of all study of language',[2] and has never sought rigidly to separate phonetics from phonology, or abstract theorizing and research from practical application. That the English phonetician should be both phonetician and phonologist, theoretician and practical teacher, and sometimes grammarian as well, is the reflection of an attitude which regards a language as a cohesive whole, with interaction at many levels, for any one of which phonetic phenomena may be of importance. It follows, therefore, that there must be constant reference back to and re-assessment of the phonetic material, since what may be irrelevant to one stage of the analysis may be highly relevant to another. It seems not unfitting that phonetic features which, though non-phonemic, are nevertheless pertinent to phonological analysis, to comparative and historical studies, and to the practical requirements of teaching, should be brought to notice by one trained in the English tradition, in a volume dedicated to the most distinguished living representative of that tradition.

## THE MID TONE

When I first began to teach Siamese phonetics, 'mid level' was a satisfactory descriptive label for one of the Siamese tones, provided students were warned that a slight fall in pitch might be expected before a pause.[3] In the somewhat slow formal style of utterance used in teaching the elements of the language, this fall was not always present, even at the end of a sentence, and was never so marked as to cause confusion with the tone labelled 'falling'. Of recent years, however, as records by younger speakers have been added to the collection of teaching material, I have had to abandon the label 'mid level' in favour of the label 'mid', since there appears to be a tendency among younger speakers to pronounce this tone with such a marked fall in pre-pausal position, even in slow formal styles of utterance, that the earlier label is now misleading to students. Confusion between the falling and the mid tones is now common among beginners. The two tones are, however, still quite clearly distinguished both by their starting pitches and by the manner of their ending. The falling tone begins on a pitch about a minor third above the starting pitch of the mid tone, and is always closed in pre-pausal position by a weak glottal stop or by glottal constriction. The mid tone is never characterized by glottal constriction of any kind at the end. In the run of an utterance, i.e. *not* before a pause, final glottal closure or constriction is frequently absent in the falling tone, but since the mid tone in the same context is level in pitch, no confusion need arise.

## THE HIGH TONE

In his notes and in his account in the Linguistic Survey of India, Professor Jones agrees with Bradley's analysis of this tone, in contexts other than short syllables closed by a stop, as beginning with a slight rise and ending with a strong fall.[4] In both Bradley's graph and in Jones's diagram in his notes, this fall is shown as reaching as low or almost as low a pitch as the falling tone. When I first attempted an analysis, the contour of the tone sounded to me like a short sharp rise in pitch, followed by a sustained high pitch, followed by a marked fall, but the fall was to a mid pitch, not to a pitch as low as that reached by the falling tone. Nevertheless, students in those days had difficulty in distinguishing the two in both pronunciation and recognition, especially as both are closed in pre-pausal position by glottal constriction or a weak glottal stop. Latterly I have become aware that there is an increasingly common variant of this tone in which there is an initial short rise, followed by a sustained high pitch, with no fall at the end. Final glottal constriction is still present. With some speakers this appears to be the only pronunciation that commonly occurs,[5] and it is the form that I now recommend to learners, since it causes them far less difficulty than the rise-fall pronunciation. Where there is a final fall in the pronunciation of this tone nowadays it is usually so slight that confusion with the falling tone is no longer likely to arise. Observation from Bradley onwards suggests that there has been a tendency over the last sixty years to curtail, and perhaps ultimately to abandon altogether, the fall in pitch at the end of this tone, the modern high level variant of which now brings the pronunciation of syllables ending with a continuant closely into line with that long observed for stopped syllables. The change has been a very gradual one, however, and is not so clearly linked to age-groups as is the changing contour of the mid tone. There are a number of instances of a pronunciation without marked final fall among the older speakers in my earlier records, whilst some of the younger speakers recorded more recently show a preference for a rise-fall contour still.

## FINAL STOPS

As in many languages of the South-East Asian linguistic area, syllable-final stops in Siamese are unexploded. In Vietnamese, where this is also the case, when the stoppage in the mouth is released there is frequently still sufficient pressure of air behind it for a weak off-glide to be audible. This is very rarely the case in Siamese except with the final glottal stop, a circumstance that appears puzzling until it is recognized that the oral closure is accompanied in Siamese by simultaneous glottal closure. This secondary closure, which effectively seals off the stream of air from the lungs, is released first so that there is no perceptible off-glide when the oral stop is released. In the case of the glottal stop, where there is only the one point of closure, the off-glide is frequently perceptible. I believe that, although I did not at first recognize it, this double closure of final stops has been the rule rather than the exception during the whole period of my acquaintance with the language. That it may not always have been so is indicated by Professor Jones's notes, which record final stops at the time of his research as being 'often exploded weakly', thus suggesting usage akin to that of present-day Vietnamese.

## INITIAL STOPS

In the pronunciation of young Siamese observed during the past five years there is a marked tendency to pronounce initial voiceless unaspirated plosives with simultaneous oral and glottal closure and release. Occasionally in the pronunciation of one of the speakers, in whom the tendency is particularly strong, there is a weak but unmistakable ejective off-glide, to be accounted for, perhaps, by a delayed glottal release. Ordinarily, however, these sounds are not ejectives, any accompanying upward movement of the larynx being too slight to build up sufficient pressure of air behind the oral stoppage to produce the typical auditory effect upon release. In short, the articulation appears to resemble closely the articulation 'à glotte fermée' sometimes described for French voiceless plosives, the Siamese sounds being of the type for which Catford suggests the description 'glottalized pulmonic pressure stop', as contrasted with true ejectives, for which the term 'glottalic pressure stop' is used.[6]

The effect of this secondary glottal articulation in Siamese is to underscore the contrast between the two series of voiceless plosives, the unaspirated ones with tense phonation and clear onset of the ensuing vowel, and the aspirated ones, articulated more laxly, with breathy release and gradual onset of the following vowel. Since the glottalization is not 'distinctive' in this context, it need not affect the conventional phonemic picture of the language.[7] It would, however, be an important consideration in the phonological analysis of the kind I attempted in an earlier article,[8] and is of considerable interest to comparatists and language historians, who have postulated a series of glottalized initial consonants for 'primitive Tai'.[9] Of particular interest here is Haudricourt's hypothesis of a series of voiceless glottalized plosives antecedent to the voiced glottalized plosives found in some members of the family nowadays.

## INITIAL SEMI-VOWELS

For many years I was puzzled by the pronunciation of Siamese initial [j], which strikes the English ear as being quite frequently an affricate rather than a fricative. I used to assume that in some articulations the tongue was probably raised high enough to touch the hard palate, thus giving rise to an affricate, which I transcribed [dj].[10] In the course of palatographic investigation, however, I was never able, despite a great many attempts, to obtain a tracing which supported this assumption. The solution has, I believe, been provided by Vichintana Chantavibulya, who in investigating her own pronunciation of a Southern Siamese dialect discovered that her pronunciation of the palatal semi-vowel in initial position is preceded by a weak glottal plosive.[11] Subsequent observation of Bangkok speakers has convinced me that this pronunciation is also current in the Siamese of the capital, and that it is the true explanation of the 'affricate' I formerly believed I heard. There is a similar pre-glottalized articulation of the labio-velar semi-vowel, which I had previously noted simply as being more vigorously pronounced than the corresponding English sound. Both sounds, once correctly analysed, are easy to recognize and to imitate.[12] Their presence in modern spoken Siamese supports the hypotheses of comparative linguists who have for the past eighteen years postulated such sounds for the earlier stages of the language.[13]

## INITIAL [t] AND [f]

Before a close front vowel the Siamese unaspirated plosive [t] and the labiodental fricative [f] are frequently 'dark' in quality, with an [ɯ]-like off-glide which suggests that there is raising of the back of the tongue. There is probably a similar modification of the sound before other vowels, but it is before the close front vowel that it is most readily perceived. The secondary articulatory feature may perhaps best be referred to for the present as 'velarization', but I am not satisfied that this is all that is involved. The flat, spread position of the tongue appears to be important, and there may be some such articulatory mechanism as that of the so-called emphatic consonants of Arabic. Once again, phonetic details which are perhaps 'irrelevant' to the phonemicist may be highly relevant to the dialectologist and historian. There are, for example, in certain Tai dialects and languages, words in which there is fluctuation between initial [khw] and [f]. Compare, for example, Sui [_fa] *right* (*side*)[14] with Siamese [ˎkhwaː], and Songkhla [ˎkhwai] and [ˎfai] *fire*, which are in free variation.[15] When it is seen that these consonantal initials can be regarded quite simply as two different arrangements of features common to them both which may be termed velarity, labiality, and breathy onset, their equation for philological purposes becomes much more plausible.

## BREATH FORCE

Difficulties encountered in teaching the tones and final unexploded stops of Siamese have compelled me to take note of the importance for their correct recognition and pronunciation of the proper control of the breath. For a pronunciation of the high tone that will satisfy a critical native speaker, the force must be increased with the slight initial rise in pitch, reaching a peak of intensity during the sustained high pitch and then decreasing quite sharply. A similar 'swell' in the breath force is sometimes observable nowadays in the pronunciation of the mid tone in isolation, as contrasted with the uninterrupted diminution of breath force heard in the other three tones. These variations in breath force may be symbolized for the five tones as follows: [ˉkhaː< >, _khaː>, ˎkhaː>, ^kha <>, \khaː>].

In the pronunciation of final unexploded stops it is important that, no matter what the tone, considerable force of breath should be maintained right up to the completion of the oral closure in order that the on-glide, which is the only means of recognizing which final stop is being pronounced, should be clearly heard, viz. [ˎmaː<k]. Students learning the language frequently make the mistake of allowing the breath-force to die away before the closure, viz. [ˎmaː>k], with the result that it is impossible to tell which stop has been made, or, in fact, whether any stop has been made.[16]

## THE PHONETIC PECULIARITIES OF PARTICLES

In an earlier article,[17] attention was drawn to sentence-final particles in Siamese, in which 'the disposition of tone and quantity is determined not by the phonetic structure of the particle itself,[18] but by the requirements of the sentence as a whole'. Greater familiarity with the usages of conversational Siamese, together with the research conducted by Terd Chuenkongchoo,[19] has pointed the way to a fuller and more satisfactory treatment of this particular aspect of Siamese pronunciation. It is clear that variations in the way in which these syllables are terminated are as important as variations in their pitch and duration. Chuenkongchoo has described and given examples of fourteen different combinations of length, pitch, and syllable-terminating features that he has observed in the pronunciation of specified particles, and it is certain that his list is not exhaustive. He has also pointed out and demonstrated experimentally that the pitch contours of particles cannot properly be equated with the five lexical tones applicable to the great majority of words in the language.[20] The pitch contours of particles generally held to be pronounced with the high and falling lexical tones, respectively, and so indicated orthographically, reach a considerably higher pitch than either of these relative to the surrounding syllables, and are further distinguished from them by the absence of final glottal constriction.[21] For example, the persuasive particle [na] pronounced with a falling pitch and a long vowel, as in the sentence [_jaː⍀phɤŋ _klap ˋnaː] 'Oh, please don't go just yet!'[22] is distinguished from the word [⍀naː] 'face', by its higher starting pitch and wider range and by its absence of final glottal constriction. It is interesting to note that when the same particle is pronounced with what Mary Haas calls the 'emphatic high tone',[23] as in the sentence [^lɛːu ʔa¯rai _ʔiːk ^naː] 'Now let me think, what else could there be?'[22] Chuenkongchoo records his own pronunciation as 'high level for most of its duration followed by a slight fall'.[22] For the lexical high tone, on the other hand, as in [^naː] 'aunt' in the sentence [^lɛːu ʔa¯rai _ʔiːk ^naː] 'And then what happened, Auntie?', he only uses the high-level variant, never the rise-fall.[24] Chuenkongchoo also recognizes for particles short rising, falling, and mid pitches which are without counterpart in the lexical tone system.

In my earlier article it was pointed out that particles admitted of stressed short open syllables without final glottal closure, a combination not found in other classes of word and one which cannot be indicated by Siamese orthography, which always implies that a short vowel without a following consonant will be followed by a glottal stop.[25] Particles with a short vowel may, in suitable social contexts, be pronounced with a final glottal stop, but are far more frequently pronounced without it, or with slight final aspiration. This latter pronunciation is particularly common in women. The final glottal stop appears to carry some implication of sharpness or incivility which is in most circumstances regarded as inappropriate to the speech of women. The transcription in my earlier article of a glottal stop after such a particle as [kha], which is a polite particle used only by women, is quite wrong therefore, and must be attributed to the fact that the examples quoted were pronounced for me by a male speaker who would never use this form himself and who was in consequence giving me a spelling pronunciation with a final glottal stop, as implied in the orthographic text he was reading from. All the female speakers I have since met have pronounced the short form of this particle and of many others, such as [si], [rɯ], and [ca], with a final breathy off-glide, and those I have asked have declared themselves unable to think of any circumstances in which they would use a pronunciation with a final glottal stop. Certain particles, such as [lɛ] and [thɤ], are found in contexts where both men and women may properly use a final glottal stop. Much useful work, preferably by native speakers of the language, remains to be done in this field.

## STRESS AND RHYTHM

Studies of Siamese phonetics hitherto have paid scant attention to the theoretical and practical phonetic problems raised by the running pronunciation of longer stretches of speech, though this is a problem which faces any teacher who has brought his pupils to the point of dealing passably with even very short utterances. It is obvious to any who care to listen to Siamese conversation that, despite the monosyllabic basis often asserted for the language, Siamese utterances are not composed of a sequence of more or less equally stressed and evenly spaced syllables, each pronounced with the tonal contour proper to its pronunciation in isolation. Variations of stress, pitch, and rhythm all play their part in the synthesis of sentences and are susceptible of systematic analysis and description, difficult though this may be. A stride in the right direction has been made by Sanit Thawisomboon in his study of rhythm and stress groups.[26] It still remains, however, for his findings, and the further extensions of which they are capable, to be integrated into a competent grammatical analysis of the spoken language. It is quite clear that many of the rhythmic groupings he describes, together with concomitant features of pitch and duration, are closely linked to grammatical structure.

*Notes*

[1] See *Linguistic Survey of India*, I, 2, 11.

[2] See Henry Sweet, preface to *A Handbook of Phonetics*, 1877.

[3] Already noted by Bradley, 'Graphic Analysis of the Tone Accents of the Siamese Language', *J. Amer. orient. Soc.*, No. 44, 1924, and by Daniel Jones in the passage already cited in the *Linguistic Survey of India*.

[4] See Bradley, op. cit., and *L.S.I.*, I, 2, 11.

[5] One such speaker is Terd Chuenkongchoo, who emphatically rejects the rise-fall analysis of this tone for his own pronunciation, which he describes as 'high level'. See his unpublished London M.A. thesis, *The Prosodic Characteristics of Certain Particles in Spoken Thai*, presented in 1956.

[6] See J.C. Catford, 'Consonants Pronounced with Closed Glottis', *Le Maître Phonétique*, No. 87, 1947; and 'On the Classification of Stop Consonants', *Le Maître Phonétique*, No. 65, 1939.

[7] For a pronunciation in which unaspirated plosives were invariably glottalized, it would of course be possible to argue with equal force that aspiration is not 'distinctive'.

[8] Eugénie J.A. Henderson, 'Prosodies in Siamese: a Study in Synthesis', *Asia maj.*, New Series I, Pt 2, 1949.

[9] See Li Fang-Kuei, 'The Hypothesis of a Pre-glottalized Series of Consonants in Primitive Tai', *Bulletin of the Institute of History and Philology, Academia Sinica*, 11, 1943; and A.G. Haudricourt, 'Les consonnes préglottalisées en Indochine', *Bulletin de la Société de Linguistique de Paris*, 46, 1950.

[10] See Henderson, 'Prosodies of Siamese', 190–191.

[11] See *The Phonology of the Syllable in Songkhla, a Southern Thai Dialect*, unpublished thesis, London M.A. degree, 1959.

[12] This revised phonetic analysis calls for a corresponding revision of the phonological statement in 'Prosodies in Siamese', particularly as regards [j]. See pp. 191, 193.

[13] See the articles by Li and Haudricourt already cited.

[14] See Li Fang-Kuei, 'Initials and Tones in the Sui Language', *Language*, 24, 1948, 161.

[15] See Chantavibulya, *Phonology*, 13.

[16] I have so far seen no description elsewhere of these variations in breath-force, which have a certain practical, if not much theoretical, importance. In his article 'Siamese Phonemes: a Restatement', *Bulletin of the Institute of History and Philology, Academia Sinica*, XXIX, 1959, George L. Trager, however, refers to an unpublished American master's thesis, *Suprasegmental Phonemes of Thai (Bangkok Dialect)*, Georgetown, 1956, to which I have unfortunately not yet had access, in which five degrees of 'loudness' are distinguished, 'the two terminal types, and three ranges of pitch-register with three accompanying loudness-volumes'. It seems probable that

the phenomena dealt with include those mentioned in this paper. In another American work *The Vowels and Tones of Standard Thai: Acoustical Measurements and Experiments*, Bloomington, 1962, by Arthur S. Abramson, the author refers to 'changes in the course of intensity with the falling and rising tones' as an aid to recognition, and urges that 'an acoustic analysis of phonetic features concomitant with the tones is needed for a better tonal perception, especially in regard to the whispering of expressions that are distinguished by tones in normal speech'. He reports that investigations he has undertaken have 'already shown that in whispered Thai, where there is no vocal cord vibration to produce a varying fundamental frequency, tones can be distinguished by features other than pitch, though there is considerable and non-uniform reduction in the distinctions'.

[17] See Henderson, 'Prosodies', 205–211.

[18] As is the case in other classes of word. See Henderson, 'Prosodies', 206.

[19] See Chuenkongchoo, *Prosodic Characteristics*, already cited.

[20] Chuenkongchoo, *Prosodic Characteristics*, 23–25.

[21] Ibid., 23–24. See also Mary Haas, 'Techniques of Intensifying in Thai', *Word*, 2, 1946.

[22] Chuenkongchoo, *Prosodic Characteristics*, 24.

[23] See Haas, 'Techniques'.

[24] Cf. footnote 5, and Chuenkongchoo, *Prosodic Characteristics*, 24.

[25] Henderson, 'Prosodies', 206, footnote 39.

[26] In his unpublished thesis, *Syllable Junctions within Stress Groups in Spoken Thai*, submitted for the London M.A. degree in 1956.

# Stress Trains in Auca

KENNETH L. PIKE

I am delighted to have the opportunity, by this article, to pay tribute to the world's elder statesman of phonetics, Professor Daniel Jones. Early in my reading I learned a great deal from his publications, both from his original contributions and, through him, from the line of earlier British and continental phoneticians to whom we all are, often unknowingly, indebted.

Here I would like to share with him some data gathered in the Auca[1] language of Ecuador, as a result of the application of some of my recent theoretical studies in high-level phonological units.[2] The crucial datum concerns a train of alternating stresses, starting from the beginning of a word, which clashes with a different wave train keyed into a mora count beginning from the last suffixual syllable. Junctures and complex vowel nuclei combine with grammatical composition of the word to affect the final result. Yet the merging pattern is predictable if all these elements are known. The data are presented, therefore, in the form of morphophonemic rules for stress placement.

RULE 1A: A wave train starts from the end of words, with final suffixual syllable unstressed, alternating backwards to penultimate stress, antepenultimate nonstress, pro-antepenultimate stress, until the stem or fourth syllable is reached. Thus the regular patterns are Cá.Ca; Cá.CáCa; Cá.CaCáCa; Cá.CáCaCáCa. In the formulas the symbol C represents any consonant or consonant cluster; the letter a, any vowel (or vowel sequence joined by ligature). The lowered dot indicates the end of the stem, both in formulas and in illustrations.

Note the following words each of which begins with the single-syllable stem /go/ and is followed by one, two, three, and four syllables, respectively.

/gó.bo/ 'I go' (/go/ 'go', /bo ~ mo/ 'I')
/gó.bópa/ 'I go' (/pa ~ mpaːmba/ 'declarative')

/gó.tabópa/ 'I went' (/ta ~ ntaːnda/ 'near-past tense')
/gó.támõnápa/ 'We two went' (/mõ/ 'first person plural', /da ~ na/ 'dual')

RULE 1B: In a chain of five suffix syllables, the stress pattern is Cá.CáCaCaCáCa.

/gó.kǽdõmõnáĩmba/ 'We two would have gone' (/kæ ~ ŋæ/ 'near-future tense', /dõ ~ nõ/ 'contingent past tense', /ĩ/ 'is')

RULE 1C: Enclitics added to the suffix train do not affect the mora count for stress placement. Compare Cá.CaCáCa and Cá.CaCáCa-Caa. The hyphen symbolizes the beginning of the enclitic.

/pố.ŋãndápa/ 'He came' (/põ/ 'come', /kã ~ ŋã/ 'third person singular'.)
/pố.ŋãndápa-dia/ 'He came – what do you think of that!' (/dia ~ niaːndia/ 'What do you think of that!')

The enclitics themselves may be unstressed, or stressed.

/ấ.ŋĩmo-to/ 'I will not say!' (/ã/ 'say', /kĩ ~ ŋi/ 'future tense', /-to/ 'disgust')
/gó.bo-táye/ 'I go!' (/táye ~ ntáye/ 'emphasis')

Note in the following illustrations that the noun is followed by that enclitic which was used with a verb in the preceding illustration:

/nẽ́mõ-táye/ 'Star!' (with the noun used as a personal name, and the enclitic added as emphatic call for attention)

RULE 2: A second wave train starts from the beginning of the word – whether noun, verb, or attributive. When the stem is made up wholly of a single root, or of a sequence of roots without derivative suffixes, this stem train begins stressed and produces an alternating stress-nonstress syllable sequence (with a few special restrictions). Thus the regular patterns are Cá.Ca, CáCaCá.Ca, etc.

/wǽ̃.ŋa/ 'He dies' (/wæ̃/ 'die')
/kíwẽɲố.ŋa/ 'where he lives' (/kíwẽ/ 'live', /yõ ~ ɲõ/ 'when, where')
/pǽdæpố̃nõ.ɲấmba/ 'He handed it over' (/pæ/ 'extend', /dæ ~ næ/ 'away from', /põ/ 'hand over', /dõ ~ nõ/ 'direction toward')
/kốõ/ 'kapok'
/bádã/ 'mother' (/dã ~ nã/ 'feminine with respect')
/bódæpóka/ 'ant-hill' (/bódæ/ 'ant', /po ~ mbo/ 'ground', /ka ~ ŋkaːŋga/ 'fastened')

Before passing to the next rule we raise the question: *What happens when the two wave trains meet at the junction of stem and suffix?* Here is the most fascinating part of the entire study. Four separate types of phenomena are observed: (a) A special set of morphophonemic rules for stress comes into play. (b) A set of juncture phonemes and rules for their occurrence become relevant. (c) Intonational relations occur across the two halves of the total phonological unit – the phonemic phrase. (d) Special rules for sequences of vowels in relation to syllable nuclei and to alternating stresses must be set up. We consider these in turn.

RULE 3A: If the two wave trains are 'in phase' – i.e., if the stem train ends with a stressed syllable and the suffix train begins with an unstressed syllable, or vice versa – then no interference with either train is observed. Illustrations of this rule are given above, in formulas such as CáCaCá.Ca and CáCaCáCa.CáCa. Note also CáCa.CáCa:

/kǽga.kã́mba/ 'His tooth hurts' (/kæ/ 'hurt', /ga ~ ŋa/ 'tooth')

RULE 3B: If the two wave trains are 'out of phase', special rules must be given. When the regular rules would cause the final syllable of the stem to be stressed, and the regular rules of the suffix train would cause the first suffix to be stressed, both stresses are retained. Note the formulas Cá.CáCa, CáCaCá.CáCa, and CáCaCáCaCá.CáCa.

/á.kã́mba/ 'He sees' (/a/ 'see')
/yíwǣ́mṍ.ŋã́mba/ 'He carves, He writes' (/yi/ 'cut', /wǣ/ 'down', /mõ/ 'state of')
/tíkawódṍnó.kã́mba/ 'He lights' (/tí/ 'touch lightly', /ka ~ ŋga/ 'fasten', /wo/ 'float, blow')

RULE 3C: When the regular stress rules would cause the final syllable of the stem to be unstressed and the regular rules of the suffix train would cause the first suffix to be unstressed, the final root of the stem becomes stressed as in the formulas *CáCa.Ca > CáCá.Ca, *CáCa.CaCáCa > CáCá.CaCáCa, and *CáCaCáCa.Ca > CáCaCáCá.Ca.

/wódṍ.ŋã/ 'She hangs up' (/wo/ 'float, blow')
/ẽ́ɲá.kãndápa/ 'He was born' (/ẽɲa/ 'to give birth, to be born')
/gã́nææ̃́mǣ́.ŋã/ 'He raised up his arms' (/gã/ 'roll', /ræ ~ næ/ 'away from', /ǣ/ 'raise', /mǣ/ 'arm')

Note that these various rules lead to phonemic contrast between stress patterns resulting from CáCaCá.CáCa vs. CáCá.CaCáCa, since the second syllable (a) is stressed if stem final but (b) unstressed if stem medial; and the third syllable is (a) stressed if it is stem final but (b) unstressed if it comprises the first of three suffixual syllables.

/ápǣné.kãndápa/ 'He speaks' (/apǣ/ 'speak', /re ~ ne/ 'mouth)'
/dádő.ŋãndápa/ 'He fished' (/da/ 'fish')

On the other hand, no stress contrasts develop between three-syllable words which have, respectively, two-syllable and one-syllable stems, since in each case the first two syllables of the words would be stressed by the regular rules: i.e., CáCá.Ca and Cá.CáCa.

/tǣ́nő.mi/ 'You spear' (/tǣ́/ 'spear', /bi ~ mi/ 'second person singular')
/bé.kĩ́mo/ 'I will drink' (/be/ 'drink', /bo ~ mo/ 'first person singular')

RULE 3D: In one special instance in which the stem is made up of three monosyllabic roots plus three following stem-formative syllables, the stem formatives are all unstressed, and very rapid.

/yǽrakǽgĩnewa.kãndápa/ 'He licked' (/yæ/ 'to stick out', /gĩnewa ~ ŋĩnewa/ 'tongue', /kæ ~ ŋæ/ 'verbalizer')

Elsewhere, these – and other – stem formatives appear to follow the regular rules for root syllables and lead to no further contrastive patterns.

/kǽgĩnéwá.kã/ 'His tongue hurts' (/kæ/ 'hurt')

In Rule 4 we discuss juncture placement. Two juncture phonemes must be postulated for these rules. The first we call 'primary juncture'. It comes at the end of phonemic phrases, which in turn are co-terminous either with grammatical words or with grammatical words plus accompanying enclitics. Secondary juncture we shall symbolize with a lowered grave accent between syllables – i.e., as CaˎCa. It comes medially within phonemic phrases.

RULE 4A: Primary juncture occurs after phonemic phrases. It is phonetically marked by one or more subtle but audible cues. A phonemic phrase containing a single syllable usually has a decrescendo during that syllable, and often falling pitch. In other instances, slight differences of timing or pseudo-pauses (extra-weak but continued articulation of a sound) force the grouping of an unstressed syllable with a stressed one before or after it in the phonemic phrase to which it belongs. When two or more stresses occur within one phonemic phrase the last is often freely – not necessarily – weakened. (I have treated this as an allophone of the primary stress phoneme, weakened by its conditioning position in the phrase.)

In addition, intonation cues are relevant here (see Rule 5).

Note primary juncture in the following phrases, symbolized by space:

CáCáCaCáCa: /wĩ́ pṍnẽmópa/ 'I do not believe it' (/wĩ/ 'negative', /põ/ 'come', /rẽ ~ nẽ/ 'causative')

CáCa CáCaCáCa: /bíwi tókãndápa/ 'younger brother laughed' (/bíwi/ 'younger brother', /to/ 'laugh')

CáCa áCáCa: /ɲówo ẽ́ɲíŋa/ 'Now she understands' (/ɲówo/ 'now', /eɲi/ 'hear, understand')

RULE 4B: Secondary juncture occurs at the end of the stem following two stem stresses before suffixual nonstress.

CáCá.⸜CaCáCa: /ówó.⸜kãndápa/ 'He stayed at home (in his hammock)' (/o/ 'stay', /wo/ 'float')

RULE 4C: Secondary juncture follows an unstressed suffix syllable which is next to the stem, when stem is totally composed of one stressed syllable:

Cá.Ca⸜CáCa: /mṍ.ŋã⸜ndápa/ 'He slept' (/mõ/ 'sleep')

RULE 4D: Secondary juncture occurs at the end of the stem, following stem nonstress, before suffixual stress.

CáCa.⸜CáCa: /gówæ̃.⸜ŋæ̃́mba/ 'He fell down'

RULE 4E: Secondary juncture follows the second of three syllables of a stem which precedes a stressed suffixual syllable:

CáCa⸜Cá.CáCa: /épo⸜káe. bópa/ 'I swim' (/e/ 'grab', /po ~ mpo: mbo/ 'hand')

RULE 4F: Secondary juncture follows the second and fourth syllables, nonstressed, of the stem before a stressed suffixual syllable:

CáCa⸜CáCa.⸜CáCa: /tówæ⸜rã́nõ.⸜ŋæ̃́mba/ 'He spit' (/to/ 'straight', /wæ tã/ '?')

RULE 4G: In a chain of five suffix syllables, the secondary juncture occurs after the second suffixual syllable:

Cá.CáCa\CaCáCa: /kǽ̃.ŋǽ dõ\monmá͜ĩmba/ 'We would have eaten' (/kæ̃/ 'eat')

RULE 5: The total phonemic phrase (i.e., the macrosegment including the sum of units between primary juncture, whether or not secondary junctures also occur) in unemotional speech has an overall intonation contour. This pattern has variants, of which the most frequent has high pitch on stressed syllables, with stressed syllables of the suffix train cascading a bit lower in a contour 'fade'. Occasional variants – especially in fast speech – have unstressed syllables on the same pitch level as the stressed ones.

More thorough study of pitch patterns in a variety of communicational and emotional contexts needs to be made, however, before the outlines of the intonational system are clarified, and contrastive pitch and quality contours identified.

RULE 6A: Within the stem, sequences of two like or of two diverse vowels act as sequences of two syllable nuclei in the mora count which affects the placement of stresses. An analog of CáCá.CaCáCa, with vowel sequences:

/ṍõ.ŋãndápa/ 'He went blow-gunning' (/ṍõ/ 'hunt with blow-gun')
An analog of CáCaCá.CaCáCa: /wóṍõ.ŋãndápa/ 'He blew his blow gun'

RULE 6B: Within the suffix train, however, sequences of diverse vowels act in the mora count as single-syllable nuclei – and morphologically-expected sequences of like vowels fuse to single ones. This rule heightens the contrast between the stem and the suffixual component of the phonemic phrase. Note:

Cá.$Ca_1a_2$ (tied) and Cá.$CaCa_1á_2Ca$ (tied): /á.bo͜i/ (/a/ 'I see', /i/ subjunctive), /wáe.kĩmo͜ĩ́mba/ 'I will cry' (/wæ/ 'cry')
*Cá.$Ca_1a_1$ > Cá.Ca: /ǽ̃.mi/ 'Take!' (/æ̃/ 'take', /bi ~ mi/ 'second person singular', /i/ 'subjunctive').

*Notes*

[1] Norman McQuown, in 'Indigenous Languages of Latin America', *American Anthropologist*, LVII, 1955, 501–570, lists Auca as equivalent to Sabela (p. 517); unclassified as to language family (pp. 512–513); and as extinct (pp. 513, 537). One

group of fifty-some speakers survives in the Upper Curaray River area, and one known somewhat larger group and a few scattered individuals, a total of two hundred or more, farther east. Gunter Tessman in *Die Indianer Nordost-Perus* lists items closely related to our Auca data under title of Ssabela.

Our informants, Dayuma, Kǽmõ ('Kimo') and his wife Dǽ̃wã with Mĩ́ŋkáyc ('Minkayi') and his wife Õmpódǽ̃ ('Ompora') have recently received world-wide attention. For biographical detail see Ethel Wallis, *The Dayuma Story*, New York, 1960.

The phonemic data were largely gathered by Rachel Saint of the Summer Institute of Linguistics. She is a sister of the late Nate Saint of the Missionary Aviation Fellowship, who was involved in the recent history of the tribe. The stress data were worked out in collaboration with her. Phonetic sequences written here as mb, mp, nd, etc., may prove to be better analysed as unit phonemes, with the homorganic nasal component as conditioned by the presence of a preceding nasal vowel.

[2] K. Pike, *Language in Relation to a Unified Theory of the Structure of Human Behavior*, II, Chapters 8 and 9, 1955, and III, 1960, Chapters 13 and 15.

# Nasal Consonants in Land Dayak (Bukar-Sadong)

N.C.SCOTT

The following notes are based on observation of the speech of Mr Andrew Salip, aged 21, whose home is in the village of Taii [tɐʔiː] in the First Division of Sarawak. He describes his speech as being of the Bukar-Sadong dialect of Land Dayak, and it will be here referred to as Buk.Sad.

The phonetic transcription is designed to give, in terms of the alphabet of the International Phonetic Association, sufficient information about the pronunciation of the words under discussion for the particular purposes of this article. The style is, in general, 'broad' (though a fuller analysis may suggest changes), but narrower renderings are used when they can be useful. Where a spelling is given for a Buk.Sad. word, it is the one used by Mr Salip. For ease of reference, the spelling of Sea Dayak words is that used for the first entry in my *Dictionary of Sea Dayak*[1]; the 'systematic spelling' following the first entry will sometimes give a less ambiguous indication of the pronunciation.

In initial and medial position in the typical disyllables, as well as in longer words, are to be found examples of simple nasal consonants, bilabial [m], alveolar [n], palatalized alveolar [ɲ], and velar [ŋ], e.g. [malu] 'strike (*vb.*)', [umɔ] 'water'; [nabur] 'sow (seed)', [ɐnak][2] 'child'; [ɲipïh] 'snake', [ɐɲap] 'nothing'; [ŋumit] 'take', [siŋau] 'cat'. As in Malay and Sea Dayak, the nasality tends to persist through the word until it is checked. In the words quoted above, the vowel following a nasal consonant has nasal quality; thus, in narrower transcription, [mãlu, umɔ̃].

In medial position frequently, and in initial position more rarely, there are found complexes consisting of a nasal consonant with a following homorganic voiceless plosive or affricate, e.g. [sampɛː] 'extending to' (cf. Malay *sampai*), [inceh][3] 'is', [suntɔk] 'in need of' (cf. S.D. *suntok*), [suŋkoi] 'cooked rice'; [mpahit] 'send', [ntakadn] 'taste'. In such cases, the plosive serves to check the nasality, and, as in similar cases in Malay and Sea Dayak, the following vowel is non-nasal.

Malay and Sea Dayak show examples of complexes of a nasal consonant with a following voiced homorganic plosive in initial and medial position, e.g. Mal. *ĕmbun*, S.D. *embun*, 'dew'; Mal., S.D., *gambar* 'picture'. Here too nasality is checked by the plosive. In Sea Dayak, the plosive element is often very weak or even absent, but the absence of nasality in the following vowel indicates that what precedes is not to be regarded as a simple nasal. Thus the words *nanga* 'straighten' and *nangga* 'set up a ladder' may be distinguished by the fact that the former, [naŋɑ̃ʔ], has, and the latter, [naŋɑʔ], has not, a fully nasal vowel in the last syllable. In Buk.Sad., complexes of nasal and homorganic voiced plosive are not heard in initial and medial position, but it is necessary to distinguish the occurrence of a simple nasal from other cases involving a nasal consonant, and the spellings given for [ramiː] 'festivity', *rami* (cf. S.D. *rami*, Mal. *ramai*), and for [gɐmiː] 'gambier', *gambi* (cf. Mal., S.D., *gambir*), are justifiable in this respect. The phonetic features involved need further investigation. They include persistence of nasality in the case of the simple nasal, and the influence of this on the treatment of final nasals will be referred to below.

As in Malay and Sea Dayak, bilabial, alveolar, and velar nasals [m, n, ŋ] may occur in word-final position in Buk.Sad., but in Buk.Sad. they occur sometimes simple and sometimes preceded by a weak homorganic stop; thus, on the one hand, [kiɲam] 'feeling', [pimain] 'a game' (cf. Mal., S.D., *main*), [pɐniŋ] 'dizzy' (cf. Mal. *pĕning*); and, on the other, [pɐlabm] 'mango' (cf. S.D. *empelam*), [kaidn] 'cloth' (cf. Mal., S.D., *kain*), [padagŋ] 'field' (cf. Mal., S.D., *padang*). The stop may be gentle, and, in the case of velars, articulated far back, so that in the last word quoted above the impression may be of [padaʁŋ]. Though the effect is in general one of voiced stops, voicing may in fact be absent, especially after long vowels.

Dunselman notes of the language of the Kendayan Dayaks: 'Slot medeklinkers *ng*, *m*, en *n*, worden meestal veranderd in *kng*, *pm*, en *tn*, wat echter een te grove weergave is.'[4] In Buk.Sad., the presence in final position of a simple nasal as against a nasal preceded by a stop depends on the nasality of the syllable as a whole. In general, the final syllable is nasal if a simple nasal consonant appears in medial position in the disyllable (in the final disyllable in longer words) or in initial position in the comparatively rare monosyllable, but there are words mentioned below in which nasality initiated in the penultimate syllable persists in the final syllable. If the last syllable of a word is nasal, any nasal consonant in final position will be simple; if nasality is checked in the vowel of the last syllable, any final nasal consonant will be preceded by the homorganic lenis stop. Thus in [tanĩn] 'story, tale', the nasality initiated in medial position persists through the whole of the second syllable, while in [mĩsĩdn] 'invite' the nasality of the initial syllable is checked by the fricative [s] and nasality is restricted to the end of the final syllable by the stop [d], as it is in the related form [pĩsĩdn], in which there is no nasality until the end. Examples of monosyllables are the particles [nan], with simple final nasal, and [padn], with stopped final nasal.

It was mentioned above that the plosive element in the complexes [mp, nt, nc, ŋk] checks nasality, and if a word with one of these in medial position has a final nasal, this last will be preceded by the homorganic plosive as in [pantudn] 'song'.

It was also mentioned above that there were words in which what was heard as a medial nasal consonant could not be regarded as simple since there was checking of the nasality that would otherwise persist. These often correspond to Malay or Sea Dayak words containing the complexes [mb, nd], etc. Thus in [ɐmudn] 'dew', corresponding to Mal. *ĕmbun*, S.D. *embun*, the nasality started in the [m] is checked, and consequently the final [n] is preceded by [d]. Other examples are [mɐnabm] 'sickness' (cf. Mal. *mandam*, 'dizzy, intoxicated'), [ɐnaːgŋ] 'prawn' (cf. S.D. *undang*), [banugŋ] 'tapioca', [girunugŋ] 'a small bell' (*girundung* against S.D. *gerunong*). With these are to be contrasted such examples as [tɐŋan] 'arm' (cf. Mal. *tangan*), [pɐniŋ] 'dizzy' (cf. Mal. *pĕning*), [iɲam] 'feeling', [rɐmin] 'house', in which there is a simple medial nasal and nasality persists. The presence of a stopped final nasal in a word that has a medial nasal consonant always indicates that this medial nasal is not simple.

Kymograms for such a word as *suntok* [suntɔk] show wave-forms between the sections for the stops on the mouth tracings, but none in the corresponding part of the nasal tracing. The word *damŭ* [damĩ] gives a kymogram in which wave-forms on the mouth and nose tracings end simultaneously, but the kymograph for *lambŭ* [lamĩ] shows the wave-forms on the nose tracing dying out before those on the mouth tracing. For a word such as *andang* [ɐnaːgŋ], in which the vowel of the final syllable is long, the mouth tracing similarly shows wave-forms persisting after those on the nasal tracing have died out before the section corresponding to the stop (after which a new set of wave forms appears for the final nasal consonant). Kymograms for words with short vowel in the final syllable, such as *kanang* [kɐnaŋ] 'posterior' and *kandang* [kɐnagŋ]

'Straits robin', may show little difference in the sections corresponding to this vowel, the stop before the final nasal in *kandang* sufficing to mark the syllable as non-nasal.

Prosodic glottal stop, as a junction feature, does not check nasality. Consequently, such words as [mɐʔan] 'eat' and [muʔun] 'go first' have nasality in both syllables and a simple nasal consonant in final position (cf. [pɐʔadn] 'feed' and [puʔudn] 'foot of a tree'). As a result of this tendency, closely related forms may differ in the treatment of the final nasal. Thus [tïʔïdn] 'place (*imp.*)' has a corresponding 'nasal form' [nïʔïn] in which the glottal stop does not check the initial nasality, and the final nasal consonant is therefore simple. The form with the infix [-in-] also has a simple final nasal, [tinïʔïn], since nasality is initiated by the [n] of the infix and is not checked. The forms [tuʔaːdn, nuʔaːn] 'open' similarly illustrate the principle.

Intervocalic [h], [j], and [w] do not in all cases check nasality. Thus we find [nïhïn] 'place (*n.*)', [simïhïŋ] 'ten', [nahan] connected with [tahadn] 'bear, endure', [pimaʲin] 'a game'; [ɲiʲum] connected with [siʲubm] 'kiss'; [ŋajun, najun[5]] connected with [ajudn] 'swing'; [nuʷaŋ] connected with [tuʷagŋ] 'pour'.

The number of words with intervocalic [h, j, w] is not large. Apart from [nuʷaŋ], no relevant example of intervocalic [w] has so far come to light,[6] but there are some words with intervocalic [h] and [j] in which nasality initiated in the first syllable is checked in the second, so that a stopped nasal appears in final position. They are: [ŋïhïbm] alongside [kïhïbm] 'capsize'; [nɐhadn] alongside [dahadn] 'move'[7]; [pinajɔgŋ] 'put an umbrella over' alongside [pajɔgŋ] 'umbrella'; [nɐjïbm] 'keep silent about' alongside [dajïbm] 'secret'; [najadn] 'make a bridge' alongside [tajadn] 'bridge'. It seems likely, therefore, that a distinction must be made between the prosodic and phonematic (consonantal) occurrences of [h] and [j] in medial position.

Borrowed words are treated like native words in respect of final nasal consonants. Thus Mal. *gandum*, from the Persian, appears as [gɐnubm] 'corn, wheat'. [bilɔdn] 'aircraft' is from the English *balloon*, [ŋubɔbm] from *bomb*, [siligŋ] 'catapult', from *sling*, and, with a simple final nasal as would be expected in view of the nasality of the last syllable, [sɐmin] from *cement*.

*Notes*

1 London, 1956.

2 Stops are exploded in final position.

3 [c] represents a post-alveolar affricate.

[4] P. Donatus Dunselman, 'Bijdrage tot de kennis van de taal en adat der Kendajan Dajaks van West Borneo', *Bijdr. Taal-, Land-, Volkenk. Ned.-Ind.*, 105, 1949, 61.

[5] Prefixed [n] takes the place of the infix [-in] when the base begins with a vowel.

[6] The expected stopped nasal appears in [kuʷadn] 'what he says'.

[7] There are, in the language, a number of instances of [ɐ] appearing in the first syllable of 'nasal' forms (and certain others) as against [a] in the 'base' (used e.g. as an imperative): [mɐcal, pinɐcal, – pacal] 'squeeze'; [nɐbĭk, bitɐbĭk, – tabĭk] 'pierce'. Compare with these [nahan, tahadn] 'bear', and [malas, balas] 'reply'.

# Observations on the Transliteration of Arabic Names into the Roman Alphabet

W.F.STIRLING

Ever since the Tower of Babel men have sought to understand one another's languages and the different alphabets which different peoples use when they write down their own particular speech. Arabs, Armenians, Greeks, Russians, Hindus, Chinese, all have their own alphabets, and these represent a small proportion of the total number; but the alphabet which is used for the transliteration of the speech-sounds of most languages is the Roman, since most of the languages of Europe and the languages of the Americas and Africa (if we except primitive written languages no longer in use) are expressed in Roman characters.[1] Consequently, to enable Romanic readers to understand the place-names and family names of people whose alphabet is Cyrillic, Hellenic, or Arabic (*et cetera*) it is necessary to transliterate these alphabets into the Roman. The reverse process is, of course, equally necessary since the average Arab reader (for example) is not necessarily conversant with the Roman alphabet. To state the problem more simply, how is the average English newspaper reader to interpret the word بغداد (printed in Arabic characters) if it appears in the date-line of a news item? And how can the average Iraqi newspaper reader be expected to recognize the equally outlandish word 'London', if it is printed in his newspaper in Roman letters?

Transliteration is not only desirable but essential if there is to be mutual understanding among nations to-day. Transliteration, however, does not mean the accurate representation of the speech-sounds of one language in the letters of the alphabet used by another language. This would, indeed, be impossible, and it has been left to phoneticians to devise a special alphabet suited to their own particular needs, a highly complicated alphabet which has a symbol for every one of the speech-sounds of nearly all languages known to-day.

Transliteration means the rendering into letters familiar to the reader of words which, being written in another alphabet, would otherwise be completely unintelligible. If an Arab business man receives a card with the words 'William Jones' printed on it he may not be able to greet his visitor courteously by name; but if the card bears the words وليم جونز, this defect is easily remedied. True, this Arabic transliteration is open to criticism; but it serves to remind the reader of the owner's name. Similarly a London banker may look blankly at the name محمد فضل, but he will certainly understand the words Mohámmed Fádhil, and be able to give an approximate pronunciation of the names. For transliteration can never be more than an approximation; and if it succeeds in this it has succeeded completely.

Many attempts have been made to romanize the Arabic alphabet, the most important attempt being that of the Spaniards who, as a result of the dominion of the Caliphate of Córdoba (which lasted for more than seven centuries), absorbed a vast quantity of Arabic words into Spanish. The great Arabic scholars and poets of Spain[2] wrote first in Arabic and, later, in Spanish – without taking into account the Mozárabes and the Mudéjares.

Since Spanish is the most phonetic of those languages which use the Roman alphabet[3] it was probably the best equipped for the transliteration of Arabic; but it lacked sounds in itself and could not therefore supply a Roman transliteration suitable to the needs of any of the great Western European languages: Italian, French, German, or English.

Probably it is the efforts of English, French, and Italian transliterators which have principally contributed to the unhappy confusion which exists to-day. The name نجيب, for instance, is variously transliterated as *Nejib*, *Nadjib*, *Neguib*, *Nedjib*, *Negib*, and so on. Now every man has the right to spell his name in his own way; but if it is a question of a student entering a School of Foreign Languages it is more likely that he will, for the first time, be obliged to write his name in such a way as to be intelligible to teachers who can only read the Roman alphabet. Why, therefore, should one student write his name *Nuri*, while his friends (similarly named) write it *Noori*, *Noury*, *Nury*, or *Noory* – when they all mean نوري? And when to one name we add two or three others, confusion is worse confounded.

What is necessary is a Roman alphabet which shall give reasonable representation to the Arabic alphabet, and yet be intelligible to all who use only one version of the Roman. To produce such an alphabet it is necessary first to summarize the Arabic speech-sounds and then to take into account Arabic word-stress.

CONSONANTS. Classical Arabic contains twenty-eight consonantal letters, two of which (و and ى) are also used in the writing of vowel-sounds, while a third (ا) can be used as a support for the glottal stop, as a vowel-sound, or as a soundless symbol. Colloquial Arabic, however, rarely reproduces faithfully all the classical consonants. In the case of normal Iraqi Arabic the spoken language (unless spoken with exceptional care) ignores the use of the glottal stop (أ) and of the voiced pharyngal fricative (ع) on many occasions: (ظ) is usually indistinguishable from (ض); and (ق) is sometimes pronounced as a voiceless uvular plosive, sometimes as a voiced velar plosive, and sometimes – strangely enough – as a voiced palatal affricate.

To these complications must be added the fact that the reader who is not familiar with Arabic will not be able, at first hearing, to distinguish between normal dental or alveolar consonants and retroflex alveolar consonants (i.e. between ت and ط, د, and ض, س and ص, ز and ظ); between the voiceless pharyngal (ح) and the voiceless glottal (ه); or between (ق) and (ك). As for the (ع) it may well escape him altogether unless it occurs intervocalically, in which case he will very probably confuse it with the glottal stop.

It is interesting to note also that a few new symbols have been introduced into the Arabic alphabet (although they are not in general use) to denote certain non-Arabic sounds: پ *p* as in English *peep*, چ *ch* as in English *church*, ڤ *v* as in English *verve*.

Bearing in mind the foregoing considerations and the exigencies of any system of transliteration the suggestions embodied in Table 1 are put forward for the Roman transliteration of the Arabic consonants as they are used in normal speech in Iraq.[4]

## TABLE OF CONSONANTS

(i) The classification given in the table refers to Spoken Arabic, not Classical Arabic. (ii) It is recommended that representation of the glottal stop be omitted unless it occurs intervocalically; even so it is popularly pronounced as a semivowel or a vowel-glide: Má'eda (مائدة) being pronounced Máyeda or Máeda. (iii) (ع) should not be transliterated unless it occurs intervocalically or finally. (iv) The feminine ending (ة) should not be transliterated if it occurs in the absolute final position; if, however, it is immediately followed by the definite article it must be transliterated *t*. (v) The assimilation of the definite article should be indicated: failure to do so would invite the mispronunciation *el-Shám* (الشام) instead of *esh-Shám*. (vi). Double consonants should always be indicated in the transliteration. Italians, to name but one

TABLE 1

| CLASSIFICATION | ORTHO-GRAPHY | TRANSLI-TERATION | COMMENTS |
|---|---|---|---|
| Plosive, Bilabial | ب | B, b | |
| Plosive, Dental | ط، ت | T, t | |
| Plosive, Dental | د | D, d | |
| Plosive, Velar | ك | K, k | |
| Plosive, Uvular | ق | Q, q[1] | |
| Plosive, Glottal | أ | , | Restricted use |
| Nasal, Bilabial | م | M, m | |
| Nasal, Alveolar | ن | N, n | |
| Lateral, Alveolar | ل | L, l | Variable in the case of أل |
| Rolled, Alveolar | ر | R, r | |
| Fricative, Labiodental | ف | F, f | |
| Fricative, Interdental | ث | Th, th | |
| Fricative, Interdental | ظ، ض، ذ | Dh, dh | |
| Fricative, Alveolar | ص، س | S, s | |
| Fricative, Alveolar | ز | Z, z | |
| Fricative, Palatal | ش | Sh, sh | |
| Fricative, Velar | خ | Kh, kh | |
| Fricative, Velar | غ | Gh, gh | |

TABLE 1—*continued*

| CLASSIFICATION | ORTHO-GRAPHY | TRANSLI-TERATION | COMMENTS |
|---|---|---|---|
| Fricative, Pharyngal | ع | ʻ | Restricted use |
| Fricative, Glottal | ح ،ه | H, h | |
| Affricate, Palatal | ج | J, j[2] | |
| Semivowel, Bilabial, and Velar | و | W, w | Consonantal only |
| Semivowel, Palatal | ي | Y, y | Consonantal only |

[1] This will probably be mispronounced by the Romanic reader as (ك). Others, however, with better ears, may wonder if the distinction is not transliterated.

[2] For the fricative pronunciation of (ج) *Zh, zh,* is recommended. In Egyptian and other dialects (ج) is pronounced [g] (voiced velar plosive).

group of users of the Roman alphabet, use them constantly, and will reproduce them accordingly.

VOWEL-SOUNDS. It is well known that Classical Arabic was based on the three vowel-sounds [i], [a], and [u], represented in the Arabic alphabet by the use of كسرة, فتحة, and ضمة, respectively, and that these three could be lengthened by adding ى, ا, and و, to corresponding short vowels. Two diphthongs were made by adding either و or ى to فتحة. As with all living languages, however, this restricted vowel-system soon developed, and there are now, in colloquial Iraqi, thirteen distinct vowels and at least nine diphthongs – although there appear to be only ten vowel phonemes (as opposed to the classical 3+3). The modern variants may be summed up for transliteration purposes in accordance with Table 2.

TABLE OF VOWELS

(i) All vowel-sounds in Arabic are affected by neighbouring consonants, particularly those noted in the preceding table. Especially subject to this is the

TABLE 2

| ORTHO-GRAPHY | APPROXIMATE MODERN PRONUNCIATION | TRANS-LITERATION | COMMENTS |
|---|---|---|---|
| كسرة | 1. Front, close, short<br>2. Front, half-close, short, retracted<br>3. Central, ultrashort | i<br><br>i<br>i | |
| كسرة + ى | 4. Front, close, long | í (stressed)<br>î (unstressed) | |
| فتحة | 5. Front, between half-close and half-open, short<br>6. Front, open, short<br>7. Back, open, short<br>3. (As above) | e<br>a<br>o | Subject to variation according to adjacent consonants |
| فتحة + ا | 8. Back, open, short | á (stressed)<br>â (unstressed) | ,, |
| ضمة | 9. Back, close, short<br>10. Back, half-close, short, advanced<br>11. Back, close, short<br>3. (As above) | o<br><br>u<br>u<br>o | ,, |
| ضمة + و | 12. Back, close, long | ú (stressed)<br>û (unstressed) | |
| فتحة + ى | 6 + 1, or 5 | ai, é, or ê | ,, |
| فتحة + و | 6 + 10, or 11 | au, ó, or ô | ,, |

(The numbers indicated in this table do not refer to the numbers properly given to the Arabic vowel-sounds by phoneticians. They are given purely for guidance in transliteration.)

vowel [a] which basically has a sound approximating to that of the letter *a* in the French word *chat*; when it is preceded or followed by a retroflex consonant, or by a uvular or pharyngal consonant it more closely resembles the sound of the letter *o* in the English word *dog*; and when followed by other consonants it tends towards an [e]-sound. (ii) The diphthong *ai* is affected in the same way after retroflex, pharyngal, or uvular consonants.

STRESS. Arabic, like English and German, is a strongly stressed language, but since there is no means readily intelligible to the Romanic reader of understanding which syllable is to be stressed it is important to mark this in any Roman transliteration of Arabic. For this purpose we must return to the system employed by the first transliterators of Arabic, to Spaniards, and note the stressed syllable with an acute accent.

There remain two important problems: (i) is عبد to be treated as a separate word or not; and (ii) should the definite article be merged with the following proper name. With regard to the first problem it is suggested that the word be separated if we are to avoid confusion in the mind of the reader; and with regard to the second problem I suggest that the article should be separated from the following name by a hyphen – this would make it easier for the Romanic reader both to speak the name and to understand something of its meaning. But we have already noted that every man has the right to spell his own name in his own way, and the transliteration of Arabic names depends ultimately on the owner of the name. It is hoped that the present observations may contribute towards a unification of such transliterated names.

## TWENTY SPECIMEN NAMES[5]

| | |
|---|---|
| Ásya Ábd ul-Láh | آسيا عبد الله |
| Amín Yásîn | أمين ياسين |
| Hasíba Mohámmed Dâúd | حسيبة محمد داود |
| Sihám Ábd el-Jabbár | سهام عبد الجبار |
| Semírat er-Rafaqánî | سميرة الرفقانى |
| Mahmúd Yúsef | محمود يوسف |
| Rasmía Hosén el Káti‘ | رسمية حسين الكاطع |
| Kámil Hádî | كامل هادى |
| Rafí‘a Ábd ul-Láh | رفيعة عبد الله |

| | |
|---|---|
| Faríha Fáuzî | فريحة فوزى |
| Ábd al-Hosén Mohámmed Álî | عبد الحسين محمد على |
| Betúl el-Háshimi | بتول الهاشمى |
| Burhán Néjm ed-Dín | برهان نجم الدين |
| Khálid Sáleh Táha | خالد صالح طه |
| Nádhif Mohámmed Álî | ناظف محمد على |
| Mohámmed el-Abúsî | محمد العبوسى |
| Fádhil el-Háj Wahāb | فاضل الحاج وهاب |
| Ráfida Ismâ'íl esh-Sheblí | رافدة اسماعيل الشبلى |
| Mejíd Áhmed | مجيد أحمد |
| Kháulat el-Háj Ábd er-Rahmán | خولة الحاج عبد الرحمن |

*Notes*

[1] In the present observations the term 'Roman Alphabet' includes all the letters of the original alphabet, together with certain extra letters (e.g. consonantal *j*), digraphs (e.g. *th*), and diacritic letters (e.g. *é*). The twenty specimen names are based on Colloquial Iraqi.

H.E. Palmer, in his *Principles of Romanization with Special Reference to the Romanization of Japanese*, Maruzen, Tokyo, 1931, includes also symbols adapted from Greek, Old English, etc., and other symbols more properly used in phonetic notation only. To use so many symbols would defeat the simplified transliteration which is the object of these observations. It would be far simpler for the Roman reader to learn the Arabic alphabet.

[2] For a full list of these cf. Hurtado y Palencia, *Historia de la Literatura Española*, Madrid, 1932. These poets and scholars though born in Spain were Arabs and carefully fostered their language; only later were their works translated and the authors' names transliterated. *Abenhabib*, *El Becrí*, *Said de Bagdad y Arramadi*, are typical of early romanized transliterations.

[3] Though by no means perfect. The use of the letter *h*, apart from many vowels and consonantal variants precludes this. Cf. *The Pronunciation of Spanish*, by the present writer, Cambridge, 1935.

[4] Other symbols would have to be introduced, and some of the consonantal symbols interchanged, for a more approximate transliteration of Arabic as it is spoken in Saudi Arabia, Syria, Lebanon, Egypt, Pakistan, and Morocco (to name the most outstanding variants). Even in Iraqi colloquial (ق) is pronounced as a voiced velar plosive [g] – but never so pronounced in names.

[5] Since all the names given are those of living people I trust that any person so-called will forgive the liberty I have taken of using his (or her) name for the purposes of scientific investigation.

# Kalenjin Phonetics

A.N.TUCKER

The Kalenjin languages are spoken by two groups of non-Bantu speakers in the Rift Valley Province in Kenya, East Africa:

(1) the Nandi Group, comprising Nandi, Kipsigis, Keyo ('Elgeyo'), Tugen ('Kamasia'), Kony ('Elgon'), Sabiny ('Sabei'), and others, covering the area: Nandi District, Kericho District, Elgeyo District, Marakwet District, Baringo District, and the slopes of Mount Elgon, and numbering 200,000–300,000 speakers;

(2) Päkot ('Suk'), spoken in two pockets – 'East Suk' in Baringo District, and 'West Suk' in West Suk District, with an overflow into Karamoja District, Uganda – by some 60,000 speakers.

There is a third group of related languages, known as Tatog, Tatoga, Barabaig – 64,000 speakers – in Mbulu District of North Tanganyika. Since, however, information on these languages is very scanty, only slight reference can be made to them.

The name 'Kalenjin'[1] was first coined locally to indicate members of the Nandi, Kipsigis, and neighbouring tribes. In linguistic circles it has been expanded to cover the three language groups.

The languages chosen here as representative are Nandi (with occasional reference to Kipsigis[2]) and Western Päkot. The material presented has been obtained in London from Messrs M.J.Seroney and A.Arap Ng'eny (Nandi), T.Arap Towett and C.Ng'elechei (Kipsigis), and E.P.Kassachon (Western Päkot) – supplemented by copious notes taken on various field expeditions.

Owing to the exigencies of space, examples will be drawn predominantly from the verbal system of these languages.[3]

The system of notation used is that of the International African Institute, supplemented by symbols from the alphabet of the International Phonetic Association.[4]

## THE CONSONANT SYSTEM

1. Here it is convenient to begin with Päkot, as the Nandi system appears in this aspect to be 'younger'.

PÄKOT

| | Bilabial | Dental | Alveolar | Palatal | Velar | Glottal |
|---|---|---|---|---|---|---|
| Explosive | p | t | | c | k | ʔ |
| Implosive | | | ɗ | | | |
| Fricative | | | s | | ɣ | |
| Nasal | m | | n | ny | ŋ | |
| Liquid | | | l, r | | | |
| Semi-vowel | w | | | y | | |

NANDI

| | Bilabial | Dental | Alveolar | Palatal | Velar | Glottal |
|---|---|---|---|---|---|---|
| Explosive | p<br>[b or ʋ] | t | [d] | c<br>[j] | k<br>[g or ɣ] | |
| Fricative | | | s | | | |
| Nasal | m | | n | ny | ŋ | |
| Liquid | | | l, r | | | |
| Semi-vowel | w | | | y | | |

2. /t/ is dental;

/c/ is a pure palatal except when final in a word, when it tends towards [tʃ]. Final /c/ in a Stem is often interchangeable with /k/, especially in Päkot.

kὲ˺lá:c or kὲ˺lá:k to wear clothes
là:câ or là:kâ Imperative

/ny/ is also a pure palatal.[5] In Päkot final /ny/ in a Stem is often interchangeable with /ŋ/.

kè˺lú:ny or kè˺lú:ŋ 'to attack'
lù:nyâ or lù:ŋâ Imperative

Note that there are many word Stems ending in /-k/ and /-ŋ/ where the sound is not interchangeable with /-c/ and /-ny/. Also, that in Nandi-Kipsigis, interchange in these categories is not so common as in Päkot. But note:

KIPSIGIS

kì˺rwɔ̂ɔ:c 'to counsel' kírwɔ̂ɔ:k 'counsel', *v.n.*

NANDI

kɛ̂ˑwáːc 'to shout' kèˑwɔ̀ːksɔ̀ 'to shout together'
ŋɛ̂ˑny, pl. ŋɛ̀ˑnyîn or ŋéˑŋwɔ́ 'salt-lick'

/p, t, c/ and /k/ occur initially, medially, and finally in Päkot; /p/ and /k/ occur only initially and finally in Nandi-Kipsigis. See § 5 below.

/r/ is strongly trilled and is often devoiced in initial position.

/w/ and /y/ may occur initially, medially, or finally, or after a consonant – but see diphthongs, § 18. They appear to be doubled in some words in Nandi-Kipsigis:

NANDI

| | | | |
|---|---|---|---|
| máyyɔ̂ | or máíyɔ̂ | (Primary form) | 'beer' |
| máyyɛ̂ˑk | or máíyɛ̂ˑk | (Secondary form) | |
| kéyyɔ́ | Pl. kéyyô | (Primary form) | 'Keyo' |
| kéyyɔ̀ˑt | Pl. kéyyêˑk | (Secondary form) | |

KIPSIGIS

| | | | |
|---|---|---|---|
| máyywá | or máíyúá | (Primary form) | 'beer' |
| máyywɛ̂ˑk | or máíyúɛ̀ˑk | (Secondary form) | |

*Grammatical Note*

3. All Nouns in these languages have a Primary (or Basic or 'Indefinite') form and a Secondary (or 'Definite') form with a Suffix.

In Päkot the Primary form corresponds roughly to the Noun with Indefinite Article in English, and the Secondary form to the Noun with Definite Article. The Primary form, however, is the one most commonly used.[6]

In Nandi-Kipsigis, on the other hand, the Secondary form of the Noun is the one most commonly used (corresponding to both 'a' and 'the' in English), while the Primary form only occurs in certain constructions or when the Noun is used in a very general sense.

4. The following phonemes are characteristic of Päkot only:

/ɗ/ is implosive and slightly retroflex. It occurs initially, medially, and finally.

kɛ̀ˑ-ɗɔ̀ŋɔ̀ 'to jump' kèˑ-kúːɗ 'to bend'
ɗàŋónyâ Imperative kùːdâ Imperative

/ɣ/ is a voiced velar fricative pronounced very softly. It often corresponds to /y/ in Nandi.

| PÄKOT | NANDI | |
|---|---|---|
| kɛ̀ˑ-ɛ́ɣ | kɛ̀ˑ-yáy or kɛ̀ˑ-yáí | 'to do' |
| kɛ̀ˑ-ɣáˀ or kɛ̀ˑ-ɣɛ̌ːɣ | kɛ̀ˑ-ɛ́ː | 'to drink water' |
| kɛ̀ˑ-ɣɔ̀ˀ or kɛˑ-ɣɔ́ːɣ | k-ìˑyɔ̀ | 'to cook' |
| kɔ́ɣ (Primary) | kɔ̀y or kɔ̀ì | 'stone' |
| mɔ́ːɣ (Primary) | mɔ̀ːy or mɔ́ːì | 'calf' |
| kîɣ (Primary) | kèy or kèì | 'thing' |
| ɛ̌ːɣ (Primary) | éy or éí | 'bullock' |

The implosive [ɗ] is also found occasionally as the result of the combination /ɣ/ + /t/.

| PÄKOT | NANDI | |
|---|---|---|
| mɔ̀ːɣtâ or mɔ̀ːɗâ (Secondary) | mɔ́ˑytà or mɔ́ˑítà | 'calf' |
| èːɣtä̌ˀ or èːɗä̌ˀ (Secondary) | èytꜵ̀ or èìtꜵ̀ | 'bullock' |

/ˀ/ (the glottal stop) occurs finally in certain Päkot words, when spoken in isolation or at the end of a breath group. It is closely associated with certain tone patterns. Thus:

| | With final glottal stop | | Without final glottal stop | |
|---|---|---|---|---|
| | Long syllable | Short syllable | Long syllable | Short syllable |
| High tone | Frequent | Frequent | Frequent | Frequent |
| Mid tone | Frequent | Frequent | Less frequent | Less frequent |
| Low tone | Frequent | Frequent | Rare | Rare |
| Rising tone | Frequent | Rare | Never heard | Never heard |
| Falling tone | Never heard | Never heard | Frequent | Frequent |

Compare in PÄKOT:

si̋wìníˑˀ 'he sees (him)'

si̋wìníˑ !tyä̂ . . . !kwáˑɣâ . . . !kírwꜵ̂ːkǐːntéː[7]
(He) sees a girl . . . a he-goat . . . the chief

si̋wìníˑ !tyä̌ˀ . . . kwàˑɣǎˀ . . . kìrwꜵ̌ːkíːntèːˀ
A girl . . . a he-goat . . . the chief . . . sees (him)

Note also:

si̋wìníˑ wóˑräˀ . . . wôˑrëːˀ He sees a boy . . . the boy
si̋wìníˑ woˑräˀ . . . wòˑrèːˀ A boy . . . the boy . . . sees him

Within the chain of speech, however, the final glottal stop is mostly elided, though sometimes preserved before a word beginning with a vowel.

The glottal stop is virtually non-existent in Nandi-Kipsigis.

*Consonants in Medial Position*

5. In Päkot /p, t, c/ and /k/ may occur initially, medially, and finally in a word or phrase. In all the languages of the Nandi Group, however, only /t/ and /c/ may occur medially; /p/ and /k/, when occurring intervocally or after /r/, are realized as [b] (or [ʋ])[8] and [g] (or [ɣ]), respectively.

NANDI

| | | | | | | |
|---|---|---|---|---|---|---|
| pír | 'Beat!' | but | kὲ˙-bír | or | kὲ˙-ʋír | 'to beat' |
| rí:p | 'Guard!' | | ri:bé | or | ri:ʋé | 'he guards' |
| kέr | 'Shut!' | | kε˙-gέr | or | kὲ˙-ɣέr | 'to shut' |
| mwǽ:k | 'Shoot!' | | mwæ:gé | or | mwæ:ɣé | 'he shoots' |
| kʊ́rgε:t | | or | kʊ́rɣε:t | | | 'door' |
| ká:-gɔ-gὲr gʊ́rgε:t | | or | ká:-ɣɔ-ɣὲr ɣʊ́rɣέt | | | 'he shut the door' |

/k/ is preserved before /w/, however:

NANDI

kὲ˙-kwέl 'to argue' kὲ˙-kwέt 'to wrestle'
là˙kwà (Primary) là˙kwέ:t (Secondary) 'child'
cf. lǽ˙gó:y or lǽ˙ɣó:y lǽ˙gô:k or lǽ˙ɣô:k 'children'

/t/ and /c/ are not softened intervocally:

kὲ˙-tɔ́:r 'to stab' su:té 'he cleans the ground'
tὲ:tá (Secondary) 'cow'

Note, however, *ded* reported in Tatog for 'cow'.

cɔ́:r 'Steal!' kὲ˙-cɔ́:r 'to steal'
wέc 'Hate!' wéce 'he hates'

6. (a) Again, in the languages of the Nandi Group (but not in Päkot), when /p, t, c, k/ follow /l/ or a nasal, they are realized as voiced explosives [b] (never [ʋ]), [d,[9] j,[10] g] (never [ɣ]), respectively. At the same time there is a tendency for some nasal sounds to be assimilated in tongue position.

NANDI

| | |
|---|---|
| pʊ́mbôn | 'soft', reduplication of pʊn |
| kε˙-la:ndá | 'to climb away' (Motion Away form of kὲ˙-lá:ny, 'to climb') |
| kε˙-tɪldá | 'to cut away' (Motion Away form of kὲ˙-tíl, 'to cut') |
| ke˙-ce:njí[10] | 'to seek for' (Dative form of kὲ˙-cέ:ŋ, 'to seek') |
| k-ì˙úŋgε̂: | 'to wash oneself' (Reflexive form of k-ì˙ún, 'to wash') |

Compare:

kɛ̀ˑwɛːktà 'to take back' (Motion Away form of kɛ̀ˑ-wɛ̀ːk, 'to return to')
k-ìˑsùpcì 'to follow for' (Dative form of k-ìˑsʊ̀p, 'to follow')
k-ìˑnɛ́ːtkɛ̂ː 'to teach oneself' (Reflexive form of k-ìˑnɛ̂ːt, 'to teach')

(b) Note also the behaviour of the Noun Formative Prefixes kɪp- (kip-), cɛˑp- (ceˑp-), and kaˑp- (kɔ̞ˑp-).[11]

NANDI (Primary forms only given)

Before unvoiced consonants

kìp-kʊ̀rgʊ̀ryà 'leg bell'
cɛ̀ˑp-swɛ́rɛ̀r 'small knife'
cèˑp-kòìgòc 'tortoise'
káˑp-kɪˑtâːny 'smithy' cf. k-ìˑtâːny, 'to forge'
kɔ́ˑp-tîc 'grazing place' cf. tîc, 'cattle'

and the place names

káˑp-sábìt 'Kapsabet' = 'place of quills'
kɔ́ˑp-túːmwɔ̂ 'Kaptumo' = 'place of circumcision'

Before vowels and /-l-/ or /-r-/.

kìb-íŋwàˑlèt or kìʊ-íŋwàˑlèt 'limping man' cf. k-ìˑŋwáːl, 'to limp'
kìp-kíràʊ̀ː or kì(b)-ràʊ̀ː 'tobacco pouch'
cɛ̀ˑb-laːŋga 'leopard'
kaˑb-arnɛ̂ːt or kaˑʊ-arnɛ̂ːt 'Kabarnet'

Elided before nasals and some other consonants

kì-máyyɔ̂ 'name of boy born during the brewing of beer'
cɛ̀ˑ-máyyɔ̂ 'name of girl born during the brewing of beer'
káˑ-máyyɔ̂ 'beer drinking place' cf. máyyɔ̂, 'beer'

7. In Päkot the first Prefix is realized as /p-/ only; there is no voicing, but elision is common.

PÄKOT

p-kòːkǎ̂c 'tortoise'
p-kʊ̀mɔ̂n 'name of boy born during the brewing of beer'
cèp-kʊ̀mɔ̂n 'name of girl born during the brewing of beer'
cèp-kɔ̀ːnã̂ˀ 'jackal'
kaːp-tı̂̊c 'place for cattle'

With elision

cɛ̀ː-sáːmpə́ʔ 'vulture' cf. sàːmpə̀ʔ, 'fur'
cɛ̀ˑ(p)-pə́rə̂m 'dove'
cèˑ-méˑryǽɔːn 'circumcized girl'
káˑ-ŋæ̀ɔːrsyä̀ʔ 'grinding place' cf. kèˑ-ŋæ̀ɔːrsyä̀ʔ, 'to grind'
káː-ꜜpǽɔryæ̂ɔːt 'battle field' cf. kèˑ-pæ̀ɔːryä̀ʔ, 'to fight'

8. In forthcoming sections of this article, for the sake of clarity and to avoid confusion in phoneme representation:

/b/ will stand for both [b] and [ʋ] in Nandi-Kipsigis;
/g/ will stand for both [g] and [ɣ] in Nandi-Kipsigis;
/ɣ/ will stand for the voiced velar fricative in Päkot alone.

## THE VOWEL SYSTEM

9. Vowels may be inherently long or short. See further under § 15.

### *Long Vowels*

10. Both language groups have a ten-vowel system of five Open and five Close vowels, which may be set out in categories as follows:

| Open category | Close category |
|---|---|
| ɪː | iː |
| ʊː | uː |
| ɛː | eː |
| ɔː | oː |
| aː | æɔː (ɑː) |

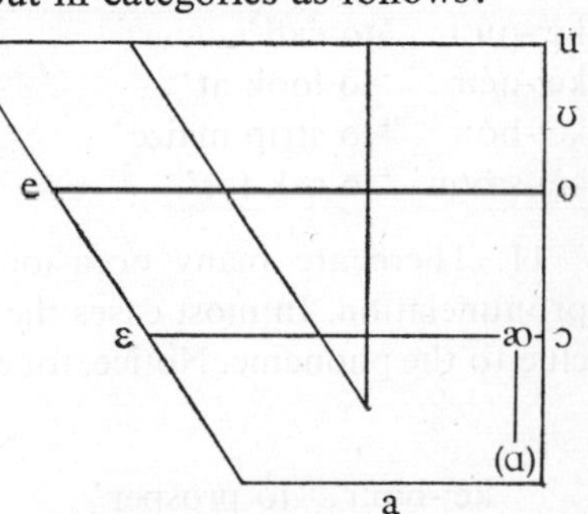


Open vowels

ɪː, ʊː, ɛː, ɔː } has a value approximating that of S. English { 'kick' (but long), 'pull' (but long), 'bed' (closer than Cardinal 3), 'law' (Cardinal 6)

aː has a value mid-way between Cardinal 4 [a] and Cardinal 5 [ɑ]

Close vowels

iː, uː, eː, oː } has a value approaching Cardinal { 1, 8, 2, 7

These four vowels are pronounced with some degree of hollowness in the voice, in contradistinction with the Open vowels, where the voice is 'hard'.[12]

/æɔː/ varies in value between Cardinal 5 [ɑ] when unstressed,[13] and Cardinal 6 [ɔ] when stressed. It has no accompanying hollowness of voice, nor any acoustic claim to be regarded as a 'Close' vowel. From its place in the sound-change patterns of the language, however, it belongs to the Close Vowel Category.

Examples of long vowels:

| NANDI and KIPSIGIS | | PÄKOT | |
|---|---|---|---|
| Open category | | | |
| kɛ̀ˑ-wíːr | 'to hit with stone' | kɛ̀ˑ-wǐːr | 'to hit with thrown stick' |
| kɛ̀ˑ-gʊ́ːt | 'to blow' | kɛ̀ˑ-kʊ̌ːt | 'to blow' |
| kɛ̀ˑ-ŋɛ́ːt | 'to get up' | kɛ̀ˑ-ŋɛ̌ːt | 'to get up' |
| kɛ̀ˑ-ɔ́ːn | 'to drive off' | kɛ̀ˑ-yɔ̌ːn | 'to drive off' |
| kɛ̀ˑ-láːny | 'to climb' | kɛ̀ˑ-lǎːny | 'to climb' |
| Close category | | | |
| kèˑ-ríːp | 'to guard' | kèˑ-rǐːp | 'to guard' |
| kèˑ-gúːr | 'to call' | kèˑ-kǔːr | 'to call' |
| kèˑ-géːr | 'to look at' | kèˑ-kěːr | 'to aim at' |
| kèˑ-bóːr | 'to strip maize' | kèˑ-pǒːr | 'to level' |
| kèˑ-sǽɔ́ːm | 'to ask for' | kèˑ-sæ̌ɔ̌ːm | 'to ask for' |

11. There are many occasions when /æɔː/ and /ɔː/ have identical pronunciation. In most cases the value of surrounding vowels gives the clue to the phoneme. Notice, for examples the Infinitive Prefix vowel in:

NANDI

kèˑ-bǽɔ́ːr 'to prosper'
and kɛ̀ˑ-sɔ́ːr 'to bring'

PÄKOT

| | | | | |
|---|---|---|---|---|
| | kèˑ-sæ̌ɔ̌ːm | 'to ask' | kèˑ-pæ̌ɔ̌ːt | 'to get lost' |
| and | kɛ̀ˑ-sɔ̌ːn | 'to cut meat' | kɛ̀ˑ-pɔ̌ːt | 'to peel' |

and the Secondary Suffix vowel in:

NANDI

| | | | |
|---|---|---|---|
| | mæ̂ɔ̂ː (Pri.) | mǽɔ́ː-êːt (Sec.) | 'belly' |
| and | mɔ̀ː(ì) (Pri.) | mɔ̀ː-ɛ́ːt (Sec.) | 'wound' |
| | sæ̀ɔ̀ː (Pri.) | sæ̀ɔ̀ː-éːt (Sec.) | 'buffalo' |
| and | sɔ̂ː (Pri.) | sɔ́ː-ɛ̂ːt (Sec.) | 'distant grazing ground' |

In some cases, however, it is impossible to guess which phoneme is involved.

*Short Vowels*

12. In the Nandi Group the same ten vowels may occur short. The short vowels of Päkot, however, are very peculiar and include three central vowels.

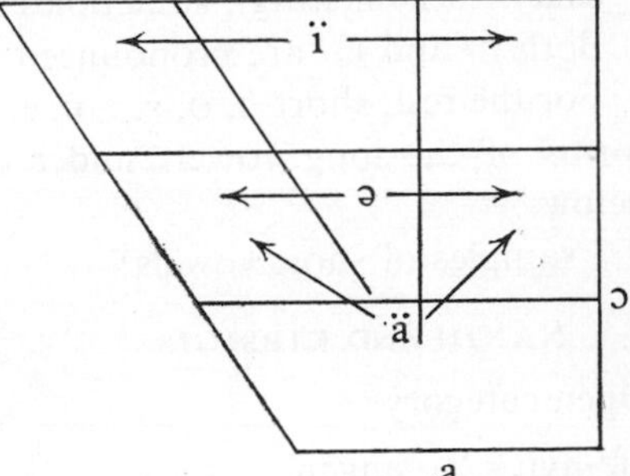


PÄKOT

| Open category | Close category |
|---|---|
| ə | ï |
| ɔ | |
| a | ä |

Open vowels

/ə/ is the most central of the vowels, and is pronounced with hard voice. In conjunction with some consonants, it has a value tending towards [ʊ], in other contexts towards [ɪ].

kɛ̀ˑ-səwáˀ, 'to see', often sounds like [kɛ̀ˑsʊwáˀ],
kɛ̀ˑ-ŋwə́n, 'to come', often sounds like [kɛ̀ˑŋʊ́n],
kɛ̀ˑ-yàːkwə̀ˀ, 'to herd', has as imperative form yaːkwə́yâ, which sounds sometimes like [yaːkʊ́yâ], sometimes like [yaːkwíyâ],

cf. kɛ̀ˑ-cə́ˀ, with imperative form cəɣá.

In the 'Motion towards' verbs, however, the final short vowel tends perhaps more towards [ʊ] than [ə].

kɛ̀ːtʊ̀ˀ, 'arrive here', from kɛ̆ːt, 'arrive'.

/ɔ/ and /a/ are as in Nandi.

*Close Vowels*

/ï/ has a value similar to that of Russian 'ы', but may also vary according to its phonetic context.

sǐwìˑníˑˀ, 'he sees', often sounds like [súwìˑníˑˀ],
kɛ̀ˑ-tǐw, 'to crush', often sounds like [kɛ̀ˑ-túː],
kɛ̀ˑ-sǐc, 'to get', often sounds like [kɛ̀ˑ-síc].

In kɛ̀ˑ-lǐˀ, 'to drink milk', and kɛ̀ˑ-yǐˀ, 'to bear', where the final vowel seems to lie somewhere between Russian 'ы' and back unrounded [ɯ], the respective imperative forms often sound like [luwä] and [yiyä].

In the 'Motion towards' verbs, however, the final short vowel tends more towards [u] and will be written so here.

kèˑ-síːkúˀ, 'to jump hither' (note imperative sìːkúː),
cf. kèˑ-síːkíˀ, 'to jump on' (note imperative sìːkiˑníː).

/ä/ has a value somewhere between those of Southern English 'but' and 'bird'. Occasionally it tends towards [o] or [e].

cä̆läy, 'it is melting', sometimes sounds like [cóläy] or [cóley].

Both /ï/ and /ä/ are pronounced with hollow voice.

For the rest, short /ɪ, ʊ, ɛ, i, u, e, o/ occur in Päkot only as shortened forms of the long vowels under conditions governed by stress. See below.

Examples of short vowels:

| NANDI AND KIPSIGIS | | PÄKOT | |
|---|---|---|---|
| Open category | | | |
| kɛ̀ˑ-nyít | 'to anger' | kɛ̀ˑ-nyə́t | 'to anger' |
| k-ɪ̀ˑbôt | 'to fall' | kɛ̆ˑ-pə́t | 'to fall', |
| kɛ̀ˑ-gɛ́r | 'to shut' | kɛ̀ˑ-kár | 'to shut' |
| kɛ̀ˑ-gɔ́r | 'to go blind' | kɛ̀ˑ-kɔ́r | 'to go blind' |
| kɛ̀ˑ-nám | 'to hold' | kɛ̀ˑ-nám | 'to seize' |
| Close category | | | |
| kèˑ-síc | 'to get' | kèˑ-sḯc | 'to find' |
| kèˑ-sút | 'to lift' | kèˑ-sḯt | 'to lift' |
| kèˑ-tép | 'to stay' | kèˑ-tä̆pä̆ˀ | 'to stay' |
| kèˑ-tór | 'to strip leaves off tree' | kèˑ-tä̆r | 'to chop' |
| kèˑ-sǽp | 'to be well' | kèˑ-sä̆p | 'to be alive' |

13. It will thus be seen that of the open short vowels:

/ə/ in Päkot corresponds to both /ɪ/ and /ʊ/ in Nandi
/a/ in Päkot corresponds to both /a/ and /ɛ/ in Nandi
/ɔ/ in Päkot corresponds to /ɔ/ in Nandi

and of the close short vowels:

/ï/ in Päkot corresponds to both /i/ and /u/ in Nandi
/ä/ in Päkot corresponds to /e, o/ and /æ/ in Nandi

14. Further examples of central vowels in Päkot:

| Open | | Close | | | |
|---|---|---|---|---|---|
| kɛ̀ˑ-sə́r | 'to bite' | kèˑ-sḯr | 'to avoid danger' | kèˑ-sä̆r | 'to help oneself' |

| | | | | | |
|---|---|---|---|---|---|
| kè˙-rɔ́s | 'to extinguish' | kè˙-rı̂s | 'to add to' | kè˙-rãs | 'to clear path' |
| kɛ̀˙-tɔ́c | 'to put foot on' | kè˙-tı̂c | 'to put on clay headdress' | kè˙-tãc | 'to notch' |
| kɛ̆˙-tɔ́c | 'to close land to cattle' | | | | |
| kɛ̀˙-tɔ́l | 'to jump over' | kè˙tı̂l | 'to grumble' | | |
| kɛ̆˙-tɔ́l | 'to begin to appear' | | | kɛ̆˙tãl | 'to explode' |

Compare KIPSIGIS[14]:

| | | | | | |
|---|---|---|---|---|---|
| kɛ̀˙-rɔ́s | 'to hit with force' | kè˙-túl | 'to be restless' | kè˙-saɔ̀r | 'to save' |
| | | | | kè˙-raɔ́s | 'to break fence' |

*Vowel Length*

15. Long vowels have already been illustrated in word stems. There are, however, many syllables in any chain of speech which must be regarded as half-long. Some of these appear to be inherently long syllables affected by shift in stress, e.g.

NANDI

kìmàgɛ̀ːt (Pri.)   kìmàgɛ̀˙tyɛ́t (Sec.)   'carnivore'

PÄKOT

ke˙-kaɔ́ːr 'to chat' ki˙kaɔ́ːrăt 'talking' ki˙kaɔ̀˙rı̆ːn 'a talker'

The assessment of vowel length in the above examples (and similar examples in the present treatise) must be regarded as purely empirical. Kalenjin informants are themselves unable to judge degrees of length.

16. Many other syllables (especially particles) never seem to be more than half-long, e.g. the Infinitive Prefixes, kɛ˙-, ke˙-, and k-ɪ˙-, k-i˙-, in the examples above.

The Tense Prefixes kɔː- (koː-) (yesterday) and kɪː- (kiː-) (time previous to yesterday) are long or half long, but ka- (kɑ-, kə-) (to-day) is always short; e.g.

| NANDI | PÄKOT | |
|---|---|---|
| kà-gɛ̀r | kà-kár | 'he shut it (this morning)' |
| kɔ̀ː-gɛ̀r | kà-kár | 'he shut it (yesterday)' |
| kìː-gɛ̀r | kɪ˙-kár | 'he shut it (long ago)' |

In the Perfect forms of these Tenses, the vowel length of the Prefixes (as well as the intonation) changes.

| | | |
|---|---|---|
| káˑ-gɔ-gɛ̀r | kâː-(kə̀-)kár | 'he has shut it (this morning)' |
| kɔ́ˑ-gɔ-gɛ̀r | kâː-(kə̀-)kár | 'he has shut it (yesterday)' |
| kíˑ-gɔ-gɛ̀r | kîː-(kə̀-)kár | 'he has shut it (long ago)' |

Owing to the frequent difficulty in distinguishing long from half-long vowels in these languages, length marks are preferred here to vowel doubling.

17. On the other hand, juxtaposition of two vowels may be acoustically indistinguishable from a single long vowel, and juxtaposition of several vowels can result in one vowel of indeterminate length, which is less, however, than the sum of all the morae of its constituent parts. The following examples show, in extreme form, the constituent parts of certain kinds of utterance, without, however, being able to indicate the real length of the resultant vowel.

NANDI

| | | | |
|---|---|---|---|
| kɛ̀ˑ-ăˑm | 'to eat' | kèˑ-óːt | 'to serve' |
| á-âˑm | 'that I eat' | òˑ-òːt | 'that you (pl.) serve' |
| ká-aˑ-aˑm | 'I ate (to-day)' | kòˑ-óˑ-òːt | 'you served (yesterday)' |
| kâˑ-aˑ-aˑm | 'I have eaten (to-day)' | kóˑ-oː-oːt | 'you have served (yesterday)' |
| ká-âˑm | 'he ate (to-day) | kó-ôːt | 'he served (yesterday)' |
| kɛ̀ˑ-ít | 'to arrive' | k-ìˑíːt | 'to count' |
| ì-ìt | 'that you (sg.) arrive' | ì-íːt | 'that you (sg.) count' |
| kìˑ-íˑ-ìt | 'you arrived' | kìˑ-íˑ-iːt | 'you counted' |
| kíˑ-ɪː-ɪt | 'you have arrived' | kíˑ-ìː-iːt | 'you have counted' |
| kíˑ-ɪt | 'he arrived (long ago)' | kíˑ-îːt | 'he counted (long ago)' |

PÄKOT

| | | | |
|---|---|---|---|
| kɛ̀ˑ-ăm | 'to eat' | kɛ̀ˑ-íɣ | 'to do' |
| á-àm-àn | 'then I ate' | í-ìɣ-nyìː | 'then you did' |
| kà-à-àm-àn | 'I ate' | kìˑ-ì-ìɣ-nyìː | 'you did' |
| káˑ-à-àm-àn | 'I have eaten' | kíˑ-í-ìɣ-nyìː | 'you have done' |
| kà-ám | 'he ate' | kɪˑ-íɣ | 'he did' |
| kâː-ăm | 'he has eaten (to-day or yesterday)' | kîː-íɣ | 'he has done (long ago)' |

### *Diphthongs*

18. Diphthongs are of two types:

(1) ending in /-i/ or /-u/ (/-y/ and /-w/ in Päkot);
(2) beginning in /i-/ or /u-/ or /w-/ (/y-/ and /w-/ in Päkot).

For examples see text, also § 2.

### *Tone*

19. The following tone marks are employed:

á = High Tone
à = Low Tone (about a minor third below High Tone)
a (unmarked) = Mid Tone
â = Falling Tone
ǎ = Rising Tone (Low to High when initial or after a High Tone, Low to Mid before a Mid Tone, Mid to High otherwise);

! before a High Tone syllable indicates 'downstep', i.e. that this syllable and all subsequent syllables are to be pronounced in a 'key' about a semi-tone lower. See § 4.

Tone is important both lexically and grammatically, but cannot be discussed in detail here.

### *Vowel Category Harmony*

20. There are many Affixes whose vowels are conditioned by the category of the vowel of the Stem to which they are attached. These Affixes are called 'weak' Affixes.

### *Weak Prefixes*

21. (a) The Infinitive Prefixes kɛ- (before open Stem vowel) and ke- (before close Stem vowel) have already been illustrated in §§ 12–14 above. The verbs given there are all Class I Verbs.

(b) Class II Verbs have a Stem Prefix ɪ- (open) and i- (close), and an Infinitive Prefix k-ɪ- (open) and k-i- (close) in the Nandi group.

NANDI

| Open vowel category | | Close vowel category | |
|---|---|---|---|
| k-ɪ̀ˑnyɪ̂ːt | 'to fill' | k-ìˑnyît | 'to recognize' |
| k-ɪ̀ˑmɔ̂t | 'to lead' | k-ìˑmûːt | 'to surround' |
| k-ɪ̀ˑnɛ̂ːt | 'to teach' | k-ìˑbêːt | 'to get lost' |
| k-ɪ̀ˑyɔ̀ | 'to boil' | k-ìˑgôːr | 'to patch' |
| k-ɪ̀ˑtyâːc | 'to untie' | k-ìˑgaɔ̂ːr | 'to purge' |

In Päkot there is no such *i*-vowel in verb conjugation, but there is a tonal difference and a difference in some of the Personal Prefixes.[15]

(c) The Conjugational Prefixes for person[16] are likewise weak:

NANDI

Class I Verbs

| | Open Stem vowel | Close Stem vowel |
|---|---|---|
| | kɛ̀ˑ-gɔ́:t 'to blow' | kèˑ-gú:t 'to smooth a skin' |
| | 'and I blew it' | 'and I smoothed it' |
| S. 1 | à-gɔ̀:t | ɑ̀-gù:t or æ̀-gù:t |
| 2 | ì-gɔ̀:t | ì-gù:t |
| 3 | kɔ̀-gɔ̀:t | kò-gù:t |
| P. 1 | kɛ̀ˑ-gɔ̀:t | kèˑ-gù:t |
| 2 | ɔ̀ˑ-gɔ̀:t | òˑ-gù:t |
| 3 | kɔ̀-gɔ̀:t | kò-gù:t |

Class II Verbs

| | | |
|---|---|---|
| | k-ìˑlâ:l 'to light fire' | k-ìˑrwɑ̂ɔ:c 'to counsel' |
| | 'and I lit it' | 'and I counselled him' |
| S. 1 | à:-lâ:l | æ̀:-rwɑ̂ɔ:c |
| 2 | ì:-là:l | ì:-rwæ̀ɔ:c |
| 3 | kɔ̀ˑ-lâ:l | kòˑ-rwɑ̂ɔ:c |
| P. 1 | kì:-lâ:l | kì:rwɑ̂ɔ:c |
| 2 | ɔ̀:-là:l | ò:-rwæ̀ɔ:c |
| 3 | kɔ̀ˑ-lâ:l | kòˑ-rwɑ̂ɔ:c |

PÄKOT

Class I Verbs

| | Open Stem vowel | | Close Stem vowel | |
|---|---|---|---|---|
| | kɛ̀ˑ-már 'to look for' | | kèˑ-mǎ̈r 'to bar the door' | |
| | 'if I looked for' | 'then I looked for' | 'if I barred the door' | 'then I barred the door' |
| S. 1 | à-màr-àn | á-màr-àn | ǟ-mǟr-àn | ǟ-mǟr-an |
| 2 | ì-màr-nyì: | í-màr-nyì: | ì-mǟr-nyì: | í-mǟr-nyì: |
| 3 | már | kə̀-mâr | mǟr | kɨ̀-mǟ̂r |
| P. 1 | kə̀-màr-cà: | kɛ́:-màr-cà: | kɨ̀-mǟr-cà | ké:-mǟr-cà: |
| 2 | à-màr-kwà: | á-màr-kwà: | ǟ-mǟr-kwà: | ǟ-mǟr-kwà: |
| 3 | már | kə̀-mâr | mǟr | kɨ̀-mǟ̂r |

Class II Verbs

| | Open Stem vowel | | Close Stem vowel | |
|---|---|---|---|---|
| | kɛˑ-lɛ́ːp 'to stalk' | | keˑ-téːp 'to make a hole' | |
| | 'if I stalked' | 'then I stalked' | 'if I made hole' | 'then I made hole' |
| S. 1 | á-lɛ̀ːp-àn | à-lɛ̀ːp-àn | ắ-tèːp-àn | ằ-tèːp-àn |
| 2 | í-lɛ̀ːp-nyìː | ì-lɛ̀ːp-nyìː | í-tèːp-nyìː | ì-tèːp-nyìː |
| 3 | lɛ̌ːp | kʊ̌ˑ-lɛ̀ːp | těːp | kǔˑ-tèːp |
| P. 1 | kíˑ-lɛ̀ːp-càː | kɛ̀ː-lɛ̀ːp-càː | kíˑ-tèːp-càː | kèː-tèːp-càː |
| 2 | á-lɛ̀ːp-kwàː | à-lɛ̀ːp-kwàː | ắ-tèːp-kwàː | ằ-tèːp-kwàː |
| 3 | lɛ̌ːp | kʊ̌ˑ-lɛ̀ːp | těːp | kǔˑ-tèːp |

Note in Päkot that the Personal Suffixes (except 2nd pers. sg.) are *neutral* – i.e. unaffected by the Stem vowel of the verb.

(d) The Tense Prefixes are likewise weak; they are:

NANDI

ka- (kæ-) 'today' kɔː- (koː-) 'yesterday'
kɪː- (kiː-) 'far past'

Open Stem vowel

| | Class I | Class II |
|---|---|---|
| | 'I blew it to-day' | 'I lit it to-day' |
| S. 1 | káː-gôːt | káː-làːl |
| 2 | kɛ́ː-gôːt | kɛ́ː-làːl |
| 3 | kà-gòːt | kɛ́ː-lâːl |
| | 'yesterday' | 'yesterday' |
| S. 1 | kɔ̀ˑ-á-gôːt | kɔˑ-áː-làːl |
| 2 | kɔ̀ˑ-í-gôːt | kɔˑ-í-ílàːl |
| 3 | kɔ̀ː-gòːt | kɔˑ-ílâːl |
| | 'long ago' | 'long ago' |
| S. 1 | kɪ̀ˑ-á-gôːt | kɪˑ-áː-làːl |
| 2 | kɪ̀ˑ-í-gôːt | kɪˑ-í-ílàːl |
| 3 | kɪ̀ː-gòːt | kɪˑ-ílâːl |

Close Stem vowel

| | Class I | Class II |
|---|---|---|
| | 'I smoothed it to-day' | 'I counselled him to-day' |
| S. 1 | kǽː-gûːt | kǽː-rwæ̀ːc |
| 2 | kéː-gûːt | kéː-rwæ̀ːc |
| 3 | kæ̀-gùːt | kéː-rwæ̂ːc |

| | 'yesterday' | 'yesterday' |
|---|---|---|
| S. 1 | kò˙-ǽ-gûːt | ko˙-ǽː-rwæ̀ːc |
| 2 | kò˙-í-gûːt | ko˙-í-írwæ̀ːc |
| 3 | kòː-gùːt | ko˙-írwæ̂ːc |
| | 'long ago' | 'long ago' |
| S. 1 | kì˙-ǽ-gûːt | ki˙-ǽː-rwæ̀ːc |
| 2 | kì˙-í-gûːt | ki˙-í-írwæ̀ːc |
| 3 | kìː-gùːt | ki˙-írwæ̂ːc |

Perfect forms (3rd pers.)

| Open Stem vowel | | Close Stem vowel | |
|---|---|---|---|
| Class I | Class II | Class I | Class II |
| 'to-day' | | 'to-day' | |
| káː-gɔ-gɔ̀ːt | káː-gɔ˙-lâːl | kǽː-go-gùːt | kǽː-go˙-rwæ̂ːc |
| 'yesterday' | | 'yesterday' | |
| kɔ́ː-gɔ-gɔ̀ːt | kɔ́ː-gɔ˙-lâːl | kóː-go-gùːt | kóː-go˙-rwæ̂ːc |
| 'long ago' | | 'long ago' | |
| kíː-gɔ-gɔ̀ːt | kíː-gɔ˙-lâːl | kíː-go-gùːt | kíː-go˙-rwæ̂ːc |

Concerning vowel junction, note that

Open Stem vowel

/ka + a/ = /kaː/ /ka + ɪ/ = /kɛː/

Close Stem vowel

/kæ + æ/ = /kæː/ /kæ + i/ = /keː/

PÄKOT

ka- (kä-) 'to-day and yesterday' kɪ˙- (ki˙-) 'long ago'

Open Stem vowel

| | Class I | Class II |
|---|---|---|
| | 'I looked for to-day/ yesterday' | 'I stalked to-day/yesterday' |
| S. 1 | kàː-màr-àn | kǎː-lɛ̀ːp-àn |
| 2 | kɛ̀ː-màr-nyì˙ | kɛ̌ː-lɛ̀ːp-nyì˙ |
| 3 | kà-már | kɛ̀ː-lɛ̌ːp |

| | | |
|---|---|---|
| | 'long ago' | 'long ago' |
| S. 1 | kyàː-màr-àn | kyǎː-lɛ̀ːp-àn |
| 2 | kìː-màr-nyìˑ | kɪ̌ː-lɛ̀ːp-nyìˑ |
| 3 | kɪˑ-már | kìː-lɛ̌ːp |

Close Stem vowel

| | Class I | Class II |
|---|---|---|
| | 'I barred door to-day/ yesterday' | 'I made hole to-day/yesterday' |
| S. 1 | kòː-mă̊r-àn | kǒː-tèːp-àn |
| 2 | kèː-mă̊r-nyìˑ | kěː-tèːp-nyìˑ |
| 3 | kă̊-mă̊r | kèː-těːp |
| | 'long ago' | 'long ago' |
| S. 1 | kyòː-mă̊r-àn | kyǒː-tèːp-àn |
| 2 | kìː-mă̊r-nyìˑ | kǐː-tèːp-nyìˑ |
| 3 | kiˑ-mă̊r | kìː-těːp |

Perfect forms (3rd pers.)

Open Stem vowel

| Class I | Class II |
|---|---|
| 'to-day/yesterday' | 'to-day/yesterday' |
| kâː-(kə̀-)már | kaː-kʊ̀ˑ-lɛ̌ːp |

Close Stem vowel

| Class I | Class II |
|---|---|
| 'to-day/yesterday' | 'to-day/yesterday' |
| kâː-(kì̊-)mă̊r | kaː-kùˑ-těːp |

Open Stem vowel

| Class I | Class II |
|---|---|
| 'long ago' | 'long ago' |
| kɪ̂ː-(kə̀-)már | kɪː-kʊ̀ˑ-lɛ̌ːp |

Close Stem vowel

| Class I | Class II |
|---|---|
| 'long ago' | 'long ago' |
| kîː-(kì̊-)mă̊r | kiː-kùˑ-těːp |

Note that /kaː/ is not affected in the Perfect, because apparently a particle intervenes. Of vowel junctions, note that:

Open Stem vowel

/ka + a/ = /kaː/ /kɪ˙ + a/ = /kyaː/
/ka + ɪ/ = /kɛː/ /kɪ˙ + ɪ/ = kɪː

Close Stem vowel

/kä + ä/ = /koː/ /ki˙ + ä/ = /kyoː/
/kä + i/ = /keː/ /ki˙ + i/ = /kiː/

(e) Certain Derivative Nouns from Class II Verbs[17] in all languages have a Prefix kɪ- (open) and ki- (close), though in Nandi ka- (open) and kɑ- or kɶ- (close) is usually preferred.

NANDI

| Open Stem vowel | Close Stem vowel |
|---|---|
| kà˙bàtɔ̀ (Pri.) } 'cultivation' | kí˙rwɶ̀˙k (Pri.) } 'counsel' |
| kà˙bàtɛ̂ːt (Sec.) | kí˙rwɶ˙gét (Sec.) |
| < k-ì˙bât 'to cultivate' | < k-ì˙rwɶ̂ːc 'to counsel' |
| | kɶ̀˙-ù˙nɶ̀ (Pri.) } 'washing' |
| | kɶ̀˙-ù˙nèt (Sec.) |
| | < k-ì˙ûn 'to wash' |

PÄKOT

| | |
|---|---|
| kí˙ɗɔ̀ŋɔ̂ (Pri.) } 'a type of dance' | kí˙rwɶ̀ːk (Pri.) } 'council meeting' |
| kí˙ɗɔ̀ŋɔ̂tâʔ (Sec.) | kí˙rwɶ̀˙kěːʔ (Sec.) |
| < kɛ̀˙-ɗɔ̀ŋɔ̀ʔ 'to jump' | < ke˙-rwɶ́ːc, ke˙-rwɶ́ːk 'to hold counsel' |
| kɪ˙tâːŋàt 'forging' | ki˙rwɶ̂ːkät 'act of ruling' |
| < kɛ˙-táːny 'to forge' | |
| kɪ˙táːnyan, kɪ˙táːŋan 'forged thing' | ki˙rwɶ́ːkän 'rule' |

(f) The three Noun Formative Prefixes, kɪp- (kip-), cɛ˙p- (ce˙p-), and ka˙p- (kɶ˙p-) are also weak. See the examples already set out in §§ 6 and 7.

Note that in Päkot the Prefix kaː(p)- is *neutral*, i.e. uninfluenced by the quality of the Stem vowel.[18]

*Weak Suffixes*

22. (a) Certain Derivative Verb Suffixes are weak. The following examples are from Class I Verbs. Class II Derivatives are similar.

KIPSIGIS[19]

| Open Stem vowel | | Close Stem Vowel | |
|---|---|---|---|
| Infinitive | Imperative | Infinitive | Imperative |
| kɛ̀·-tɛ́m | tɛ́m | kè·-mwɔ́:k | mwɔ́:k |
| 'dig, cultivate' | | 'shoot' | |
| kɛ̀·-tɛ̀mdà | tɛ̀mdɛ́·n | kè·-mwɔ̀:ktɔ̀ | mwɔ̀:kté·n |
| 'dig away from speaker' | | 'shoot away from speaker' | |
| kɛ̀·-tɛ̀mɛ́:n | tɛ̀mɛ́:n | kè·-mwɔ̀:gé:n | mwɔ̀:gé:n |
| 'dig with' | | 'shoot with' | |
| kɛ̀·-tɛ̀màk | tɛ̀mágɛ́·n | kè·-mwɔ̀:gɔ̀k | mwɔ̀:gɔ́gé |
| 'be diggable' | | 'be shootable' | |
| kɛ̀·-tɛ̀mà:n | tɛ̀mâ:nʊ́n | kè·-mwɔ̀:gɔ̀:n | mwɔ̀·gɔ̂:nún |
| 'come this way digging' | | 'come this way shooting' | |
| kɛ̀·-tɛ̀mà:t | tɛ̀mâ:tɛ́n | kè·-mwɔ̀:gɔ̀:t | mwɔ̀·gɔ̂:tén |
| 'go that way digging' | | 'go that way shooting' | |
| kɛ̀·-tɛ̀mà·nʊ̀nɛ́:n | tɛ̀má·nʊ́nɛ́:n | kè·-mwɔ̀·gɔ̀·-nùné:n | mwɔ̀·gɔ́·-núné:n |
| 'come this way digging with it', etc., etc. | | 'come this way shooting with it', etc., etc. | |

PÄKOT

| Open Stem vowel | | Close Stem vowel | |
|---|---|---|---|
| Infinitive | Imperative | Infinitive | Imperative |
| kɛ̀·-wɪ̌:s | wɪ·sá (Cl. I) | kè·-ɣǐ:m | ɣi·mã̂ (Cl. I) |
| 'leap' | | 'tilt' | |
| kɛ̀·-wɪ·sʊ̀ʔ | wɪ·sʊ:ná | kè·-ɣì·mùʔ | ɣi·mu:nã̂ |
| 'leap this way' | | 'tilt this way' | |
| kɛ̀·-wɪ̀·stàʔ | wɪ̀·stɛ̌:ná | kè·-ɣì·mtã̀ʔ | ɣì·mtě:nã̂ |
| 'leap away' | | 'tilt away' | |
| kɛ̀·-wɪ̀·sà:nʊ̀ʔ | wɪ̀·sǎ:nʊ·na | kè·-ɣì·mɔ̀:nùʔ | ɣì·mɔ̌:nú·nã̂ |
| 'come leaping' | | 'come tilting' | |
| kɛ̀·-wɪ̀·sà:tàʔ | wɪ̀·sǎ:tɛ·na | kè·-ɣì·mɔ̀:tã̀ʔ | ɣì·mɔ̌:té·nã̂ |
| 'go leaping' | | 'go tilting' | |
| kɛ̀·-wɪ·sáʔ | wɪ̀·sɛ̌:ná | kè·-ɣi·mã̂ʔ | ɣì·mě:nã̂ |
| 'leap by means of' | | 'tilt by means of' | |
| kɛ·-wɪ́:s | wɪ̀:sâ (Cl. II) | ke·-ɣí:m | ɣì:mã̂ (Cl. II) |
| 'cause to leap' | | 'cause to tilt' | |

(b) Certain Derivative Noun Suffixes are weak. The following examples are from Class I Verbs. (For examples from Class II Verbs see § 21e above.)

NANDI

| Open Stem Vowel | Close Stem vowel |
| --- | --- |
| kɛ̀ˑ-sáː 'to pray' | kèˑ-tyén 'to sing' |
| kɛ̀ˑ-cám 'to love' | kèˑ-géːr 'to see' |
| sàɔ̀ (Pri.) } 'prayer' | keˑrùˑteˑt (Sec.) 'a sight' |
| sàɛ̂ːt (Sec.) } 'prayer' | tyên (Pri.) } 'a song' |
| | tyéndæ̀ (Sec.) } 'a song' |
| cáman (Pri.) } 'favourite' | kéˑræn (Pri.) } 'something seen' |
| camanɛ́ːt (Sec.) } 'favourite' | keˑrænéːt (Sec.) } 'something seen' |

and the Participle:

| | |
| --- | --- |
| nyɪˑtáːt 'full' < kɛ̀ˑ-nyíːt 'to become full' | keˑrǽːt 'seen' |

PÄKOT

| Open Stem vowel | Close Stem vowel |
| --- | --- |
| kɛ̀ˑ-pán 'to bewitch' | kèˑ-tŭːm 'to sing' |
| pàn (Pri.) } 'a charm' | túːm (Pri.) } 'song' |
| panɛ̆ːˀ (Sec.) } 'a charm' | tŭːmtâ̆ˀ (Sec.) } 'song' |
| pànàt 'act of bewitching' | tŭːmâ̆t 'act of singing' |
| pànàn (Pri.) } 'bewitched one' | mâ̆râ̆n (Pri.) } 'a barred (door)' |
| pànànɛ̆ːˀ (Sec.) } 'bewitched one' | mâ̆râ̆nĕːˀ (Sec.) } 'a barred (door)' |

and the Participle:

| | |
| --- | --- |
| nyəɣɪˑtáːt 'full' < kɛ̀ˑ-nyəɣə́ˀ 'to fill' | wæ̀ːnyæ̌ːt 'ended' < kèˑ-wæ̌ːnyâ̆ˀ 'to come to an end' |

(c) Category Harmony is also to be found in many of the Primary Number Suffixes of Nouns, also in the Secondary Suffixes, but cannot be discussed here.[20]

*Vowel Category Shift*

23. This is a process by which the Stem vowel of a word (and any attached weak affix) changes to the corresponding vowel of another

category. In most cases the shift is from open vowel to corresponding close vowel, and may be represented as follows:

| Long Vowels | Short Vowels | |
|---|---|---|
| NANDI and PÄKOT | NANDI | PÄKOT |
| ɪː > iː | ɪ > i | ə > ï (i) |
| ʊː > uː | ʊ > u | ə > ï (u) |
| ɛː > eː | ɛ > e | |
| ɔː > oː | ɔ > o | ɔ > ä (o) |
| aː > æː | a > æ | a > ä |

In Päkot short /i, u/ and /o/ may occur as the result of category shift from /ə/ and /ɔ/, but never in original Stems.

24. Category Shift is best exemplified in the Verb Stems in the Continuous Aspect.[21]

Thus from the Class I Stem kʊːt with open Stem vowel (= to blow), is obtained:

| | NANDI | PÄKOT |
|---|---|---|
| S. 1 | æ̀-gúːté, á-gúːté | ä-kúːt-aːn 'I am blowing', etc. |
| 2 | í-gúːté | i-kúːtä-nyiː, i-kúːtéː-nyì˙ |
| 3 | kuːté(y) K. kúːtè(y) | kúːtäy |
| P. 1 | kí-gúːté | kï-kúːtä-caː, kï-kúːtéː-càː |
| 2 | ó-gúːté | ä-kúːtä-kwaː, ä-kúːtéː-kwàː |
| 3 | kuːté(y) K. kúːtè(y) | kúːtäy |

Close Stem vowels are not affected, so the above paradigm could equally represent 'I am smoothing, you are smoothing', etc., (< -kuːt), and only the semantic context will tell the hearer which verb is intended.

Note that the personal Prefixes, being weak, have close vowels. Note also that the Päkot personal *Suffixes* (except in the 2nd Pers. Sg.) are *neutral*, i.e. unaffected, and retain their open vowels.

Similarly, from the Class II Stems (N) ɪlaːl (= to light) and (P) ɪlɛp (= to stalk) are obtained:

| | NANDI | PÄKOT | |
|---|---|---|---|
| | I am lighting etc. | I am stalking etc. | |
| S. 1 | æ̀ː–læ̌ːlí | ä–léːp–aːn | |
| 2 | íː–læ̌ːlí | iː–léːpä–nyi˙, | iː–leːpéː–nyi˙ |
| 3 | íɭæːli | lèːpäy | |
| P. 1 | kíː–læ̌ːlí | kiː–léːpäː–caː, | kìː–leːpéː–caː |
| 2 | óː–læ̌ːlí | ä–léːpä–kwaː, | ä–leːpäː–kwaː |
| 3 | íɭæːli | lèːpäy | |

25. Similarly, the Continuous Stems of the other verbs listed in § 10 are (3rd Pers. forms given):

| NANDI | KIPSIGIS | | PÄKOT | |
|---|---|---|---|---|
| wiːré(y) | wíːrè(y) | 'hit(s) with stone' | wíːräy | 'hit(s) with thrown stick' |
| ŋeːté(y) | ŋéːtè(y) | 'get(s) up' | ŋéːtäy | 'get(s) up' |
| oːné(y) | yóːnè(y) | 'drive(s) off' | yóːnäy | 'drive(s) off' |
| lɔːnyé(y) | lɔ́ːnyè(y) | 'climb(s)' | lɔ́ːnyäy, lɔ́ːŋäy, | 'climb(s)' |
| riːbé(y) | ríːbè(y) | 'guard(s)' | ríːpäy | 'guard(s)' |
| kuːré(y) | kúːrè(y) | 'call(s)' | kúːräy | 'call(s)' |
| keːré(y) | kéːrè(y) | 'look(s) at' | kéːräy | 'aim(s) at' |
| poːré(y) | póːrè(y) | 'husk(s)' | póːräy | 'level(s)' |
| sɔːmé(y) | sɔ́ːmè(y) | 'ask(s) for' | sɔ́ːmäy | 'ask(s) for' |

and in § 12:

| NANDI | KIPSIGIS | | PÄKOT | |
|---|---|---|---|---|
| nyíte(y) | nyítè(y) | 'anger(s)' | nyĭ́täy | 'anger(s)' |
| íbutí | íbùti | 'fall(s)' | pĭ̀tă̂y | 'fall(s)'[22, 23] |
| kére(y) | kérè(y) | 'shut(s)' | kắräy | 'shut(s)' |
| kóre(y) | kórè(y) | 'go(es) blind' | kắräy, kóräy | 'go(es) blind'[23] |
| nɔ́me(y) | nɔ́mè(y) | 'hold(s)' | nắmäy | 'seize(s)' |
| síce(y) | sícè(y) | 'get(s)' | sĭ́cäy, sĭ́käy | 'find(s)' |
| súte(y) | sútè(y) | 'lift(s)' | sĭ́täy | 'lift(s)' |
| tébe(y) | tébè(y) | 'stay(s)' | tắpɔː | 'stay(s)' |
| tóre(y) | tórè(y) | 'strip(s) leaves' | tắräy | 'chop(s)' |
| sɔ́be(y) | sɔ́bè(y) | 'is/are well' | sắpäy | 'is/are alive' |

26. All weak Affixes, i.e. Personal or Tense Prefixes and Derivative Suffixes, will naturally now have their close forms, e.g. (compare paradigms in § 21d).

NANDI

| | Class I | Class II | |
|---|---|---|---|
| | 'I was blowing it' *or* 'I was smoothing it' | 'I was counselling him' | 'I was lighting it' |
| S. 1 | kɔ́ː-gúːté | kɔ́ː-lɔ̆ːlí | kɔ́ː-rwɔ̆ːcí |
| 2 | kéː-gúːté | kéː-lɔ̆ːlí | kéː-rwɔ̆ːcí, |
| 3 | kɔ-guːtẹ | kêː-lɔ̆ːli | etc. |

| | | |
|---|---|---|
| S. 1 | kòˑ-ǽ-gúːté, kòˑ-ɑ́-gúːté | koˑ-æ̂ː-læ̆ːlí |
| 2 | kòˑ-í-gú-té | koˑ-îː-læ̆ːlí |
| 3 | kòː-gùːté | koˑ-ílæːli |
| S. 1 | kìˑ-ǽ-gúːté, kìˑ-ɑ́-gúːté | kiˑ-æ̂ː-læ̆ːlí |
| 2 | kìˑ-í-gúːté | kiˑ-îː-læ̆ːlí |
| 3 | kìː-gùːté | kiˑ-íllæːli |

Perfect forms (3rd Pers.)

| | |
|---|---|
| kǽˑ-go-gùːté | kǽˑ-goˑ-læːli |
| kóˑ-go-gùːté | kóˑ-goˑ-læːli |
| kíˑ-go-gùːté | kíˑ-goˑ-læːli |

Note that /æ + æ/ = /æː/ /æ + i/ = /eː/

PÄKOT

| | Class I | Class II | |
|---|---|---|---|
| | 'I was looking for' *or* 'I was barring the door' | 'I was making a hole' | 'I was stalking' |
| S. 1 | koː-mă̂r-aːn | koːléːp-aːn | koː-téːp-aːn |
| 2 | keːmă̂rä-nyiː | kiː-léːpä-nyiˑ | kiː-téːpä-nyiˑ |
| 3 | kă̈-mă̂räy | kèː-leːpäy | kèː-teːpă̂y |
| S. 1 | kyoː-mă̂r-aːn | kyoː-léːp-aːn | kyoː-téːp-aːn |
| 2 | kiː-mă̂rä-nyiː | kiː-léːpä-nyiˑ | kiː-téːpä-nyi |
| 3 | kiˑ-mă̂räy | kiː-leːpă̂y | kiː-teːpă̂y |

Perfect forms (3rd Pers.)

| | | |
|---|---|---|
| kâː-(kĭ̂-)mă̂räy | kâˑ-kùˑ-leːpă̂y | kâˑ-kùˑ-teːpă̂y |
| kîː-(kĭ̂-)mă̂räy | kîˑ-kùˑ-leːpă̂y | kîˑ-kùˑ-teːpă̂y |

Note that /ä + ä/ = /oː/ /ä + i/ = /eː/ or /iː/ /i + i/ = /iː/

27. Category Shift may be attributable to the influence of an Affix, here called a Strong Affix, and may then be designated 'Umlaut'. Where no apparent phonetic reason for the change is found, it is here designated 'Ablaut'. In many instances one cannot be certain which process is involved.[24]

28. Category Shift also occurs in the following conditions:

(a) In certain Derivative Verbs.

*Umlaut*: Strong Suffixes

KIPSIGIS

| Infinitive | Imperative | |
|---|---|---|
| kɛ̀·tɛm | tɛ́m | 'dig, cultivate' |
| ke·temjí | tèmjí·n | 'dig for or at' |
| ke·temjine·cí | temjí:nê·cín | 'dig on behalf of' |
| ke·temji·nɔ̂ɔ̂:n | temjí·nɔ̂ɔ̂:nún | 'dig for this way' |
| ke·temji·nɔ̂ɔ̂:t | temjí·nɔ̂ɔ̂:tén | 'dig for that way' |
| ke·temí·s | temî:syén | 'dig occupationally' |
| ke·temi·sye:cí | temí·syê:cín | 'dig occupationally for' |
| ke·temi·sye·cine:cí | temí·syê·cine:cín | '. . . on behalf of' |
| ke·temi·sye·cinɔ̂ɔ̂:n | temí·syê·cinɔɔ·nên | '. . . this direction' |
| ke·temi·sye·cinɔ̂ɔ̂:t | temí·syê·cinɔɔ·tên | '. . . that direction' |
| etc. | etc. | |
| kɛ̀·tíl | tíl | 'cut' |
| ke·tiljí | tiljí·n | 'cut for' |
| tílɔɔksê | | 'it is cuttable' |
| kɛ̀·wá:c | wá:c | 'shout' |
| kè·wɔ̀ɔ̀:ksɔ̀ɔ̀ | ɔ̀wɔɔ:ksé | 'shout together' |

Close Stem vowels are not affected.

| | | |
|---|---|---|
| kè·tíny | tíny | 'nurse' |
| ke·tinjí | tinjí·n | 'nurse for' |
| etc. | etc. | |

*Ablaut*: Certain Derivative Verb Stems without apparently the aid of any strong Affix.

NANDI

| Infinitive | Imperative | |
|---|---|---|
| kɛ̀·bál | bál | 'to dig' |
| kè·bɔ̀ɔ̀l | bɔɔlú | 'to dig up' |

KIPSIGIS

| | | |
|---|---|---|
| kɛ̀·tɛ́m | tɛ́m | 'to dig' |
| kè·tèm | temún | 'to dig in this direction' |

This seems to be the main way of expressing the 'Motion towards' idea, otherwise expressed by means of the weak Suffix -ʊ(n), -u(n).

(b) Certain Derivative Noun Stems with and without the aid of strong Affixes.

*Umlaut and Ablaut*

### NANDI

| Class I | | Class II | |
|---|---|---|---|
| kɛ̀ˑ-bán | 'to bewitch' | k-ìːbât | 'to cultivate' |
| | | k-ìˑtâːny | 'to forge' |

| Singular | | Plural | | |
|---|---|---|---|---|
| Primary | Secondary | Primary | Secondary | |
| pɔ́ˑnîːn | pɔˑníːndèt | pɔ́ːn | pɔ̀ˑnîˑk | 'witch' |
| kìːtɔ̀ˑŋíːn | kìːtɔ̀ˑŋìˑndèt | kìːtɔ́ːŋ | kìːtɔ̀ˑŋîːk | 'smith' |
| kɔ̀ːbɔ̀tíːn | kɔ̀ːbɔ̀tìːndèt | kɔ́ːbɔ́tîn | kɔ̀ːbɔ̀tîːk | 'cultivator' |

### PÄKOT

| Class I | | Class II | |
|---|---|---|---|
| kɛ̀ˑ-cɔ̌ːr | 'to steal' | kɛˑ-yáːkwə́y | 'to herd' |

| Singular | | Plural | | |
|---|---|---|---|---|
| Primary | Secondary | Primary | Secondary | |
| coˑríːn | coˑríːntêː | coˑrı́ʔ | coˑrı́kâ̂ | 'thief' |
| kìyɔ̀ːkwı̀yı̌ːn | kìyɔ̀ːkwı̀yìːntéː | kìyɔ̀ːkwïyı́ʔ | kìyɔ̀ːkwïyíː | 'herdsman' |

### KIPSIGIS

Compare k-ìàgá 'to tend cattle' giving:

| | | | | |
|---|---|---|---|---|
| kɔ̀ˑyɔ̀gíːn | kɔ̀ˑyɔ̀gìːndét | kɔ̀ˑyɔ́k | kɔ̀ˑyɔ̀gík | 'herdsman' |

with k-ìɔ́ːk 'to send' giving:

| | | | | |
|---|---|---|---|---|
| kɔ̀ˑyɔ̀ˑgíːn | kɔ̀ˑyɔ̀ˑgìːndét | kɔ̀ˑyɔ́ːk | kɔ̀ˑyɔ̀ːgík | 'apostle' |

(c) Category Shift is also to be found in Singular-Plural relationships of many nouns, and in Primary-Secondary relationships of a few nouns[25].

Cases of Reversed Category Shift, i.e. Close vowel to Open vowel, have been found sporadically in the above relationships, and also in certain genitival relationships,[25] but no examples have as yet been recorded in verbal behaviour.

*Notes*

[1] The word means 'I tell you' in Nandi.

[2] The two languages are so close as, linguistically, to be regarded as local variants of the same idiom.

[3] The phonetic behaviour of nouns is discussed in 'Noun Classification in Kalenjin', by A. N. Tucker and M. A. Bryan, *African Language Studies*, 3, 1962.

[4] See Tucker and Bryan, op. cit.

[5] IPA [ɲ]. Note also that /y/ here corresponds to IPA [j] and /j/ here to IPA [ɟ].

[6] In Eastern Päkot the Secondary form is less used than in Western Päkot.

[7] The small exclamation mark in these examples indicates a 'step down' in intonation, i.e. a slight lowering of the general pitch of the sentence. See Tone, § 19.

[8] [b] is occasionally heard even initially in words. Further, in words such as bál, 'Dig!', an implosive rather than an explosive [b] has been heard from time to time. This variety of the /p/ phoneme is, however, only to be heard at the beginning of stressed syllables.

[9] This is the only context in which [d] is heard in these languages.

[10] Here pronunciations such as [-ceːncí] are not uncommon.

[11] The underlying meaning of these Prefixes would seem to be: kɪp-, masculine or big; cɛp-, feminine or small; kap-, place. The first two Prefixes, however, may extend to the names of many animals as well, with no reference to sex or size. Note that in the above examples, a 'limping woman' or a 'small tobacco pouch' would have the Prefix cɛp-.

[12] In a few areas (the Southern Kipsigis area of Mr. Ng'elechei is one) there is a tendency for Open /ɪː/ and /ʊː/ to merge with Close /iː/ and /uː/ acoustically, though not in category behaviour, e.g. words containing such vowels still take Open vowel Prefixes and Suffixes as in the examples given here.

[13] Rarely heard in the long variety, but more frequent in the short variety.

[14] There are probably more Nandi correspondences than given here; further research is needed. Note that some centralization of /i/ and /ɪ/ has been heard with some Nandi-Kipsigis speakers.

[15] See below. Note that the Prefix kɪ- (ki-) is to be found in certain nouns derived from Class II Verbs.

[16] The 3rd pers. sg. and pl. are identical.

[17] For Class I Derivative Nouns see § 22b.

[18] It is neutral in some forms of Kipsigis also.

[19] Kipsigis forms are fuller than Nandi forms, which omit the final /-n/.

[20] See Tucker and Bryan, op. cit.

[21] There are two Aspects in verbal conjugation in these languages, describing 'Momentary' and 'Continuous' action respectively – the latter Aspect involving Category Shift from open Stem vowel to corresponding close Stem vowel. Stems with normally close vowels do not undergo Category Shift.

[22] Class II Verb.

[23] Short /o/ occurs in Päkot only as the result of Category Shift from short /ɔ/.

[24] In the paradigms just cited, for instance, one might argue that the Suffix -e, -ey, or -äy is a strong Suffix causing Umlaut of the Stem vowel, or, alternatively, that the Category Shift is purely grammatical (like the Tense forms of Strong Verbs in English and German, and, therefore, an example of Ablaut), and that the Suffix, being weak, takes a close vowel accordingly.

[25] See Tucker and Bryan, op. cit.

# Syllabication in the Kashmiri Language

SIDDHESHWAR VARMA

The purpose of this paper is to point out a few notable trends in the syllabication of Kashmiri. The interest of the present writer, who is not a Kashmiri speaker, has been roused for years by this feature in Kashmiri, a feature which distinguishes Kashmiri remarkably from many Indian languages.

We shall consider this subject from two points of view, syllabic structure and syllabic catenation.

## SYLLABIC STRUCTURE

'The pivotal principle of syllabic structure is the contrast of successive features within the syllable.'[1] This contrast usually concerns the succession of vowels and consonants. Now the first notable point in this connection is that a consonant cluster at the end of a syllable (CC) is unknown to Kashmiri, e.g. Kashmiri (ˈkhʌrĭtʃ][2] 'expenditure', Hindi [xʌrtʃ]; Kashmiri [ˈnjarʌkh] 'rate', Hindi [nɪrx]; Kashmiri [nʌkʌd] 'cash', Hindi [nʌkd]. Another sequence, peculiar to Kashmiri, is CVCV, but the last vowel, in dialectical speech, is not heard, though it is definitely articulated, e.g. Kashmiri [koru̥] 'did', [ˈpo˔pu̥] 'ripe', [ˈto˔nu̥] 'thin'. Compare also a final consonantal vowel in [ˈphʌtʃo˔ŭ̥] 'was split'. The present writer actually observed the rounding of lips when these four words were pronounced by Kashmiri speakers, but he never heard the final vowels. This phenomenon has been called 'non-acoustic articulation' by the present writer in his writings on the subject.

Now we come to a very peculiar feature of Kashmiri syllabication, viz. the occurrence of glides. If we symbolize a glide as G, we find in the language the following schemes: GVC, VGVC, or CGVC. In connection with GVC, as in Kashmiri [jɪs] 'such', it may be pointed out that no Kashmiri word begins with the vowel [i], that this 'initial' [i] is always preceded by [ĭ] or [j] and that the present writer has heard the English phrase 'in the room' pronounced as [ĭin ðə ru˙m] by many Kashmiri speakers. VGVC may be illustrated by the Kashmiri pronunciation of the English word 'out' (in a cricket match) as [ˈʌ˙ʊuṭ]. Even two glides, viz. [j] and [i̥], occur in the Kashmiri word for the Dewali festival, viz. [djʌˈʊɜ˙i̥li̥] (CGVCVGCV). CGVC may be illustrated by Kashmiri [ljʌd] or [ljäd] 'dung of ass or horse', for which Panjabi has [lɪd], with no glide.

The complications in syllabication, created by such glides, which have been called 'parasitic vocalic elements',[3] will be particularly appreciated when we take into account the fact that they enter the nucleus of a word, as in Kashmiri [ˈpɜ̣˙i̥tlɜ̣] 'kettle', Panjabi [pəˈti˙lɑ], so that the determination of the *minimum* prominence in the syllable concerned becomes difficult.[4] Now the question arises: in a Kashmiri word like [mʊˈzu˙i̥ri̥] 'wage', Panjabi [mʌˈzu˙ri], what could be the phonetic function of the glide [i̥] after [zu˙]? Jones suggests that 'diminution of prominence between two syllables is generally supplied by the glide which connects them'.[5] Another function, which our 'tenacity' principle will presently suggest, is also possible, viz. the glide serves as a separator of the two syllables [zu˙] and [ri̥].

It is curious that the languages adjacent to Kashmiri do not show any traces of such tendencies. Grierson, in his *Linguistic Survey of India,*[6] mentions a dialect Lōdhāntī (a sub-dialect of Bundēli) spoken in the very distant Gangetic plains, in which, to the literary Hindi word [mōrā] 'my', corresponds [mūărau].

## SYLLABIC CATENATION

But in view of the fact that the syllable, by itself, is more or less an abstraction, the proper study of the syllable in any language should concern that syllable in connection with another. As regards this point, the present writer's investigations show that Kashmiri syllabication exhibits a remarkable co-existence of two apparently conflicting principles, viz. tenacity and fluidity.

(1) TENACITY. That Kashmiri syllables tend to be kept apart from each other, each syllable tenaciously maintaining its individuality, could be illustrated by the following examples:

(a) The English word 'glass' (tumbler) is pronounced as [gɪˈlɑ˙sɜ̣] with three full, almost even, syllables, though the prominence of [lɑ˙] is a little greater than that of the other two.

(b) The English word 'football' is pronounced [phuʈɜ̣ˈbaḁlḁ], with four nearly even syllables.

(c) The word for 'Panjabi', which Webster renders as [pŭn-jä'bē̇], is [ˈpʌ̃ˑʤeˑbḁ]. The nasalization in [pʌ̃ˑ] dissociates it from the succeeding syllable. On the other hand, the pronunciation of this word in many adjacent Indian languages indicates the adhesion of the first syllable to the second by the nasal consonant [ɲ], as in [ˌpʌɲˈʤɑbi] or [pəɲˈʤɑˑbi].

(d) The Kashmiri word for the numeral 75 is [ˈpʌ̃ˑsʌtʌth], while Hindi has [pʌˈʧhʌttər], Panjabi [pəɲʌˏttər]. In both of these forms the first two syllables are on the border-zone, syllabic division being difficult.

(e) For this tenacious separation, Kashmiri often uses the mechanism of quantity, e.g. the word for 'banana' is [kɛːəl] or [ˈkɛːlɜ̣], with fully long vowels in the initial syllables, while the neighbouring languages Hindi and Panjabi have [kelɑ] or [kellɑ]. Jespersen, distinguishing two kinds of syllabic junction, could call the Kashmiri one a 'tenacious junction', 'fester Anschluss',[7] the vowel firmly adhering to the consonant.

(f) The Kashmiri correspondences for medial consonant-clusters reveal the same tendency, e.g. for the word 'Kashmir', we have [ˌkɜ̣ˈʃɪːr], so that [ʃm] as a consonant-cluster will be impossible in Kashmiri. This aversion may perhaps be ages old, for the Chinese traveller Hieven-Tsang names Kashmir as [kiɑ-shi-mi-lo].[8] Again, for a 'Brahmin', the Kashmiri word is [ˈbrɛhɛmun], differing remarkably from Panjabi [bàmˑəɳ] and Hindi [brɑhmʌn].

(2) FLUIDITY. The fluidity of Kashmiri syllables is remarkable. A Kashmiri syllable, though very tenacious, is quite sensitive to a succeeding [i] or [u]. Cf. the following examples:

(a) The plural of [ˈmɜ̃zɪm) 'internal', is [ˈmɜ̃ḁzḁmḁ]; the final [ḁ], being the plural termination, has 'generated' two more [ḁ's] in the other two syllables, so that all of them have [ḁ].

(b) The word for 'sweet' is [ˈmʊdʊru̥], literary Panjabi and Hindi [mʌdhʊr].

(c) In some Kashmiri dialects, a final [u̥] or a succeeding [ɔ] has stimulated the emergence of labio-velar and labio-dental plosives, e.g. Banihal Kashmiri has [ˈkᵘɔkuru̥] 'cock', [dᵘɔd] 'milk', Hindi [duˑd], Panjabi [dʊ̀d].

This study appears to indicate: (1) that Kashmiri is one of those languages which, by virtue of 'tenacious junction', can offer object lessons on syllabication; and (2) that, this strict syllabication being mostly confined to Kashmir dialects, it is of international importance to survey these dialects in the near future, for they are rapidly disappearing.

*Notes*

1 R. Jakobson and M. Halle, 'Phonology in Relation to Phonetics', *A Manual of Phonetics* (ed. L. Kaiser), Amsterdam, 1957, 226.

2 The mark [ˈ] before a syllable in the transcriptions in this paper stands for prominence, and not for stress in particular.

3 O. Broch, *Slavische Phonetik*, Heidelberg, 1911, 217.

4 Cf. D. Jones, *An Outline of English Phonetics*, Cambridge, 1956, 55.

5 Ibid., 57.

6 Vol. IV-1, 465.

7 O. Jespersen, *Lehrbuch der Phonetik*, Leipzig, 1920, 202.

8 J. N. Ganhar, *Buddhism in Kashmir and Ladakh*, New Delhi, 1956, 92.